Kokoda

Paul Ham
Kokoda

HarperCollins*Publishers*

HarperCollins*Publishers*

First published in Australia in 2004
by HarperCollins*Publishers* Pty Limited
ABN 36 009 913 517
A member of the HarperCollins*Publishers* (Australia) Pty Limited Group
www.harpercollins.com.au

HarperCollins*Publishers*
25 Ryde Road, Pymble, Sydney NSW 2073, Australia
31 View Road, Glenfield, Auckland 10, New Zealand
77–85 Fulham Palace Road, London W6 8JB, United Kingdom
2 Bloor Street East, 20th floor, Toronto, Ontario, M4W 1A8, Canada
10 East 53rd Street, New York NY 10022, United States of America

National Library of Australia Cataloguing-in-Publication data:

Ham, Paul
    Kokoda.
    Bibliography.
    Includes index.
    ISBN 0 7322 7693 4.
    1. World War, 1939-1945 – Campaigns – Papua New Guinea.
    2. World War, 1939-1945 – Participation, Australian.
    3. World War, 1939-1945 – Participation, Japanese.
    4. Kokoda Trail (Papua New Guinea). I. Title.
940.542651

Cover and internal design by Mark Gowing Design
Cover photograph courtesy of the Australian War Memorial: AWM013287 (frame enlargement from the
film *Kokoda Front Line!* by Damien Parer, featuring Salvation Army Chaplain Albert Moore lighting the
cigarette of a wounded soldier, Lieutenant Valentine G. Gardner, D Company, 2/14th Battalion)
Front cover quote by an unnamed Australian soldier
Author photograph by Justin Mclean
Maps of the Pacific Theatre, Papua and New Guinea, and the Kokoda Track by Laurie Whiddon,
Map Illustrations. Other maps adapted from Dudley McCarthy's *South-West Pacific Area — First Year,
Kokoda to Wau*, by Natalie Winter, HarperCollins Design Studio, with kind permission of the
Australian War Memorial
Typeset in 11 on 15pt Bembo by Kirby Jones
Printed and bound in Australia by Griffin Press on 90gsm Fine Offset

6 5 4 3 2   04 05 06 07

For my son, Ollie; my brother, Ian;
and the poor, bewildered bloody infantry

'... I mean the truth untold,
The pity of war, the pity war distilled.'
— Wilfred Owen, 'Strange Meeting'

Contents

Part One — Landing

Part Two — Invasion

Part Three — Withdrawal

Part Four — Counteroffensive

Part Five — Annihilation

List of Maps

Author Note
Kokoda Track or Trail?

I glimpsed a kind of hell during the writing of this book. The Kokoda campaign — by which I include the battles of the Kokoda Track, Milne Bay and the Papuan beaches — is exceptional in military history. In terms of casualty numbers, of course, it was insignificant alongside the huge pitched battles for Europe and the Soviet Union. But such quantitative judgments mean little to the mother, father, wife, brother, sister or child of a dead soldier. What made this campaign uniquely grim was the proximity of the fighting and the extraordinary terrain over which the two armies clashed. It was indeed, at times, a 'knife fight out of the stone age', as historian Eric Bergerud wrote. The Kokoda campaign is distinguished for three other reasons: it was the first land defeat of the Japanese Imperial Army; it marked the start of the great roll-back of the Japanese troops from the southernmost point of the Pacific empire; and it was the battle that saved Australia from certain isolation — and possible invasion, as it was perceived at the time — in the Pacific War.

Against this backdrop, the heated argument over the correct name of the jungle path along which the Australians and the Japanese fought seems trivial. To my mind, a track is little different from a trail or path, and I have used these terms interchangeably. Where I formally identify it, I use 'Kokoda Track', because that is the preferred name of the Isurava Memorial and most soldiers. Incidentally, a research paper by Peter Provis on the subject, commissioned by the Australian War Memorial, concludes that 'Trail' is technically correct, but concedes that either may be used — for which clarity one is, I suppose, thankful.

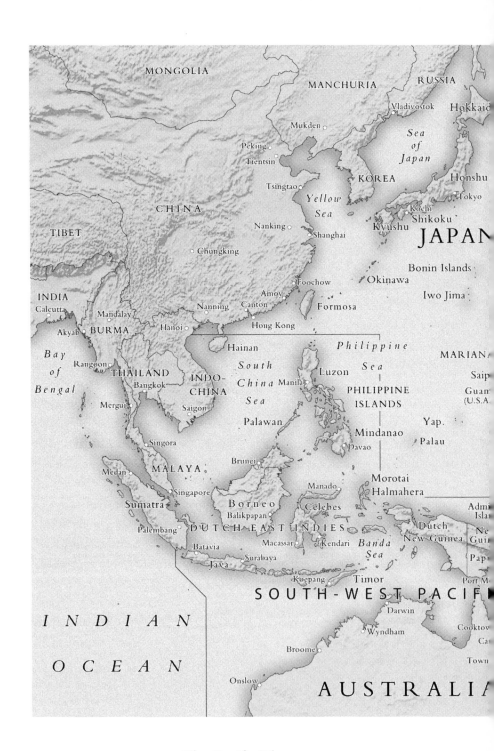

The Pacific Theatre

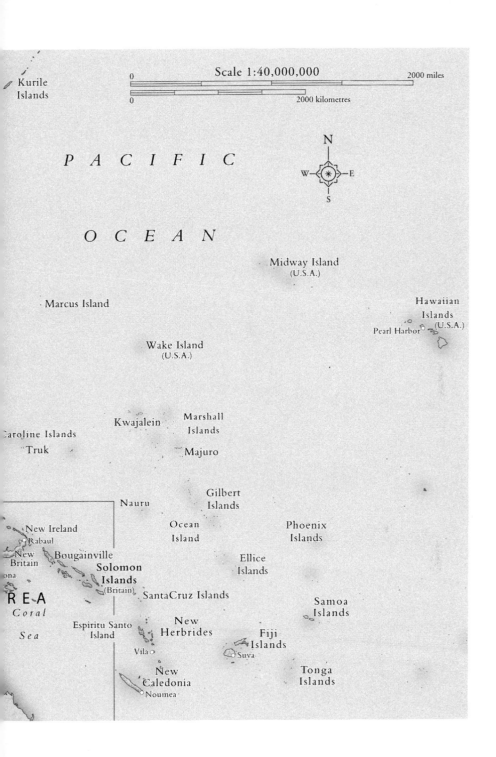

Papua and New Guinea

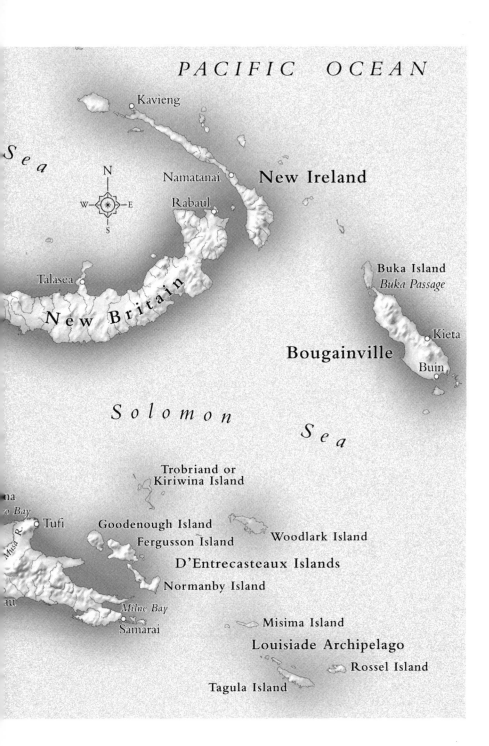

PACIFIC OCEAN

Kavieng

Sea

N

W—✦—E

S

Namatanai

New Ireland

Rabaul

Buka Island
Buka Passage

Talasea

New Britain

Bougainville

Kieta

Buin

Solomon

Sea

Trobriand or
Kiriwina Island

na

o Bay

Tufi

Goodenough Island

Fergusson Island

Woodlark Island

D'Entrecasteaux Islands

Normanby Island

Milne Bay

Samarai

Misima Island

Louisiade Archipelago

Rossel Island

Tagula Island

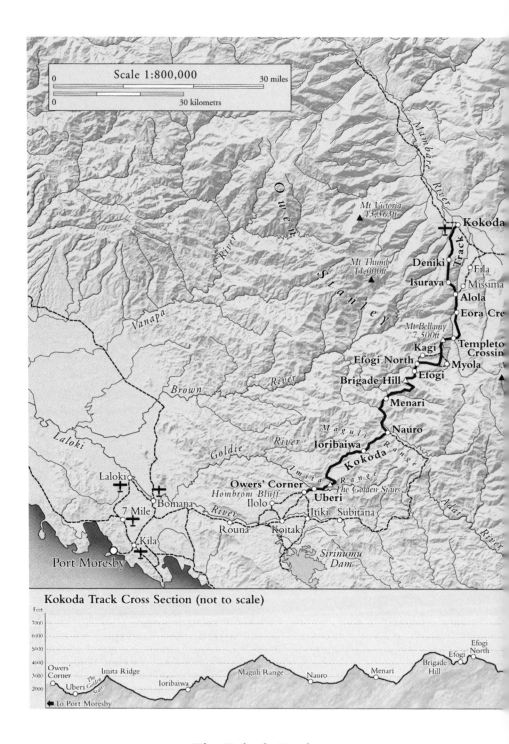

The Kokoda Track

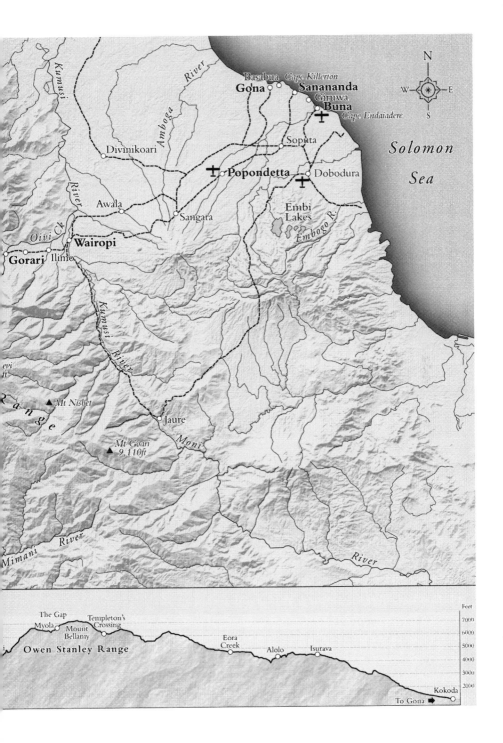

Part One
Landing

Chapter 1
Missionaries

'Dry your tears. Perhaps they are *otao naso*, our friends'
— *Father James Benson to a Papuan boy, on seeing the Japanese ships*

On the afternoon of 21 July 1942, a humble Christian missionary was fixing his deckchair in his shed by the Solomon Sea. Father James Benson enjoyed pottering about with his tools at Gona Mission, on the north coast of Papua. The little deckchair served a special function for this Yorkshire-born clergyman: he would perch himself upon it aboard the native outriggers that plied his coastal parish.

Benson, the Anglican missionary at Gona since 1937, was a respected local figure. He'd devoted himself to the spiritual wellbeing of his small flock, many of whose ancestors were head-hunters; and while not every Papuan had converted to Christianity as enthusiastically as he might have hoped, Benson could not complain. His parish numbered several hundred, and those parishioners who had not 'gone bush' were models of zealous attentiveness.

Two decades earlier their tribes had been warriors and cannibals who solved tribal disputes with bloodshed, and whose trophies of war were the shrivelled heads of their real or imagined enemies. They were the Orokaiva and Binandere people, with a reputation for being 'bellicose in the extreme' and 'the most rampant and obstinate savages', in the view of the Australian Governor of Papua in 1923.[1] No doubt their thorough head-hunting raids on neighbouring villages were 'uneconomic',[2] as he also observed.

The flaxen-haired Orokaivans, whose oiled ringlets grew into a mass of tails, pencil-thick, and fell about their shoulders 'in the manner of a Chief Justice's wig'[3] were notoriously superstitious, and the Australian Government deemed it seemly to stamp out an interesting snake ritual in which the village witch doctor induced in his patients 'paroxysms of a peculiarly horrible nature'.[4]

Yet in time these powerfully built people adapted to white rule, and agreeably sheathed their scalping knives to participate in the less dangerous diversions introduced by the colonial power: chiefly cricket and football. Western controls were introduced. The Orokaivans who joined the local constabulary gained a reputation for 'cheerful bravery', transmuting the ferocious warrior ethos of 1920 into a force for order and relative stability. Notwithstanding Governor Murray's appeal for 'less Christ and more cricket',[5] some eschewed sorcery for Christianity and, in 1942, some three hundred parishioners welcomed the familiar sight of their white-haired preacher who, sitting up in his outrigger, came by sea to spread the word of the white man's god.

At about 4.00 p.m. that day, Benson heard loud cries from Gona beach. An assistant ran up to the door of his shed: 'Father! Great ships are here!'[6] Benson put aside his deckchair and emerged from the shed into the sunlight to see, less than a mile offshore, a 5000-ton Japanese transport ship flanked by two destroyers. 'My mind must have been numbed,' he later wrote, 'for in the next few minutes I did several foolish things.'[7] He stored his deckchair and packed some odd items in a canvas satchel: a cheap watch, a few sticks of tobacco, a notebook and pencil, some spare handkerchiefs and a compass. He then walked the few hundred yards from his mission compound down to the grey, palm-shaded sands of Gona beach. A tearful little Papuan boy stood there, crying and shaking with terror, and pointing at the great black ships that loomed offshore.

The Japanese fleet had penetrated the network of shallow tropical reefs and was 'almost on the beach'.[8] The biggest ship the boy had seen, apart from his father's toy-like canoe, was Benson's 50-ton mission boat, *The*

Maclaren King. But the monsters anchored off Basabua Point, their hulls shimmering in the afternoon sun, were from another world.

'Dry your tears,' said Benson. 'Perhaps they are *otao naso* — our friends.'[9] The reverend instructed the boy to rejoin his people at Jenat, some two miles up the beach, and went to confer with the senior Papuan teacher and the mission's two young Anglican Sisters: Miss May Hayman and Miss Mavis Parkinson.

Benson had been alert to the Japanese threat since December 1941. That month the Australian Government recommended the compulsory evacuation from Darwin, Papua and New Guinea of all women and children 'other than missionaries who may wish to remain and nurses'.[10]

New Guinea was a colony of Australia, which had been granted a mandate over the northern region, New Guinea, and the nearby islands, at Prime Minister Billy Hughes' behest during the Paris Peace Conference in 1919. Papua and New Guinea would form 'ramparts' to be held from 'the hands of an actual or potential enemy'.[11] Only 1500 white people lived in Papua, the southern half of the island, and 4500 in New Guinea, in 1939. The local people numbered around 1.8 million, representing a huge variety of ethnic and language groups for whom extreme violence tended to be the chief mode of dispute settlement until European guns, the rule of law and the church (chiefly the Seventh-Day Adventists) arrived to pacify them in the early twentieth century.

Most white civilians had left Papua by July 1942. At Gona, Benson and the two young women elected to stay. Mavis Parkinson, a teacher who ran the three schools in Gona, got permission from her parents back in Ipswich, Queensland, to remain. Elsewhere in Papua and New Guinea, 689 foreigners, including 121 missionaries with 26 children, decided similarly against evacuation, and remained in their villages.[12]

Benson was under no illusions about Japan's intentions. He'd seen hundreds of refugees fleeing the Japanese attacks on Salamaua and Lae pulling up on the beach; he'd witnessed the occasional dogfight in the sky. He prevailed upon the two young women to leave Gona, but they refused. They bossed him about in a cheerful way, and were unyielding in their determination.

Benson's dwindling Papuan flock were less stubborn and needed no encouragement to go. Fearful of the Japanese — or perhaps in the grip of a less benign god than Benson's — most had already evacuated along the coast, or fled to the foothills of the Owen Stanley Range. The village people streamed along the bush tracks and across the swamps, which ran parallel to the beach strip. They carried all they could: sleeping mats, clay cooking pots, little pigs and babies.

A handsome, easily dominated man of 57 with bright, compassionate eyes behind round spectacles, Benson stood on the beach and contemplated the Japanese convoy. It was time to leave, he thought, to abandon all this. He turned and surveyed his little paradise one last time: Gona Mission, whose green lawns, little cricket pitch, carefully groomed gardens and paths lined with flowers — hibiscus and yellow crotons — seemed to him a corner of the world that would indeed remain forever England.

The mission's tin-roofed house — marked today by a little white cross — a school with sago-stalk walls and a little church of woven sago leaves, surrounded by native huts on stilts, were as dear to Benson as the services they performed. On balmy nights, he remembered, the missionaries would entertain visitors, chiefly the bishop, beneath swinging hurricane lamps on the lawns by the sea. Indeed, the Yorkshireman's eye beheld something of exceptional beauty in Gona whose 'tropical garden', he wrote, was 'set above a lovely sweep of grey sand and blue water, with a couple of coral islands to the east … I don't think the Garden of Eden could have been more beautiful.'[13] Unless, of course, one looked inland, where an altogether less reassuring spectacle met the eye: a coastal plain of jungle, swamp and rough grassland merging with coconut groves and crisscrossed by flood-prone creeks and rivers. To the east, a few miles along the beach, were Buna and Sanananda. The three villages marked out one of the wettest, most malarial regions on earth; the swamplands offered a perfect breeding ground for the anopheles mosquito.

Benson hoped the Japanese might spare a Papuan village and religious community. He was swiftly disabused. At about 4.45 p.m. on 21 July the destroyers bombed Buna beach and then Gona. 'Hundreds of guns were spitting fire, and the deep woof! crump! crump! of bursting bombs a mile away gave me a queer feeling in the pit of my stomach.'[14]

The sight thrilled the two hopelessly naive Anglican Sisters. Mavis

Parkinson clapped her hands and cried, 'Scrummy! A real naval battle and here we are watching it. I do wish we knew if they are our ships.'[15]

The softening up lasted several minutes, after which, at about 5.00 p.m., hundreds of Japanese troops slid down ropes thrown over the ships' sides into barges. The sound of rifle butts stamping on the hulls accompanied their shoreward advance, according to one native witness.★

The Orokaivan outriggers that normally plied the coastline lay abandoned on the beach. The tribes had deserted their villages. A nervous Benson decided he, too, must lead his little white tribe into the jungle: 'Miss Hayman, in a brisk manner, was putting tins of food into an empty kerosene case. I put two mosquito nets, some old blankets and a square of calico into a blue canvas bag. Miss Parkinson put a change of clothes and some other odds and ends into a small suitcase.'[16]

The first Japanese troops stepped ashore near Basabua, about a mile east of Gona, and the advance troops — the Tsukamoto Battalion — set off immediately inland. At about this time Benson's party left via a path to the rear of the mission compound and into the jungle, 'our nice hot dinner — Miss Hayman's daily delight — still in the oven, and . . . soldiers' shirts and trousers awaiting repairs laid out neatly on a side table.'[17] The uniforms awaiting the Sisters' needlework were those of two officers of the Papuan Infantry Brigade, the indigenous army led by Australians.

The missionaries walked over hard country towards the Siai region, where the local Papuans 'constructed a small bush hut for them a little way up river'.[18] Their destination was Popondetta, the largest town in northern Papua; they were accompanied by a few Australian soldiers and two wounded American airmen. But the advancing Japanese cut off Benson's route, and forced his party off the track. At one point, within yards of the enemy, Benson offered to approach the Japanese commander, to which the girls said, 'That is impossible. We will never give ourselves up to the Japanese.'[19] They plunged into the jungle with only a compass and Benson's prayers — the gently lilting Itinerarium and The Lord's Prayer — to guide them: 'Lighten our Darkness, O Lord,'[20] the missionary prayed, as he led the group into the Papuan night.

★ As told to Frank Taylor, director of Kokoda Treks & Tours. The native witness may have confused the sound, or imagined it, as the Japanese veterans who landed at Papua have no recollection of stamping their rifles on the barge hulls.

Chapter 2
Yokoyama

'From today, we are entering an area subject to air attack . . .
Those who are slow will be regarded as cowards. If sunk, remain
calm until the water touches the feet. When in the water . . .
platoons should gather together to sing military songs'
— *Colonel Yokoyama Yosuke, to the Nankai Shitai advance landing force*

Imanishi Sadaharu was among five of 60 candidates who gained an elite
position in the Imperial Japanese Army. Aged 21, he was immensely proud
to join the 44th Regiment — precursor of the unit that would fight
Australia along the Kokoda Track — as an A-grade soldier. It was 1936, the
dawn of Japan's military empire, and Imanishi's family doted on their clever
son who marched off in his new uniform to his regimental barracks in
Asakura, in Kochi City, his home town.

A short, wiry, pugnacious man, with a loud laugh that erupts at
unexpected moments, Imanishi spent eight years fighting in some of the
grimmest battles of the Pacific campaign. By the time he stepped ashore at
Gona in 1942, he'd had long experience of combat and beach landings.
Having rehearsed and perfected their speciality — the coastal invasion — at
the river mouth near Kochi, his regiment was chosen to lead the invasion of

Shanghai in 1937, losing 700 dead and 1600 wounded in that action. He fought for another three years in China, after which he was promoted to staff sergeant.

He did not fight at Nanking, the scene of the mass rape and slaughter of civilians by the occupying Japanese forces, the scale of which Japanese historians continue to deny. While en route there his unit was diverted to Taiwan, and he returned to Japan in February 1941. To this day the 88-year-old veteran and former provincial mayor wonders why 'not a single bullet hit him under intense firing'.[1]

In 1941, he resumed his career as a schoolteacher, but declined to marry because he feared that 'Japan was going to go to war against the United States'.[2] Indeed, in July 1942, he found himself aboard a Japanese transport ship as one of the crack infantrymen of the Yokoyama Advance Force, the forward troops of the Japanese invasion of Papua.

Imanishi was one of 2000 advance troops who streamed ashore at Gona and Basabua on the Papuan coast. In addition to the standard pack, he carried a bag of rice weighing 50 pounds, 180 bullets, two grenades, a steel helmet and a toothbrush — an astonishing load for this diminutive man.[3] 'There was little resistance,' he recalls. 'Soon after we landed, Australian aircraft attacked, but we escaped into the jungle. We headed straight for Kokoda.'[4]

When the Yokoyama Advance Force landed at Gona, no Allied army lay in wait on the shore; no navy contested the Japanese control of Papuan waters. American ships were occupied near the Solomon Islands and elsewhere in the Pacific, where they were soon to assist the invasion of Guadalcanal.

A small formation of Allied bombers and P-400 Airacobras — not '100 aircraft', as one Japanese history claims[5] — did attack the convoy. While dozens of shells plopped into the sea, the inexperienced Allied pilots scored a couple of direct hits. The burning transport ship *Ayatozan Maru* ran aground, and the black hulk was dubbed the Gona Wreck.

'The enemy planes impudently evaded [our] fire,' wrote one Japanese soldier, 'and calmly soared over the *Ayatozan Maru*, dropping countless bombs [which] screeched as they fell ... almost lifting the ship out of the sea.' Then, 'like a typhoon came the low-flying Spitfires!'[6] (In fact, these were the Airacobras; Churchill's long promised Spitfires arrived belatedly.)

Allied aircraft were no match — yet — for the Japanese Zero. The famous Mitsubishi fighter won most dogfights over Papua and New Guinea at this stage of the war. Undaunted, the Australian airmen had a go. Pilot Officer Warren Cowan, of 32 Squadron, Royal Australian Air Force, dared to attack enemy ships leaving Buna in an aged Hudson. Nine Zeros, one of which was piloted by the legendary Japanese ace, Saburo Sakai, shot him down over the jungle.

Darkness soon obscured the targets, Allied aircraft flew away, and the Yokoyama Advance Force continued its disembarkation through the night. The Japanese had secured the Papuan beachhead by dawn on the 22nd. It was the southernmost point of the Imperial Army's great arc of conquest of 'Greater East Asia', stretching from Manchuria to New Britain, through Thailand, Burma, Singapore and the Dutch East Indies, and virtually isolating Australia.

News of the landing panicked the inexperienced Labor Government of Prime Minister John Curtin. Within a day of the Japanese landing on Australian territory, Curtin met a storm of criticism over Australia's woeful military preparedness. Though it was unfair, given Curtin's brief period in office, William Morris Hughes was unrepentant. As the prime minister during the Great War, who had represented the nation at Versailles, Hughes denounced the lack of resistance in withering terms. 'We must wake up to the fact that we are fighting an enemy that is not afraid to die,' he told Australians, 'an enemy who is on the offensive everywhere. To reach [Gona], the Japanese had to come in a convoy, with barges and troopships. We have an airforce on duty there, day and night. The Japanese ought not to have got there. Every day they are creeping nearer and nearer. Soon they may have established sufficient bases to make a major attack on Australia itself.'[7]

If the wily old fox Billy Hughes was not the only one alarmed by the absence of an Allied military response, he was certainly the most devastatingly outspoken.* On 5 August, Hughes once again bludgeoned 'our military leaders' for 'a lamentable lack of vision, of initiative, or coordination of

---

* In his memoirs of captivity, Benson recorded Japanese surprise at the absence of Allied resistance: 'Susuki [an interpreter] told me the Japanese had been puzzled at the lack of ground opposition to their occupation of Gona and Buna.' Benson noted that for ten days in August he had neither seen nor heard an allied plane. (Benson, *Prisoner's Base and Home Again*, p.49.)

control'.[8] His remarks enraged Curtin and the military establishment, and fired the public mood. The blame could not be laid at the feet of John Curtin, who inherited, and sought desperately to reverse, the state of a near defenceless nation.

Yokoyama's troops were not the first to land on the mainland of New Guinea. The Japanese had already captured, in February, Lae and Salamaua, and penetrated the Sepik region to the west, where they clashed with Kanga Force, an Australian guerrilla unit that would survive in the jungles for months without relief.*

The native response there presaged similar terror on the coast. Drums in the Sepik villages beat out, '*Japan 'e come. White man 'e go bush*'.[9] Anarchy gripped the Highlands. Masterless farm labourers went on a recidivist rampage. Some highlanders rediscovered their taste for human flesh. As recently as the 1900s, the tribes had cannibalised the bodies of defeated warriors and invaders. The grisly practice of consuming 'living meat' — keeping prisoners alive to preserve their flesh — is well-documented: 'The well-fleshed,' so an older Papuan told Benson, 'used to be tied by their hands to a tree; then, as meat was needed, slices would be cut from their legs and buttocks ... So for days the poor tortured bodies would hang, mercifully fainting from time to time.'[10]

'Plantation houses were looted and burned by roving bands,' reported the war correspondent Osmar White. 'Even the nails were wrenched from the timbers and thrust triumphantly for adornment into the ear lobes and distended septa of the raiders. Lonely prospectors, several of them Chinese, were speared or shot to death with arrows. Their heads were taken to the main houses and their entrails ceremonially eaten.'[11]

The spore of chaos landed on the Papuan coastline. Terror of the Japanese drove communities into the jungle. Order broke down and loyalties — to the Australian or Japanese army — divided native communities. Tribal informers were punished, on both sides, with summary execution.

This coastal region was 'the area of greatest violence in the history of the Australian pacification of Papua'.[12] Warfare was the default method of

---

* Kanga Force might be considered an early Australian example of the umbilically severed commando units pioneered by the British military genius, Orde Wingate; a later, less effective example, in the Owen Stanleys, was Chaforce.

settling disputes on the grey sands of the Huon Gulf and along the banks of the Kumusi River in the nineteenth and early twentieth centuries. The Orokaivan people needed little provocation to come to blows with outsiders in the early 1900s. Then the intruders were neither barge-loads of Japanese troops nor Australian Government-backed goldminers and mercenaries — nor indeed Anglo-Saxons bearing crosses — but Melanesian explorers landing from long canoes. Those clashes were alive in the oral history of the Orokaivan tribes in 1942, and the memory rekindled the bloody history of the coastal communities.

Who were the Japanese invaders, and what were their intentions? It is worth nailing a few myths. In July the Japanese did not intend to invade Australia. Premier Tojo Hideki, the Japanese leader, had contemplated and, on 15 March 1942, rejected a land invasion of the great southern land. But the idea was discussed, and entertained, by soldiers who dreamed of celebrating New Year in Sydney.

Asked after the war if Japan had intended to occupy Australia, Tojo replied: 'We never had enough troops to do so ... We did not have the armed strength or the supply facilities to mount such a terrific extension of our already overstrained and too thinly spread forces. We expected to occupy all New Guinea, to maintain Rabaul as a holding base, and to raid Northern Australia by air. But actual physical invasion — no, at no time.'[13]

The Imperial Army's plan was to isolate and neutralise Australia as an American base for offensive action. This meant commanding the air space and waters around Australia; and the best place from which to achieve this was Port Moresby. Its capture became a vital piece in the jigsaw of the Imperial Army's strategy.

So on 11 June, darkly brooding after the lost Battle of the Coral Sea, Imperial General Headquarters in Tokyo considered a different line of attack. The commander of the Japanese 17th Army in Rabaul, Lieutenant-General Hyakutake Harukichi, was ordered to examine the viability of an overland invasion of Port Moresby.

Hyakutake proceeded without bothering with a reconnaissance of this bitterly obstinate country.[14] He chose Major-General Horii Tomitaro, a commander of unusual stubbornness and unflinching obedience, to lead the elite invasion force, named the Nankai Shitai, or South Seas Detachment.

The forces that bombed Benson's Gona Mission were Horii's advance troops, led by Colonel Yokoyama Yosuke, who personally instructed his men three days before their departure, to 'occupy a strategic line south of Kokoda ... Push on day and night to the line of the said mountain range ... Have the infantry battalion reconnoitre the route to Moresby ... as quickly as possible ...'[15]

Imanishi was listening. Within moments of running up the Gona beach, the sergeant remembers carrying his bicycle along the muddy track toward Kokoda. The Japanese clocks left no room for error.

Yokoyama's troops were an amalgam of elites. The core infantry were drawn from the Tsukamoto Battalion, part of the 144th Infantry Regiment, raised in Shikoku. In addition there were mountain and anti-aircraft artillery units, Yokoyama's own 15th Independent Engineers Regiment (engineers in the Japanese army doubled as combat infantry), and a company of shock troops, the Sasebo 5 Special Naval Landing Party. In total there were nearly 2000 men most of whom, like Imanishi, were veterans of the invasions of Shanghai and Rabaul. In addition, there were 100 Formosan (Taiwanese) troops, 52 horses, and some 400 Rabaul natives, press-ganged into service as carriers.

They sailed from Rabaul on 19 July over rough seas that made pre-invasion deck exercises difficult. As the convoy entered coastal waters, Yokoyama addressed his men with a cheerless premonition of doom: 'From today, we are entering an area subject to air attack. Hereafter ... any attack will be the real thing. Those who are slow will be regarded as cowards. If sunk, remain calm until the water touches the feet ... Those who hurriedly jump will drown. When in the water ... platoons should gather together to sing military songs. All must be calm, even when awaiting rescue, for perhaps two days and nights.'[16] Singing in a catastrophe was a common Japanese trait: civilians would sing encouraging songs to each other during the Tokyo fire bombing; the crews of bombed ships — for example, the *Zuikaku* at Leyte — stood to attention and bellowed traditional naval songs as their boats sank.[17] It seemed the karaoke spirit came alive in the most inauspicious circumstances.

The troops were spared that ordeal on this occasion and Yokoyama's force landed safely off Basabua on that cloudy afternoon, 21 July. The convoy comprised two cruisers, two destroyers, and two transport ships (the *Ryoyo Maru* and *Ayatozan Maru*). They were fully disembarked by 6.00 a.m. on 22 July. The infantry were dispatched inland the moment they set foot on Gona's dark sands. Tsukamoto Hatsuo, a grouchy middle-aged Lieutenant-Colonel with a great fondness for *sake*, led the advance toward Kokoda. Back on the beaches, anti-aircraft guns were installed at intervals along the coast; the unit HQs were built, and a system of fortified bunkers was begun. The engineers worked round the clock, readying the beachhead for the arrival of the full invasion unit, the 10,000-strong Nankai Shitai, which was to leave Rabaul in mid-August.

Speed was the catchcry, drummed into the men at every moment. Colonel Yokoyama had told his officers: 'Have the infantry ... reconnoitre the route to Moresby in the occupied forward zone as quickly as possible. Reports of its value must be made, as well as reports on how quickly construction of roads for packhorses, light and heavy traffic ... can be carried out. Report also on whether or not the main force of the detachment could capture Moresby by overland route. Guard particularly against "defeat by detail" by the enemy.'[18]

The advance troops were phenomenally energetic. While Tsukamoto's 900 infantrymen swept inland towards Kokoda,[19] the transport battalions mowed down the jungle with crushing thoroughness. Consider the astonishing progress of the Sakigawa Transport Unit: by 24 July, two days after landing, these indefatigable troops had cleared six miles of rough track between Buna and Soputa. They worked by the light of the moon, through pouring rain, laying palm logs over mud. A Japanese soldier said of his unit's superhuman effort: 'Our duty to reach the front line would not let us rest for one moment.' That day, 'black clouds, hiding the moon',[20] deposited torrential rain on the road-builders, but the Japanese engineers continued working through the night. The next day they reached their destination, a mile south of Soputa, where they built a heavily camouflaged vehicle base, and trucked in a radio station from Buna.

Mud and rain stalled the motorised units, whose vehicles got hopelessly bogged in the log road. 'All personnel covered with mud and sweat and needing sleep, bravely carried on,' wrote one soldier. 'Since the night before landing we have not slept. The difficulties of the roads and their repair are beyond description. All officers and men realised their duty and proudly carried on.'[21]

As the terrain worsened, the vehicles were discarded, and the men were turned into packhorses. The troops, like Imanishi, shouldered heavy bags of rice, in addition to their usual kit, over miles of difficult country.[22] 'I am completely exhausted,' wrote Private Watanabe Toshio, of the Tsukamoto Battalion, 'because I walked 40 ri [about five miles] with 1 TO 9 SHO [7.54 gallons] of rice and miso on my back.'[23]

Chapter 3
Intelligence

'GHQ consistently belittled suggestions that this [Japanese] force could make any attack on Port Moresby and correspondents were encouraged to talk glibly about the "impassable barrier of the Owen Stanley Range"'

— *Chester Wilmot, Australian war correspondent in New Guinea*

Why did the Allied army fail to resist the Japanese landing on the Australian-mandated territory of Papua? It wasn't for lack of knowledge. Allied High Command had been aware of Japan's intentions for four months. They owed this intelligence to Ultra, the name for the Allied code-breaking system that had successfully cracked Japanese and German wireless codes.

The code-breakers were among the most brilliant cryptographers, mathematicians, linguists and computer experts in Britain, America and Australia.[1] They worked day and night, deciphering signals using IBM punch card computers and the 'Purple' decoder, a mirror image of Japan's secret diplomatic keyboard. General MacArthur treated this intelligence with the greatest respect; it usually formed the core of his strategic thinking.

As early as April 1942, a team of code-breakers working in a block of Art Deco flats in Melbourne had confirmed fears of a Japanese plan to capture Port Moresby — from the sea. Lieutenant Rudi Fabian's Fleet Radio

Unit Melbourne (FRUMEL) — one of two code-breaking units — managed to break the Japanese naval codes that warned of a seaborne attack on Port Moresby. FRUMEL sent the brief intelligence: 'Suggest an early enemy offensive against Port Moresby before the end of April.'[2]

Not only did FRUMEL confirm this suggestion, on 4 May they calculated the precise route of the sea invasion. Immediately the American fleet steamed to the Coral Sea, and the first battle of aircraft carriers was joined. The Japanese were forced back, but not without the loss of one US carrier and a destroyer. The Battle of the Coral Sea was a qualified victory; FRUMEL even intercepted the Japanese wire that signalled defeat: 'Moresby Occupation Force is to proceed [back] to Rabaul.'[3]

Allied intelligence had broken the Japanese navy's codes; but what of the Japanese army? Could the code-breakers crack its strategy, too? A separate Allied decoding unit was established to decipher the army signals. These proved elusive; each word or phrase was embedded under a double layer of numeric codes. 'The result was an apparently meaningless set of unconnected numbers.'[4]

Persistence yielded results. The Allies' Combined Operational Intelligence Centre warned on 25 April of 'an offensive move against the eastern New Guinea area before the end of the month ... the major [Japanese] objective is to control the New Guinea–Torres Strait area involving the occupation of Port Moresby.'[5] This didn't mention an attack over the mountains, but the code-breakers were getting very warm. Then, on 19 May, they revealed the contents of a signal that said the Japanese army planned to invade Port Moresby via a mountain route from the north coast. One wireless section built up a detailed picture of the Japanese troops 'attempting to cross the Owen Stanley Range'.[6]

In short, the cryptographers served up Japanese intentions to MacArthur on a platter. ★

....

★ It wasn't until January 1944 that the Australians conclusively broke the Japanese army codes, with the discovery in Cape Huon, in a bomb crater full of water, of a metal box full of Japanese code manuals, says the military historian Lex McAulay. 'The Japanese had fled into the mountains, and the code man had received a message to destroy all code books. He said he'd done it.' When they dried out the books, the Australians realised their significance, and sent copies to London, Washington and Brisbane. 'Macarthur just couldn't ask for anything better,' said McAulay. It changed the course of the war: the Allies were henceforth able to pre-empt every Japanese intention. Indeed, the invasion of the Philippines was brought forward because of the new capability to read Japanese wires.

Even Australia's conventional intelligence led High Command to conclude accurately, as early as 5 March, that Japan's main object was to cut the air and shipping lines of communication between the United States and Australia.

Whoever controlled Port Moresby controlled Australia's development as a base for offensive operations against Japan, so it would be natural for the Japanese 'to attempt to eliminate Port Moresby or at least to neutralise it as early as possible', said Allied GHQ.[7] Their 'best forecast'[8] was that Japan would attack Darwin again in early April; Port Moresby in the middle of March; and the east coast of Australia in May. They erred only in predicting Port Moresby's invasion three months too early.

Even if these warnings went unheeded, less scientific intelligence was shouting to be heard. Australia's coastwatchers, a unit of extraordinarily brave men who constantly scrutinised the Papuan coast and Rabaul for signs of enemy activity, alerted Allied commanders to repeated sightings of Japanese ships in the Solomon Sea.[9] 'The Jap had beaten us to the punch,' noted Eric Feldt, the coastwatchers' commander, when Yokoyama landed.[10]

There were strong anecdotal warnings as well. Rabaul natives who deserted the Japanese after landing in Papua described the magnitude of loads they were expected to carry inland.

Why then did the Allies not respond to the overwhelming evidence of a Japanese attack? The answer is simple: MacArthur refused to believe that the Japanese would commit large forces to an overland invasion of Port Moresby. It was sheer folly, military madness. The Owen Stanleys — the central mountain range — formed an inviolable natural shield, he believed. MacArthur gainsaid his own intelligence sources. When Yokoyama's men did in fact disembark, MacArthur dismissed them as a minor threat, 'so deep-rooted was the belief in the effectiveness of the mountains as a barrier against invasion'.[11]

There was a related reason: MacArthur's head of intelligence, Brigadier-General Charles Willoughby, persuaded his boss that the Japanese couldn't possibly advance over the Owen Stanleys. The ill-advised Willoughby was still banging on about the impossibility of an overland attack — 'in view of logistics, poor communications and difficult terrain'[12] — as late as 12 August, days before the 10,000-strong Nankai Shitai landed at Buna.

Willoughby was neither a respected nor highly intelligent man, of whom MacArthur witheringly said, 'there are three great intelligence officers in history and Willoughby is not one of them'.[13] Nonetheless, Willoughby stayed by his boss's side throughout the war, and exerted an influence on events that, with hindsight, seems remarkably disproportionate to the respect afforded his opinions at the time.

'Willoughby got the intelligence wrong,' concluded one military expert. 'The Japs were landing large numbers of troops on the north coast. And Willoughby said they're not coming far; they're just coming a little way inland to build airfields.'[14]

There were no accurate maps of the area; people would land at Port Moresby with outdated Shell road maps. The press were tamed. War correspondents were told a tiny force of 2500 or less had landed and posed no threat. 'GHQ consistently belittled suggestions,' wrote the reporter Chester Wilmot, in one of his blistering critiques, 'that this force could make any attack on Port Moresby and correspondents were encouraged to talk glibly about the "impassable barrier of the Owen Stanley Range".'[15]

In any case, MacArthur's mind dwelled on loftier stratagems than the Papuan sideline: chiefly his great northern offensive, the immediate goal of which was the recapture of the Philippines to whose people he had famously promised — after being forced to flee the archipelago — 'I shall return.'

He had one niggling concern, however: the little government station of Kokoda. No mountains stood in the way of the Japanese taking Kokoda, a strategically vital airfield situated on the northern foothills of the Owen Stanleys, a few days' march from the sea. Certainly, the Allies couldn't risk the loss of it; and in June this fear prompted MacArthur to wire Major-General Basil Morris in Port Moresby for details of his strategy to protect the vital Kokoda area.

Morris, the commander of Allied forces in New Guinea, didn't have one. He answered that the Papuan Infantry Brigade was patrolling the area (actually many of the PIB had already deserted). His reply was the kind of lame assessment GHQ had come to expect from Morris who 'readily admitted he had no pretensions to being a tactician'.[16] But perhaps Morris, a fundamentally decent man, did not deserve one general's description of him as 'a very good scout — no brains but ... stout-hearted'.[17]

At least Morris had his finger on the pulse of the problem (even if it was partly a problem of his own making). His troops were hardly trained at all and did not look forward with confidence to facing the enemy. It was something of an own goal, since Morris was ultimately responsible for training the odd assortment of misfits, drunks, rabble-rousers and looters who then made up Australia's only defence against invasion.

Chapter 4
Chocos

'These blokes came around and said they wanted to make a battalion up to guard the tropics. They said "you can take your tennis racquets and cameras and all sorts of things". So all six of us in my tent said, "Oh yeah, we'll go."'
— *Private Laurie Howson, 39th Battalion*

Laurie 'Smoky' Howson joined the 39th Battalion at the age of nineteen. A tall, skinny, amiable bloke, Smoky belonged to that rowdy, iconoclastic breed of Australian men who scythed their way through tall poppies over last rounds in the local. He was raised in difficult circumstances, in Oakleigh, Melbourne, one of nineteen children: 'Yes, twelve boys and seven girls, and the rest are better looking than me!'[1]

The family expanded at a terrific pace, and soon found itself in a state of extreme poverty. During the fag end of the Great Depression, Smoky worked 60 hours a week on his father's small garden allotment, the family's chief source of food. He was fourteen. 'We ate a lot of vegetables,' he recalls. 'We were so poorly educated that we believed babies came from under cabbages.'[2]

He enlisted to escape this crushing existence and break the hold of a dominating, dipsomaniac father. In 1940, aged eighteen, Smoky ran away to sea. But the navy rejected him because, he claims, 'I was too old.' They advised him to join the army.

Smoky took their advice, and volunteered. He joined the Australian militia, a kind of national home guard. He had no idea how he would be used; he knew as a militiaman he could not be sent outside Australian territory. One morning, 'These blokes came around and said they wanted to make a battalion up to guard the tropics. They said "you can take your tennis racquets and cameras and all sorts of things". So all six of us in my tent said, "Oh yeah, we'll go", which was stupid. It was all propaganda.'[3]

Howson was one of 4000 militiamen who departed Sydney's Woolloomooloo docks aboard the *Aquitania*, a converted troopship, in December 1941. Like Smoky, none had combat experience, or any proper training. Few had fired a gun in anger; most had never fired a gun. Some thought they were bound for Brisbane or Townsville, or surely Darwin, whose harbour Japanese Zeros would destroy in February. A few did bring their tennis racquets, anticipating a spot of R&R in Australia's northern climes.

As 'militia', the law limited them to the defence of Australian soil. That did not exclude the territories of Papua and New Guinea, which were then part of Australia. At sea, the troops learned their destination, a nearby country of which they knew little. The *Aquitania* crossed the Coral Sea untroubled by Japanese submarines and on 3 January 1942 moored in Basilisk Bay, Port Moresby.

Osmar White witnessed their arrival: 'issued with weapons they hardly knew how to fire, 2000 of them poured from the decks of a single transport onto Moresby's solitary T-jetty. They were charged with the defence of a base vitally important to the fate of their homeland.'[4] In truth, they were little more than a token force, a tremulous gesture towards the defence of Port Moresby from an anticipated seaborne invasion.

The first of many supply disasters struck at once. Tents, medical equipment and extra clothing, mistakenly or indifferently stored at the bottom of the ship's hold, would not be unpacked for ten days. Smoky and his mates — the Zorro Gang — slept in the open bush, on the Seven-Mile aerodrome, or near the wharf. They ate with their fingers and they stank. They had no mess tins, plates, pannikins or mosquito nets.[5] Some lacked waterproof groundsheets, in a place where torrential rain was a near daily occurrence, even in the 'dry' season. Such conditions had a grave effect on morale 'and contributed in no small measure to the disorderly and undisciplined conduct'.[6]

It was as though they were expected to fail, and the disdain in which the Australian authorities held them seemed to hasten the inevitable. The militia was 'grossly undervalued', observed Sir Paul Hasluck.[7] The Australian Quartermaster's store did not concern itself with jungle camouflage and tropical hygiene: the troops were issued with khaki shorts easily visible in the jungle (no jungle greens or green dye were then available). Mosquito nets were scarce; quinine was unavailable for the initial weeks; and malaria tablets were reduced to mush by the damp conditions.

'We camped in the middle of a paddock,' said Smoky, 'out in the scrub, with no mosquito nets, no tucker, nothing. The tucker when it did come was dumped in a heap, in the hot sun.'[8] Two hundred men drew washing and drinking water from a single ¾ inch pipe. Within five weeks, a third had succumbed to disease.[9] Clouds of mosquitoes tormented them day and night: 'Their faces and arms and legs became grotesquely swollen and infected . . .'[10] Within a month, dengue, malaria, dysentery and tropical ulcers had reduced their effective strength by 25 per cent.

Where were Australia's main forces? Two years earlier the nation's most experienced soldiers, the Second Australian Imperial Force (AIF), had been sent to fight the Germans and their allies in Africa, Greece and the Middle East. In their country's darkest hour, 60,000 of Australia's best troops were abroad. Men who did not enlist for overseas service were eligible for, or conscripted into, the citizen militia. This 'two-army' structure was deeply divisive, organisationally unsound and poorly administered: 'the greatest mistake of the Australian war effort', concluded military historian David Horner.[11]

The militia were almost sent abroad too — such was the clamour for men in the European war, and the public enthusiasm for the mother country. On 2 May 1942 the House of Representatives, after a heated seven-hour debate, rejected by just four votes a conservative motion that the Government should have the power to send the militia overseas.

The press, too, supported the dispatch of the militia to the Middle East. It was 'an intolerable anomaly' that these men should stay in Australia, declared the *Sydney Morning Herald*: 'We could not honourably ask others [the Americans and British] to help us in our extremity, and then withhold any part of our strength which might contribute to victory.'[12]

The *Daily Telegraph* curiously seemed to think sending the militia overseas was the best way of saving Australia: 'Are we fools? A populous, powerful enemy is about to invade our country. Yet we refuse to change one word of a law which prevents our own soldiers from hitting the enemy outside our own soil ... Instead of saying, "We will kill the German, the Jap or the Wop wherever we can find him", our own politicians insist on a law to restrain the greatest part of our army from killing its enemies anywhere except in our own backyard ...'[13]

Curtin rubbished these and the Opposition's arguments with the simple observation that the line of true defence of Australia should not be established a long distance from Australia. Curtin saw, as few did, that the defence of the nation depended on bringing home the troops and uniting them.

Of the many damaging consequences of a divided army, the worst — at troop level — was the impact on morale. The Australian Imperial Force ridiculed the militia. This went beyond mere cajolery. The militiamen were branded 'chocos' — chocolate soldiers, who would melt in battle — or 'koalas', because in the 1930s you couldn't shoot the cuddly, endangered marsupial.

True, many militiamen laughed this off in the Australian way. But the stigma stayed, and the insults stung. The militia were derided as cowards and somehow unAustralian for refusing to volunteer to fight for the mother country. The chocos, it was felt, were sub-standard, poorly trained, without the stomach for combat.

Tom Keneally, the Australian novelist, remembers growing up in Kempsey in New South Wales, when the militia were camped at the town's showground. 'My father and my older cousin — who were volunteers in the army — used to get me to go out on the verandah as these militia blokes passed by, and yell "choco".' Keneally was a little boy at the time and, later, when the facts of Papua emerged, his father said he was ashamed of having 'wound me up to do it'.[14]

Many civilians derided the militia in Australia — notably the World War I veterans who were too old, and pugnacious boys who were too young, to fight. Women, too, were disdainful of these apparently half-formed troops. Chocos like Smoky Howson were acutely conscious of their second-rate status, painfully revealed in the ballad 'The Unwrapped Chocolate Soldier':

> You saw him in the town, a'strolling down the street
> You saw him in his uniform that always looked so neat,
> You heard him in the dance hall, with your hand upon his shoulder,
> Cursing fate and his bad luck; 'The Unwrapped Chocolate Soldier'.
>
> You labelled him a choco because he did not fight;
> You thought he didn't have the guts to stick up for the right;
> You heard him in the bar, and if you felt a little bolder,
> You didn't hesitate to say, 'another chocolate soldier'.

Yet these were the only men available to defend the country against the Japanese. Australia's national security relied on a motley crew of untrained reservists, volunteers and boyish conscripts, in whom the nation's military leaders had little, if any, confidence. Indeed, the most vicious condemnation came from the military itself. The generals who consigned the bewildered young men of the militia brigades to the New Guinean jungle openly belittled them. They were treated with a sort of arm's-length embarrassment all the way to the top. Generals MacArthur and Blamey, who never set foot on the Kokoda Track, were dismayed by the quality of the militia. Not once did they observe the peculiarly awful conditions into which they were soon to send these scorned young men to die — and not until the final phase of fighting did Blamey acknowledge the militia's courage. By then the survivors were too disgusted with the Australian army to care.

A gallows humour grew among the militia ranks in those early months in Port Moresby. In January 1942 their self-confidence, never strong, hit rock bottom.

'The Mice of Moresby', as the 49th Militia Battalion were called — a play on the name, if not the military example, of the famous Rats of Tobruk★ — dreamt up mad plans for escape in the event of a Japanese invasion. They half-jokingly envisaged a flight of 400 miles west to Daru — the Daru Derby — across the impassable swamps of the Fly River Delta. The evacuation plan reflected the mood of despair, as did their sad self-image in the poem:

> *Rats of old 'Tobruk'*
> *Or merely 'Moresby Mice',*
> *We've had our fill of fighting*
> *And of hardships — once or twice . . .'*[15]

Few had seen any fighting when this was written. Nonetheless, Major-General Basil Morris, commander of New Guinea Force in Port Moresby, was prepared to give his troops the opportunity to show their mettle. In February, in case of seaborne invasion, he assembled his dubious officers and issued their orders: 'No position is to be given up without permission . . . even the smallest units must make provision for counter attack . . . We have the honour of being the front line defence of Australia. Let us show ourselves worthy of that honour.'[16]

It was a generous display of confidence in their fighting condition. But a cursory glance at the Australian militia suggested Morris's confidence was wildly misplaced. The troops were better equipped to serve the nation as wharfies than jungle fighters. Most had spent their time unloading ammunition and food from vessels moored at Port Moresby's jetty and digging holes around the aerodrome, both of which soon became daily targets for Japanese Zeros.

There was one full-strength militia brigade, the 30th, in Port Moresby in January 1942, containing three battalions each of about a thousand men, none of whom had combat experience.★★ The battalions were the 39th, the 53rd and the 49th. We need not inquire into the historic meaning of these apparently arbitrary numbers. Suffice to say, they emerged from an earlier

---

★ The name was given to the early garrison troops of Port Moresby by the Japanese entertainer Tokyo Rose, in her radio propaganda (see *Reveille*, 7 December 1979).

★★ Part of the 14th Militia Brigade were sent to Port Moresby later in 1942.

reordering of men and machines. Numbers festoon military organisations, and behind every number is a mob of anxious, impatient, bored and apprehensive troops.

The militia tended to come from inner city, working-class backgrounds in Melbourne and Sydney, during a time of extreme economic hardship. 'We weren't over-educated because from the age of fourteen we had to leave school and go out and work,'[17] said Don Daniels, a veteran of Kokoda and retired interior designer from Melbourne. He volunteered at the age of seventeen — 'I put my age up a year.' So did George Cops, who similarly left school at fourteen. Both volunteered for the 39th.

While most militiamen volunteered, a large minority were conscripts. Conscription for the militia came into force in 1941, in call-up waves of about 9000. (The Second AIF was an army of volunteers, like its Anzac predecessor.) His conscription papers gave the recruit five days' notice before departure to army camp: 'You will report to Drill Hall, Area X ... prepared to proceed to a Camp of Continuous Training ... PLEASE SHOW THIS NOTICE TO YOUR EMPLOYER IMMEDIATELY.'[18]

On entering camp, the men received a uniform and a free issue of singlets, underpants, socks and a towel. They were advised to bring toiletries and kitchen utensils, and sufficient food for two meals. Most received perfunctory lessons in parade ground etiquette and how to salute, and were bussed to the docks for shipment to Port Moresby.

Their average age was not eighteen, as many claim. It is impossible for any unit to have an average age of eighteen because the delay between call-up and action is usually a year, as Hank Nelson patiently explains.[19] Only three of those killed in the 39th Battalion were under twenty. Their average age was closer to 23 or 24 — and not only due to the skewing effect of a few fiftyish AIF officers too old to serve in the Middle East. There were quite a few 30-somethings. Indeed, a spin-minded statistician could easily construe some militia units as a Dads' Army as much as a boys' brigade. Some lied about their age. In the 39th Battalion, a handful were sixteen, and there was one fifteen-year-old, Arthur Bury, born 2 January 1927.*

---

* On 19 October, New Guinea Force decreed that no one under nineteen could be sent into combat: 'No member of any combatant unit under the age of nineteen years shall be permitted in the forward areas. When any such Unit is ordered into a forward area, all such men shall be withdrawn and will remain with rear details ...' (Blamey Papers).

'There were quite a number who really shouldn't have been there,' said Daniels. 'They were just very slow — not retarded — but slow. They should have been a cook's off-sider. They should never have been at the front line.'[20]

The men enlisted for a variety of reasons. Many simply yearned for adventure. The allure of war as an antidote to boredom is gravely underestimated. A few were of the 'biff the Jap' school of patriotism; the notion of 'King and country' persuaded others. The King's shilling was a more tangible incentive to the sons of the Depression. Some wanted a chance to prove themselves to hard-bitten fathers, veterans of the Great War, or to escape the family's poverty.

Don Daniels and George Cops were both 'Depression kids' who, like Howson, enlisted because anything seemed better than the drabness of the 1930s. Signing up 'was glamorous', recalled Daniels. 'And of course, they were calling out on the radio and in the streets, "Join Up! Join Up!"'[21]

A powerful motive was mateship — it was a time when the term meant something and had not been politically bowdlerised. Mates of the Australian stamp, circa 1942, got drunk together, chased girls together and ruined their lives together. It was a stamp of honour to stand by your mate through the worst excesses of peacetime. They enlisted together, too — and only in war did the term come to mean dying for your best friend. Smoky Howson's Zorro Gang were six drinking mates who volunteered for the 39th. Gangs like Smoky's were the binding that held the Australian army together.

Despite their inauspicious start, the 39th Battalion forged an unusually strong sense of camaraderie. They identified as a unit. This transcended their civilian friendships, and took the shape of an emerging *esprit de corps*. 'The bond formed very quickly,' said Daniels. 'The ones I joined with in my hut I still see today [i.e. 2003]. And it's still the same today as it was then. A very very close association.'[22]

There is no single reason why this should have happened to the 39th; no doubt the devotion and respect they owed to their brilliant leaders in battle would have a powerful influence. But that came later. From the earliest moment a mysterious bond seemed to form between these men. It was partly patriotic. They shared an impression of themselves as the first troops to defend Australia on Australian soil — a delicate flower of an idea for men unaccustomed to seeing themselves as heroes or saviours. If they thought about it at all, their self-identity was founded on negative role models and influences: they were chocos, the ne'er-do-well sons of remote fathers, the products of harsh experience, poverty and military indifference.

They spent eight months unloading ships, rolling drums onto the aerodrome and doing very little that might prepare them for combat. 'We had no training whatsoever — no shooting, nothing,' said Daniels. They had a couple of goes at throwing grenades — 'but most had forgotten how to pull the pin out'.[23]

Some of the 39th troops were 'cast offs' from other Victorian units; the battalion was a disorganised mob when they first formed up. A leavening of excellent AIF officers with combat experience in the Middle East perceived the unit's gathering self-confidence, and built on it. One such officer was Lieutenant-Colonel Ralph Honner, who commanded the 39th along the Kokoda Track and at Gona. Honner was an unusual example of superb leadership under whose inspiration the men of the 39th would discover something else within their ranks: a stoic quality, a rare self-overcoming, and, in time, a burning sense of their place in history as the first battalion to resist the Japanese on Australian soil.

The 53rd Battalion was not destined to share the glory of the 39th. The story of this unfortunate unit is one of the sadder episodes of Australian military history, and rarely told in the gung-ho accounts of the Kokoda campaign. They were similar men, with similar backgrounds, as those in the 39th. And many were as brave and as committed. But incompetent leadership and a splinter group of malcontents fatally compromised them.

The battalion's hopes were poisoned from the start: in November 1941, eighteen existing militia battalions were ordered to supply a quota of men for 'a new unit' designated for a special task. Again, this was seen as an opportunity to cast off dregs and misfits. The result was a unit with a reputation for hard drinking, rebelliousness and chronic ill discipline — unfairly, in many cases, the label stuck. When their December 1941 embarkation date arrived, 'many ... were illegally absent, bitter because they had been given no Christmas leave'.[24]

To make up for the AWOL losses of the 53rd, a mob of vagrants and drifters was shanghaied off the streets of Sydney and virtually frog-marched to Woolloomooloo wharves for immediate departure. Many were refused leave to farewell their loved ones. Roy Wootten, padre of the 53rd, was obliged to write letters to their mothers to explain where they were, he said. Married men were excused; that was the only concession to civil society. It was a method of conscription the Elizabethan press gangs would have envied. 'The whole incident,' observed Lex McAulay, was 'what members of the western democracies believe is normal in totalitarian regimes, not in our own armed forces.'[25]

If Curtin's Labor Government spotted the irony, they didn't act to prevent this injustice. At Garden Island wharves in Sydney, amid scenes of hysteria and anger, hessian walls were reportedly slung up to seal off the tearful eyes of families from the doomed, departing troops.[26]

'These poor devils had no idea what was happening to them,' observed a sergeant as the men of the 53rd came aboard the *Aquitania*. 'They had received no final leave, were given no chance to let their families know what was happening to them . . . Most of them had never seen or handled a rifle.'[27] They were crowded into F deck or G deck, in the ship's boiling hold. Wootten recalls that no-one knew where they were heading. Even then, volunteers such as Daniels and Cops felt sorry for the conscripts of the 53rd: 'They were shanghaied. The poor lads didn't have a chance to say goodbye to their families. They didn't know what was going on,' said Daniels.

They were, in fact, lambs to the slaughter; and though they were unaware of how they would be used, many of the 53rd Battalion nursed a deep grudge against the Australian authorities. Unchecked by the morale-building influence of good leadership, this festered in their minds, and would soon find tragic expression along the Kokoda Track.

Chapter 5
Port Moresby

'I suppose the Japs will try to capture Port Moresby, because
it would give them a marvellous striking base for air blows
against the Australian mainland. If it becomes necessary,
we must be prepared to make Port Moresby the Tobruk of
the Pacific'
— *Major-General Basil Morris, commander of Allied forces in Papua
and New Guinea after the fall of Singapore*

A mood of lazy sullenness prevailed in Port Moresby in early 1942. If this
was the 'last chance saloon' there was little to be cheerful about.
Entertainment amounted to the occasional cinefilm and a drinking binge.
There were no mixed bars, no brothels on the European model, none of the
traditional forms of R&R to relieve the troops. Apathy reigned.

One militia battalion, the 49th, was in Port Moresby when the
Aquitania dropped anchor; this unit had garrisoned the town for twelve
months. They inspired less confidence than the arriving ranks, if that were
possible: the bored troops lolled about, drinking and sleeping in a state of
bemused inertia. Disease — mostly malaria and dysentery — had spread
through the battalion, and 'tropical breakdown' was alarmingly frequent. As

late as 11 July, ten days before Yokoyama landed at Gona, the Chief of the General Staff, Lieutenant-General Vernon Sturdee, described the 49th as 'quite the worst battalion in Australia'.[1]

The new arrivals swiftly sank to the level set by the 49th. They received no jungle training and were 'in the charge of inexperienced officers who appeared to have little or no control over them'.[2] Brawling and looting were commonplace. In one instance, drunken troops ransacked one of Port Moresby's two pubs, for which a senior officer of the 39th was 'reposted'.

The first Japanese air raid on Port Moresby, at 3.00 a.m. on 3 February 1942, stunned the troops and terrified the native population. A 'wholesale exodus' ensued,[3] as the locals 'went bush'. Native police fled with their prisoners; desertions temporarily immobilised seaborne communications. 'By today no native servants will be left,' wrote Group Captain William Garing. It seemed to him that Port Moresby would be abandoned, in the same way as Rabaul.

The remaining civilians — the women had been evacuated in December — panicked: 'They thought the end of Port Moresby had come. The general feeling was that Port Moresby was going,' the troops observed.[4]

Three hours after severe air raids on the 5th, the looting of Port Moresby began in earnest. The militia simply stole whatever they felt they needed. It degenerated into wholesale theft. After the last civilians evacuated the town on the 18th, 'savage looting' became an 'open go'.[5] The troops thought they might as well salvage the spoils of defeat before the Japanese arrived. The battalion history of the 49th defends this behaviour: 'The troops took the view that these things were going to be destroyed anyhow — no civilians were left — so they took furniture, goods, refrigerators ...'[6] The army led the charge, with the navy and air force mopping up. The native people did little stealing, but quite happily indulged in some 'receiving'.

Threats of punishment had no effect whatsoever. The military police were too feeble to restrain them; the indigenous constabulary had gone bush; and the militia's own guard were utterly powerless. Indeed, some indulged in the orgy of snatch and grab.[7] Hundreds of items were sent home to Australia: 500 packages arrived by post from soldiers at Port Moresby and about 350 from members of the air force, according to the Brisbane police commissioner. They contained rolls of cloth, table and bed linen, apparel, glassware, and many other articles.★

General Morris was ordered to conduct an inquiry.[8] His findings revealed why so many troops were used for manual labour: after the air raids, they were the only labour available to fortify the town. Most of the civilians and natives had evacuated Port Moresby in terror. Between January and June 1942, a thousand troops a day were engaged in unloading ships or working on the roads.

The Australian militiaman may have acquired his first fridge, but he was 'inadequately equipped in every way' for combat.[9] The weapons were ancient, World War I issue .303 rifles and clapped-out Lewis machine-guns. The troops would not be shown how to use their Bren guns until days before they went into battle. They received no jungle training. The training they did get was half-hearted. Few could fire their rifles properly; some men were not even shown how to clean and dismantle their weapons. None had any experience of anti-aircraft fire, except aboard the *Aquitania*, where they 'shot down' box kites meant to symbolise low-flying Zeros. Bill Guest, a 39th veteran, recalled that '. . . the kites were hauled in and there were found to be a total of three holes in them . . . as usual, many of our antiquated guns did not function due to stoppages'.[10]

There was a blimpish charm to lessons in the use of the new 'Tommy guns', the hip-fired Thompson submachine-gun beloved of Chicago gangsters. Some units first laid eyes on the weapon in Port Moresby in February 1942. During a lecture, Captain Bill Merritt explained the correct firing pose: 'You take an aggressive stance, an expression of pugnacity and determination on your face . . .' To which a private inquired, 'Are we supposed to frighten [them] to death, Sir?'[11]

★ Looting was not restricted to Port Moresby: there was extensive looting at Darwin. Ships would often sail away packed with contraband. One man, Ingraham, a ship's steward, was found to have in his possession: 'An electric refrigerator, a sewing machine, a typewriter, one set of snooker balls, six golf sticks [sic], 26 lady's hats, four lady's handbags, three lady's stoles, four Chinese cummerbunds, seven lady's umbrellas, 18 dozen lady's hairnets, 360 pearl buttons, 31 pairs of child's bloomers, 28 lady's frocks, 49 pairs of lady's bloomers, 24 lady's belts . . .' (*Inquiries into Looting at Darwin and Port Moresby*, CBS A5954 256/3).

From mid-February Japanese air raids on Port Moresby were a near daily occurrence. The Zeros, Mitsubishi 97s, flew over the mountains from the north like tiny 'silver butterflies'; they made 'a noise like millions of bees'.[12] The Australians responded with unprotected ground artillery. After an attack they would rush out, shake their fists and jeer at the Japanese pilots. But the pathos of their condition troubled them. 'Where the *hell* are our planes?' was a constant refrain. Allied fighters were then unavailable. As late as December 1941 Australia's home air defences amounted to two squadrons, each with two Empire flying boats and six or seven Catalinas and little else.

Dreadful mistakes were made in this dazed environment. When, on 20 March, four strange fighters zoomed across the Seven-Mile drome the troops ran out, waving their mess tins ... and were promptly strafed. 'In our eagerness to see the Kittyhawks we had welcomed Zeros!' said Corporal Jack Boland.[13] The next morning, four more aircraft appeared, at the same time and from the same direction. The ground troops would not be fooled again, and opened fire. Two planes were hit, including the squadron leader's. Then the troops noticed to their horror the blue and white markings of the Allies: the Kittyhawks had arrived.

That afternoon brought heartening news: the full complement of Australia's 75 Squadron landed safely; thirteen more Kittyhawks taxied into their hangars. In coming months, dozens of P-40 fighters, bombers and transport and supply planes, from American and Australian units, landed at Port Moresby. Few of the Australian pilots had more than a handful of flying hours in the Kittyhawk, but at least their planes were in New Guinea at last.

All this time, from January to June 1942, not a single unit reconnoitred the Owen Stanleys; not a single jungle patrol went up the Kokoda Track. Everyone presumed the Japanese would take Port Moresby by sea or air; they believed, like MacArthur, that the Owen Stanleys protected them from overland attack.

Meanwhile, the returning troops of the AIF were held back in Queensland to build fortifications and train in country 'in no way resembling the jungle and mountain terrain of New Guinea'.[14] Not even advance parties, or staff officers, were sent to Port Moresby to study the actual conditions. A seemingly wilful ignorance imbued High Command, and trickled down to the most gormless private.

In April 1942, a new commander arrived to invigorate the garrison. Brigadier Selwyn Porter, the hard-driving hero of the Syrian campaign, emerges as one of those bull-headed officers who function in a realm of slight, if authentic, eccentricity. It is probably an unfair exaggeration to compare him to the demented but hugely effectual Captain Grief, of George MacDonald Fraser's Burmese classic.[15] On the other hand, the English novelist Evelyn Waugh would surely have placed Porter in the biff 'em school of command alongside Brigadier Ritchie-Hook.[16] Porter, like Ritchie-Hook, had a habit of issuing stern advice to the troops, the response to which was surely one of fascinated hilarity.

Porter knew a thing or two about New Guinea, as shown in his December 1941 paper, 'NOTES ON NEW GUINEA'. It is a document of surpassing grimness relieved by flights of prosaic exuberance. No one could accuse him of opacity. Porter's 'OBJECTIVES' for the Australian militia were clear: 'Kill the invader, give him no rest, no peace, no resources . . . harass him, deceive him, the role of all ranks will be fashioned towards these ends once he has landed.'[17]

His tips under 'HEALTH' left little hope: 'Malaria is common; as are dengue fever, and bacillary dysentery and pneumonia . . . in addition, tropical ulcer, amoebic dysentery, sycosis ringworm, dhobi itch, syphilis, prickly heat etc, are also encountered.' Porter revealed no more of his thoughts on the subject.[18] In his section headed 'NATIVES' Porter wrote, 'Languages are many and varied. [Between] the tribes or clans, having sought each others' heads for generations, little social communication exists.' Porter's 'OTHER HINTS' included: '(i) Don't go without footwear. (ii) Don't drink alcohol until the late afternoon. (iii) Don't take advantage of the honesty of the Chinese. (iv) Wear head-gear during the day when not in the shade. (v) Give cuts and sores immediate attention.'

Scenes of sloth and inebriation greeted the brigadier on his arrival in Port Moresby. Drunk, bare-foot troops somehow fashioned an existence in this bomb-shattered town strewn around the grimy waterfront, on which a single jetty was supposed to feed MacArthur's vaunted defence of Australia. Brown hills denuded of vegetation rolled northward; when it rained, muddy yellow streams deluged the low-lying areas. Tattered, shirtless men stood idly about the roadsides, their faces expressionless, their movements listless.[19] At the sound of air raid sirens they would rush to their trenches in an undisciplined rabble. The town's 'defences' amounted to 'red scars of excavated earth' that easily betrayed their position on the ridges to Japanese bombers.[20] The atmosphere was like living in a vast open-cut mine.

Morale was virtually non-existent. Senior officers supinely obeyed distant orders, when they should have been pleading for reinforcements. As Major-General Morris explained, his *raison d'être* was to transform Port Moresby into an air base, not an infantry training camp. One officer appeared before Porter 'emaciated and almost transparently thin from dysentery'.[21] He was sent home for a prolonged rest.

Porter, having quietly absorbed this hapless environment, gathered his officers together. The brigadier fumed: 'The Brigade is not in a fit state to fight a battle. Officers and men are so obviously backward that the training programme will go on around the clock. I will make no allowance for the weather.'[22] In a country in which the weather made no allowances for men, Porter was taken seriously. At once he set in motion a wholesale reorganisation of New Guinea Force.

One of his innovations was a school for 'junior leaders'. The brigadier launched a competition for the 'best defensive post', with the prize of a fortnight's leave. The excellence of the response amazed him. One section of the 39th Battalion produced a superbly camouflaged post, went home, and promptly disappeared. Later found AWOL in Melbourne, they were arrested and court-martialled.

Nonetheless, the timing of Porter's reinvigoration was fortuitous. On 8 May, Ultra code-breakers intercepted Japanese wires, and confirmed the imminent threat of a seaborne invasion of Port Moresby. From his Melbourne HQ, General Sir Thomas Blamey, the commander-in-chief, Allied Land Forces, warned that 'a serious attack against you ... will develop in the immediate future . . . Australia looks to you to maintain her outposts, and is confident that the task is in good hands.'[23]

The threat exposed profound flaws in the organisation of the Australian army in New Guinea. It was, in a word, chaotic. With no time to reshape the town according to his desires, Porter ordered his troops back to their old defence lines — those prior to his shake-up. A traffic jam resulted as soldiers and machines scrambled to find their old posts; maps were lost; unreliable telephone lines confused the units; great breaches in perimeters opened up as soldiers thinned and dispersed. Many fled to the hills.

Amidst the chaos, Porter found a reason to be cheerful. The men of the 39th, alone among the Australians, seemed to be pitching for a fight. They dug in and pleaded for more mortar bombs than the official issue. The brigadier happily obliged them. Why restrain a unit from wanting to kill more Japanese? he reasoned.[24]

To Porter's relief, the danger passed. In the Battle of the Coral Sea, the ships never met; the battle was fought in the skies, and the Japanese withdrew. This deflection persuaded General MacArthur that Australia was secure from attack. He pronounced victory. It was an early example of the supreme commander's tendency to declare victory before thousands of casualties confirmed that his declaration was premature.

A deceptive calm prevailed in the aftermath of the sea battle. Disappointed by the shambles, Porter moved to shake up the garrison: fresh, young AIF officers replaced the militia's ageing World War I commanders. New orders were distributed. Efficiency and duty were stressed.

The brigadier couldn't resist issuing his 'LESSONS RESULTING FROM THE RECENT THREAT OF INVASION'. This said as much about the want of discipline as it did about Porter's vibrant personality (the capitals are emphatically his):

1. Disobedience of Orders & Instructions . . . there are instances which appear to prove that certain elements of the Brigade have to be shocked into action . . .

Orders have been issued that the troops will shave, pay ordinary courteous compliments, wear their colours with pride, work under camouflage when digging and so on. The fact that these orders need repeating is deplorable . . . It is an indication of bad leadership and bad organisation of the chain of command . . . Shaving and saluting will NOT win a war; but, they are signposts of other features that will NOT win a war . . . Look to the discipline of British troops who saved the situation in FLANDERS, LIBYA, SYRIA and ABYSSINIA, because minor discipline was a habit and major discipline became a matter of course. You are not merely required to obey. You must go further. You must SEEK improvement . . . Do not consider the 'Battle of MORESBY' over and won. It has NOT commenced.[25]

It was sound advice; the war could not be won by a mob of bearded men who didn't know how to salute. Nor could it be won by sick, understrength, untrained troops, as Porter acknowledged in July, days before the Japanese landed at Gona. He noted that one regiment had not arrived; a battalion was understrength and 'backward in all respects'; a brigade, the 14th Militia, had forfeited two companies; the rest were understrength and disabled with sickness; and both the 30th and 14th Brigades were 'NOT' properly trained for likely operational tasks. 'Deduction: At best . . . a much mutilated [i.e. fragmented] force of inadequate and uncertain strength . . .'[26]

Worse, the 30th Brigade HQ was 'badly organised' and incapable of acting or moving in the field. It possessed only one civilian car, useless on any but first-class asphalt, and three one-ton trucks. Of the transport facilities, the vehicles were of poor quality and the workshops, overworked and understrength. One transport officer had been 'conscientiously working himself into a state of nervous and physical collapse', as did many technicians.

Of the troops' training, Porter rated it as 'Practically nil . . . Officers know nothing of recent campaigns . . . This is a very serious shortcoming.' As far as an understanding of the topography went, the Australians had no maps or aerial photos of vital areas.

Porter had correctly assessed his failure to invigorate the garrison. Nonetheless, he had flashes of insight that cut through the murkiest thinking in Brisbane. He believed an attack overland from the north coast 'was the most likely . . . option', of which he concluded: 'It would be an admirable threat to be carried out as a distraction, in conjunction with an attack on our position from the sea.'[27]

Porter could be eminently pragmatic. The state of the men's personal kit was, not surprisingly, 'BAD'. Porter made a list of hints necessary to combat mosquitoes, vegetation and humidity. He recommended tightly woven mosquito-proof shirts, ventilated hats and gaiters of the American kind. It would have been even better had the Australian Q-store made these items available. Porter wrote with searing finality of the quality of his jeeps and troop carriers: 'I wish to report that the time has arrived when the transport as a whole must be regarded as being below the lowest degree of serviceability.'

This ineluctable truth applied to the men as well as their machines. The Australian militia would never be combat-ready. In April 1942, three months before Yokoyama's veterans set foot at Gona, the Australian militia battalions in New Guinea received the lowest 'F' grade in a report on combat efficiency. 'Unit training is not complete,'[28] was the blunt conclusion of Major-General George Vasey. Port Moresby, the most important air base in the South Pacific, found itself garrisoned by the worst troops in the Australian army, 'stationed in the most threatened area'.[29]

Into this scene of incompetence walked a man who merits profound gratitude for his contribution to the Australian war effort. His name was Bert Kienzle, a tough Australian plantation owner of Teutonic roots who knew the country like the proverbial back of his hand, understood the local dialects and could competently organise and lead the mountain tribes.

This old New Guinea hand was a godsend. Kienzle saw immediately the vital importance of the indigenous people — as carriers and stretcher-bearers — and on 1 July took charge of all 'native labour', under the control of ANGAU (the Australian New Guinea Administrative Unit). His job was to turn the Papuan natives into an army of willing workhorses able to conquer on foot the insuperable supply — and medical — problems posed by the Kokoda Track.

Kienzle met his first team of Papuan workers at the native labour camp at Ilolo: 'I found the natives numbering about 600 ... very sullen and unhappy. Conditions in the labour camp were bad and many cases of illness noted. Desertions were frequently being reported,' he wrote in his diary on 3 July.[30]

It was an inauspicious beginning to a wonderfully heroic working relationship between Kienzle, the Papuan people and the extraordinary Captain Geoffrey Vernon, who was responsible for the carriers' medical needs. Without the compassion and organisational abilities of Kienzle and Vernon, the legendary fuzzy wuzzy angels may never have found their wings — or more appropriately, their war legs.

Kienzle was given his first big logistics job on 1 July 1942, three weeks before the Yokoyama Advance Force landed at Gona. It was a task of sublime absurdity: he was ordered to build 'a road from Ilolo to Kokoda', the deadline for which was the end of August 1942. A road over the Owen Stanleys would have taken the finest engineers, using the best technology, years to construct. None exists to this day.

The idea that the Owen Stanleys could be made roadworthy in a month revealed the depths of Allied ignorance of the terrain; it might have been laughable, had it not been so dangerous. But Kienzle adopted his usual, wry insouciance in the face of the impossible. He accepted the order, as was his duty: 'A colossal engineering job and not to be taken lightly!' he wrote. One can see the smile on his face, as he added, 'I was one of the very few men who knew the country to be traversed and had walked over it recently on foot.'[31] Work started on the road on 5 July; earthworks never got further than Uberi, half a day's march from Owers' Corner, the jump-off point of the Kokoda Track.

It was about this time — early July — that Major-General Morris sent a company of the 39th Battalion over the mountains to guard the Buna and Kokoda airfields and collect supplies being sent around the coast by boat. Kienzle was asked to guide them: 'I was informed that a company of troops ... had been waiting for someone to guide them across the Owen Stanley Range for several days.'

They had to be guided across the mountains before he could start the road in earnest. As he led this little band of some 120 troops over the Kokoda Track, Kienzle made some telling entries in his diary. They would have been of great use to the generals in Brisbane:

10th July. With the exception of Uberi, no camp or staging place on track to Kokoda had sufficient accommodation for a company of men ... shelters for native carriers were non-existent.

19th July. The track to KOKODA takes eight days, so the maintenance of supplies is a physical impossibility without large-scale co-operation of plane droppings.

24th July. One of my last requests ... was for the laying down of a telephone line from HQ to Kokoda or 'the front' where the enemy were being contacted.[32]

Chapter 6
Kokoda

'We were very good at executing night attacks. We had
experience of this in China. We kept shooting all night'
— *Imanishi Sadaharu, of the Tsukamoto Battalion,*
which launched the first attack on Kokoda

Captain Sam Templeton was a quiet, considerate man in his early fifties,
of great mental and physical stamina. He had been a naval reserve
gunner in World War I, and was reputed to have fought in the Spanish Civil
War. 'Uncle Sam', as the troops called him, was too old to serve abroad in
the Australian Imperial Force. He spoke rarely, with a slight Northern Irish
accent, usually after the hurricane lamps had been doused. Darkness
loosened his inhibitions.[1] Remote and enigmatic, Templeton's age and
combat experience were reassuring to younger troops, who looked on him
as a father figure. They would follow him anywhere, and indeed they did.

Templeton led the first company of Australians over the mountains,
with Kienzle as his guide. This was B Company of the 39th Battalion. The
march was less arduous than it would later prove for the AIF troops who had
to carry full packs and ammunition in pouring rain. The Papuan climate in
early July was relatively benign, being the end of the 'dry' season; the daily

monsoonal deluge would start promptly in September. And Kienzle's carriers were on hand to shoulder much of the equipment. Even so, it was an exhausting initiation to the Owen Stanleys.

The less fit troops couldn't carry their loads and Warrant Officer Jack Wilkinson, an AIF veteran of the Greek campaign, lent a hand. He and Templeton shouldered four rifles and three haversacks between them up one ascent. 'Uncle Sam insisted on carrying all my gear as well as that of others,' Wilkinson wrote in his diary. Wilkinson's drinking habits were interesting: 'Made a brew of rum and lime and hot water, which revived some. Many non-drinkers among these kids. Rum turned out to be mostly metho ...'[2]

Perhaps an exaggerated rumour, or poor communications, led to Port Moresby's bleak report on the state of these troops. General Morris wired Brisbane on 17 July that '33%' of the men were unfit for action after their hike to Kokoda: 'request urgent advice aircraft for troop carrying to Kokoda'.[3]

On the contrary, Uncle Sam's men reached Kokoda in fairly good shape; only one fell by the side of the track due to dysentery. En route, they ate bananas and pawpaws, and at Kokoda Kienzle shared out food from his farm in the Yodda valley. In any case, Morris received no advice on airlifting the men to Kokoda, nor any explanation for the lack of planes. Brisbane simply ignored him.

Twenty tons of stores awaited Templeton at Buna. His company arrived there on 19 July, two days before the enemy landed. He loaded up a long line of carriers, and set off back to Kokoda. As his patrol rested, on the 21st, he heard a distant rumble on the horizon. He gazed over the green apron of palm groves that spread to the sea. The sound seemed to issue from a thundercloud at the base of a tropical storm. But there was only light cloud cover that afternoon.

At Buna Government Station — which was being attacked — Sergeant Barry Harper relayed the message: 'A Japanese warship is shelling Buna ... to cover a landing at Gona or Sanananda. Acknowledge, Moresby. Over ...'[4] Harper received no reply from Port Moresby. But three coastwatchers — all soon to be killed by the Japanese — picked up the message at Ambasi, 40 miles north-west of Buna, and relayed it to Moresby. Templeton soon learned the cause of the boom. He ordered a platoon (of about thirty men) forward. He had no idea of the scale of the landing, and continued back to Kokoda to meet his battalion's commanding officer, Lieutenant-Colonel William Owen.

The lone platoon, led by Lieutenant Arthur Seekamp, marched through the night and reached the village of Awala at 11.00 a.m. on 22 July. They dumped their packs and prepared to meet the enemy. Within hours the first of Tsukamoto's forward scouts, moving nimbly south from the coast, appeared and, in a lightning manoeuvre, encircled Seekamp's platoon. The speed and physique of the Japanese troops astonished the Australians, who had been led to think of 'the Jap' as a 'little yellow, bespectacled fellow': 'The first Jap I hit was six feet two inches and 15 stone ...' recalled a stunned Lieutenant Doug McClean of the 39th Battalion. 'Their movement in the bush had to be seen to be believed ... they'd just vanish. Their field craft and movement was magnificent.'[5]

The enemy were not, in fact, all fleet-footed sumo wrestlers; the point was that the Australians perceived them as larger that the clichéd image in their minds. There were a few extreme cases among the crack troops of the Yokoyama infantry. But most were simply well-built, well-trained men. Later, a shorter, clumsier Japanese soldier — closer to the stereotype — appeared, but that didn't dispel the rumour of thousands of Japanese supermen crashing through the undergrowth towards Port Moresby.

Okada Seizo, the *Asahi Shimbun* war correspondent attached to the Yokoyama Advance Force, described the advance troops in more pedestrian terms: '... the unit continued to walk with single-mindedness ... day and night. Each man was required to carry provisions for thirteen days in his backpack, comprising 18 litres of rice, a pistol, ammunition, hand grenades, a spoon, first aid kit, [approximately 100 pounds] ... The backpacks loaded with this luggage rose about 30 cm above the heads of the soldiers. They would walk step by step with staff in hand, using it as an extra leg to propel them along.'[6]

Some slept in riverbeds, and a few troops drowned when flash floods surged through their camp sites. They knew little of the terrain and had had little jungle experience — contrary to what most Australian sources had maintained. Senior Japanese intelligence officers misread maps and photos, and most seemed to think a road connected Kokoda to Port Moresby.

———

What they had in speed and experience, they lacked in firepower. Their light arms were inferior to the Australians'. They did not possess automatic weapons of the quality of the Bren and Tommy guns, both of which were relatively light and efficient.

Imanishi said his troops typically carried a Type 38 bolt-action rifle that shot five rounds, and was designed in the Meiji period. Their grenades were left over from the Russo–Japanese war of 1904–05; they would not explode unless struck on the ground at a 45-degree angle (later, some Japanese would commit suicide by striking these against their heads). They did have, however, two remarkable weapons: the wheel-mounted mountain artillery (carried in pieces) and the Juki heavy machine-gun, both of which inflicted terrible casualties on Allied forces. Astonishingly, they lugged these weapons over the mountains. Both far exceeded in destructive power anything in the Australian arsenal during the first phase of the battle.

Another weapon the Japanese deployed in droves was the human bullet. Suicide squads hurled themselves at the enemy to draw their fire and frighten them into submission. The Japanese outnumbered the Australians by ten to one at Kokoda and at least three to one at Isurava. There seemed no shortage of volunteers for suicide squads, at least at the start of battle, and Australian veterans remember night attacks by squads of human bullets — the Japanese excelled at night attacks — as the most terrifying experience of the war.

Seekamp's little Australian patrol fell back to the Kumusi River, at Wairopi (pidgin for 'wire rope' bridge) in the early hours of 24 July. The river is about sixty yards wide here; the depth depended on the rains, which could turn a gentle current into a swirling torrent. At 9.00 a.m., they received Templeton's signal to pull out: 'Reported on radio broadcast that 1500–2000 Japs landed at Gona Mission Station ... in view of the numbers I recommend that your action be contact and rearguard only — no do-or-die stunts. Close back on Kokoda.'[7] Accordingly, they ripped up the footboards, slashed the cables, and sent the wire bridge crashing into the river. Twenty men — two sections — remained on the southern shores of the Kumusi, and two machine-gunners set up either side of the little bridge spanning Gorari Creek.

The Japanese waded the river, and the advance troops walked into the Australian ambush; fifteen were shot dead. The setback did not detain them long. Snipers, scurrying up trees, poured fire onto the Australian gunners, who retreated back to Templeton's company at Oivi. The resistance briefly surprised, but did little to dent, Tsukamoto's push to Kokoda.

'There was some resistance and a few casualties,' said Imanishi. 'But I was a bit behind. I had to carry my bicycle on my shoulders across the Kumusi.' He threw it away further up: 'I thought there'd be a road; I saw it was useless.'[8]

Lieutenant-Colonel Owen flew into Kokoda on 23 July. A survivor of the invasion of Rabaul, he was under no illusions about the determination of the Japanese soldier. He listened closely to Templeton's report and signalled Port Moresby for reinforcements: 'must have two companies ... must have fresh troops ... to avoid being outflanked'.

Military jargon is full of anodyne phrases the purpose of which is to normalise the process of killing the enemy. To be outflanked along a jungle path meant, in effect, encirclement and probable destruction. This was the danger at Oivi, an elevated strip of land where Templeton's troops were being comprehensively outflanked. They dug a trench with their bayonets and steel helmets, and waited. Behind them were the foothills of the mountains, in front, the coastal plain.

Owen wanted at least 200 men. He got 30. The first fifteen flew into Kokoda in the morning of 25 July, and he sent them off straightaway. One sergeant asked the way. Owen pointed, bellowing, 'Follow that track and you'll get there!'

The reinforcements never got there. Templeton's men were trapped in a classic Japanese pincer movement — a miniature precursor of the vast outflanking manoeuvres to come. Unaware of the extent of their predicament, Uncle Sam set off alone back up the track to warn the arriving reinforcements not to come forward. He was never seen again. His men heard only a machine-gun burst in the forest behind them. Stories later went that he was badly wounded and died in Japanese captivity. Indeed, Templeton is cited as the source for the Japanese belief that they faced a thousand Australians at Kokoda — an exaggeration, possibly elicited under threats or torture, to dent Japanese self-confidence. 'Templeton's Crossing', a camp site by the banks of Eora Creek, now bears his name.

General Douglas MacArthur and Prime Minister John Curtin at their first Advisory War Council meeting, on 26 March 1942. Those who condemn Curtin as a minor figure, sidelined by the generals, fail to appreciate his immense effort in securing much-needed American support and bringing the troops home to defend Australia.

The heart of darkness: the Owen Stanley Range, viewed from Owers' Corner, the jump-off point of the Kokoda Track. The first summit is Imita Ridge; and beyond, Ioribaiwa Ridge, the southern-most point of the Japanese advance.

An Australian infantry patrol crosses a creek through dense jungle on the Kokoda Track. Often the enemy couldn't be seen through the undergrowth, and hand-to-hand combat was common. The wounds inflicted at such close proximity were horrific and many troops died of blood loss while awaiting evacuation.

Japanese crack troops depart Rabaul for the invasion of Papua. They were the Nankai Shitai, the South Seas Detachment, led by Major-General Horii Tomitaro, whose parting instructions were to capture Port Moresby by land. It was a task about which he had grave misgivings.

The Nankai Shitai crosses the Owen Stanleys towards the Australian lines at Isurava. Their orders were to, 'Lay in wait and go around the flank…Harass them and exhaust them by ceaseless activity. Finally, when they are completely exhausted, open the offensive.'

Lieutenant-General Sydney Rowell, commander of New Guinea Force, in August 1942, at the height of the crisis in the Owen Stanleys. Stubborn and high-minded but with a brilliant military mind, Rowell was later sacked by Blamey, whom Rowell accused of making him 'eat dirt'.

Lieutenant-Colonel Ralph Honner was rushed over the Owen Stanleys to lead the 39th Battalion at Isurava. He later led the same unit at Gona. His citation for the Military Cross described him as the best company commander in this war or the last.

Major-General Cyril Clowes, known as 'Silent Cyril', soon after leading Australians at the battle of Milne Bay, the first land defeat of the Japanese. Blamey and MacArthur grudgingly credited Clowes with the victory, described by the British Field Marshall William Slim as the battle that broke the invincibility of the Imperial Japanese Army.

Brigadier Arnold Potts (far left), who'd been awarded a Military Cross in World War I aged 19, commanded the 21st Brigade in Papua. He was sacked and sent home in disgrace after leading the fighting withdrawal over the Owen Stanleys. The troops loved him as the hero of the Kokoda Track who salvaged their self-esteem in terrible conditions. Today, Australians have largely forgotten him.

Doomed youth: young officers of the 2/14th battalion a week before Isurava. (L to R) Lieutenant George Moore, Lieutenant Harold 'Butch' Bissett, Captain Claude Nye, Lieutenant Lindsay Mason and Captain Maurice Treacy MC. All were killed in action in Papua except Mason, who was badly wounded.

October 1942: 'Biscuit bombers' — Douglas C47 transport planes — were the main source of supplies over the Kokoda Track. Ammunition, food and weapons were dropped onto marked clearings. Parachutes weren't always used, causing bales to smash apart where they fell, and mortar bombs to fuse on impact and later explode in their cannons, killing the crews.

Native porters carried huge loads to the forward Australian troops. It is a popular fiction that they volunteered willingly for this exhausting job; the carriers were indentured labour, poorly paid and at times badly treated.

An advance patrol of the 25th Brigade crosses the Brown River towards Menari, in pursuit of the retreating Japanese; relieved troops bathe in the background.

The first jungle-trained Australian troops joined the war in New Guinea in October 1942, when these soldiers of the 16th Brigade set off over the mountains. Veterans of Africa, Tobruk, Greece and Crete, they had been rigorously exposed to jungle conditions while garrisoning Ceylon (Sri Lanka).

A poster produced for the Department of Aircraft Production in 1942. The map is ringed by Japanese ships and aircraft, an impression that owed more to the imagination of Australian propagandists than the reality. Japanese intentions were to cut off Australia from its US ally, not to invade.

Japanese propaganda leaflet. A well-dressed American officer, standing on a map of Australia, molests an Australian woman. The point touched a raw nerve: many troops fighting in Papua were anxious about their wives and girlfriends back home, where 90,000 well-paid American troops were stationed.

Cut off without a leader, the troops cursed themselves for letting Uncle Sam leave unaided. As night fell, the Japanese taunted the remaining Australians — young, leaderless militia. They hacked through the scrub, banged their mess tins and shouted orders in English: e.g. 'Come forward Corporal White!'[9] The 39th replied by rolling grenades down the hill.*

It was dark when a native police boy, Lance-Corporal Sinopa, led the unit to safety along the Oivi Creek, a feat for which he won a Military Medal. Each man held the bayonet scabbard of the man in front, and some reportedly used the phosphorescent fungus on the jungle floor as 'headlights'.[10] From behind came a burst of machine-gun fire, as the Japanese poured into the empty clearing.

The retreating troops reached Kokoda at dawn, and found the plateau deserted. Stores and huts were burnt down and still smouldering, supplies destroyed: the result of Owen's rash scorched-earth policy. The battalion commander had hastily abandoned Kokoda for Deniki, a village a few hours' south-east, just forward of Isurava. Owen's sudden withdrawal was a mistake: it handed the Kokoda airstrip to the invaders without a shot being fired. Realising this, the commander of the 39th returned to Kokoda the next day, to defend the vital airstrip. He atoned for his error with the supreme sacrifice.

Kokoda is an orderly government station set on a tongue-shaped plateau protruding from the Owen Stanley Range at the northern end of the eponymous track. The tongue juts out over a wide valley, and the area has a reassuringly open feel for troops about to enter, or emerge from, the jungle-clad mountains to the south. In 1942, Kokoda's little huts, gardens, school, airstrip and hospital — the few oddments of civilisation — seemed thrown together in meek defiance of Nature's encroaching chaos. Strategically vital for its airstrip and commanding location, Kokoda marked the link with civilisation in an otherwise inhospitable land, and the troops held this outpost in great affection — as do hikers today.

To the north-east, the short escarpment falls away to the Mambare River and the coastal plain of the Gona–Sanananda–Buna littoral. To the

---

* The Australian troops later chose passwords unpronounceable on the Japanese tongue, such as Woolloomooloo. The AIF troops sometimes issued orders in pidgin Arabic they'd picked up in the Middle East, which baffled the enemy.

Battle for Kokoda: First Battle, 28 – 29 July 1942

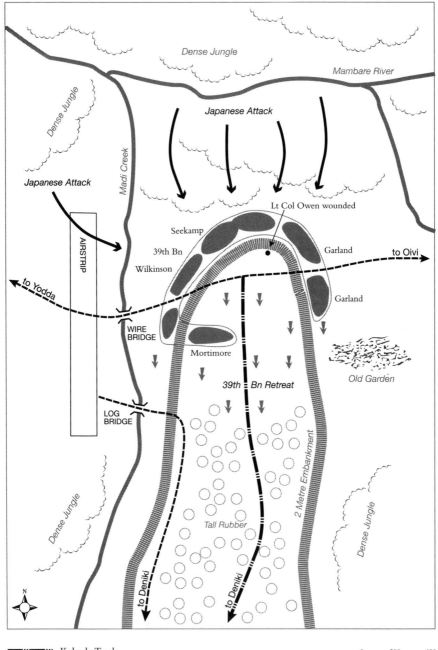

Dense Jungle

Mambare River

Japanese Attack

Dense Jungle

Japanese Attack

Madi Creek

AIRSTRIP

Lt Col Owen wounded

Seekamp

39th Bn

Wilkinson

Garland

to Oivi

to Yodda

Garland

WIRE
BRIDGE

Mortimore

39th Bn Retreat

Old Garden

LOG
BRIDGE

2 Metre Embankment

Dense Jungle

Tall Rubber

Dense Jungle

to Deniki

to Deniki

N

Kokoda Track
Australian Positions
Australian Movement
Japanese Movement

| 0 | 200 | 400 |
Approx. Yards

south-east Fiawani Creek, a tributary of Eora Creek, feeds into the Mambare River via a narrow gorge; west is the airstrip, and beyond it, dense jungle rising to a high ridgeline which eventually becomes the Naro Ridge.

Leading out of Kokoda heading south is a lane, lined in 1942 by a rubber plantation (and today, by ginger plants and palm groves). After a few miles the lane narrows into the famous little track (or trail, or path) bearing the name Kokoda, which gradually ascends the first mountain in the Owen Stanley Range towards the villages of Deniki and Isurava.

'To us [Kokoda] was paradise,' said Jack Lloyd of the 39th Battalion. For one thing, the lush gardens supplemented their dreary ration of bully beef, biscuits and baked beans with delicious fresh fruit, bananas, pawpaws and wild passion fruit.

Owen strode about the edge of the Kokoda plateau in apparent command of the situation; he deployed his meagre force — the same men of B Company, of the 39th Battalion — along the tip of the escarpment, where he expected Tsukamoto's advance unit to attack. The invader soon did. At 2.00 a.m. on 29 July, about 400 of Tsukamoto's 900-strong force charged up the short, steep slope. It was a classic nocturnal charge; they shouted and sometimes chanted, and fell on the Australians with apparent unconcern for their own lives. 'We were ordered to occupy the airfield at Kokoda,' recalls Imanishi. 'No one knew there was a hill; we knew nothing of the terrain. But we were very good at executing night attacks. We had experience of this in China. We kept shooting all night.'[11]

The shocked 39th responded with a couple of machine-guns, grenades and rifle fire; they had not expected anything like this. Their resistance briefly delayed the enemy, whose front-line troops soon scrambled onto the plateau. Both sides merged in a melee of hand-to-hand combat.

The gathering mist obscured the moonlight, and bloody chaos ensued. Men were bayoneted in the darkness. One Australian officer shouted for help to his neighbouring troops; they happened to be Japanese, and hurled grenades at the voice in the darkness. A sniper's bullet hit Owen in the head. He fell off the edge of the escarpment into a weapon pit. Captain Geoffrey Vernon, then the battalion's medical officer, climbed down the slope with stretcher-bearers. They found Owen 'propped up in a narrow place struggling violently yet more than semi-conscious, quite unable to realise where he was ...'[12] They hauled him up the escarpment. The 'Japs [were] moving and whispering in the grass', recalled Jack Wilkinson, as he assisted Vernon. The bullet had penetrated Owen's skull above the right eye. There was no exit wound. The dying commander looked strangely on the faces of his men. Brain tissue protruded from the wound. He fell unconscious, his body convulsed, and settled. 'A hopeless case,' Wilkinson recorded.[13]

Vernon and Wilkinson worked desperately in their medical hut — dressing wounds and sending the wounded back through the rubber plantation — as scores of fresh Japanese troops stormed the plateau in the forward area. As Vernon recalled: 'Wilkinson held the lantern for me and every time he raised it a salvo of machine-gun bullets was fired at the building.'[14]

They stayed with Owen, who lay in a coma, until the last moment: 'We fixed up the Colonel,' said Vernon, 'who was now dying, as comfortably as possible, moistening his mouth and cleaning him up. Then I stuffed our operating instruments and a few dressings into my pocket, seized the lantern, and went out toward the rubber.' Owen lasted perhaps fifteen minutes.[15]

The Australians managed to salvage most of their weapons, although the Japanese did capture 180 grenades, 1850 rifle rounds and five automatic weapons, according to an enemy sitrep. It added: 'The [Australians] are skilled marksmen and expert grenade throwers.'[16] No doubt there were quite a few good cricketers in the militia. An enemy Intelligence Report observed that the Australians 'have greater fighting spirit ... [than] English, American and Filipino troops'.[17]

The 39th retreated along the Kokoda Track; the walking wounded hobbled to safety. The early morning mist, like billowing smoke, spilled off the Kokoda plateau to the Mambare River: 'Thick white streams ... stole between the rubber trees and turned the whole scene into a weird combination of light and shadow,' wrote Vernon, who had a poet's command of the language. The troops climbed by the moonlight, which occasionally shone on the path through the mist. With the Japanese in control of Kokoda, the Australians withdrew to the village of Deniki, on the first ascent of the Owen Stanleys.

During the pre-dawn retreat to Deniki, Captain Vernon lingered beneath a rubber tree on the Kokoda plateau. It had been 'dinned' into him that the place of a medical officer was at the end of a retreating column.[18]

This gentle Sydney doctor, on whose grave is inscribed the words 'A friend to all men', took his responsibilities to the letter. As he waited, his mind curiously contemplated the 'weirdness' of the natural world around him, and the sadness of the soldiers' place in it. He later wrote this beautiful passage, oft-quoted because it evokes the very mood of the place: '[there was] the mysterious veiling of trees, houses and men, the drip of moisture from the foliage, and at the last, the almost complete silence, as if the rubber groves of Kokoda were sleeping as usual in the depths of the night, and men had not brought disturbance'.[19]

Vernon remains unsung. He was a hero of the Kokoda campaign, chiefly for his unusual devotion to the care of the troops and the Papuan carriers. Born on 16 December 1882 in Hastings, England, he immigrated to New South Wales where his father was made government architect. He attended the Sydney Church of England Grammar School and Sydney University.

During World War I he was concussed by enemy fire, probably at Gallipoli, where he served as a captain in the Australian Army Medical Corps. He suffered partial deafness for the rest of his life, of which he later wrote: '... being very deaf, from concussion ... on Active Service 1915, I do not gather much information from others. I therefore miss much that goes on, including the many rumours and false reports that constantly passed along the line, and the absence of these may be an advantage.'[20]

As regimental medical officer of the 11th Light Horse, he won the Military Cross for 'conspicuous gallantry' at the battle of Romani in 1916. Though wounded, 'he went beyond the Australian lines at night to attend and bring back an injured man'.[21]

The outbreak of World War II found him, a rubber planter, in the hills of west Papua, where his tall, khaki-clad frame and tanned, leathery skin was a familiar sight. He volunteered for the Papuan Infantry Battalion in February 1942, aged 60, and established a hospital at Ilolo, near the start of the Kokoda Track.

Vernon crossed the Owen Stanleys in July 1942 to make himself useful. Passing through Efogi, on his way to Kokoda, he heard from a tribal police runner that the Japanese had landed at Gona. 'I'll go on,' he said. 'There's no medical officer with those 39th youngsters.'

In the months ahead, Vernon quietly allotted himself the job of caring for the fuzzy wuzzy angels, the native stretcher-bearers who would carry out

Australia's wounded. Most officers had little time to think of their needs. Yet their villages and gardens were plundered and destroyed, and their people displaced, as the war crashed across their land. Vernon requisitioned blankets, medicines and food for them, and helped to ease their terror of bombardment and machine-gun fire. He spoke to their souls and found a beautiful and willing response.

Hank Nelson wrote of Vernon:

> . . . with his white hair and body so thin there seemed only a
> sheet of brown paper covering his bones . . . he became one of
> the most remembered men on the Trail. He doctored and
> comforted black and white, boosting the morale of the carriers,
> protecting them from over-work and ensuring they were properly
> fed and clothed. His own frailty was partly because he gave his
> rations to the carriers. Vernon was one of the few Australians
> present at both the fall and recapture of Kokoda. 'This' he said of
> the Kokoda Campaign, 'should bind us to the Papuan race.'[22]

The doctor continued smoking under his rubber tree, awaiting stragglers. Two soldiers passed, Major W.T. Watson and Lieutenant Peter Brewer, and urged him to join them. He stayed.

'Snowy' Parr, and another private, were in fact the last soldiers out. Parr, a young Bren gunner who had just learned to use his weapon, had watched the death throes of Owen, his respected commander, with a silent rage. Parr then hid on the threshold of Kokoda and waited until two dozen Japanese troops stood around celebrating. From a range of 60 yards, toting the weapon at shoulder height, he emptied a full magazine at the crowd, killing about twenty Japanese. He then hastened cheerfully back through the rubber plantation. 'You couldn't miss,' Vernon heard him say to his mate as they passed.

Vernon then withdrew, the last man out. At Deniki he was relieved as the 39th Battalion's temporary medical officer by Captain John Shera. He went back to the Eora Creek field hospital, where he took charge of the casualties there — both sick and wounded, black and white.

———

The first battle for Kokoda was, in terms of casualties, tiny. Yet the count revealed a Japanese readiness to tolerate huge losses. Of the Australians, there were just six killed and five were wounded. For these, 40 Japanese died, according to one captured Japanese document.[23] Another source counted eighteen Japanese dead, and 45 wounded. Lieutenant Noda Hidetaka, of the 3rd Kuwada Battalion, summed up: 'our Advance Force has been engaged in battle with 1,200 Australians and has suffered unexpectedly heavy casualties ...'[24] The Yazawa and Yokoyama Battalions respectively reported 1000 and 1200 Australian troops at Kokoda. There were in fact 77 Australian troops at the first battle of Kokoda.

Yet the 39th had lost its commander, Owen, and a company commander, Templeton, within days. The loss of much-admired senior officers deeply depressed the younger troops. Unlike the Japanese, who were inured to battle and bloodshed, few of the Australians had ever seen a corpse. A number ran away when their officers fell. Others, such as Parr, experienced a general hardening of the mind. To the untutored soldier of the 39th, revenge became the battle cry, the revenge of fallen mates. Mateship was not contrived or clichéd, it was real. Laurie Howson, recalling later how his sergeant, 'Bunny' Pulfer died, said, 'Your mate alongside you became your mother, father and God all rolled into one.'[25]

Chapter 7
Kokoda Lost

'I pinned one Jap to the ground with my bayonet and screamed with laughter'
— *Warrant Officer Jack Wilkinson, 39th Battalion*

'Kokoda lost from this morning. Blow the drome and road east of Oivi,' urged the Australian wire to Port Moresby on 29 July. The Allied aircraft obliged, and swooped on Kokoda's airfield.

A new commander, Lieutenant-Colonel Alan Cameron, briefly succeeded Owen on 4 August. An aggressive, uncompromising man, Cameron had escaped the invasion of Rabaul with twelve others aboard a little boat. He looked dimly on deserters. On his way over the mountains to Deniki he encountered a few wild-eyed young privates of the 39th Battalion's B Company who'd fled after the deaths of Owen and Templeton. Cameron was 'very bitter towards [these] men. Says they are cowards,' according to one soldier's diary.[1] Cameron ordered the troops who'd 'shot through' back to Isurava.

The colonel's orders were to recapture the Kokoda airstrip, which had suddenly assumed the highest strategic importance at GHQ in Brisbane. General Blamey, no less, had exuberantly confided to the American air commander that he'd recapture Buna in a few weeks.[2]

The deflated spirits of the 39th rose before the battle. Deniki, now a bustling camp site, commanded the high ground above Kokoda. Sixty-six miles of telephone line had been laid over the Owen Stanleys. Kienzle's carrier lines were operational. These things diminished the troops' acute sense of isolation, of being cut off by the Japanese in front, and by the rainforest and mountains to the rear.

A greater boost to morale came with the arrival on 6 August of the full complement of the 39th Battalion. They had been rushed over the mountains when Kokoda fell with the most basic cartographical support: before he left Port Moresby each man was given a little bit of paper naming the villages he would encounter en route, and the approximate marching time between them. Such was the state of Allied map-making. A few got a swift lesson in the use of the Tommy gun — a parting shot, as it were, with a weapon many had 'never seen in their lives'.[3]

The only good news in early August came from Kienzle. He single-handedly solved the most pressing logistical problem: how to airlift supplies to the troops. The carriers were simply unable to deliver the vast amounts of food and ammunition needed to sustain a combat infantry, whose numbers would soon enter the thousands.

Kienzle found the solution while flying over the Owen Stanleys in July. Then he'd noticed a crater-like depression near the Kagi Gap, at the highest point of the Owen Stanley Range. His diary tells the story:

> 31st July. I was determined to find an area suitable for dropping supplies somewhere on the main range ... I knew of an area of 'two dry lakes' right on top of the main range ...
>
> 2nd August. I descended east through very heavy jungle and followed a native hunting pad, using village policeman and three local Koiaris as guides, who were reluctant to show me the area. A Taboo existed on the place except for a few, who used it as a hunting ground ...
>
> 3rd August. We broke camp at 0700 hrs and arrived at first dry lake at 0725 hrs. It presented a magnificent sight — a large patch of open country right on top of the main range of the

Owen Stanleys. It was just the very thing I had been looking for to assist us in beating the Japs.[4]

Kienzle's 'dry lake' is an eerie, windswept plain more than a mile long and half a mile wide. It has the desolate look of a blasted heath — more Scotland than New Guinea. A creek runs through the middle, with swamps on each side covered in sharp reeds. Kienzle observed quail and bush pigs running about. Elsewhere grassland obscured the swampy ground; the bed was too rough and sodden to be converted easily into a landing strip, and the lip of the crater was a perilous obstacle for aircraft. So it would serve as a drop zone. 'It is an excellent area for dropping supplies,' wrote Kienzle. 'I erected shelters during the afternoon and stayed the night.'[5]

Kienzle dubbed the lakebed 'Myola' after the wife of Major Sydney Elliott-Smith, an ANGAU commander. Myola is also an Australian Aboriginal word meaning 'dawn'. It swiftly became a daily drop zone for food, ammunition and medical supplies, and spared the native carriers the exhaustion of bearing all this over the mountains on their backs. By 14 August, thanks to Kienzle's phenomenal energy, Myola was nearly operational. He knew what could and couldn't be done in this hostile land — and made an interesting aside in his diary at this time that 'the prospect of quietly building a road from Port Moresby to Kokoda ... was an impossibility from the start'.[6]

Cameron had a 'three-pronged' plan for recapturing Kokoda. It nearly didn't happen. His junior officers resisted; they thought it unworkable. Captains Symington and Bidstrup scorned the idea of marching back down the track, without any idea of Japanese positions or strength. Symington condemned the plan as 'ill-conceived and highly dangerous'.[7] Bidstrup believed it exposed his troops to needless crossfire. 'All [the Japanese] had to do was to enfilade that track — and that's it!'[8]

Cameron, an inveterate moustache chewer, overruled their objections, and the men moved out at 6.30 a.m. on 8 August. They soon came under intense enfilading fire — as Bidstrup had predicted — from a mountain gun on the valley's eastern side. When a Japanese sniper picked off another highly popular officer,[9] a whisper of rage — 'the skipper's gone' — flew among the troops like 'a flame in sun-scorched grass'.[10] The Australians completely lost their reserve and trepidation and charged down the valley straight into Japanese fire. The Japanese fell back in shock. For an instant a weak point in the enemy's famous psychological armoury was laid bare.

It was a mere spasm of reflex aggression. But the charge showed that the 39th could mount an offensive. The momentum soon collapsed, however. Bidstrup's ambush near Pirivi, the second prong of three, failed. Pressed in from both sides by superior numbers, his company suffered eleven deaths for which he claimed twenty Japanese casualties. One of his platoons, driven deep into the jungle, did not emerge for days, and their captain despaired of the claustrophobic fighting conditions: 'All of my platoons were almost within voice call. I sent two runners from one platoon to another . . . I've never heard or seen them since.'[11]

Captain Symington, however, actually succeeded in retaking Kokoda. His men had moved down the mountain, crept through the rubber trees and, to their amazement, walked straight into Kokoda, unopposed.

Tsukamoto had presumed Kokoda secure, and sent most of his men up the mountain ridges in an attempt to outflank the Australians. So the dozens of slouch hats that advanced across the plateau stunned the little group of Japanese who had stayed to guard the airstrip. They screamed and ran into the jungle, according to witnesses. A captured Japanese notebook and map, showing some knowledge of the Kokoda Track, were sent to Port Moresby.

Immediately the 50-year-old Sergeant-Major Jim Cowey, winner of the Military Cross in World War I, fired a flare, as ordered, to signal the recapture of Kokoda and to request supplies and reinforcements. The flare went unseen at Deniki — Cameron must have been chewing his moustache again. In fact, no one in Cameron's HQ at Deniki saw the flare they were supposedly anxiously awaiting.

Assuming help was coming, the Australians reoccupied the battalion's old trenches on the tip of the plateau, and awaited the return of the Japanese. As they gazed down on the Mambare River, and west to the coveted airstrip, they kept watch for signs of any movement, or any shape, in the gathering dusk.

———

The big, bellowing Japanese commander of the 1st Battalion, 144th Regiment, provoked strong feelings in his troops. One described Lieutenant-Colonel Tsukamoto as 'that thundering, bawling old man'. Others admired his courage, and his capacity for *sake*. Tsukamoto had 'such a dynamic way of drinking sake', observed Imanishi, who served in his unit. 'And he was such a daring man.'[12]

Tsukamoto rewarded the troops with *sake* if they fought well. He drank copious quantities of the stuff himself, as he staggered up the track. It didn't always help — he later saw fit to send crates of *sake* to the front lines, at a time when the troops were starving. Crapulence on an empty stomach did little to assist the Japanese war effort. In the end, the men seemed either to admire or despise him.

Tsukamoto wasted little time redressing the grave error of losing Kokoda, the seriousness of which required an extreme response. He would not be forgiven if he failed. He ordered a counterattack through driving rain at 11.30 a.m. on 9 August. Their faces smeared with mud, their uniforms festooned in vegetation, his troops crept back through the jungle toward the Australian lines. They met raking fire, and withdrew. Symington's unit was extremely well dug-in, with rows of light machine-guns trained on all approaches. On his most vulnerable wing he'd placed thirteen automatic weapons in groups of three, every twenty yards. They plugged out a wall of lead covering a 250-yard perimeter, into which the Japanese charge had little hope of success. Indeed, the Australian Bren and Tommy guns were proving their superiority over the Japanese rifle and unwieldy Juki with devastating effect.

Tsukamoto ordered a second attempt at dusk. Two hundred Japanese troops stormed the escarpment and threw themselves at the first Australian platoon. Again, they were repulsed. The Australians resisted two more attacks that night, at 10.20 p.m. and 3.00 a.m. The heavy rain and mud helped to thwart the Japanese advance.

'We went back to Kokoda in order to recapture it,' wrote Watanabe Toshio. 'We fought all day and night. We had still not captured it by midday of the 10th.'[13] Tsukamoto's men seemed to grow confused; this wasn't supposed to happen. Discipline slipped. 'The men were not properly assembled,' wrote Second Lieutenant Hirano, one of Tsukamoto's platoon leaders and an unusually candid diarist. 'Valuable time was wasted in the torrential rain and darkness. Even the section leaders could not be lined up.'[14]

In the heat of battle, even the usually alert Hirano 'turned in the wrong direction ... within 40 [yards] of the Australian lines, and grenades were thrown at us'. Hand-to-hand combat at night was chaotic: 'Suddenly encountered enemy guards in the shadow of large rubber trees. Corporal Hamada killed one of them with bayonet and engaged the others, but enemy fire forced us to withdraw. The platoon was scattered. First class private Hirose was killed ... the soldier I grappled with was wounded in the leg by a hand grenade thrown by Corp Hamada.'

Hirano fell back, stunned by the resistance: 'Every day I am losing my men. I could not repress tears of bitterness. Rested, waiting for tomorrow and struggled against cold and hunger.'[15]

Daylight discouraged combat. The troops withdrew into their trenches like small nocturnal creatures. Furious at their failure to dislodge the enemy, the Japanese waited until dusk for another try. This time they would unleash their speciality, honed in China: a night attack in force. 'No enemy can withstand ... this stirring and dauntless charge,' Hirano wrote.

At sunset a low chant, a primitive dirge, rose from the jungle below the escarpment. It paused. Then a Japanese voice shouted out, 'That should frighten you!' The Australians swore back. Smoke candles burst on the edge of the jungle, and through the cloud the Japanese came. The screams of Tsukamoto's warriors split the night. 'Our grenade discharger began to roar ... we advanced to within 70 [yards] of the Australians ... we fired a smoke candle with excellent results.'[16]

But Hirano's dauntless charge came unstuck. As he jumped over a tree, he recounted: 'I caught my foot in something and fell flat.' He resumed the attack on his hands and knees. But this time Tsukamoto's forces prevailed. After resisting one last burst of Australian fire, they streamed across the plateau — and found it deserted. Symington, short of ammunition and food and easily outnumbered, had withdrawn along the western edge to Deniki.

The Australian veterans similarly recall direct personal experiences: the sudden proximity of the enemy, moments of searing pain or numbing fear; often they knew nothing of things happening yards away in the rain, smoke and darkness. 'Everything happened so quickly,' is a soldier's constant refrain.

'The order came to fix bayonets,' said Smoky Howson, 'and it was then, for the first time, that I became really frightened.'

Some of the wounded, shunning help, wandered off into the darkness: Lieutenant Hercules Crawford, 'limping along the track with head swathed in blood-stained bandages', refused carriers and forced his escorts at gunpoint back to their units. He hobbled off into the jungle and was never seen again.[17]

Private Vic Smythe, though shot through the upper arm, managed to keep firing his Bren for 24 hours. Another private, Trothe, hit in the face by a bullet and minus two fingers, held his position and continued firing for eight hours during the night.[18]

The extreme strain of battle, the loss of friends, the unyielding nature of the Japanese soldier — all contributed to a murderous hatred of the enemy felt among the Australians. At Pirivi village, Wilkinson recalled: '[I] pinned one Jap to the ground with my bayonet and screamed with laughter ... one of my police boys went back to nature and used his rifle as a club.' Later, he reverted to his old, caring self — putting hot stones around a dying mate to warm him. 'Sucking wound of back,' Wilkinson wrote on 8–9 August. 'Holding rosary and crucifix all the time. No rations at all.'

The loss of Kokoda was a strategic disaster for the Allies, redeemed by the extraordinary verve of a few Australian militia troops. A mere 80 men had recaptured and held Kokoda for two-and-a-half days against successive waves of 400 Japanese. During this time, they received no fresh supplies or reinforcements. About twenty Australians died; enemy casualties were far higher.

The battles for Kokoda were small, scarifying flash points; the full invasion of Papua had not yet begun. Their significance was perhaps psychological: not since the start of the Pacific War had the aggressor encountered such fierce resistance. Lieutenant Onogawa, commander of a detached unit of Tsukamoto's battalion, was magnanimous: 'Although the Australians are our enemies, their bravery must be admired,' he wrote on 11 August.[19] Indeed, Kokoda immortalised the name of the 39th Battalion — the first to fight the Japanese on Australian territory.

———

Wilkinson reached Deniki 'totally buggered' and found Cameron 'chewing his whiskers'.[20] The survivors of the 39th withdrew to Isurava, a village on a precipice with a panoramic view of Kokoda and the Mambare River flood plain. Here they dug new trenches — with bayonets and their steel helmets (there were no shovels) — in anticipation of a fresh onslaught. Meanwhile, making his way over the mountains came their new commander, a man of singular coolness and immense courage, the rapidly promoted Lieutenant-Colonel Ralph Honner.

And so they waited in their trenches, high in the mountains at Isurava, for a leader and reinforcements. It was the lull before the storm. Scorned by their own country, poorly trained and supplied, these men formed Australia's front-line defence against the perceived threat of a Japanese invasion. There was no immediate hope of relief and, at that time, they didn't envisage the possibility of retreat.

In Kokoda, meanwhile, the Japanese fortified their positions — and no doubt themselves, with a swig of Tsukamoto's *sake* — and awaited the arrival of the rest of the Nankai Shitai, the South Seas invasion force of the Imperial Army.

Chapter 8
The Sasebo 5 Special Naval Landing Party

The killing of the missionaries was 'very brutal'; and 'a little cruel'
on the part of the battalion commander
— *Japanese POW to Allied interrogators*

No one could have guessed the fate of the Anglican missionaries by observing the Japanese treatment of the Papuan people. Initially, the invader dealt with the local tribes firmly, but not brutally. There is no evidence that the Japanese raped the Orokaivan women or bayoneted the men when they landed at Gona.

On the contrary the Japanese came ashore presenting themselves as freedom fighters, sent to avenge the cause of Asian liberty on behalf of the struggling Papuan. The troops were told by their superiors to behave as though they were the natives' 'equals'.[1] No Japanese soldier believed this, of course. Nor did such crude propaganda persuade the Rabaul natives press-ganged at bayonet point into labour columns and shipped to Gona. Even so, a Japanese–English phrase book found at the beachhead gives an idea of the intention:

Pacification (to the people):

Japanese army has come here with the view of restoring your freedom and giving you independence.

It is for the purpose of restoring liberty for the races in Asia. There is nothing for any of you to get scared at.

Whenever we use your property, you shall be well paid for it.[2]

Not all of this was nonsense. Japanese veterans insist vigorously that they did not mistreat the local people in Papua.[3] And this was, to some extent, true: the Japanese rewarded Papuan collaborators and those willing to work with food or cash. It was deemed expedient to get on with the natives — the Japanese relied on them as guides and carriers. A few friendly relationships flourished between the invading army and the coastal communities. One involved the future Prime Minister of New Guinea, Michael Somare, who remembers the benign influence of the Japanese on his village near Wewak, largely through the enlightened influence of one man, Lieutenant Shibata Yukio, who built houses and helped to educate the children (in one lesson, they learned how to use bamboo sticks as spears). He appears to have been an exception.[4]

Most New Guineans had a different experience of Japanese occupation; they saw their villages destroyed and their plantations plundered — largely through the severity of the Japanese supply failure. As the war in New Guinea progressed, the tribal communities experienced a catastrophic rupture. But at that early stage Japanese intentions were relatively benign.

Major-General Horii Tomitaro himself issued instructions before the invasion on how to deal with the indigenous population: 'Do not wantonly kill or injure them,' he wrote. 'In battle we must overwhelm and destroy the enemy ... however, the natives are those whom we must lead in the future in order to rebuild East Asia. Wantonly to kill ... unresisting natives is to mar the honour of the Imperial Forces ...' He appealed to the troops not to treat the natives as 'pigs'.[5]

A phrase-book of Japanese orders in English perhaps more truthfully reflects the Japanese army's methods of dealing with the natives. The orders listed below were translated from Japanese and handed out to officers in Papua. The subordination of the tribes to the status of slaves is revealing:

Hey! Call one hundred of the villagers together.
Dig in along this line.
Dig a little bit deeper.
Put the sand in [the bags].
Pile them up here.
Bring the stone.
Bring shovels.
Bring here pick axes.
Fifteen minutes rest!
Bring bamboos and logs here.
Try harder.
You carry the gravel.
You carry the pebbles.
Take off that big stone.
Build a new road here.[6]

The road to Greater East Asia was going to be long and hard.

The Japanese found no such uses for the white civilians in New Guinea who, whenever caught — with rare exceptions — were ritually slaughtered. The fate of Benson's party served a grisly early warning of the treatment Australian troops could expect from some Japanese officers. After several days in the jungle, they were betrayed to the Japanese by a Papuan collaborator named Embogi, the village councillor at Upper Dobodura. Embogi was later captured by the Australian army and hanged.

The Japanese caught Benson and incarcerated him in Rabaul for the duration of the war. The Australian soldiers and wounded American airmen were shot, and May Hayman and Mavis Parkinson received no clemency either. Imprisoned for days in a coffee mill near Popondetta, they were taken to a plantation near Buna on 13 August and bayoneted to death.

'Mavis was the first to die,' wrote Dr Tony Matthews. 'A Japanese soldier grasped her from behind and attempted to embrace her; she struggled, almost managed to break free, but the soldier took a step backwards and plunged his bayonet deep into her side. She screamed and sank to the ground. May was ordered to cover her face with a towel; as she was doing so she was bayoneted in the throat.'[7]

When they heard of the ritual slaughter of defenceless women the Australians struggled to articulate their hatred and incomprehension. Padres and chaplains wrestled with their deity to account for such arbitrary cruelty.

Canon Charles Sherlock, an RAAF chaplain who'd known Mavis Parkinson at university, said: 'One found a sense of hate coming in your own mind. One couldn't help feeling a sense of revulsion, and I suppose hatred, because you'd known those two people ... And one wouldn't be human I suppose if one didn't have that kind of reaction.'[8]

The murder was not an isolated incident. The Japanese bayoneting of civilians — and prisoners, as the murder of 160 Australian troops in Rabaul bears witness — was common in the Pacific War. On 12 August, the same fate befell another Anglican mission party, from Sangara, betrayed to the Japanese by people of Perambata village.

The Rev. Henry Holland and Rev. Vivian Hedlich, two teenage girls and two half-caste mission workers were beheaded one by one, with a single stroke of the sword, on Buna beach. 'Before they were killed their grave was dug. The prisoners were made to kneel down by the grave, and were killed one by one,' said a witness.[9] A six-year-old boy and his mother were near the end of the line. The little boy buried his face in his mother's breast. Both were shot in the head, perhaps a merciful concession to the child's terror. The execution of one girl, aged sixteen, was bungled, according to several Japanese witnesses. 'They held her down screaming and crying out while they cut off her head,' said Sato Toshio, a translator attached to the Sasebo 5 Special Naval Landing Party. 'The soldier who told me this said the sight was more than he could stand.'[10]

Such massacres were perfunctorily entered in Japanese diaries; for example, that of first-class seaman Shin Shunji was typical:

'13 August: Natives brought Australian prisoners — five men, three women and a child.

14 August: About 8.00 a.m. decapitated or shot the nine prisoners.'[11]

Junior officers eager to show off their credentials as compassionless warriors tended to perform these executions; the ordinary troops were expected to stand and watch their performances. But many were privately ashamed of such cruelty. One POW who witnessed the killing told his Allied interrogators that he thought such treatment very brutal. The death of the child, in particular, was pitiful. He said he thought it a little cruel on the part of the battalion commander.

Many Japanese troops witnessed these events, as their diaries attest. Yet no War Crimes Tribunal punished the perpetrators and the Japanese Government has paid no compensation to families. One reason is that those responsible were part of the unusually brutal Sasebo 5 Special Naval Landing Party (5SNLP) led by Tsukioka Torashigo, most of whose troops later died in the Pacific War, making identification of the culprits difficult.

The naval landing parties were the Japanese equivalent of the marines or the commandos — crack troops of exceptional courage and strength. In the Japanese case they were often men of innate callousness rendered monstrous in the hands of training officers brutalised beyond redemption. The Japanese commando was trained to think little of human life; any act of cruelty was justified in the name of the imperial will and the rehabilitated Code of the Warrior.

Such were the methods deemed acceptable by many, but by no means all, of the Japanese officers who led the invasion of Papua and New Guinea — and who, borne along on the mantra of the Imperial Rescript, their swords dangling by their sides, drove the Nankai Shitai from the Kokoda plateau into the heart of the Owen Stanley Range.

Part Two
Invasion

Chapter 9
Defenceless

'Why cannot one squadron of fighters be sent out from North Africa? Why cannot some positive commitment be entered into regarding naval reinforcement of Singapore? At this stage misty generalisations will please ... the Japanese and nobody else'
— *Sir Robert Menzies, Australian Prime Minister,* 1939–41

A few hundred Australian militia troops stood between the Japanese and Port Moresby. This was the miserable state of Australian arms in the first week of August 1942. The nation was near-defenceless on the eve of the invasion of its mandated territories. The main causes were the gross neglect of national security and the blind subservience to Britain that had driven prewar defence policy and denuded Australia of arms and troops. The remedy was to be found in the quiet fortitude and extraordinary determination of one man.

That man was not Robert Menzies. When Britain declared war on Germany, Menzies, then Australian prime minister, reluctantly decided to send an expeditionary force abroad. He was deeply suspicious of Japanese intentions. But he received assurances from Britain that the Japanese threat was not serious; in any event, Fortress Singapore would defend Australia. And he was answerable to the local press, who reflected the popular itch to 'bash the Hun' — after all, hadn't little New Zealand just raised an expeditionary army?

The decision chimed with Menzies' personal prejudices. He was an Anglophile and imperialist of the old school.* 'Australians are ... good Australians because they are unhesitatingly British,' he said in a radio broadcast, in the context of the war effort. In any case, the dispatch of Australian troops acquired an irresistible logic once war broke out. Menzies told the Australian people that it was his 'melancholy duty' to inform them that 'they were at war with Germany' within hours of Neville Chamberlain committing Britain. There was no parliamentary or public debate. And so, 25 years after the carnage of Gallipoli, a few men too old to fight sent a new generation of young troops to a foreign killing field. Menzies' decision was extremely popular at home, and reflected the cloying Anglophilia of a nation deeply obeisant to British demands.

To feed the British war effort, Australia unquestioningly sent most of its core army, navy and air force to the European and North African theatres of war. The nation was essentially unprotected. The facts speak with deadening force: throughout 1939–40 Australia dispatched to the Middle East and Singapore four divisions (about 80,000) of its fittest young men. Even on 8 December that year — the day the Japanese bombed Pearl Harbor** — 118,129 Australian Imperial Force troops were serving overseas, up by almost 10,000 on the previous fortnight.[1] Just 31,951 remained at home.*** Not until January 1942 — and the invasion of Rabaul — did the flow cease. According to Sir Paul Hasluck, the historian and former governor-general, 120,945 Australian military personnel were overseas that month. The home

....

* Menzies even fancied himself a future prime minister of Britain. In this odd project, Menzies was dangerously deluded. He misread the march of history. On the eve of its dissolution, he spoke of the indissolubility of the British Empire. Of course he was no 'blind, unthinking imperialist', and did not wish to be bounced into a decision to send Australian troops to Britain (see *High Command*, by David Horner, p. 31). But, ever the artful politician, he couldn't fail to see the electoral support at the time for such a move — support that swiftly turned when the Japanese threat became real.

** 7 December American time. Here the Australian date has been used.

*** These figures refer to the Australian Imperial Force — the volunteer army formed for overseas service. The homeguard, Civilian Militia, exceeded 200,000 at this time — but most were part-time, untrained troops.

guard — the militia — were neither trained nor equipped to make up for this colossal loss of manpower. One splenetic Labor backbencher described this exodus as a 'traitorous act', and laid the blame squarely at the feet of the Menzies Government.★

Home air and naval defence were virtually non-existent in 1939–41. The Royal Australian Navy became a mere appendage of British sea power; Australia's few warships were placed under the command of the Admiralty in the Mediterranean; our six destroyers handed over in exchange for a promised two British cruisers, neither of which reached Australian waters. Swathes of the Australian coastline were left vulnerable.

Witness the navy's 'Coordinated Plans' of 29 August 1941 for the sea defence of the vast eastern seaboard: just eighteen minesweepers, 34 auxiliary minesweepers, and 34 motor patrol boats were on duty guarding Australian waters. The naval shield might have apprehended a balsa canoe, but little else.[2]

The Royal Australian Air Force offered no conceivable domestic deterrent because Australia's best young pilots were absorbed into Britain's air force, the Royal Air Force, via the Empire Air Training Scheme. In January 1941, 23 air squadrons were either serving abroad or earmarked for dispatch; and by September 1941, 12,000 Australian pilots had either been sent or were in training for overseas service. At a stroke, this severely reduced the nation's air defence capacity. Abroad the Australian airmen were the forgotten 'Few': the RAAF's 460 Squadron, for example, flew more Lancaster missions and dropped a greater tonnage of bombs over Germany than any other squadron in Britain's Bomber Command. Back home, on the day Japan bombed Pearl Harbor, Australia had just two air squadrons, each equipped with two flying boats and six Catalinas.

With Australia's best trained soldiers, sailors, and pilots abroad, who was left behind on the eve of the declaration of war with Japan? 'A core of several thousand regulars supplemented by … part-time militiamen,' notes historian David Day. These were the disdained chocos, 'equipped for combat in the style of the Great War'.[3] The nation's home defences were

★ The Labor MP was Eddie Ward, who had a reputation for making intemperate attacks and famously and unfairly accused the Menzies Government of contemplating the abandonment of Australia north of the so-called Brisbane Line (see Hasluck, *The Government and the People*, Volume 1, p. 209; and Day, *The Politics of War*, p. 494).

'unprepared, muddled and confused', stated the *Daily Telegraph*.[4] In June 1940, the defence chiefs could not envisage raising a trained and equipped home army of 130,000 men and bleakly conceded that were Japan to invade, Australia's guns and ammunition 'would not last the defenders more than a month'.[5]

'That is what you cannot tell the public,' warned Sir Keith Murdoch, father of the media tycoon Rupert Murdoch, and then Menzies' Director-General of Information.[6] Menzies heeded this advice, and the nation's defencelessness remained a well-kept secret. The press were muzzled or editorially hijacked, and Murdoch found himself the target of ridicule in the newspapers he did not control, until his resignation from the post of chief censor in December 1940.

Australia needed weapons as well as men. By 1939, the country was virtually unarmed. Its defence spending was a mere 1.06 per cent of national income in 1936–37, far less than Britain's. Even when the money was available, it wasn't spent. By 1939, not a third of the £25 million earmarked two years earlier for capital defence equipment had been spent.[7] As late as 1939–40, Australian war spending amounted to a mere 4.9 per cent of gross national expenditure. To put this in perspective, the figure reached 36.8 per cent in 1942–43 under Prime Minister John Curtin, a demonstrably reformed pacifist.

The gravest weakness was aircraft, a flaw to which Curtin repeatedly drew attention as Leader of the Opposition. At the declaration of the war in the Pacific, the aircraft reserved for home defence numbered 101 Wirraways, normally used for training; 53 Hudson bombers; twelve Catalinas and nine Seagulls. There were not enough fully trained crews to man the 'first line aircraft' — most pilots were then fighting in Britain. To make up the shortfall, 32 fresh squadrons had to be built — a mammoth task that fell to Essington Lewis, nicknamed the 'Steel Tzar', the brilliant former BHP head whom Curtin appointed Director-General of Aircraft Production at the end of 1941.[8]

Even if Britain had sent a Spitfire squadron when initially requested, Australia had only a fifth of the aviation fuel necessary to fight an air war.[9] In January 1942, there were no anti-aircraft guns.[10] Dozens of aircraft ordered from America were diverted to Britain during the evacuation of Dunkirk.

The nation had no effective tanks, fighter planes or heavy bombers, and none in prospect.[11] When Japan attacked Pearl Harbor, there were just ten light training tanks in the country — and 70 light tanks on order.

The nation's light arms industry was a joke. Of the prized Vickers machine-guns manufactured locally at the rate of 200 a month, 125 were destined for the British army in India; of the rest just twenty found their way into the Australian army.[12] Rifles were in short supply; anti-tank weapons and light machine-guns — mostly the old Lewis World War I models — would equip the army at merely half-strength. As late as April 1941, there were no mines to protect the nation's ports — an open invitation to the enemy.

Even by 1942, the situation was dire. In February, after the fall of Singapore, Australian arms production showed a deficiency of 32,000 rifles; 250 heavy and 1000 light anti-aircraft guns; and 7000 light machine guns.[13] In the same month, only 300 Bren guns were produced, and just 1590 were in stock.

Oddly, 80 per cent of the required bullets were available; there just weren't sufficient guns to fire them. Most seriously, as late as April 1942, Australia had a mere 185 tanks to defend the largest island on earth. It is true that arms production would soon rise dramatically, and that American firepower would arrive. Even so, when the Japanese attacked Darwin in February 1942, Australia was a nation on its knees.

We need not delve too deeply into the seeds of this feeble legacy. Suffice to say Menzies' belated efforts to re-equip Australia failed to arrest decades of neglect. In 1933, the state of the defence force 'had reached its lowest point for 20 years', observed Hasluck. The rearmament policies of the late 1930s were too little, too late. Successive governments during the 1930s ignored warnings of the grave risks of Japanese aggression and 'demonstrated a chronic lack of self-reliance'.[14]

Menzies was made painfully aware of the Japanese threat, but did little about it. Only the most blinkered could miss the signs: the Manchurian Incident of 1932; the invasion of Shanghai and the rape of Nanking in 1937; the emergence of a belligerent martial regime; and the drumbeat of propaganda championing Japan's right to an Asian empire and supremacy over the white imperialists. On 27 September 1940 Japan signed a mutual cooperation pact with Germany and Italy, recognising their leadership in Europe in exchange for recognition of Japan as the ruler of 'Greater East Asia'. Alert to these warnings, Menzies turned constantly to his imagined saviour and cherished mother country, which looked askance at its importunate offspring like an embarrassed parent.

In this polarising world, Menzies sought assurances from Britain of the inviolability of Singapore; these were summarily scotched on 13 June 1940 when a British cable 'of apocalyptic character' denied that it would, after all, send reinforcements to Singapore.[15]

In response, Menzies ratcheted up defence spending and pursued a 'craven policy of appeasement' of the Pacific aggressor.[16] He sought to trade with Japan when virtually no one else would; America had shut its door on most trade with Japan partly in protest at the latter's refusal to withdraw from Manchuria. A Menzies olive branch to Japan — Australian scrap iron — earned him the incorrect nickname, 'Pig Iron Bob'.★ His government turned a blind eye to Japan's conquest of China — an ugly precursor of the Labor Party's disgraceful collusion with Indonesia after the invasion of East Timor. Indeed, had Menzies not emerged as the nation's most successful post-war leader he would surely have been remembered, with Chamberlain, whom he admired, as an appeaser of fascism.

Menzies shunned the Americans, perversely insisting on a defence 'between Australia and Britain, not Australia and America'.[17] A gaping void thus lay at the heart of defence policy, to which Sir Frederick Shedden, then the powerful secretary of Australia's Defence Department, responded by

---

★ It was scrap iron, not pig iron, that Menzies exported to Japan, as he archly put it in a radio broadcast on 10 April 1942: 'My term of office was from April 1939 to August 1941. So, far from the Menzies Government being a "pig-iron-for-Japan Government" the records show that, during my term of office, no pig iron was exported from Australia to Japan, nor was any iron ore. In the whole of the two years the exports of steel to Japan from Australia did not reach fifty tons. It is true that over the same period there was an export of one hundred and seven thousand tons of scrap iron to Japan from Australia, while in half that period, namely the year 1939 alone, the United States of America exported to Japan two million tons of scrap iron and the like material. During my term of office Australia exported to Japan one hundred and ten million pounds' weight of wool, valued at £8,000,000, and £1,700,000 worth of wheat. About these last two items I have heard no complaint, though it is obvious that the maintenance of any army depends upon food and clothing just as much as it does upon guns and ammunition.'

recommending the production of as many aircraft as could be built, as quickly as possible.[18]

As a last resort, Menzies pleaded for military help from Churchill. His pleas were met with polite obfuscation. A year before the fall of Singapore, Menzies plaintively wrote: 'Why cannot one squadron of fighters be sent out from North Africa? Why cannot some positive commitment be entered into regarding naval reinforcement of Singapore? At this stage misty generalisations will please . . . the Japanese and nobody else.'[19]

Menzies' own party eventually turned on him, for various reasons, not least of which was the rudderless handling of national security. The Prime Minister complained that he spent a third of his time 'warding off blows aimed at me . . . from those who are supposed to be my supporters — "snipers", people who shoot from behind'.[20] In August 1941, to sustain the metaphor, they shot him.

In 1940–41, however, Australians comforted themselves that, if attacked, Britain would immediately send ships and planes to the rescue. Menzies justified the dispatch of more than 100,000 Australian troops overseas on these grounds. The Australian people rather naively imagined their country was a sacred priority in the British schema. In truth, Churchill thought India the jewel in the imperial crown; Australians, he once intemperately muttered, were a people of 'bad stock'.[21]

Yet this sense of closeness between the two nations was understandable — on racial, cultural and historical grounds. Most white Australians called themselves 'British' in the 1933 census. The emotional link with the mother country was strong and real. The official statistician observed that Australians had the 'essential characteristics of their British ancestors, with perhaps some accentuation of the desire for freedom from restraint'.[22]

'The idea that Britain was "home",' noted historian David Day, 'was a long time dying in the harsh climate of the distant dominion.'[23] Such feelings underlay the White Australia Policy, officially in place since Federation, and firmly applied during World War II. Of course, this fed through to anti-Japanese propaganda, and ratcheted up hatred of the Japanese to hysterical heights. Elsewhere it had unexpected consequences. In one disgusting application, black American troops sent to help defend

Australia were refused permission to disembark. An Emergency War Cabinet later overturned the ban, and the Negroes, as they were then known, were hidden away on manual duties in the Northern Territory.*

The strongest emotional argument for British military help was the mother country's historic debt to Australian arms. The point has been thrashed out many times — tediously, no doubt, to British ears. Perhaps this is because it is uncomfortably true. From the birth of (white) Australia, at Federation, in 1901, to the crisis of 1942, the nation put the defence of the British Empire ahead of her own.

No country proportional to its population gave so many lives fighting for British interests as Australia did in the twentieth century. Three hundred thousand young Australian men were sent to Europe during The Great War, in a country of then 4 million people; 61,000 of them died on foreign soil, at Gallipoli and the Western Front; Pozières alone claimed 23,000 Australian casualties within weeks. Australian troops won 63 of the 577 Victoria Crosses awarded in World War I, most posthumously. They were all volunteers. Indeed, Australia suffered the greatest proportional loss of any nation.

The people — from the ordinary man and woman to Menzies himself — naively supposed Britain would demonstrate a reciprocal obligation. Prime ministers instinctively exploited the emotional power of this argument. John Curtin famously declared that Britain would be 'gravely indicted' if it failed to help Australia, 'which sacrificed 60,000 of its men on overseas battlefields in the last war and, at its peril, has sent its naval, military and air forces overseas to fight in this one'.[24]

It had not escaped Churchill's notice that the Australians would fight. At the battle of Bardia in January 1941, the Second AIF raised the standard of Gallipoli, charged five hundred miles across the western deserts of Africa, destroyed nine and a half Italian divisions, and captured 130,000 prisoners, 40 tanks and 1290 guns. It was an auspicious start to a campaign that ended with the Siege of Tobruk.

---

* Interestingly, Britain was even more hostile to black troops, and permitted even fewer to enter their country during the war than the number allowed into Australia.

Australia pressed Britain for a guarantee of military support, and its ambassadors in London extracted what they supposed to be a watertight commitment. The wording should have alarmed Menzies' sharp legal mind: 'If … Japan set about invading Australia … on a large scale,' Churchill wrote in August 1940, 'I have explicit authority of Cabinet to assure you that we should then cut our losses in the Mediterranean and proceed to your aid, sacrificing every interest except only [the] defence position of this island on which all else depends.'[25]

In short, the Japanese would have to be charging up Bondi Beach before Britain would send a fleet to the Pacific. Churchill's assurances were 'militarily worthless'.[26] The words 'large scale' and 'except' were heavy hints. If the point penetrated Menzies' sharp, legal brain, it did not show in his actions. He deemed it perfectly safe to keep tens of thousands of Australian men in the Middle East. He held this line, in a steadily weakening form, until his ejection from office in August 1941.

In this light, Britain did not betray Australia. Churchill had offered a heavily qualified guarantee. His paramount loyalty, in their extreme peril, was to the British people. Churchill recognised that the 'first duty of any Government is to its own country'.[27] Menzies might have taken a leaf out of this remedial political text.

The United Kingdom Chiefs of Staff, in rejecting Australia's representations for greater forces in the Pacific, stated their guiding principle: 'It is vital to avoid being weak everywhere.'[28] The war against Germany was exhausting British military resources. They had little to spare for the Far East. In 1941, British weakness 'on all fronts', made it 'impossible to denude them any further to meet a possible [Japanese] threat', said one British commander.[29] Churchill had diverted a division of British troops to Singapore, in response to an Australian plea, thousands of whom perished.

Churchill knew, in the end, that Britain couldn't save Singapore: 'I do not see how anyone could expect Malaya to be defended once the Japanese obtained command of the sea and while we are fighting for our lives against Germany …'[30] While British circumstances had profoundly changed, Australians were locked in a dream world based on fading assurances from the past. The 'steel walls of the British navy'[31] proved rather more brittle than Menzies' scrap iron.

Australians, in truth, were betrayed not by Britain so much as by their political and military leaders (with the notable exception of Curtin), whose appalling neglect of the most basic duty of government — national security — directly led to the crisis in the Owen Stanleys. And it is possibly true that the Australian people, in their wistful nostalgia and denial of the Japanese threat, betrayed themselves.★

One act of Churchill's was unforgiveable, however, and it was directly linked to the battle for Australia. The British leader stubbornly resisted the return home of two divisions of Australian troops, and actually ordered their diversion to Burma while they were at sea, without informing the Australian Government. No doubt the loss of British soldiers in Singapore had affected his judgment.[32] Yet no nation, least of all Britain, would have tolerated such grotesque interference in domestic security by a foreign power. The episode formed the crucible of a heroic struggle by Australia's new prime minister, in a crisis not of his making, for the return home of the Second Australian Imperial Force — the very men who would soon relieve the militia in the Papuan mountains.

★ The case for an orchestrated 'betrayal' of Australia by Britain is not easily made. It seems rather that British ministers were unable, or refused, to see the war through Australian eyes. In January 1942, Churchill ordered the redirection of an entire division of British troops, which had been bound for Burma, to Singapore, in response to the Australian claim that the evacuation of the island fortress would be an 'inexcusable betrayal'. With the fall of Singapore, thousands of these British troops died. Churchill never forgave the Australian Government for the loss, argues David Day. At other times, Churchill spoke sincerely of British gratitude to Australia for her military support. Churchill constantly reassured Curtin of Britain's intended support, despite Britain's own grave situation. He restated Britain's commitment to send immediate troops and ships at the expense of India and the Middle East if Australia were *invaded in force* by Japan. It was an effective caveat. Whether these reassurances were hollow or sincere depends on one's measure of the British leader. Curtin never openly condemned Churchill for 'betraying' Australia. It is noteworthy that Evatt, and not Curtin, penned the intemperate cable that described the evacuation of Singapore as an inexcusable betrayal of Australia. Davids Horner and Day, the titans of Australian World War II military and political history, disagree on whether Britain betrayed Australia during World War II. David Horner does not recognise a betrayal, stating that British inability to help Australia was forced on Churchill by the fact that it was fighting a total war. David Day, however, in his books *The Great Betrayal* and *The Politics of War* makes plain his view that Britain betrayed the dominion. Churchill himself perhaps spoke the truth of Britain's position, when he said that a government's first duty is to its own country (see *The Politics of War*, p. 307). It was just as well that Curtin took the same view.

Chapter 10
Curtin

'Dear Mr President ... We are now, with a small population in
the only white man's territory south of the equator, beset
grievously ... we now lack adequacy for the forces of our
homeland in the defence of our own soil'
— *Prime Minister John Curtin to President Franklin D. Roosevelt,
early* 1942

John Curtin became Australian prime minister in October 1941. He
travelled a long, hard road to this perilous height, as leader of a free nation
at war with Germany and under the perceived threat of invasion by Japan.

A brief biographical sketch shows an idealistic young man of pedigreed
working-class origins, who abandoned the Catholicism of his birth for a
humanists' paradise, 'a paradise created in this world by the will of men and
women sufficiently courageous to fight for it'.[1] This wistful dream
underscored his life's work and prophesied his own political destiny.

Curtin looked a quiet, bookish man. With his elliptical black-rimmed
spectacles and intense concentration, he seemed to resemble a Left Bank
literary don, a Joycean doppelganger, rather than a shrewd political operator
and formidable thinker.

It was not always so. In his younger days as a fiery unionist and determined alcoholic, he rose through the Labor Party at times 'elevating and inspiring',[2] at others, a comatose wreck. He could be found darkly 'boozing in quiet corners' before making a campaign speech 'in an alcoholic daze'.[3] An avowed anti-war campaigner at the outbreak of World War I, there is a story that he presented himself drunk to the recruiting officers. He beat his addiction, and abandoned the extreme socialist dogma of his youth. A profoundly tortured soul, a genuine man of the people, he later shocked his left-wing colleagues by supporting a limited form of conscription. In time, he re-acquired a Christian, if not Catholic, understanding of the world.

As the Japanese threat intensified, Curtin appeared to undergo a transformation. The exigencies of the hour seemed to envelop him, and he responded with extraordinary gusto and determination, despite his own frail health. His humility and quiet compassion never left him. No doubt he was prone to indecisiveness and forgiveable naivety — and later fell too far under the American wing. But accusations that he handed control of the defence of Australia to MacArthur need strong qualification. The circumstances were forced upon him: he inherited a near-defenceless country, and in the absence of a British saviour, America was Australia's only hope. Inevitably, the price of freedom was US control of the war effort.

Curtin's great wartime achievement was to articulate — through his actions, by securing the return to Australia of Australian troops, and in his inspiring oratory — an independent destiny for a nation that had scarcely loosened its grip on the coat-tails of the mother country. He did this despite ferocious criticism from elements of the Australian press, and opposition from some of his own diplomats, who seemed bewitched by Churchill's charm.

In sum, Curtin overcame deep personal failings to lead a nation at war with decency and humility. He deployed a shrewd intellect and an appealing pragmatism. And he could be very tough, demonstrated repeatedly in the manner in which he dealt with the unions. Some union leaders tried to buy Curtin off — demanding the promise of a post-war blueprint for social change in return for their cooperation. They mistook his decency for weakness. He scorned their demands, telling the wharf labourers in his own electorate of Fremantle, on 28 January 1941, 'We have to concentrate on one supreme task which the enemy has imposed on us. We have to defeat him or die. It is no use preaching ... the precepts of the Apostles to the enemy. The whine of bullets is the only epistle he will understand.'[4]

He dealt with strikers by threatening to withdraw their exemption from military service if they refused to work in their protected industries. When wharf workers refused to unload ships, Curtin sent in the navy to do it, then shamed the strikers into resuming their jobs: 'The men who are not in the fighting forces and who ... will not work are as much the enemies of this country as the ... legions of the enemy.'[5] Strong stuff; it shamed many workers into rejoining the war effort in defiance of their union bosses. Indeed, by 1942, Curtin took the podium of a nation at war with the unquestionable moral authority of a man for whom many Australians felt something akin to love.

It was a painful rite of passage for the Australian people. The milestones are worth charting in order to understand how, in a very tangible way, Curtin may be seen as the politician who saved Australia. His policy decisions — made under extreme pressure, in the teeth of great resistance from Churchill and Roosevelt — delivered the manpower and weaponry necessary to banish the Japanese aggressor from Papua and New Guinea. And there is no doubt that the reinforcements he secured from the Middle East saved the militia, stranded in the Owen Stanleys.

On assuming office, Curtin read the mood, noted the disastrous state of Australia's armed forces, observed the Japanese peril, and powerfully formulated the national response. The war with Japan was a 'new war', not 'merely another incident in the present war', he declared.* Curtin resolved upon a 'revolutionary' course for Australia. No longer would young men be sent to die at the beck and call of the British. No more, the humiliation of Australia's diplomatic supplicants, prostrate on the stairs of Whitehall. The men would come home and the domestic arms industry would be revived.

---

* The words were, in fact, Shedden's, whose acute sense of timing outshone the 'scrappy and meagre' performance of the Australian Chiefs of Staff (see Horner, *High Command*, and Day, *Curtin*, p. 432).

On 8 December 1941, close to 200 Japanese Mitsubishis took off from aircraft carriers anchored beneath the Pacific horizon. They burst out of the dawning sun and dive-bombed the American fleet at Pearl Harbor. Within a morning, America lost the pride of her navy. Churchill said he was 'well content' with the news; America at last would be forced to enter the war. Curtin responded with simple, noble melancholy: 'Well, it has come.'[6] Japanese Premier Tojo Hideki was free to pursue Japan's Greater Asian war unchecked by the guns of US warships.

Curtin declared war the next day: 'We are at war with Japan. That has happened because, in the first instance, Japanese naval and air forces launched an unprovoked attack on British and United States territory.'[7] He did so without getting the green light from London, as was normal procedure for the dominions. It was a sign of his impatience with Britain, and growing confidence in the Americans. In rapid succession, Thailand, Hong Kong and the Philippines fell to the Japanese war machine. As the threat to the nation rose, Curtin urged an 'all-in' war effort 'to resist those who would destroy our title to Australia'.[8] Workers would sacrifice their holidays; employers would curtail their golfing parties; Christmas would be a Spartan affair.

Curtin's near-exhausted arsenals meant that only American or British help could save Australia. In Opposition he'd argued for years for local over imperial defence. As prime minister, he now firmly set Australia's course in a powerful letter to Roosevelt and Churchill, on 23 December 1941:

> Our men have fought and will fight valiantly. But they must be adequately supported. We have three divisions in the Middle East. Our airmen are fighting in Britain, Middle East and training in Canada. We have sent great quantities of supplies to Britain, to the Middle East and to India. Our resources here are very limited.
>
> It is in your power to meet the situation. Should the government of the United States desire, we would gladly accept an American Commander in the Pacific Area . . .'[9]

The offer drew a line in the sand with Britain, and pointed Australia towards a new military and political alliance with America.

The public statement of this intention flashed out of a hot summer's day, 27 December 1941, when Curtin played his American hand to the Australian people. The paddock, the beach and the backyard were unprepared for the impact of the Labor leader's New Year's message, which was said to 'reverberate around the world' (insofar as Australian political messages were capable of global reverberation). It was a mere newspaper article (in the *Melbourne Herald*), but its historic significance lay in his defiant appeal for American military help.

Declaring that Australia should jettison its historic military dependence on Britain, Curtin struck at the heart of Australia's 'Britishness'. To the disgust of Churchill, who found the remark insulting, Curtin unapologetically bound Australia's destiny with America's: 'Without any inhibitions of any kind, I make it quite clear that Australia looks to America, free of any pangs as to our traditional links or kinship with the United Kingdom.'[10]

Curtin's article was a 'clarion call to Australian nationhood'.[11] His appeal to America transcended crude party politics. It was a statement of Australia's new place in the world and, ultimately, a plea for help. He envisaged the creation of an Australian–American military alliance powerful enough to defeat the Japanese in the Pacific. In this sense, his New Year's message was also a call to arms, an exhortation aimed at 'revolutionising ... the Australian way of life' in which 'every citizen' was expected to 'place himself, his private and business affairs, his entire mode of living on a war footing'.[12]

There was a bit of genius in this unashamed appeal to Australian patriotism in alliance with America, the citadel of capitalism, from a man of the Left. Few Liberals possessed such breadth of vision, while Labor's communist sympathisers — Stalin's 'useful idiots' in the West — were aghast. Neither fussy conservative Anglophiles nor militant left-wing ideologues had a place in the national emergency to come.

Curtin revealed the gravity of the situation in a letter to his wife, Elsie, on 5 January 1942:

The war goes very badly and I have a cable fight with Churchill almost daily. He had been in Africa and India, and they count before Australia and New Zealand. The truth is that Britain never thought Japan would fight and made no preparation to meet that eventuality. [Britain] never believed airpower could outfight seapower and now they will not risk ships uncovered by air support and there is no probability of air support. In Australia we have to produce our own aircraft. Notwithstanding two years of Menzies we have to really start production. But enough, I love you, and that is all there is to say.[13]

No statement better captured the isolation of Australia, and the transcendent humanity of its leader. Curtin had no doubt where the blame for the lack of aircraft lay. On 11 December, after the Japanese sank the British warships *Repulse* and *Prince of Wales*, he reminded the nation that for years he'd insisted the navy and army — however strong — relied on maximum air defence. 'Now we are faced with the reality.'[14] Indeed, Australia had no aircraft remotely capable of meeting the Japanese threat. An 'absolute concentration' on the war effort was decreed.

The rate of arms and aircraft production was cranked up to an unprecedented level under the robust guidance of Essington Lewis. Aircraft were 'the first degree of priority'; the goal, to produce 60 squadrons. Thanks to Lewis' energy and Curtin's unstinting support, Beauforts, Tiger Moths and Wirraways were coming off the assembly lines at a rate that would meet the required quota within six months.[15]

But the southerly advance of the Japanese demanded a swifter response. Australia would soon turn in despair to America. The Americans had already discussed the country's value as an offensive base. But assistance would not be forthcoming yet, because of 'inadequate naval strength' in the region,[16] noted the Australian War Cabinet on 20 January.

Nor was Japan Roosevelt's first priority — despite Pearl Harbor. Churchill and Roosevelt had agreed to defeat 'Germany First', as enshrined in a secret pact code-named WWI. It didn't take a forensic expert to glean the essence of the deal. For months, media and political circles understood

'Germany First' as the guiding theme of the war. Churchill had suggested as much to Curtin in an earlier Christmas correspondence.

Yet Australia's blinkered diplomats in London and Washington failed to see the wood for the trees — until they were standing inches from the bark. Indeed, Page, Bruce, Casey and Evatt* were incapable of drawing Whitehall's and Washington's attention to the extreme vulnerability of Australia. These men seemed to misapprehend the brutal truth that their country was, in fact, expendable. And they were excessively prone to Churchill's charms. In one case of clear disloyalty, Page took the British line against Curtin's instructions.

Curtin was ill at ease with the aristocratic flamboyance and condescending humour of his British counterpart. For example, Churchill on 10 January presumed to tell the Australian leader, 'the defence of Australian soil ... rests primarily with you ... It is quite true that you may have air attacks but we have had a good dose already in England without mortally harmful results.'[17] Yet mutual respect — and an odd, mutual curiosity — nonetheless bound the two men, and they got on well despite the growing friction.

On 23 January 1942, 5000 Japanese troops captured Rabaul, the capital of New Britain, causing widespread panic in Australia. The RAAF commander at Rabaul pleaded for bombers and fighters. GHQ, then based in Melbourne, replied, 'If we had them you would get them.'[18] No event more gravely underscored Australia's helplessness in the skies. The Japanese Zero, if it chose, virtually controlled the air space as far south as Townsville. New Britain would soon become Tojo's South Sea base, hosting one of the largest concentrations of Japanese troops outside Japan. The threat of a Japanese invasion of Australia was seen as real, and imminent. Quoting Byron's 'Night

---

* Sir Earle Page, special envoy to British War Cabinet; Stanley Bruce, a former Prime Minister and High Commissioner in London; Richard Casey, Australian Minister in Washington; Dr H.V. Evatt, Minister for Foreign Affairs. Evatt managed to elicit the most patronising of British put-downs. A stuffy English intelligence officer, observing that Churchill had worked hard 'to educate and mellow' Evatt, described the Australian as 'this parochial, restless, rude, ambitious, indefatigable and by no means unintelligent creature whose brain and energy one cannot help respecting and to some extent liking in spite of his drab appearance, dreary droning voice with its nazal [sic] whine, and unattractive personality'. (Day, *The Politics of War*, p. 321.)

Before Waterloo' — 'Nearer, clearer, deadlier than before/The cannon's opening roar' — Curtin warned the nation, 'Anybody who fails to perceive the immediate menace which this attack constitutes for Australia must be lost to all reality.'[19]

He immediately agreed to US leadership of what would be called the South-West Pacific Area. As negotiations progressed, the defence chiefs quietly decided which parts of the country must be defended from invasion. Lieutenant-General Sir Iven Mackay, commander of the Home Forces, in a memo sent on 4 February to the Minister for the Army, identified the coal-rich arc of Port Kembla–Newcastle–Lithgow; the cities of Sydney and Melbourne; and the burgeoning US military base at Brisbane. Three divisions of militia were available to defend this vast region, extending a thousand miles from Brisbane to Melbourne. In purely military terms, it made sense to concentrate the small number of available troops behind the so-called Brisbane Line, yet the Government did not officially adopt Mackay's recommendation. All the same, the retention of AIF troops for months in Queensland, the fortifications north of Brisbane, the concentration of defence facilities in Newcastle–Sydney–Port Kembla, and the failure adequately to reinforce Western Australia gave the infamous legend a great deal of plausibility.*

Australia's darkest hour came sooner than Curtin feared. On 15 February 1942, the Australian people awoke from their pleasant dream to an awful reality. Singapore had surrendered. A few thousand Japanese troops landed, captured the island's water supply, and forced the most ignominious

---

* MacArthur would later claim that when he arrived in Australia the defence of the south-east corner of Australia, and a readiness to abandon the north to the Japanese, was official policy and that only through his insistence was it withdrawn: 'That was the plan when I arrived, but to which I never subscribed and which I immediately changed to a plan to defend Australia in New Guinea' (AWM 3DRL/6643 47 of 141). It is hard to find an Australian military expert who agrees with this statement. The situation was constantly changing, they argue, and Australia's defensive shield extended as resources came home from the Middle East. No government officially adopted the policy — despite the claims of the Labor MP, Eddie Ward, that the Menzies Government first proposed the Brisbane Line. Even so, the idea that Western Australia, the Northern Territory, South Australia and most of Queensland were apparently dispensable did not impress a people animated by the idea of a fair go. It transgressed every principle of mateship for which Australians prided themselves. Forde, the Minister for the Army, was nonplussed, to say the least; members of his electorate lived in northern Queensland. The furious Western Australians would later contemplate secession from the Federation.

capitulation in British military history — precipitating General Arthur Percival's sad walk towards the Japanese lines bearing a white flag.★

The fall of Singapore was 'Australia's Dunkirk',[20] Curtin declared; 'the Battle for Australia' would commence.[21] Japan was now at liberty to invade Australia 'should she so desire', noted the Australian Chiefs of Staff, masterfully perfunctory as always. Of three possible invasion plans, Japan was most likely to attack Port Moresby, 'thence the mainland of Australia', they concluded.[22]

In four days their fears were realised. On 19 February 1942, as Curtin lay sick in bed with gastritis, scores of high-altitude Japanese bombers flown by Pearl Harbor veterans bombed Darwin, killing 250 people and destroying Darwin's port, nine ships and twenty aircraft.[23]

A month earlier Churchill appeared to have acceded to Australian demands for the return of two divisions of the Second Australian Imperial Force. 'I am sure we all sympathise with our kith and kin in Australia,' he told the House of Commons on 27 January, 'now that the shield of British and American sea power has ... been withdrawn from them so unexpectedly and so tragically and now that hostile bombers may soon be within range of Australian shores ... We shall not put any obstacles to the return of the splendid Australian troops, who volunteered for Imperial service, to defend their own homeland ...'[24]

Churchill did not mean they should go home; he meant they should go to India or Java or the Malayan barrier — defending British as well as Australian interests — as he deftly hinted: 'the Japanese are more likely to [secure] their rich prizes in the Philippines, the Dutch East Indies and the Malayan Archipelago ... than to undertake a serious mass invasion of Australia ...' This was consistent with his proposal in December 1941 to return 40,000 Australian troops to the Dutch East Indies (Indonesia), but emphatically not to Australia.

★ On the day Singapore fell, a letter of singular befuddlement floated into Curtin's office: 'My dear Prime Minister,' Menzies wrote, 'would we be ... better off in this war by concentrating all available forces in the north of Australia to carry out a Continental defence and not an island one?' Menzies was now advocating the concentration of Australian troops in Australia, and presented the idea as though it were a novel one. 'There are undoubtedly naval and military and air considerations of which I am ignorant,' the former PM conceded. To which a weary Curtin replied, 'The evolution of [your] opinion towards a policy which has long since been advocated by me ... is not without interest.'

These islands fell successively to the Japanese in January–February. So Churchill insisted that the fleet then in the Indian Ocean, and carrying 20,000 Australian troops, should be diverted to Rangoon, to defend the Burma Road.

Roosevelt, the Australian Chiefs of Staff, most of the Australian press, Menzies, (Sir Keith) Murdoch, even Curtin's own diplomatic representatives in London, all agreed with Churchill. Page was the most vocal of a posse of Australian diplomats and generals who supported the diversion of Australian soldiers to Burma.[25] They argued, in essence, that it was vital to keep the Burma Road open, in order to supply China; China, they claimed, was the linchpin of the Pacific War.

Curtin, virtually alone, disagreed. He demanded that the troops be returned home. He found himself in the extraordinary position of having to defend the most basic duty of a prime minister: to procure an army and protect his country from possible invasion.★

His desperation and bristling indignation can be painfully felt in the exhaustive cable sent on 19 February to the British General Wavell (who had recommended to the Pacific War Council that Australian troops be diverted to Burma):

In no respect whatever, have calls upon AUSTRALIA for assistance elsewhere remained unanswered. When state of land and air defences in MALAYA was revealed by the first SINGAPORE conference we did NOT hesitate to send the bulk of an AIF division and three squadrons from the RAAF. The AIF formation and additional reinforcements despatched have now been lost … We have sent AUSTRALIAN land and air forces to AMBON, KOEPANG, PORTUGESE TIMOR, NEW CALEDONIA and SOLOMON islands. There are 6250 empire air scheme personnel abroad. Our resources are NOT only strained but are desperately

---

★ Curtin seemed to be surrounded by ineffectual men, stooges for Churchill, and plain disloyalty. He had to reprimand Earle Page sharply, after Page failed repeatedly to stress Australia's predicament to London, 'We fear that you cannot have sufficiently emphasised the very unsatisfactory state of our own defences … We lack adequate air support. We have little naval strength … Japan has command of the relevant sea approaches. We have no fighters whatever and our bombers and reconnaissance planes have been reduced to about 50. Our militia is small and is very short of equipment.'

small. Equipment which we could NOT reasonably spare was made available at the request of the British Government ... we would be completely failing in our duty to the people of AUSTRALIA if we agreed to diversion of any division of AIF ... [Our] object [is] to stop JAPAN's thrust south. That object can now be achieved only by allocating AIF to Australia ... it should come to AUSTRALIA with greatest possible expedition.[26]

Churchill would not abide this truculent dominion. He tried to intimidate Curtin, with a meanly phrased wire the next day, 20 February:

I suppose you realise that your leading division, the head of which is sailing south of Colombo ... at this moment ... is the only force that can reach Rangoon in time to prevent its loss and the severance of communication with China? I am quite sure that if you refuse to allow your troops to stop this gap ... a very grave effect will be produced upon the President and the Washington circle upon whom you are so largely dependent ... We must have an answer immediately as the leading ships of the convoy will soon be steaming in the opposite direction from Rangoon [to Australia] and every day is a day lost.[27]

Churchill had indeed carefully harnessed the support of Roosevelt, the aristocratic, liberal US President, who weighed into the transcontinental debate with a cable to Curtin of persuasive dignity, on 21 February. It is worth quoting at length:

I fully appreciate how grave are your responsibilities in reaching a decision in the present serious circumstances as to the disposition of the first Australian division returning from the Middle East.

I assume that you know now of our determination to send, in addition to all troops and forces now en route, another force of over 27,000 men to Australia. This force will be fully equipped in every respect.

We must fight to the limit of our two flanks — one based on Australia and the other on Burma, India and China. Because of our geographical position we Americans can better handle the reinforcement of Australia and the right flank ...

... you may have every confidence that we are going to reinforce your position with all possible speed. On the other hand the left flank simply must be held. If Burma goes it seems to me our whole position, including that of Australia will be extremely strained. Your Australian Division is the only force that is available for immediate reinforcement. It could get into the fight at once and ... save what now seems a very dangerous situation.

While I realize the Japanese are moving rapidly I cannot believe that ... your vital centers are in immediate danger.

While I realize that your men have been fighting all over the world, and are still, and while I know full well of great sacrifices which Australia has made, I nevertheless want to ask you in the interest of our whole war effort in the Far East if you will reconsider your decision and order the division now en route to Australia to move with all speed to support the British forces fighting in Burma.

You may be sure we will fight by your side with all our force until victory. Roosevelt.[28]

It is worth reminding ourselves that these exchanges of words between the most powerful men in London, Washington and Canberra were dealing with the fate of some 20,000 men — the 7th Australian Division — then at sea, in enemy waters, for whose repatriation Curtin fought down to the wire in order to reinforce Australia.

Curtin stood firm: the troops would come directly to Australia, and not go to Burma. In the manner of his stand lay the mark of political greatness. Was not his first duty to the Australian people, to use Churchill's own words?

His was not an emotional plea; Curtin wrapped his case in trenchant argument: China was not the linchpin in the war; Australia was extremely vulnerable; American troops, who did not share the digger's patriotism, could not adequately defend the nation, he argued. Indeed, the Australian soldiers abroad and at sea were clamouring to get home to fight.

Curtin saw that Japan controlled Burmese air space and waters. It was the decisive factor in the loss of Burma.[29] Any troops landing there were certainly doomed, as Curtin reminded Churchill: 'In view of superior Japanese sea power and air power, it would appear to be a matter of some doubt as to whether [the Australian troops] can be landed at Burma . . .

'The movement of our forces [to Burma] . . . is not considered a reasonable hazard of war . . . its adverse results would have the gravest consequences on the morale of the Australian people. The Government therefore must adhere to its decision . . .'[30]

His bargaining chip was his very country, the only free nation in East Asia that offered a suitable base for an American-led counteroffensive. America knew this. Curtin's mind was made up. He wrote gratefully but firmly to Roosevelt the next day, 22 February:

> Dear Mr President . . . We are now, with a small population in the only white man's territory south of the equator, beset grievously . . . we now lack adequacy for the forces of our homeland in the defence of our own soil.
>
> You have indicated an appreciation of the gravity of our responsibilities in reaching a decision on the matter referred to in your message. It has affected us profoundly . . . our vital centres are in immediate danger.

Roosevelt accepted Curtin's decision as that of a sovereign country entitled to direct its troops to where it saw fit: 'Well, if they have made their minds up, that is the way it is.'[31] (He graciously added that it would not affect the movement of US troops to Australia.)

Churchill did not. The British leader ignored the Australian Government's wishes. On 20 February 1942 Churchill, of his own volition, without informing Australia, re-directed the convoy to Burma — with 'callous disregard'[32] for Australia's defence needs. Privately Churchill never forgave Australia for the loss of thousands of British troops at Singapore. This weighed on his mind and spurred his action virtually to commandeer Australian defence policy, and order a division of Australian troops to what he knew would be their likely doom.

He defended his incredible action to a furious Curtin, on 22 February, on the grounds that 'we could not contemplate that you would refuse our request'. 'We knew,' Churchill explained, 'that if our ships proceeded on their course to Australia while we were waiting for your formal approval they would either arrive too late at Rangoon or ... be without enough fuel to go there at all. We therefore decided that the convoy should be ... diverted northward ...'[33]

It was a jaw-dropping moment. Even dear old Stanley Bruce, then in London, was 'appalled'.[34] Curtin took a brief walk. He then replied, with tightly controlled fury: 'you have diverted the convoy towards Rangoon and ... treated our approval to this ... as merely a matter of form. By doing so you have established a physical situation which adds to the dangers of the convoy and the responsibility of the consequences of such diversion rests upon you ...'[35]

Churchill relented. The convoy refuelled at Colombo and steamed for Australia with the 7th Division on board. The bewilderment of the troops — pawns in the great game of political power — can be imagined. Had the convoy landed in Rangoon 20,000 men would surely have been captured, many killed, and the Japanese given a free run at Port Moresby. Curtin had surely saved their lives, and his defiance of Churchill fulfilled his obligation 'to save Australia' for itself and as a base for 'the development of the war against Japan'. It was surely his finest hour.[36]

The convoy came home over the shimmering vastness of the Indian Ocean. Their voyage was a dark journey of the soul for Curtin. For a man who strongly empathised with the pain and suffering of others, the thought of thousands of young lives strung out across enemy seas was intolerable. Curtin's mind sometimes 'writhed in tortuous struggles with its own honesty and power of reasoning', observed Sir Paul Hasluck.[37] In his extremity, the Prime Minister saw through the logic of his decisions with terrifying clarity: Who, he surely asked himself, would be answerable to the boys' parents were the convoy sunk?

His racked, exhausted face, the sleepless nights and silent vigils made colleagues fear he was close to breakdown. Under the immense stress,

Curtin's health severely deteriorated. A 'peculiar and devouring strain ... used to burn up his nervous and emotional reserves', recalled one friend.[38] He felt personally responsible for every soldier at sea, so great was his fear of Japanese submarines — indeed, empty Australian vessels were sent into the Indian Ocean to rescue any survivors of a possible attack.

Borne down under the weight of such private contemplation, Curtin's war, necessarily shrouded in secrecy from the Australian public, would soon kill him.*

Some 20,000 Australian troops safely disembarked at Perth and Adelaide over several weeks, starting on 9 March 1942. Curtin 'was a man released from great darkness and unhappiness', recalled one MP.[39] Their R&R was cut short in the national emergency. A 'Special Order of the Day' from Lieutenant-General Sir John Lavarack denied the soldiers immediate leave: 'We disembark in Australia today under conditions which demand that we be ready and available to fight at short notice. All our training and experience abroad is now disposable for the defence of our native land, which is menaced by the advance of an exultant enemy. In these circumstances I know you will realise that the safety of Australia precludes your immediate dispersal to your homes on leave.'[40]

Not all took the news well — these men had been away for two years. Some 350 troops of the 2/16th Battalion went AWOL upon their arrival in Fremantle. Military discipline had its limits.

They were soon railed to Queensland, ostensibly for jungle training. In fact, most were dubiously employed fortifying the coastline, and weren't shipped to Port Moresby until 8 August 1942 — the week the militia withdrew to Isurava high in the Owen Stanleys.

Australia did not get all its troops back. Most of the 6th Division garrisoned Ceylon (Sri Lanka) until returning to Australia in September 1942, and Curtin acceded to Britain's request — under shameful pressure from his own diplomats — to delay the return of the 9th Division and other

---

* Rangoon fell to the Japanese on 8 March. The Australian troops, had they survived Japanese air strikes, could not possibly have been battle-ready to save it. Java fell on the 12th, with the capture of 3000 Australian troops.

personnel, some 38,000 Australians, from the Middle East. A further 8000 Australian pilots and air force personnel and 2700 sailors remained in Europe. These did not appease British demands for Australian cannon fodder, and Churchill and his generals privately expressed their bitter resentment of Curtin's government and the Australian people, who were 'the most egotistical, conceited people imaginable'.

One measure of a man is the depths to which he will sink to scorn those who defy him. These grubby accusations redounded to the extreme discredit of Churchill and his government. Were not the Australians simply exercising their right to defend themselves — as Britain had so ruthlessly exercised its own? It is interesting to speculate how Britain may have behaved had the roles been reversed — that is, had Curtin ordered two British divisions to stay in the Pacific and on Australian soil in defiance of the wishes of Churchill and the British people.

Chapter 11
Commanders

'Sensual, slothful and of doubtful moral character ... [but] a
tough commander likely to shine like a power light in an
emergency. The best of the local bunch'
— *General MacArthur on General Blamey*

The Second Australian Imperial Force was coming home. The 'two-army'
system was about to collide, geographically and culturally. Yet the lines of
command were confused and the senior officers muddled. A whiff of
incompetence hung over High Command in Australia. The nation urgently
needed a single, supreme commander with overarching powers to direct the
land war. Instead, it had a muddle of hyphenated generals clamouring for a role.

This glaring deficiency was revealed in January 1942, when the
Australian army's top echelon decided to reshuffle itself. Like butchers
advancing on a lush side of beef, a gallimaufry of elderly generals and
brigadiers carved the nation into regional zones of command, and appointed
themselves regional commanders. Lieutenant-General Mackay claimed the
east coast; the incompetent Morris was handed New Guinea.

When Australia required a leader with full executive control, it got the
elevation of uninspiring old men rewarded for long service, unpaid favours

and old courtesies. Something more than war by committee was needed to match the Japanese, as Curtin saw.

With its peculiar skill at articulating the truth in a crisis, the press echoed the Prime Minister's view, and condemned the reshuffle. 'We have taken a step back towards disunity, more muddle and red-tape ... the latest move is completely retrograde,' blared *The Sunday Telegraph*.[1]

The *Sydney Morning Herald* published a monumental denunciation of the nation's rudderless armed services:

> We have then a picture of Australia facing the near approach of a
> remorseless enemy, frantically striving to make up lost time in the
> last hours given to arm herself — facing the situation with
> neither a single army nor a single commander; but with at least
> two separate and basically distinct organizations of incompletely
> trained soldiers; a sharply divided command, and, as supreme
> directing authority, a committee or board, partly departmental
> and almost wholly lacking practical knowledge of modern
> warfare.[2]

The remedy, concluded a pungent editorial, was to appoint a commander-in-chief without delay and invest him with complete powers. The paper recommended General Sir Thomas Blamey, deemed the Australian soldier best suited to unite the militia and the AIF in 'a homogeneity of command'.[3]

Curtin had earlier reached the same conclusion. The day after the destruction of Darwin, he cabled Blamey in the Middle East and ordered him to return to Australia 'as speedily as possible'.[4] The Advisory War Council, on 11 March, confirmed Blamey's appointment as Allied Commander, Land Forces.

Blamey returned from the Middle East that month to a generally favourable press. He was cheerful, and gung-ho, though he clearly disapproved of the Australian attitude to the war. They were lazy and complacent. He was shocked by the indiscipline of the home guard, and warned the nation: 'We have to be prepared for fighting in Australia ... We must be ready to hit the enemy hard whenever we can ... Australia has a rough time ahead, but I believe the people realise now that this is total war.'[5]

Who was this grenade-shaped Australian appointed to lead the Allied Land Forces? Born near Wagga Wagga on 24 January 1884, Blamey was a gruff, stocky, often tactless man with huge ambition, a sharp intellect, a ruthless and somewhat craven political mind, and deep-set, wandering eyes. He admired orchids and drank whisky.

Throughout his life Blamey displayed an unusual talent for making enemies. Curtin would later describe him as a great hater.[6] Blamey was once heard to say, 'You know, a Commander-in-Chief must be prepared to have breakfast with his brother and shoot him before lunch.'[7] In 1910, as a 26-year-old instructor at an officers' training course, he so irritated the trainees — many of whom were older than he — that one night they 'raided Blamey's tent and deposited him, bed and all, into a horse trough'.[8]

The first Australian to graduate from Britain's famous Quetta officers' school in India, in 1913, Blamey was an 'astute, first class'[9] staff officer under General Monash at Gallipoli. His unusual ability promised rapid, high promotion.

He seemed cool under fire — especially when the risks were calculable. Those working with him qualified this impression. He avoided returning to Gallipoli for the big attacks on Lone Pine and the Nek, claimed his assistant, Major Gellibrand, by delaying a minor operation for haemorrhoids. He had them removed after the troops had left. In Greece during World War II, when he refused to lie down during a bombing raid, his usually admiring adjutant, Norman Carlyon, observed, 'I ... thought his coolness was exaggerated.'[10] When in serious danger — during the Australian withdrawal from Greece, for example — Blamey was prone to panic.[11] Blamey himself decided a front-line role was not for him. He never led a unit in combat, though he reportedly shot a Turk with his revolver.

Between the wars he served, with a less than fragrant record, as Victorian police commissioner. In this capacity, he was inscrutable and, frankly, creepy. In the 1920s he was rumoured to command the League of National Security, a secret military wing of the white establishment, also known as the White Army. He was thought to have privately favoured the setting up of a military dictatorship during the Japanese crisis. Not surprisingly, he was a ferocious anti-communist and a loud hater of the 'yellow races'. At the time, such opinions were common among the educated Australian establishment as well as the working class. Left-wing intellectuals inevitably damned him as a proto-fascist.

Blamey cared little. He detested the media and, in time, the feeling was generally reciprocated. He withdrew the press accreditation of war correspondents he didn't like. 'Blamey would never hear a word spoken against him,' wrote Carlyon.[12]

Those for whom he worked roundly admired his ability as a superb staff officer and a brilliant army administrator. This he clearly showed as Commander-in-Chief of the Australian Military Forces between the wars. He organised the field troops into coherent units. 'The efficiency of field formations went up by leaps and bounds ... the value of his services to the nation in this capacity is beyond question,' remarked the military historian Colonel E.G. Keogh.[13]

At the outbreak of World War II, Blamey was sent to the Middle East to command the Second Australian Imperial Force, whom he led with exceptional mental toughness. He steadfastly refused British pressure to hand Churchill's armies a leavening of Australian troops, for which he earned the label 'most hated man in all the Middle East' by his British counterparts. He thus preserved the unity of the Australian army, and his role in their safe return to Australia won lavish praise from Curtin.

Perhaps Blamey's finest hour was his insistence on the relief of the Rats of Tobruk: 'Gentleman,' he told General Auchinleck and other British officers who'd resisted their relief, 'if I were a French or an American making this demand what would you say about it?' 'But you're not,' replied Auchinleck. 'That is where you're wrong,' said Blamey. 'Australia is an independent nation. She came into the war under certain definite agreements. Now, gentlemen, in the name of my Government, I demand the relief of those troops.'[14]

Blamey was a politician's commander, with a chilling appreciation of the oleaginous nature of political power. British Air Marshal Arthur Tedder described him as 'really a rather unpleasant political soldier'.[15]

This had its advantages — Blamey was the only person in the military who could stand up to the politicians, because he understood the nature of the political game. He was also dealing with inexperienced Labor men who rose through the trade unions and suddenly found themselves running a war.[16] It put him in an enviably powerful position, which upset many Labor MPs.

On the downside, his political antennae seemed not to pick up signals from the army. Blamey excelled at protecting his own hide and nuzzling up to those more powerful than he. He was a great schmoozer among those who mattered. But he failed to get on with many of his field commanders — with disastrous consequences. He engaged in titanic struggles with senior officers. He would rudely forget, or simply fail to find out, the names and achievements of key officers. Shamefully he failed to recognise Lieutenant-Colonel Ralph Honner, an undisputed hero of the New Guinea campaign, when Honner returned to Port Moresby after leading the 39th on the Kokoda Track.

There were suggestions that a 'cabal' of officers had tried to remove him in the Middle East, one of whom Blamey violently smacked in the face at a dinner in Benghazi, according to Lieutenant-General Sydney Rowell.★

He was exceedingly ruthless in the application of power, which seems to have stemmed from a rather disturbing psychological source. He confided in Lieutenant-General John Lavarack that he had a bad inferiority complex, which 'had been his constant companion in life . . .'[17]

There were endless 'Blamey stories', of course — of graft and corruption and self-indulgence. Scrupulous officers disapproved of a man who used his influence to secure pleasures unavailable to others. Blamey insisted on his wife joining him in the Middle East, a perk no other officer enjoyed. He wrote to his brother: 'Those who control our destinies at Home seem to have a great objection to sending out our womenfolk.'[18] He was accused of fixing his younger son's early evacuation from Greece. Perhaps this was unfair: his elder son was killed in an air accident in 1932, three years before the death of his first wife, who suffered a long illness. Blamey showed little outward emotion at these losses, according to colleagues; one can only surmise that he internalised deep personal trauma.

★ John Hetherington gave the letter Rowell wrote to him describing this incident to the Australian War Memorial on condition that it not be made publicly available until after Rowell's death; he died on 12 April 1975.

Indeed, Blamey was a complex man, often misunderstood, and a ripe target for poppy loppers. He was certainly Australia's most accomplished soldier — becoming the nation's first, and only, field marshal before his death, in 1951. But we need to delve a little deeper to understand his actions during Japan's southward thrust towards Australia.

Blamey began his working life nurturing an unattainable purity of purpose. The nineteen-year-old had designs on a clerical career, and wrote intensely personal religious poems. One began: 'O Lord lead thou me on/I grope and struggle in my darkness Lord'.[19]

He told his brother in 1905, 'I would be a minister whose power would be felt and whose sagacity and sympathy would be Christlike, such is my ambition.'[20] Blamey's ambitions were never modest.

A self-flagellatory asceticism animated this religious zeal. He confided in his brother that he hadn't 'given a real thought to a girl for eighteen months. What's more I don't want to'[21] — surely an unusually punishing regime for a nineteen-year-old.★

Out of the shell of this trainee priest crept a ruthless self-promoter and political operator. The monastic young Blamey metamorphosed from a soldier of Christ into a Christian soldier. His decision to join the army was less a change of heart than a psychological extrapolation. The Christian church and the army were thoroughly reconcilable in 1942. Both demanded order and obedience; both relied on a strict moral hierarchy; both were fighting the same enemy. Notwithstanding Stalin's awkward alliance with the West, World War II is often crudely seen as a neat delineation of the forces of good and evil. The idea of 'Christian soldiers' was not only plausible but also thoroughly commendable for men such as Blamey. And military service conveniently offered more money and earthly power than the church.

★ One girl to whom Blamey reportedly took a shine as a young man was the sister of a young officer called Arnold Potts, later a hero of the Kokoda Track. She did not reciprocate Blamey's affections, and it has been suggested that the memory influenced Blamey's disgraceful treatment of Potts in New Guinea. This seems unlikely at so great a distance, but Blamey was known to hold awesome grudges.

There was an all too human side to Blamey. Throughout his life he nourished an insatiable appetite for pleasure. This was evident in his relations with women. Younger, pretty women easily smote the 58-year-old general. Carlyon, Blamey's most intimate observer, divulged, 'Blamey was attracted by young and pretty women. When opportunity arose, he had no inhibitions, enjoyed himself to the full — and then moved on.'[22]

Lex McAulay commented: 'Like Bill Clinton he had weaknesses of the flesh — in those days it was far more a bad thing. He didn't personify what the Australian soldier wanted in a leader.'[23]

This had moments of high farce. He unwisely visited at least one prostitute while commissioner for police in Victoria in the 1920s — and was famously identified by the badge he left in the bordello — and pursued 'short-lived intimacies with accommodating women'[24] in Egypt and Palestine.

Avowed prudes found fault in Blamey's enthusiasm for a belly dancer in Cairo. The poet and war correspondent Kenneth Slessor wrote of Blamey 'jazzing fatuously with a blowsy Egyptian girl ... surrounded by junior officers sitting at tables'.[25] Slessor later lost his press accreditation, though not for his views on the general's enthusiasm for belly dancing.

Blamey's love of whisky, orchids and beautiful women — not always in that order — supported MacArthur's view of him as 'sensual, slothful and of doubtful moral character'. Another American officer dismissed him as a 'non-professional Australian drunk'.[26] These were harsh words. But MacArthur also happened to think Blamey 'a tough commander likely to shine like a power light in an emergency. The best of the local bunch.'[27] Curtin agreed. When challenged about Blamey's disreputable past, the Prime Minister robustly defended him: 'I hired a soldier, not a Sunday school teacher.'[28]

How good a soldier he was depends on whose opinion one seeks. 'Blamey men', such as General Ned Herring, found little to criticise. But most of the military–political establishment (and even Blamey, in the end) disapproved of his dual role in 1942 — as commander of the Australian Military Forces and commander, Allied Land Forces. It led to conflicts of interest and placed Blamey under huge pressure (though he seemed to wear it lightly).

Of the quality of his command, Blamey found his most damning critic in Chester Wilmot, the ABC's war correspondent. Wilmot never got on with Blamey. But the reporter cannot be dismissed as grudging, politically motivated or ignorant. He possessed a brilliant insight into the military aspects of the campaign. His unofficial reports were highly regarded by the army's top echelons, notably Major-General Sydney Rowell, Blamey's sworn enemy.

In the Middle East, Wilmot wrote of the 'widespread lack of faith in Blamey ... In two years I have heard him denounced in the strongest possible terms ... in private conversations by senior officers, who had no interest in supplanting him, by junior officers and by ordinary Diggers.'[29]

Blamey should in the end be judged by his own standards. And what were those? In 1935 he wrote the closest thing to a personal manifesto. 'My philosophy,' he said, 'is to do that thoroughly which I have to do; to be just and fair always ... it would be a great grief to me to know I had done an injustice to any man. I think above all I am one of those who do not care much what others think so long as I know what I think. And what I expect of my men I expect of myself.'[30]

Few would disagree with Blamey's assessment that he did not care what others thought of him — as historian David Horner has observed. But to what extent would Blamey honour these intentions? What of his actions?

On 18 March, an announcement upstaged Blamey's appointment as commander, Allied Land Forces, and provoked a national celebration. General Douglas MacArthur, one of America's most famous soldiers, was named supreme commander of all Allied Forces in the South-West Pacific Area.

'St George, having killed his dragon, could not have been hailed more fervently ... than this distinguished military leader who had come to extinguish the Rising Sun,' wrote Hasluck.[31] Politicians drooled over this dashingly handsome, four-star American hero in his well-pressed uniform. Women were ecstatic. Forde, the Minister for the Army, spoke admiringly of this 'well-proportioned man' who 'kept in the very best physical form'. He had an aquiline nose and a tall, trim frame that conveyed a 'sensuous, fine, almost feline quality'.[32]

One man was less than ecstatic. Blamey heard the news while travelling across Australia by train from Perth, and was deeply apprehensive about his new American superior officer.

MacArthur stepped off the train at Melbourne's Spencer Street Station at 9.30 a.m. on 21 March, like 'a grand entry in opera'.[33] John Curtin's first words, as he stretched out his hand, were, 'Hello, Doug'. The greeting cut through the pomp and circumstance, and the pair settled down to a fruitful working relationship of great mutual respect. They had a lot in common: both were at the pinnacles of their careers, both were immensely hard-working, austere men.

The Australian War Cabinet rejoiced at MacArthur's 'inspiration'; the local press were 'jubilant'. The popular headlines pealed through the land: 'MacArthur! MacArthur! MacArthur!'[34] *The Bulletin* exceeded its jingoistic norms: 'In sending their national hero to Australia, [the Americans] have charged themselves with the responsibility of saving it as a free white English-speaking nation, as far as it lies within their power, for it is not in the nature of that great people to let MacArthur down.'[35]

For Curtin, it seemed a dazzling reward for his long cultivation of the USA. With MacArthur in Australia, the Prime Minister's vision of an American military alliance seemed to have materialised in the most sensational manner conceivable.

'You have come to Australia to lead a crusade,' Curtin told MacArthur on 15 April, when assigning his command, 'the result of which means everything to the future of the world and mankind . . . You are being placed in Supreme Command of [Australia's] Navy, Army and Air Force, so that with those of your great nation, they may be welded into a homogenous force . . . Your directive . . . instructs you to prepare to take the offensive.'[36]

MacArthur's character provoked extreme responses. In some he summoned the deepest loyalty and admiration; others responded with infrangible hostility.

Major-General George Brett, who served under MacArthur in Australia, wrote of 'a brilliant, temperamental egoist; a handsome man, who can be as charming as anyone who ever lived, or harshly indifferent to the needs and desires of those around . . . Everything about MacArthur is on the grand scale; his virtues and triumphs and shortcomings . . .'[37]

Colonel G.H. Wilkinson took a different line, writing of MacArthur in 1943: 'He is shrewd, selfish, proud, remote, highly strung and vastly vain. He has imagination, self-confidence, physical courage and charm, but no humour about himself, no regard for truth, and is unaware of these defects. He mistakes his emotions and ambitions for principles. With moral depth he would be a great man: as it is he is a near-miss, which may be worse than a mile.'[38]

His strengths overawed many of these weaknesses. One of America's most decorated soldiers, MacArthur ended the Great War as a divisional commander on the Western Front, aged 38. He subsequently held a string of top jobs — superintendent of West Point, America's top military academy (1921), Chief of Staff of the US Army (1930) and later military adviser to the Philippine Government.★

MacArthur was more than a highly successful career soldier; he was the supreme innovator and military strategist, who 'laid the foundation for the development of an American armoured force'.[39] In time he would become, with Eisenhower, the most popular soldier in American history, the man credited — justly or not — with rolling back the Japanese Empire.

There were caveats. MacArthur persistently sought scapegoats for his own mistakes. He blamed others for the Philippine catastrophe when the responsibility was mostly his. He unfairly condemned Australian commanders and troops on the Kokoda Track, a travesty of the truth.

'I came through and I shall return,' MacArthur told the Australian people. He meant he would return to the Philippines — and gave an heroic account of his flight from Corregidor. The American President, he declared, had ordered him to 'break through the Jap line' and proceed to Australia 'for the purpose of organising American offence against Japan'. Not for the first time would MacArthur describe the largely Australian offensive in New Guinea as American.

Indeed, his notion of truth was elastic even by today's lurid standards of spin. In Papua and New Guinea MacArthur approved the dispatch of a

★ The Philippines were critical in containing Japanese expansionism, and MacArthur devoted himself to building its defences. It was a conveniently isolated post, for political reasons. Roosevelt suspected MacArthur of harbouring presidential designs, though MacArthur later claimed he had no such ambition.

regiment of lies in the form of doctored communiqués that invariably presented him in the best possible light. These were known by the troops, with smiling contempt, as 'Doug's Communiqués'.

A depressing example was the communiqué that announced, on 8 January 1943, victory in Papua — Washington was impatient for good news. In fact, the war ground on for a bloody fortnight, with a huge casualty rate. Such cavalier disregard for the truth inspired the popular lampoon that circulated throughout the Allied armies:

> *Here, too, is told the saga bold*
> *of virile deathless youth*
> *In stories seldom tarnished with*
> *the plain unvarnished truth.*
> *It's quite a rag, it waves the flag,*
> *Its motif is the fray,*
> *And modesty is plain to see in*
> *Doug's Communiqué. . .*
>
> *'My battleships bombard the Nips from*
> *Maine to Singapore;*
> *My subs have sunk a million tons;*
> *They'll sink a billion more.*
> *My aircraft bombed Berlin that night.'*
> *In Italy they say*
> *'Our turn's tonight, because it's right in*
> *Doug's Communiqué. . .*
>
> *And while possibly a rumour now,*
> *someday it will be fact*
> *That the Lord will hear a deep voice say*
> *'Move over God — it's Mac'.*
> *So bet your shoes that all the news*
> *That last great Judgement Day*
> *Will go to press in nothing less than*
> *DOUG'S COMMUNIQUÉ!*

MacArthur, like Blamey, was accused of cowardice. He was said to have 'turned on his heels' when serving on the Western Front.* He earned the nickname 'Dugout Doug' for the prolonged periods he apparently spent in bomb shelters in Corregidor. And he was heavily criticised for his flight from the Philippines on 12 March 1942 before its surrender to the Japanese. In this, he had little choice; Roosevelt personally ordered MacArthur to flee (or, in MacArthur's phrase, 'break through') to Australia. He was too important. Less forgiveably, MacArthur visited his doomed troops at Bataan just once before their capture — and the Bataan Death March that followed.** And he had an irritating way of implying that he led from the front in New Guinea and elsewhere — notoriously at Buna, when in fact he was 120 miles away from combat.

Curtin gave his two commanders complete freedom to conduct the war as they saw fit, with an assurance that 'neither governments nor politicians' would interfere.[40] The generals were constrained only by their resources; these were not promising.

To his horror MacArthur discovered, on the train from Darwin to Adelaide, that just 25,000 US troops — mostly national guardsmen — were then in Australia. The news 'literally stunned' him: 'He turned deadly white, his knees buckled, his lips twitched,' observed one witness.[41]

'I have never seen him so affected. He was ... heartbroken,' said an officer who'd known him for twenty years. The single division of US troops was not enough to defend the country, much less propel a counterattack. After a long silence, MacArthur whispered miserably, 'God have mercy on us.'[42] He spent the whole night pacing the train.

News of the dispatch of a second US division contingent on some Australian troops remaining in the Middle East cheered him up, and he arrived in Melbourne to declare: 'My faith in our ultimate victory is

---

* MacArthur fled the frontline when fighting in northern France during the 1914–18 war, according to 89-year-old Ned Putzell (as told to Petronella Wyatt; see *The Spectator*, 1 February 2003, p. 48).
** The memory clearly tormented him. Determined constantly to remind himself of his responsibility to the victims — and perhaps the shame of defeat — MacArthur named his private plane, HQ and telegraph codes, 'Bataan'; and his secretaries were instructed to answer the phone, 'Bataan'. He even dubbed his staff, the 'Bataan Gang', which had the effect of sharing the responsibility.

invincible ... There can be no compromise. We shall win or we shall die, and to this end I pledge you the full resources of all the mighty power of my country and all the blood of my countrymen.'[43]

But his presence did not galvanise US support for Australia as Curtin hoped. The future allocation of US support — 338 bombers, two infantry divisions, one artillery brigade and two anti-aircraft brigades — was not enough to defend Australia; in any case, their 95,000 officers and men would not be available for combat until late in 1942.

Curtin realised that MacArthur, a Republican, was outside the Washington loop. Roosevelt looked coldly on him; Generals Marshall and Eisenhower were never fans; and Admiral King would later refuse MacArthur's pleas for naval support. Indeed, it was left to Curtin to plead with Roosevelt for more troops, a plea that largely fell on deaf ears. He tried force of numbers — 607,000 of 1,529,000 Australian men aged between eighteen and 45 had enlisted. He wrote to the US President, 'We have two of your splendid American Army divisions in Australia ... We are deeply grateful ... but I would respectfully point out, Mr President, that Australia's capacity to help herself has been limited by the fact that 48,000 men are still serving overseas [in the Middle East] and our casualties in dead, missing and prisoners of war total ... an aggregate of 85,000.'[44]

Roosevelt bluntly refused — 'Germany First' came first. Shipping commitments made it impossible to move more troops to Australia 'now or in the immediate future ...'[45] An early and decisive defeat of Germany, Roosevelt said, must come before an 'all-out' effort in the Pacific. The limits of MacArthur's powers came hurtling into focus: he would have no naval support and no marines in the battle for Papua.

Of the Japanese commanders in the South-West Pacific Area, little is known publicly. Most did not survive the war, doomed to commit suicide as the Allies thwarted and then destroyed their armies. Some had fleeting roles in the battles to come, and emerge as blurred figures with little control over the terrible events that convulsed them.

While many were publicly disgraced for shaming Japan, or abandoning their troops, some are still remembered in little, awed ceremonies held in the Japanese provinces: the front-line commanders in Papua — Horii, Kusunose,

Oda, Tsukamoto, for example — are seen today by some Japanese veterans and their families as warriors and heroes.

These men, whose characters emerge in the coming actions, were answerable to High Command in Rabaul, personified by the imposing figure of Lieutenant-General Hyakutake Harukichi, who gave the order for the invasion of Papua. He would later be sent to Guadalcanal, and the command of the troops in Papua transferred to General Adachi Hatazo, commander of the Eighteenth Army.

Hyakutake's impulsive personality sowed the seeds of the coming Japanese debacle. He rose to his new command in April 1942, when His Imperial Majesty the Emperor Hirohito summoned him to the palace in Tokyo. The Emperor was pleased to bestow upon the bowing Hyakutake a promotion: commander of the Seventeenth Army, of which the Nankai Shitai was to form part.

Hyakutake swiftly imposed his new powers; he delivered his first message to the troops that month. With hindsight, his rhetoric carries a deep pathos, given the disastrous military adventure he was about to launch:

> I have now been appointed commander of the 17th Army by his Imperial Majesty the Emperor and, with the co-operation of all of you, I am about to carry out the important duty of completing one stage in the War of Greater East Asia . . .
>
> All of you, like myself, will be deeply impressed by this honour. You will make practical use of the personal experience gained in many successive victories and, girding your loins, you will assume a new resolve. You will promote still further your military discipline and perfect your training. Using outstanding initiative to overcome every hardship, you will display the true worth of a god-sent army and god-sent soldiers . . .
>
> Hyakutake Harukichi
> Commander, 17th Army[46]

On 2 May he ordered Major-General Horii to prepare the Nankai Shitai for the invasion of Papua. Hyakutake was initially sceptical about sending troops over the Owen Stanley Range to attack Port Moresby, a view Horii shared.

To quell these doubts, Hyakutake ordered Yokoyama's Advance Force Unit to land at Gona on a reconnaissance mission. Their job was not to invade, but merely to see whether an attack on Port Moresby over the mountains were possible.

Then Hyakutake suddenly threw caution aside. An envoy purporting to represent the Emperor arrived from Staff HQ in Tokyo. This man was Lieutenant-Colonel Masanobu Tsuji, who flew into Rabaul on 15 July 1942. He bore a dramatic piece of news. He told Hyakutake that the Emperor was very eager to occupy Port Moresby, as soon as possible.

This was a lie, but Hyakutake believed Masanobu, and decided to change Yokoyama's reconnaissance mission into an actual invasion — which went ahead at Gona on 21 July 1942. Hyakutake learned the truth four days later, when his Seventeenth Army HQ received a telegram from the Deputy Chief of Staff for Military Operations, Colonel Takushiro, in Tokyo. It said that Army HQ in Tokyo were awaiting the result of the 'research' mission. The result never came; the invasion had begun.

So the invasion of Papua was ordered on the strength of a lie, believed by a man who placed the Emperor's pleasure ahead of the lives of 13,000 troops.[47] Masanobu lied to Hyakutake, it appears, to hasten the southerly advance of the Empire. That he was not punished suggests he had the backing of Army HQ in Tokyo, which often presumed to speak for the Emperor without the latter's knowledge.

Already the catastrophic consequences of Hyakutake being misled were becoming visible: the Nankai Shitai had little time to prepare their supplies. They were consigned to the jungles with scarce resources — just two weeks' rations.

Chapter 12
Emperor

'Commit suicide rather than dare to shame me by returning
home as an ex-prisoner ...'
— *The mother of a Japanese soldier*

In 1940, Kochi City was a large rural town set in lush, green hills at the
mouth of the Niyodo River, which flows through the mountainous island
of Shikoku. The 144th Regiment was raised here. Keen volunteers, the sons
of rice farmers and tradesmen, they were ordered to form up at the nearby
village of Asakura, on 1 August. Many — such as Imanishi (who would join
the Yokoyama Advance Force) — were experienced troops who had
participated in the invasion of Shanghai in 1937.

The soldiers of the new regiment were trained to excel at beach
landings. They practised night and day, using local boats and old weaponry,
on Katsura-Hama Beach, a place of scenic beauty. The training started in
March 1941, and the regiment swiftly grew expert at the mock-invasion of
its home town.

The Kochi combat troops joined an amalgam of carefully chosen units
— mountain gun artillery, engineers, supply and transport troops — to be
later joined by the 41st Infantry and 15th Independent Engineer Regiments.

The force was called the Nankai Shitai — the South Seas Detachment — and commanded by the diminutive figure of Major-General Horii Tomitaro. Crack naval landing units, such as the Sasebo 5 Special Naval Landing Party would support the Shitai's southern trajectory, especially during beach landings. At this stage, there was no plan to attack Papua, according to the 144th Infantry Regiment Official Record; the Shitai's mission was to occupy Rabaul and Guam Island. The 3500 troops of the 144th Regiment formed the Shitai's core infantry — formal recognition of the famed courage (known as *Tosa-jin Kishitsu*) of the Kochi soldier, whose ancestors had helped depose the Shogunate and restore the Emperor. His performance in Shanghai had impressed Tokyo — not least his expertise at beach landings.

The Nankai Shitai had a special status, being the only Japanese force to come under the direct control of Imperial Headquarters in Tokyo, and not, initially, answerable to any single army division.

Called up in the strictest secrecy, the troops were ordered to wear mufti to their first parade and hide their military possessions in a cotton bag. Local curiosity was to be discouraged. The troops were told little — only that they were heading for the South Seas, the furthest outpost of the Japanese Empire. It is unclear exactly when the Japanese Navy pressed the case for the invasion of Papua, and possibly Australia. But in early 1942, the shadow of the idea had little impact on the Army, whose commanders would reject it as a bad idea of the Navy's (the two services did not get on well). It was not until 2 February 1942 that General HQ in Tokyo approved the overland attack on Port Moresby.

The Shitai left Osaka Port on 27 November 1941 and sailed on a southerly course; the troops knew not where. In early December the Shitai occupied the island of Guam, with little resistance, and on 23 January, they ran their barges ashore at New Britain. After fierce resistance by a small Australian force, they overran Rabaul and captured about a thousand Australians, 160 of whom were tied to coconut palms at Tol Plantation and bayoneted to death[1] — 'combat training' for young Japanese warriors.[2]

Bayonet practice on live victims was common, and appeared to have been officially sanctioned.* It 'eradicated the sense of fear in raw soldiers', says the Kure Naval Station's 'Notes for Unit Commanders': *Chi Matsuri* [literally 'Carnivals of Bloodshed'] are most effective,' it advised. 'Killings with the bayonet should be carried out whenever an opportunity occurs.'[3]

Surviving veterans of the 144th claim not to recall the Tol Plantation massacre. Yet the execution of prisoners was routine. Imanishi says he personally intervened to stop the execution of an Australian medical officer. He asked for it to be delayed a day. Over his last meal, the Australian spoke of his family back home, and Imanishi persuaded the executioner to let the man live.[4]

Private Hisaeda Akiyoshi seemed a model Japanese warrior. In his diary he reminded himself of the need for 'Resolution to death' and 'Necessity of victory'. At all times he would 'Be loyal to Emperor's orders' and 'Strictly enforce military discipline'.[5] He would not 'needlessly kill or injure the local inhabitants'; nor would he rape women or burn local property in enemy territory 'without permission'. This was all in accord with his copy of the 'Guide to Soldiers in the South Seas'. This pocket guide is a disturbing read because one senses that, with permission, or under orders, some Japanese troops might readily burn, rape, loot and kill — such was the brutal code of obedience imposed on the Japanese soldier. That they were obeying an order, of course, hardly excuses Japanese atrocities – of which there were many committed against civilians. That should be set against the fact that Australian soldiers raped Japanese women in Kure City after the war, and Americans raped hundreds of Okinawan women (including twelve-year-old girls).

Many Japanese soldiers, like Hisaeda, were unusually sensitive to their environment and conditions, but rarely is this latent humanity noted — such

---

* In the war with China, Japanese soldiers commonly bayoneted live Chinese guerrillas. One Japanese POW, a superior private, recalled that new recruits were ordered to bayonet hundreds of blindfolded victims between March '41 and October '43; he himself was ordered to cut down Chinese captives. 'He said it was very inhuman and he resented the cruelty of it, but was forced to comply with the commanding officer's command,' notes his Allied intelligence dossier. The ferocity of Chinese reprisals later discouraged the practice. When Chinese guerrillas captured one notoriously cruel Japanese officer, they cut off his ears, tongue and nose, gouged out his eyes, then 'killed him by degrees' (ATIS Research Report, *The Warrior Tradition*).

is the intensity of condemnation of a minority's war crimes. Reading their diaries, it is clear that many ordinary troops were decent men caught up in extraordinarily violent circumstances over which they had no control. That one feels the need to remark on this at all is perhaps a comment on the banal uniformity of Western perceptions of the Japanese people. Like many soldiers, Hisaeda wrote innocuous poetry and drew exquisite landscapes of the invaded territories. In his diary of 28 May 1942, he drew the Rabaul volcano, under which he penned haiku, the Japanese verse form of three lines and seventeen syllables, which tended to describe the natural world:[6]

The full moon
Reflects my home village
Like a mirror of water

Pacific Ocean
Enemy ship disappearing
Quiet waves[7]

Hisaeda was one of about 10,000 troops of the Nankai Shitai who garrisoned Rabaul in August 1942 and impatiently awaited the order to invade Papua. Their advance force — the Yokoyama — had already captured Kokoda. Lae and Salamaua were occupied in February. After the Japanese navy's failure at the Battle of the Coral Sea (May) and crushing defeat at the Battle of Midway (June) — losing four aircraft carriers and 250 planes — the seaward invasion of Port Moresby was abandoned. Instead, Imperial Headquarters hastened plans for the overland invasion of Port Moresby, and alerted Lieutenant-General Hyakutake in Rabaul. The Nankai Shitai was promptly transferred from General HQ in Tokyo to his command, as part of the 17th Army.

Who were the soldiers of the Nankai Shitai? Were they the monstrous fanatics as portrayed in the West? How far did they conform to Allied propaganda posters of 'loathsome, buck-toothed, little yellow savages'?[8]

The cliché is well known: the Japanese soldier was a fanatical, sword-wielding warrior, heir to the samurai code, for whom surrender was unthinkable. His training inculcated a sense of unquestioning obedience within the collective will of a vast military machine. His destiny was to die fighting for his Emperor, or to terminate his life in captivity. He was entranced by the 'divine cause' of imperial conquest, and thoroughly imbued with the righteousness of his mission, for the sake of which any act appeared justified, however cruel or barbaric.

That is the Western image of the Japanese soldier, and to some extent it was true. But there are heavy qualifications, and exceptions. For one thing, the troops of 1942 bore little resemblance to their samurai antecedents. The vast majority of the twentieth-century Imperial Army were not of the original warrior class; they were typically conscript peasant farmers or public servants. Their most-likely ancestors were the proletarian ranks of the new army formed after the Meiji restoration, in the late nineteenth century, when the samurai were in a state of terminal decline.

These intense young men sent off to fight the White imperialists and conquer the Pacific were fashioned as an 'Army of the Gods, liberating a billion people in East Asia'.[9] It appeared that any act that expanded the Japanese Empire, crushed resistance and served the imperial will would be exonerated. Their attacks on defenceless civilians in China, notably in Nanking[10], can be seen as the barbaric manifestation of this expansionist policy.

In building their new army, successive regimes ruthlessly appropriated the Spartan traditions of the old warrior code. In two respects did the modern soldier resemble the samurai: burnt into his being was utter obedience to his superior; and scored on his heart was the wish to die for his country and Emperor. Of course, there were varying degrees to which Japanese soldiers were receptive to such relentless propaganda; many questioned and later resisted their brutal indoctrination. But even the samurai were not so blindly obedient as the Japanese troops of 1942, as one son of a samurai family explained: 'If his lord did a wrong or shameful thing, the samurai had to scold and correct his lord to choose a better way. If his lord was stupid enough not to listen to him, then the samurai should commit Hara-kiri to make his lord understand.'

In the eyes of the new government, however — most of whom were from the samurai class — the Imperial Army would be like no other, an army for whom duty was weightier than a mountain and death lighter than a feather (in the words of *The Imperial Rescript to Soldiers and Sailors*). Under the blazing red orb of the Sun God would march the ultimate expression of the art of war. The Japanese military machine would conquer Greater East Asia — and the world — by virtue of one ineluctable truth: Japanese troops, unlike their all too human Anglo-Saxon enemies, were not afraid to die.

The typical Japanese soldier welcomed death, thirsted for a glorious end, and volunteered eagerly for suicide missions. (Again, there were degrees: not all pleaded for the chance to sacrifice themselves — many despised the regime that demanded their corpses.) Suicide was state-ordained; schoolchildren were told to write to soldiers, urging them to 'die gloriously'.[11] There are many stories of very young officers weeping at being denied the opportunity to steer a human torpedo into the belly of an enemy battleship or fly a rocket onto the deck of an aircraft carrier. The *kamikazes* were revered as living gods at the end of the war. The army, too, had its suicide squads — 'human bullets' — the supply of whom seemed inexhaustible. Australian veterans recall the uniquely terrifying experience of facing waves of such troops rushing from the jungle with bayonets raised, yelling '*Banzai!*' or '*Yaruzo!*' ('Let's do it!') or '*Chiesuto!*' ('Damnation!' in the Kagoshima dialect).

The single lightning strike, the unexpected body blow, followed samurai tradition. It would never cease until the enemy capitulated. One Japanese instruction manual stated: 'each man must go into battle with the firm conviction that he would not stop unless the enemy had been completely annihilated'.[12]

The soldier gave his life for his Emperor. There was no greater glory than to die for Hirohito, whose divine presence would one day rule over *Hakko Ichiu*, 'Eight Corners of the World Under One Roof'.

The soldier's sacrifice was absolute, as conveyed by a popular song of the day (originally a poem by Otomo no Yakamochi [718–785 AD], to which music was added in 1937):

If I were to go to sea
I will become a water soaked corpse
If I were to go to the mountains
I will become a corpse sprouting from the grasses
Even far from our Emperor
I will give up this life
I have no regrets
There will definitely
Be no looking back.[13]

Many Japanese troops did see themselves as the appointed emissaries of the imperial will. It might have been a scorned, or laughable, piece of indoctrination, were it not so sincerely believed. Others simply acknowledged their duty, for the sake of *Tatemae*, or 'making a public impression'. In practice, however, most Japanese soldiers were heavily armed puppets. They blindly did what they were ordered to do. Realms of power weighed on the ordinary soldier's mind, and his notebooks and diaries reveal little dictatorships of thought, packed with self-warnings, chastisements, and personal checklists: 'I must be worthy of the Emperor', 'I must be resolute unto death', 'I must be a better soldier'.

The notebook of Okamato Shigeo, who was captured at Milne Bay, is typical: 'To serve is loyalty to the Emperor which is being loyal to your parents,' he wrote. During a field lecture entitled 'Imperial Instructions' he noted: 'Emperor — Parent — Leader. Emperor is Aragitogami — Personification of the Way.' He reminded himself to 'Be thoroughly prepared for your duties; reflect and examine things before doing it; be reliable.' He told himself: 'To exterminate the enemy in the attack is to become a warrior.'[14]

Senior officers' and staff diaries carried endless lists of the aims of their 'Sacred Campaign':

1. The establishment of the Greater East Asia Co-Prosperity Sphere;
2. Exclusion of the White Race from East Asia;
3. Establishment of peace in the Orient;
4. Promotion of the welfare of mankind in the world ... to extend the light of Imperial Power to the south.[15]

In theory the Emperor enjoyed absolute temporal and spiritual power under Article III of the Japanese Constitution; in practice Hirohito was a figurehead, the amanuensis of Tojo's military junta. In many troops' minds, nonetheless, Hirohito occupied a sacred place of transcendent purity. Never would their devotion falter, not in the worst extremes of battle.

The summit of the Emperor's spiritual power was his incarnation as the Shinto Sun God, which apparently beamed down on the Japanese soldier wherever he may be: 'The Imperial Army is an immortal army,' Major-General Okabe told the Nankai Shitai on 29 December 1942, 'and we are immortal soldiers'.[16]

The person and power of the Emperor were placed constantly 'in the forepart of the troops' consciousness'.[17] Acts of worship were conducted daily. Troops in their bomb shelters and foxholes would bow in the direction of the Imperial Palace before battle; few failed to honour Japanese memorial days.*

Many officers of the Nankai Shitai clearly saw themselves as leaders of an army 'on a mission to free East Asia from the yolk of white colonialism'.[18] Their exuberance matched that of their comrades at the fall of Singapore, who sang:

This day we have waited for! The history of aggression, blood-stained by the whip of America and Britain burning with selfishness! Look up, as the sun sets on their withdrawal from their positions: the Sun of East Asia rises. Ah! This deeply stirring morning! Singapore has fallen.

Raise both hands high! Shouting the victory of East Asia, vowing the union of blood, the great march now goes on. May its rhythm echo through the world! Ah! This deeply stirring Greater East Asia! Singapore has fallen.[19]

Copies of the song were found on the bodies of soldiers in Buna.

---

* Lafcadio Hearn, an authority on Japan at the turn of the nineteenth century, explains Shinto: 'It is not all belief, nor all religion; it is a thing formless as a magnetism and indefinable as an ancestral impulse. It is part of the Soul of the Race. It means all the loyalty of the nation to its sovereign, the devotion of retainers to princes, the respect to sacred things ... the whole of what an Englishman would call sense of duty; but that this sense seems to be hereditary and inborn. I think a baby is Shinto from the time its eyes can see ...' (ATIS Research Reports 12/53).

The Nankai Shitai were similarly embarking on a divinely inspired crusade. The Western 34th Butai of the 144th Regiment sang*:

Of Heavenly Japan,
The Emperor's power is clear
We must build a new World Order,
Everlastingly, all nations under one Roof.
While we have this weighty Mission,
Even if in the waters, grass-grown corpses soak,
Let us go, Comrades, with hearts united —
The Western 34th Regiment![20]

How were such soldiers produced — insofar as an individual is the product of his environment? The Japanese boy's training in obedience and his exposure to the culture of self-sacrifice started at junior school. It was no coincidence that several ministers for education were army generals. Japanese schools were run like little armies. The Japanese boy was a piece of malleable metal to be hammered on the military anvil. He was ferociously disciplined, and routinely beaten.

Children were exposed to death as ritual from a very early age. *Tales of Hara-Kiri*** was on the junior school curriculum in 1940. It tells a story of the first year of the Meiji era (1868), when clansmen of the Tosa tribe assaulted the crew of a French vessel. Twenty men were obliged to commit *hara-kiri* to atone for this disgrace. This group disembowelment was performed in the presence of a French minister, who stopped it after the eleventh man died: 'He could not bear it any longer.'[21]

---

* Major-General Horii himself penned a jollier verse; he called it 'The South Seas Marching Song':
Vigorous youths of the Southern Seas
Who have been reared by the sea,
The time to test your strength has come.
It is delightful to leave a wake behind,
Cleaving the black sea.
Where are you Japan? Your light cannot be seen.
** *Hara-kiri* was seen in Japan as the supreme embodiment of human courage and self-control: the practitioner, squatting on a mat, slashed his stomach with his ceremonial dagger, disgorging his guts, in which the spirit was said to reside (AWM 55, ATIS IR No 9).

The punishment regime immeasurably hardened when the boy reached the age to attend military training school. One leading private told his Allied interrogator: 'The first three months of military life were hardest. Whether they were right or wrong, recruits were kicked and knocked about.'[22] He knew of one or two suicides. Another, Sakamoto Eizo, stated that he was sometimes hit so hard he was unable to eat for days.[23]

Watanabe Fukuichi, Second-Lieutenant with Yazawa Butai, survived the special officers' training school. He reported that some of his tutors seemed to enjoy watching him stumble through his duties. Reveille was at 6.00 a.m., when he and his comrades were taken out for 'warming up exercises' which consisted of rubbing down their naked bodies with a sharp brush or towel. Manoeuvres in the snow were frequently held; some went all night and into the next day.

Japanese officers treated their own troops sometimes worse than they treated prisoners. The cruelty to which Allied POWs were subjected 'partly reflects the brutality to which their captors were subjected', notes an Allied intelligence report.[24]

The troops of the Nankai Shitai had experienced the full rigours of Japanese military training by the time they left Kochi. The officers were the products of a grinding daily regime of study, exercise and punishing indoctrination, animated by a 'will that knows no defeat'.

The cult of ritual suicide served the modern army, too: an army that fought to the death was believed to be unconquerable. So the military junta resurrected the samurai ideal that a dishonourable life was not worth living.★ A soldier must destroy himself rather than submit to capture. If he failed he would be severely punished on his return to Japan — executed, as happened to repatriated prisoners from China, or gaoled. A Manual of Military Law,

---

★ Perhaps the most cynical example of the repackaged warrior was the reinvention of Bushido. Bushido — literally 'the way of the warrior' — was tremulously invoked as the ancient, spiritual source of Japan's military power. Japanese propaganda summoned misty-eyed visions of a glorious Imperial past, of squat warlords brandishing enormous swords. In this sense, Bushido was devised to whip up Japanese courage. For hundreds of years Bushido had formed the core of the samurai code. Yamamoto Tsunetomo (1659–1719) of Saga City, Kyusyu, in his book *Hagakure* (*In the Shadow of Leaves*), instructed the samurai in how to live. An early sentence states, '*Bushido towa Shinukoto to Mitsuketari!* ('I have found the essence of the Bushido way to die!').

read out to the 144th Regiment before they left Kochi, noted that, depending on rank, or other extenuating circumstances, the death sentence that normally applied to returned POWs may be commuted to a maximum of 30 years' imprisonment.[25]

Elite troops needed no such encouragement. The Nankai Shitai, as befitted a crack unit, were determined to commit suicide if caught; many left Rabaul eager to give their lives for the Emperor. One POW said: 'Each soldier kept one grenade or bullet to be used by him for taking his own life.'

Imanishi, Yamasaki and Shimada agreed that, if captured, they would certainly have killed themselves. To this day, belief in the tradition survives. Indeed, one survivor of the Cowra break-out — a 144th veteran — returned to Kochi, joined the New Guinea Veterans' Association, and helped organise their annual reunions. Some families are still angry that the man did not kill himself in captivity, and refuse to attend the reunions.

A persuasive incentive for a Japanese POW not to return was the attitude of his family to his capture. Many wives and mothers believed their husbands and sons would kill themselves, if captured, rather than return to disgrace the family. On his departure, one POW's mother told her son to kill himself rather than 'dare to shame [her] by returning as an ex-prisoner'.[26] There are numerous similar examples. Another POW emphatically declined a suggestion that he might write to his wife, as being a prisoner was to him the greatest shame imaginable. However, evidence suggests that much of this apparent pressure from mothers and wives was mere lip service paid to the new regime.

Shame could ruin the family. Fathers of imprisoned sons lost their jobs or citizenship; children of imprisoned fathers were ostracised at school. 'If it were known in his neighbourhood that he was a POW,' noted the dossier of POW Kunisawa Yuki, a 27-year-old private in the Kusunose Butai, 'his children would have no chance in life. He himself would lose his citizenship.'[27]

An especially pathetic case was that of Matsuoka Kazuo, a 25-year-old superior private, captured near Gona on 12 December 1942. He failed to blow himself up with his last grenade because he was shot in the hand before he could pull the pin. He told his interrogator he would have to commit suicide if sent back to Japan.[28]

First Lieutenant Horiguchi Tsugio, a medical officer and veteran of the Russo–Japanese war, used to visit the homes of those who died in action. The families would rejoice and shed tears of happiness if their son had died an honourable death. But those whose sons had disappeared were inconsolable: they feared their sons had been taken prisoner, 'which is the worst thing that could happen to a soldier'.[29]

Yet, as we shall see, not all Japanese soldiers were deaf to the call of life, nor were they all blindly obedient. Many resisted the compulsion to kill themselves. At the appointed time they simply couldn't squeeze the trigger or drown themselves or pull the grenade pin. The will to live overwhelmed the lessons of their indoctrination. Under interrogation, some soldiers, in their despair, rubbished the regime that demanded their lives.

Tsuno Keishin, a Japanese POW, said that Japanese officers, especially junior ranks, treated the men very badly, and therefore, he said, 'it is not uncommon … for an officer to be shot from behind by his own men'.[30]

In captivity, Japanese troops — especially older, more experienced men, and fathers — occasionally vented their extreme anger at the regime. An extraordinary example was a 35-year-old first class seaman captured at Milne Bay on 17 October, whose name Allied interrogators transliterated as Katsukara Kanemidzu — not a recognisable Japanese name and probably an alias. In a remarkable outburst, he told his interrogators that few of the men, young or old, had much interest in the war. They resented being called up, and preferred to stay at home with their families, he said. 'None of them liked war and all were far more interested in getting back to Japan.' Katsukara vehemently criticised the war, and complained of vague orders and lack of food. But he said he could not return home 'as he would be killed'. He personally knew of few young men who went willingly to war, but they had no choice, and accepted their three years in the armed forces 'with the best grace possible'.[31]

Clearly not all were robots of the regime. Many ordinary troops were privately disgusted by the cruelty they were expected to inflict on the orders of brutal officers. Some openly resisted, for example, orders to bayonet live victims:

'It did not last, as the men could not stomach it ... Many found they could not sleep at night because of the nightmares,' said one POW, whose name is given as Nakino Tokuhashi — again, not a familiar Japanese name, and probably an alias. Another stated that he and his comrades, in disgust at what they were doing, deliberately missed the victim, or penetrated the side of the body; which only made it worse, because it took several thrusts to kill him.

Such was the psychological diversity of the 10,000-strong Nankai Shitai, who sailed from Rabaul to Papua in mid-August. As they crossed the Solomon Sea, the troops sang their favourite military song, *Futsuin Dayori*, to the tune of *Tidings from French Indochina*:

Just below the Equator
We are under the Southern Cross
The warrior's blood runs hot
As the Rising Sun flag advances.
Ahead the enemy pleads for his life under a white flag.
A brisk divine breeze blowing
Towards Australia at the limit of the south.
The ultimate place to reach.
The dawn of a new world...[32]

Chapter 13
The AIF Arrives

'The people were in a complete panic ... They believed that the Japs were going to invade any day and they were completely defenceless except for the untrained militia. We were the first battle-trained troops to be back in Australia'
— *Corporal Frank McLean, MM, 2/27th Battalion, Second Australian Imperial Force*

The mood at Advanced Land Headquarters (Landops) in Brisbane on the morning of 4 August 1942 did not inspire confidence. The freshly painted rooms of the newly opened Queensland University, commandeered by Landops for the duration of the war, seemed full of disconsolate Australian Women's Army Service soldiers 'sitting on typewriter boxes'.[1] The officers tried to remain calm before the cool example of their boss, General Sir Thomas Blamey.

Blamey had a keen eye on the big picture. So it was regrettable that certain details vital to this morning's big picture had escaped his attention. One was crucial: Blamey had forgotten or simply failed to alert Morris in Port Moresby that reinforcements and a fresh commander were being dispatched immediately.

The job was left to Major-General George Vasey, who arrived at Landops that day as Blamey's chief of staff. Vasey, an unstuffy, popular officer, promptly wired Port Moresby with the cryptic note: 'Syd is coming.'[2] The dispatch of this intelligence was helpful. To his great relief, the embattled Morris was being replaced as leader of New Guinea Force (he became commander of the Australian New Guinea Administrative Unit). He welcomed the arrival of 'Syd'. It meant things were about to change.

'Syd' was Lieutenant-General Sydney Rowell, the new commander of New Guinea Force. His reputation preceded him: a clever, pugnacious, somewhat prickly senior officer, with a brilliant academic record and an impressive tour of duty in the Middle East. This was his first senior command of a combat unit.

Sent to Gallipoli aged nineteen as a lieutenant with the 3rd Light Horse Regiment, Rowell's World War I service was cut short by accident and serious illness — he was said to suffer from an 'enlarged heart'. He recovered and in the 1930s completed with high distinction the senior army commander's advance training course at Britain's Imperial Defence College, one of few Australians to do so.

His peers held him in the highest esteem. Lieutenant-General Lavarack praised his strength of character, intelligence, judgment and loyalty.[3] 'Every Australian,' wrote war correspondent John Hetherington,[4] 'who served under, or knew, Rowell in the black days of the Middle East in 1940 and 1941 is aware of his quality as a soldier and a man ... I never saw him slightly rattled in the grimmest situation.'

At the outbreak of World War II, he led a brigade of the Australian 6th Division in the Middle East. A consummate strategist, he is credited with planning the evacuation of Australian troops from Greece — in which two-thirds of the force was extricated from an extremely sticky situation — and the defeat of the Vichy French in Syria. Hetherington described the withdrawal from Greece, under German attack, as 'brilliantly executed'.[5] For men of such overweening ambition as MacArthur and Blamey, Rowell's light perhaps shone too brightly.

Blamey well knew Rowell's Achilles heel — the pair fell out badly over the Greek disaster. Rowell was high-minded, did not respond well to criticism and suffered from an over-fastidious concern for form. He refused to play the high-stakes political game evidently relished by Blamey. Rowell was a soldier. One officer remarked that he was 'Proud, very austere and sensitive.'[6] 'The trouble with Syd is that he expects everyone else to act like a saint,' said another.[7]

When he arrived in Port Moresby on 10 August, Rowell faced the toughest challenge of his career: to take the offensive to the Japanese. His first task, as he immediately saw, was supply. Never had he studied a battle in which the outcome would be so mercilessly dependent on the quality of his supply lines.

He could not rely on native carriers alone. The Myola drop zone was vital, and mindful of this Rowell was angry to find, on 16 August, that his transport planes — some 28 of them — were parked wing-to-wing on the tarmac of the Seven-Mile drome, sitting ducks for a Japanese air raid. He promptly ordered them to be removed, camouflaged and protected.

Rowell made it his business to see the country. He visited the jumping off point of the Kokoda Track, and subjected it to a mind highly trained at seeing the natural landscape as a theatre of war. He scanned the distant mountains of the Owen Stanleys to the north. He noted the jungle canopy and the misty valleys. The sight profoundly affected him. He 'instinctively judged the claustrophobic influence of jungle country on troops entering it for the first time'.[8] There was nothing like this in Queensland.

Rowell momentarily doubted the sense of sending men over the mountains. With grim prescience, he told the journalist Osmar White: 'As far as I'm concerned I'm willing to pull back and let the enemy have the rough stuff if he wants it. I'm willing to present the Jap with the supply headache I've got. But there are those who think otherwise. We need a victory in the Pacific and a lot of poor bastards have got to get killed to provide it.'[9]

Under Rowell's command were the newly arriving troops of the 7th Division's 21st Brigade, veterans of the Middle East. These battle-hardened soldiers of the Second Australian Imperial Force, for whose return to Australia John Curtin had lost so much sleep, had spent the past three months training in light rainforest in Queensland and desultorily building coastal defences north of Brisbane.

Their jungle training was unimpressive. The brigade had attempted a major jungle exercise in Queensland. Not a single unit in the 'attacking force' had reached its objective within the two-day deadline; communications collapsed; and the evacuation of the 'wounded' was a catastrophic failure.

As for training manuals, 'There was one book written about jungle fighting. In it there was a diagram of a jungle track, kind of a single wobbly line running down the page, with defensive positions marked. Well, that was a load of rubbish,' said Major Geoffrey Lyon.[10]

Nor were Porter's 'NOTES ON JUNGLE TRAINING' illuminating: 'What is jungle?' he began. 'At the equator, the temperature is consistently high and the rainfall consistently heavy … This results in rapid, intense growth of vegetation — trees, vines, fleshy shrubs and grass. The rainfall produces voluminous rivers, creeks and swamps with the resultant prolific animal and insect life. All these go to produce jungle.'[11]

If not jungle-trained, the men were at least combat-ready. Unlike the militia in the mountains, they'd fought in the Middle East. Why, then, were they withheld in Queensland for months after their return? Blamey had instead dispatched another militia unit, the 'inexperienced and poorly trained'[12] 14th Brigade to Port Moresby. This decision almost 'made us weep',[13] said Rowell, who was aghast at the deployment of a unit 'in which we had no confidence'.[14]

One reason cited was that MacArthur wanted the AIF to finish the construction of Australian airfields and coastal fortifications before sending them to New Guinea. In other words, the nation's most experienced soldiers were kept in Queensland as virtual manual labour, while the Japanese advanced on threadbare militia units at Isurava. In this light, MacArthur's boast that it was he who decided to take the fight to New Guinea sounds absurd — and the Brisbane Line suddenly acquires a palpable reality.[15]

In early August it was deemed expedient to send up the AIF troops. Some 3000 men of the 21st Brigade boarded the *James Fenimore Cooper* and the *James Wilson*, on 6 and 8 August, to a huge heroes' farewell (in striking contrast to the rather sad send-off for the militia nine months previously).

A few who'd gone AWOL were rounded up and put in steel cages on the deck.[16] The brigade disembarked on 8 August and sailed undisturbed through calm seas.

Albert Moore, of the Salvation Army, led a church service on the deck of the *James Fenimore Cooper*: 'I have never heard a company of men sing as these men sang that Sunday morning,' he said. 'We were surrounded by the great expanse of the Pacific Ocean. And I am sure that never before or since have I been so moved by a gathering of people as I was this morning. It seemed that every man felt that he was on the precipice of the great unknown.'[17]

They marched into Port Moresby with the chutzpah of a conquering army. A cavalcade of jeeps, buggies, motorbikes, anti-aircraft guns, batteries of 'snub-nosed' 25-pound guns and truckloads of men bristling with rifles, Bren and Tommy guns, grenades and bayonets roared through town and rattled up the drab brown hills. 'All day they rolled up the road from the harbour in open trucks, bound for foothill camps,' observed White from the porch of Correspondents' House. The troops' bodies were 'burnt ... the colour of leather by desert winds'.[18]

Port Moresby had been transformed. The Seven-Mile drome was a giant military base. All day American bombers roared overhead. On the ground the air was thick with dust and the smell of diesel fuel, rifle grease, human sweat and plumes of exhaust. A vast military machine was taking shape; tent city had spilled into tent suburbs.

To the north, like some dark, Gothic horror, the Owen Stanleys cast a great shadow on these Lilliputian endeavours, at the head of which Allied sappers impudently persisted in trying to carve a road through the jungle from Owers' Corner. Dozers, power shovels, graders and rollers gouged out a lane to the base of the Golden Stairs, where the first serious ascent of the Kokoda Track begins. Thousands of tons of 'metal, crushed coral, pumice, logs and gravel were poured into the endless belly of the road's foundations'. The results were puny: 'it was still a river of mud in which every wheeled vehicle but the unconquerable jeep ... stuck fast or skidded into the ditch'.[19]

Within days, the first AIF troops were preparing to march over the Owen Stanleys. The correspondent Osmar White witnessed the men preparing to depart. Hundreds rested 'in a green meadow flanked by rubber trees'. They had their shirts off, and their backs were 'sun-tanned, rippling with muscle'. Some sang songs, others wrote letters home. There was much rowdiness and joking — perhaps too loud for comfort; a few were quietly introspective. One group cheerfully sharpened hundreds of bayonets on a grindstone, their slouch hats 'pulled rakishly down and their eyes bright and reflective',[20] and laughed as they honed the razor-sharp tips.

Though mostly in their twenties, they had something of the severity of old soldiers. They did not 'cheer and catcall' — 'They knew what fighting meant and they were going to fight.'[21] Their muscular frames distinguished them from the gangly militia. They were also older. The average age of one battalion was 29, with the oldest, 55, and the youngest, who lied, fifteen.[22] A less obvious difference was their minds: they were conscious of their status as saviours of the nation. Rushed back from the Middle East, they were welcomed home with ticker tape parades in all the capital cities.

'Everywhere we went,' said Frank McLean of the 2/27th, 'we were met by huge crowds, cooking meals for us at the station, hugging us at every opportunity. I don't know how many hundreds of girls' addresses were thrust into our hands. The people were in a complete panic ... They believed that the Japs were going to invade any day and they were completely defenceless except for the untrained militia. We were the first battle-trained troops to be back in Australia.'[23]

White, the war correspondent, saw chinks in the armour, however. Their equipment weighed about sixty pounds, he quietly observed; their uniforms were khaki — not jungle green — and their webbing 'shone white from long bleaching in the desert suns'. Their semi-nakedness displayed an ignorance of, or foolhardy indifference to, the risk of mosquito bite and malaria. 'For the first time, the shadow of doubt crossed my mind. I dismissed it. Lesser fighters might fail, but not these — not the best assault infantry in the world!'[24]

The best assault infantry in the world answered to the obligatory roll call of Australian nicknames: 'Pop', 'Butch', 'Bubba', 'Junior', 'Runt', 'Lefty', 'Nugget', 'Curley', 'Snowy', 'Doc', 'Sandy', 'Wog', 'Tarzan', 'Dusty', 'Baldy' and so on. 'Blue' was usually a redhead; 'Tiny' tended to be a giant. They came from all backgrounds: working and middle class, educated, illiterate; 'men of all creeds and political beliefs ... blended into something of strength, unity and endurance'.[25]

The brigade's three battalions were raised in Victoria (2/14th Battalion), South Australia (2/27th Battalion) and Western Australia (2/16th Battalion).* Each contained 1000 men. Mates and brothers chose the same units: in the 2/14th there were dozens of pairs of brothers, as well as three groups of three brothers. Many had transferred from militia units. The battalion had one Aboriginal soldier, Harry Saunders, who was very popular — and later killed.

Gangs joined up together. One was the Goldfields Mob of the 2/16th Battalion. They were machine-miners, boggers and truckers from the tough gold mining towns of Western Australia. Like Smoky Howson's Zorro Gang, the Goldfields Mob decided to enlist while drinking in their local pub. Unlike the Zorro Gang, they claimed they were sober at the time. Indeed, after their final binge in the Court Pub in Boulder, Western Australia, the Mob soberly nailed various personal items to the pub walls — socks, underpants, boots — and set off for Northam training camp. They carried little. The biggest, and the lightest, suitcase was that of Frank 'Runt' Reed, the smallest member of the Mob. On arrival at camp, a sergeant asked Runt what his outlandish luggage contained. Lifting it with exaggerated ease, Runt declared, 'There are exactly 53 articles in that case, sarge.' 'Fifty three?' replied the sergeant, finding the case unusually light. 'Yes,' said Runt, 'a pack of cards and a toothbrush.'[26] Runt Reed died of wounds in 1943.

Sometimes a man's physique decided his place: heavily built soldiers were encouraged to join the mortar platoons. The weediest bloke in the 2/27th Battalion's mortar platoon was Sergeant 'Shaggy' Clampett, six-foot and twelve-stone, whose nickname was given to Shaggy Ridge.[27]

Each battalion was 'in effect a fair sized town', with cooks, carpenters, blacksmiths, builders, mechanics, bandsmen, drivers, fitters, tailors, postmen, telephonists, sanitation experts, drain-diggers, electricians, butchers, bakers, grocers — 'and a lot of other people besides fighting men'.[28] While bandsmen were of little use in the jungles of New Guinea, mechanics and sanitation experts would prove helpful.

....

* The number '2' denotes the Second Australian Imperial Force, to distinguish these battalions from their WWI predecessors.

The brigade had a smattering of the sons of World War I veterans. One was Corporal John Burns, a baker from Adelaide, whose father won the Military Medal in the Great War. Burns would soon match his father's achievement in the most harrowing circumstances imaginable.

After a few days of hasty jungle exercises, the brigade assembled at Itiki on 15 August. Before them stood the amiable, crew-cutted Brigadier Arnold Potts, their new commander, a solidly built World War I veteran a few weeks shy of his 46th birthday.

Potts delivered their battle orders: some 1500 Japanese troops had landed at Gona. The enemy had captured Kokoda. They were to cross the Owen Stanley Range, relieve the 39th at Isurava, recapture Kokoda and drive the enemy into the sea. Potts chose less vivid language, but the message was clear. In short, the men concluded, 'we were to wipe them out'.[29]

Even at this late stage, the Allied generals dismissed the notion of an overland invasion of Port Moresby. It seemed at best a profound error of judgment; at worst, a mad fantasy. They held this belief until well into August. Neither MacArthur nor Blamey 'could credit the Japanese with planning to attack Port Moresby by way of the tortuous Kokoda Track'.[30] Willoughby repeatedly scorned the idea of a land invasion; he held this view until as late as 18 August, a week before the decisive battle of Isurava.

No one seemed aware of their illogical position. If the mountains were supposedly unassailable, why were the Australians being sent to fight a war across them? If the mountains would so assuredly block the Japanese invasion from the north, why would an Australian offensive from the south so readily succeed? Only Rowell saw the yawning contradiction at the heart of Allied thinking. Japan had conquered most of Asia, yet GHQ seemed always to underestimate the Japanese soldier.

The men were not entirely ignorant of the terrain: maps, crude as they were, did show elevations, walking times and distances between villages.[31] And they had the 39th Battalion's sketches. But there were no contour maps of New Guinea, only 'pitiful quarter-inch-to-the-mile sheets'.[32]

The intelligence was pretty woeful. The departing 2/14th listed its knowledge about the Kokoda Track as: a little ANGAU information, one air photo, and an inaccurate track report.[33] In sum, the Australian army had 'virtually no military knowledge of the region and no appreciation of the tactical and logistical problems it would pose in a war'.[34]

The Australian ignorance of the Kokoda Track is baffling. There was a great deal of information about the track, had Allied Intelligence bothered to find it. It was not a 'little known jungle path', as it is so often described. Since 1904, when the Kokoda station was established, it had been a well-trodden trade and communication line over the mountains.[35]

At the outbreak of war, the Koiari people at Kokoda, Isurava, Efogi, Menari, Nauro and Ioribaiwa farmed the land along its winding route. Today, the villagers subsist much as they did in 1942, on the produce of their market gardens, growing bananas, yams, pawpaws and taro.

The track had been well known for decades. In the 1890s Australian gold prospectors took the Kokoda trail to the Yodda goldfield on the upper Mambare. 'It was the main path to the goldfields and the gazetted mail route,' said John Rennie, a former policeman in New Guinea.* An Australian government surveyor mapped the track in 1899 — and was attacked by Orokaiva tribes north of Isurava. Gold was not the only lure: rubber, coffee and Seventh-Day Adventism — which established a mission at Bisiatabu in 1908 — all brought white men over the track before the war. The first white woman to walk it was probably Miss Philippa Bridges, in 1923. She described it as a 'splendid experience', records Hank Nelson.[36]

Tom Grahamslaw, an ANGAU captain, had sent hundreds of his men over the mountains in April 1942. Civilians escaped south using the Kokoda route. And the Papuan Infantry Brigade walked it many times before the Japanese landed — first setting off under Lieutenant Harold Jesser in February 1942.

Several of these people could have disabused the Allied commanders of their wilder notions about the Owen Stanleys — had they been consulted.[37] As Hank Nelson explains: 'The track, then, so often described as a native pad and said to have been used infrequently by the occasional missionary ... was well known in Port Moresby.'[38] As early as 1917, Richard Humphries, a patrolman, described the Kokoda crossing as the 'most important' in all of Papua.

---

* John Rennie played a vital role in the development and completion of the Isurava Memorial, which was unveiled in 2002.

It is astonishing, then, that such bizarre notions of the Kokoda Track should have gripped the imagination of GHQ in Brisbane. The Americans in particular seemed to be in the thrall of images more appropriate to a cartoon strip, or a boy's own adventure story. Was the track roadworthy, they wondered? Was 'the Gap' defendable with a handful of men, like the Greeks at Thermopylae? The Gap had insinuated itself into the commanders' minds in the form of a narrow mountain pass flanked by steep cliffs, in which a few men could hold thousands of rampaging warriors. In fact The Gap is a seven-mile-wide, U-shaped valley suspended in the mountains, and paradoxically one of the few places where more open battles were possible.

The high-water mark of Allied blockheadedness came when Major-General Pat Casey, the American engineer-in-chief, suggested that the mountain pass could be blown up. In fact, on 13 August, New Guinea Force was ordered to select 'points where the pass may be readily blocked by demolition . . .'[39] A wall of rocks would presumably hold back the Japanese invader, to which Rowell caustically replied: 'It is respectfully suggested that such explosives as can be got forward would be better employed in facilitating our advance than for preparing to delay the enemy!!!'[40] The three exclamation marks are revealing of Rowell's temperament. In his memoirs, he noted: 'I sent [the order] back asking whether it was this week's funny story.'[41]

GHQ showed extraordinary little interest in the terrain that so richly fed their imaginations. The exception was General Vasey who had, in fact, flown over the Owen Stanleys in July, and flew into Kokoda on the 18th — three days before the Japanese landed at Gona. Oddly, he did not inform Blamey of his useful insights until 7 September, with a devastatingly casual aside: 'apparently, our ideas of topography in the area of the Gap were all wrong'.[42]

The day before their departure, the troops lavished special care on their equipment and weapons. Machine-gunners and mortar platoons doubly checked their equipment. The rifle companies dismantled and cleaned their rifles, and sharpened their bayonets. The troops cut mosquito nets to half-size; studded or placed leather straps on the soles of boots for extra grip; and dyed their khaki uniforms green using extract from local plants. It washed out. Four hundred and fifteen pairs of American gaiters were issued.

They packed their haversacks as lightly as possible; they even cut their towels and toothbrushes in half. The standard pack contained: two shirts, a pair of shorts, underpants, a pullover, equipment pouches, six days' rations of bully beef and biscuits, one dehydrated emergency ration and one chocolate emergency ration, a dixie and mug, anti-malarial cream (i.e. insect repellant), seven days of quinine tablets, water purifying tablets, toilet gear (including half a toothbrush), a ground sheet, long khaki drill trousers, half a blanket, half a towel and half a mosquito net. It weighed about 40 to 45 pounds.

Each soldier carried a rifle with bayonet and 50 rounds of .303 ammunition (unless he was a machine-gunner or mortar-bomber), and three hand grenades.[43] The total weight of pack, rifle and ammunition exceeded 55 pounds. Bill Russell of the 2/14th Battalion remarked, 'Never before had white men, or native carriers for that matter, attempted to carry such loads over those towering ranges, in the humidity of the tropics.'[44]

The Bren and Tommy guns, with 100 rounds and twelve magazines per gun respectively, plus two grenade discharger cups, were to be shared among the stronger men. The best light machine-guns — the Vickers — were too difficult to carry and left behind. Three 108 wireless sets, five field telephones, a quantity of three-inch mortars and a set of medical gear were borne by the signals and support troops, and native carriers.

Crucially, 40,000 fresh rations, four two-inch mortars, four miles of field cable, three magazines per light machine-gun, blankets, picks, shovels, and other vital supplies were to be dropped by plane at Myola, while the troops crossed the mountains. Rowell assured Brigadier Potts the biscuit bombers would deliver the supplies to the lakebed in time. There was little room for error in this immense exercise. Everything needed to feed and fuel a combat unit of 1200 troops would be dropped from the air or carried on the backs of the men.

The brigade held a church service on the eve of their departure. Some 500 men assembled in the camp clearing at Itiki in the Owen Stanley foothills. Chaplains C.W. Daly and Fred Burt[45] bestowed the blessings of Christ on soldiers about to fight the apostles of a living god.

That night, a message confirmed that a further 1800 Japanese combat troops had landed at Gona. Brigadier Potts shrugged: 'It appears to be just a question of killing more Japs.' As long as his supplies arrived at Myola, and his reserve force, the 2/27th Battalion, went up on time, his men would defeat the enemy. And so they set off.

Chapter 14
The Track

'Surely no war has ever demanded more of a man in fortitude.
Even Gallipoli, or Crete or the desert ...'
— *Osmar White, Australian war correspondent*

After four days in Port Moresby the fresh Australian battalions boarded trucks for Ilolo, near the start of the Kokoda Track. At 9.00 a.m. on 16 August the first AIF troops marched off. Company by company — logistically only about a hundred men could move up at a time — they departed; first the 2/14th Battalion, then the 2/16th the following day.

The forest closed behind them, as the little army of 1200 Australians slowly disappeared into the mountains. The long thin line of soldiers 'was swallowed up by the jungle'.[1] Hundreds of native carriers wound like a great serpentine tail slowly behind them. Never had war been waged in such conditions. And as the last units moved off, Rowell was heard to remark, 'I don't think that I've ever given any troops a tougher job than this.'[2] Their destination was Isurava, some six days' march north, where the 39th Battalion held the mountain pass.

An arsenal of superlatives has been hurled at the Kokoda Track. The notorious jungle path was 'the world's worst killing field', a 'green hell', 'the steepest', 'toughest', 'most treacherous', and so on. The track silenced the usually loquacious writer Raymond Paull: 'There is no language equipped ... to portray its many perversities.'[3] And no doubt the jungle path has exhausted — perhaps reduced to tears — many modern-day trekkers, celebrities and executives attired in the latest hiking gear.

In fact, the Kokoda Track breaches one of the less forbidding sections of the Owen Stanleys, crosses many delightful streams and passes through a landscape of raw, excrescent beauty. No doubt it is a 'regular orgy of hill climbing', as Vernon said, though in places it settles into little more than a hefty bush walk. As Hank Nelson observed, 'it was a long way from being the worst track in Papua and New Guinea — it was not broken-bottle limestone country, it did not require a day or two wading in swamps and sleeping in trees'.[4] Pretty little tribal villages appear at welcome intervals along the route, offering native fruit and vegetables.

None of these facts, however, addresses the barely imaginable horror of fighting a war here. No war had ever been fought in such country. The wounded would suffer unspeakable agony on their struggle back over the mountains. Long after the war, Lieutenant-Colonel Ralph Honner confided sadly to his son Brian, who then led an Australian unit in Vietnam, 'if we'd had helicopters we could have saved half the men we lost in the Owen Stanleys'.[5]

The track followed a slightly different route in 1942, and the jungle has reclaimed several of the original villages; their inhabitants disappeared — some say to escape the evil spirits of war. Isurava and Efogi have relocated. The original Nauro was abandoned in 2002 after a local feud, and a second Nauro established, high on a spur. Eora Creek and Ioribaiwa have simply ceased to exist — and serve as mere camp sites for trekkers.

Between the lowest point, at Uberi, and the crest of the range, the Kokoda Track climbs more than 20,000 feet. The altitude at its highest point is 8500 feet. For every 1000 feet gained the track falls 600 feet to the foot of the next ascent.[6]

In 1942, the track officially started at McDonald's Corner, the plantation owned by the McDonald family. A narrow road runs from here to Owers' Corner, where the track plunges off a precipice to Uberi — where a flying fox was later set up — and follows the Goldie River for a mile or so, before turning up the steep spur of Imita Ridge. Into this slope Australian engineers had cut some 2000 steps — the infamous 'Golden Stairs', a tough prelude to far more difficult ascents ahead.

When the first troops reached the Golden Stairs, rain had washed away the steps leaving a skeletal crossbeam — a small log — suspended above a pool of mud. The logs tended to snap under the percussive footfall of hundreds of heavily burdened soldiers. Rain made the ascent exceedingly difficult. At the summit — the razor-sharp Imita Ridge — the troops beheld with dismay 'another ridge like the one he had scaled, and another beyond, and more farther on, each clad in jungle'.[7]

These 'false summits' were frustrating in the extreme. The track rises, from crest to trough to crest, in ever-ascending stages; the peak you stood on this morning seems a stone's throw from the one you're on this evening.

It is worth quoting Colonel Kingsley Norris's famous description of the track, written in 1942:

Imagine an area of approximately 100 miles long. Crumple and fold this into a series of ridges, each rising higher and higher until 7000 feet is reached, then declining in ridges to 3000 feet. Cover this thickly with jungle, short trees and tall trees, tangled with great entwining savage vines.

Through an oppression of this density, cut a little native track, two or three feet wide, up the ridges, over the spurs, round gorges, and down across swiftly flowing mountain streams. Where the track clambers up the mountainsides, cut steps — big steps, little steps, steep steps — or clear the soil from the tree roots.

Every few miles, bring the track through a small patch of sunlit kunai grass, or an old deserted native garden, and every seven or ten miles, build a group of dilapidated grass huts — as staging shelters — generally set in a foul, offensive clearing.

Every now and then, leave beside the track dumps of discarded, putrefying food, occasional dead bodies and human foulings. In the morning flicker the sunlight through the tall trees, flutter green and blue and purple and white butterflies lazily through the air, and hide birds of deep-throated song, or harsh cockatoos in the foliage.

About midday and through the night, pour water over the forest, so that the steps become broken, and a continual yellow stream flows downwards, and the few levels areas become pools and puddles of putrid black mud.

In the high ridges above Myola drip this water day and night over the track through a foetid forest grotesque with moss and glowing phosphorescent fungi. Such is the track which a prominent politician described as 'being almost impassable for motor vehicles'.[8]

It is a lurid portrayal, and largely correct — with the caveat that in mid-August dead bodies were not seen along the track.

On the first day, the Australian troops saw through the canopy two formations of Japanese Zeros and heavy bombers soaring high overhead towards Port Moresby. They dismissed them as another air raid on the poorly defended town. But this time the bombers' targets were intricately involved in the fate of the troops. They destroyed or seriously damaged 28 Allied aircraft, Rowell's entire available fleet of transport planes, then parked on the tarmac at Seven-Mile drome. These were the planes requisitioned to drop Potts's 40,000 rations and supplies at Myola — the same fleet Rowell had ordered to be dispersed and camouflaged. The American brigadier-general responsible had failed to execute Rowell's order.★

The mangled wrecks lay burning under a great cloud of black, oily smoke. Delayed action bombs exploded, fuel dumps burst into great clouds, petrol barrels 'kept popping', and an ambulance on Hellfire Corner overturned, killing the occupants. 'The strip was a tragic sight,' observed White. 'The entire runway was ankle-deep in debris — fragments of blackened and twisted duralumin, shattered motors, parachute packs ripped open and the silk blasted into pieces the size of a pocket handkerchief.'[9]

★ This was Brigadier-General Ennis Whitehead, who had earlier agreed with Rowell's concern about the vulnerability of the aircraft.

It is unclear when Rowell got this news, because on 23 August he believed adequate supplies had been previously dropped at Myola.

The destruction of the fleet was a death sentence for the army then trudging over the mountains. Rowell wired Blamey with the disastrous news. Worse was to come: only five days' supplies were reported to be at Myola instead of the supposed 25, according to one of Rowell's staff officers who'd gone there on 11 August. They were either lost or pilfered, or they'd never been dropped.

'Once more,' concluded Lex McAulay of this fiasco, 'it was the frontline soldier who had to pay for the stupidity, mistakes and bloodymindedness of those in the rear.'[10]

Unaware of the looming catastrophe ahead, the troops trod on, stamping the rough trail into a wider passage. Most had acquired long wooden walking sticks, slashed from the trees. In the afternoon, the rains usually came, pouring onto the slopes, steaming the canopy, dripping off the trees, and draining rivulets of yellowish mud down the track. The march in such conditions turned into a grinding series of skids and slides. On the second night they scrambled up to the village of Ioribaiwa, the last section, in places a hand-over-hand climb.

'I saw what the country could do to raw troops,' observed White at Ioribaiwa. 'Most of them were big men and fit ... They made the last few 100 feet climb out of the valley in 5- or 10-yard bursts. Half of them dropped where they stood when they reached the plateau. Their faces were bluish grey with the strain, their eyes staring out. They were long beyond mere breathlessness. The air pumped in and out of them in great, sticky sobs; and they had 100 miles of such travelling ahead.'[11]

This ritual repeated itself for six days and nights: stragglers, swearing breathlessly, would stumble into camp after dark, where hundreds of men lay on wet, muddy groundsheets in cramped clearings on the slopes and tops of razorbacks. The rain fell in blinding sheets, and drenched everything through. Fires were initially banned.

At dawn, advance patrols rose from their drenched lean-tos and ground sheets and set off to prepare the forward camp for the day's incoming lines of men. One of these dawn starters was Stan Bissett, an intelligence officer (and former Wallaby) who seemed to be everywhere at once — goading and willing the troops, encouraging the die-hards and even singing — he had an excellent voice, and, on one occasion, entertained the camp site. His brother, Harold 'Butch' Bissett, was also a highly popular member of the battalion. The pair were the epitome of the tall, rugged, sports-loving Australian; it seemed nothing could diminish their optimism, cheerfulness and determination.

The Owen Stanley Range was a peculiarly terrifying environment in which to fight a war. The troops — on both sides — fought a constant mental battle against the unknown and the unseen. Night was so dark as to seem corporeal.

'The strange small noises took hold of the imagination, and were transferred into the stealth of some lurking beast or the enemy at one's elbow,' wrote Paull.[12] Geoffrey Lyon, a young officer with the 21st Brigade, said: 'It was a war of shadows. I can distinctly remember before I went up the track a chap came down who was wounded. He said, "I haven't seen a Japanese yet." That's how it was. The nefarious war of shadows.'[13]

'The intense jungle,' concluded a 7th Division medical report, 'induced feelings of claustrophobia. The intolerable quietness was rent by eerie sounds, and occasionally, the crashing of enormous rotting trees.'[14]

Every shadow hid a potential danger for troops not yet 'jungle conscious': 'A withered bush may hide a Jap sniper,' observed Honner, 'a fresh palm frond, or banana leaf in an unnatural position is probably being used for the same purpose.'[15] For now, they were safe from such dangers — the Japanese had not yet advanced beyond Deniki — but the process of acclimatisation involved constantly scanning the jungle for the slightest aberration.

Birds of paradise — the national emblem of New Guinea — were rarely seen. Most often the troops rose to the loud, harshly slurred note of the friarbird, a 'large, slim-necked drab bird with pugnacious habits and a raucous call' that 'often perches atop dead branches'. Its cry went 'keeyo keeyoway'.[16] But the sounds and sights of the local fauna were incidental ephemera consigned to the subconscious by men on the watch for a very different species.

The terrain did offer one advantage: concealment. The troops were always on the hunt, or being hunted. The jungle provided cover for, and from, infantry patrols, and a natural shield against frontal attack. It enabled lethal flanking manoeuvres. The dense canopy blocked the flight of mortar shells (and sometimes sent them crashing back down onto mortar crews).

The terrain, it could be said, actually saved lives — unlike Gallipoli, where the Turkish hillside commanded a murderous view of the beach; or the Somme, a gentle plain across which men were ordered to march into German machine-guns. And while obscenely hot in the lowlands, bitterly cold at the peaks, and miserably wet throughout, the Papuan climate did not kill with the thoroughness of the blackened finger of Russia's winter, nemesis of the armies of Hitler and Napoleon. But the one thing this country did inflict with deadly consistency was sickness, hunger and utter exhaustion.

Chapter 15
Nankai Shitai

'Lay in wait and then go around the flank. Lure them. Harass
them and exhaust them by ceaseless activity. Finally ... open the
offensive ... the enemy must never be allowed to escape'
— *Major-General Horii Tomitaro to his troops on the eve of the
Japanese invasion of Papua*

Allied commanders were still dismissing the possibility of an overland
invasion when the Japanese launched one. On 10 August the land
invasion of Papua — Operation Order A-10 from 17th Army HQ in Davao,
the Philippines — began. Major-General Horii received his instructions that
day in Rabaul, and issued the Nankai Shitai order for the invasion of Papua
and the capture of Port Moresby. His 10,000 troops — Shimada and
Yamasaki among them — prepared to board the transports, but the US
attack on the Solomons delayed their departure until 17 August.

Horii personally had grave doubts about the enterprise. He had done
his own arithmetic, and calculated that securing his daily three-ton supply of
food and ammunition would require 230 carriers a day to the front line. The
twenty-day round trip from Buna to the end of the Kokoda Track at Owers'
Corner would demand 4600 carriers; if the front line were extended to Port

Moresby, an impossible 32,000 carriers would be needed.[1] The hope, by that stage, of course, was that Port Moresby would yield up their needs; and there was the expectation of 'Churchill supplies' scavenged off the local tribes and abandoned enemy camps. Each man received a two-week supply of rice.

The Japanese commander even warned Army HQ in Tokyo about the logistical problem; it made the attack on Port Moresby extremely difficult, if not impossible, Horii is reported as having said. 'He was a very gracious and strong back-boned man,' remarked Nishimura Kokichi. 'And I admired him for complaining to Tokyo.'

In fact, in July Horii told Tokyo that 20,000 Allied troops were stationed in Port Moresby. According to Lieutenant-Colonel Tanaka Kengoro: 'He was not confident of victory despite the atmosphere of success after previous victories in the war.'[2] Horii perhaps confided in his most trusted officers, but said nothing to his troops, of course, who were itching to depart and brimming with self-confidence.

Horii's orders offer a fascinating insight into the Imperial Army's preparation for battle. The coming battle would be fought 'in an extensive jungle', he said, 'in sparsely settled, uncivilised country, the roads of which are very poor'. The Australians numbered at least 4000 (the figure, attributed to Australian prisoners captured at Kokoda, refers to supply troops at Port Moresby). In fact there were 350 Australians at Isurava, and 1200 marching over the mountains.

Of the Australians' fighting quality, Horii wrote: 'In comparison with the American infantry, the fighting spirit of the Australian infantry is strong. In the Kokoda and Rabaul battles, winding roads ... and natural objects were ably utilised. Their use of automatic small arms at close range, their sniping and grenade throwing were good.' The Shitai must 'advance unexpectedly quickly' to avoid enemy impediments such as destroyed bridges and defiles. 'It is of vital importance not to allow the enemy any time ...Where there are no bridges, swim across rivers ...'

Before contact with the enemy, his battalions would 'take advantage of the natural features of the land'. It was the smartest advice Horii gave. He elaborated: 'One unit will attack from the front, while the main force will venture a bold, resolute and prompt flanking envelopment and charge the enemy's rear flank ... a frontal, headlong and reckless advance ... will cause our forces great losses.'[3]

Most of Horii's troops had not had jungle combat experience, contrary to the widely held belief in Australia that they were the greatest jungle fighters in the world. They were certainly highly experienced in warfare, but none of the 144th Regiment — his core infantry — had fought in mountainous jungle like this. 'We had never experienced combat in jungle,' said Shimada.[4] On the other hand, they had invaded Guam and Rabaul, albeit with relatively little resistance, and had spent months in New Britain, training extensively in similar country. Morale building and jungle exercises were a daily regimen.★

The terrain would not dissuade them from deploying the night charge, as Horii explained. He gave his troops last-minute, step-by-step instructions in night attacks:

A. After flanking approach by crawling.
B. Attract the enemy with smoke, firing or shouting from the front, then charge from a different direction.
C. If nightfall is 20 or 30 min off, utilise the night for the charge.
D. Utilising rain and fog charge when the enemy is off-guard.
E. Charge when the enemy's attention is diverted by bombing ...
F. Charge suddenly from positions which the enemy believes to be unapproachable, such as cliffs, rivers, streams ... and jungles.

The Imperial Army were warned, 'not to allow overzealousness to cause grouping together at vital points' during night charges. 'Supply,' Horii added briefly, 'will be difficult.'[5]

★ The 144th official regimental history tells the story of Colonel Kusunose participating in an athletic carnival in Rabaul prior to the invasion of Papua. He believed it would boost morale and generate a great cooperative spirit. His men were ordered to climb up one of the mountains in Rabaul and return to the base camp at nightfall. Kusunose was very impressed with the soldiers' enthusiasm. The last race was a relay between officers and sergeants of the regimental HQ. Kusunose himself accepted a request to join the race. He ran dead last, which delighted the troops. One witness, First Lieutenant Fujita Motoshige — who sensed Kusunose's pessimism towards the Owen Stanley operation — resolved 'to fight to the utmost of his power in the battlefield in order to reciprocate Colonel Kusunose's sincere concern for the soldiers' (see *The 144th Infantry Regiment Official Record*, p. 79).

The tactical imperative of surprise and encirclement was drummed into every man: 'Never engage the enemy in combat without having concealment,' instructed one soldier's notebooks (later found on a Japanese corpse). Horii urged his troops: 'Lay in wait and then go around the flank. Lure them. Harass them and exhaust them by ceaseless activity. Finally, when they are completely exhausted, open the offensive ... You must fire with accuracy from cover and the enemy must never be allowed to escape.'[6]

At 9.20 a.m. on 17 August the Nankai Shitai paraded at Rabaul Harbour, bowed twice in the direction of the Imperial Palace in Tokyo, and marched aboard the 5960-ton *Ryoyo Maru* transport and other smaller vessels. The convoy left Rabaul at 6.00 p.m. bound for the Papuan beachhead.

'The military operation for the occupation of Port Moresby' had begun, wrote the exhilarated Warrant Officer Sadahiro. 'After seven months' preparation and training, at last the time has come to rise and strike dauntlessly with the iron maul.'[7] The troops, however, experienced a very rough crossing. Throughout the night the weather worsened; the ships heaved on a gathering swell. A horse was washed overboard. Lieutenant Horibe stood on the deck as dawn approached, and the wind and rain howled around him: 'The waves started to roar,' he wrote, but the weather saved them from air attacks.

The grumbling Lieutenant Noda complained that it was 'unspeakably hot and humid. If this goes on for another day I shall be ill.' Later he whinged, 'The rain came down and the wind rose, and having spent my time on deck I know I shall catch a cold.'[8]

Allied aircraft and warships offered no resistance — they were occupied in Guadalcanal — and the Nankai Shitai were allowed another unchallenged passage across the Solomon Sea.[9] Indeed, the beachhead was well supplied throughout August, with the Japanese completing five safe trips between Rabaul and New Guinea that month. They delivered tons of rice, arms, medical stores and ammunition to the beachhead and for transfer to Kokoda. The invading force was, at this stage, properly fed, fit, and, with two weeks' rations per man, confident of a swift descent on Port Moresby.

The first barges of the Kusunose Butai landed at Buna at dawn, 18 August, in motor-propelled mobile landing craft, each holding 50 men. The trip from ship to shore took twenty minutes. All day, and the next, the barges ran ashore at Buna. The scene resembled the arrival of a colonising power: two battalions of the 144th Regiment — about 1600 troops; the full complement of the 55 Mountain Artillery and cavalry regiments; several companies of the Sasebo 5SNLP and support units; 700 Rabaul natives; and 170 horses.

Within days several more battalions, of the Yazawa 41st Infantry Regiment and other units, as well as another 175 Rabaul natives and 230 horses, came ashore.[10] By 22 August about 6000 Japanese combat troops, of a total force of 10,000 — including six infantry battalions and one mountain gun unit at part-strength — had landed, or were advancing to Kokoda. That did not include Yokoyama's 2000 troops then at Kokoda–Deniki. With reinforcements the total would later exceed 13,000.

The combat troops set off immediately to join Yokoyama's men. Each soldier received a fifteen-day ration, consisting of about thirty pounds of rice, miso (bean paste), shoyu sauce in powdered form and salt, according to Yamada Kuzuo, a first class private. His basic kit consisted of a rifle, 60 rounds, a spare uniform, a water bottle, two hand-grenades, a steel helmet and a camouflage net. Extra food rations and supplies made the total load as heavy as 50 pounds, and sometimes at lot more.

The diary of Watanabe Fukuichi, 26, offers a snapshot of a typical Japanese junior officer. He was Second Lieutenant Watanabe, a primary school teacher in civilian life, and now a machine-gunner in the Koiwai Battalion, Yazawa Butai, (41st Infantry Regiment). He was five feet, two inches tall. His company had 110 men, twenty per platoon. All officers wore their swords; Watanabe's sword, at two feet, six inches long, was almost half his height. He also carried a six-chamber revolver, a map case, a compass, a bottle of creosote and ten days' supply of 'anti-malaria medicine'. An orderly carried his rations.

Each company had two heavy machine-guns (Jukis) with a crew of eight men each. There were four boxes of ammunition, each with 600 rounds (twenty brass strips of 30 bullets). During the march these were packed into canvas bags, and each man carried a number of bags, in addition to normal kit, depending on his weight.

Watanabe complained that his Juki often jammed and required a complete overhaul. Being a heavy machine-gun, it was particularly awkward to use. The firing rate, he noted, was twenty rounds every four or five seconds.

The riflemen had old Meiji 38s. Only half the troops had hand grenades, due to a shortage. These were fragmentation grenades, with a four to five second fuse. To ignite it, 'the safety pin was removed with the teeth, then the grenade tapped sharply on something hard, and thrown on the count of three'. One knew they were live by a hissing sound.

Soldiers usually wore jungle-green uniforms (though some wore khaki), and all held their trousers up with the 1000-stitch belt (the *Senninbari Haramaki*) presented by family or friends before their departure. On his feet Watanabe wore hobnailed boots, and rubber-soled shoes during landing (others had webbed-toed boots, which were light and offered better grip). A string loin cloth (the *Fundoshi*) completed Watanabe's attire.*

Watanabe and other officers would probably have seen the latest secret intelligence assessment of the enemy that came in just before he set off. It warned: 'The Australian soldier has a greater fighting spirit than the English, American or Filipino.'[11]

---

* He was shot through the chest and captured on 27 November on the road to Gona.

Chapter 16
Jungle

'Must have 14 days' reserve of rations by 26th August, also
100,000 rounds small arms ammunition, 3600 four-second
grenades, 1000 seven-second grenades, and 2-inch mortars'
— *Brigadier Arnold Potts to Port Moresby, on finding no supplies*
at Myola

Meanwhile, the Australian troops were trudging towards Myola. The
long line of light khaki wound over the mountains like an ant-trail.
They had bully beef, army biscuits and a cup of tea for lunch and dinner.
Tobacco was their greatest pleasure and morale-booster.

The terrain divided the stronger from the weak, and sub-units struggled
to stay intact as stragglers fell back. The older, and bigger soldiers couldn't
keep up, but gradually the troops grew used to the fatigue. Though 45 years
old, the inexhaustible Potts cheerfully drove his men on towards Myola,
where, he'd been assured, the supplies for his offensive had been airdropped.

On the 18 August the forward troops reached the foot of the third
range, the Maguli, some 2200 feet high, into which the engineers had cut
3400 steps. 'Impossible for white men carrying loads; natives may carry up to
15 pounds,' warned one track report.[1] This was the longest ascent, and took

the slower soldiers seven hours. 'Gradually men dropped out utterly exhausted — just couldn't go on. Many were lying down and had been sick,'[2] observed Captain Phil Rhoden, later to command the 2/14th Battalion. 'I went backwards and forwards encouraging the stragglers to get up and move,' he recalled. 'You slept in the open, you slept where you fell.'[3]

From the Maguli, the men dropped to the Brown River, and crossed at two places over single tree trunks. Up ahead, beyond a black swamp, was the village of Nauro — old Nauro. Here, and in forward villages, supply stations and medical posts were supposedly anticipating their arrival with fresh rations.

This was false: the village administrators were usually surprised at the sudden arrival of an army, and some of the forward ANGAU patrols treated the troops with careless inattention. At Nauro, ANGAU officers were barely able to offer a cup of tea.[4] Potts later spoke bitterly of the incompetence of the forward stations, whose staff generally 'displayed little interest [in us] and gave the minimum of help'.[5]

On the third and fourth days the Australians reached the pretty village of Menari, at the junction of two creeks. Menari is still a 'pleasant midday halting place ... both peaceful and prosperous ... inhabited by men and women leading the old life of Papuan mountain folk'.[6] Here the friendly Koiari people offered fruit and vegetables, and the soldiers replenished their water. Of all the forward stations, Menari was the only one 'where everything possible was done to assist the troops', Potts wrote.[7]

The next morning they crossed a stream 'on a huge log jamb, and passed across ... a cliff face on a scaffold of saplings',[8] leading to the foot of Mission Ridge, some 5000 feet high, at the top of which they reached an oval-shaped clearing, covered in kunai grass. The summit would later be called Brigade Hill (or Butcher's Hill), in memory of the battle fought there. The clearing straddles a magnificent 360-degree view of the ranges, dominated in the north-west by Mount Victoria, at 13,363 feet (the height of which had been wrongly calculated, resulting in several plane crashes). At the peak, the troops 'were in very high spirits ... Each man regarded the fact that he had reached this spot as a personal triumph, which gave him confidence in his ability to endure even greater hardships.'[9] In the evening fires were lit in the chilling alpine air and they sang songs as they shivered around the flames. 'We warmed ourselves, and we sang and we sang and we sang,' Phil Rhoden recalled. 'We sang a lot of rugby songs. The morale was high. It was great. You felt you were a member of something good.'[10] Stan Bissett led the chorus of voices, and during the singing he remembers catching his brother Harold's eye: 'I felt at that moment,' Stan recalled, 'that he was not going to make it; I had a premonition that he was going to die.'[11]

On 20 August they reached the village of Efogi, perched on an exasperating knoll, and encountered the first of the 39th Battalion's wounded coming back down the track. They nursed gunshot and bayonet wounds wrapped in old field dressings.

White recalled two 'walking wounded' edging along the path: one was shot through the foot, the other through the skull — the bullet had entered just below the left eye, and emerged behind the ear. He complained of a headache. A third was shot clean through the thigh, and another carried a badly shattered hand. 'They had walked 113 miles in 16 days,' White reported. If so, these men must have been involved in the skirmishes at Wairopi. They were 'jubilant', because their wounds ensured home leave. None spoke of the fighting. They were 'desensitised . . . completely inured to suffering. They accepted it as an integral part of living [like] eating and sleeping.'[12]

On the last ascent the men passed through The Gap, supposedly a narrow defile; in fact, aircraft could easily fly through it in fine weather. Had the Spartan army encountered this at Thermopylae they would surely have poured through and crushed the Persians.

Near the highest summit, at 8500 feet, they entered a dark, moss-covered forest, a cathedral of trees that dwarfed the forward troops. It is a cold, cavernous place — the bizarre, botanical manifestation of an alpine climate on the equator.

Gathered there are the freaks of nature, alien, triffid-like flora: great figs, startling ferns and the giant pandanus trees, whose colossal roots hang at eye level as though ripped out of the earth by a giant's hand. Fronds as long as ten feet fall from the canopy, channelling the rain to the forest floor. The long, sharp leaves of the cycads, a prehistoric remnant, explode in perfect, radial symmetry. On the forest floor vines, roots and shrubbery seem to have coagulated in a frozen state of serpentine violence. Bright green moss sheaths the lower tree trunks; and phosphorescent slime clings to their buttresses, where fans of cream fungi grow. Anomalously lining the trail are little ginger plants, as though perversely planted here by some mad, lost gardener.

There are no carnivorous animals or deadly insects. Rarely do the indigenous birds of paradise or the ostrich-like cassowaries appear, although members of the parrot family are common, and there is the occasional snake. The track is nonetheless a paradise for butterfly catchers and orchid lovers. An incurable orchid fan, Blamey later found many to distract him near Moresby and wrote to his wife of their voluptuous beauty.

The troops took a track to the right and on 21 August, in weary ones and twos, emerged from the forest onto the vast crater of Myola. Here Potts expected to find a bustling camp full of freshly dropped supplies — 40,000 rations and a huge arsenal of ammunition — with which to relieve the 39th at Isurava and launch his counteroffensive.

He found virtually nothing: a few makeshift huts, and a totally inadequate supply of rations and ammunition: 'Nothing [had been] dropped since August 16th although the weather had been good.'[13] There were just 80 blankets and 6000 rations — about four days' worth.[14] Worse, only two days' reserves were held ahead of Myola. As for firepower, there were 10,000 rounds of Tommy gun ammunition and 75,000 rounds of .303 ammunition, less than half the amount required — 'and the 21st brigade was expected to take the offensive!'[15] bitterly remarked Frank Sublet, a brave, ruthless officer impatient to defeat the enemy. Nor had the small force at Myola, which included Kienzle, been told of the timing of the brigade's arrival.

A furious Potts contained himself and questioned the uncomprehending ordnance officers in charge. No, they had not received any airdrops for at least a week. No, they had not been informed of his arrival — and so on.

Potts was bewildered. The supply arrangements at Myola were 'appallingly lax', noted the 21st Brigade War Diary. Of course, the scale of the cock-up can be easily seen with hindsight; at the time, Potts knew little of the size of the army he was about to confront, and the extent to which the supply failure would cripple his offensive. But from his vantage point it was a grave crisis — Potts never underestimated the importance of supply. He maintained an outward calm, as his battered sense of military precision cast around for a solution.

All around him the windswept lakebed, suspended like a great dish in the heart of the mountains, rolled away to the peripheral clouds; and the silent emptiness seemed perhaps to reflect the forlorn state of the Australian army. They were stranded in the mountains without adequate food or ammunition. Over the next range was Isurava, where the few hundred men of the 39th were dug in; far below them, at Kokoda, the forward troops of the Nankai Shitai had arrived and were steadily absorbing Yokoyama's men into their ranks.

Potts signalled Port Moresby and demanded, immediately, nine days' reserve rations for 2000 troops — the figure included the 53rd Battalion, which was then coming up the track — and several hundred native carriers.

His wire to Rowell that day — 23 August, the very day Potts became commander of Maroubra Force* — was perhaps the most vital of the campaign: 'Must have 14 days' reserve of rations by 26th August, also 100,000 rounds small arms ammunition, 3600 four-second grenades, 1000 seven-second grenades, and 2-inch mortars.'[16] He then dispatched a trusted officer, Major Cameron, back to Port Moresby to press the unit's needs.

A shocked Rowell relayed the news directly to Blamey in Brisbane, and wired Potts the next day with emergency instructions: '... It is possible for the rations to have been moved forward from MYOLA. Until the matter is cleared up and an adequate reserve established you will not repeat NOT make any fw'd move.'[17]

The response was swift; Potts would get some rations and ammunition. Rowell, with the help of General Arthur 'Tubby' Allen**, organised the immediate dispatch of several planeloads of supplies. Between 23 and 24 August, some 5000 emergency rations, 4480 pounds of biscuits, 1500 balanced rations, assorted ration components, and — unnecessarily, since the mountains were

* Maroubra Force was the name of the combined Australian units — militia and AIF — then stationed in the Owen Stanleys.
** Then the popular 7th Division commander.

mosquito-free — 21,000 quinine tablets, tumbled out of the rear doors of Dakota biscuit bombers and bestrew the lakebed.

The airdropped arsenal included: 237,000 rounds of .303 bullets; 1050 four-second grenades; 140,000 rounds of Tommy gun ammunition; two 3-inch mortar cannons and 120 mortar bombs. Sent the next day were 4000 grenades, 714 mortar bombs, 1000 blankets, 1000 sweaters, 1000 green-dyed uniforms, 2000 packets of cigarettes and a quantity of soap.[18]

It was not enough, but it was something. The blankets were welcome; in the alpine climate, the troops had used their groundsheets to keep warm. The green-dyed uniforms, albeit better than light khaki, were one tone of green, but the jungle tended to be mottled-green. It seemed Australia's Quartermaster's store misunderstood the concept of camouflage. War correspondent Chester Wilmot threw in his usual withering assessment of the incompetence around him: 'It is strange that six months after the return of ... General Blamey there should be no green uniforms in Australia.'[19]

With packages raining down, the problem was retrieval. Hundreds of heavy great bales suddenly littered Myola. There were not enough tribesmen to gather them — despite Kienzle's unceasing efforts. Potts needed at least 2000 carriers for the job; there were only 933 (including the sick) shuttling between Myola and Isurava at that time. About a third had deserted — protesting their lack of pay, fear of the Japanese and exhaustion. 'The carriers' spell of two half-days a week was merely a cherished memory ... and none forgot that his contract had long since expired.'[20]

The broken carrier lines drew hostile criticism. Little or no foresight, thundered the brigade's operational report, had been shown 'by those responsible' for calculating the number of natives needed to maintain Maroubra Force and pick up from drop zones.[21]

How was Potts to commit his troops to battle? As little as 30 per cent of his emergency supplies would survive the plunge into the Myolan lakebed. Parachutes were not yet attached to airdropped packages, many of which were lost, pilfered or damaged. The consequences of the supply failure cannot be overstated. It fatally delayed Potts's planned offensive: he lost his momentum, and had to rethink his entire strategy. The recapture of Kokoda and the thrust to the sea were impossible without a huge arsenal and a reliable food supply.

The catastrophe undermined Potts 'even before he met his enemies' and altered his mission from an offensive to defensive one. 'He should not have been given orders which, through no fault of his own, he could not fulfil'[22] — thus Australia's official war historian, a writer subject to military censorship, condemned the logistical disaster. Others were less polite. The disaster at Myola exposed an ill-equipped Australian infantry to the full brunt of the Japanese invasion.* The great cost of such spectacular incompetence was the loss of time. It delayed for seven days the relief of the 39th, whose exhausted survivors had been dug in at Isurava for weeks, fighting off sporadic Japanese patrols.

Stalled at the highest point of the Owen Stanleys, unable to advance, with barely enough ammunition and food to sustain the most threadbare resistance, Potts could only wait as his supplies were hauled in.

Meanwhile, Horii's troops were streaming into Kokoda. His patrols had alerted the Japanese commander to the weak Australian resistance at Isurava. The Japanese knew nothing, yet, of the two AIF battalions then marooned at Myola.

Horii saw no reason to change his schedule. Officially he planned to reach Isurava within two days, and Moresby within five.[23] No doubt he still had deep misgivings. But his orders of 18 August were to 'advance to the southern slopes of the Owen Stanley Range and destroy enemy troops there'.[24] And orders were orders.

His biggest headache, similarly, was supply. Horii's vast supply line extended to Buna–Gona (by human carrier) and then by transport ship to Rabaul. If Allied air raids destroyed the ships the loss rippled all the way into

---

* It was a mystery why so little had been dropped at Myola before the transports were destroyed. Rowell later accepted technical responsibility (see Rowell, *Full Circle*). It seems that the American pilots missed their targets — 'US navigational ability was a longstanding joke among the Australian forces' (see McAuley, *Blood and Iron*, p. 116). Others argued that the rations were never dropped at all, and blamed the catastrophe on 'inexperienced and ignorant' staff (see McCarthy, *South-West Pacific Area*, pp. 196–199). This infuriated Rowell, whose order to clear the Moresby airstrip had been disobeyed, and whose wires to Blamey went unheeded. Not until 24 August did MacArthur authorise six Douglas Dauntless dive-bombers, one Flying Fortress bomber and two transports to be sent to New Guinea.

the heart of the mountains, and broke Horii's tenuous lifeline. For now, the line seemed to be working relatively well, and Kokoda had a large stockpile.

But there was no room for error; his troops had no emergency rations. A Japanese soldier's usual prescribed daily field ration, according to Lieutenant-Colonel Tanaka Kengoro, was two pounds of rice and tinned meat. In the Owen Stanleys, they received twenty pounds of rice to last fifteen days, and no tinned meat — 'a reduction of one third in the normal daily rice ration'.[25]

Their famous spirit would see them through; that was a constant refrain. Many Japanese soldiers carried little tomes of spiritual succour; one military pamphlet issued during training (and later found on several corpses), said: 'The spirits of over 100,000 warriors are guarding us.'

The Shitai's camp site reading was never light: 'In this war ... after landing, a small detachment may have to march deep into the enemy country. Be prepared to abandon your dead ... Be ready to die at any time and any place',[26] the pamphlet continued. It is hard to imagine the troops actually reading these grisly documents. But presumably they'd acted on one snippet of advice before leaving Rabaul: 'Make the necessary will, and have your hair and nails cut' — locks of hair and nail ends were sent to the soldier's home before departure in case his remains were not forthcoming.

The Shitai were briefed on the correct treatment of prisoners and natives. On the face of it, the rules (in their unit war diary) seemed civilised — and certainly some soldiers observed them, in spirit if not to the letter. For example, the troops were not to harm prisoners, women or tribal inhabitants: 'If we, in a moment of excitement, kill a man who has thrown away his arms and surrendered, this will not be the true warrior spirit. Particularly are the natives to be respected, for they are included in the unification of East Asia. To harm non-resistant natives is to shame the banner of the Imperial Army ...'[27]

No 'senseless counter-measures' were to be taken against Australian POWs; these included 'useless murder caused merely by anger ... or cruelty caused by a man seized by emotion'. Australian officers, especially, were to be spared 'the third degree'. This was totally ignored, of course: the Japanese bayoneted or shot all Australian and American prisoners in the Papuan campaign, from Templeton on.

Indeed, other 'instructions' contradicted the rules of the Shitai's war diary, and suggest the extent to which they were honoured in the breach. These were the 'Essentials' of Japanese interrogation, for example:

Tie up four or five men at a time . . .
Inform them that they will be shot if they cause any disturbance.
Officers will be placed in a separate room . . .[28]

The degree of severity towards the Papuans seemed to differ from soldier to soldier. Yamasaki said his unit treated the local people very well, always gave them food, and enjoyed 'good relations' with them.[29] One readily believes this small, smiling man, who recalls being ordered to carry a 180-pound bag of rice to Kokoda. So, too, Shimada and Imanishi are convincing when they say they never hurt the tribal people. Yamasaki has a black sense of humour. When he heard that some of the Papuans were former cannibals, he asked a local, 'Would you care to eat a Japanese man?'

By 26 August, Potts had salvaged whatever supplies he could, and ordered the 2/16th Battalion up to Myola. The two Australian battalions continued along the track towards Templeton's Crossing. It is a dark, gloomy place, perpetually wet, 'with a general air of depression'.[30] It was the first point on the track to be named after a dead Australian officer. In time ridges, corners, track junctions, and even single rocks and trees would be named after dead Australian and American troops, evoking the macabre impression that an army of ghosts had conquered and then colonised this primeval land.

Over a series of short, precipitous slopes, the troops descended into the Eora Creek gorge, a deep ravine into which the track seems to plunge headlong so that a soldier has to clutch at hanging branches for support. The men edged along feeder streams and reached the brink of 'rushing water thick with white and yellow spume'.[31] Little whirlpools swirled around huge boulders, and the backwash sent a film of spray into the air.

On the misty banks was the last Allied base before Alola and Isurava: a little cluster of huts thatched with palm leaves. Eora Creek was destined to become briefly the busiest Australian field hospital on the Kokoda Track. As the troops approached, files of wounded militiamen passed by like so many plaintive ghosts, 'walking skeletons ... their eyes ... bright with fever'. They would shuffle forward a few yards, in little bursts, then pause for relief.[32]

On the banks scores of men stood about 'in mud to their shins ... slimed from head to foot, for weeks unshaven, their skins bloodless under their filth'.[33] The village itself looked as though it were submerged in a sea of mud. Discombobulated native carriers sat on logs on the edge of the clearing eating 'muddy rice off muddy banana leaves', their eyes shining with exhaustion. The stretcher cases lay in rows, wrapped in dirty, blood-soaked bandages, waiting to be lifted upon the shoulders of tribesmen. The ubiquitous Vernon and his medical officers constantly attended them. When morphia ran its course, the wounded lay prostrate, numbed with pain, Vernon observed. When a soldier died, he was swiftly buried with a short service.*

Vernon's diary offers a Rabelaisian glimpse of the hospital:

At Eora Creek I took over all white casualties as well as sick carriers with the aid of a rather untrained orderly. There were cheerful patients and grumpy ones, and the latter did not scruple to voice their complaints, but considering the extreme lack of comfort and the spent condition of the men, they were really a very patient and long-suffering crowd ...

The kitchen was the best spot in the hut; there was a roaring fire there day and night and one of the most cheerful cooks I have ever come across, a sergeant with a badly inflamed leg who had volunteered to cook for the boys in spite of being a cripple. He managed to knock up some very artistic dishes, which we ate from any receptacle we could find.

The space around his fire was hung with muddy shirts and pants steaming with moisture; beneath the empty (petrol) drum that served as a stove was a heap of boots that never dried out, and all around the hearth lay men in the last stages of exhaustion, very thankful to get close to the blaze. The cook did not seem to mind how many men he had to shove through to get to his billy cans.[34]

---

* After the campaign ended, battlefield clearance parties would exhume and return the bodies to Bomana Cemetery near Port Moresby for a proper burial.

Those with relatively light wounds faced the long walk back to Owers' Corner. The 39th Battalion's Lieutenant Alf Salmon had received a bullet through his pectoral muscle, 'a nice little charmer in my right breast just missing the nipple', as he described it in a letter to his wife. 'My dear Gwen,' he added, 'don't go rushing about sending a big bundle on ... Honey, don't worry about me and don't worry about the mail not being regular as you have no idea what a job it is to get it in and out again.'[35]

On the eve of the battle of Isurava Brigadier Arnold Potts wrote to his wife, Dawn, from his tent in the Owen Stanleys:

> My lovely lady,
>   Some paper to hand at last ... My dear, there are such
> interesting things to see ... not the least being gorgeous waterfalls
> ... Give both my daughters a big hug and kiss ... I love you
> darling and want you close to me as always. What fun when this
> row is finished ...'[36]

It was 25 August. Potts was in good spirits despite the supply disaster. The day before he had succeeded Porter as commander of Maroubra Force. His troops (many of whom, as a battalion commander, he'd led in the Middle East) were at last approaching the combat zone.

No one doubted Arnold Potts was a fine choice to lead the first major land offensive against the Japanese. This short, tough, nuggety farmer from Western Australia, whose piercing blue eyes seemed to 'flash and twinkle',[37] was an original Anzac with an outstanding military record.

He was born in the Isle of Man in 1896; his family emigrated to Australia when he was eight and settled in the Perth suburb of Cottesloe. He attended a private cadet school. In World War I, he fought at Gallipoli and in France, where, promoted to captain, he became the youngest company commander in the Australian forces — aged nineteen — and won the Military Cross. He was twice wounded; once a sniper's bullet passed within an ace of his spine. Between the wars he became a grazier, married, and had children. He enlisted for the Second Australian Imperial Force, aged 44, despite family hopes that he may have been too old. Potts kept extremely fit (though his war wound prevented him from touching his toes).

Potts was an intriguing mixture of romantic idealism and ruthless pragmatism — a devoted husband, sensual letter-writer, and fastidious commander. He was also pragmatic. He shocked a unit padre by advocating the use of 'French letters' over the muzzles of machine-guns, to keep out mud and water, and later joked to his wife that it would 'protect their weapons'.

After their last weekend together before he sailed, Potts wrote to his wife:

Belovedest of women, It was delightful to hear your voice this morning . . . it is torture Beloved though very sweet torture. You're such a delicious girl that the voice alone is most unsatisfactory and I can't pretend that the 'half loaf' satisfies me. What a marvellous weekend you gave me Heart's Delight . . . Even though I squeezed my memory I couldn't dig up anything but dreams — splendid dreams — all woven around a valiant heart and a wonderful woman — my wife.[38]

That day, he'd departed for the Middle East, as commander of the 2/16th Battalion. Again he proved a superb soldier, earning the Distinguished Service Order at the battles of Sidon and Damour. The citation reads: 'Major Potts was particularly outstanding not only for his personal bravery in going forward under fire . . . but in his own personal leadership and example.'[39] Promoted to brigadier, he returned to Australia with the 7th Division — the very unit Curtin had fought so hard to repatriate — to command the forces in the Owen Stanleys. Potts was the genuine article: a war hero and a brilliant leader.

There was something eminently sensible about Potts the soldier. Very much his own man, he always did what he thought right for the troops. He decided, for example, to establish his base camp in the hills above Port Moresby, in defiance of New Guinea Force's instructions. Here, he reasoned, the men would have a few days to acclimatise to the jungle, and the risk of malaria was less.

One anecdote tells a great deal about his gutsy resourcefulness. When he got to Port Moresby he met the resigned mentality of 'can't', as in, 'You can't carry more than 15lb in this country; you can't move without carrier lines.'[40] He dismissed this as tropical inertia, and within a day secured a promise that 40,000 rations would be dropped at Myola before his men arrived there (the fact that it was unfulfilled perhaps vindicated the 'can't' brigade).

He was said to care too much for his men. He led from the front; he instinctively shared their ordeal over the Owen Stanleys: 'There was great strength in his thickset frame, despite his 46 years, and even greater strength of spirit behind the round cheerful English face which smiled from beneath grey hair cut *en brosse*.'[41] His startling blue eyes smiled on everyone under his command, whatever their rank or status. On the track he seemed to be 'everywhere', recalled one private.

It was unusual to find a free spirit so highly ranked in the Australian army. Potts was politically artless and highly critical of incompetence, a dangerous mixture in any human organisation. Sometimes, his blasts unwittingly indicted his superior officers. 'He could cut a man down in just a few words. If he thought it was wrong he'd say so, even to his superiors. That could be a problem at times,' concluded Bill Edgar, Potts's biographer.[42]

The brigadier put the lives of his men ahead of the approbation of his superiors. His desire to save his army and thwart the Japanese invasion led him to adopt new tactics in response to the terrible circumstances. As Lex McAulay said, 'he could simply have retreated; instead he chose a fighting withdrawal'.[43] Potts may have become 'bogged in the soft sands of other people's logistical errors';[44] but he resolved to fight his way out.

Uppermost in Potts's mind at Isurava was whether the 39th Battalion could hold on — at least until his reinforcements were combat-ready. The militia's condition so shocked him he alerted Rowell to the state of the men: 'weak due continuous work ... wet every night ... Morale good but troops useless for holding job.'[45]

They'd performed a holding job for five weeks: lost, recaptured and lost Kokoda; withdrawn to Deniki; then to Isurava, which they'd held for the past ten days against Japanese attacks. They were highly praised: '... at no period has this unit lost its cohesion ... and there has been no complaint whatever from it apart from ... the difficulty of removing stretcher cases', concluded one report.[46]

Unfortunately, the same could not be said of elements of the 53rd Battalion, whose disgruntled troops pulled up at Isurava a few days before Potts's men. The fresh militia were 'the most spent and disheartening looking of our troops I had yet seen', observed Captain Vernon, as they passed him at Efogi.[47] On 25 August, Porter, their temporary leader, described the officers of the 53rd as lamentably weak and the men, 'in a state of bewilderment'.[48] Potts sent them into battle that day.

Chapter 17
Isurava

'The Nankai Shitai ... have succeeded in completely surrounding the Australian forces ... The annihilation of the Australians is near'
— *Major-General Horii Tomitaro, commander of the Japanese troops at Isurava*

A scene of grotesque beauty surrounds what was Isurava. The 'forces of nature gone berserk' was one apt description.[1] The original village stood on the great spur jutting out over the Kokoda plateau. It is possible to imagine this place as a huge, north-facing amphitheatre. To the east, Eora Creek rushes heard but unseen down the deep gorge, and high up the far side, on the eastern 'dress circle', is the village of Abuari, shrouded in the mist of a waterfall. To the west, the great Naro Ridge curves around the Isurava spur like the gods of an opera house, the whole effect of which is to thrust the eye forward to the 'stage', the Kokoda plateau far below, where the Japanese army massed.

The Australians had a strong geographical advantage. The corvette-shaped valley offered a brilliant defensive position. The country immediately beneath the spur is a steep, heavily forested slope, up which Horii's troops were forced to climb. To reach the high flanks — the 'arm-rests' east and west — from where they could enfilade the Australians, they had to ascend mountainsides through virgin jungle.

Indeed, it is tempting to speculate that when they spoke of 'The Gap', Allied GHQ actually meant Isurava (so poor were their maps). Lieutenant-Colonel Ralph Honner perhaps unwittingly made the allusion: 'Isurava could yet be Australia's Thermopylae,' he wrote.[2] It was 'as good a delaying position as could be found ... If the enemy ... should try to outflank us they would face a stiff uphill climb from the Eora Valley on our right or a tedious struggle through the dense jungle round our left. And if they should choose the easy way in from the flanks they would walk into our waiting fire.'[3] Honner was among the few to realise that somehow the Australians had to use the jungle to their advantage, to make tactical moves that allowed 'the jungle itself to do the killing ...'[4]

Numerically, the Japanese had a massive advantage — but not as great as many think. The legend of Isurava holds that one tiny, ragged Australian unit withstood 10,000 or even 13,000 fanatical Japanese combat troops, at a ten to one advantage, for weeks.[5] The truth avers that about 6000 Japanese combat troops confronted some 1800 Australians, of whom 600 were untrained militia (the 39th and 53rd) and 1200 were AIF (the two battalions fought at half-strength or less). At the height of the battle, 28–30 August, there were perhaps three or four Japanese to one Australian.[6] At no point along the track did the Australians face 10,000 Japanese.[7]

Honner, rushed over the range in mid-August to lead the 39th, looked on his men with sympathy and dismay. He found them sitting in drenched dugouts in their mud-caked uniforms, shivering 'through the long chill vigil of the lonely nights'.[8] They were worn out by strenuous fighting, and 'many of them had literally come to a standstill'. 'We were as wet as shags,' said Smoky Howson, 'and most of the fellas were crook with dysentery.'

On Sunday the 23rd a Protestant chaplain, Jack Flanagan, held a church service outside a hut in Isurava. Hymns were sung in the cool jungle air. Hundreds bowed their heads at prayer. 'Everyone was in full battle dress and on the alert for an attack.'[9]

Of three possible strategies, Potts decided on the one that seemed the least costly in terms of casualties; paradoxically, it also seemed the riskiest. He planned to relieve the 39th with one fresh AIF battalion (the 2/14th), which would attack along the centre and west, up Naro Ridge. He decided also to commit the 53rd along the fork in the track towards Abuari, high up on the eastern ridge.

Potts's over-reliance on the 53rd Battalion was the plan's biggest flaw.[10] To lose Abuari meant exposing his HQ to fire from the east. Indeed, though Potts privately doubted whether the 53rd could do the job, it was his only 'battle-ready' unit. They had rested at Alola for a week. It was humanly impossible to send into battle men who were just arriving over the mountains.

Early signs of the coming conflagration could be seen in the valley below, where the Japanese 'were moving as purposefully as soldier ants'[11] to the flanks — the beginnings of a vast pincer movement. In previous days, Japanese night patrols had more frequently attacked the militia's perimeter. There were occasional suicide squads.★ Selected with ritual solemnity from the Japanese ranks, such men were ordered to 'be a messenger unto death ... strive to reach your objective to the last man'.[12] When Jack Boland's section ambushed Japanese troops who 'hadn't fired a shot', he felt certain 'they'd sacrificed their blokes to draw our fire'.[13]

In the Japanese camp, supplies were faltering, some bags of rice had started to putrefy, but the men seemed to thrive on an apparently bottomless reserve of Japanese 'spirit'. 'The day was beautiful and the birds sang gaily. It was like spring,' wrote Lieutenant Hirano, an officer in Tsukamoto's unit at Deniki. 'Cooked sufficient rice for three meals.'

Hirano, a Kokoda veteran, was a vivid chronicler: when six guards accidentally 'let the natives escape', he witnesses his commander 'ragingly threaten them with court-martial'. When a friend was killed, he openly

---

★ The suicide squad, Kesshi Tai (literally 'Determined-to-Die Unit'), became a depressingly familiar feature of the Pacific War, as were booby-trapped corpses, and corpses used as decoys. An Australian patrol found the body of Private MacGraw, a 53rd Battalion scout, propped up against a tree. 'The patrol got within a few yards of the body when the Japanese brought heavy fire to bear' (see Budden, *That Mob*, p. 25). Sometimes the corpses were horribly mutilated, as happened elsewhere in the Pacific. In New Georgia the severed penis of a dead American soldier was found in his mouth, an act designed to infuriate and demoralise the marines. Nor was it unusual for Allied troops to desecrate or booby-trap the Japanese dead, later in the war.

wept, and thought of their parents. It is tempting to read Hirano's diary entry of 20 August as a rare example of Japanese irony: '20th Aug. Our new Coy Commander, 1st Lt. Hatanaka Seizo, arrived. Summary of his lecture: "In death there is life. In life there is no life."'

That, however, would put a Western interpretation on a deeply earnest man. The triumph of death over life obsessed Hirano, as revealed in his chilling entry the next day: 'I will die at the foot of the Emperor. I will not fear death! Long live the Emperor! Advance with this burning feeling and even the demons will flee!'[14]

A new arrival was Warrant Officer Sadahiro. He believed utterly in the triumph of the Japanese spirit. He led a company and carried the unit's standard: 'the highest honour a soldier can achieve'. He goaded his men harshly during the long march from the beach. Few of these seemed the super soldiers of Western mythology: 'Scolding and shouting at confused subordinates, I again led the march,' Sadahiro boasted. They marched all night. Of his 120 troops, at least 40 stragglers fell out from exhaustion. Sadahiro bemoaned their want of spirit: 'Stragglers seem to be increasing daily. Is it because of the absence of daily training, or is it a lack of physical energy? What we need is spiritual strength!'[15]

Major-General Horii himself reached the heights above Kokoda on 24 August. He surveyed the battlefield, and distributed sketches of the Australian positions. He issued his last orders before battle with the gruff, perfunctory tone of a man for whom defeat was unthinkable and victory, an apparent formality (of course, Horii's precise emphasis may be lost in translation). The word 'annihilate' was a personal favourite: 'On the 26th the Shitai is to attack the enemy and advance towards Moresby,' he decreed. The Kusunose Butai was ordered to 'advance along the eastern side of the valley, deploy to the south of Isurava, cut off the Australians' withdrawal and annihilate them'.[16] It seemed all too simple. Horii's main force, meanwhile, would charge up the centre and up Naro Ridge to the west, 'surround the enemy and annihilate them'.

On the morning of the 25th a detachment of the 53rd Battalion set off on their crucial mission to Abuari, on the eastern flank, as ordered. As they trudged off, Potts had serious misgivings. He'd seen these youths coming up the track, slouching towards a maelstrom for which not even Australia's most experienced soldiers were prepared. But Potts had no choice. They were his only rested unit.

Their first contact with the Japanese revealed a glint of steel. A forward patrol led by Lieutenant Alan Isaachsen, a South Australian bank clerk, reached the village of Kaile. As night fell, two Japanese platoons attacked with mortar bombs and machine-guns, killing him. But his men held their position and hit back with a barrage of fire. 'Heavy casualties' were later reported. At the time, Lieutenant-Colonel Kenneth Ward, the 53rd's brave if inexperienced commander, couldn't get through to Isaachsen's men. This was because the Japanese had killed or scattered Australian signalmen at Missima, and 'a Japanese officer, wielding his sword with theatrical fervour' had smashed the radio set.[17]

Ominous news arrived. That afternoon, a 53rd officer was brought before Potts. The man had led an 'unarmed patrol' of 30 men towards Missima, to assist the Australian signalmen. Potts was aghast. *Unarmed?* The officer explained that they were to use the signal platoon's rifles, but the (presumably heavily armed) Japanese had forced them back. The soldier's attitude shocked Potts, who ordered Lieutenant-Colonel Ward 'at first light tomorrow' to recapture Missima and Abuari and restore the position on the eastern flank.[18]

Potts's worst apprehensions were being horribly realised. He wired Port Moresby for urgent reinforcements: '53rd battalion training and discipline below the standard required.'[19] It was imperative, he said, that his reserve troops (the 2/27th Battalion) leave Port Moresby at once. This demand was not met.*

This, then, was the state of Potts's force as battle began: his supplies were inadequate; he had no troop reserves; and he faced an enemy four times the size of his exhausted force, almost half of whom were virtually untrained.

Horii's heavily camouflaged troops moved up the mountain in swift bursts; some were so thickly adorned in vegetation they resembled moving shrubs. An unending line scaled the Naro Ridge above Isurava; to the east, they advanced towards the Abuari waterfall; and in the centre they came up the Kokoda Track from Deniki.

---

* The Japanese that day landed troops at Milne Bay, on Papua's east coast, and the 2/27th Battalion was withheld in case of a new attack on Port Moresby.

Sadahiro led the night movement on the 25th: 'Today [we] became a flanking party ... Faces of the warriors were tense. At 1400, while advancing up a breath-taking cliff, No 5 Company encountered and fought the enemy ... Fully realised that the enemy is not to be underrated. At 1700 [we] became the advance party. Slashed ahead through the jungle all night long.'[20]

Dawn the next day found Australia's 39th Battalion — of whom there were about 300 left — 'crouching like pale ghosts'[21] in their dugouts at Front Creek, near Isurava village, atop the main spur. Honner deployed B Company — accused of desertion at Kokoda — up the Naro Ridge, 'the most dangerous sector' (in defiance of Porter's view that they were 'finished as a fighting force'[22], and worthy only of disbandment).★

The opening salvo in the four-day battle of Isurava struck at 7.00 a.m. Japanese Jukis spat round after round across the valley. A mountain gun sent shells crashing into Isurava village, killing two Australian soldiers. All day sporadic bursts crackled across Isurava. Fresh Japanese infantry, under cover of high grass, entered the native gardens at Front Creek. An Australian patrol returning at 5.00 p.m. 'hunted them down through the long grass while the light lasted' and killed eight.[23]

Night came. Two militia platoons a few hundred yards forward of Isurava were cut off by a 'silent tide of attackers' flowing undetected through the darkness. Then 'all hell broke loose', as the Japanese 'stormed over the two staunch platoons, lurching around the gnarled tree-roots and leaping over the ambuscading pits, shooting, stabbing, hacking, in a sudden surge of blind and blazing fury that broke and ebbed back into the darkness from which it sprang, leaving its jetsam of death stranded before it'. Thus Honner captured the fury of the first Japanese night attack at Isurava.

The Australian wounded were helped back to the village. The dead were unreachable. The Japanese soon reclaimed the native garden. By the night of the 26th they'd captured Missima village; and were deploying thousands of troops along the high Naro Ridge.

★ Honner later justified his decision: 'To replace these unfortunates with another company could be the final lethal act of contempt, destroying when I should be building.' B company were to be given a chance to 'erase forever that early slur' (*Stand-To*).

That evening the 39th received a 'providential blessing':[24] the first platoons of the Australian Imperial Force moved up to Isurava. The sight of these fit, experienced troops, who used their weapons with habitual ease, and who fell into the dugouts with calm unconcern, startled the militia: 'Who are you? Where are you from?' one of the 39th men asked. 'We're the 2/14th Battalion, AIF,' one replied.[25] The rift dissolved; the men embraced. It was the first time the 'twin armies' had fought together. 'I thought Christ had come down again,' the 39th Battalion's Sergeant John Manol exclaimed.[26] 'We all did. We thought of them as gods, these blokes. They were tall and they were trained ... [with] clean uniforms.'

The AIF gazed at the cadaverous troops they were relieving. 'Gaunt spectres with gaping boots,' one soldier said, 'and rotting tatters of uniform hanging around them like scarecrows ... Their faces had no expression, their eyes sunk back into their sockets. They were drained by [disease], but they were still in the firing line ...'[27]

'I could have cried when I saw them, they looked terrible,' said Jim Coy of the 2/14th. 'But they were terribly pleased to see us,' said Phil Rhoden, of the 2/14th. 'The divisions faded at once. We were Australians fighting for Australia. The mood was electric.'[28]

The next day disaster struck the 53rd, on the eastern flank. In line with Potts's orders, Lieutenant-Colonel Ward sent 200 men to recapture Missima. They set off along the track at 10.00 a.m., led by Captain Cuthbert King. Near Abuari they walked into enemy patrols, and King's companies 'scattered'. Then an Australian — no one seems to know who — gave the order: 'Go for your lives — the Japs have broken through.'[29] The cry went up — and most of the men bolted into the jungle. A few held their ground, or were immobilised by fear. Fifteen Australian bodies — the victims of an ambush — were later found slung in the jungle. Some 70 Australian troops were absent for days, having 'gone bush'.*

'The Australians were seen ... to be retreating to the mountain top,' observed Japanese machine-gunner Lieutenant Sakomoto. Another Japanese

---

* They would not emerge until the 28th, followed by eighteen survivors of Isaachsen's earlier patrol, haggard and hungry, whose brave stand at Kaile would offset to some degree the unit's disgrace. But the damage was done. A 53rd diarist later blamed 'the nature of the country' and 'lack of offensive spirit and physical condition of the troops' for their flight.

soldier said bitterly, 'The Australians won't fight!' — as though he'd been cheated of a long-awaited stoush.[30]

By 2.00 p.m. Ward, with no word from King, followed with his entire HQ staff. At 3.30 p.m. they skirted the Abuari waterfall and walked straight into a Japanese ambush. Ward was the first to die: 'Senior command of the 53rd battalion was wiped out in a matter of minutes.'[31]

A runner alerted Potts to the debacle: the Japanese now occupied Abuari, within artillery range of brigade HQ. Disgusted, Potts ordered the 53rd back to Port Moresby* and rushed up the 2/16th Battalion; company by company were sent in to recapture the eastern flank, now gravely exposed.

What became of the 53rd? The fittest were assigned to labour details at Myola. One unit went back under armed escort:[32] 'Their "execution" was completed when they arrived in Moresby,' wrote Porter, who had the decency to qualify the disgrace of the 53rd: 'Some AIF units have suffered similarly; but there has always been someone sufficiently interested to smother the stigma attached.'[33] Had someone been sufficiently interested in this battalion they might have directed their ire at the Australian military authorities who'd sent untrained, deeply stigmatised young men into battle.

Captain Merritt of the 39th was famously shaving in a creek at dawn on the 28th when a runner raced up with news from the Isurava front. Honner turned to Merritt and calmly said, 'Captain ... when you've finished your shave will you go up to your company. The Japanese have broken through your perimeter.'[34] Merritt was 'off like a racehorse'; he arrived to find his

---

* The full repercussions of the debacle can be found in the Australian War Memorial archives. Four officers were singled out for severe reprimand. According to the charges, one had 'broken down and evacuated'; another had 'reported back to HQ without his company'; and a third had 'lost control of company'. A major was accused of dumping ammunition on the track because it was too heavy, and was moved forward only after aggressive coercion. 'The area vacated [by the major's company] was littered with ammunition, clothing, food and weapons. I would have NO confidence in this Offr under active service conditions,' concluded a post-mortem report. One captain 'returned to his Bn feeling ill. He was in such a bad state of nerves when I saw him that I ordered ... him evacuated.' The most criticised offender, another captain, had refused to advance citing the excuse 'the country was too rough'. 'His action allowed the enemy to work behind the waterfall and another company had to be admitted to protect the right rear. My impression of this officer was that he could not be trusted to carry out orders' (see 'Confidential Report on Officers 53 Bn. During Operations 'Alola' Area' 20/31 Aug. '42, in Porter Papers, AWM PR00527 Box 10).

men resisting a series of ferocious attacks. All day the 39th held, shored up by fresh AIF troops then pouring into their dugouts.

Mortar and machine-guns again opened up across the valley that afternoon, from Naro Ridge to Missima. A fastidiously time-conscious Japanese diarist noted: 'At 1538 our guns all joined in together and the advance began along the whole front.'[35]

'Mortar bombs and mountain gun shells,' observed Honner, 'burst among the tree tops or slashed through to the quaking earth, where the thunder of their explosion was magnified in the close confines of the jungle thickets. Heavy machine guns — the dread "woodpeckers" — chopped through the trees, cleaving their own lanes of fire to tear at the defences ... bombs and bullets crashed and rattled in an unceasing clamour that re-echoed from the affrighted hills ...'[36]

All night, Japanese patrols probed the Australian lines. They tried to bayonet troops on the camp fringes and at least five Australians were wounded or killed by enemy bayonets that night. Scouts would cry out in English 'Johnny! Johnny!' Some taunts were lost in translation, such as, 'You die! Good morning!'* Less amusing was the cold voice in the darkness, 'You die tonight!'[37]

Combat was unbearably close. In one peculiarly harrowing incident, a Japanese soldier managed to slip a lasso made of vines around an Australian's ankle, and tried to drag him into the jungle. 'I had the presence of mind to fit my bayonet ... stretch out and stab him in the eye and cut the vine rope,' said the soldier.[38]

The Japanese preferred the worst conditions — moonless nights through driving rain — to attack. They used flares, and smoke candles, banged tins, and shouted 'simply to keep us awake', thought one Australian private. The Australians, however, learned to use the enemy's noises against them by listening closely for the direction of the sound, often with deadly precision. One AIF soldier claimed to have lobbed a grenade into the horn of a bugle, silencing the bugler.[39]

---

* The Americans heard the same taunts in Guadalcanal and elsewhere. On the island of New Georgia, Japanese troops shouted 'Fuck Roosevelt', to which the marines shouted back 'Fuck Tojo'. The Japanese then cried, 'Fuck Eleanor', to which a marine shouted, 'No way, you fuck her!' Both sides roared with laughter. (See Bergerud, *Touched with Fire*, p. 399.)

The weird dirge heard at Kokoda often preceded a charge: '... a shouted order from the rear, echoed by subordinate commanders further forward, and then succeeded by a wave of noisy chattering ... Then right along the front the final, urgent order rose ...'[40] There were loud cries of '*Banzai!*' — 'Long live the Emperor!' — the banging of tins, and the wail of bugles. (One Japanese ruse was to burst through a smoke cloud yelling, 'Gas! Gas!') Then 'Nippon's screaming warriors' dashed towards the Australian lines.[41]

All day reckless waves of Japanese tore down Naro Ridge and into the Australian perimeter, 'regardless of the casualties that soon cluttered that short stretch of open ground'.[42] 'They just kept coming,' recalled Sergeant George Cops of the 39th. 'You just could not stop them. A lot of us thought Moresby would fall.'[43] The 39th were virtually overrun — 251 out of 700 men were left — when a fresh batch of AIF troops, under Captain Claude Nye, rushed up to Front Creek, grabbing mortar bombs and grenades as they came. 'I do not remember anything more heartening,' said Honner, 'than the sight of their confident deployment.'[44]

Fierce hand-to-hand fighting ensued, as Honner witnessed at Front Creek, and rendered in his scorching passage: 'Through the widening breach poured another flood of the attackers ... met with Bren gun and Tommy gun, with bayonet and grenade; but still they came, to close with the buffet of fist and boot and rifle-butt, the steel of crashing helmets and of straining, strangling fingers. In this vicious fighting, man-to-man and hand-to-hand, Merritt's men were in imminent peril of annihilation.'[45]

The Australian light machine-gunners still held the line beyond which lay a rising pile of corpses. To their relief, a single bugle note would sound, and the attackers would melt back into the jungle (sometimes encountering stray Australians in sudden, shocked encounters in the darkness).*

---

* In fact, three platoons were cut off behind enemy lines that day; two, led by Lieutenant Sword, got lost along the track to Deniki with their signal wires slashed; another, sent to thrash a trail up Naro Ridge, got stuck in forest 'alive with Japanese'. Badly wounded, the latter's patrol commander Arthur Davis attempted to struggle back alone. He was captured and tortured, and his body dumped some hours later in a clearing, as a decoy to draw out the Australian troops. Only the strictest discipline prevented them. Potts later recalled such harrowing incidents: 'We had to sit in the jungle listening to the screams of comrades tortured by the Japanese in an attempt to provoke an attack.' A chaplain and a medical officer rushed off with a stretcher toward the noise of fighting, and soon brought in Davis's guide, who had a shattered thigh.

A strange calm fell over the eastern flank on the 28th and 29th. The Japanese oddly faltered. They could easily have broken through from Abuari, destroyed Potts's HQ and cut the Australian army in half. Instead, Horii diverted most of his eastern force across Eora Creek to attack Isurava village. His sudden change of plan remains 'one of the mysteries of the Papuan campaign'.[46] Perhaps he believed stronger enemy reinforcements had arrived at Abuari, than in fact had. Just two companies, under McGee and Sublet, were available; they crossed the waterfall and entered the village at sunset, unopposed.

A low mist shrouded the valley, and the air was heavy with moisture — perfect conditions for a Japanese charge. Later that evening, 'amid wild yelling', the Tsukamoto and Kuwada battalions rushed the Australian dugouts at Front Creek, in waves of a hundred at a time. The Australian Bren and Tommy guns chattered away as crowds of warriors fell before them. In one attack, an estimated 90 Japanese infantry were shot.

Potts's situation reports on 29 August bear out his rising anxiety (his password to Port Moresby that day was, suitably, 'FILTH'):

29 Aug 42
    SITREP to 2100 hrs. ISURAVA. Front and left flank 2/14 Bn
    broken. Attempt to restore unsuccessful . . . Weak coy 53 Bn sent in
    support of 2/14 Bn. Unable to dislodge. 39 Bn effective strength
    down to 16 offrs 235 Ors. No amm[unition] at MYOLA. No
    droppings today. Shortage green uniforms lack of rifle grenades severe
    handicaps . . . Apparently enemy strongly reinforced last two days.[47]

General Horii had not expected such strong resistance. His planned five-day march to Port Moresby was already three days late. His officers were alarmed. Lieutenant Noda, of the Kuwada Battalion, wrote: 'The Australians are gradually being outflanked, but their resistance is very strong, and our casualties are great. The outcome of the battle is very difficult to foresee.' Some Japanese vented their frustration with startling bursts of suicidal violence. George Woodward, a Tommy gunner, remembers a Japanese officer charging down the track, waving his sword. The Australian Bren guns almost chopped him in half. The officer fell at Woodward's feet, his binoculars dangling from his neck, and his sword stuck upright in the earth.

At sunset on the 29th the Japanese commander committed his men to an attack in full strength that would 'shatter the Australian resistance beyond hope of recovery'.[48] He called on no less than five Japanese battalions, including two fresh units of the Yazawa Butai (41st Regiment). The attack would start that night and continue the next day, across the whole breadth of the valley.

The Japanese commander's progress report was precise:

> The Nankai Shitai since 24th August have succeeded in completely surrounding the Australian forces . . . The annihilation of the Australians is near, but there are still some remnants . . . and their fighting spirit is extremely high.
>
> The enemy's defeated 39th battalion has been reinforced, and . . . they appear determined to put up a serious resistance. The Shitai will make night attacks and will be expected to capture the Australian positions . . .[49]

The Kusunose and Yazawa units were ordered up to execute the last Japanese offensive at Isurava.

It was a long night. It did not result in the Australians' annihilation. At troop level, doubts were creeping in. Hirano noted in his diary, 'enemy seems to have lost their fighting spirit', but added, 'Many of our number were killed or wounded.' They included his old friend First Lieutenant Hatanaka Seizo with whom 'only this morning I was gaily talking over a cup of sake from the canteen. Now it is only a memory. How cruel and miserable this life is!'[50]

The sun rose on two armies eating a brisk breakfast: a handful of rice for each Japanese soldier; bully beef for the Australians. The last battle for Isurava erupted at dawn on the 30th. It started with a Japanese diversion on the east flank, at Abuari, where a detachment of the Australian 2/16th Battalion moved to encircle a 100-strong Japanese force. Neither side gained ground, and the Australians suffered heavy casualties, not least from the Japanese ambush technique: 'They climbed into the dense foliage of the trees and . . . attacked from all sides and on top — a terrifying experience.'[51]

Isurava: Afternoon, 29 August 1942

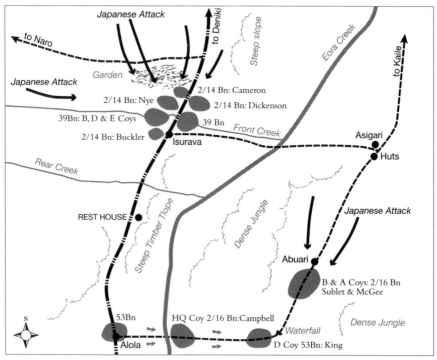

Isurava: Afternoon, 30 August 1942

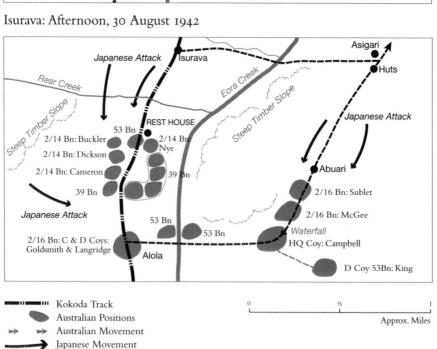

The sources we have present a confused chronology of that day. We do know that the battle continued long into the night, along the whole front, from Abuari to Naro Ridge. But the precise order of events is difficult to confirm. No one on the ground knew exactly how the next section along was faring.

Signal lines were invariably faulty, or 'being cut all the time', recalled Phil Rhoden.[52] Signalmen were constantly repairing the wires that linked forward troops with unit HQs. Major Geoffrey Lyon, among the first of the AIF troops up the track, recalled that the radios were useless. 'Each man [was] totally reliant on the others, almost blind in the concealing grass.'[53] So they resorted to runners, but these men took an hour through dense jungle to get across the main battle area, which was about 100 yards deep by 750 yards wide, Rhoden estimated.

Then the waves came. The Japanese charged all day, racing up to the Australian dugouts with bayonets fixed. All over the field, Australian machine-gunners and riflemen, amazed at the enemy's willingness to die, kept firing. The Australian troops thought this madness, not bravery.

It was 'like a brawl on a football field, things just got totally out of control', said Rhoden.[54] This brawl had guns and bayonets as well as fists. One AIF platoon[55] repulsed 'eleven enemy attacks, each of about company strength' (i.e. about 120 men), inflicting 250 casualties.[56]

The Australians had neither the numbers nor the ammunition to withstand the onslaught. They were gradually overwhelmed, but not without a string of extraordinary last stands, which yielded more Allied decorations than in any other single battle in the Pacific.

These were not blind heroics; they were calculated initiatives by Australian privates, corporals and platoon commanders determined to hold off the enemy as their units withdrew. Thus Private Wakefield, a Sydney wool worker, held up a Japanese charge as his section fell back; he won the Military Medal. Thus Captain Maurice Treacy, a shop assistant, 'parried every thrust levelled at him'.[57] He got a Military Cross. Though wounded in the hand and foot, Corporal 'Teddy' Bear, a die-cast operator from Moonee Ponds, killed a reported '15 Japanese with his Bren gun at point blank range'; he was later awarded the Military Medal and the DCM.[58] Lieutenant Mason, a draftsman, led his platoon in four counterattacks that afternoon; as did Lieutenant Butch Bissett, a jackaroo, whose platoon fought off fourteen Japanese charges.

At noon that day, the Japanese tried to run straight up the centre, towards the site of the present-day Isurava Memorial. It was an astonishingly audacious move, as anyone who has seen Isurava will acknowledge. The steep gradient shows why a few Australians were able to resist them for so long. By the early afternoon, 'the breakthrough was menacing the whole battalion position'.[59] A 2/14th HQ detachment rushed up to meet the emergency. Privates Alan Avery and Bruce Kingsbury latched onto this last attack.

Kingsbury was an average, outgoing young Australian of apparently modest ambitions. After leaving school, he took various jobs around New South Wales and Victoria — real estate salesman, station hand, farmer — before returning to work for his father's property business in Melbourne. He enlisted in the AIF on 29 May 1940, and served in Syria and Egypt — then came home with the 7th Division to fight the Japanese. Avery and Kingsbury were childhood friends; they'd enlisted together, and maybe Avery best knew what ran through Kingsbury's mind at that moment: Calculated courage? Conscious self-sacrifice? Or the thoughts of a young soldier anxious not to be seen to fail? Perhaps all three combined to produce Kingsbury's next action, as recorded in his citation for the Victoria Cross, the Commonwealth's highest military honour:

> . . . one of few survivors of a Platoon which had been overrun and severely cut about by the enemy, [Kingsbury] immediately volunteered to join a different platoon which had been ordered to counterattack. He rushed forward firing the Bren gun from his hip through terrific machine-gun fire and succeeded in clearing a path through the enemy. Continuing to sweep enemy positions with his fire and inflicting an extremely high number of casualties . . . Private Kingsbury was then seen to fall to the ground shot dead by the bullet from a sniper hiding in the wood . . .[60]

He died instantly, aged 24. His was the first VC won on Australian soil. 'Kingsbury's Rock' stands to the right of the Isurava Memorial, and a roadside rest area between Sydney and Canberra also bears his name.

VCs are not awarded for blind heroics; the action must tangibly improve the unit's position. Kingsbury's saved his battalion headquarters by halting the enemy advance. 'He stabilised our position; he just made up his mind he was going to do it, and he did it,' said Rhoden.[61] If the Japanese had broken through they would've overrun and destroyed the Australians, and no doubt 'streamed on down to Port Moresby', said McAulay.[62] His action inspired his mates to follow: Kingsbury's section — ten men of the 2/14th Battalion — remain the most highly decorated in military history, winning a Victoria Cross, two Military Crosses, three Military Medals and several Mentions in Dispatches.

It was a brief respite. The Japanese kept surging up the mountain and down the sides of Naro Ridge. The Australian body count rose. In a day, C Company of 2/14th Battalion sustained dozens missing or dead. The death of Harold Bissett deeply saddened the battalion. He was a popular officer. Carried to safety by four volunteers — fighting off the enemy as they went — Bissett sustained severe abdominal wounds. He died at 4.00 a.m. on the 30th in his brother's arms. 'I held him in my arms for four hours,' said Stan Bissett. 'We just talked about our parents, and growing up, and ... good things.'[63]

Among the last gestures of useful Australian defiance at Isurava was that of Corporal Charlie McCallum, a farmer of South Gippsland, Victoria. At the risk of sounding dangerously flippant, his action seemed more Schwarzenegger than Anzac. After the order came to pull out, he remained behind to cover his platoon. He sprayed the enemy with his Bren; when it ran out of ammunition, he swung up a Tommy gun grabbed from a dead mate. While he checked their advance with this weapon, he slammed a full magazine into the Bren with his right hand. When the Tommy ran out, he resumed firing with the Bren until his platoon were safe. He was wounded three times during this performance, in which he literally found himself firing amidst a crowd of Japanese troops so close that one, lunging forward as he died, tore off McCallum's utility pouches. McCallum was reported to have killed 25 Japanese and saved his platoon. He was recommended for the Victoria Cross; he received a Distinguished Conduct Medal, and died in a later battle on the track.[64]

Japanese survivors remember that day as the defining battle of the Kokoda campaign. 'For eight hours ... the Australians offered fierce resistance without withdrawal, resorting to hand-to-hand combat. There were numerous point-blank hand grenade exchanges.'[65]

Yamasaki recalls that every officer in his company was killed or wounded. 'The resistance was very strong. The Australian position was very good; they were high up. Even when men were killed, we had to keep going, to keep attacking in waves.' He participated in a bayonet charge, and was hit in the wrist and hand by shrapnel: 'My rifle was thrown ten metres away. I saw white flesh in my hand and I was ordered to go to the rear.' He stayed a week in the Kokoda field hospital 'with no morphine. It was extremely painful.' Were the Japanese scared? 'We were not scared at all, not of the jungle or the enemy. We were trained to attack — we were told if we didn't attack we'd be killed.'

Shimada looked slightly incredulous when asked the same question: 'We were never afraid,' he said quietly. The idea was inconceivable to this 86-year-old warrant officer. However, Yamasaki remembers one man being so frightened he refused to fight; he was sent to the rear. 'I brought him back when he had recovered his nerves.'[66] He never informed the man's superiors — cowardice was severely punished, often by execution.

In the late afternoon it started to pour with rain, and the flattened jungle became a steaming wasteland. The little bomb craters and weapon pits filled with water. Lanes of devastated vegetation lay in the spectral aftermath of concentrated machine-gun fire. Platoons all along the Australian lines were being infiltrated and overrun. Some 'stood ringed by a scattered rampart of the enemy dead'.[67] Some 250 Japanese corpses were later counted in front of Harold Bissett's position.

In total the Japanese had lost 550 men killed, and more than a thousand wounded.[68] The Australians lost about 250, with many hundreds wounded. The most depleted unit was the 2/14th Battalion, able to field only 230 men after Isurava, half its initial force.

The Australian survivors withdrew in a state of shock. The recapture of Kokoda a mere pipedream, Potts was now fighting to save his army.

In despair he sent into battle about a hundred remaining troops of the 53rd, who'd been resting at Alola. They got no further than the Isurava Rest House where, 'weary of the march', they decided to rest.[69] With no intention of advancing, some commandeered native carriers to help carry their weapons back to Port Moresby.★ Potts's leadership could not undo the damage. The unit had imploded — physically and psychologically.

Their unfortunate experience sits uncomfortably alongside the incredible decision of 30 wounded men of the 39th Battalion, then sitting in Eora Creek (waiting to return to Port Moresby). All except three got up and stumbled back into battle. Lieutenant Stewart Johnston, a huge 24-year-old with a handlebar moustache, led this 'weak and tottering cohort of the crippled and sick' past the few 53rd survivors, then sitting 'in peaceful unconcern by the track'.[70] The three who didn't go back were forgivably 'minus a foot; had a bullet in the throat, and a forearm blown off'.[71]

So, too, the ghosts of troops thought lost or dead in the jungle returned in corporeal form to fight. One 'grimy bearded figure' saluted Honner and announced, 'Sword, Sir, reporting in from patrol'. Sword's platoons had been cut off behind enemy lines for three days. Their appearance prompted a corporal to observe, 'It was enough to make a man weep to see those poor skinny bastards hobble in on their bleeding feet.'[72] They too rejoined the battle.

However selfless and brave they were, Potts's men were near-spent. The 2/16th Battalion summoned a last counterattack at Abuari, which failed. Perhaps fittingly, one Australian soldier, shot in the buttocks, dropped his trousers to inspect the wound and asked a mate, 'Are you sure that's blood?'

After some fierce fighting, with dozens killed, the Australians fell back to Eora Creek in disarray. Potts was forced to abandon 25,000 small arms bullets, 1500 Tommy gun rounds and 500 grenades at Alola.[73]

....

★ Frederick Shedden wrote on 3 October 1942: '[Lt-Gen Rowell] was very critical of the quality of the Militia brigade despatched to Port Moresby ... One infantry battalion at Milne Bay refused to unload ships, and another refused to fight near Kokoda. On its retreat it encountered a large number of porters who were carrying supplies to the front, and the troops commandeered the services of a large proportion of these porters to carry their rifles and equipment back ...' (*Defence of Port Moresby*, NAA A5954, Box 587).

Rowell was clearly unaware of the disaster when he wired Blamey on 31 August:

To: Landops
31 August 42
From: NG Force
Personal for Commander in Chief from ROWELL:

...POTTS HAS FORCE WELL IN HAND AROUND
ISURAVA AND I HAVE NO DOUBT AS TO HIS ABILITY
TO CLEAR THE POSN. IT IS AS WELL THAT AIF
TROOPS WERE SENT UP AS OTHERWISE I FEEL WE
MIGHT HAVE BEEN PUSHED OFF THE RANGE ...WE
ARE EXERTING ALL OUR ENERGY TO MAINTAIN
OFFENSIVE ACTION BUT YOU WILL APPRECIATE
THAT ADMINISTRATIVE FAILURE WOULD BRING
DISASTER.[74]

Potts disabused Rowell that evening, with his last two messages of the 31st:

31 Aug: 1215 Air strafing urgency requested ALOLA village ...
SITREP TO 1830 hrs. Force withdrawn on IORA CK area.
53 Bn MYOLA. 39 Bn approx 250, 2/14 Bn approx 230 ...
holding posns vicinity IORA Ck ... Enemy obviously in
considerable strength ... Still desire rest of 2/27 Bn.[75]

Thus ended one of the most bitterly fought infantry battles of the Pacific War. For the Japanese, it was a truly pyrrhic victory, won at great cost in terms of time, ammunition, supplies and lives. They were a week behind schedule. Isurava fatally wounded them, but the bleeding beast crashed on towards Port Moresby. The losses eclipsed Horii's judgment. A defiant stubbornness now seemed to possess him and overrule his more sensible counsel. He intended to press his entire force over the mountains; his men cut a nine-foot mule track from Eora Creek in the direction of the main range to Myola. He drove them on into the depths of the Owen Stanleys, deaf to the howling reminder of every failed military excursion in history: a vastly overextended supply line.

The Australians had been 'outfought and outmanoeuvred,' according to an official report on Isurava. Their officer ranks were severely depleted. 'Five platoon commanders died in those four days,' concluded Rhoden.* 'When they died, sergeants took over; when the sergeants died, corporals took over; and then the ordinary soldier. It was incredible. To this day I would do anything for the ordinary soldier.'[76]

What made Isurava uniquely wretched in the annals of war was the devastating closeness of combat. The armies were fighting within earshot and, unlike their medieval forebears, with guns and grenades. 'When the Japs were about ten feet away ... I shrivelled up into almost nothing,' recalled one private. Near the end of the Pacific War, a US army medical team examined the effects of near point-blank fighting in jungle conditions. It found that more than 50 per cent of the casualties were struck at 25 yards or less, and nearly 85 per cent at 50 yards or less.[77] The wounds inflicted by a high velocity bullet at this distance can be imagined. Abdominal injuries were always fatal; shattered knees and limbs left the victim stranded. There were no helicopters. Hand-to-hand combat with fixed bayonets made the battle seem like 'a knife fight out of the Stone Age'.[78]

Smoky Howson was haunted for the rest of his life by the sight of a Japanese soldier 'with both legs chopped off from the trunk of his body' by machine-gun fire. Ordered to 'finish off the dying Nip', Howson hesitated. He noticed that the man's eyes were still open. 'He had a terrified expression and he was still moaning, and I have lived to this day with those eyes staring at me.'[79] Howson said this in an interview on 23 March 2003, a few months before he died, aged 85.

The Australian nightmare was just beginning. Potts somehow had to stop the rampaging Japanese army from reaching Port Moresby. Another question was extremely vexing for this brigadier who concerned himself so much with his men: How, Potts wondered, were the sick and wounded to survive?

---

* Rhoden, who succeeded Key as commander of the 2/14th, died in 2003.

Chapter 18
Milne Bay

'If you were going to give the world an enema — you'd push it in at Milne Bay'
— *Pilot Officer B.E. 'Buster' Brown*

'Of all the allies, it was the Australians who first broke the invincibility of the Japanese army'
— *Field Marshal Sir William Slim,* Defeat Into Victory

There is a quiet sort of Australian man who, in obscurity, achieves great things for which a few people are eternally grateful; he then fades away unsung and is soon forgotten. You can see him on weekends tinkering in his shed, or sanding a little boat, or pursuing an odd hobby. He does his duty, fails with dignity and, when he succeeds, succeeds without trumpeting his success. He is remote, and self-absorbed, and is liked by his grandchildren. His life is one of ceaseless curiosity within his chosen field, of which he is a supreme expert. He is scarcely comprehensible to women — one of whom, tolerating his self-absorption, rewards his devotion and loyalty with her unstinting love.

'Silent' Cyril Clowes, the Australian commander at Milne Bay, seems to have been such a man. No biography exists of this extraordinary commander; few Australians will have heard of him. After Duntroon Military College, where his classmates were Rowell and Brigadier George Wootten, he pursued a long and successful career as a professional soldier and rose to the rank of major-general. He won a swag of medals and decorations (CBE, DSO and MC) in both world wars, and earned the reputation of being oblivious to personal danger.

A brilliant artilleryman — some say the finest the Australian army has produced — Clowes was a decisive, steadfast, pipe-smoking general with a conspicuous personal trait: he rarely spoke. Even his best friends called him Silent Cyril. 'He was a very good commander in my book,' observed Colonel Fred Chilton, his staff officer, 'but he wasn't a good communicator.'

Yet Clowes's friends saw the value of this honest soldier in a world of incipient spin: 'The only thing I think he can be criticised for,' added Chilton, 'is his lack of public relations — for not sending back phoney reports about what a wonderful job he was doing and how many Japs they'd killed ... he didn't give the boys [in GHQ] what they wanted ...'[1]

Clowes quietly led the first land defeat of the Japanese, in any war. He deployed 4000 infantry troops, two squadrons of Kittyhawks and few words against 2400 Japanese naval commandos armed with tanks.[2]

The Battle of Milne Bay was a complete Australian victory. This statement is not intended to be crudely triumphalist; it is meant simply to distinguish the battle from MacArthur's boast of another 'Allied' triumph on this semi-elliptical bay at the eastern tip of Papua. Undeniably the Americans offered logistical and engineering troops (fourteen of whom were killed). But the infantry blood spilt at Milne Bay — as in the Owen Stanleys — was Australian.

The victory came at a critical moment: just after the battle of Isurava, from which Potts had been forced to withdraw. The effect on morale was incalculable: Milne Bay is said to have broken the spell of Japanese invincibility, no less. It is not churlish to point out, however, that the Japanese were outnumbered two to one and lacked airpower; yet they did have tanks. Australia's 75 and 76 Squadrons were crucial to this victory: early in the battle their pilots did irreparable damage to the Japanese supply lines. Even so, the infantry largely won land wars in those days, and the Australian infantryman at Milne Bay fought with phenomenal courage.

A lesser-known fact about Milne Bay is the unspeakable cruelty the Japanese unleashed against the native people and Australian prisoners, as later documented by the Webb Report on Japanese war crimes.

Both sides saw this vile waterway at the eastern end of the New Guinea mainland as strategically crucial. Blamey and MacArthur were determined to hold Milne Bay. Not for nothing had the Allies built two narrow, steel-matted runways here. The Japanese similarly valued it as a crucial air base, from which their Zeros could fan out over northern Australia, encircle Port Moresby and link up with the Nankai Shitai, which were then fighting in the Owen Stanleys.

From a distance it seemed like paradise. Up close, in 1942, Milne Bay was a disease-ridden basket case of interminable rain and steaming heat, and the most malarial region on earth. All the troops caught malaria or dysentery or both.

The bay is a natural deepwater harbour. The entrance is seven miles wide, and the depth westwards, about twenty miles. Steep, jungle-covered mountains rise to 3500 feet on three sides, leaving only a narrow strip of mangrove swamps, coconut groves and boggy tracks to which the few human inhabitants clung.

The mountains drew 200 inches of rain a year, which splashed down the sides and drenched the coastal villages. The Australians complained endlessly of their discomfort. One wrote: 'Even without the war Milne Bay would have been a hell hole ... The sun hardly ever shined and it rained all the time. It was stinking hot and ... very marshy, boggy country ... It was a disease-ridden place — it was terrible.' Not only that, coconuts tended to fall on them from high palms; the men were told to wear steel helmets in the plantations after one coconut broke an officer's collarbone.

Allied intelligence was vital. FRUMEL decoders in Melbourne intercepted Japanese signals[3] that detailed the enemy's invasion plan, in response to which MacArthur and Blamey sent up the 18th Brigade to hold the bay. Militia units had garrisoned Milne Bay since early August; on the 21st, the last of the AIF reinforcements landed there aboard little fishing luggers — Milne Bay had no wharf. They negotiated the reefs in tiny dinghies, one of which sank under the weight, and a soldier drowned. Ashore, the men drew lots for the best tents; these were of little use. On the first night, six to eight inches of rain fell.

Clowes established his HQ near the village of Gili Gili, on the north-western corner of the bay where the coastal plain is widest (facilitating the construction of the two airstrips). From here a twelve-foot wide, mud-gorged track — previously covered in soft coral and contemptuously described as a road — ran several miles along the north shore through creeks and swamp. It linked the settlements of Rabi and KB Mission to Ahioma, where the Japanese landed.

They landed by moonlight on 25 and 26 August. Their orders, from Rear Admiral Matsuyama, were uncompromising. They must 'strike the white soldiers without remorse. Unitedly smash to pieces the enemy lines and take the aerodrome by storm'.[4]

Some 2400 Japanese leapt ashore and ran up the beach into the shelter of jungle. Most were commando-style troops of the notorious special naval landing parties — but not all. Sakaki Minoru, First Class Seaman of the Kure 5 Special Naval Landing Party, had no jungle training and scarcely any rifle practice. He carried two days' rations, of biscuits and 'bento'.[5] A bank clerk in civilian life, married with two sons, then aged four and five, he seemed thoroughly disinterested in the whole exercise.

Most showed greater determination than Sakaki. The navy, arch rivals of the army, needed to redeem their failure to capture Port Moresby at the Battle of the Coral Sea. Milne Bay afforded them that chance. 'Milne Bay would make a good jumping-off point for an attack along the south coast,' according to war historian Peter Londey.[6]

The stakes were extremely high. By landing at Milne Bay, the Japanese hoped to open a second front in their attack on Port Moresby. Already they had met severe setbacks: 350 Japanese troops died when Australian Kittyhawks strafed their landing barges at Goodenough Island. And on two mornings after they disembarked at Milne Bay, Australian pilots destroyed their barges and most of their supplies. Instead of moving down the shoreline by barge — as they'd planned — they were forced to march along the swampy coastal strip.

Milne Bay: 25 August 1942

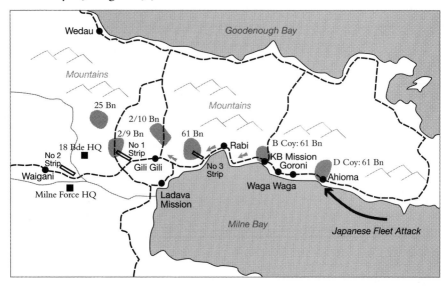

Milne Bay: 28 – 31 August 1942

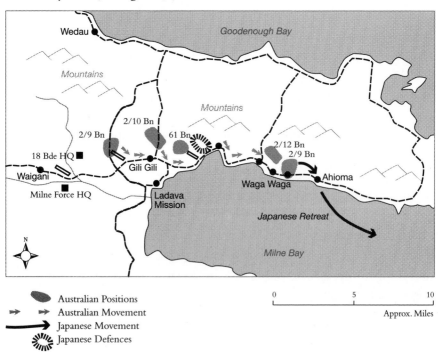

Clowes did not know how many Japanese had landed on those gloomy tropical shores; his staff estimated 5000. In fact, the enemy numbered half that. For their part, the Japanese fatally underestimated the size of the Australian garrison. And yet, Keith Hinchcliffe, part of an Australian radar unit, was not alone in feeling premonitions of doom the night the Japanese convoy entered Milne Bay: '. . . there was no future for us at Milne Bay. Singapore had fallen. The Japs had landed at Buna and occupied Gona and Lae and were fighting their way towards Moresby . . . We had our bags packed and were anticipating a walk . . . along the coast to Port Moresby. Our mood changed within 36 hours . . .'[7]

Though outnumbered, the Japanese had one advantage: tanks. Their tanks were light, high-turreted machines vaguely reminiscent of a Dalek, the tottering robots from *Dr Who*. At night on the 27th several Daleks — the spearhead of clusters of creeping troops — trundled along the coast over streams and through deep mud towards the Australian lines.

Clowes had sent one AIF battalion[8] into the coconut plantation at KB Mission, a tiny settlement halfway along the north shore. The first tank advanced with its dazzling headlights shining through the pouring rain, at which one Australian soldier shouted, 'Put out that fucking light!'[9] Alas, it was not an Australian torch.

Then, from behind the tanks, came an extraordinary sound: the choir-like note of a single voice — 'and a beautiful voice it was' — in Japanese. Hundreds of others soon joined in, singing 'in sonorous unison'.[10] The war chant rose to a crescendo, and then the Japanese charged. The tanks drove straight into the Australian lines, floodlighting each other's sides for protection from grenade runners. 'The enemy tanks were fitted with brilliant headlights, with the aid of which they cruised around amongst our troops inflicting many casualties,' wrote Clowes.[11]

Bayonets flashed, and dreadful screams could be heard in the darkness. The adrenalin of hand-to-hand combat shut out the peripheral noise in the troops' ears. One group of grappling bodies spilled into the sea, so narrow was the battlefield. The tanks charged into small parties of troops, trying to flatten them. The Australians leapt out of the way and hurled 'sticky bombs' — anti-tank grenades packed with nitroglycerine. Most bombs rolled off or, damaged by damp, failed to explode. 'From close range they threw them but they did not stick,' wrote Frank Allchin, a battalion commander.[12]

The Japanese forced the Australians back beyond Gama River, where militia units[13] held the line — a rare instance of the militia covering the withdrawal of the AIF.

GHQ peered into the glass darkly. Blamey and MacArthur couldn't abide a Japanese presence on the eastern Papuan seaboard, and pressed Clowes to clear the enemy from Milne Bay immediately.

Urgent cables tapped back and forth between Clowes's tent, Port Moresby and Brisbane. GHQ demanded news from Silent Cyril, whose silence, at this time, was due rather to the genuine dearth of information on Japanese strength than to his natural reticence. Clowes's apparent lack of offensive activity agitated MacArthur extremely. Nor were the Americans pleased with Clowes's laconic sitreps, which lacked the tendentious verbosity of their own battle reports written in what George Vasey smilingly called 'Americanese'.

Vasey — then Deputy Chief of the General Staff— meanwhile warned his friend Rowell of the 'wrong impression' the troops at Milne Bay were creating 'in the minds of the great'. In fact, Milne Bay exposed gathering fault lines in the minds of the great, which was epitomised by Vasey's arch question: who, he breezily wondered, in a private letter to Rowell, was commanding the Australian army — MacArthur or TAB (Blamey)?[14]

For three days sporadic skirmishes — a neat military euphemism for bloody lunges by hate-filled enemies staggering through mud in pouring rain — seemed to confirm MacArthur's poor opinion of the Australian troops. He felt he must explain the causes of the delay to Washington, in case of doubt about who was responsible. He alerted Roosevelt, 'I ... am not yet convinced of the efficiency of the Australians.'[15]

Vasey anxiously awaited good news. As the first to see Clowes's sitreps cabled in morse to Brisbane, Vasey longed for a breakthrough to throw in MacArthur's face. He told Clowes: 'I'm dying to go back to those bastards [at GHQ] and say "I told you so — we've killed the bloody lot."'[16]

Slowly, Vasey's wishes materialised. On 29 August Clowes sent in two battalions of the 18th Brigade — the crack unit that would inflict such misery on the Japanese at Buna. By day, Australian pilots strafed Japanese positions on the north shore, as the infantry gradually forced the Japanese back over their occupied ground towards KB Mission.

The gruff, thickset Brigadier George Wootten — soon to lead his men with awesome finality at the battle of the beaches — sent up reinforcements. Bit by bit the Australians clawed their way along the muddy track. They inflicted hundreds of Japanese casualties. At the night battle of Gama River, a Japanese unit came jogging along the track straight into Australian machine-gunners, who were alerted by a lookout perched in a coconut tree. Within minutes, 92 Japanese were killed and hundreds wounded. Aerial bombardment meanwhile cratered the shoreline in readiness for the final clearance.

At this moment, Clowes received an oddly peremptory message. It was 7.00 p.m. on 1 September, and he was preparing for a final thrust (in battle, it seems, the next thrust is usually final). Instead, GHQ warned: 'Expect attack JAP ground forces on Milne aerodromes from West and North-west, supported by destroyer fire. Take immediate stations. MACARTHUR.'

This intelligence had the smack of Ultra-decoded authenticity; it wanted to be taken seriously. So Clowes put his eastern offensive on hold. All that night the Australians kept watch for an attack from the most unlikely direction, over the mountains behind them. Nothing happened. The intelligence was baseless, and the delay, immensely frustrating. Clowes questioned whether MacArthur's decoders had translated accurately. Later he wrote that these 'decodes of "most secret" Jap signals were of little use to us and served merely to hinder and hamper the development of our counter-attack ...'[17] At dawn the men resumed the grinding battle eastwards, along the north shore.

Hideous, flyblown atrocities formed before their astonished eyes. In the villages and along the track appeared the first signs of the enemy's gruesome handiwork. One Australian captain found the body of a native boy, bound with wire, a bayonet up his anus and half his head burnt off with a flamethrower; nearby a native woman lay bound by her hands and legs, with her left breast cut off. Both victims, mercifully, were dead. Nor did the Japanese spare two Australian militia troops, on whom they had practised bayonet attacks; one, tied to a tree, had deep bayonet wounds in both arms, and a bayonet jutting from his stomach. They were the first in a revolting catalogue of Milne Bay war crimes.

Revulsion turned to anger; anger to cold fury. News of the atrocities put the Australians in a mood of murderous rage. No prisoners would be taken. A measure of this attitude were the bullet wounds found in the body of a Japanese sniper, dangling from a tree: every time an Australian platoon came up the track and saw the hanging corpse, they riddled it; 500 bullet holes were later found in the body.

In coming attacks, dozens of men on both sides died fighting in conditions of ghastly proximity. On one especially dark night, Sergeant Jim Hosier, on a mine-laying patrol, felt a Japanese hand run over his face.

The Australian 18th Brigade soon recaptured KB Mission. They walked through clearings strewn with Japanese bodies. One sergeant, concerned about fakers, told his platoon, 'Look — I want you all to make sure these Japs are dead. As you go through, stick them.' A rather quiet, introspective soldier refused. He was told, 'It's for all our safety' — and he was reminded of an incident when an apparently dead Japanese had shot a passing Australian. The quiet soldier said 'Okay', and lunged his bayonet into the nearest Japanese body, which groaned and crawled forward. The Japanese had been hiding his rifle. The Australian shook with revulsion and never quite recovered from the incident. He died later in the campaign.[18]

In the jungle nearby the Australians found the burnt-out shell of a Kittyhawk and the body of the legendary pilot, Squadron Leader Peter Turnbull, who had flown dozens of air raids against Japanese positions. The sight brought home to the infantry the reality of the air battle. Their reliance on air power at Milne Bay cannot be overstated, as Blamey said.*

The man largely responsible for the air victory was Group Captain William Henry Garing, the RAAF's commander at Milne Bay. He had won the Distinguished Flying Cross (DFC) in Europe, for engaging five German bombers. Garing was a brave and forceful officer, whose nickname 'Bull' accurately described his personality. The historian Dr Alan Stephens praised

---

* Turnbull was replaced as commander by the Australian ace 'Bluey' Truscott, famous for shooting down fifteen German planes in the Battle of Britain. Forced to bail out over the English Channel, Bluey's parachute got caught, and released him just 400 feet from the sea. He lived.

Garing's 'expert planning and inspirational leadership at Milne Bay and the Bismarck Sea'.[19]

Into the melee beyond KB Mission crept ten Australian troops led by 'the quietest and most unassuming man you could ever see',[20] an apprentice hairdresser from Crows Nest, Queensland, named John French. On 4 September, this 27-year-old veteran of the Siege of Tobruk stopped his men short of three enemy machine-guns. If they rushed in together they would surely all die. So, 'as their leader', French decided, 'it was his duty to attack on his own'.[21]

French ordered his men to take cover, then advanced on one of the machine-guns and silenced it with grenades. He then killed the second machine-gunner with his Tommy gun. Badly wounded, he stumbled forward and fell in front of the third gun pit; later all three enemy gun crews were found dead.

French saved the lives of his section, cleared the path for the Australian advance, and won a posthumous Victoria Cross, the second on Australian territory. He and Private Bruce Kingsbury are buried at Bomana Cemetery in Port Moresby.

The terrain did the job the sticky bombs couldn't: tanks got bogged in deep, treacly mud and torrential rain, or ran off the road, where they were easier prey to Australian firepower.

The cooperation between the Australian army and the air force delivered the *coup de grâce* at Milne Bay. 'Australian fighters forced the Japanese to move entirely at night.'[22] Kittyhawk pilots strafed any visible Japanese activity: 'Palm fronds, bullets and dead Japanese snipers were pouring down with the rain,' one witness remarked.[23]

The wounded died where they fell, or dragged themselves back to the beachhead, half a mile to the east. Another Japanese convoy sailed into Milne Bay on the night of 6 September to evacuate the troops — some 1400 of them escaped. The fleet bombed and sank the *Anshun*, an Allied supply ship and twice bathed another Allied vessel, the hospital ship *Manunda*, in searchlight, and spared it — a rare example of restraint.

Many Japanese troops fled into the mountains, doomed to long excursions through the bush before starvation, disease or Australian patrols claimed them. An anonymous Japanese diary, captured at Milne Bay, tells of one soldier's end: 'Hid and lived on the ground for about 25 days. Ate coconuts, papayas, apples and mountain potatoes ... Even though I am lost I cannot give myself up ... it is hard to believe I am still alive ...'

The diarist escaped a machine-gun attack, but wrote that he had lost 'my helmet, canteen and my mess gear'. 'In case I am killed please forward my pass-book number to [a Japan address].' His last entry was: 'Received a bullet in my back. Have live ammunition in my back ... '[24]

The aftermath of Milne Bay brought home the extremity of the Pacific War. Japanese ground troops left a trail of cruelty, 'such as to shock and dismay the feelings of every decent human being', observed Evatt, Australia's wartime Minister for External Affairs.[25] Of the 95 atrocities documented by the Webb Royal Commission on war crimes, 59 were perpetrated against native people and 36 against Australian troops. Justice Webb conceded that, in a few instances, the same case may have been described several times. That did not diminish the horror. To say the Japanese *flouted* The Hague Convention at Milne Bay is a cruel understatement. The prolonged torture and apparent pleasure with which they dispatched their victims suggests the Australians were fighting, not soldiers, but a criminally insane mob of serial murderers and rapists. The Japanese at Milne Bay demonstrated none of the restraint of trained professional soldiers, but rather the barbarity of rampant Visigoths.

Cynics and pacifists may scorn the notion of 'civilised war' implicit in the rules of war drawn up at The Hague. Indeed, the cumulative horror of the twentieth century consigned the notion of a 'gentleman's war' to its deserved dustbin. But there are clearly boundaries. If not, who were the rules devised at The Hague aimed at? The atrocities at Milne Bay help to answer this question, which is the only case for describing them here.

The Japanese bound and bayoneted dozens of tribesmen who refused to cooperate with them. Women were raped, sometimes with bayonets. One native woman was pegged down and slit from her throat to her vagina; a teenage girl was nailed to the ground with a bamboo stake through her chest. The genitals and anuses of several native men and women were mutilated; the breasts of several women were chopped off and left on or beside their bodies. One woman was disembowelled, and one man's buttocks were hacked off. At Moteo the Japanese tied a man's hands with signal wire and shot and bayoneted him several times. At Wanadela, three young women were bound, raped and mutilated. Near Waga Waga, two hundred yards from where the Japanese landed, two men and a young girl were found tied up and bayoneted; the girl had been raped. Australian sworn affidavits describe a dead native woman tied by her hands and legs to a hut, with 70 condoms lying around her.

Webb listed 36 atrocities against Australians troops. Many were the victims of bayonet practice, repeating the outrage of Tol Plantation. Several soldiers were bound to trees and repeatedly stabbed. At least two were disembowelled, one decapitated, and one bayoneted in the rectum. The heads of several were crushed in. One soldier's fingers were cut off. Another soldier was tied by a long rope and used as a running target, as shown by his torn shirt and stab wounds in the back. Two men were bound, one on the ground, one to a tree, and slowly mutilated. In Justice Webb's unsparing language, 'The man on the ground had his hands tied in front of his chest below his throat ... He had wounds each side of his chest and on his forearms. His arms were cut as though he had been trying to protect himself. His buttocks and genitals were cut to ribbons. The tops of his ears were cut off. His eye sockets were missing. He had about twenty knife or bayonet wounds in his body.'[26]

The victims died slowly, dimly conscious of the use to which their bodies were being put. 'It took them a long time to die,' said a sign placed on the bayoneted bodies of Australian troops in New Britain; the same could be said of the victims at Milne Bay.

Webb described the perpetrators as 'sadists' and 'fiends' who had committed 'savage' war crimes in breach of Article 46 of The Hague Convention. Judges rarely seem able to find the language to fit the crime. In this case, perhaps words were unavailable. Four Special Naval Landing Parties — Sasebo 5, Yokosuka 5, Kure 3 and 5 — and 10 Pioneer Unit were held responsible for the atrocities.

———

Those who are determined to hate the Japanese no doubt relish evidence of behaviour that seems to support the most vicious racial stereotype. They are wrong. Most of the Japanese army did not mutilate natives and prisoners, and many ordinary Japanese soldiers were revolted by the cruelty of officers. It is, however, a lame response of revisionist Japanese academics and military historians — who refuse to acknowledge that the rape of Nanking happened, for example★ — to bundle up the cruelties of war with the dismissive, 'all sides committed atrocities'. This won't do. No doubt the Allies took very few prisoners and, on occasions, committed massacres. But there is no evidence that they subjected individual prisoners — and civilians — to a slow, deliberate and agonising death.

The perpetrators were the navy's advance landing parties, shock troops brutally trained to subdue any resistance using methods designed to terrify and demoralise the enemy and their suspected native collaborators. What can be said of these men? What can be said of the people who trained them? One searches in vain amid the atrocities of Milne Bay for some sort of explanation. In the absence of any from the Japanese Government, one is left to agree with Evatt: '[Webb] reveals not only individual and isolated acts of barbarity but also practices which are beyond the pale of accepted human conduct, and which could not have become general without connivance, encouragement and direction of superior officers up to the highest.'

'If those responsible,' Evatt added, 'for these outrages are allowed to escape punishment, it will be the grossest defeat of justice and a travesty of principles for which the war has been fought.'[27] Most of those responsible died in coming battles; meanwhile, no Japanese government has officially acknowledged the war crimes or apologised to or compensated the victims' families.

Of the 2400 Japanese troops at Milne Bay, 612 were reported dead — most of whom the Australians buried — and 535 wounded, a total of 1147. Of the Australian casualties, 161 troops were killed and 212 wounded.

There were very few prisoners. The Australians took a handful. A footnote to a letter appended to the Clowes Report states, 'The reference to

★ See *The Alleged 'Nanking Massacre'* by Takemoto and Ohara, the latest revisionist history.

"no prisoners" is not true as eight or nine were captured.' The Japanese killed all prisoners at Milne Bay.

Of those eight or nine — in a battle involving 6500 troops — one was Sakaki Minoru, a family man and reluctant soldier, who was captured on 6 September suffering from 'foot trouble'.[28] He had lost touch with his unit. He told the Australians that he expected them to kill him. He said he did not mind dying, and would have preferred to commit suicide 'but had no weapons available to him'. His greatest concern was for his wife.

Months after the fighting ended, unburied Japanese bodies were still rising from the swamps, or bobbing along the banks of the creeks. Many skeletons were found in coral caves along the coast.

A fitting epitaph to this disastrous Japanese affray is the image of two troops found wandering the grasslands by Papuan natives, who pelted them with rocks whenever they tried to rest. At dusk the two soldiers hanged themselves from a tree.[29]

The Milne Bay defeat had wider ramifications. It was considered extremely hazardous for Horii to attack Port Moresby unsupported by air power from Milne Bay, and on 28 August 1942, Rabaul ordered him to halt 'at a strategic line south of the Owen Stanley Range' and await further orders.[30] Horii sensed his growing isolation, but pressed on into the mountains.

Victory was sweet for Silent Cyril, to whom 'the great' offered grudging congratulations — then later relieved him of his field command. Clowes's star had risen high enough in the firmament. High-ranking military officers seemed inordinately jealous of each other's success. Clowes reported on the battle with generous understatement: 'The troops performed admirably in the face of very adverse conditions.'[31]

Had the battle for Milne Bay not ended, an enemy deadlier than either side, the anopheles mosquito, would soon easily have exceeded the capacity of men to kill one another. Up to a thousand Australian troops per week caught malaria in the month after the battle, according to Colonel Speight, OBE. By the end of October, virtually the entire Australian garrison at Milne Bay had symptoms of the disease.

Part Three
Withdrawal

Chapter 19
Wounded

'I want every man who is capable of walking ... to start off for the top of the hill. We haven't got enough bearers to carry everybody, but this place must be cleared tonight'
— *Captain Rupert Magarey, 2/6th Field Ambulance, to Australian stretcher cases*

The Australian evacuation from Isurava continued through three days and nights of pouring rain. The walking wounded bumped and shuffled along the trail towards the Eora Creek gorge. Those unable to walk — the stretcher cases — lay at Alola awaiting bearers.

Stretchers were hastily constructed by torchlight out of poles, vines and blankets. Kienzle and Vernon brought up new stretcher-bearers from Myola to help carry out severely wounded men. As they withdrew, shock turned to silent despair. The Australian army appeared to have 'fallen to pieces' amidst the 'bloody, disintegrating, invisible confusion'[1] of defeat. In the darkness behind, the Japanese were in full pursuit; ahead lay only the mountains and the jungle, for 80 miles. Australian stragglers and the wounded left behind in enemy-held territory were bayoneted.

The elusiveness of the Japanese soldier infuriated the Australian troops. 'You couldn't see the bastards!'[2] muttered a frustrated twenty-year-old private with severe abdominal wounds. His last words were a plea for a gun, to kill the enemy before he expired.

'Almost all the troops I've seen,' Chester Wilmot wrote at the time, 'reported either that they didn't see the enemy at all, or else that they could not see him till he was within a few yards …'[3]

As they pulled out, the Australians wearied of the enemy's incessant nocturnal taunts. Near Abuari, the Japanese muttering provoked an Australian to shout, 'Go to bed you silly bastards and let us get some sleep!'[4] One Japanese scout crept up to Lance-Corporal Alex Salvaris and whispered in English, 'Where are you, digger?' Salvaris, who was virtually next to the Japanese soldier, politely replied, 'Here I am,' and fired into the scout's face.[5]

The Australian stretcher cases at Alola lay within range of Japanese guns. The Eora Creek field hospital was a six-hour walk from Alola, down one of the steepest sections of the track. Somehow these men had to be carried back over such country.

Medical orderlies crept on hands and knees along the muddy stretcher lines, applying dressings and administering morphine. Bullets flew overhead. None of the wounded wept, recalled Major Henry 'Blue' Steward, confirming the observation of the war correspondent Quentin Reynold: 'The wounded don't cry.'[6] 'They die quietly', observed Ralph Honner, of the men under his command in the 39th Battalion.

To help carry them out, fresh teams of native porters were sent back into the battle zone. They were terrified; of 140 new carriers dispatched to Alola from Eora Creek on 30 August, only twenty arrived. Many deserted; others were among those commandeered to carry the packs and rifles of troops then returning down the track.

Even so, some 900 brave carriers were already doing the job. Carrying out the wounded demanded immense endurance, courage and agility — and manpower. On 29 August 42 badly wounded men were brought in, requiring 336 carriers, according to Kienzle. On 31 August another 300 native carriers were urgently sent up from Myola.

In the end, Papuan Infantry Brigade and Australian troops had to assist the evacuation. Their progress was agonisingly slow. 'Carrying [the wounded] by Europeans,' wrote Captain Rupert Magarey, of the 2/6th Field Ambulance, in his diary, 'over even moderately hilly tracks at anything like a reasonable rate is impossible.'[7]

A small composite unit (of 2/14th and 2/16th troops) protected the evacuation with covering fire, buying time for stretchers to be made. During this respite, they saw a chance to inflict a brief counterattack on the Japanese troops arriving at Alola. Shouting hoarsely, they rounded on their tormentors and charged with bayonets across open country. The pursuers momentarily fled. This small victory was immensely heartening — the AIF hadn't yet seen Japanese soldiers running away.

The wounded crowded into Eora Creek field hospital on the night of 30 August. One side of the camp was set aside for the dying or dead; the other for the operating theatre: a hut with a canvas awning, set in mud. Amputations were performed by torchlight; the surgeons worked through the night, kneeling over their operating tables, which were canvas stretchers soaked in disinfectant and draped with blood-soaked sheets.

Soon the Japanese advance patrols had scaled the high moss forest above the Eora Creek gorge, and the hospital was ordered to evacuate. Medics swiftly packed up their most vital supplies. Doctors were told to stop operating — fracture alignments and amputations ceased — and only to stem blood loss in cases deemed 'absolutely necessary for the immediate saving of life'.[8] One medic, Captain Wallman, was busy amputating a man's hand when this order came through. He gave the wound a ligature, liberal sprinklings of sulphonamide powder and a new dressing, and sent the man and his half-amputated hand up the track in a morphine-induced daze.

Medical officers Magarey, and Steward, of the 2/16th Battalion, had the hellish job of deciding who must be carried and who could walk. A limb wound, unless exceptionally severe, was not thought worthy of a stretcher. Abdominal wounds were written off as hopeless cases — 'no abdominal or thoracic surgery was possible at any time'.[9] The medics could only nurse these doomed youths, many of whom lay whispering for their mothers and girlfriends before they expired.

On the night of 31 August — one that 'will never be obliterated from the memories of those who endured it'[10] — the walking wounded trudged across Eora Creek and up the steep bank toward Templeton's Crossing. It rained incessantly, drenching their bandages and reducing the trail to a mudslide on which they slipped and crawled in agonising confusion. Some troops assigned to a stretcher refused it, and hobbled or dragged themselves up the track. Men with smashed legs and sucking chest wounds were seen crawling from the hospital. Private John Wilkinson observed sadly: 'The war would have been different if we'd had helicopters.'[11] Honner later mourned the huge losses that modern technology might have averted.

The jarring journey over the mountains would take two weeks. There were incredible stories of survival. One private, John Blythe, was literally riddled: shot in the chest, chin, back, right hand and leg. Steward bluntly told him: 'I've bandaged you up and you've got no chance of reaching Moresby. Goodbye.' 'Thanks very much,'[12] Blythe cheerfully replied, and he was carried away. The journey took twelve days; he weighed six stone on arrival, half his normal weight. They amputated his arm, but somehow he lived.

The troops' apparent imperviousness to pain amazed the medics. Two 2/14th corporals — Lindsay 'Teddy' Bear, shot twice in his right leg, once in the left foot and once in the hand, and Russ Fairbairn, shot in the stomach — managed to will themselves unaided, back over the track. Bear's wounds had reduced him to a crab-like scuttle, and Fairbairn helped push him over the mountains to Myola.

The war correspondent Osmar White encountered a soldier whose leg had been blown off just below the knee: 'He'd ligatured the stump, applied two shell dressings, and wrapped the remainder of the leg in an old copra sack.'[13] Two days later White saw the same soldier at Templeton's Crossing, to where he'd crawled and hopped in excruciating pain. White offered to find a stretcher, to which the man angrily replied, 'If you can get bearers, then get them for some other poor bastard. There are plenty worse off than me.'[14]

The Sisyphean resolve of such men formed the substance of the Kokoda legend. And they were thankful in one respect: none would swap their limb wounds, however horrible, for ADSO — 'A Dick Shot Off'.

But these were the walking wounded, the relatively fit. What about the stretcher cases?

———

At Eora Creek on 30 August there were not enough natives — many of whom fled as the Japanese drew near — to carry the rising number of Australians who couldn't walk. These men were in danger of being surrounded and massacred where they lay. Magarey addressed the dozens of besmeared faces blinking up from the mud: 'I want every man who is capable of walking ... to start off for the top of the hill. We haven't got enough bearers to carry everybody, but this place must be cleared tonight.'[15] The stretchered troops were told to drag themselves out. 'A personal appeal was made to the men to walk, even if only for a few 100 yds without assistance.'[16]

'Like slave drivers we urged them on, some hobbling, some staggering like drunks,' remembered Steward. 'They slithered, crawled and clawed their way through the mud, faces twisted with effort ... Men can rise from dreadful pain to superlative heights ...'[17]

The guns of the surviving remnant of the 39th Battalion covered the doctors as they strove to save the wounded. The AIF battalions fell back under the same protective fire. It was the second time Australian militiamen had covered the withdrawal of an AIF unit, and the poignancy was not lost on Smoky Howson, who found himself posted near a deep pit in the clearing near the Eora Creek village (the pit is still there): 'The Japs chased us back to Eora Creek and in a bloody great hurry ... We took up positions there, but no-one knows why, because Eora Creek is down in a valley with bloody great mountains on all sides ... my Bren was right alongside a deep hole. I kept thinking, "If I get hit I'll go straight into that pit".'[18]

About 200 or 300 yards up the southern slope of the gorge several carrier teams, terrified by the encroaching fire, abandoned their wounded on the side of the track. The patients lay there, dazed and staring into the darkness. Australian troops ran back to retrieve these stretcher cases, grabbing the hewn handles of the stretchers by torchlight.[19] Steward helped to carry some of the last out — 'till then we never knew the effort needed, nor fully appreciated the work the carriers were doing'.[20]

All but three stretcher cases were evacuated from Eora Creek that day. These badly injured men — two with abdominal wounds, one with an open chest wound — were given up for dead. Magarey calculated they had half an hour to live. Later a medical patrol returned and found one of these men miraculously alive. The youth opened his eyes and asked an officer, 'You're not going to leave me here, sir? I won't be left behind?'[21]

Magarey arranged to get the boy out — which was done — and he lived for several days on the shoulders of the fuzzy wuzzy angels.

The Japanese wounded faced a less arduous ordeal: a one-day journey downhill to Kokoda, where air evacuation was possible (though rarely used due to frequent Allied air raids). That did not help the Japanese stretcher cases, hundreds of whom were strewn through the forest, awaiting bearers. The worst cases were left to die; it was impossible to spare carriers for men who were doomed anyway. The Japanese were nothing if not practical in these matters.

The wounded found themselves crowding into the Kokoda field hospital, optimistically built for 150 patients. In early September, they 'packed in like sardines'.[22] There were no beds; the men lay on sapling leaves. The tiny wards were 'lined up like pigsties'; their roofs made of 'blackened rotting banana leaves', supported by thin poles, from which water dripped interminably. There was no morphine; the Japanese soldier was expected to bear his pain. A fresh graveyard of little white sapling markers stood appropriately near the hospital entrance.

Takita Kenji, an officer in a Naval Propaganda Squad, visited the patients:

[They] lay strewn in their blood-stained, blackened uniforms. Large drops of water fell on their faces ... they didn't even have the energy to avoid them. They were ... tormented from the pain of their injuries, or distressed by high fever. Were they praying for life? Or just waiting for death? Some several hundred of these inmates were probably embraced by unbearable torment. The hospital, where not a word was uttered, had sunk to the pit of a deathly silence.[23]

The Japanese army tended to deny the seriousness of disease; they treated it as shameful, a blot on the Imperial Army. The indomitable Japanese spirit would conquer pain, wounds and sickness. Medical resources suffered accordingly. One patient, a 24-year-old soldier, remembered the Kokoda field hospital but could not remember seeing any doctors: 'When patients went to the hospital,' he told his Australian captors, 'they got worse instead of better. Food was worse than that received by troops. They ate grass roots part of the time.'[24]

The army's medical services were woefully equipped, and their guidelines to troops, highly inappropriate. A *Handbook of Hygiene in the Tropics* (found on a Japanese corpse) suggested precautions against leprosy and plague. Its 'Strict encomiums to cleanliness' advised troops on horseback to wash and dry the 'inside of thighs and posterior' to stop saddle sores; all troops were to 'prevent the decay of teeth by cleaning them before going to bed'.[25]

Takita left the field hospital in deep dismay. He accurately foresaw that 'epidemics and deficiency in diet' would destroy the soldiers' fighting strength. 'High command cannot by any means understand this.' He gave the army 'less than one month' without food and medical support.[26]

The Australian field hospitals in the Owen Stanleys were little better: mere cordoned-off clearings, perhaps with a tarpaulin, in which the stretcher cases were lined up in rows. What else could be done in such terrain? They were slightly less abysmally equipped. Captain Allan Hogan, a regimental medical officer, reckoned medical services were virtually non-existent during the Australian withdrawal. They did, at least, contain morphine.

Medical supplies often didn't arrive. Don Barnes, an ANGAU medical assistant, held 'a small roll of plaster and a pair of nail scissors' with which to treat the wounded streaming into Deniki after the fall of Kokoda.[27] No salt tablets were issued until late in the campaign — 'the Army had not yet grasped that salt was needed by soldiers sweating in the mountains'[28] — and the wonder of penicillin did not arrive to comfort the armies in New Guinea until 1944. In the Owen Stanleys, medical science seemed at times to have degenerated into a helpless, medieval state in which a doctor's role was merely to ease the pain of inevitable death.

Japanese-inflicted rifle wounds were small bullet holes — the enemy did not appear to use explosive bullets (though there is some suggestion they were used later). The wounds inflicted by mountain gun and mortars were of a different order — deep flesh wounds, shattered bones — and usually fatal. Open wounds became quickly infected, and sometimes gangrenous. Lieutenant Alf Salmon's chest wound, the 'little charmer' with which he'd earlier walked back over the Owen Stanleys, turned out to be a bullet hole five inches long, requiring many stitches. '[The wound] is pretty open and will take a long while to heal,' he told his wife on 19 August 1942. 'The medical orderly made a bit of a mess of it ... They had lost their needles and sewed me up with an old needle — the one and only needle they had.'[29]

Steward used morphine for those in dreadful pain; sulphonamide tablets for oral use, and powder on open wounds. The main problem was blood loss; wounds haemorrhaged constantly on the bumpy stretcher journey. To support broken limbs, he made splints out of bayonet scabbards 'or a branch off a nearby tree'.[30] He added ruefully that 'imparting hope' was the best medicine for a wounded soldier in such conditions.

Or a fag. Cigarettes were a wonderful relaxant. Pain suppressants, with the exception of morphine, were non-existent. Valium and Serepax were then unknown; alcohol was usually only available to officers. So the troops smoked — all the time. 'Cigarettes have crippled and nearly blinded me,' said Bill Crooks many years later. 'But without cigarettes there would have been no success in the war ... awake 24 hours on end men ... would smoke sixty or seventy a day.'[31]

Surprisingly few lost their minds. Mental collapse was quite rare; Bob Iskov of the 2/14th Battalion recalls only a few cases during the retreat, of 'blokes throwing in the sponge'. Not until after the war did many experience serious psychological damage.★

A few troops were accused of self-inflicted wounds. 'The unfortunate men,' said Magarey, who disbelieved the claims, 'received scant sympathy and treatment.' Yet cases of small hand and foot wounds did flow into Queensland hospitals in suspiciously large numbers. Captain John Oldham claimed that between 10 and 25 per cent of these were intentional. There has been no investigation.

Nor were the Australian doctors spared accusations of being overprotective. So great was the need for fighting men, Frank Sublet criticised the medics for wrongly diagnosing dysentery. 'They haven't all got dysentery!' he boomed. 'Some of them are putting it over you!' To which

----

★ See Raftery, *Marks of War — War Neurosis and the Legacy of Kokoda.*

Steward countered, 'I say they have got dysentery, but if you expect me to look up every arse to make sure you're making a big mistake.'[32]

Almost every man had some form of bowel disorder, varying from mild diarrhoea to bacillary dysentery, with the passage of blood and mucus. Vernon tried to reduce the prevalence of dysentery by improving latrine sanitation. He observed that a number of latrines 'were too shallow, roughly dug and finished, and were already being prospected by flies'.[33] He ordered them to be dug again, but was ignored. On his return to Ioribaiwa on 25 August, 'I found the same pits breeding myriads of flies and dysentery rife'.

By the end of the first week of September the long file of walking wounded, like the creeping queue at a soup kitchen, was strung out for miles over the Owen Stanleys. All night, Osmar White and the photographer Damien Parer passed lines of dazed troops heading for Myola (where, they hoped, light aircraft might evacuate them).

'They shuffled at a snail's pace, holding onto each other in long pitiful strings ... They kept sorting and re-sorting themselves,' White observed. The stronger overtook the weaker, and at the end of each 'string' men would 'drop off and lie face down in the mud. Some died there. Some recovered ... and [joined] the tail of another string.'[34] Others collapsed on 'pyres of heatless embers' — the phosphorescent fungus that grew along the trail, whose light they found heartening. Parer, the ubiquitous photojournalist who filmed the campaign (and won an Academy Award for his documentary*), remarked to his colleague, 'An Army in retreat, my boy? Not very pretty is it? I've seen so many retreats. Greece was a picnic compared to this.'[35]

Of all their torments, the darkness was peculiarly disturbing. Night in the Owen Stanleys seems to have a substance so dense you imagine you can touch it. Preying on their minds was the thought of the enemy somewhere in the jungle, and some men reverted to a childhood horror of the 'chasmic blackness': 'Tell them to send a light down the trail, will you? Tell them to send a light, digger!' a plaintive voice cried out one night.[36]

Osmar White produced an old torch, and a line of wounded a hundred yards long formed up behind him. Now and then he flashed the light back

---

* See McDonald, *War Cameraman*; and McDonald and Brune, *200 Shots*.

down the line, and the beam shone over the troops. One, White noticed, was shot twice in the chest; the next soldier had shrapnel wounds in his forearm and thigh. White's battery lasted two hours, flickered out, and the wounded vanished in the enveloping darkness. The soldier with the sucking chest wound lay down, mumbling, 'I'm pretty tired. I think I'll wait till daylight.'

White, a pretty hardened reporter, lost his composure at this sight: 'I gave him a nip out of my brandy flask ... and he was asleep, lying in the arsenic weed ... I started to cry ... Now there was no light. The line fell away, disintegrated. I was alone.'[37]

When they reached Myola — with hopes of air evacuation dashed — new stretchers were built, wounds dressed, and they were sent on their way, back through Efogi, Menari and Nauro, to Uberi. They were either limping along or on the shoulders of the fuzzy wuzzies.

There was neither time for sleep nor long rests. Magarey pressed them harder. 'Every man who could walk had to ... It was necessary to be quite ruthless in this respect ... over and over again men arriving at medical posts could be given only short rests and then pushed on again.'[38] The endurance of those with leg wounds was 'almost incredible', he noted.

For days they continued in this state. The sight deeply moved Colonel Kingsley Norris, the 7th Division's chief medical officer, who came up the track as far as Nauro: 'It is impossible to resist the feelings of a slave driver ...' he said.[39]

On 9 September about two hundred wild-looking men walked into Ilolo near the start of the Kokoda Track. They were skinny, hungry, dirty, unshaven, dressed in rags, some without shirts or trousers. Many were wounded. All had dysentery. Fresh troops preparing to march off over the mountains 'just stood and stared'.[40] These survivors of the 39th Battalion, who'd been fighting in the mountains since July, stripped, threw their rags onto a bonfire, and took a 'glorious wash' in the river.

Soon, the stretcher cases started coming in. They were transferred to field hospitals near Owers' Corner, and later flown back to Queensland. The 2/9th Australian general field hospital, near Rouna Falls, had 600 beds in

October. By December it would hold 2000 patients, so overcrowded that stretcher cases were slid under bunks.[41] Sister Murie was solely responsible for 120 patients, of whom 40 to 50 were very ill or seriously wounded. So crowded was the hospital, she reached those on the tent's edges by lifting the tarpaulin from the outside, standing shin-deep in mud with a lantern to guide her way. 'We dreaded the moonlit nights,' she said.[41] On one occasion a bomb fell on the hospital but failed to explode.

In the eyes of returning troops, these pretty young nurses were visions of angels descended. 'To them, it seemed as though we were Heaven-sent,' said Sister Murie, aged twenty.

The troops were given a while to recuperate. Many were sent to the stinking 'Lightning Ridge' Dysentery Hospital, where each man was issued on arrival with a baked bean tin in which to pass his daily sample — 'just slime', observed Private Kevin 'Spud' Whelan. Smoky Howson was sent to a base camp hospital in Port Moresby where doctors bored into his 'upstairs department' to relieve fluid from a head wound.

Within weeks, the 39th Battalion was sent back over the mountains to fight at Gona.

Chapter 20
Fuzzy Wuzzy Angels

'We sat down by his stretcher and cried for him. And then we buried him'
— *Lubini Helia, fuzzy wuzzy angel, of Alola village in the Owen Stanley Range*

Havala Laula is probably 76 years old this year (2004), but he may be older. He's not sure.* Havala lives in the village of Kagi, in the Central Province of Papua. Sixty-two years ago, aged perhaps fourteen, he carried his first wounded Australian over the Owen Stanley Range.

Havala was one carrier in a team of eight and possibly the youngest fuzzy wuzzy angel on the Kokoda Track. Today he proudly wears the tunic of the Papuan Infantry Brigade and the badge of an Australian flag, and he's happy to discuss his memories standing on two broad, flat, roughly calloused feet that carried Australian servicemen to safety.

---

* Many fuzzy wuzzies did not know their ages when they were recruited. The fuzzy wuzzy recruiting procedure was fairly crude. Frank Taylor, one of the more experienced Kokoda guides, tells how the Australian administrators called in all the men from the villages and asked them their age. If a man didn't know, they'd lift up his arms. If he had hair under his arms he was made a carrier.

'When Australians were wounded we took them from here to Owers' Corner,' he said, casually waving a hand towards the mountain range, as though he does this every day. 'We took off their bandages and rubbed their wounds with bush medicines. And then we wrapped leaves around their wounds. That made them feel better — they felt all right ... When a wounded soldier died we'd bury him on his stretcher.'[1] As Seventh-Day Adventists, Havala's people gave the dead troops a Christian burial. The men were not the only ones helping, he insisted: 'The women carried the food, too. All of the village people took part.'

His bright smiling face darkens as a memory intrudes. 'It was a very sad time for us, when the war came to Kagi.' The day the Japanese passed through the region, he said, 'They destroyed the villages, ruined the gardens and killed all our livestock. But the Australian troops treated us well, they gave us food and supplies.'

Up ahead, at the village of Alola, is Lubini Helia, a farmer like Havala, whose feet are twisted so far around he walks on the outer edges. Lubini, too, was a carrier — nor does he know his age — and he speaks with similar clarity of the war. His villagers hid in hills and caves when the Japanese army arrived; they returned to find their homes destroyed, their pigs shot, and two villagers lying dead, with their throats cut.[2] Lubini thinks the Japanese did these things because his village refused to cooperate as guides.

He remembers giving the wounded Australians water and food (and bush medicine): 'We'd light their cigarettes and give them anything they wanted.'

How hard was the journey? 'It was very, very hard. We wanted the soldiers to be alive; we didn't want them to be dead. So even though it's steep down and up we went as fast as we could.'

Havala and Lubini were two of about 3000 tribesmen needed to carry out the Australian wounded and feed the army. Each man carried a 40-pound load (excluding his own food) from Myola to the forward stations at Templeton's Crossing, Eora Creek and Alola. During the supply crisis, they rushed huge quantities of ammunition, grenades, rations, blankets, medical supplies, rifle grease, tobacco, papers and wax matches up to the troops.

Having deposited their loads, they were converted into human ambulances, and shouldered the wounded back to Myola. Some carrier teams continued to Owers' Corner; others were part of a relay. Most worked until they dropped. Vernon complained that they were overworked and overloaded — 'principally by soldiers who dumped their packs and even rifles on top of the carriers' own burdens' — and suffered from exposure, cold and malnourishment. 'Every evening scores of carriers came in, slung their loads down and lay exhausted on the ground ...'[3]

The legend of the fuzzy wuzzy angels, as the tribal carriers were affectionately and deservedly known, holds that they were angelic, devoted stretcher-bearers and the saviours of the Australian wounded. Many were, but a little perspective is needed. In early 1942, Australian colonial interests employed about 10,000 labourers in Papua and 35,000 in the Mandated Territory.[4] When war broke out they were harnessed as porters and then stretcher-bearers, and by September, 20,000 natives were thus employed throughout Papua and New Guinea.[5] Many were recruited from the labour depots around Port Moresby, with as little knowledge of the mountains as the Australians had, notes Hank Nelson. About one in ten were Koiari people, the tribe that lived along the track and on the Sogeri plateau.

They were not all smiling natives who benignly nursed the troops without complaint (though a lot were). Many had been 'hard used' by the Australian Government before the war, and forced to carry huge loads to plantations and goldfields.* Some were bitter. The first teams of carriers were badly treated and 'desertions were frequently reported'.[6] Nor did they simply drift down from their villages and happily give their time — and sometimes their lives — to save the white man. Very few were volunteers (though Havala and Lubini, whose villages were sacked, probably were, as they state). The native people understandably dreaded the war.

In fact, they were indentured labourers, a form of paid slavery. On 15 June 1942, Australia's National Security (Emergency) Control Regulations Act

---

* There were prewar cases of carriers being ordered to carry 100-pound bags of rice over the mountains. In 1942, the Australian Government introduced a maximum threshold of 50 pounds, subsequently reduced to 40 pounds.

provided for 'the conscription of whatever native labour might be required by the [Australian armed] Services'.[7] This gave near dictatorial powers to the quasi-military regional officers of ANGAU,[8] who could harness 'any native upon such work and subject to such conditions not inconsistent with the order as he may see fit'.[9] The clause was open to wide interpretation by bored white 'old New Guinea hands' and latent slave drivers.

Natives who refused to work, deserted, absented themselves 'without leave' or worked in 'a careless of negligent manner' faced severe fines and imprisonment. The grinding reality of carrying broken men over the Owen Stanleys rendered these petty, officious terms absurd. They worked like Trojans. They responded to perks and incentives, and one reason they liked the Australians had nothing to do with their putative affection for their white colonial masters: it was simply that they were allowed to take any damaged goods dropped at Myola back to their villages as a kind of bonus.[10]

Some Australians treated them abominably. Natives were rounded up and 'held' for service — they were corralled into pens. Many were pushed to the limits of physical endurance. Vernon was shocked by the weight of the load on the back of a decrepit old native man, a father of eight, who tottered into his field hospital at Eora Creek and promptly collapsed. 'The age of this old chap showed me how desperate was the call for carriers.'[11]

A large number were expected to work long after their contracts expired, without pay. Nor were their rations always reliable. Wilmot, a torchbearer for the fuzzy wuzzies, wrote sternly to the authorities: 'The native ration is pay, and he regards it as his RIGHT. Any whittling down he regards as a breach of faith.'[12]

Both Japanese and Australians routinely plundered their gardens. 'The native regards his garden ... very jealously,' Wilmot reported. 'They would, I'm told, give the troops fruit, if they had it, but we will lose their faith if the troops loot.' He cited a few 2/14th men who hacked down young pawpaw trees at Menari in an act of 'sheer vandalism'.

The terms of native 'contracts' were imposed with brutal, if necessary, efficiency. The Australians hunted and summarily executed those accused of betrayal and collaboration. An Alola man was hung as a traitor in Isurava, according to Lubini. There was a cruel catch-22: the natives were executed by the Japanese if they refused to collaborate; and imprisoned or executed by the Australians if they were found collaborating.

Havala remembers the Japanese arriving at Isurava, and asking the way to Port Moresby. When the Isuravan people gave no reply, 'the Japanese got these Isurava people and killed them'.[13]

The natives were mortal, not superhuman; many fled the bombs — the hellish sound of which was so alien to their world — and rejoined their villages. Others 'chucked a sickie', in the Australian vernacular, to avoid duty — 'a typical Fuzzy trick',[14] that no doubt resonated with their Australian bosses on a bad day.

A large minority dumped their loads and simply gave up. After the battle of Isurava, for example, the desertion rate was said to be 30 per cent; many supplies were left by the track, including 18,000 rifle rounds, on 31 August. And there was the rare case during the explosive evacuation of Eora Creek when a few terrified angels flew away, leaving their wounded beside the track. 'The carrier position is very precarious,' Wilmot warned at the time.[15]

There is another side to the truth, however, which befits the angelic legend. At their best, the fuzzy wuzzy angels were 'magnificent', said Magarey, who worked closely with them. They saved the lives of hundreds of Australian soldiers. This went well beyond the call of duty. 'Every need which they can fulfil is fulfilled. [At night] they will find a level spot beside the track, and build a shelter over the patient. They will make him as comfortable as possible, get him water, and feed him if any food is available.'[16]

Many felt a deep personal responsibility for their patients, and close friendships developed between fuzzy wuzzies and the Australian wounded. The sight of their powerful back and leg muscles, hoisting their patients aloft, gave hope to men who had utterly abandoned hope.

'The Fuzzy Wuzzies performed all tasks asked of them, tasks that few white men could have stood up to,' concluded an official 21st Brigade report.[17] And the tribeswomen, it is rarely observed, helped too, carrying lighter supplies and distributing food at village stations.

———

They shunned the standard army canvas stretchers, which rotted and tore. They made their own by doubling a blanket around two long poles and tying the edges together with native string. The poles were kept apart by spreaders lashed across them at each end. These were deeper, thus avoided spillage, and were far tougher.

Though sure-footed, the fuzzy wuzzies could not avoid jolting their heavy human cargo. Sometimes, the stretchers collapsed; or the carriers slipped. The pain was extreme and soldiers passed out. With every jolt, blood seeped from wounds and stumps. Amazingly, few of the stretcher cases died from blood loss; such was the care with which they were borne over the rivers and steep slopes.[18]

One soldier, Hamlyn Harris, witnessed the stretcher-bearers 'picking their way ... softly and silently ... handling their stretchers with surprising deftness in rough places, to save their human burden the slightest jolt ...'[19] No amount of care could ease the pain of horribly wounded cases, but a surprising number survived the journey through mud and slush, over razorbacks and across rivers. The rhythm of the movement rocked some men asleep.

At night, the fuzzy wuzzies slept four to each side of the stretcher, in a protective ring, and assisted the patient's every call and need: 'The natives practically never left the patient until they had brought him to his destination,' said Magarey.[20]

The fuzzy wuzzy angels were hailed as heroes; many were decorated or rewarded with gifts. The legend adorns Australian schoolchildren's textbooks, and some Australians continue to honour them on Kokoda Day,* as they did in 1942. A well-known wartime poem reads:

> ... For they haven't any halos,
> Only holes slashed in their ears,
> And their faces worked by tattoos,
> With scratch pins in their hair.
> Bringing back the badly wounded

---

* Australian gratitude seems to have been more vocal than material — surviving fuzzies quietly note the absence of a war pension, and very little compensation for their villages. Though in fairness this may be an issue for the New Guinean, not the Australian Government, which has been lavish with war reparations and aid to Papua and New Guinea.

Just as steady as a hearse,
Using leaves to keep the rain off
And as gentle as a nurse.
Slow and careful in bad places
On the awful mountain track
The look upon their faces
Would make you think that Christ was black.[21]

The stretcher-bearers felt a deep sense of personal loss if their patient died, such was the bond formed during the ordeal over the mountains.

'We were very, very sad when we saw the wounded Australian soldiers,' said Havala. 'When a patient died, we were tearful,' he said.

'We sat down by his stretcher and cried for him. And then we buried him,' Lubini remembers, of one Australian soldier.

The Japanese treated the native people variably: sometimes well, at other times with brutal impatience. Rabaul carriers said they were compelled at bayonet point to join the Japanese convoy to Papua. Certainly many were starved and beaten along the Kokoda Track.

The Japanese sought to confute this impression. 'Rabaul natives entertained no animosity against Japanese troops,' Superior Private Iwasa Koji told Allied Intelligence officers. 'They were well treated and were always paid in Military Notes for anything they supplied. Severe penalties were imposed for striking a native or for robbery ... while rape was punishable by death. The Gendarmerie was very strict about correct treatment of natives.'[22] Surviving veterans are adamant they did not harm the Papuans.

Some coastal villages did cooperate with the Japanese, and initially relations were good. There were great carrots on offer to those who collaborated. The Japanese portrayed themselves as long lost relatives, returning to liberate the tribes from the white imperialist. They promised equal rights, and a smorgasbord of impossible rewards after the war: cars, planes, investment, and so on.

A 'warm spiritual reception' for the Papuans was vital, noted a Japanese military guide, *The Handling of Natives*: 'There must be no racial discrimination.

Suitable awards and punishments must be made ... If it is at all avoidable they must not be beaten ...'[23] Troops were told not to respond to native complaints with, 'You are only a dirty native': 'Do not treat them as pigs for they resent it,' the handbook warned. Uneaten rice should be given to native carriers, but 'do not be too generous ... as it spoils them'.[24]

Japanese troops were never to forget that carriers were 'also human and that there is a limit to their endurance'.

In reality, the Japanese were rather less caring. Desertion was severely punished, and collaboration an immediate death sentence. Native rations were gradually cut to about a third of the troops' ration, and were barely enough to sustain sedentary human life. Many exhausted Rabaul carriers were later found starving on the side of the track, with bayonet wounds.

'This ... propaganda had very gratifying effect at first but generally had to be supported by threats of decapitation after a month or so,'[25] observed Keiko Tamura.

As well as carrying supplies and wounded, their work involved cutting sago, and building bunkers, roads and airstrips, according to Hiromitsu Iwamoto, who later interviewed many tribal elders of the Sepik and Madang regions.[26]

The Japanese did not recruit Papuan carriers in an organised manner; individual officers tended to press-gang native labour when and where it suited them (they usually dubbed the tribal chiefs 'Boss Boy'). In this the Australians, as the colonial power, had the advantage of local familiarity. Some villagers took the view, 'better the devil we know', after exposure to the firmer Japanese methods; Kienzle's rigorous propaganda helped persuade them.

Any goodwill the Japanese enjoyed with the villages utterly collapsed later in the war, when the starving invader plundered their plantations on a scale that dwarfed the worst excesses of the Australians. They would sweep through villages like 'a typhoon', stripping out the slightest morsels of food.[27]

Horii's carrier desertion rate soared as he advanced over the Owen Stanleys, putting immense strain on his supply lines. The Japanese commander would rely mostly on his loyal Formosan conscripts, Korean labourers and his own troops as both porters and stretcher-bearers. So few carriers were available, the bearers had to work in teams of four to a stretcher, with no relief. It was a gruelling regimen, hardened by the fact that they were not as sure-footed as the Papuans. The Japanese wounded had to be 'firmly tied to the stretchers with vines to prevent them rolling off...'[28]

Chapter 21
Buckler

'To save a further call on stretcher-bearers he has actually crawled
on his hands and knees for days'
— *Captain Ben Buckler, of Corporal John Metson*

After Isurava, 170 Australian soldiers were cut off behind enemy lines in
the jungle. Many were badly wounded and couldn't walk, or keep up;
their mates stayed back with them.

The most senior example was Lieutenant-Colonel Arthur Key,
commander of the 2/14th Battalion. Key and his entire HQ staff had been
caught in friendly fire during the last fighting at Alola and forced off the
track. Key, who would later win a posthumous DSO for his leadership at
Isurava, struck south along the Eora Creek bed, hoping to find his men at
Abuari. After ten days of pushing through the jungle, his party were caught
by the Japanese. They were taken back to the northern beachhead.

'Captured Lt-Col K and four others,' noted one Japanese soldier.
'Though questioned they stubbornly refused to speak.'[1] A witness during the
interrogation, Keishin Tsuno, was so impressed by Key's silence that he, too,
tried to keep silent when the Australians captured and questioned him.

It was a fitting epitaph for Key's party; few suffered in silence under Japanese interrogation methods.

It seems they took Key to Buna where James Benson, then a prisoner of the Japanese, recalled seeing 'a tall gaunt Australian with the star and crown of Lieutenant-Colonel' brought into camp with a bad leg wound. He was emaciated and exhausted.

If this was Key — as seems likely — his fate, and that of his men, was decapitation, either in Buna, or in Rabaul.[2] A Japanese prisoner later stated: 'An Australian 2nd Lieutenant was captured ... After examination he was beheaded that night ...'[3] Key was the third Australian battalion commander to die within two months of fighting on the Kokoda Track. To put this in perspective, only one battalion commander had been killed in the Middle East during five substantial campaigns fought over two years.[4]

One astonishing story of lost troops survives in all its haunting pathos, thanks to a diary of surpassing descriptive power belonging to Captain Ben Buckler, whose 42 men were severed from the main body of their battalion[5] at Isurava Rest House.

Tending the wounded had delayed their withdrawal, and they were stranded behind Japanese lines. They built stretchers out of timber and blankets and struck out alone, hoping to circumvent the enemy. To begin there were two stretcher cases, three walking wounded and one 'crawling case': the young corporal John Metson, a St Kilda salesman, who was shot in both ankles. Eschewing a stretcher, Metson got along on his hands and knees, which he'd bandaged up. In this manner he dragged his useless legs over the ranges for three weeks. Buckler observed: 'To save a further call on stretcher-bearers he has actually crawled on his hands and knees for days.'[6]

On 4 September, Buckler dispatched a platoon commander, Captain Maurice Treacy, to get help while he waited with the wounded at a native garden on the hills above Eora Creek, which was now in enemy hands. Here Buckler's party lived for six days on sugar cane and sweet potatoes. While reconnoitring an abandoned Japanese camp nearby, he encountered nine Australian bodies — 'had the unpleasant task of removing identity discs from the week old corpses'[7] — and salvaged 21 tins of bully beef from their haversacks.

Help did not come in time: on 11 September, the day before Treacy reached an Australian base, Buckler spotted Japanese boot prints — the telltale webbed toe — in the garden, and ordered his men to move out. They pressed three carriers, who had earlier deserted, into service, and headed north-east toward the coastal village of Tufi. By this time the party numbered 47: two officers, 37 others ranks and eight wounded, four on stretchers, three 'limping cases', and the crawling Metson. Of the stretcher cases, Privates Yeo and Mayne were both shot through the knees, which were badly fractured; Sergeant Knights had a bullet lodged in the thigh and a deep flesh wound.

On the 17th a soldier shot a wild pig. They dismembered and stewed it, and poured the blood off into a mess tin. 'Nothing was wasted ... the three carriers divided up the entrails.'[8] The hide was carried for two days, scorched and eaten. At a nearby village members of the Biagi tribe provided sweet potato, sugar cane and bananas, and the troops regained their strength. But the Biagi refused to work as stretcher-bearers, so the troops offered 34 shillings and threepence in silver and copper coins to entice them.

Seven days later Buckler's band, 'like white apparitions', entered the village of Sangai, where friendly villagers supplied shelter and food. Some huntsmen carried 'huge 12 foot pig spears'.[9] Buckler decided to leave the wounded here and press on for help. Two village chiefs, Faria and Ewoki, gave assurances they would look after the seven sick and wounded troops.

Before he left, Buckler dutifully listed their names, rank, next of kin and addresses in his diary. Corporal Metson and Privates Mayne, Hunter, Snelgar, Knights and MacDonald were from Victoria; and Private Yeo from Perth. It makes eerily melancholy reading, the little list of 'next of kin' written in Buckler's pencil beside each soldier's name: 'father, cousin, father, mother, father, wife, father ...'

Private Thomas Fletcher volunteered to stay with the stretcher cases, for whose care he had two shell dressings, fourteen field dressings, towels and soap. There was no morphine. Their pain was intolerable and two of the wounded, Buckler later reported, 'went mental ... these men lost their senses and had no confidence in coming through. They had to be left at Sangai.'[10]

Buckler's patrol departed, passed perilously close to the Japanese-occupied track between Buna and Kokoda and crossed a swinging rope bridge high over the lower reaches of the Kumusi River. The natives assisted by piggybacking their weapons across: 'It is a queer sight,' wrote Buckler, 'to see an old warrior of the spear age place down his weapons and shoulder a Bren gun over the waters.'[11]

There were lighter moments, as on the night of the 23rd when a full moon sparkled on the stream, and Buckler felt moved to sing, 'Roaming in the Gloaming', to an unrecorded response.

At this stage, the captain was experiencing exceptionally vivid dreams of food and home: 'I ... walked through a maize crop and there came to our home. There was my family sitting around watching my mother cook and butter some steak!'[12] Unable to sink his teeth into it, he awoke, gnashing the air. At Ilomo he paid the natives five shillings for fruit and vegetables. The men dreamt of a plate of hot bully beef. 'Funny,' Buckler observed, 'how circumstances alter tastes — sometimes bully is rather despised as a dish.'[13]

Anxious about Fletcher's party, Buckler left his men at Kuru on the 26th and pressed on alone. He passed Jaure and Suweri where, at the foot of the Owalama Divide, he tried to recruit a guide. The Suweri locals initially refused as the alpine moss forest, like Myola to the Koiari people, was named *diriva gabuna*, a place of ghosts. Buckler shrugged and pressed on. Eventually they agreed to send a small native boy, who ran after the lone Australian into the haunted mountain pass.

They camped in a high forest, where 'all I could do was huddle up in half a blanket and gas cape and listen to the moans of the little native who was covered only by a small thin piece of beaten pig skin'.[14]

At 1.30 p.m. on 28 September, a month after he left the track at Alola, Buckler rounded a corner and walked into an American camp at the Oidobi Rest House. His relief must have rivalled Stanley's, on finding Dr Livingstone. The Americans 'seemed to have been conjured up by a spiteful Papuan mountain djinn ... or an image of wishful thinking to a man who had endured a month of strain and vicissitude', wrote Raymond Paull.[15] After sharing a plate of bully beef, the Americans — the recently arrived 126th Regiment — guided the exhausted captain to Dorobisolo, half a day on.

Here, Buckler met the press — some sixteen war correspondents. A war artist sketched his face. Commando patrols were sent immediately to retrieve the stragglers. Some 33 survivors were brought into camp. A *New York Herald Tribune* correspondent, Lewis Sebring, witnessed their return:

Sunken eyes looked at us from bearded faces as the Australians, in tattered uniforms, painfully shifted from sitting positions, rising to reach for outstretched hands ... the crowd parted as the Aussies crunched up the gravel.

The men who had not yet been in the fight looked in awe at those who had. Two ambulances received a half-dozen wounded who had walked through the jungle with the rest. One limped from a piece of shrapnel in his back. Others had bandaged legs and arms. A colonel watching every move of the men commented that despite [their] condition ... they carried all their firearms, ammunition and equipment. That is a great tribute to the leadership and discipline of these troops.[16]

Fletcher's stretcher party was still at Sangai, and on 6 October, Buckler flew back over the mountains in an American bomber, with food and medical supplies. The plane circled the village, but found no sign of Fletcher and the seven sick and wounded. On the 7th Buckler tried again; and his plane dropped two packages. Again, no sign of the men. The answer lay in the dust of the deserted village. A Japanese patrol had got there first, shot Fletcher, and bayoneted the sick and wounded where they lay. Metson received a posthumous British Empire Medal for his epic feat of endurance in dragging his broken body over the mountains for three weeks.

The story has an intriguing epilogue. Buckler greatly admired the American can-do attitude, and sought their support for his idea of forming an Orde Wingate-style Australian parachute regiment: 'Now equipped as a Yank and living with 126th Regiment,' he wrote, soon after he recovered.[17]

The idea had been burning in his mind as he walked over the mountains, and he approached Colonel Lawrence Quinn, of the 126th.

Quinn told GHQ, '[Buckler] has in mind trying to obtain certain items of our uniform and possibly some of our equipment . . . I thought we might be able to lend him a hand.'[18]

The captain was brought back to Brisbane to explore his paratroop plan. He was asked to list his ideas for defeating the Japanese. In this, Buckler revealed a gift for parade ground prose that rivalled Porter's. Some of his ideas were excellent. Beards, he said, were 'a natural camouflage', and more effective than painting their faces green. 'I would suggest that all infantry be allowed to retain their whiskers for camouflage purposes.' This would have the added benefit of reducing kit weight 'by deletion of shaving material'. He claimed that a sniper had once picked out the only clean-shaven officer in his battalion. One of his more inventive tips was the development of a triple-purpose stick for use on the Kokoda Track: it would be 'a walking stick, camouflage screen and umbrella'.[19] This did not get up.

He urged a course in native customs and languages, as well as a lesson in Japanese phrases to counter their English jibes. He suggested, as a first step, that all Australian troops learn the Japanese for, 'Stop there', 'Come forward' and 'Japanese bastard'. Most radically Buckler recommended that dehydrated meat, bacon rashers, and vitamin pills replace bully beef. The jury is still out.

Chapter 22
Myola

'Potts's tactic was to keep us between the Jap and Moresby. He had a wonderful attitude, was completely fearless'
— *Keith Norrish, 2/16th Battalion*

The Japanese converged on Eora Creek on 1 September and found only abandoned hospital huts, destroyed weapon pits and scattered food. A few corpses lay in their stretchers. Potts's men had either carried stores away, or punctured the cans and bags, and dumped their contents in the creek.[1] It was the first phase of a scorched-earth policy he planned to employ all the way back over the mountains.

The Japanese had eaten deeply into their two-week rice ration, and they were hungry. Their rations approached depletion after the delay at Isurava. They were already supplementing the food they carried with native garden produce and 'Churchill supplies'.

Major-General Horii clearly understood the danger of advancing at the end of a faltering supply line without adequate resources. On the night of 1 September, he issued an urgent instruction. 'All Tai commanders and those in authority of whatever rank,' he ordered, 'must exercise the most painstaking control ... so that every bullet fells an enemy and every grain of rice furthers the task of the Shitai.'[2]

The daily rice ration was cut to an average of about 1½ pints per man, and troops were ordered to collect fruit and vegetables from native gardens. Discipline lapsed. Japanese casualties at officer level were mounting, and several companies now lacked commanders or even qualified officers.

During the first week of September, Potts's much-needed reserve force, the 2/27th Battalion, set out from Owers' Corner to join Maroubra Force. With the threat of seaborne invasion removed after the victories at Milne Bay and in the Coral Sea, they were no longer needed in Port Moresby.

It was just as well, because Potts's force was 'pathetically depleted'.[3] Most of his men were unfit for action. Five hundred were dead, wounded, sick or missing. After the loss of Key, Captain Phil Rhoden, a Melbourne solicitor, took command of the 2/14th.

Potts rallied his men. The one thing in his head was to keep an Australian fighting force between the Japanese and Port Moresby. He aimed to turn a terrible setback into an opportunity and gathered his officers together. His battalion commanders (then Rhoden and Lieutenant-Colonel Albert Caro of the 2/16th) were given the grave responsibility of executing a set of new tactics immediately.

The Australian army was not going to retreat, Potts said. They were going to withdraw fighting. They would fight the Japanese every inch of the way back over the mountain; resist the aggressor at every opportunity; draw in and then strangle his supply lines. Every bend in the track, every creek, copse and spur would serve as an ambush and attack opportunity. Potts knew well the difficulty of trying to supply an army over the mountains. Now the Japanese would learn the same lesson: he devised a fighting withdrawal that would reverse the equation, and subject the Japanese troops to constant harassment and their supply lines to the full trauma of this merciless country.

Australian patrols were given a crash course in jungle combat. They were to use the jungle to advantage, plan ambushes, and fan out around the enemy through virgin forest. They were not to cling to the track. These instructions were adopted immediately, with promising results. An Australian ambush above Eora Creek succeeded in killing ten Japanese soldiers, and the advancing enemy were stopped dead. Japanese officers had to wave their swords to get their men moving. Some refused. The Koiwai Battalion's diarist noted, 'The Australians resisted stubbornly; we have failed to defeat them.'

This phased skirmishing continued all the way back to Myola. 'Had Potts not withdrawn, we would have been completely encircled by 7000 Japs,' said Keith Norrish, of the 2/16th Battalion. Norrish vividly described how the fighting withdrawal worked:

> Potts knew the only way to survive was to withdraw, to set up ambushes — and withdraw. So we'd send a patrol out every 15 minutes to face the Japs. The patrols were armed with two Tommies and a Bren gun.
>
> They'd eliminate the first Jap patrol, and then our fellows would withdraw, and come back to the main force. Then we'd attack in force, with a pincer movement on either flank. We'd give them a fair hammering, and withdraw again. Potts's tactic was to keep us between the Jap and Moresby. He had a wonderful attitude, was completely fearless, and always had a word for anybody.[4]

The tactic was repeated again and again, using fresh troops each time. 'One lot would hold, the next lot would dig in; when the first lot couldn't hold any more they'd fall back through the next lot, and leapfrog their way back,' explained Frank Taylor.[5]

At Templeton's Crossing the Australians destroyed everything they couldn't carry — the carriers cheerfully slashed heavy bags of rice and punctured tins of bully beef — and on the night of 3 September they reached Myola. Hot food and a change of clothing awaited the troops here. Mail was distributed. Some men hadn't removed their boots in a week, and 'exposed their puffed and leprous-looking feet to the sun'[6] — and to the brigade's 'chiropodist', one Corporal Clark, a window dresser from Victoria. Clark found himself paring away rotten foot tissue from crumbling, waterlogged socks.

The respite didn't last, and soon Myola itself was threatened. It seemed the enemy never slept; true, Horii deployed his fresh troops while resting others. His total forward combat strength exceeded 3000. Potts had only 500 men — the 39th and 53rd battalions had returned to Port Moresby — and most of these were unfit to fight (his reserve battalion had not yet arrived).

Little of this was properly appreciated in Port Moresby, or Brisbane, as revealed in Rowell's wire to Blamey on 3 September:

> ...I have told ALLEN to order POTTS to hold MYOLA at all costs ... Every yard the enemy makes increases his own supply difficulties, which we hope to accentuate by air action. Unfortunately some of our bombs fell among our own troops today at KAGI, but that is always possible ... The enemy is resourceful and well trained, and is not afraid to die. His defeat is not going to be a walkover, but will only come from the most stubborn and bitter fighting ...[7]

With so few men Potts could not hold Myola — which, being a wide-open space was, in fact, indefensible — and he abandoned the vital drop zone. Had he chosen to stay and fight, his army would assuredly have been wiped out. He saved his men's lives, but would incur the wrath of Brisbane. Rowell and Allen could only sit and read Potts's wires with rising anxiety:

> 4 Sept: to ALLEN from POTTS:
> ...country utterly unsuitable for defended localities. Regret necessity to abandon MYOLA intend withdrawing EFOGI ... men full of fight but utterly weary ... remaining companies of 2/27th battalion too late to assist.

They withdrew hastily: demolished the supply depot, spoiled the food supplies, and fell back to Efogi. The decision infuriated Brisbane. The loss of Myola handed the main Allied dropzone to the Japanese (though this didn't help them, since the Allies virtually controlled the air). 'The abandonment of

Myola must have sickened Potts,' writes the official historian Dudley McCarthy. 'More than any other man he knew its importance.'[8]

Rowell and Allen were literally between a rock and a hard place. They were under extreme pressure to arrest the withdrawal. On one hand, Blamey and MacArthur breathed orders down their necks to regain the offensive; on the other, they began to understand Potts's problem (in fact, the dimmest civilian standing on Lake Myola can see why Potts couldn't defend it, even with fresh troops, but none of the high commanders had seen the country).

Allen was reduced to sending mild encouragement. He alerted Potts's attention 'to the desirability of assuming the offensive'. Potts ignored this, and stuck to his guns. He technically disobeyed orders, and continued the fighting withdrawal — a stroke of inspired disobedience. He saw that his little army were better off alive, held together as a barrier, than dead in a heap on this 'place of ghosts'.

On 5 September, during a violent squall, the Japanese poured into the abandoned Myola. They feasted on leftover rations, which had been deliberately spoiled, and 'yielded a prolific crop of gastric disorders'.[9] The mass outbreak of food poisoning caused another day's delay, to Horii's fury.

An extremely brave Japanese machine-gunner emerges as an influential commander at this point. Lieutenant Sakomoto — who never shirked his duty, not even *in extremis* — chronicled the Japanese experience in excruciating detail. He kept a furtive diary. On reaching Myola, he wrote, '. . . discovered large quantities of enemy rations such as corned beef, milk, jam etc. First taste of milk for a long time.' He shared it with his men, who were still feeling the side effects the next day: 'Many suffered diarrhoea by over-eating captured provisions.'[10]

That afternoon Potts rendezvoused with the long-awaited 2/27th Battalion at the village of Efogi. Colonel Geoff Cooper, their commander, was a scion of Adelaide's Cooper brewing dynasty. The brigade's three battalions were united for the first time in the mountains. Cooper related an unfortunate incident on the way: at Nauro, biscuit bombers had missed their targets, and dropped their loads onto the thatched huts sheltering the men, which killed one and injured five.

Potts sent the fresh troops to the front position on the track, and continued the phased withdrawal. But New Guinea Force HQ back in Port Moresby was unimpressed. The next day Potts received a stern order from Tubby Allen, which reflected the alarm in Brisbane: 'Absolutely essential you give no further ground,' Allen barked, 'and that you lose no opportunity to hit the enemy with strong, offensive patrols. Contact will be regained at earliest. 2/14th and 2/16th battalions will be rallied at once.'

The order was impossible to fulfil. Potts had one combat-ready battalion (itself at half strength), and the Japanese were reinforced. The Australians were now fighting an army about five times their size. He replied to Allen at once:

> 6 Sept: to ALLEN from POTTS:
> Situation not sufficiently stable ... 2/14 and 2/16 very little physical reserves ... enemy appears able to follow up his advantage for at least 4 days. 2/27 bn only tps in condition to fight. Please expedite foot powder, boots, socks, methylated spirits and bootlaces. Urgent need.[11]

He resolved to stick to his new tactics. They had the advantage of letting him choose his battlefields. Imperceptibly to those in Brisbane, Potts's men were drawing the enemy into a death trap. They had shored up their losses, regrouped and struck back. By 6 September, Potts had converted his 'inspired disobedience' into a brilliant defensive manoeuvre, more accurately described as 'calculated disobedience'.

Chapter 23
Butcher's Hill

'You'd have to be a qualified mountain goat to be able to do
physically what they did'
— *Private Bert Ward, 2/27th Battalion, on the Japanese at Efogi*

That night the Australians dug in high above Efogi saw an
extraordinary sight in the valley below: a line of twinkling Japanese
lanterns seemed to be guiding the enemy down the steep slope from
Myola, bobbing along in a macabre suggestion of festivity. In truth the
'lanterns' were flaming lengths of rubber-coated signal wire, abandoned by
the Australians.

'Conceited bastards!' grunted the intelligence officer, Ray Watson. The
lanterns were within range of a Vickers machine-gun, but these had not
been brought up — a source of intense frustration for Potts. He wired Port
Moresby for air attacks: 'Quiet night but lights observed coming down
MYOLA track into EFOGI from 1830 on 6 Sep to 0200 this morning ...
Turn all you've got from air on EFOGI and MYOLA at earliest tomorrow
morning ...'[1]

At dawn eight bombers and four Kittyhawks bombed and strafed the
Japanese positions. A suspiciously exact 100 Japanese were said to have died in

the raids; but both sides confirm the figure.★ Australian satisfaction was short-lived. The jungle canopy offered protection from air raids, and the Allies could not defeat Horii by air power alone. Scorning the bombardment, some 1500 Japanese troops occupied the deserted village of Efogi later that day, and Horii moved his HQ there.

All night the Japanese consigned their dead to funeral pyres that burned in the hills near Efogi. About this time, Colonel Kusunose Masao, the much-admired commander of the 144th Regiment and Horii's second-in-command, succumbed to severe illness. That day his men had been selected to lead the pursuit, and Kusunose was forced to issue orders from his stretcher, carried forward like a sultan aboard a palanquin.

Fifteen hundred miles away General MacArthur strode about his Brisbane headquarters in high dudgeon. The Allied supreme commander railed at the Australians between puffs on his corncob pipe. MacArthur and the 'Bataan Gang' of Americans were forming a bleak assessment of the antipodean army.★★

MacArthur persisted in presenting the Japanese land invasion as a sideshow, an irritating irrelevance, as if a junior demon had merely dared to spoil the handiwork of Zeus. The enemy would never succeed over the mountains.[2] Privately, MacArthur saw the enormity of what was happening, and not only to the Australian forces: the Japanese advance threatened his career. The flipside of MacArthur's self-aggrandisement was a gnawing

----

★ One soldier who survived the bombardment was Sergeant Morita Masura, of the 144th Regiment. He recalled being strafed as they walked along the ridgeline; he fell off one side of the ridge. Only eight of his 40-man unit survived the attack. He was captured later in the war, at Oivi, and imprisoned at Cowra, New South Wales. On his return to Japan, he became president of the Kochi New Guinea Association (whose reunions some veterans still refuse to attend because they disapprove of Morita's failure to commit suicide while in captivity).

★★ MacArthur's downplaying of the Japanese threat provoked a strong complaint from Rowell, who wrote to Landops on 6 September: 'ABC news broadcasts presumably with approval central censorship continue give completely misleading impression NG operations ... Forces here hearing broadcasts feel Australian public being hoodwinked ... and tend disbelieve all repeat all official announcements ... This eventually have most damaging effect on morale ...' (Landops, Vasey papers, 2/9). A 24-hour delay in communicating the fast-changing events was blamed. But the real reason for GHQ's press pantomime was that, 'MacArthur will not admit that any serious operations are going on in New Guinea' according to Lieutenant-Colonel Howard, press relations liaison officer at GHQ (McCarthy, p. 226).

preoccupation with personal failure. To be forced out of the Philippines only to lose Papua and New Guinea would cause irreparable damage to the American general's tightly coiled ambition.

Skilled at engineering a scapegoat, MacArthur latched onto the Australian officers. On 6 September, he told General George C. Marshall: 'The Australians have proved themselves unable to match the enemy in jungle fighting. Aggressive leadership is lacking.'[3]

In this judgment MacArthur cast a dangerous hostage to fortune. The withdrawal from Myola can be directly traced to errors beyond Potts's control: the catastrophic supply failure; the insistent denial of Japanese land invasion plans (despite Ultra's warning); the underestimation of enemy strength; and the gross ignorance of the terrain. This trail of incompetence led ultimately to GHQ in Brisbane.

The fall of Kokoda, Isurava and now Myola were admittedly disturbing, MacArthur allowed. From his perspective, the enemy seemed able to conquer at will. The mood at GHQ swung 'like a bloody barometer in a cyclone', quipped Major-General Vasey, as an element of panic gripped the command structure. MacArthur's press-release writing team were put on full alert.

'[GHQ] is like the militia — they need to be blooded,'[4] Vasey remarked. In Blamey's absence (on another interstate troop inspection), Vasey had the job of relaying MacArthur's concerns to Port Moresby. He did not relish the task; he and Rowell were old friends. Veterans of the Great War, the two Australian generals had fought three campaigns in the Middle East. They were bemused, to say the least, at the inexperienced Americans' handling of the situation.

That day Vasey signalled Rowell of the 'grave fear' felt by GHQ that the Japanese may capture the Port Moresby airfield. MacArthur 'feels that present withdrawal policy is wrong and I know it is against your instructions. He urges greater offensive actions against Japs.'[5] Rowell was instructed to 'energise combat action'.[6]

Amid his tentage on the scorched hills above Port Moresby, Rowell, commander of New Guinea Force, needed no such reminders. Nor did it help to be told that Potts's withdrawal technically went against orders. Rowell knew better than any in Brisbane the seriousness of the situation.[7] He was, after all, defending three fronts in Papua and New Guinea: at Milne Bay, in the Owen Stanleys, and at Lae–Salamaua.

While he insisted later that he never believed the Japanese would capture Port Moresby, the possibility they might get close to the Seven-Mile drome focused his mind. Rowell had the authority to order the destruction of Port Moresby, the airstrip and all unwanted supplies, and head for the hills, as it were, in the event the Japanese reached the coast. He dismissed such a course. He would not countenance a policy that conceded defeat in advance. He resolved, if the Japanese broke through, to 'drive [the enemy] back by offensive action ... the guns must be fought to the muzzle'.[8]

Brigade Hill is a natural citadel, apparently inviolable, at the summit of Mission Ridge, just south of Efogi. The summit and jungle-clad flanks command a strong defensive position. Seeing this, Potts installed his HQ below the knoll at the southern end of the summit, seemingly suspended in the clouds.[9] To the west is a steep, thickly forested slope, a near-cliff, the kind of natural barrier to which any commander might feel comfortable turning his back. Across the clearing, like the ancient sentinel of a forgotten creed, stood the ruin of a wooden shack that once housed a Christian mission.

Potts's troops were strung out ahead, between the summit and the ridge's north-facing foothills, overlooking old Efogi, a distance of about one mile or so along the track. The fresh 2/27th Battalion was at the vanguard, on the hills near the approaches to the enemy-held village.

Potts was in the habit of writing to his wife on the eve of battle. 'Sweetheart,' he addressed her on the 6th, 'Have I neglected you so very badly? ... Sorry I can't talk more ... but the main thing is I love you always ... Did I comment on the possibility of bringing back a grass skirt? Judy would look ripping in one, and so would her mother ... It rains every day ... with the little yellow devil being a perfect nuisance ...'[10]

He grabbed a few hours' fitful sleep. The guns were silent, and the clear night moonless and cool. The alpine air carried the smell of smoke and wet vegetation. Across the valley burned the fires of battle, bombed villages, and Japanese funeral pyres.

Well before dawn on the 8th, Cooper's troops above Efogi were on the alert for a powerful Japanese offensive. His men were destined for an especially nasty war. Already, he'd lost dozens in two days of fighting, during which they'd held off sporadic Japanese attacks by rolling grenades down the slopes: 'I don't know to this day how many thousands of grenades went down that hillside,' wrote Corporal Frank McLean, MM.[11] In fact, during those two days, the battalion had fired 100 rounds of ammunition per man and thrown 1200 grenades, almost exhausting their entire supply.

Grenading the enemy in the darkness was a precise business. The troops used grenades with seven-second fuses. They pulled the pins, counted to four, and then tossed them down the slope. The bombs were meant to explode at the bottom of the valley, after three seconds. It didn't always work out that way, said one soldier: 'It was like Russian Roulette in the dark hoping there weren't any four-second grenades among them.'[12]

All that night, they heard the Japanese chopping at the vegetation and yelling to each other in the valley below. Suddenly, just before dawn, five enemy companies charged up the hill towards the Australians. This tremendous barrage was, in fact, a diversion from Horii's real plan — another wide-flanking movement, this time, one of exceptional audacity.

It began the night before. At sunset on the 7th Horii had sent a company led by Lieutenant Sakomoto[13] on a wide encircling march to the west. At about midnight, the patrol were halfway up the apparently unassailable western slope to Brigade Hill — site of Potts's HQ — laden with a Juki heavy machine-gun. 'Started to climb a steep mountain which takes 11 hours. Detoured in order to come out at enemy's rear,' Sakomoto wrote. 'Slashed through the jungle aided by engineer Tai.'

Without seeing the terrain, it is hard to imagine what happened there. In sum, Sakomoto led about ninety men up a near 45-degree incline, with a machine-gun, through thick forest. It took them most of the night.

Brigade Hill: 5–9 September 1942

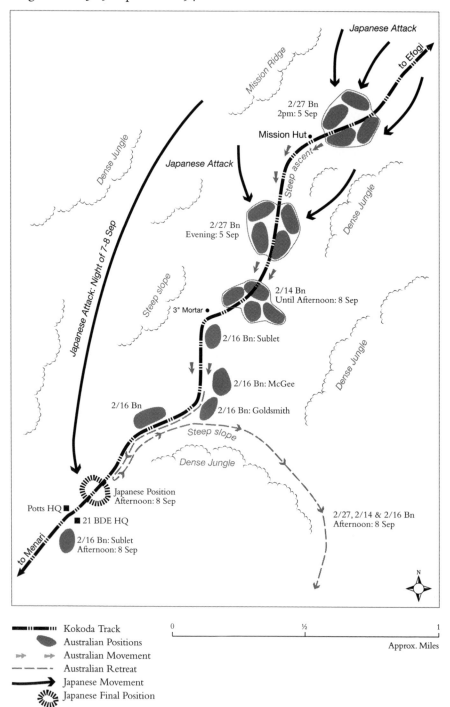

Japanese Attack

Mission Ridge

to Efogi

2/27 Bn
2pm: 5 Sep

Mission Hut

Steep ascent

Japanese Attack

Dense Jungle

2/27 Bn
Evening: 5 Sep

Dense Jungle

Japanese Attack: Night of 7-8 Sep

Steep slope

3" Mortar

2/14 Bn
Until Afternoon: 8 Sep

2/16 Bn: Sublet

2/16 Bn: McGee

2/16 Bn

2/16 Bn: Goldsmith

Dense Jungle

Steep slope

Dense Jungle

Japanese Position
Afternoon: 8 Sep

Potts HQ

21 BDE HQ

2/16 Bn: Sublet
Afternoon: 8 Sep

2/27, 2/14 & 2/16 Bn
Afternoon: 8 Sep

to Menari

N

Kokoda Track
Australian Positions
Australian Movement
Australian Retreat
Japanese Movement
Japanese Final Position

0   ½   1

Approx. Miles

Understandably it never occurred to Potts that an attack would come from this direction.

At 5.30 a.m., Sakomoto's men reached the summit. Potts was returning from the latrine — a pit dug on the far side of the clearing — when he heard a crack, and saw Private Gill, a sentry, slump forward with a bullet in the head. The sniper reportedly just missed the brigadier, who dashed back to his HQ. There was a moment of silence — then suddenly the Japanese were pouring over the threshold. They slammed their machine-gun into place on the summit, and attacked the Australians on both sides — the rear guard of the 2/16th Battalion to the north and Potts's HQ to the south.

A Dads' Army of Potts's staff — cooks, signallers, clerks and batmen, whose average age was over 30 — ran forward with revolvers, rifles and grenades, and fired at a range of fifteen yards. One officer rustled up a mortar, and fired it in a near-vertical trajectory.[14] But they were forced back by the intensity of the machine-gun fire.

Within moments, the Australian army was cut in half. Potts and his HQ were severed from their forward infantry. Hearing the fire behind them, the Australian rear companies rushed back down the track, and tried to break through the Japanese blockade. The attempt failed. 'They encircled us at Efogi in an area like that ... Well, you'd have to be a qualified mountain goat to be able to do physically what they did', said Private Bert Ward.[15]

A saving grace was that Potts's radio worked (though the Japanese had quickly slashed the telephone line to his forward troops). He alerted his battalion commanders to the encirclement; they ran back down the track. Potts guessed he was probably doomed, and issued what he thought would be his last order: in the event that the enemy 'wiped out' Brigade HQ, Albert Caro was to take charge, he said.[16]

Three Australian companies, led by Nye, Captain Douglas Goldsmith and Sublet, returned to Brigade Hill determined to breach the Japanese positions. Nye's men burst from the jungle straight into Sakomoto's machine-gunner, who had trained the weapon on the point where the track broke from the forest. The 'jungle seemed to vibrate hotly from the ... hail of machine-gun fire'.[17] Dozens of Australians fell dead across the grass. Further attacks were thought to be suicidal.

On the HQ side of the summit, Captain Bret Langridge, one of Potts's staff, volunteered to lead a counterattack. Knowing he was going to die, he handed in his identity disc and paybook. He then dashed out, and was shot in the chest within a few yards. As he fell to his knees, he 'yelled encouragement to his men'.[18]

The Australian army suddenly found itself sandwiched between Sakomoto's gun on the summit, and thousands of Japanese troops who were advancing along the track from Efogi. The Australians had two choices: to die in the enclosing vice, or pitch into the jungle. They chose the latter. Elements of three battalions — about 300 men — spilled down the eastern sides of Mission Ridge. The wounded were dragged and piggybacked into virgin rainforest. They included Private Kevin Tonkin, a golf coach from Western Australia. Tonkin was 'my saddest sight', said Blue Steward, the 2/16th Battalion's medical officer: 'He had a ghastly, gaping wound of the throat, and although my eyes could see only darkness and death, he saw light and hope. They were asking me something with all the mute urgency that eyes can convey ... the hardest thing is not to flinch from the gaze of the man you know is going to die.'[19] There was neither helicopter nor donkey to spirit Tonkin away. He was carried to safety on the shoulders of his mates, and died four days later on a stretcher, lost in unmapped country.

Seventy-five Australians died in the battles of Efogi and Brigade Hill that day. Japanese losses were 200 killed, and 150 wounded. 'Corpses were piled high ... it was a tragic sight,' wrote Sakomoto.[20] The last diary entry of company commander Lieutenant Noda noted hopefully: 'Death is a fate. It is no use being pessimistic.'[21]

Potts's fighting withdrawal had become a rout. The Australian troops were 'no longer of any importance as the vital ground in the defence of the brigade position had been captured,' said one battalion history.[22] Their supply and signal lines were severed, and their commander cut adrift from his troops. 'No orders from [Potts] could be received.'[23] No ammunition or rations could get through. The defeated battalions were, 'cut off without certainty of getting out at all'.[24] The lost troops embarked on a wide detour to the east in the hope of reuniting with their commander.

Private Bruce Steel Kingsbury VC, 2/14th Battalion, real estate agent. He was awarded the Victoria Cross posthumously for leading an extraordinary counter-attack at Isurava. He rushed forward, firing his gun from the hip through heavy machine-gun fire, and succeeded in saving the position.

Corporal John Alexander French VC, 2/9th Battalion, apprentice hairdresser. French won the Victoria Cross posthumously after he single-handedly silenced three Japanese machine guns at the battle of Milne Bay, thus saving his men's lives and clearing the path for the advance.

Kokoda War Cemetery, 1944: Signalman R. Williams tends the grave of Private Kingsbury. These graves (pictured) were later moved to the Bomana Cemetery outside Port Moresby. Kingsbury's VC was the first won on Australian territory.

The famous image of Private George 'Dick' Whittington being led by Raphael Oimbari along a track through the kunai grass towards a field hospital at Dobodura, northern Papua, on Christmas Day 1942. Whittington recovered from his wounds but died of scrub typhus at Port Moresby on 12 February 1943.

Up the steepest slopes, down precipitous descents, the fuzzy wuzzy angels bear their human cargo in stoic silence. They often became personally attached to the wounded troops, and deeply aggrieved when a soldier died in his stretcher.

The Japanese were not as well served by carriers, many of whom were press-ganged into service from Rabaul. On occasions, they had to shoulder their own men through awful conditions.

Australian troops of the 55th Battalion approach Milne Bay (below), regarded as the most malarial region on earth. It was here, in August 1942, that Australian troops fought in a battle marked by horrific war crimes.

The counter-offensive begins, October 1942: Generals MacArthur and Blamey break for tea near Owers' Corner after seeing the 16th Brigade march off in pursuit of the Japanese. It was MacArthur's first visit to New Guinea; he would later lie about the date he officially moved his HQ there. Neither man saw the conditions into which a few untrained Australian militiamen had been sent to confront several units of experienced Japanese troops.

The battered survivors of the 39th Battalion, being addressed by Honner after weeks of fighting on the Kokoda Track. The militia went to Papua derided as 'chocos' and cowards; they returned to Australia as genuine heroes. Their legend has withstood the harshest scrutiny.

September 1942: having winched it to the summit of Imita Ridge, the 14th Field Regiment, Royal Australian Artillery, fire their 25-pounder gun across the valley towards the retreating Japanese.

Troops of the Second Australian Imperial Force sharpen their bayonets before going into action against the Japanese in the Owen Stanleys. They were still wearing khaki uniforms — easily visible in the jungle — as late as September 1942. General Blamey refused to accept the argument that mottled jungle greens provided better camouflage.

A break during the counter-offensive: men of the 2/31st Battalion take a swim in the Brown River, between Nauro and Menari. It was their first wash for about five days, during the pursuit of the Japanese back over the mountains. The Bren gunner (at left) watches for any enemy stragglers who may still be in the area.

One of the first Japanese prisoners taken by the Australians in October 1942, found exhausted and starving near Nauro; he apparently received medical care, food and a stretcher. Others were not so lucky; very few prisoners were taken by either side.

An Australian officer tries to communicate with a Japanese prisoner captured in the Kokoda area. The flag is one given at a farewell party before the Japanese left for active service, and bears the signatures of friends who attended.

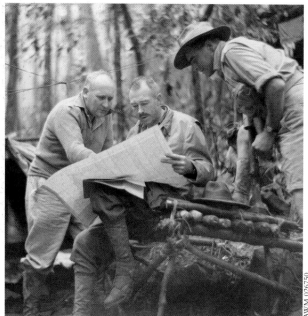

Major-General Arthur 'Tubby' Allen, commander of the 7th Australian Division (left) and Brigadier Ken Eather, commander of the 25th Australian Infantry Brigade (centre), plan an attack in deep jungle at a forward position on the track. Allen's counter-thrust was plagued by supply failures, largely the result of incompetence and negligence in Port Moresby and Brisbane.

Kokoda, November 1942: medical personnel make last-minute adjustments to ensure that a sick or wounded Australian soldier is secure for an air evacuation flight to Port Moresby. Colonel Frank Kingsley Norris stands to the left (with a hand on his helmet); Captain Geoffrey Vernon, the partially deaf medical officer who cared so much for the Papuan carriers, leans on a walking stick. The recapture of Kokoda meant the wounded could be airlifted safely to Port Moresby for the first time; until then, most were carried out on the backs of fuzzy wuzzy angels.

Meanwhile, Potts and his few surviving staff — plus some forty troops who had breached the Japanese positions — retreated down the trail to Menari, from where he sent a bleak message to Port Moresby (the telephone line was still linked south of Brigade Hill): '9 Sep: No communications with Battalions since attempted breakthroughs ... Attempt failed ... CARO previously instructed if BRIGADE HQ wiped out to assume command.'[25]

Back in Port Moresby Rowell was fully apprised of the catastrophe, and summed up his feelings in an intensely personal letter to his friend, Vasey: 'Today,' he wrote on 8 September, 'has been my blackest since we came ... Potts said yesterday "I intend to bash him here" ... yet he does nothing except get bottled up ... I have thought over my own position in the past few days ... I think I must have killed a black cat without knowing it. If I felt I'd mucked things up I would not hesitate to say so, but I feel any decisions I've made on major problems have been right & I've been knocked back by natural difficulties, by failures in leadership or fighting capacity or by a superior enemy ...'

Rowell could be murkily self-indulgent. Yet from the earliest he had consistently argued that Horii would not capture Port Moresby: 'I hope I'm not wrong this time in saying I'm confident the enemy has no hope of getting MORESBY from the North. His difficulties will now start and I trust we can get him on the rebound ...'[26]

The bad news went straight to the top. Vasey duly informed Blamey on the 9th that Potts's situation 'took most serious turn yesterday morning'. The Japanese had succeeded in planting themselves on the track between 'BATTALIONS and BRIGADES HQ'.[27]

Rowell readily imagined the groan issuing from Brisbane.

That evening, high in the Owen Stanleys, the Japanese hero of the day, Sakomoto, sat eating a plate of rice. It was the first time he'd eaten rice in three days, he wrote. He rested his triumphant troops at Brigade Hill, later dubbed Butcher's Hill, and at 4.20 a.m. the next day set off in pursuit of the Australian army, 'climbing breath-taking cliffs and wading through muddy swamps'.[28]

Chapter 24
Rout

'The tension, the excitement, the flow of adrenalin, all ebbed, and
I was not the only man to fall deeply into a great gulf of despair
and gloomy introspection'
— *Major Henry 'Blue' Steward, of the 2/16th Battalion*

His victory at Brigade Hill was General Horii's most decisive. The
Japanese soon controlled the Kokoda Track as far as Menari, with a
virtual free run to Ioribaiwa, 25 miles from Port Moresby. Their 'mastery of
movement' in the jungle was the key to Japanese success, wrote Wilmot: 'the
track is NOT of such tactical importance to the enemy as it is to us.'[1]

Yet Horii overreached himself. He pressed south for Port Moresby
heedless of the near collapse of his supply lines. Allied strafing, the desertion
of carriers, and the bombing of ships from Rabaul had wrought havoc with
the fragile human chain across the mountains.

Sheer bloody-mindedness, it seems, was one factor in the strange
psychological brew that drove Horii on. The losses at Isurava and Brigade
Hill would be avenged. The infernal Australians enraged the Japanese
commander, who sought their total destruction. '[Horii] wanted to be
forever rid of them. Their annihilation obsessed him.'[2] Nowhere down the

great swathe of conquest — in China, Thailand and Singapore — had the Japanese encountered such an impudent foe. Failure was unthinkable, and not only for the sake of the Emperor. A defeated commander was obliged to expiate his unit's disgrace with ritual suicide.

Horii pushed his men hard. They were ordered, 'to carry as large a quantity' of rice as possible.[3] Most had nearly exhausted their fourteen-day rations, and relied on abandoned, usually spoiled, Australian supplies and native crops. Dysentery was endemic. 'Port Moresby' — synonymous with food, shelter and victory — exerted a terrific hold on their minds. It was as if they could already smell the sea.

Menari is the prettiest of Papuan villages, standing between two mountain ranges on a relatively mild section of the track, just a few miles south of Brigade Hill. As Maroubra Force's walking wounded arrived here, their eyes lit up. Strewn on the village square were dumps of food, tobacco, boots, chocolate and clothing. Mountains of supplies suddenly appeared when they were least needed. The troops gorged themselves on the food lying about, 'making them all very happy ... and sending them [away] more cheerfully', observed Vernon.[4]

Suddenly this happy atmosphere soured. News of the disaster at Brigade Hill came in. The Japanese were bearing down in force, with Menari naked to the storm. In panic, some of the wounded took to the bush, in the hope of finding a safe route back to Port Moresby. They wandered for days, to be later retrieved 'in a state of colourful disorientation'.[5] It was a traumatic awakening for the stretcher cases, jerked onto the carriers' shoulders, and bundled off along the track.

In the forest east of Brigade Hill, meanwhile, hundreds of Australian troops cut off during the battle moved through virgin jungle in a wide arc towards Menari. The survivors of two battalions, the 2/14th and 2/16th — a mere 307 men — were the furthest south.[6] They used their bayonets as machetes, and that night stuffed luminous fungi into their belts as 'torches'. Their normally upbeat mood deserted them.

'After the battle of Butcher's Hill,' wrote Steward, 'a deep reaction set in. The tension, the excitement, the flow of adrenalin, all ebbed, and I was not the only man to fall deeply into a great gulf of despair and gloomy introspection. I was troubled not only by the memories of that awful day, but weighed down by premonitions of coming disaster: that we would never reach Menari; the Japs would get ahead and cut us off; that tomorrow would see the end of every one of us.'[7]

They reached Menari, where Potts awaited them, a day before the enemy, at 11.30 a.m. on 9 September. Virtually every man had dysentery, and many wore 'khaki kilts' — with the crotches cut out of their trousers. Their feet were monstrous curiosities: 'Smelly, soggy socks had to be cut from pulpy blotched flesh that was starting to disintegrate.'[8]

Scores, perhaps hundreds, were still missing, doomed to wander the jungle for weeks until one strange day a mob of wild-eyed, bearded cavemen would fall upon the pity of an Allied camp. 'All through the mountains were parties of stragglers making their painful, hungry way to friendly territory.'[9]

Ominously there was no sign of Cooper's 2/27th Battalion — the 'lost battalion' — which had been furthest north when Brigade Hill fell.

A farcical element — more catch-22 than Clausewitz — entered Potts's war. Orders with no connection to reality started coming in. One wire instructed him to establish a firm base and drive the Japanese back to Kokoda. He should contemplate no further withdrawals, it insisted.

'What firm base? I haven't got one here. I think they'd better send one up,' the exasperated brigadier told Major Geoffrey Lyon, who accompanied him back to Nauro. Of the 300 troops who reached Menari, none was fit enough to resist the 2500 to 3000 Japanese troops (allowing for losses due to sickness and battle casualties) then streaming down the track.

An air of surreality descended. Out of the blue Potts received a long, tedious signal requesting the prompt return of all expendable stores. Potts's response is unrecorded; a weaker commander would have been reduced to howling at the moon at this demand. It was as though no one had yet alerted the Australian supply depot to the fact that a war was being fought on the sides of mountains, in dense jungle. 'Expendable stores' (of which a substantial amount had to be abandoned at Menari) could simply not be got out.

Potts mucked in with the men on the journey back, and had some tragicomic encounters. On the trail to Nauro, he came across one Private Clarrie Maskiel, who was barely conscious, face down in the mud, with a shattered arm tied to his bayonet scabbard. After a dose of whisky, Maskiel stirred but wouldn't rise. Potts thought provocation the best medicine: 'If you weren't so yellow you'd do something to help yourself. You're yellow, Maskiel. And you're holding up your mates!' the brigadier yelled. Maskiel, so the anecdote goes, struggled to his feet, swung a weak punch at Potts, and walked. He reached Nauro as Patient No. 40.

Potts encountered Maskiel again — slumped by the track just before Ioribaiwa. Impressed, Potts ordered a stretcher for the wounded man. Maskiel was carried back to Uberi, where he attempted a second swing at the brigadier, lost his footing and collapsed.[10]

GHQ's extreme displeasure caught up with Potts at Nauro. The brigadier was told to report immediately to Generals Rowell and Allen in Port Moresby. You are being relieved, not replaced, Rowell insisted. Though sympathetic, the generals reckoned the severe strain was beginning to affect Potts's judgment. The poor man needed a rest.

The trigger was a blunt summary of the disaster at Brigade Hill by the liaison officer, Major Geoffrey Lyon. It stated, 'we have not sufficient troops to prevent outflanking ... troops from Port Moresby would have to fight into us'.[11] The message was the last straw for Port Moresby, not least because it had Potts's imprimatur.

Potts's temporary successor was the extraordinary Brigadier Selwyn Porter, who arrived at Nauro at noon on 10 September. Potts briefed him. The men were 'unfit for further operations', he said, and could endure no more.[12] Porter made his own mind up. He examined the exhausted line of sick, half-dressed men, stumbling along in a bleary-eyed daze. Many could barely walk. 'They hardly knew they were marching,' recalled Steward. 'Some had peculiar dreams or hallucinations. Others actually dropped into a doze, shuffling along in the line ...'[13]

The absence of potassium weakened the muscles and 'played a part in the mental confusion many of us experienced', the doctor advised. Medically speaking, he told Porter, the men 'had almost had it'. Porter decided instead that they were merely in a state of 'general demoralisation', a verdict deeply resented.[14] Whatever their condition, Porter realised he lacked the resources to defend Nauro — and continued the retreat (this could no longer be called a fighting withdrawal). On the 11th he organised his meagre force into a composite battalion of the 2/14th and 2/16th, and fell back to the Maguli Range.

As they neared Ioribaiwa, their spirits revived. The proximity of relief raised the battered Australian morale, and the few who were able to fight, did so. They turned and inflicted a series of deadly ambushes and assaults on their assailants. Potts's 'fighting withdrawal' flickered to life. The healthier troops picked off enemy scouts, and blunted the enemy advance, the evidence of which can be seen in the myriad dugouts between Ioribaiwa and Nauro. Occasionally, Japanese dressed in Australian uniforms tried to infiltrate the lines. A few sword-carrying suicide squads marched brazenly into Australian fire. The ambushes caught the exhausted Japanese off-guard.

In one example, Corporal Brian 'Bluey' Malone left tins of rations lying around as bait. When hungry Japanese approached, he opened fire.[15] British officers sent to learn 'jungle tactics' later asked Bluey, 'And tell me, corporal, how close do you let them get?' 'About six feet, sir. Any closer and the bastards'll fall on top of you.'[16] Corporal Bluey Malone was killed at Wewak.

Up ahead, rounding a bend in the trail at Uberi, the walking wounded beheld a strange vision in a jungle clearing, of smiling faces and roasting scones beneath a fluttering red shield. It was a canteen offering tea and cakes and cigarettes, emblazoned with the words 'Salvation Army'.

If this was a godsend, one man, Major Chaplain Albert Moore, was His most indefatigable messenger. When he got to Papua, neither the Red Cross nor the YMCA — which otherwise did a brilliant job — was able to get him a glass of water. Moore thought, 'I could see a grand opportunity here' for the Salvos.[17] He set up several canteens along the track, news of which passed from man to man, as Moore's diary describes: 'Monday Sept 7th, 1942: Rose early and got coffee etc ready, and from 8.30am a steady stream of wounded and sick came along, and were they delighted to see the …

Salvos on the job. Men arrive here in a state of utter exhaustion and move on revived.'[18] That day the Salvos' hut at Uberi served 39 stretcher cases.

Throughout September, Chaplain Moore achieved prodigious logistical feats. He mysteriously rustled up biscuits, tea and coffee from the ends of the supply lines, distributed thousands of sheets of writing paper, and baked hundreds of scones, with varying success. He served 4200 gallons of coffee during the whole campaign; his one-day record, 106 gallons.[19] He slept with a phone by his ear, in case of emergency, and his staff were on call 24 hours a day.

Moore closely observed the state of the troops as they came in. 'One fellow,' he wrote, 'weary, sick, all spirit sapped from his broken body, took the cup I offered him, sat on the track with his back against the embankment. His head drooped and ... the tears coursed down his cheeks.'[20]

Of the hundreds of stretcher cases who passed through his care, one soldier suffering from deep chest wounds stuck in Moore's mind: 'I could seem to hear the pulsating of his lungs through the wounds. The Natives who carried him camped alongside the wounded man ... In the morning I gave him a little nourishment, and as the Natives lifted him to their shoulders I put my hand on his and uttered a prayer ... He said to me, "You are worried about me Padre, don't worry, I will be OK."'[21]

'Never in my life', Moore later wrote, 'have I felt so compensated for service rendered.'[22]

Chapter 25
The Lost Battalion

'Whilst the [use of maggots] was uncomfortable in the extreme
for the patient, many men are alive today because of Captain
Viner-Smith's ingenuity'
— *The 2/27th Battalion history*

The last survivors of the withdrawal were Colonel Cooper's 'lost
battalion', the 2/27th. Cooper and 310 officers and men had been
forced off the track near Efogi, after the battle of Butcher's Hill. There were
46 wounded, of whom fourteen were stretcher cases.

A dearth of carriers made the retreat through enemy-held territory
painfully slow. Stretcher cases were carried over the steepest gradients along
human chains, but on the night of 11 September the last nineteen native
carriers abandoned the battalion. The troops then shouldered the wounded.
'Most were wounded in the stomach, neck or head,' wrote Corporal Frank
McLean. 'We lost about six on the trip; some we even carried for most of
the day, not even knowing until we stopped that they had died.'[1]

Heat and flies had turned the wounds gangrenous, and the battalion's
medical officer, Captain Keith Viner-Smith, devised an ingenious, if ghastly,
remedy: maggots were to be left in the wounds. The creatures preferred

rotting to healthy flesh, and flourished in gangrenous wounds. This saved several limbs from painful bush amputations — without anaesthetic, and with the likelihood of death from infection or blood loss. 'Whilst the [use of maggots] was uncomfortable in the extreme for the patient, many men are alive today because of Captain Viner-Smith's ingenuity,' records the battalion history.[2]

Cooper despaired at finding Menari and Nauro in Japanese hands. His troops were so hungry he thought of attacking for the sake of food. Between 5 and 21 September, each man had lived on one tin of bully beef and one emergency ration. Fortunately a patrol recovered a box of broken biscuits and dried fruit from an airdrop. The same day fortune smiled on them: they found two garden huts filled with fruit and vegetables; patrols filled their haversacks and went back to the wounded.

By 18 September, half the stretcher cases had died. Cooper decided to leave the survivors near a village garden several miles east of Nauro, and pressed on to Iawarere, where a runner had been sent to fetch help. On the 25th, after a week of solid walking, he and about three hundred men walked into the Allied camp at Iawarere, amid scenes of profound relief. The survivors had lost on average two stone each. Cooper immediately set in motion arrangements to bring out the wounded.

Earlier Corporal John Burns and Private Alf Zanker had volunteered to stay behind with the seven stretcher cases and nine walking wounded in the village garden. Their supplies were ten shell dressings, a bottle of morphia, a syringe and a garden of yams.[3] At the slightest noise Burns and Zanker stood to, their weapons raised, ready to defend this circle of helpless men.

These eighteen troops — two of whom were fit — remained in the jungle for three weeks, as related in Burns's diary:

> 0810 hours on September 19, 1942, found Private Zanker and myself in charge of the wounded ... Zanker and I built shelters to help protect the lads from the terrific heat and rain ...
>
> Wednesday 23rd ... Corporal Williams spent a terrible night and when Zanker and I had washed the lads we decided to put him on a new stretcher and put the first fresh dressings on his

wound. It was a terrific job but we succeeded in the end; both Zanker and I had a couple of blackouts during it.

Diarrhoea broke out . . . and we were lifting the poor lads for the next 24 hours without respite.

Friday dawned with a blazing hot sun and millions of flies. Again I spent the night with Corporal Williams and at 0800 hours he had a drink and at 0810 hours we found him dead. We immediately dug a grave [with] a tin hat and a machete . . . at 0930 we buried him with just a little prayer.

The 25th arrived . . . after what seemed the longest and hardest night of my life. Zanker and I managed about two hours' sleep, but the poor lads on the stretchers couldn't get off. Private Burke had taken a definite step towards the end . . . and lapsed into semi-consciousness . . . There was nothing we could do for him except a dose of morphia to put him out of agony . . . It took Zanker and I all our time to hold him on his stretcher when he started throwing himself around . . .'[4]

Private Burke endured a second day of convulsions. 'He was going through a living hell.' Mercifully, Burke died on the 28th, and they buried him alongside Williams.

By then the walking wounded felt strong enough to walk to Itiki, and paid a native guide ten shillings for his trouble. Burns and Zanker stayed with the five remaining stretcher cases. To pass the time Burns gave lectures on the 'finer points of baking' — he was a baker — and the men 'debated the merits' of the books of the New Testament.

On 2 October an Australian patrol found them — 'You have no idea,' Burns wrote, 'how the boys' spirits came to life' — and they were carried out on the shoulders of native carriers. This journey across the mountains took seven days.

A doctor accompanied them and food was available, and on 9 October — after a month in the jungle — Burns, Zanker and their five surviving stretcher cases were led into Subitana. The wounded were given a hot bath, pyjamas, and rushed to hospital; the 'hero bearers' received a huge meal. Burns and Zanker were awarded the Military Medal and Mentioned in Despatches.

Chapter 26
Ioribaiwa and Imita Ridge

'Never in my life, in the worst part of Gallipoli, or anywhere, had
I seen soldiers who looked so shocked and so tired and so utterly
weary as those men.'
— *Brigadier John Rogers, Australian director of military intelligence*

Anxiety in Brisbane fuelled the alarm in Canberra. The War Cabinet
sensed that something was rotten in Papua. Some ministers' electorates
were panicking at rumours of an imminent Japanese invasion.

The Advisory War Council, which included the Chiefs of Staff of the
Australian Army, Navy and Air Force, met on the morning of 9 September.
They referred unsmilingly to earlier ideas of the inviolability of the mountains.
Menzies recommended that MacArthur or Blamey be sent to Port Moresby, to
reassure the nation. Curtin replied that his Minister for the Army, Frank Forde,
had already proposed that Blamey be sent to confer with Rowell.[1]

Blamey's first visit to New Guinea on 12 September was a carefully
orchestrated event. That the Japanese were a mere 30 miles away on the
threshold of Ioribaiwa seemed not to trouble the Allied land commander.
His discussions with Rowell that day were wide-ranging and, by all
accounts, positive. Blamey agreed that the 39th should remain intact; the

53rd, however, should be merged with the 55th Battalion. On his return he would express his faith in Rowell and New Guinea Force.

There was one blot on proceedings, which said much about Blamey's breezy disinterest in his senior officers. Honner, commander of the 39th at Isurava, was told to report to the Allied land commander. He 'spruced himself up' and presented himself at Blamey's tent at the appointed time.

'Good morning, Honner,' said Blamey, glancing up casually, 'you've just arrived from Australia, have you?'

'No, sir,' said Honner, 'I've been in Papua for some time.'

Honner, who'd led the 39th at Isurava, never forgot the exchange, not least for what it said about Blamey's attitude: 'I'd been his commander of the Australian forces opposing the Japs. He didn't know who I was. He didn't know, he didn't care.'[2]

The next day Blamey held a press conference. Were jungle-green uniforms superior to the regulation khaki? Chester Wilmot wanted to know. 'They were not,' Blamey gruffly replied. 'The khaki had been designed in India as the ideal camouflage for the jungle.' The general added that 'this jungle' was 'no different from that of India', to which Wilmot offered to provide him with 'several thousand witnesses who thought otherwise'.[3]

Even as Blamey spoke, Australian troops were dyeing their khakis green or changing to green uniforms — within a week the 25th Brigade would go into battle in jungle greens.[4] Those who missed out on the new jungle greens stripped and dumped their khaki uniforms in large Sawyer stoves, then retrieved any uniform about their size, now mottled with green dye. The dyed uniforms were not ideal: they proved intolerably hot because the material couldn't breathe; the dye blocked the holes in the fabric.[5] American knee-length gaiters replaced the Australian web anklets. Steel helmets and sprigged boots would complete the picture. The slouch-hatted, baggy-shorted Anzac was slowly metamorphosing into an American-style combat trooper.

General Tubby Allen later summed up Blamey's colour blindness as 'a simple example of apathy, ignorance, and not the keenness to find out'.[6] Blamey flew back to Brisbane expressing himself pleased with the visit, and confident that the Japanese could be held and Moresby saved.

In September, Australian reinforcements poured into Alola, at the foothills of the Owen Stanleys. Four fresh battalions — three AIF units (of the 25th Brigade) and a militia battalion (the 3rd) arrived on 8 and 9 September. They found an 'atmosphere of desperate defeatism', and were regaled with terrible accounts of the enemy: 'Japs attack at night.' 'They crawl silently up to your position and bayonet you while you sleep.' 'They scream in the night yelling in English to "come and help me, Jack".' 'You can't see them until a bayonet is in your guts.' 'The jungle is a bloody nightmare, everything that moves turns out to be Japs trying to surround you.'[7]

'Never in all our war years,' Bill Crooks, a sergeant in the 25th Brigade, recalled, 'were we to hear such panicky versions of the usual soldiers' rumours and enlarged half-truths ...' He later discovered 'the stories were certainly based on facts, as we were to learn'.[8]

At midnight the new brigade assembled under their tent flies for a final briefing. A 'bombshell order' came: the troops were told not to attempt to rescue the wounded. The wounded were to be abandoned. Too many able-bodied men had been sacrificed in needless heroics rescuing the wounded — and the Japanese preyed on the Australians' determination to save their mates. So ran the explanation for this strongly resented instruction.

The order was 'a sickening one,' recalls Crooks. 'Whatever lay ahead we were prepared to face. But the ... information that [the] wounded would have to fend for themselves, received in the darkness of a tent at midnight, to men just awakened from their sleep, was shattering.'[9] Of 65 Australian Victoria Crosses won in World War I, thirteen went to troops who rescued the wounded under enemy fire. 'Now the men were told that if hit ... they would have to get back as best they could.'[10] It shredded the one insurance policy in the back of the soldier's mind: that his mates would help him if he fell. Years later, Crooks remembered that night as 'the low point of the war'.[11]

At 4.00 a.m. on the 9th the first units of the 25th Brigade boarded trucks bound for Owers' Corner and the Kokoda Track. They had two types of maps: one was 'an expanse of green colour, with blue rivers and black tracks' — even at this late stage, no contours or even heights were marked;[12]

the other, was simply a collection of 24 hand sketches, in which the officers were required to fill in information as they went along — a bit like a child's dot-to-dot puzzle. This was the extent of Allied intelligence about the track.

So another long line of Australian troops marched back into the Owen Stanleys.

The Japanese officers were in a gung-ho mood on 12 September, and readied their troops for the final rush down to the Coral Sea. Not all were convinced of the success of the mission. At 8.00 a.m., Sakomoto dryly recorded the facts, as he saw them: 'Arranged weapons, stored forage ... and prepared for an attack on Moresby. Information received: Enemy strength at Moresby — 20,000.'[13]

Three days later Horii, from his tent near Ioribaiwa, issued 'Operations Order A-115', his final invasion order. He observed that the Australians were 'in a state of utter confusion, and to a great degree have lost the will to fight'.[14] He set the advance on Port Moresby for 20 September. All units were to 'replenish fighting strength' in readiness for the thrust to the Coral Sea.

Privately Horii did not believe the attack would go ahead — at least, not until his supplies were replenished. He realised the war in Guadalcanal — the American marines had invaded — would deplete his resources; air support had been diverted to the Solomon Islands. A sense of being isolated, even abandoned, began to prey on Horii's mind. His men had reached the most southerly point of the Japanese Empire at great cost. Were they now to be forgotten? Would their lives be given in vain? Such questions consumed this proud, supremely stubborn man.

The fresh Australian troops merged with those pulling back, and the combined unit fought — in some confusion — the last confrontation of the Australian withdrawal. The formidable Brigadier Ken Eather, commander of the 25th Brigade, relieved Porter as temporary commander of Maroubra Force (Porter would continue to pop up and then fade from view throughout the campaign).

The battle for Ioribaiwa Ridge lasted from 13 to 16 September. The Australians set ambushes and booby traps on the northern approaches. Food was used as bait. Lieutenant-Colonel Alan Cameron reportedly ordered his men to spread bully beef on the banks of a creek. When some forty hungry Japanese warily tasted it, a barrage of Australian Bren guns opened fire from the surrounding grass; twenty Japanese died and the rest fled. Infuriated by these losses, the Japanese again hurled themselves at the Australians. They charged up the ridge through a torrential thunderstorm. Many died. A whole platoon was annihilated, wrote Sakomoto.

The survivors rushed between two Australian companies, and occupied the high ground to the east, a topographical feature that Eather's maps mysteriously failed to record.[15] From here they fired at will on the Australian positions lower down the slope, and drove the defenders off the ridge.

Porter was devastating in his criticism of the Australians on the eastern flank. In an echo of the 53rd's performance at Isurava, the fresh troops were literally caught without their weapons:

> 15 Sept: The ENEMY managed a 'breakthrough' between nearest high peak on R flank and the village ... the unit as a whole had NOT dug itself in efficiently ... the Commanding Officer had insisted on ... deeper slits ... At the time of the encounter, they were digging ... but their arms and equipment were out of reach and sentries were NOT observing from concealed positions — were NOT observing at all, in fact.
>
> The Jap stalked up to them; and, with a rush, positioned himself astride the ridge, between two coy positions ... untouched. At the same time, fire was brought to bear on the diggers, who could only seek the shelter of their slits — still out of reach of their weapons.[16]

The Japanese sustained heavy casualties, however: Lieutenant Hayashi of Shitai HQ later spoke of the 'tremendous litter of the dead' at Ioribaiwa. 'The stench ... is almost unendurable.'[17]

On the last day of the battle for Ioribaiwa a Japanese shell landed squarely on an Australian trench. The occupants were blown apart. The victims —

highly popular troops of Potts's unit — were within a day of relief. The display of open grief at the burial — soldiers wept and two fainted — suggested a severe weakening of the surviving army's composure.

The Australians were indeed showing signs of 'mental, nervous and physical breakdown', concluded the 2/14th Battalion historian.[18] The toughest soldiers had reached breaking point: normally extroverted men had grown 'withdrawn, morose and silent'.

One morning the 'hardest case' limped into Steward's tent and said he couldn't take any more. 'I told him to sit down and take a rest,' Steward recalled, 'and assured him that if he really felt he couldn't face it, then I would not send him back to duty with his platoon.'[19] Steward gently reminded the man that he'd stuck it out during the Syrian campaign, in the same state. Reassured, the soldier went back to his platoon by a circuitous route to avoid the shame of being noticed. He ran into troops of the new militia battalion coming up the track, one of whom nervously mistook him for the enemy, and threw a grenade. The soldier died of wounds a few days later.

With the loss of Ioribaiwa, Eather urgently requested permission to fall back to Imita Ridge. He explained that he needed a 'firm base for the start of my offensive, and it doesn't exist [at Ioribaiwa]'.[20] Eather's request stunned New Guinea Force HQ. Imita Ridge is the last razorback in the range before Port Moresby. Hadn't Eather just received a fresh brigade and a new militia battalion? Further reinforcements — the 16th Brigade — were on the way. Why the need for yet another withdrawal, demanded Rowell and Allen.

Eather, with Porter's assent, pressed the demand. He needed time, he repeated, and a firm base on which to consolidate his forces.

The last retreat to Imita had a deeply unsettling effect on Rowell. 'We are now so far back,' he told Tubby Allen, 'that any further withdrawal is out of the question and Eather must fight it out at all costs.'[21] Allen relayed the warning to Eather, adding: 'There won't be any withdrawal from the Imita position, Ken. You'll die there if necessary. You understand that?'

'Yes,' Eather said. 'I understand that.'

The Japanese troops scrambled onto Ioribaiwa Ridge, elated. Three weeks after landing in Papua the Imperial Army beheld the lights of Port Moresby and the distant sparkle of the moon on the Coral Sea. The sight elicited an emotional response: officers were reduced to tears and embraced. There were the usual *Banzai!*'s — 'Long Live the Emperor!'

'Gazing out from the summit [in daylight],' wrote Captain Nakahashi, of the 55th Mountain Artillery,

> ... there was not even one mountain to obstruct our range of vision. A dense, overgrown ... forest, rising and falling like ripples on the water, and far off one was able to see, as the sun's rays came through a break in the clouds a glitter and a sparkle, without doubt it was the sea! Over there was Port Moresby, the object of our invasion, which had become an obsession. Officers and men alike embraced one another overcome by emotion.[22]

Of the Nankai Shitai's 6000 combat troops, only 1500 — at most — remained. At least half had withdrawn sick or wounded. Some were missing and more than 1000 were dead. Japanese sources place the losses far higher. During his three-week slog over the mountains, Horii lost 80 per cent of his fighting force, according to the incisive war correspondent Okada Seizo, whose hatred of the war perhaps rendered him prone to exaggeration.[23] (Certainly, by the end of the Papuan campaign, total Japanese losses approached 95 per cent.)

'The line of captured positions more than atones for their blood,' wrote a defiant Nakahashi. 'They will never be able to gaze on this splendid spectacle ... At night we are able to see the lights of Port Moresby, and the beam of the searchlight of Seven Mile Airfield on the outskirts.'[24]

The sight fixated them, held their attention as though it were a place of mystical splendour, an El Dorado whose long-sought treasures were not jewels and doubloons, but plentiful supplies of food. The front-line troops clung to one idea: 'Victory meant food.' Private Uehara Tetsunosuke shared the general hope that if they fought for another two or three days they could fill their stomachs to their hearts' content.

The troops' self-confidence, for a brief while, overrode their pangs of hunger. They were within sight of their goal and for a time, their faith in victory seemed to rise in inverse proportion to the extremity of their condition. The sick and wounded were carried forward in the vain hope they would get food and medical aid at Moresby — just as the Australian patients, lying at Alola, had hoped that the recapture of Kokoda would save them.[25]

As always, the ordinary troops were utterly unaware of the higher designs that lay in store for them. The state of Japanese food supplies was dire. Horii had cut the daily rice ration to 150 grams per man during September, in order to stretch his dwindling reserves.[26]

Horii, meanwhile, knew of the imminent order to withdraw, but as yet gave no indication to his men, who worked day and night on near empty stomachs to fortify the position. This was their first real rest since Isurava; but many were impatient for the green light to advance on the shimmering stronghold in the distance.

They dug in on the summit of Ioribaiwa. Despite their hunger, their talent for field engineering had not deserted them. They built air raid trenches, camouflaged their tents and dug latrines. They erected a low fence, and excavated and timbered a connecting network of weapon pits. Fields of fire were cleared, and guns positioned all along the ridge.

The Australian withdrawal to Imita Ridge provoked panic in Port Moresby. Comparisons with Singapore plagued the town, and many 'timid souls' contemplated evacuation. Some Australian and American servicemen planned to escape along the coast to Daru, the closest town to the Australian mainland. The journey would have killed them: Daru lies beyond the vast swamp of the Fly River Delta.

Stronger constitutions were ready to fight for Moresby. They need not have bothered: senior commanders rightly believed that the Japanese were an almost spent force. Australian reinforcements were pouring into Port Moresby, and heavy artillery was being winched up the Golden Stairs to Imita's summit.

Mobilising his counteroffensive was Rowell's top priority; the furthest thing from his mind was capitulation. He had growing concerns for his career, too — and desperately needed good news. 'Our heads will be in the basket over this, Tubby,' he told the commander of the 7th Division, when he learned of the pull-back to Imita.[27]

Eather hunkered down on the last razorback, a mere 25 miles from Port Moresby. By 16 September his fresh brigade had fully relieved Potts's battalions. His officers were told they must defeat the enemy here, or die.

Brigadier Eather was a tough, composed man of immense fortitude. He was also a curiously lateral thinker, exemplified by an odd exchange at the height of the emergency. Vernon happened to be passing through Imita 'on the way home'. He was summoned to the brigadier's shelter, a mere strip of canvas 'stretched over a boulder in a sea of mud'.[28] Eather asked the elderly medic, 'How do you think we ought to reward the carriers after the war?' Vernon was taken aback. 'The end of the war,' he thought, 'seemed so remote that all I could think of saying ... was, "Give them all the food and smokes they could wish for ..."'[29]

Potts returned to Port Moresby to an atmosphere of simulated cordiality. Some plainly treated him as an ignominious failure, and his men were to share this odium. Potts wouldn't hear a word said against them in his round of top-level debriefings, from which he emerged as the convenient scapegoat for a layer of incompetents, seat-warmers, and seasoned backstabbers. It suited few people actually to defend Potts, or to inquire too deeply into the true circumstances of his withdrawal. The brigadier was, in some circles, deemed untouchable.

He needed calming down when he arrived at Port Moresby on 11 September. Generals Rowell and Tubby Allen withheld judgment — the brigadier had had 'a very gruelling time'. They desired to hear him out 'before condemning'.[30]

Others rushed in to judge him. Over lunch MacArthur's engineer-in-chief, Major-General Pat Casey, hectored Potts about the withdrawal. Rowell leapt to Potts's defence: 'I thought it injudicious of [Casey] to be needling Potts and ... I asked Casey whose bright idea it was to blow up the mountain. He said "it was mine".'[31]

The next day Potts was summoned for a debriefing at 7th Division HQ, in Bisiatabu.[32] It was a searching interview. Rowell and Allen grilled him about tactics, supplies, and relative army strengths. Potts unburdened himself of his grievances: the lack of a reserve force, the supply failure at Myola; the absence of Vickers machine-guns; the air force's refusal or inability to evacuate the wounded; the 53rd Battalion's weakness. Any criticism of the rest of the troops 'stung him fiercely'.[33]

'I don't know the bastard who sent the 53rd up the track,' Potts reportedly said.[34] Rowell, who did know the bastard, chose to ignore this implied criticism. Potts continued, 'There's no better way of killing men in large numbers than sending raw and undisciplined troops to fight a jungle war against troops of seven years' experience.'[35] He dismissed any suggestion that the armies were numerically matched (MacArthur still thought the Australians outnumbered the Japanese). 'My own estimate is that we had about five-to-one against us, and the number killed is four-to-one in our favour.'[36]

The two generals were sympathetic. They admired Potts's tenacity under the most trying conditions. Rowell recommended that he be returned to his brigade. The Japanese army's greater numbers, better camouflage and higher standard of jungle training were the causes of the Australian withdrawal, not Potts, he noted (tactfully avoiding the supply disaster, for which he accepted technical responsibility).[37] Tubby Allen later observed that Potts had 'saved Port Moresby from invasion by forces superior in number and had prevented the catastrophe nearly brought about by the neglect of New Guinea by the authorities ...'[38]

Sir Keith Murdoch in his influential newspaper column echoed these sentiments. The media baron refused 'utterly to accept any easy explanation of the Kokoda disaster. [No] slur shall be cast upon the men who fought there or upon their battalion officers. Of course some failed; but they were NOT the cause of the great failure.'[39]

Nobody in MacArthur's office shared these generous verdicts.

Blamey seemed coolly unperturbed by the crisis in the mountains. He barged around Landops in ebullient mood. He had repeatedly expressed confidence in Rowell — on his visit there on 12 September, in a national broadcast on the 15th, and again on the 17th, when he told the Advisory War Council that the Japanese 'would not be able to take Port Moresby from the land'.[40]

Yet Blamey was privately vexed. On the 16th he got alarming news of the retreat to Imita Ridge. Rowell, guessing how this would be received, explained that Potts's replacement, Brigadier Ken Eather, needed time to consolidate his force at Imita Ridge. Rowell added emphatically: 'I had NO repeat NO alternative but to confirm [the decision to withdraw].'[41]

Despite this disastrous news, Blamey remained sanguine. On the 17th he deluged the War Council with details of progress: for the first time, the Australians outnumbered the enemy; the 25th Brigade was deployed; the 16th Brigade was on its way, as well as two squadrons of light tanks, three field regiments, a mountain battery and one horse transport unit. The supply advantage had shifted overwhelmingly to the Allies. No more nonsense about unassailable mountains: here were raw military facts that should have persuaded everyone of Allied supremacy.

The War Council was not persuaded. Their ignorance of the campaign was profound. Forde, the Minister for the Army, believed the Japanese could still capture Port Moresby. Billy Hughes demanded to know why the Japanese did not appear to have the same supply problems. Others wondered why the Allies had failed to take the fight to the Japanese.

With silken emphasis, Blamey gently explained that when he'd returned to Australia in March the only troops at the nation's disposal were untrained militia. It was a deftly delivered self-acquittal, tinged with the subtlest suggestion that the home forces, and by definition the Government, were to blame for a crisis not of his making.[42]

MacArthur's GHQ had become a lightning rod for ill tidings. News of the withdrawal to Imita shocked his staff. General Kenney warned on his return from a visit to Port Moresby that the town would be lost, and that Rowell's attitude was 'defeatist'. MacArthur was apoplectic — and, as usual, sought someone to blame.

The supreme commander told a disturbed Curtin by secraphone that he'd lost confidence in the Australian command and the Australian troops. They lacked efficiency. The fresh troops were 'only two days out from Port Moresby ... the Japanese have the same troubles as our troops, but they are not withdrawing'.[43] He decided American troops could do a better job, and ordered their dispatch to New Guinea by air or by sea.

MacArthur invoked the spectre of Singapore. If the Japanese advance continued, the Allied defensive 'would duplicate the situation of Malaya'.[44] Or the Philippines? MacArthur confronted the memory and, with his unerring nose for a scapegoat, quickly found another. He recommended that Blamey, as Commander-in-Chief of Allied Land Forces, be sent to Port Moresby to 'energise the situation'.

The survivors of the 21st Brigade reached Koitaki in the last week of September. Those who saw the line of men enter camp never forgot the sight. Brigadier John Rogers, Blamey's director of military intelligence, observed: 'Never in my life, in the worst part of Gallipoli, or anywhere, had I seen soldiers who looked so shocked and so tired and so utterly weary as those men.'[45]

Potts's men were somehow set apart from their fellow troops. Their condition was shocking; many looked stupefied, with the 'bulkhead stare' of stunned infantry. They were dimly conscious of failure. They'd neither recaptured Kokoda, nor held the track between Isurava and Ioribaiwa. Most humiliatingly, the Japanese had driven them into the jungle at Brigade Hill.

Yet they'd successfully delayed a far bigger army, fatally thwarted its advance and inflicted far more casualties, perhaps three times as many. They'd fought a brilliant withdrawal between Eora Creek and Efogi, and rallied towards the end with a series of attacking patrols that punctured Japanese morale. Horii had planned to capture Port Moresby by the first week of September. It was now the 19th; and the Japanese had lost most of their men — either killed, wounded or sick. His army, now abysmally resourced, tottered at the end of a 150-mile supply line.

On 3 October the health of the Australian survivors was examined, to assess when they would be fit for combat again. Of 295 survivors of the 2/14th and 2/16th battalions, 189 would be 'fit in one week', the medical report said. These men were diagnosed with 'Avitaminosis ... including oedema of the legs, neuritis and loss of sensation ... feelings of lassitude and breathlessness ... cases of glossitis and dyspepsia ... a number of cases complaining of arthritic pains in the knees ... dyspepsia is very widespread ...' Sixty-two men were classed as 'permanently unfit for operations over mountain country'. Of these, 22 were over 35 years old. 'A number of cases had already "cracked up" when sent out on patrol ...' the report concluded.[46]

Chapter 27
Press

'[Doug's communiqués] bewilder the public by making it
impossible for them to reconcile such a series of crushing
victories'
— *Sir Keith Murdoch and Warwick Fairfax, in a letter to Curtin*

Days before Blamey left for Port Moresby, the international press reports
were as hysterical as they were inaccurate. Their confusion did not
help the mood of defeatism. No paper reported the true state of the Japanese
and their near-exhausted supply lines at Ioribaiwa; no paper found anything
to praise about Potts's delaying tactics.[1] On the contrary, 'Another Singapore'
was about to engulf Port Moresby. The American newspapers suggested that
Australian troops were to blame for the likely fall of Port Moresby, and that
only American reinforcements could save the day.

A *New York Times* editorial (22 September) warned that the Kokoda
campaign bore a disquieting resemblance to the disastrous defence of
Malaya; that the Japanese, without risking a battle, had driven the Australians
back. *The Herald Tribune* (22 September) criticised the leadership of the
Australians, who were forced to surrender their positions in the Owen
Stanley Ranges. The article concluded that the troops lacked adaptability —

and no explanation would excuse the loss of Moresby. Earlier, the *Chicago Daily Tribune* (11 September) said the Australian soldier had been driven back by an enemy with fewer advantages, and that American reinforcements were needed. A leading column in the *Washington Post* (19 September) reported the crisis in the Owen Stanleys under the headline, 'Another Malaya'.

A trawl through Australian newspapers suggests that civilian Australia lived in fear and ignorance. When in doubt — as they so often were — the Australian press exaggerated the danger to the Australian mainland. Or they underplayed the fighting conditions. Little of the true horror of this war permeated the public mind. Hugh Dash of the *Daily Telegraph* described the withdrawal as 'Lilliputian ... the fighting has never exceeded the limits of sniping duels and patrol ambushing'.[2] This was a direct echo of MacArthur's communiqué. The victory at Milne Bay was trumpeted; but a smokescreen hung over the war along the Kokoda Track. Not for years would the Australian public learn the truth.

There was no television, of course. Censorship laws of almost totalitarian severity throttled the local press. In September, the Japanese were 25 miles from Port Moresby, yet most Australians went about their lives in sanguine ignorance. Very little news — and only that of a vague and dream-like quality — survived the censors' pen.

Osmar White, Chester Wilmot and other correspondents reported as accurately and bravely as they were able (after the war, White wrote a brilliant memoir). They were at the front line briefly — and none witnessed the battles of Isurava or Brigade Hill. Nobody outside a closed military circle saw Wilmot's series of blistering critiques. Damien Parer and George Silk, the officially approved photojournalists (and the only two photographers on the track) took superb sequences of footage and film, which were subject to intense scrutiny by censors. Their brilliant imagery was sanitised; the bodies of dead Australians were excised from Silk's harrowing photographs.

A glimpse of the spectacular cock-ups, the breathtaking incompetence, the squalid treatment of the militia and the sheer horror of this war would await the correspondent Raymond Paull's *Retreat From Kokoda* in 1958, a well-written, deeply partisan treatment (and thinly disguised apology for Rowell). Dudley McCarthy's encyclopaedic official history, *South-West Pacific*

Area — First Year, appeared a year later. Blamey commissioned his own brief pamphlet, *The Jap Was Thrashed,* a self-celebration cobbled together by his PR team. David Horner exposed the breakdown in command in his magisterial *Crisis of Command* (1978) and in *High Command* (1982). Many battalion histories appeared, but they tended to be privately published and thinly circulated among families. Not until Peter Brune published *Those Ragged Bloody Heroes* in 1991 did Australians hear a word from the ordinary soldier about his experiences.

MacArthur bludgeoned the first casualty of war beyond recognition. The Australian civilian's notion of Kokoda groped about the dimly lit world of 'Doug's Communiqués'. The Allied supreme commander decreed in May 1942 that war correspondents must write only what his daily summaries contained. They were reduced to the supreme commander's copy boys. All articles passed through two censors, one in New Guinea and one in Australia. Criticism of commanders, any speculation, unauthorised photos, and even hostile cartoons, were banned. These conditions did not apply in Britain and America; only the Australian Government acquiesced.

Doug's communiqués usually stated that 'Allied' or 'American' soldiers were doing the fighting, when in fact no American soldier saw combat until mid-November. Battles fought entirely by Australians were Allied even when only a few American engineers were present in the rear. The battles of Isurava, Brigade Hill and Ioribaiwa were described as mere patrol skirmishes. MacArthur would not dignify the Japanese advance as a land invasion, so little had he credited its chance of success. The truth ran a distant second to the importance of preserving MacArthur's reputation.[3] His press officers had mastered the art of spin long before the grubby practice reached its apotheosis in the early twenty-first century.

Australia's media laws were so strict that Captain Henry Steel, an army public relations officer based in Townsville, took the unprecedented step of complaining on the journalists' behalf. He protested that his office was superfluous under such a regime. With extraordinary effrontery he told Blamey that the censorship regime had 'decimated' the media's efforts to present an honest picture of war: 'No correspondent is serving the vital function he is supposed to be, by simply repainting the daily communiqué. If his activity is to be limited to that, there is no need for his presence here.'[4]

In disgust, foreign correspondents left the country, to work in comparatively liberal America and Britain. Irvine Douglas, London editor of the Australian Associated Press, described Australian censorship as 'the most dangerous in the world, outside the Axis countries' — a rather disturbing irony. Australian censors had 'poisoned' the outlook of foreign reporters to the Allied war effort. 'Australia's name has suffered very badly,' he wrote.[5]

'The fact is it is useless our writing anything,' remarked an exasperated *Melbourne Herald* journalist, on his return from New Guinea, 'unless it conforms to the communiqué though the communiqué be false.'[6]

Reports were held up for days or weeks, and stamped, 'To await release with appropriate communiqué'.

Furious editors wrote to their readers in self-exculpatory tones: 'MacArthur should tell America — and us!' thundered the *Daily Telegraph* (7 August 1942): 'The Australian people are perplexed,' it said, 'because the meagre and platitudinous communiqué tells so little.'

Again, on 10 September, the paper railed at the censorship regime: 'Thoughtful people feel that something important is pending or happening. Communiqués, which give the impression the fighting is confined to small patrols, do not ... put the facts adequately ... All the signs suggest that the enemy is developing a big operation against Port Moresby ...'[7]

A fortnight later one of Doug's communiqués contradicted the paper. The editor was ropeable: 'One week [Australians] are told that the Owen Stanley Range is impassable. The next week they learn that the Japanese have crossed the range'. His readers, he mourned, were very upset at such 'inconsistency between prophecy and fact'.[8]

This frustrating situation drove editors mad. Some decided to take political action. A furious Ralph Simmonds, editor of the *Herald*, pleaded with John Curtin several times between August 1942 and June 1944 for the right to send photographers to film the war.[9]

Only Damien Parer and George Silk — the brilliant, if heavily censored, official photographers — were allowed in the combat zone. The

Government upheld the ban, sniffily concluding: 'Press photographers concern themselves with subjects of transitory importance, which are likely to win popular appeal, while Official War Correspondents ... are imbued with the necessity of building up a permanent pictorial record of war ... preserved for posterity in the Australian War Memorial.' This was mere obfuscation — and arrant nonsense.[10]

Heavyweight media identities entered the fray. Warwick Fairfax Snr, managing director of the *Sydney Morning Herald*, and Sir Keith Murdoch, press baron and former government censor, sent a list of heated demands to the Prime Minister on behalf of the Press Advisory Committee. They called for an end to the disastrous 'cumulative effect' of communiqués that led the public further from the truth, day after day, week after week. 'They bewilder the public by making it impossible for them to reconcile such a series of crushing victories.' Murdoch and Fairfax insisted that criticism of the war was 'a fundamental democratic right'.[11]

The concerns of the press barons were ignored — even criticism of the censorship laws was censored. A cartoon in *Smith's Weekly* — depicting the shocked reaction of members of a gentlemen's club who had just learnt of Australian Federation — was disallowed. 'This ... can only be ascribed to a humourless and pedantic outlook, such as [we] would not have expected to find outside Germany or Japan', said Fairfax and Murdoch.[12]

Curtin was unmoved. He supported the generals' wishes to ban 'blanket speculation': a catch-all phrase that pretty much outlawed any reporting of the war, if the censors so wished.[13] It was a shameful resort to totalitarian press control.

One voice calling for more media openness came from an unusual quarter: Curtin's own Minister for the Army, Frank Forde. After his return from New Guinea, Forde couldn't help noticing the distortion of the news: 'One of the outstanding conclusions of my visit,' he mused, 'is the lack of really authentic news ... I have no hesitation in stating that an incorrect impression has been created in the minds of the public in Australia'. No doubt he also observed that the white things in the sky were clouds.

Forde proposed to remedy the situation. He recommended the appointment of an official government reporter of the calibre of Charles

Bean (the legendary Australian World War I correspondent and historian). Blamey contemptuously slapped down the idea, thereby underlining the powerlessness of the Minister for the Army in times of war.[14]

Ironically, the Government itself was left in the dark. MacArthur's censorship regime had in fact frozen out the chief censor and therefore the Australian Government — from access to the truth, a sign of how far the generals controlled the dissemination of news: 'The Government has been considerably embarrassed,' Forde wired Blamey, 'by the absence of reliable news from the battle fronts apart from your official communiqués.'[15] No reports on the land operations had reached the War Cabinet, the Prime Minister observed on 14 October. Curtin, like the nation's newsmen, was at times dangerously out of the loop.

Forde was told to act. But how? Australia's Minister for the Army didn't exactly thirst for facts about his army. A fortnight later, in no apparent hurry, Forde wrote a meek letter to Blamey. It revealed the staggering ignorance of the War Cabinet about the state of Australia's troops: '...it would be appreciated,' Forde pleaded, 'if you could furnish me with your advice as to the possibility of supplying all periodical despatches, say weekly, of the progress of [the war in New Guinea].'[16]

The Japanese press were tightly controlled, with threats of automatic gaol sentences and closure of newspapers to those who transgressed. The staggering irony was that totalitarian Japan did have a war correspondent at the front lines: the brilliant reporter and closet pacifist Okada Seizo. Okada slogged over the mountains — 'embedded' is not the word — with Horii's troops right into the combat zones. He walked over Brigade Hill and reached Ioribaiwa.

Okada's dispatches were heavily censored, of course, but later he wrote an unsparing account of the collapse of the Japanese army, called *Lost Troops*.[17] Here is what he said of the state of the Japanese army as they approached Ioribaiwa:

We had lost a considerable portion of the troops wounded or killed in action. Besides, a growing number of men were suffering from malaria, colonitis, weakness of eyesight amounting to night blindness, pneumonia and other fevers of undetermined causes, nervous breakdown, diet deficiency diseases, fainting — illnesses brought about by insufficient supplies ... extreme shortage of food, exhausting march ... and other indescribable hardships under which we had been marching along.[18]

Okada despised militarism, and said so out loud during his interview with Benson, when the missionary was imprisoned at Buna (at first Benson assumed this was a trick, then realised Okada was sincere).

It is safe to assume that had Okada been an Australian reporter, his accreditation would have been promptly denied. Indeed, in their effect on news availability, Japanese censorship rules did not differ much from those in Australia. The citizens of both countries were utterly ignorant. The only real distinction lay in the fact that a Japanese editor faced harsher punishment than his Australian counterpart — possibly several years in gaol — for a breach.

The Japanese censors banned troops from writing in combat zones. The army virtually dictated the few postcards that got through. The Japanese soldier was not allowed to mention anything that suggested his location, including 'climate conditions, lack of food, use of terms such as "coconuts" and "natives"'. He was permitted to write: '(a) Am fighting south of the Equator. (b) The enemy is weak. (c) Am fighting fiercely. (d) Living under conditions similar to those of the regular residents. (e) Am safe and happy.'[19]

In any case, most troops conformed willingly. Exultant Emperor worship was a common theme of letters home: 'I shall smilingly undertake the Emperor's great mission. Long Live the Emperor!' and 'The sacred souls of my dear comrades who died became the hallowed guardians of the country ...'[20]

In a twist of the knife into the demoralised army, the regime refused to allow the soldiers' families to write to them, except under very strict circumstances. 'No mail from home. Why don't letters come?' wrote one soldier at Ioribaiwa. 'I have the right to receive mail from the homeland. I've written home but not a single reply!'

Most soldiers received nothing for more than a year, and letters tended to arrive months old, torn and opened. 'Received postcard and did not recollect the sender's name,' remarked one soldier in Papua on reading his mail.[21]

A remarkable letter by a twelve-year-old girl to her brother did reach him at Buna on 15 October. The little girl wrote:

> In the place, where you are now there will be plenty of
> pineapples, bananas, coconuts and other fruits, I think. I want to
> go and see the South Seas myself sometime. Our teacher always
> says to us ... that we must study well so that we can all go South
> to teach when we have grown up. Where you are, there will be
> not only various kinds of fruits, but also various kinds of animals,
> I think. What kinds of animals are there?[22]

Chapter 28
Blamey and Rowell

'Moresby is going to fall. Send Blamey up there and let him fall
with it!'
— *John Beasley, Minister for Supply, Australian Government*

In Blamey, MacArthur had found his 'biggest scapegoat'.[1] The supreme
commander resolved to shoehorn the only Australian general on his staff into
the most politically dangerous job in the war: commander of New Guinea
Force. Blamey would be released into the wild at a critical moment: if he
succeeded, MacArthur would bask in the accolades of an inspired appointment;
if Blamey failed, Blamey would get the blame. There can be few less edifying
examples of powerful old men worrying about their reputations and careers,
while the nation's youth were giving their lives in battle.*

The Australian Labor Government dutifully acquiesced. Curtin's Cabinet
displayed an embarrassing strain of sycophancy towards the American
commander. There were several toe-curling examples. One Australian minister

---

* In one of the richer ironies of the war, MacArthur let it be known that he, in fact, had gone to Port
Moresby at this time, in a book written by his staff members. In fact, MacArthur first set foot in New
Guinea on 6 November, and only with great reluctance. He never once visited the front line. (See
McCarthy p. 235.)

drooled over 'this best-dressed and most handsome military leader I'd ever seen', in whom there was such confidence that 'we should comply with what MacArthur requested in the special circumstances'.[2] John Dedman, Minister for War Organisation, described MacArthur as 'one of the greatest generals thrown up in WW2'.[3] The general's charm captured Curtin, too, though the Prime Minister's willingness to suspend disbelief at least had the honourable intention of securing the American lifeline to Australia.

The decision to send Blamey to Port Moresby was well received. MacArthur explained that the Allied land commander should be in the vicinity of the main land offensive, since the decisive US victory at the Battle of Midway had removed any naval threat to Australia. The idea impressed the War Council: one cabinet minister later unwittingly echoed MacArthur's own personal insurance policy: 'Moresby is going to fall. Send Blamey up there and let him fall with it!'[4]

The job was a poisoned chalice, and this explained the politicians' glee. Many in the Labor Party — with the notable exception of Curtin — despised Blamey, whom they viewed as an oafish conservative, the lapdog of the Right. The Blamey haters derived a perverse pleasure from holding Blamey against the blowtorch of defeat.

His political antennae on alert, Blamey saw he was entering an extremely volatile and dangerous situation. The Allied land commander obviously knew that Macarthur had set him up as a scapegoat. There was tremendous backpressure on Blamey, explained historian Lex McAulay.[5] His career was in great danger.

Blamey didn't believe he was necessary in Port Moresby. He dismissed Canberra's eagerness to fall in with MacArthur's knee-jerk demands, in three words: 'Canberra's lost it.'[6] And initially he dragged his feet. Curtin was reduced to threats — 'if you value your position!' — to get him on the plane. The Allied land commander departed the next day, 23 September, 'to take personal command' of New Guinea Force.[7]

None except Blamey foresaw the real ramifications of his new appointment: the private impact it would have on the proud, prickly Rowell. And as he flew over the Coral Sea he reflected on their bitter past relations, notably in Greece. The scene was set for a supremely ugly clash of the generals.

Blamey landed in New Guinea, cornered and dangerous. In Australia, baying members of the War Council and jumpy American commanders relished the prospect of his demise; there, the exhausted, irate Rowell, commander of New Guinea Force, deeply resented his second coming.

'[Blamey's] every move is watched,' William Dunstan, VC, general manager of the Melbourne *Herald*, warned Rowell. 'He had made ... statements which neither the Cabinet nor the public will swallow.'[8]

Curtin was unaware of the military repercussions of confirming Blamey's appointment (and later acknowledged his own naivety). As he saw it, he was giving Blamey a last chance to redeem the Australian army and save Port Moresby. In so doing, the Prime Minister unwittingly helped to ignite a titanic confrontation between two of Australia's most important soldiers — at a time of grave military crisis.

With baying politicians and the knives at his back, the beast within Blamey stirred. He shed the affectation of unhurried calm that had so irritated MacArthur in Brisbane; the jolly assassin and ruthless troubleshooter emerged.

Blamey knew exactly what was at stake: he was being sent to replace his most senior field commander in whom, days ago, he had expressed his full confidence. Blamey's very presence in Papua, he knew, would 'outrage Rowell's precise ideas of how the command system was intended to function'.[9]

The two generals went back a long way; unfinished business smouldered between them. Rowell had lost all respect for Blamey after the withdrawal from Greece. He'd refused to join the hasty evacuation until Blamey sharply reminded him 'to obey an order'.[10] After Greece Rowell said, according to Sir Keith Murdoch, that he would never again serve on General Blamey's staff.[11] Blamey wrote of Rowell at the time, 'I found him very difficult ... and, as Commander, had to exercise considerable tact. Rather a reversal of what it should be ...'[12]

Whatever tact Blamey once possessed, it had worn thin since Greece. He wrote portentously to Rowell before he left for Papua: 'The powers that be have determined that I shall myself go to New Guinea ... I hope that you will ... not think that it implies any lack of confidence in yourself ... it arises from the fact that we have ... politicians who are inclined to panic.'[13]

To a character as sensitive as Rowell's the message implied a total lack of confidence in him — which was possibly Blamey's intention.

Rowell succumbed to dark, melancholy moods ahead of the inevitable clash. His very language presaged his fall. He confided in his close friend Cyril Clowes 'that [Blamey] hasn't enough moral courage to fight the Cabinet on an issue of confidence in me ... He comes here when the tide is on the turn and all is likely to be well. He cannot influence the local situation in any way, but he will get the kudos, and it will be said, rather pityingly, that he came here to hold my hand and bolster me up. Shades of Greece in April 41!!'[14]

Rowell's rather petulant nature assumed a self-destructive trajectory. The war seemed to fade into the background as the generals moved into each other's orbit. For Rowell, dealing with Blamey posed 'a problem more difficult to me than fighting the enemy'.[15] He wasn't being flippant: Blamey arrived in Port Moresby just as the Japanese army showed every sign of physical collapse.

The Japanese threat had dramatically receded since Horii captured Ioribaiwa Ridge in mid-September. Horii's battered supply line — under constant danger of Allied air raids — writhed and twisted like a headless snake. Australian reinforcements were moving up the trail. And in the Solomons the Japanese were facing strong resistance from the US marines.

Blamey arrived with a small entourage — he intended to use Rowell's staff — on 23 September and pitched his tents some distance from Rowell's on the hillside near Rouna Falls. The icy atmosphere 'belonged more to arriving in Antarctica than the tropics', observed Blamey's adjutant, Norman Carlyon.[16] After dinner, Blamey immediately repaired for talks with Rowell.

He began with the chilling assurance that Rowell's difficulties in New Guinea were the first 'bumps' in an otherwise exemplary career. Rowell, not a man to endure damnation with faint praise, swiftly concluded, 'for all practical purposes I was being supplanted in my command'.[17] The mood rapidly deteriorated.

Rowell suggested that Blamey's faith in him no longer existed. Blamey silently agreed. He could not have found a better amanuensis in Rowell who, though a superb soldier, was no politician.

Blamey could be insufferably upbeat. Much as the tyrant moulds history in his image, it was not beneath him to construe the latest good news as a consequence of his arrival. In fact, the day Blamey got to Moresby was 'the key date in the entire South West Pacific campaign', his PR men would write. On this day, they claimed, the 'elimination of the enemy' began, leading to the 'eventual re-conquest of the whole of New Guinea'.[18]

An ugly and drawn-out command crisis resulted. Officer morale plummeted; lines of command got confused: to whom should the brigadiers report, Blamey or Rowell? To whom should the battalion and company commanders look to as their ultimate leader? As Rowell wrote, 'The position had to be made clear to my subordinates, who were as much in the dark as I was.'[19] For five days the leadership lurched in limbo, as the two generals thrashed out their understandings of power.

The clash cannot be dismissed as the grandstanding of vainglorious men with one eye on their place in the history books. Nor can their battle of wills be reduced to a crude question of who gave orders. Blamey, as the most senior officer in New Guinea, indisputably wore the purple. Their feud was subtler, and the repercussions, immense. Blamey and Rowell both had brilliant records. They were two of Australia's most accomplished soldiers, utterly dedicated to the nation's defence. They understood the consequences of military power; the lives of millions of people ultimately hinged on their making the right decisions.

The row was ostensibly about military etiquette and intelligence. Would Blamey work through Rowell, as he proposed, or bypass him completely? Would Rowell ensure all intelligence went straight to Blamey? Why did Blamey not bring his own support staff? In truth, these flash points were superficial manifestations of the deepest personal animosity.

From the start an upbeat Blamey seemed intent on tapping this raw nerve. Rowell was furious when, on 25 September, Blamey 'suggested' to the commanding officer at Milne Bay that a battalion be flown to Wanigela on the north-east coast of New Guinea. Blamey planned to open an easterly line of attack on the northern beachhead, and capitalise on the Allied victory at Milne Bay. Rowell interpreted this move as a deliberate provocation that circumvented the proper chain of command — in a word, him.

When Blamey 'bounced in' to Rowell's office and announced the Wanigela decision, Rowell, who happened to be removing his boots, got so angry he almost hurled one at the general.[20] 'I fairly rose. I then got off my chest what I've been storing up since April 1941. I told him he'd already dumped me twice and was in the process of doing it a third time, as I hoped he would.'[21]

Rowell did not help himself. He failed to control his temper and seemed to be willing his own demise. To be fair, this underestimates the excruciating effect of Blamey's unprincipled, transparently self-seeking personality on an exhausted, high-minded man.

Blamey fired a second shot on the 26th. It was a 'directive', which laid down the new law of the land: '1. I have been directed by the Prime Minister and the Commander-in-Chief, South West Pacific Area to take control of the forces in the NEW GUINEA area.'[22]

Blamey would 'exercise command' through Rowell's own HQ. Whatever it gained in efficiency, the usurpation of Rowell's staff crudely underlined the latter's subordination. Contemptuously sidelined to the meaningless role of 'deputy field commander', Rowell felt humiliated in the eyes of his hand-picked staff. Blamey added a string of demands: 'I would be glad,' he wrote, 'to be promptly furnished with all tactical, supply and administrative information'.[23] Brittle hopes of a *modus operandi* forming between the two men collapsed. Though their tents were within walking distance, they often chose to communicate by hand-delivered mail.

This then, was the state of Australia's High Command with the Japanese not 30 miles from Port Moresby. Both men were under huge pressure: they were defending three fronts: the Kokoda Track, at Wau and at Milne Bay. They were answerable to the nation; and responsible for the lives of tens of thousands of soldiers. And they were, of course, proud, arrogant, ruthless commanders.

It got worse, far worse. Rowell refused to accept Blamey's terms. If so, said Blamey, early retirement was the only option. It was a crude provocation, but Rowell took the bait — interpreting it as a threat, not a warning. Had he swallowed Blamey's demands he may have survived, and completed the job of defeating the Japanese to which he was dedicated.

Instead, Rowell became openly insubordinate and nakedly contemptuous of Blamey. This eased his executioner's task. On 27 September, after 'three first class brawls', Rowell confided in a colleague, 'I would never have believed a senior officer would have taken what I said to him.'[24]

On the morning of the 28th the generals clashed for the last time. It was an argument of such ferocity that neither would speak to the other for years. Rowell, driven to his limit, exploded. Something of unmentionable squalor passed between them. It seems Rowell accused Blamey of cowardice in Greece; if true, it was an astonishing accusation to level at a superior officer.★

Blamey responded that afternoon with a peremptory missive, the clipped tone of which suggests the clash had ended thoroughly to his satisfaction. Having tormented Rowell to the limit, Blamey put him out of his misery:

> Dear General Rowell,
>   ...I regret that I feel it my duty to relieve you of the
> Command of New Guinea Force. You will please arrange to
> return to Australia at your early convenience ...A copy of the
> message sent to the Prime Minister and the Commander in Chief
> dealing with the matter is available ... at my office. I would be
> glad if you would ... initial it. [Signed] T.A. Blamey[25]

Blamey's subsequent message to the Prime Minister and MacArthur was nothing short of a character assassination: 'Rowell has taken my coming here as personally against himself ... he would be seriously disruptive influence if retained here ... Rowell is ... of a temperament that harbours imaginary grievances. He has had very limited experience of command ... In view of circumstances I have relieved him of command ...'[26]

A proud officer, Rowell felt acutely Brisbane's loss of confidence in him. It was doubly wounding to be relieved of your command just as the war turned in your favour. But to have your career casually jettisoned in such terms was intolerable to a man who placed such store by his professionalism and sense of duty.

The charges contained in the 'dreadful document ... could not be justified', protested Rowell, to whom Blamey, with infuriating smugness, replied, 'I don't have to justify it to anyone.'[27]

★ According to David Horner in an email to the author: 'My guess is [Rowell's remarks] referred to Greece and Rowell's claim that Blamey was a coward, but this is just speculation.'

By now a visceral hatred simmered between the two men. His sacking was just the beginning of a long feud, as Rowell revealed to Clowes: 'Well the blow descended . . . I am sacked. So the fight is on and one of us will go down. I pray that . . . this bad man and his rotten influences will be put out of public life forever. Like all crafty gangsters he got his blow in first . . .'[28]

He was ordered home, 'to what job I do not know, if any,' he told Tubby Allen. 'I have tried not to let personal matters get on top . . . but I am not able to go beyond a certain point in eating dirt.'[29]

In sum, one of Australia's finest military strategists was put out to graze in the nation's hour of crisis.

Dissatisfied with merely sacking Rowell, Blamey sought to destroy him. In a private letter to Curtin on 1 October, Blamey accused Rowell of refusing to cooperate; failing to develop the new offensive; and persisting in a line of attack along the Kokoda Track that was 'so difficult that it will be months before a force of 2000 could be supplied by this route. There is no hope of achieving victory along this route alone.'[30] Rowell's intelligence section 'was very deficient in energy, initiative and enterprise'.

Rowell's defence is well documented and just, if fatally flawed. He conceded his limited experience of combat command, but how, he asked, did this square with Blamey publicly praising him days before he was sacked, and the fact that his successor, Herring, had even less experience? On his loss of temper, he felt that 'two statements, made in the heat of the moment, [were] divorced from their context . . .'[31]

On one point, however, Blamey drew blood. Rowell had withheld information vital to the prosecution of the war, Blamey claimed: 'I had the greatest difficulty in obtaining information from the Intelligence Section', he told Curtin. 'It operates as though we were at peace.'

Rowell later conceded that Blamey's accusation 'may have had some degree of truth initially'.[32] If so, this was certainly a sackable offence. For a short period — perhaps two days — the Allied land commander had not received the relevant intelligence. It looked like 'a deliberate attempt to isolate Blamey',[33] and no matter how boorish the method, Rowell's sacking seemed justified on this basis alone. Perhaps Rowell's fury paralysed his judgment, and he allowed himself to be goaded into committing a sackable offence. In the terse conclusion of one brigadier, 'Rowell sacked himself.'[34]

Banished to the Unattached List — 'a veritable Sargasso Sea of the army's unwanted'[35] — Rowell confined himself to his Melbourne garden until he received fresh orders.* There can be few more humiliating experiences for a career soldier than to find himself pruning his hedge while his country is at war. Rowell waited for weeks as the War Council, in a manifest failure of political will, delicately negotiated his future.

Blamey pursued a bitter personal vendetta against the man. He literally sank his teeth into Rowell's carcass and refused to let go. He demanded that Rowell be demoted. He vetoed Rowell's chances of several senior overseas appointments. He refused to temper his animosity, inveighing against Rowell at every opportunity; 'it would be quite impossible for me to accept him as a Commander in the field under me, and he would be a continual source of evil if he held an appointment in Australia', Blamey told Curtin on 27 December.[36]

Blamey recommended Rowell's early retirement and that he revert to his prewar rank of colonel.** Blamey was indeed 'a great hater', as Curtin dispassionately observed.***

----

* On his way back, Rowell dropped in on MacArthur, who bluntly said that Rowell 'had not prosecuted the campaign as vigorously as he would have liked. His Intelligence system had not been good ... He would be absolutely opposed to his return to New Guinea' (see Rowell, *Full Circle*).

** In 1943, Rowell found himself 'exiled' to a post in the Middle East. He later assisted in drawing up the plans for the D-day landings. Britain, and not Australia, received the benefits of his experience. Before his departure he wrote a conciliatory letter to Blamey. The tone is intriguingly contrite: 'Had you suspended judgement for perhaps a day I feel sure I would have gone a long way in withdrawing statements ... which were made in the heat of the moment.' Rowell added, 'I know you considered that I was merely batting for myself and not for the team, but this was not so ...' (see *Full Circle*, p. 134). Blamey did not reply.

*** Military historians, officers and battalion reunions are still dissecting this extraordinary row. David Horner has slightly changed his views. In *Crisis of Command* (1978), he concludes: 'Rowell did not fail as a commander in New Guinea, despite Blamey's later claims. His only failure was his inability to work with a man towards whom he felt only loathing and disgust.' Blamey was the more culpable, Horner argued, not least for his unwillingness 'to risk his own position by an affirmation of loyalty and trust in his subordinate' (*Crisis of Command*, p. 187). Horner latterly argues, in his biography of Blamey, that, 'Rowell took an unduly pure view of the responsibility of a higher commander to shield a lower commander from political interference. In practical terms that is just not always possible. Therefore, it was Rowell's responsibility to get on with his superior' (see *Blamey: Commander-in-Chief*).

Chapter 29
'Rabbits'

'Remember ... it is not the man with the gun that gets shot; it's the rabbit that is running away'
— *One account of General Blamey's speech to the troops at Koitaki*

With Blamey in charge, and the completely loyal General Ned Herring installed as his deputy, the war was allowed to resume. This is not meant flippantly: some certainty prevailed after a week of confusion. Troops were apprised of their new lines of command; fresh orders issued; and US regiments deployed along tracks parallel to Kokoda to the east. A stream of 'Rowell men' left Port Moresby, casualties of Blamey's 'purges'. The most prominent scalps were Brigadier Arnold Potts and Chester Wilmot.

Wilmot, the acclaimed Australian war correspondent, made the mistake of writing an honest analysis of the Kokoda campaign.[1] Rowell had appended it to a sitrep, unwisely noting that he'd be happier if more officers understood the war as well as 'this civilian observer'. Blamey was unimpressed.

A marked 'Rowell man', Wilmot complained about press censorship and was overheard criticising Blamey's 'profitable rackets' in the Middle East. And, of course, he dared to ask irritating questions about the lack of jungle greens. Wilmot had to go. Blamey activated a simple expedient: he withdrew Wilmot's press accreditation, and thus froze him out of the Pacific War. Australia's finest war correspondent went to Britain, where he covered the greatest story of the war in Europe, the D-day landings, for the BBC.

Potts met a swift and ignominious end. It saddened the troops, who looked on this man as a father figure, and a hero. He'd salvaged their self-esteem as soldiers in a desperate situation. Brisbane had a different opinion. Potts had failed, Blamey concluded. MacArthur, who 'needed scalps',[2] agreed: his own scalp was looking decidedly vulnerable. In October the Americans were hard-pressed at Guadalcanal; if the Japanese gained control of the island, they could sever the vital US–Australia link and throttle the Allied counteroffensive. MacArthur had to clear Papua and New Guinea of the enemy as soon as possible. In this atmosphere, brigadiers whom MacArthur perceived as having failed were finished.

Before his dismissal, Potts wrote a series of fascinating letters to his wife, Dawn, in which he shared his contempt for Blamey (Dawn was aware of Blamey's youthful attraction to Potts's sister): 'He's a difficult cove and hard to talk to, as he butts in to any statement and sidetracks with savage criticism ...' And in a letter on 11 October: '[Blamey] screams and interferes terrifically and the axe is held over any head that doesn't bow to superior wisdom. I'd love to have one hour of authority and ask who is running the bloody war ...'[3]

The axe was for Potts. There are various accounts of his dismissal. The most credible tells of Blamey simply phoning Potts on 22 October, with a few blunt words: 'Change of climate for you, Potts. You go to Darwin. Your successor ... will meet you tomorrow and take over.'[4]

Lieutenant-Colonel Ken Murdoch gave a more dramatic, if unconfirmed, account: Blamey visited Potts's office on 23 October and ordered everyone out. Murdoch, working in an adjacent room, did not hear the order. He did hear the conversation, and claims that Blamey said, 'failures like the Kokoda Trail ... could not be tolerated — the men had shown that something was lacking ...'

Blamey, so the account goes, added that he was 'relieving Potts forthwith'. During the row Blamey reportedly barked, 'I'll see you're finished in the army!' To which Potts is said to have replied, 'Good! I can go back and tell the country what a mess you've made of things!'[5]

Potts was not permitted to meet his successor Ivan Dougherty; he was ordered to 'make himself available' immediately for transfer to Darwin.

The news raced through the brigade. The troops were outraged. Many officers tendered their resignations, which the brigadier, deeply moved, refused to accept.

Potts wrote a brief farewell message to 'Officers, NCOs and men' on 23 October 1942: '... saying goodbye is the hardest job in my life ... This much I can say: that I regard this Brigade as the best fighting formation in the AIF and second to none in this war or the last ... I'm proud that I was one of you, Thanking you and goodbye.'[6]

Not all senior commanders deserted Potts. General Tubby Allen later bravely commended Potts's fighting withdrawal — 'with the resultant extension of the enemy's line of communication' — as the right decision in appalling circumstances. This infuriated Blamey, who complained that he'd never heard of a reversal on the field of battle 'explained away so ingenuously'.[7]

Regardless of who, ultimately, was to blame for the circumstances that led to Potts's retreat, the brutal facts, as Bill Edgar points out, were these: Potts had gone backwards when he'd been told to go forwards, he'd disobeyed orders; and he'd been innovative (perhaps his most dangerous tendency).[8] He'd also saved the lives of many young men (for which, no doubt, their parents were later grateful).

In this, Blamey's actions must be seen within the context of the army culture of the day. 'That an officer should be sacked when he has done his best,' explained Australia's official historian, Dudley McCarthy, 'may be cruel, but it is merely one of war's cruelties ... The only way to stop it and to stop the other cruelties ... is to stop having wars. To protest against it is like protesting against the Laws of Gravity.'[9] In the dignified manner of his exit, Potts understood this.

———

Blamey inflicted one last indignity on the 21st Brigade. On 9 November, he ordered Maroubra Force to assemble at Koitaki Cricket Ground, near the starting point over the mountains. Some troops anticipated a message of congratulations, or perhaps individual decorations. They felt they'd exhausted the aggressor and saved Port Moresby.

The men formed up in ranks, resplendent in slouch hats and their best uniforms. Blamey appeared in his broad-rimmed hat, long khaki coat and baggy shorts, with a handkerchief at hand to wipe his sweating brow. Droplets of moisture gathered on his moustache as he prepared to speak from a little wooden dais.

Norman Carlyon, Blamey's loyal ADC, stood beside the platform, and remembers, despite the intense heat, breaking out 'in a cold sweat': 'I realised that [Blamey] was in a most aggressive mood.'[10]

Blamey spoke without notes. He got straight to the point. Carlyon recalls him saying: 'The men had been defeated, I had been defeated, and Australia had been defeated ... this was not good enough. Every soldier ... had to remember that he was worth three Japanese. In future he expected ... advance at all costs.'[11] With every word, the troops grew restless.

There are several accounts of what he said next: 'Remember ... it is not the man with the gun that gets shot; it's the rabbit that is running away',[12] is one version.

The troops thought they were being compared to terrified rabbits. Some dared to protest, to shout out. Blamey 'couldn't believe anyone would interrupt him', recalled one lance-corporal.[13] The feeling among the troops approached mutiny, said Frank Sublet. Major Steward described the men as 'almost molten with rage and indignation'.[14] Only the officers' restraining influence prevented an ugly scene.

Nor were the officers spared. The same day Blamey summoned the 21st Brigade's senior brass to a private meeting (several refused to attend, including Steward). He began, 'I wonder if you are worthy of commanding such magnificent troops?'[15] They emerged severely demoralised. They were inadequate to the task, Blamey told them. They had let down their men and, by implication, their country; some had failed miserably. They were not worthy of the troops, he said.

Extreme resentment met these charges. One lieutenant swung a punch at Captain Robert Porter, a Blamey staff member. The wrath of the men pursued

Herring out of the camp. After tactlessly lobbing in his tuppence worth — 'soldiers must not be afraid to die' — the startled Herring ran the gauntlet of 'a booing and jeering exit'.[16] Blamey himself went 'strangely quiet' as his staff car drove away. He was on the point of weeping, observed his ADC.[17]

The charge of cowardice was an intolerable psychological burden for young men who'd endured the Kokoda withdrawal. They were not cynics; they believed in noble motives such as courage and self-sacrifice.* They saw themselves in heroic terms, as the saviours of their nation. Friends had died in their arms; they'd witnessed the wounded crawl off into the jungle. Posthumously decorated mates had flung themselves in the path of the enemy. They were in their twenties.

The brigade boiled with indignation. A deep disrespect for the commander rippled through the ranks. Blamey's 'rabbit speech' spread like 'a grass fire borne on a summer gale'.[18] When he heard of it, Potts said that he'd fry Blamey's soul in the next world for 'passing the buck'. The wounded heard of the speech in their bunks at the Australian General Hospital in Port Moresby. When Blamey visited, the men nibbled on lettuce leaves and sang 'Run, Rabbit, Run!' as he walked down the lines of beds. Blamey gave no sign that he'd heard them.[19]

No copy of Blamey's speech survives, only the recollections of those who were there and the muted reinterpretations of those who were not. The speech is glaringly absent from battalion histories, whose associations were threatened with the loss of their War Memorial grants if they mentioned it. The 2/14th's battalion history derisively alludes to Blamey's 'lectures of considerable interest'.[20] There were attempts to leak the speech to the press, but wartime censorship forbade publication. Men vented their bitterness in other ways.

Padre Fred Burt (2/16th Battalion), on his return to Perth in 1942, delivered a sermon about the injustice of Koitaki. Summoned to Army HQ in Melbourne on suspicion of a breach of security, Burt told Major-General

---

* It would have tragic repercussions in the battle of Gona, where many Australian troops would die seeking private redemption from the charge of cowardice in suicidal acts of bravery — a phenomenon Ralph Honner dubbed the 'Koitaki Factor' — see Part 5.

C.E.M Lloyd, the adjutant-general, 'You can put me out of the army; I'll resign my commission.' To mollify the angry cleric, Lloyd explained that 'mistakes are always made' in war, to which Burt replied: 'On this occasion, the men who saved Australia in spite of your mistakes, are the men who are blamed.' The padre then got up and walked out.[21]

Could it be that Blamey was misunderstood? Or misheard? This possibility is often raised. Some attempts have been made to exonerate Blamey. Brigadier Ivan Dougherty, Potts's successor, believed the men misinterpreted him; their sensitivity to criticism had led them to draw conclusions that weren't intended.[22]

He claimed Blamey was referring to the Japanese, and killing them was 'like shooting rabbits back home'. Dougherty added that 'listening to him I thought what he said was quite a good description of the tactics needed to deal with the Japanese. It never occurred to me that he was having a crack at the brigade ...' The official historian Dudley McCarthy used a tangle of zoological metaphors to portray Blamey as misunderstood: '[Blamey] said the Jap was like a gorilla; he would get into a hole and he would not surrender ... he had to be got out of his holes and put on the run. Blamey added that it was like shooting rabbits.[23]

Perhaps the last word ought to go to the man least likely to embellish, edit, fabricate or mishear Blamey: his adjutant and friend, Lieutenant-Colonel Norman Carlyon, a most fastidious man, who stood beside his boss during the speech. 'The rank and file assumed that they were being described as rabbits. It amazed me that Blamey should deal so insensitively with the men ... Blamey had spoken, as usual, with complete candour. I see this as one of the rare times when his judgement was hasty and wrong.'[24]

Whatever the truth, Blamey's 'rabbit' speech lives on in the minds of a dwindling number of war veterans. Time has not healed their bitterness. Every soldier interviewed for this book expressed hatred and bitterness towards the man — only a few senior officers were forgiving.

Part Four
Counteroffensive

Chapter 30
Civilians

'Australian men of the better sort are resentful of the loose
behaviour of many Australian women, whose husbands are
serving abroad ... In particular they do not like the way
Americans "paw" them and embrace them in public. Australians
of other types are annoyed when Australian girls refuse their
company, but soon afterwards are seen to accept the advances of
the first Americans that offer'
— *From an inquiry into the street fighting between Australian and
American troops in Queensland*

The 'yellow hordes' of government propaganda — the ghastly, buck-
toothed beasts that were about 'to rape your sister, your mother or your
grandmother'[1] — did not intrude on the Melbourne Cup in 1942. The
crowd, at 35,942, was a third of the norm. But they weren't going to let the
war diminish their delight in seeing the four-year-old Colonus win, at 33 to 1.
The social Cup-goers, though fewer in number, were determined to deny the
proximity of the Japanese and relive the usual gala event, as young women
swanned amidst the neatly uniformed American troops, whose square-jawed
smiles filled their society magazines.

At the Sydney Rugby League Grand Final two months earlier, in September 1942, 26,000 people watched Canterbury-Bankstown beat St George 11–9. Meanwhile, the Japanese army stood at Ioribaiwa and gazed upon the Coral Sea. The Australian people seemed to revel in the oblique threat of invasion. None knew the actual state of the men in the Owen Stanleys; the full truth had not impinged on the civilians' frivolity. Professor Clunies-Ross earlier observed on his return from London: 'Australians on the whole are distinctly complacent about the war. They congratulate themselves on having a record crowd at the Melbourne Cup; they resist petrol rationing, the control of civilian spending — anything, in fact, that interferes with the ordinary life of the community. They are ... too interested in political faction fights and industrial disputes and strikes to realise that their country is in danger.'[2]

In condemning their 'astounding complacency' in a broadcast on 10 November 1941, Blamey more bluntly told Australians: 'You are leading a carnival life. But if you do not take your part you'll find your homes overwhelmed as were the homes of people in France and Belgium.'

Blamey had 'a most extraordinary feeling of what you might call helplessness', on his return from the Middle East.[3] He likened the people to 'a lot of gazelles grazing in a dell near the edge of a jungle, while the beasts of prey are working up towards you, apparently unseen, unnoticed. And it is the law of the jungle that they spring upon you, merciless.'[4] It was vintage Blamey. He even scoffed at the 'deplorable crowds' turning out to watch football. Sports commentators were jolted from their daze. This was tantamount to blasphemy in sports-mad Australia. Could the nation really be at risk?

Nor did the war crack that great mirror of the national mood, the letters pages, to any great degree. In late July 1942, with the Japanese at Gona, a lively debate erupted in the *Telegraph*'s letters pages over the battle of the sexes. The issue was women's rights. Louise Ashley, of Rose Bay, observed: 'To flourish figurative rolling-pins will rouse resentment in men. For all their pious pre-marital resolutions, they remain dictators at heart, and so they must be assailed through the heart rather than the head.'[5]

Deep within the *Sydney Morning Herald*, at the time of Miss Ashley's letter, there appeared a one-paragraph news brief about a speech by the

Japanese Premier, General Tojo: 'Australia,' Tojo declared, 'is now completely isolated and is hopelessly awaiting reinforcements from America. If she persists in her useless resistance, there is no need to reiterate that the Japanese will show no mercy in crushing her.'[6]

Just how true were these snapshots of a nation of sports-loving lotus-eaters? During 1942, the crisis year, many Australians evacuated the cities and headed for the hills. A rush of 'some thousands' from Sydney fled to the Blue Mountains, Bowral, Mittagong and Bathurst, according to contemporary reports.[7] When a submarine shelled the eastern suburbs of Woollahra, Bellevue Hill, Rose Bay and Bondi in June, many home owners sold their harbour-side properties at knockdown prices and fled west. A want of fortitude met the attack on Darwin in February 1942: government ministers were seen to run about 'like a lot of startled chooks'; the people of Darwin fled their homes, some heading as far as Adelaide; and 'looting and desertions' were commonplace.[8]

The evacuation of northern Australia began on 8 March: some 10,000 to 14,000 civilians abandoned their homes in Townsville and Cairns.* Lex McAulay was one of three children from Innisfail, south of Cairns, who was evacuated along with thousands. He recalls husbands sending instructions to their wives about what to do, where to go: 'Go to aunt Edna's place, go inland!'[9]

Elsewhere, Australians built air raid shelters in their backyards; others hatched elaborate plans to escape the rape and pillage of the invader. Thousands went bush, a few terrified souls committed suicide.[10]

Curtin beat the austerity drum until people wearied of the Government's doom mongering. The constant refrain of self-sacrifice inoculated elements of the nation against the reality, and apathy set in; others appreciated the sincerity with which Curtin sought to organise 'a non-military people for

---

* Japanese propaganda exploited these fears. On 3 March, a Japanese radio broadcaster thanked the Americans for laying on hot water at the Queen's Hotel in Townsville, and for building a new aerodrome and headquarters: 'We will soon be using them ...' It also correctly anticipated the arrival in Townsville of troops from Melbourne (see Horner, *Crisis of Command*).

the purposes of complete war'. It necessitated 'a revolution in the lives of the people,' the Australian leader warned.[11]

The Prime Minister invoked terrifying images to rouse the masses, most memorably in his speech to mark the third anniversary of the outbreak of war in Europe:

> If we do not strip ourselves to save our country, then the enemy
> will do it with a ruthless efficiency and with a maximum of
> misery that can have a counterpart only in the imagination.
> Consider our fate should he be victorious! What will we have
> then? ... Today Port Moresby and Darwin are the Singapores of
> Australia. If those two places fall, then, inevitably, we are faced
> with a bloody struggle on our soil when we will be forced to
> fight grimly, city by city, village by village, until our fair land may
> become a blackened ruin ...'[12]

The Government's austerity drive intruded upon every corner of life. Australians were asked to eschew 'every selfish, comfortable habit, every luxurious impulse, every act, word or deed that retards the victory march'.[13] Christmas holidays were reduced to three days, from the usual week or so. The unions protested (many workers resigned, took the normal holidays and then reapplied for their jobs). Evatt chastised them for their selfishness — the fighting forces needed every ounce of materials that may be produced, he said. That meant less consumption, and shorter holidays.[14]

Boats were impounded, rifles impressed, supplies of hand tools were frozen. Cigarettes were limited to military canteens — and satirists joked about a strange rare substance called tobacco.

Military phrases peppered civilian language: mates spoke nervously, or mock-seriously, of 'infiltration', 'guerrilla tactics', 'scorched earth', 'ack-ack', 'strafing', and so on.[15] People got fed up with hearing 'war effort', 'unity', 'new order' and 'liberty' on the radio.[16]

Clothing restrictions were announced on 27 July, as part of the 'Fashions for Victory' campaign. A no-frills wardrobe awaited men and women. Double-breasted suits, waistcoats, cuffs or other fancy accessories were outlawed. When John Dedman, Minister for War Organisation, posed in one of the new suits, the nation howled with laughter. 'It was an unattractive advertisement,' observed Paul Hasluck the future Governor-General.[17]

Dedman became the unfortunate face of the Government's austerity drive, which acquired the name 'Dedmanism'. Dedmanism reached a high-water mark at Christmas 1942, when he banned advertising. 'Dedman kills Father Christmas' ran the headlines.

Dedmanism imposed fifteen prohibitions on women's fashion. Evening wear, cloaks, fur coats, dinner gowns, and children's party frocks were among the items banned. Many luxury goods ceased to exist. In this category the Government placed lawnmowers, as well as fur coats and jewellery — though not wedding rings.

Silk stockings were a noticeable casualty of Dedmanism. Young women evaded the restrictions by painting their legs and pencilling a seam down their calves.[18] An elastic shortage meant the banning of bloomers; swimsuits were, of course, outlawed. Celebrities and 'bright young things' had a dreadful time: editors were asked not to publish glamorous photos of wealthy party-goers.

Most alarmingly, sport was restricted. A ban on mid-week sport, with horse racing — the Melbourne Cup excepted — limited to Saturday afternoons, provoked uproar. 'The government had touched upon a sacred subject,' noted Hasluck.[19] This was tantamount to closing Lourdes to pilgrims, or introducing a no-wash zone in the Ganges.

Sport, observed one social commentator, was the yardstick by which men and women were judged.[20] Not to entertain an obsession with sport — any sport — seemed unAustralian and somehow redolent of a worrying character flaw. Dedmanism had gone too far, and there were universal appeals for commonsense.

Many Australians — by no means a majority — reacted against this strange new culture of modesty and restraint. The 'orgy of betting' continued. SP bookmakers flourished. On the first 'raceless Saturday' — 4 October 1942 — the secretary of the Timber Workers' Union (John Curtin's old union) warned that restrictions on sport and racing would impair the morale of the people.[21]

Meanwhile, loud protests met the decision to cut drinking hours to a mere seven a day. The alcoholic content of beer was reduced. People responded by drinking in a more concentrated manner. 'Drunkenness in public places continued to be a common feature of Australian city life throughout the war,' Paul Hasluck wearily concluded.[22]

Parties flourished in the hedonistic atmosphere. Melbourne streets were teeming with crowds 'from dawn till midnight'.[23] It was 'dance, dance, dance all the time', remembered Elaine Hope, an ambulance driver in Sydney.[24] If this was the end of the world, Australians were going out with a bang.

Of course, not everyone indulged, and hundreds of thousands quietly sacrificed pleasure and toiled away for the war effort: working for veterans' charities, hospitals, and in factories. Women thronged the assembly lines. But a very substantial number of people ignored the Government, and carried on guzzling beer and petrol, placing bets and seeking pleasure with cheerful abandon. Perhaps their selfish sanguinity may be seen as strength: the careless indifference of a people who felt they knew better than their political masters.

People simply became inured to the shrill encomiums to self-denial. The Government had protested too much, insisted Eleanor Dark, an Australian novelist: 'We are being lectured, scolded, bullied, alarmed and even taunted about it.' She feared the emergence of 'a morbid and hypochondriac interest' in self-sacrifice among the powers that were.[25]

In fairness to Curtin, the Government's measures appealed to restraint and responsibility, not total self-abnegation; few activities or enjoyments were banned outright. The Prime Minister was in the lonely position of comprehending precisely the implications of total war with Japan.

Visually the war transformed the cities. A brownout introduced in December 1941 plunged the nation in brownness for eighteen months. In order to conserve coal and power, display advertising and late night shopping were prohibited, and daylight saving introduced.

Disused windows and doors were bricked over or sandbagged; councils dumped heaps of sand in public places for residents to use against incendiary bombs. Car headlights were masked, and windows draped. Air raid shelters were built in public parks; householders dug their own slit trenches in their backyards with picks and shovels. Barbed-wire rolls appeared on the beaches. Cars — not yet a source of mass mania — were seen less and less, with the petrol ration cut by 20 per cent. Air raid guidelines warned people not to crowd in doorways to watch dogfights (should they occur overhead).

Ghost towns proliferated, as did signless cities. Signboards, place names and street names were removed; even harmless tourist names such as Lyre Bird Glen in the Blue Mountains were pulled down. Households were told to destroy their roadmaps lest they assist the conqueror. Presumably many people got lost.

Total war transformed the economy. The Treasurer, Ben Chifley, launching the austerity campaign in his budget speech on 3 September, warned, 'the spending of every shilling must be avoided wherever possible'.[26] No capital could be sold or invested without government permission; profits were to be pegged at 4 per cent on capital, and those in excess to be taken in tax or passed on to consumers — so much for the unions' claim that capitalist profiteers were driving the war.

Farmers were dismayed to learn of their scorched-earth policy. Rural newspapers offered lists of what they were required to kill and wreck should the Japanese invade. One imagines few hardened station owners taking this seriously. Yet cows and sheep joined the people heading south: drovers herded 80,000 head of cattle distances of more than a thousand miles during 1942.[27]

Australians had no experience of total war, and many simply refused to recognise the threat. Union leaders sledgehammered the workers into believing they were victims of a capitalist plot. Strikes soared, as pay and conditions deteriorated. Almost six million working days were lost due to strikes during World War II; 4,462,925 were lost in New South Wales alone, due to that state's high proportion of civil servants and coalminers.[28] While the number of lost working days fell during 1942, the number of industrial disputes doubled on the previous year.[29]

Wharf workers struck at critical times. Troops bound for Port Moresby sometimes had to load their own ships because Australian dockers were on strike. At Hamilton Wharf in Brisbane, finding no one to load the supplies and ammunition on board, the disgusted commander of the 2/1st Battalion shouted, 'We'll load the bloody thing ourselves.'[30]

Communists and 'irresponsibles' fanned the flames of union action. They blamed the war on the capitalist bogey and employers. Their madder conspiracy theories did not dent every worker's sense of duty to the fighting men, and many honourably resisted the order to strike.

For an old socialist, Curtin might have been expected to sympathise with union claims. Instead he showed robust good sense, and shut down any argument that compromised the war effort. Strikers, drunkards, bright young things — anyone who refused to accept the sacrifice — were 'not true citizens of the Commonwealth'.[31] 'I ask you,' he said to the Australian people on 19 August, 'to ... think about [the troops] a little more and think about ourselves a little less.'[32] Curtin himself gave everything, assuming 'the whole weight of care of a nation at war'.

The heightening sense of danger stirred the human libido. A potent mixture of sexual attraction and a sense of fear saw many Australian women fall into the arms of American servicemen. A number had husbands or boyfriends at the front — provoking fury among Australian men.

Women who experienced the war tend to remember the Americans, 90,000 of whom were based in Australia during 1942 (their combat units did not move to New Guinea until late that year).[33] They were seen as handsome, charming, well-paid soldiers in neatly pressed uniforms. The Australian men, in contrast, seemed slovenly in their baggy shorts and slouch hats, and they were markedly less well paid.

The Americans were 'attentive' to Australian women, said one woman, modestly. Olga Masters recalled a group of 'very smart, very handsome' Americans passing her, one of whom said, 'Excuse me, but you're beautiful.' Never had she been so openly complimented, she said. On the other hand, Vera Harding of Newcastle slapped one American soldier who 'didn't know what "no" meant'.[34]

There were huge brawls between the Australian and American troops. Street fights and stabbings erupted in Townsville, Brisbane and Melbourne in November. The 'girl' question was a major cause, concluded an inquiry into street fighting:

Australian [men] of the better sort are resentful of the loose
behaviour of many Australian women, whose husbands are
serving abroad, with American Service men ... In particular they
do not like the way Americans 'paw' them and embrace them in
public. Australians of other types are annoyed when Australian
girls refuse their company, but soon afterwards are seen to accept
the advances of the first Americans that offer.[35]

There were other motives for fights. Americans got special treatment in hotels, shops and cafes; Americans were better paid. Mobs of Australians sometimes went after them; fifteen attacked two Americans for no other reason than a refusal to hand over money. On Thanksgiving Day, 26 November, several hundred men went on a rampage; one Australian soldier was killed and at least sixteen wounded, in the 'Battle of Brisbane'.[36]

At the front, Japanese propaganda leaflets crudely exploited Australian troops' concerns about their wives and girlfriends back home. One depicted an American soldier having sex with an Australian girl, with the caption, 'Take your sweet time at the front, Aussie. I got my hands full right now with your sweet tootsie at home.'[37]

The Australian press was reliably jingoistic and colourfully apocalyptic. 'War has ceased merely to be on Australia's doorstep,' wrote Ek Dum of *The Bulletin* on 11 March. 'It is on the mat reaching for the knocker.'[38] The Government launched a propaganda campaign to incite hatred of the Japanese, which fitted snugly into the *Daily Telegraph*'s existing editorial policy. It was a pointless exercise, which did not reflect well on Curtin. In one of his most dignified and courageous speeches, Menzies lambasted the Government's 'use of hatred as an instrument of war', and it is worth quoting at length:

The last advertisement I saw ended by announcing, apropos of the Japanese, that 'We always did despise them anyhow.' Now, if I may take that last observation first, it does seem to me to be fantastically foolish and dangerous. It is, in my opinion, poor policy to try to persuade people to despise the Japanese ...

Their courage is admitted; their skill is much greater than we thought; their resource and ingenuity and capacity for devising novel means of warfare have been at times staggering ...

To despise such people is absurd. Such an attitude is merely of a piece with the constant underestimation of our enemies, which has been one of our great handicaps in this war ... we are not dealing with a contemptible enemy whom a second-rate effort will serve to overthrow, but with a tremendously powerful enemy whom we will have to go at full stretch to defeat ...

But this is only one aspect of the problem. The real thing that troubles me about this campaign is that it appears to proceed from a belief, no doubt quite honestly held, that the cultivation of the spirit of hatred among our own people is a proper instrument of war policy ...

We all — and very naturally at a time like this — have our moments of burning hatred. But the real question is whether we should glorify such a natural human reaction into something which ought to be cultivated and made a sort of chronic state of mind.

It is conceded the world over that the Australian soldier is a good fighter. But I have never heard it suggested that he was a good or persistent hater. He has very frequently respected his enemy though he has fought him, and fought to kill.

Do we want to change him, or are these campaigns directed to the civilian? Is it thought that Australian civilians are so lacking in the true spirit of citizenship that they need to be filled artificially with a spirit of hatred before they will do their duty to themselves and to those who are fighting for them?

It is an offence to an honest citizen to imagine that the cold, evil and repulsive spirit of racial hatred must be substituted for honest and brave indignation if his greatest effort is to be obtained.[39]

What of the Japanese civilian?

The average Japanese civilian had little idea of the conditions under which their front-line warriors were fighting. New Guinea, Papua, Guam, Rabaul ... were so many exotic islands. The starving, disease-racked troops in the Owen Stanleys would have been unrecognisable to a nation weaned on the myth of martial supremacy. Even so, they were aware of the severe food shortages, and the harshness of military life, and drew their own conclusions.

The Spartans would have found much to admire in the stoicism, self-denial and utter lack of civil rights of the Japanese people during World War II. Most Japanese people unquestioningly obeyed their political masters. But there were dissenting voices, and to describe Tojo's Japan as a grim military dictatorship overlooks the existence of a vocal, if ineffectual, political opposition.

The Government awarded itself the powers to set prices, ban strikes, confiscate property, seize newspapers, impose new laws at will, and do many other things under the Civilian Mobilisation Law of 1941. Article 31 ominously added, 'anyone who violates the mobilization law will be punished by fines of up to 50,000 Yen and penal servitude of up to 10 years'.[40]

The vast majority willingly hunkered down to a long period of extreme austerity. Nowhere was this better and more entertainingly demonstrated than by the nationwide competition to find the most perfect example of 'curtailed living'. The winning entries provided a unique snapshot of civilian Japan: 'I have curtailed living as much as possible,' wrote one young female finalist in Kishiwada City. In her household, orange peel had replaced sweets, fish guts were applied as fertiliser, and wild mugwort used to ward off colds and clear the bowel. She preferred walks in the mountains to shopping — 'the fine air of the fields is free' — and proudly salvaged a pair of discarded boots as an umbrella holder. 'I should like to wipe the word "throw away" from the earth,' she said.

The judges were impressed: 'Discovery of a person like you gives a feeling that the future will be bright for Japan.'

Sugiara Toshiro, a father in Nagoya City, introduced a regime of dawn exercise for his family who, he thought, tended to oversleep. He was disgusted at himself for not rising until 7.30 a.m., which was clearly out of sympathy with the troops at the front line: 'Henceforth the family will rise at half past six sharp. All must join in callisthenics before the radio. If by any chance one does not join in, he goes without a meal. This was the iron rule adopted for the family. It would be a calamity for me as head of the house to be first to miss a meal.'

The judges read this 'with a faint smile', but praised Sugiara's regimen.

Farming communities stretched their rice rations to the limit. One tenant farmer had heard of soldiers gnawing tree roots while fighting in Guadalcanal, and duly introduced a fixed daily ration of 1¼ pints rice for his family of five. Another farmer wrote that he'd strictly curtailed the rice consumption for his family of eight, which greatly impressed the Government's judges: 'This piece of writing is a fine example which all persons, particularly farmers, will wish to read.'

The better off Japanese were similarly restrained. Yoshiko Kuwada, the wife of a landowner, reduced her 'two maids to one', stopped using sugar, and ate only home-produced food. Her husband, she said, a touch optimistically, had 'cut out sake and tobacco altogether', while her daughter now made her own clothes.

The judges were delighted: 'Housewives of landowners are usually indifferent to economics,' they noted. 'Your resolution to abandon your former way of life . . . is most commendable. If people from all walks of life have a spirit like yours, the home front of Japan is in excellent shape.'

One typical household each night would empty their wallets and put all the spare coins into a bamboo tube. If any of them indulged in some lazy activity, they had to put more money down the tube, as a 'punishment tax'. 'When I simply had to go to the movies I dropped a fine of 50 sen into the bamboo,' said one child. Though an excellent entry, the judges regretted they were unable to publish it due to a lack of paper.[41]

But perhaps the most abstemious Japanese civilian was the exemplary Yamashita of Nagasaki, who felt the Government's slogan 'Until Victory I Shall Desire Nothing' deeply inadequate. He said it should be revised to,

'I Shall Desire Nothing At All Times'. After the defeat of America and Britain, Japan's '100,000,000 leaders of Greater East Asia' should desire nothing further, he suggested.

Not everyone in Japan shared these curtailed lives, of course. The cities had all the usual distractions. Returning troops were disgusted to find men queuing up for *sake*, rampant shoppers, and women 'primping themselves like dolls', as one wrote.[42]

Chapter 31
Hunger

'Not a single grain of rice left. Taroes sufficient for only another day. From tomorrow we will have to chew grass or bark'
— *Lieutenant Sakomoto, at Ioribaiwa*

The war correspondent Okada Seizo stood on Ioribaiwa Ridge in mid-September and witnessed the Japanese troops pouring onto the summit, 'wild with joy' and 'stained all over with mud and blood'. They embraced and wept.

As the invader's triumphant glow faded, their predicament began to dawn on Horii's officers. The silent pacifist within Okada found a voice: 'They knew nothing,' he later wrote. They knew nothing of the bigger picture: the diversion of resources to Guadalcanal, the destruction of transport ships from Rabaul, the sudden need for reinforcements at Buna. 'They had simply done the best they had been taught to do, and reached the top of Ioribaiwa,' he wrote.[1]

Horii knew what was happening. Perched on the dripping summit, the Japanese commander realised the advance on Moresby was doomed. He had overshot the southern-most point of his advance, as defined by Rabaul HQ on 28 August. His supply lines were dangerously over-extended.[2] Ahead,

20,000 Allied combat and support troops were assembling; behind, his line of battered carriers — Formosans and Koreans, as well as Rabaul natives — stumbled up the track, harassed daily by Allied aircraft. And ominous news was coming in about the situation at Guadalcanal.

Horii allowed his men to labour under the delusion a little longer.

The Japanese troops had been promised an extra rice ration when they took Ioribaiwa. Most were disappointed. The machine-gunner Lieutenant Sakomoto did manage to reward some of his men with saturated Australian rations. But for most, there was nothing. 'Not a grain of rice left,' he wrote on 17 September.[3]

The Australians had left a little ammunition and signal gear, as well as about a thousand spoiled rations consisting of punctured tins and scattered food, the rotting detritus of spent ration packs.[4] Australia's 25th Brigade had burnt clothes and blankets, bayoneted cans of bully beef and strewn biscuits and rice through the bush. Booby traps — grenades poised to explode — were placed in piles of rubbish, in old boots and the cold ashes of extinguished fires.

With rising anxiety the Japanese scratched about the Australian dugouts for a morsel, wary of spoiled food after their terrific bout of food poisoning at Myola. 'We were indeed in a hopeless position. The only thing that kept up the morale was the thought of Port Moresby,' wrote Okada.[5]

As the first flush of victory dissipated, the men began to comprehend their peculiarly hellish circumstances. Some soldiers grew disorderly and angry. Military discipline lapsed and a mob mentality spread. The hungriest tore at tree roots and gnawed on native taro plants and sugar cane sticks. They were caught in a closing vice.

Even so, it was an exaggeration to suggest, at this point, that 'In the scramble [for food] ... the warrior spirit evaporated.'[6] Most of the troops remained stoic in the face of extreme adversity. Mutiny and desertion were unthinkable, as remote from their minds as questioning the divine will of the Emperor.

To calm the troops, Major-General Horii appealed to their martial pride. Were they not the legendary South Seas Detachment, the Nankai

Shitai, conquerors of Rabaul and the Owen Stanleys? Had they not driven the Australians back to Port Moresby? After all this, must they capitulate to the mere demands of their stomachs?

A string of morale-boosting declarations were distributed to platoon commanders. Horii had announced on 11 September, just before the charge on Ioribaiwa: 'The Shitai has completed the pursuit of the enemy ... these troops are in a state of utter confusion, and to a great degree have lost their will to fight ...'[7]

Three days later, from his tent on the heights west of Wamai, Horii issued an order of brazen mendacity — a plan for the capture of Port Moresby: '... you will kindly take note of the following,' he told his officers, '... First the South aerodrome [Kila Kila airport] is to be captured ... Next our main force will capture Moresby peninsula and the town of Moresby. Only one battalion will then be assigned for guarding this area and mopping up ...'[8]

The Japanese commander was either pre-emptively defying orders he knew were imminent, or wilfully deceiving his men to sustain morale. He knew the advance was impossible. Yet, junior officers effusively relayed his instructions. First Lieutenant Akiyama told his unit that the enemy 'have only been putting up resistance on a small scale during their retreat ... They are thought to have abandoned their last key position ... in order to defend Moresby.'*

By mid-September, news of the landing of US marines at Guadalcanal came from behind, 'as if borne by the wind'. While the troops thought little of this — preoccupied as they were with the advance on Port Moresby — many officers realised the dire consequences: 'So that was why no Japanese planes nor supplies came to New Guinea!' wrote Okada, with devastating simplicity.[9] 'An atmosphere of uneasiness stole over their positions on the mountain like the fog that gathered noiselessly every morning.'[10]

Horii could not face defeat. He'd driven his men into the heart of darkness; many had survived. The idea of abandoning Port Moresby, for

---

* Citing 'prisoners' statements', Akiyama claimed that the Australians had suffered 'enormous losses'. He appears to have been well informed. One company in the 2/14th Battalion (A Company) whose normal strength was 120, 'numbered only 50' and another (B coy) had been reduced to 28 men, as at 9 September. The losses, a result of deaths, wounds and disease, were about right.

which thousands had been killed or wounded, was intolerable. For Horii, the deeds of the dead were more important than the lives of the living.*

In many ways, Horii had only himself to blame for the supply failure. One POW, Lieutenant Inagaki Riichi, said that Horii had always expected his troops to eat off the land. Another fatal error was his decision to commandeer the powerful Formosans (known as the Takasago**) for mountain use, when they were supposed to be delivering supplies from the Buna beachhead to Kokoda. So the crucial section over the Kumusi River was left to weaker carriers.

Horii stubbornly clung to the advance. He sent Japanese patrols to reconnoitre enemy positions, with a view to launching an attack on Port Moresby on 'about the 20th September'.[11] The Kusunose Butai — whose leader arrived on a stretcher — would form the front line, with support from the apparently inexhaustible Yokoyama Independent Engineer regiment.

In readiness, the officers tried to fortify their depleted ranks. Orders flew down the lines for the immediate requisitioning of native food. All captured arms and supplies were to be instantly reported. A strict rationing regime controlled the consumption of salvaged Australian and native food. Resource Collecting Tai were dispatched to gather taro, yams, sugar cane, pumpkins and green vegetables. The daily rice quota was cut to under a pint on 11 September, and two days later, 'men involved in great physical exertion' were to get two thirds of a pint, and the rest, even less.[12]

The Tomita Battalion's discovery of an abundance of sugar cane, taro, yams, pumpkins, melons and vegetables relieved this crippling regime, to some extent (it didn't help the Rabaul carriers, who received a mere one-third of a pint of rice a day — barely enough for an inactive man to survive on).

---

* One prisoner later claimed that officers criticised Horii for 'unnecessary waste of lives during the Stanley campaign'. Some of Horii's top ranks had recommended an earlier retreat to the coast to await reinforcements, 'but Horii roughly refused to listen to advice' (ATIS Interrogation Report 211).

** The Formosans, former headhunters, had a reputation for utter fearlessness and astonishing endurance. Some still carried their bolo knives, which in early times were used to severe their victims' heads. Most had volunteered for the Japanese army, claims Inagaki Riichi, and some wrote their enlistment applications in their own blood. The Formosan government explicitly requested of the Japanese not to pay their bonuses 'as big wages might spoil them in future' (ATIS Interrogation Report 54).

'The fullest use must be made of taro, wheat and other local produce and captured food in order to maintain fighting strength,' one captain told his unit in a hastily scrawled note.[13] He sternly added: 'The eating of captured food between meals is forbidden.' Nor were the men allowed to prepare their 'rice substitutes' in their tents, as they pleased. Officers had been ordered to report in writing whether they believed their food would last until 23 September.

In mid-September a few fitter Japanese troops attempted to pursue the Australians into the valley between Ioribaiwa and Imita Ridge. It was here that the Australian 2/33rd Battalion mounted the most lethal Allied ambush of the campaign. They lay in wait in the tall grasslands. At 6.45 a.m. on the 15th some 50 to 70 Japanese troops led by a sword-bearing officer marched into the area 'carrying tins of Aussie food'.[14] Bunched together in two files, none seemed on their guard. They marched along 'chattering and laughing' in a 'wanton suicidal move'.[15]

Captain Larry Miller shot the swordsman, and 80 Australian rifles, Tommy guns and mortars opened up in a barrage of fire. For two minutes, 3000 rounds were shot into 'this screaming, writhing heap of humanity'.[16] The Australians withdrew, planting booby traps along the track and observation posts in the treetops.

After the ambush, the Japanese sent no more troops forward. They were, literally, at the end of the line — and daily showed signs of physical and mental collapse.

The Japanese soldiers did not openly complain. It was deemed unworthy of the Imperial Army to whinge about hunger and sickness. This severe, if medically disastrous, tradition permeated the armed forces. Troops were not to lose their martial spirit merely because they were hungry.[17] To fall ill was seen as disloyal. Japanese soldiers were imbued with the idea that succumbing to sickness and hunger was a disgrace and 'a dereliction of duty to the Emperor'.[18]

A soldier did not simply get sick, he 'allowed himself to become sick' through 'negligence of the body'.[19] Those guilty of deliberately neglecting their health faced imprisonment, according to the official *Extracts from Court Martials and Punishments*. Mindful of the shame of illness, many soldiers tried to suppress the signs until it was too late; then they simply collapsed. Casualties multiplied. Some commanders saw this, and tried to encourage the men to report symptoms early.

It was an extraordinary paradox that, while Japanese medical science at home was highly advanced, the quality of medical care at the front reverted to the Dark Ages. Doctors doubled as combatants, carried weapons, and were obliged to prod and harry the sick and wounded back to the front lines as quickly as possible. Medical orderlies did not wear the Red Cross insignia (it was merely displayed on their satchels).[20]

The wounded were operated on without anaesthetic or painkillers — 'as a soldier he should be able to endure pain unflinchingly'.[21] The most hopeless stretcher cases were left to die, ordered to commit suicide or shot.* Such was the fate of the seriously wounded in the last battles of Ioribaiwa.

Some Japanese doctors were ashamed of this affront to their duty of care, and disturbed by the woeful quality of army medicine. Of course, this didn't help the victims, or arrest the decline. Doctors were powerless: 'The medical personnel, unable to appease the hunger of the wounded lying in agony at the front line, feel deeply their responsibility as hospital officials,' said army medical officer First Lieutenant Okubo Fukunobo.[22]

Captured diaries and documents dated towards the end of September portray an army slowly starving to death: 'We gave some dry bread to the Engineer Tai at the foot of the hill. They had not eaten anything for two days, and said it was delicious,' one entry records.

---

* Ueda Masami, captured in August 1944, 'had had malaria so badly that he was among those ordered to commit suicide, since they were neither able to work or fight', noted his interrogators. 'He did not obey this order, he said, because he felt that the Emperor would prefer that he remained able to fight' (ATIS Research Report 76 [VI], AWM 12/53). Ueda's case was typical, according to one Allied informant, an Indian medical captain who became a Japanese POW in February 1942 and served in a Japanese medical unit until 1944: 'The Japanese believe that a sick man is of no service to the Emperor,' the Indian doctor said. 'If a doctor thinks a patient may, after treatment return to active service, he will [receive] attention, but if really ill medicine and treatment will not be wasted on him; he may even be shot.' Later in the war, the Japanese sick and wounded were always the first to suffer the deprivations of an army on its knees. In Bougainville, for example, the medical orderlies were repeatedly ordered to shoot the seriously sick. In the Philippines in 1945, the hospitalised received two rice balls a day, compared with six for fit troops. They were considered simply not worth feeding, and slowly starved to death.

Within a few days Sakomoto fully comprehended the fate of his men: 'How will we live in our present position without food?' he wrote on the 18th. 'Inspected tents and noticed scarcity of food. Entire company turned out to find food.' That day he went to his HQ to report the food crisis and to order supplies: 'Returned empty handed,' he noted.

He dared to suggest High Command were responsible: 'Wonder what General HQ are doing? Patients will die and we will soon starve. How can we fight against this?'[23]

Again, on the 20th, the machine-gunner articulated the despair of the whole force: 'Never till now, did I realise the true meaning of the saying "A full belly counsels well". Not a single grain of rice left. Taroes sufficient for only another day. From tomorrow we will have to chew grass or bark.'*

Sakomoto wrote this on the day Horii had earlier fixed for the supposed invasion of Port Moresby.**

Towards the end of September, the human chain that stretched over the mountains to Kokoda and the coast, where boats fed it from Rabaul, was in chaos. The sentient Japanese soldier knew it was near collapse: he had only to view the pitiful result at his end.

Allied air attacks were getting more accurate, and persistent. The American General George Kenney, Allied air commander since 3 September, boasted that his massive air bombardment had halted the Japanese advance. This was not true. More often than not, his pilots missed. The jungle canopy

---

* Sakomoto never seemed to lose faith in the invasion: 'The battle we are fighting now is an important one. The eyes of the whole world are upon us,' he wrote that day.

** The Shitai's medical department, such as it was, had issued a set of orders to 'high ranking medical officers' aptly titled, 'Matters pertaining to health during period of waiting'. It was singularly unhelpful. Defecation 'in the open' and drinking unboiled water 'after eating biscuits' were forbidden. There was the peculiar rule, 'even during an action, troops are forbidden to relieve themselves in the vicinity of roads'. There were no roads, of course; these orders were drawn from a standard text. Stream water should be divided into water for drinking, cooking and cleaning, it instructed, sensibly. Wooden floorboards should be placed on tent floors, and any draughts blocked with vegetation. Malaria sufferers were to receive 'internal medicine', and those who had not contracted the disease should be wary of the anopheles mosquito, which 'is found in the valley areas'. Many of the Shitai's 'health tips' revealed the gross ignorance of the medical department. A similar disregard for biological truth coloured their advice on leeches. The harmless, if ubiquitous, bloodsuckers were 'the most terrible things. There is no method of avoiding them ... their bite is not usually fatal to human beings' (ATIS Enemy Publications No. 38).

obscured the targets, and the topography made low-level missions perilous. Often they strafed the Australian ground troops. Even visible targets eluded them. When Australian troops requested the bombing and strafing of Ioribaiwa, a 'village ... easily found from the air', the pilots failed to find the ridge.[24]

It was not for want of trying — and many sorties bombed open targets on the beaches. Throughout September and October 'Ken's Men' (the 43rd Bombardment Group of the Fifth American Air Force, apparently named after Kenney himself) attacked the Japanese lines over the Owen Stanleys and the boats arriving at Buna. Australian pilots from the 75 and 76 squadrons, vital to the defeat of the Japanese at Milne Bay, were equally active.

Consider a few days in the life of Ken's Men during September. On the 3rd, they bombed and strafed Kokoda airfield, Alola, Isurava and Missima. On the 5th, P-40s machine-gunned Kokoda, Kaile, Isurava, Alola, Buna, Sanananda, and the Buna–Kokoda trail. On the 7th, A-20s and P-40s attacked Japanese positions at Myola and Efogi. On the 11th, A-20s and B-26s again struck Efogi and Menari. The next day, a huge squadron of P-40s, B-26s, A-20s, and B-17s bombed the airfield and strafed supply barges at Buna; further barges were destroyed at Sanananda on the 16th.[25]

October was a virtual turkey shoot. Enemy camps, huts, barges, ships and troop formations were targeted. How many were actually hit is unclear. The bridge over the Kumusi at Wairopi — vital for getting Horii's supplies in — was bombed as frequently as it was patched up, and destroyed altogether on 2 October, thereby denying Horii an escape route across the river.[26]

On the ground there was mayhem. Native carriers deserted in terror, taking whatever food they could; the wounded scrambled into holes under the jungle canopy; soldiers' attempts to direct anti-aircraft fire were useless. Koreans and Formosans — and Japanese transport troops — were left to man the supply line when the natives deserted.

If the food survived Allied air raids, it did not escape theft and sabotage. The Rabaul carriers and Korean labourers who bore most of the loads stole a huge quantity. They knifed open bags of rice, bored holes into bread packages, and pocketed tins of beef. Much of what reached the hungry troops at the front was half-eaten, or spoiled. The Korean carriers, whom the Japanese tended to view as 'a lazy, shiftless and thieving lot', were generally blamed and severely punished if caught.[27]

In one case, 'only 5 tins of beef remained out of 33'.[28] Bread parcels were bayoneted, rice pilfered. Half-cooked rice was found strewn along the track. Native carriers were also blamed for any theft and punished, even though evidence suggested Japanese troops were the more likely culprits. The carriers were given a third of a pint of rice daily, half that of other transport personnel. Stragglers, Horii noted with disgust, had 'thrown away ammunition … used cleaned rice in excess of their ration, and consumed biscuits etc'.

Much rice got wet and putrefied. To combat this Horii issued a long list of cooking instructions. Wet rice must be separated from dry rice, wrapped in special containers, laid out to dry whenever the unit halted, and consumed first; or roasted and turned into hard-dried *hoshii*.

Rations were slashed. Combat troops received one mess tin of rice per day, and were told to complement their diet with taro and other native vegetables. The natives got a third of this, if they were lucky.

The native carriers collapsed or deserted under this regime, and the Nankai Transport Corps were forced to double their efforts to get the rice over the mountains. But they, too, yielded to temptation. 'We worked desperately to get it to the front line,' said one transport officer.[29] An eighteen-litre bag of rice had typically lost as much as four or five litres to pilfering and wastage by the time it reached Efogi; it was virtually empty by Ioribaiwa. The Transport Corps were ordered to salvage the losses, and adopted the motto, 'Even if it's just one grain of rice, let's get it to the front!'

But they were ravenous — their two cups of rice a day was not enough to sustain them — and they couldn't help nibbling on their loads. When bags split, 'these fallen grains were a source of uncontrollable temptation', said the transport officer. 'Though we focused on the fact that we must not let the front line starve, in our hearts, we couldn't but be aware that we ourselves would die [on two cups of rice per day].'

'Our commander repeatedly issued the order that fallen rice be collected and sent to the front, but the increasingly starving rear-guard corps felt that this was virtually impossible ... By the time we arrived at the front, much of the rice had seemingly evaporated into thin air.'[30]

By late September no supplies were getting through to Ioribaiwa. Horii ordered that every man must try to capture enemy provisions and 'make the fullest use of taro and the like'.

His army had received just two airdrops — on 23 and 29 September — at Kokoda.[31] Allied planes were close to cutting off all seaward landing at Buna and Gona. Nor could he communicate adequately with Kokoda to fix the supply lines. There was a tendency, he stressed, for troops to slash 'our own, yellow wiring', mistaking it for Australian communication lines.[32]

By the last week of September some 1500 to 2000 survivors of the Nankai Shitai were cut off — by air, sea and cable — in the mountains.

Chapter 32
Retreat

'I'm not going back, not a step! How can we abandon this
position, after all the blood the soldiers have shed and the
hardships they have endured? I cannot give such an order'
— *Major-General Horii Tomitaro to his staff officer at Ioribaiwa*

Horii's deadline for the invasion of Port Moresby, 20 September, passed
without a movement. Torrential afternoon rains drenched the ridge,
and the Japanese troops sat and contemplated their position. The scale of the
anti-climax engendered a deep depression. Reality came seeping in. 'Every
company is reduced to about half its strength,' wrote Private Watanabe of the
Tsukamoto Battalion. The bodies of the Japanese who'd died storming the
ridge remained on the northern slopes; the troops hadn't the strength to
burn or bury them. Lieutenant Hayashi Hiroyuki of Shitai Headquarters
couldn't endure the stench 'of the tremendous litter of the dead'.

Horii issued a message to the troops that day. It can be read as the last
gasp of a proud general indulging in memories of battles of dubious merit,
in order to prepare his army for the shock of retreat. He makes no mention
of the immense losses, delays, and the pointlessness of the advance despite
how much he knew about his supply failure:

Message of instruction:

It is now over one month since we took over from the Yokoyama Unit ... We first reduced the strong position at Isurava, and continued on crushing the enemy's resistance ... at The Gap, Eora, Efogi, etc ... We smashed his last resistance in the fierce fighting at Ioribaawa [sic] and today we firmly hold the line on the heights of that area, the most important point for the advance on Port Moresby.

For more than 20 days ... every unit forced its way through deep forests and ravines, and climbed over ... high peaks in pursuit of the enemy. Traversing mud more than knee-deep, clambering up steep precipices, bearing uncomplainingly the heavy weight of artillery ammunition, our men overcame the shortage of our supplies, and we succeeded in surmounting the Stanley Range. No pen or word can depict adequately the magnitude of the hardships suffered.[1]

Conceding that the Americans at Guadalcanal and Tulagi had 'not yet been annihilated', Horii urged his men to 'strike a hammer-blow at the enemy stronghold of Moresby ... in front of us, the enemy still crawls about ...'* (He claimed the Shitai had killed 300 Australians at Isurava and 320 at Brigade Hill; the actual figures were about 250 and 77).

If Horii believed this message, he'd possibly lost his mind — or suffered from Captain Ahab syndrome, with Port Moresby transmogrifying into the white whale. His own officers, notably Tanaka, saw the writing on the wall: the severe setback at Guadalcanal, the diversion of reinforcements to the Solomons and the defeat at Milne Bay meant that the order to withdraw was imminent.

Sunset on 24 September found the Japanese commander sitting 'solemnly upright on his heels, his face emaciated, his grey hair reflecting the dim light of a candle, that stood on the inner lid of a ration can'.[2] The flickering light

---

* Another translator rendered this last phrase, 'the enemy is still squirming forward'.

played on his worn face. Lieutenant-Colonel Tanaka sat opposite him, a rigid silhouette in the orange glow of twilight — 'two lonely shadows' against the wet canvas.

Up ahead the Japanese forces clung to the summit of Ioribaiwa like a little medieval village isolated by some terrible disease. With weary inevitability the rain came down in heavy, spitting droplets. Torn tents and hastily built lean-tos served as pathetic shelters for this doomed fragment, whose gaunt faces peered out on the steaming jungle, tormented by thoughts of their next meal.

That day a wireless message had arrived from General Imamura Hitoshi, commander of the Southern Army in Rabaul: 'Stop attacking Port Moresby,' it said, 'and wait for further instructions at present position.'

Later a second message came: 'Withdraw from present position to some point in the Owen Stanley Range which you consider best for strategic purposes.'[3]

Horii, stubborn to the end, reacted angrily. 'I'm not going back, not a step!' he shouted at Tanaka. 'How can we abandon this position, after all the blood the soldiers have shed and the hardships they have endured? I cannot give such an order.'

There are melodramatic flourishes in Okada's account of what happened next. Apparently Horii 'grasped his samurai sword', drew up within inches of Tanaka, and added in a biting tone: 'I will not retreat an inch. I'd rather disguise myself as a native of these mountains and stay here!'

Tanaka was silent, 'watching the burning wick of the candle as though to avoid the commander's eyes, when a rustling sound was heard in the thicket outside'.[4] Then the signal squad commander came in with another wireless message, from the army commander at Rabaul, who instructed the Nankai Shitai 'to withdraw completely from the Owen Stanleys and concentrate on the coast at Buna'.

In case any doubt remained, another wire immediately followed, reported Okada. It carried the imprimatur of the divine — sent directly from Imperial HQ in Tokyo: 'It was now beyond doubt that the order . . . had been authorised by the Emperor himself,' the journalist claimed. It seems incredible that Hirohito should have taken a direct interest in the welfare of this tiny, hungry cog in the vast Japanese military machine.

Perhaps the news that his South Seas Detachment had almost reached Port Moresby impressed him. Whatever the reason, His Majesty must be obeyed.

'A terrible grief cut deep into our hearts,' remembers Takita Kenji. 'This must be what is meant by "*namida o nomu*" that is, to drink or swallow one's tears.'[5]

For the Imperial Army, it was a new experience. The Nankai Shitai had never retreated from a battleground. 'No one knew what was going to happen — they didn't know how to retreat,' said Imanishi.[6]

At 9.00 a.m. the next morning Horii ordered his officers to withdraw. They responded with great bitterness. Hungry men within sight of the sea could not fathom the decision. 'Hot blooded battalion commanders advocated a desperate single-handed thrust into Port Moresby,' reported Okada.[7]

'The order came like a bolt from the blue,' said Captain Nakahashi, 'causing an overflowing ... of emotion, which could not be suppressed; it was compounded by feelings of anger, sorrow and frustration. The purpose, the dreams and the desires of the officers and soldiers of the South Seas Force had vanished in an instant.'[8]

Horii's staff officer Tanaka — apparently a man of inexhaustible patience — tried to reason with senior ranks angry at being told to abandon their heavy guns: 'I know how you feel,' Tanaka said gently, 'but it can't be helped. Guns are valuable but soldiers are more valuable. Leave your guns and ammunition and all that. We must take every living soldier with us — every living soldier, sick or wounded.'[9]

The Japanese top brass passed the order down the ranks. Many of the ordinary troops were motionless with shock — 'stupefied among the rocks' in Okada's vivid phrase. Sakomoto noted briefly: 'Received orders to withdraw to Isurava. Regretted leaving an area captured with brave warriors' blood.'[10]

A few available native carriers were press-ganged into lines, supplies that could not be carried were destroyed, and the battalions formed up.

On 25 September, at precisely 11.00 a.m., an Australian heavy artillery cannon fired its first shells towards the Japanese positions. The troops lining Imita Ridge cheered on every blast. Even Albert Moore of the Salvation Army delighted a little guiltily in the arrival of the first artillery piece.

It had taken seven days and 50 Australian sappers using a powerful pulley system to winch the gun up the Golden Stairs — an amazing engineering feat.[11] Though the shells fell short of the Japanese across the valley, the sound of their crumping explosions on the southern approaches to Ioribaiwa sent a clear message to the enemy: heavy cannon had arrived for the first time in the campaign. If Horii had any remaining plans to disguise himself as a native and stay, they were swiftly expunged.

Sakomoto rose early on the 26th to prepare for the day's departure. The sick and wounded were assembled at 8.30 a.m.; the dead were buried. 'It is truly regrettable,' he wrote, 'having to leave . . . the bodies of our comrades and the ground that we won so dearly. Sleep peacefully my friends. Farewell. We shall meet again in Heaven.'[12]

The Japanese prayed to their Shinto gods under a fresh deluge that drenched the heights from which they watched the gathering Australian forces across the valley. As a last gesture of defiance they fired a few rounds of their little wheeled mountain gun — dwarfed by the Australians' 25-pounder — 'thereby uplifting our downcast spirits and those of our dead comrades' and formed up. A few, too weak to stand, stayed on Ioribaiwa and died there.

The retreat began at 5.00 p.m. that afternoon, and continued 'all night through the woods under the moonlight' to avoid air attack.[13]

An odd thing happened as the Japanese moved out. Their bitterness gave way to feelings of relief. The fitter troops were suddenly animated by the will to live. The general oppressiveness seemed to evaporate. They were on a northern route for the first time in the war. They no longer faced the Allied guns. They were heading, geographically at least, home. To men inured to the harshest military tradition, the idea of actually surviving the war perilously entered their minds. Had the will to live survived the cult of death? Okada witnessed the moment:

... once in retreat they fled for dear life. None of them had ever thought that a Japanese soldier would turn his back on the enemy. But they were actually beating a retreat! There was no denying that. As soon as they realised the truth, they were seized with an instinctive desire to live. Neither history nor education had any meaning for them now. Discipline was completely forgotten. Each tried for his life to flee faster than his comrades.[14]

The Horie and Kuwada battalions pushed north under a clear night. Some of those too sick or hungry to keep up were left by the track: twelve men too weak to continue remained at Nauro, and soon died of starvation or sickness. Dozens more suffered a similar fate a little further up the track.

Those with foot rot, fever, or malaria moved a few inches at a time, shaking violently and leaning with both hands on long wooden sticks. Few survived. 'Here and there along the path soldiers were seen lying motionless, unable to walk any longer,' reported Okada.[15]

The Japanese, however, did try to carry out the remaining stretcher cases. Since native stretcher-bearers were scarce, the troops attempted to shoulder their own wounded, an impossible task for a malnourished army: 'The wounded not only had to bear their wounds,' witnessed Captain Nakashima in early October, 'they were under a great mutual strain caused by the unremitting toil of their comrades ... the stretcher cases overcome with emotion would cry out, "Please leave us here", "Let us die". The stretcher-bearers kept their emotions under control and in an effort to encourage the sick and wounded, spoke harshly to them ... If the situation remained unchanged both patients and stretcher-bearers would die together.'[16]

It was decided to save the lives of the bearers by putting the hopelessly wounded out of their misery. They were shot in the stretchers. 'The matter was settled and before long rifle shots reverberated throughout the jungle.'[17]

Up ahead, Okada and a fellow journalist called Sato walked day and night — 'on walking depended our lives' — under threat of daily air attack. They scrounged for food in market gardens, and found not a single potato. Small plantations had been stripped, and the stems of papayas had been 'rooted out and bitten to the pith'.

Aggressive Australian patrols had been probing the enemy at Ioribaiwa for several days; one, led by Sergeant Bede Tongs of the 3rd Battalion, had slashed the Japanese communication line and killed several enemy troops. The absence of a strong response emboldened the Australians, and the entire 25th Brigade was ordered to attack Ioribaiwa at dawn on the 28th.

The three Australian battalions moved off on the 26th, the day officially marked as the start of the counteroffensive. They dropped to the valley floor, crossed the Goldie River, and pushed up the Ioribaiwa razorback towards the Japanese camp. On the night of the 27th 'our ... guns harassed the whole ridge and at dawn ... swept it from the right to the left'.[18]

'H hour' for the attack was 9.00 o'clock the next morning. Two Australian companies, about two hundred men, walked onto the ridge unopposed, and radioed their HQ, 'not a Jap ... sighted'.[19] At first, Brigade HQ didn't believe this: perhaps the troops were in the wrong place, they thought.

A battalion commander, Lieutenant-Colonel Alfred Buttrose, hurried forward: sure enough, the enemy had gone. Much abandoned equipment lay scattered about. The Australians especially admired the enemy's giant tripod-mounted observation binoculars, with which they clearly viewed their own positions, back across the valley.

Sakomoto, the machine-gunner who led the attack on Brigade Hill, chronicled the Japanese retreat in his diary. It is a unique portrayal of the Imperial Army in decline:

September 27, 1942: Men are searching in the moonlight for
food. Sickness increased.
    October 1: Rations reduced again due to bombing of ...
supplies.
    October 3: Dried wild berry grass to smoke as cigarettes ...
Men under rank of NCO ... are getting disrespectful.
    October 4: Woke up and made a fire, but not one man got
up to assist me, everyone is so egotistical. It is damp and dark

here. We have no more than a handful of rice left. If we remain until the end we will all die ... What is the army doing?

0500: Twenty men left for Isurava to dig for potatoes.

October 7: 0700 ... Did not feel well. Diagnosed by a doctor as beri-beri.

1800. Our company commander was sent back with a large supply of rations. He seems unconcerned whether we starve or not. Takes his exercise by riding a horse, and yet he could not come to the front! Kokoda has been bombed daily.

October 8: Spent all day gathering Australian rice. I was amazed at the various ways one is able to prepare tainted rice ... Two thirds of the men are suffering from beri-beri. Their visual powers and physical strength are weakened ... Our life here is worse than a beggar's. Wish the people back home could see our condition.

October 10: Arose and spent few moments meditating. Cruel nature, God take us to paradise. Each day, we are nearing our death ... We seem to have been left behind, no order has come out yet ...

October 11: ... A man consciously shows his true character when faced by hunger and hardship; he becomes rowdy and rude.

As the condition of his men worsened, Sakomoto's thoughts darkened. He shed his usual deference to High Command, and seemed even to lose faith in the Code of the Warrior:

October 13: Had only a sip of rice gruel for breakfast and half a package of dried bread for lunch. What will we eat for supper? Complaints of discontented soldiers were heard continuously, the effect of inefficient administration and management by the Butai at the rear ...

October 17: Attitude of 2nd Lieutenant Nagano is disgusting ... His only concern is his own safety ... Enemy active again. According to reports from our scouts, enemy troops were groggy, possibly from lack of food. Better men than we are.[20]

Chapter 33
MacArthur

'...by some act of God your brigade has been chosen for this job. The eyes of the Western world are upon you. I have every confidence in you and your men. Good luck and don't stop'
— *General Douglas MacArthur to the departing Australian troops*

A cavalcade of generals, politicians and military police accompanied by 'war correspondents galore'[1] drove up the muddy road to Owers' Corner. From this point, above the Goldie River Valley, the Kokoda Track starts its winding route over the mountains. Deceptively, the first step is down; the trail plunges to Uberi, on the riverbank, and then ascends the Golden Stairs to Imita.

It was the morning of 3 October 1942. General Douglas MacArthur sat imperiously in his open jeep, serene and apparently unshaken, notwithstanding the severely potholed road. The supreme commander's first appearance in New Guinea achieved its goal of demonstrating to a sceptical world that Port Moresby was safe, and the Japanese in retreat. As a publicity stunt, it was impressively timed. The American correspondents were obliged to tone down their panic-stricken reports of September. Perhaps Port Moresby wasn't going to be 'another Singapore'.

The only Australian journalist at this historic media outing was a photographer from the Department of Information — the rest had slept in or missed the bus. When they woke up they officially complained that MacArthur's PR men had failed to alert them to the event.*

Singularly out of the loop, the Australian media were unable to correct one politician who was quoted in the Sydney papers as saying, 'Australians were now fighting in country almost impassable to motor transport'.[2]

The entourage climbed out of their jeeps and mingled with the troops. They were not here merely for appearances. MacArthur had come to Owers' Corner to energise the counteroffensive and to witness the departure over the Owen Stanleys of Australia's 16th Brigade. He and Blamey briefly scanned the country from the precipice across the valley to Imita Ridge beyond which successive razorbacks melted into the blue-green haze. The heavy guns at Imita were silent now, as the Japanese had retreated as far as Myola.

Grinning jovially in his pith helmet, the Minister for the Army ingratiated himself with the troops, promised them the world, and posed for photographs. Frank Forde cut a blimpish presence: 'It was indeed an inspiring sight,' he noted, 'to see these lads stripped to the waist and toiling in the tropical heat and rain to keep the roadway continuously open ...'[3] The troops later had some fun with this slightly ridiculous figure; Forde went away burdened with the idea that the Japanese soldier's 'peculiar manner of waging warfare' involved donning 'a suit of body armour which is invulnerable to submachine gun fire'.[4]

Lieutenant Dalrymple Fayle kept an entertaining diary of the morning's photo opportunity:

The civilians in the party caused much mirth. They were clothed in semi-military clothing which fitted in a very unmilitary

---

* The chief publicity censor, E.G. Bonney, deemed the vehemence of the Australian war reporters' complaint worthy of prime ministerial attention, and told Curtin: 'It is possible that you may hear from Canberra pressmen a complaint that Australian Newspaper men in Moresby were not given an even break with American correspondents on General MacArthur's activities there ... I feel sure that our Newspaper men missed the bus through their own lack of alertness. Colonel Diller could hardly have been expected to take time off to round up all Australian correspondents' (CRS M1415).

manner and they were arrayed in tin hats and pistol belts of air force pattern ...

The politicians spent their time getting about amongst the troops promising them all sorts of impossible things and promising to write to their folk etc. They certainly admired the scenery and got frightfully sunburnt, especially behind the knees, but as far as we could see did nothing much but waste a lot of valuable time and use jeeps which were vitally needed for some real purpose.[5]

The dignitaries were a long way from the front line. Australia's 25th Brigade had by then reached Nauro, and advanced 'by double pincers and central block'.[6] General Tubby Allen, commander of the 7th Division, was bored by the whole occasion. He muttered that he'd far prefer to be slogging over the Kokoda Track with his men than milling about for a photo opportunity and talking to the press. His wish would soon be granted.

At 10.30 a.m. the entourage took morning tea. 'Gen MacArthur impressed everyone ... extremely friendly and considerate and very much a leader,' wrote Fayle. Army Minister Forde was, however, 'a washout, but we all hope he can do at least some of the things he promised.'[7] After tea, the generals inspected the departing troops.

Australia then had no fitter soldiers than the 16th Brigade. It comprised some 3000 men (divided among the 2/1st, 2/2nd and 2/3rd battalions) of the 6th Division. They were highly trained, experienced combat infantry, veterans of the Middle East and North Africa, with an average age of 25. 'They looked like the greatest specimens of soldiers we'd ever seen,' said a few militiamen who witnessed a bayonet charge.[8]

Most had been trained in the jungles of Ceylon (Sri Lanka); they garrisoned Colombo on their way back from the Middle East. Their jungle training was thorough. They had been taught to use the jungle to advantage: to 'melt' into the foliage; to retrace their steps at night; to use camouflage properly; to detect human presence by crushed twigs and disturbed leaf mould; to move silently over undergrowth; to build shelters; and to discern human from animal sounds. They were taught even to detect the enemy's peculiar smell, 'an unpleasant dank odour which is most persistent'.[9] They were repatriated on 4 July to ticker tape parades in the capital cities at which the people welcomed them home as conquering heroes. Thirty-six days later, they were dispatched to Port Moresby.

Colonel (now Major-General) Paul Cullen, DSO, AC, CBE, ED, led the 2/1st Battalion. Cullen was a veteran of the Middle East and Crete, where he met the English novelist Evelyn Waugh. When attacked by German dive-bombers, Cullen recalled, 'We all dashed to take cover under the nearest twig. Waugh remained standing on the road. After the attack, we asked why he did not take cover like the rest of us. "I have got such a large arse that it makes no difference whether I am standing up or lying down," Waugh replied.'

In 2004, at the age of 95, Cullen was sharp as a tack and still riding his horse around the family farm near Goulburn. A great, rambling raconteur, he interrupts his stories with loud, foghorn laughter:

And they [journalists] asked another question . . . what happens when your friend is wounded or killed? Well, two thoughts happen, I said. One was you're bloody glad that it wasn't you . . . and the other was the joke. I remember at the battle of Bardia, Geoffrey Cox [loud laughter] was hobbling off, and he was shot in the arse, and we said, 'You're a lucky bastard, Cox, you've got five arse holes' [uproarious laughter]. I mean, this is the cynical humour engendered by casualties in war. A few hours before, one of my friends, Scott Jones, was the first officer killed in my battalion, and I'll always remember that one, because he was lying with his hand like that [clutches glass] holding the glass — he was a bit of a drinker you see. But you laugh at that . . . you think that's funny, holding a glass when you're lying there dead. That's what you think about, you have to laugh don't you? [laughter]

That was after the Western Desert. You see, one of the factors why the 6th Division did so well in Kokoda was that we'd fought in three different continents in the first six months of 1941, three different continents against three different European nations; in the

Western Desert against the Italians [laughter]...Greece and Crete against the Germans, where we lost but were not disgraced ... and then against the Vichy French in Syria which we won, and we were pretty bloody experienced soldiers ... I mean what other division fought in three different continents against three different European nations in six months? We were perfectly equipped ...

If anyone was going to beat the Japs you were?

Absolutely. It was wonderful preparation.

Did you feel confident about victory at Kokoda?

Well, we were confident about everything. I was always confident about anything, that's been the tragedy of my life ... I don't have any complaints; I've had a wonderful life [laughter]...We really weren't frightened of anybody. We were light, headstrong, impulsive. We were pretty bloody good. That's the whole secret of leadership, you've got to convince yourselves that you're the best.

We just got on and did it ... like Private McDonald. The doctor said he'd got appendicitis, you might die from it, and we'll have to operate. He had no anaesthetic you see, so I said to McDonald, you've got to have this out without an anaesthetic. I'll hold your hand. So we took him and laid him on the table, I held his hand, we gave him a bottle of Scotch, and took his appendix out. But that was life, I wouldn't dare do it today, you wouldn't have had to ... but our lives then were like that — you had to, you had to.[10]

Cullen distilled the art of war into three inviolable principles: 1. No bad soldiers, only bad officers; 2. Woolly orders get woolly results; 3. That which is not inspected is not done.

For once, the digger looked the part: no more the khaki-clad, baggy-shorted Anzac in a slouch hat. The 16th Brigade wore a steel helmet camouflaged with a Hessian net; long-sleeved shirt and trousers dyed 'streaky green' (shorts were acceptable in malaria-free areas, so long as all bare knees were stained green); and American green gaiters and boots fitted with sprigs, of 'first class condition'. The soldier carried a green veil to cover his face. Underpants and singlets were at the soldier's discretion.

All badges of rank were removed to avoid detection by Japanese snipers. The 25th Brigade had taken the same precaution. 'Jap snipers had an unhappy knack of choosing as a target any soldier who seemed to be in a position of authority,' wrote one lieutenant. 'We were told if we wanted to survive ... we must not draw attention to ourselves.' Pistols were carried not on the hip but slung around to the back. Officers were told not to wave their hands about or shout orders to the men.[11]

In his haversack the soldier carried a green beret (the slouch hat was on the wane); a 'golf jacket', or windcheater; foot powder; a featherweight, waterproofed sleeping bag; half a towel, half a dixie, six tins of bully beef, six packets of biscuits, a spoon, tea, sugar, quinine and powered milk. All webbing equipment was dyed green. In his large front pockets he carried a field dressing and emergency rations. One entrenching tool, or shovel, in a green bag was allocated to every three men. Ammunition included 100 rounds of .303 bullets for each rifleman; or ten magazines (300 rounds) per light machine-gunner, plus two grenades per man. Each soldier also had 'a good supply of salt'.[12]

The Anzac had changed utterly: 'On Kokoda,' said Hank Nelson, 'the Australian army transformed itself from the image of the World War I digger to the green-clad jungle fighter, an image ... the Australians were to retain for the next sixty years.'[13]

Their mentality was different, too. They were prepared for the onslaught. They were jungle-trained, and confident. They'd closely studied the enemy's tactics, and had heard all the usual horror stories. To say they hated the enemy is inaccurate; it implies they recognised the enemy as human. On the contrary they were trained to see the Japanese as inhuman: 'The Jap' was something bestial, an unspeakable brute to be hunted down and systematically slaughtered. The Australians had become predators; the Japanese, the prey.

With his inimitable grasp of metaphor, General George Vasey drilled the message into unit commanders, in a circular on 23 September:

The Japanese are well trained in jungle warfare. In this form of warfare they are like tigers, cunning, silent and dangerous. Like tigers, too, they are vermin and like vermin they must be destroyed. One does not expect a live tiger to give himself up to capture so we must not expect the Japanese to surrender. He does not. He must be killed whether it is by shooting, bayoneting, throttling, knocking out his brains with a tin hat or by any other means our ingenuity can devise. Truly jungle warfare is a game of kill or be killed and to play it successfully demands alertness of all senses but particularly of ears and eyes. The latter must not be focused on the next footstep but continually looking all about including upwards at the trees.[14]

Vasey's words resonated with senior officers. The 16th Brigade's commander, Brigadier John Edward Lloyd (DSO, MC) said his men 'would clean up the Jap in quick time. They have ... a complete hatred of the Jap and what he stands for.' Echoing Vasey, he added, 'They ... realised it was a matter of KILL or be KILLED and that it was TOTAL WAR with a vengeance [Lloyd's capitals].'[15]

The troops were trained to think as conquerors, not defenders. It was essential to dislodge the crippling idea that the Japanese troops were somehow superior. The warrior myth must be utterly vanquished from their minds. 'The Jap' must be ruthlessly dehumanised. 'Any illusion that the Jap is a superman leans strongly towards the ridiculous,' wrote Lloyd. 'His minor tactics, by our standards, are unsound, ie, he bunches during the assault, chatters during the approach, and his forward patrols blunder into ambushes ...' But, Vasey warned: 'The Jap soldier has, however, the cardinal virtue of all soldiers. He will fight to the death ...'[16]

Lloyd, a veteran of World War I, had led the 2/28th Battalion at Tobruk before being promoted to command the 16th Brigade. Described as a genial leader with the manner of an English regular officer, he was 49 when he set off over the Owen Stanleys. His orders were to relieve the 25th Brigade, drive the Japanese over the mountains, recapture the Kokoda airfield and, with two American regiments and fresh Australian units coming up from the east, destroy the enemy in detail.

MacArthur fixed his eyes on the brigadier and his men as they marched past, and famously declared: 'Lloyd, by some act of God your brigade has been chosen for this job. The eyes of the Western world are upon you. I have every confidence in you and your men. Good luck and don't stop.'[17]

Company after company poured off the edge of Owers' Corner to confront the southernmost arrow of the Japanese empire. MacArthur's tall frame and flashing eyes worked their magic. There was a real sense that this was the start of the rolling back of the Imperial Army. At that moment the Japanese controlled all East Asia and Oceania, with the exception of Australia, southern Papua, and parts of the Solomon Islands. The very sight of the gilded general and his posse of powerful commanders had the desired effect, and the troops disappeared off the edge of Owers' Corner 'eager for action'.[18]

MacArthur spent an hour at Owers' Corner, returned to 'A' Mess for lunch, and left for Brisbane the next day. His brief appearance was nonetheless rousing stuff. On this occasion, the supreme commander hit the mark. He spoke with the pomp and circumstance of a leader of greatness, a fact lost on those unable to comprehend the grandeur of MacArthur's vision. Alone among commanders, he grasped the essence of what needed to be done: to force the Japanese juggernaut, island by island, back to the heart of Tokyo. MacArthur was that rarity, a man who believed his thoughts and actions were integral to the fate of the world. Only Churchill and Hitler — for good and evil — appeared to share the same colossal self-definition and sense of personal destiny.

The troops' field commander followed, on 8 October. Tubby Allen was a portly veteran of great resilience and quiet courage much liked by the troops. Like Potts, he got too close to his men, and was willing to put his career on the line in their interests. His superiors were not persuaded that he had the necessary drive and aggression to lead the counteroffensive. But his superb record as a brigadier in the Middle East gave them pause for thought.*

---

* Perhaps he'd been promoted above his talents, mused David Horner: Tubby Allen was 'a good brigade commander who had been spoilt by being made a divisional commander' (Horner, MA Thesis p. 56).

The track swiftly wore him down. Allen's chosen prophylactic was eminently in character: 'Very difficult up to Ioribaiwa,' he wrote on 9 October. 'Camp pitched in pouring rain. Natives made a lean-to ... Camp was on a narrow razorback with practically no movement possible off the track ... It turned very cold during the night and whisky was a real lifesaver.'[19]

The enormity of the supply problem troubled Allen. There were no supplies at Nauro, the first depot on the track, nor were any found at Efogi on 9 October. There was a critical lack of carriers, and the job of finding them fell again to Bert Kienzle. The Australian army needed 5000 native men in fit condition to supply them; but sickness and desertion had depleted their ranks. There were about 900 carriers working on the track: these men had served as human ambulances and packhorses for fourteen weeks without a break.

In early October Kienzle rounded up as many 'A' class natives 'as I could muster from Bisiatabu and the Base Camp Depot'.[20] He needed many more. One method was to disseminate stories of how the Japanese had treated the Rabaul natives, who were found starved and beaten along the track. 'They gave harrowing accounts of Jap brutalities ... They were glad to be with us,' said Kienzle. He used their testimonials to persuade the local people that their lot was far better under Australian than Japanese control. 'This stiffened their morale ...'[21]

The new troops acclimatised swiftly to the conditions. Their training in Ceylon had proved useful, and they moved with comparative ease, even finding time to admire the 'beautiful butterflies'.[22] Their sprigged boots offered better grip on the muddy slopes. They progressed rapidly over the first few ridges.

The track wound through the steaming aftermath of battle. It was as though the fresh troops had entered a lifesize diorama of war modelled out of the bodies of real men. Here and there, on the slopes and in dugouts and then, suddenly, in grotesque clusters where an ambush occurred, the corpses of Australians and Japanese could be identified — sometimes only a few yards apart from one another. The tactical pattern of pitched battles, ambushes and bayonet charges were readily discernible from the position of the dead and the kind of wound; the slashed trails through virgin jungle marked a flanking movement or an escape route.

The grassy clearings, creeks and forests disgorged the unwanted baggage of a retreating army: spoiled rations, tangled signal wires, field binoculars, logbooks, swords, papers, diaries, maps and punctured tins. Potts's recently manned perimeters, shallow trenches and machine-gun posts, dug with helmets and machetes, were littered with spent cartridges, rusting weapons and the dead. In places, the bodies of Japanese snipers dangled from the branches of trees. At night, the moon shone on the bones of skeletons, eaten white by bull ants. Blackened stumps stood like lonely sign-posts amid the delineated lanes of fire, where heavy machine-guns had mown down the vegetation. There were areas where the whole canopy lay fallen and mangled across the wasteland like a great net thrown over an exhausted animal.

Booby traps were a constant worry for troops arriving at abandoned camps — both armies had set grenades primed to explode when disturbed in camp fires and rubbish. Near Menari, two carriers who lit a fire over a Japanese booby trap were blown up, but fortunately the ubiquitous Vernon was there to dress their wounds and to administer morphine.

The half-deaf doctor came forward a third time, to attend the wounded and assist the carriers. His presence seemed to hover over the track like Dante's Virgil passing through the lower circles of hell. He seemed everywhere at once, assisting, inquiring and generally making himself useful. He crossed the mountains several times. Though short of a donkey, he deserves the recognition accorded to the famous Simpson of the Gallipoli campaign in World War I. Vernon observed in his diary, 'many dead Australians still lying about' alongside 'piles of ammunition in the grass . . . It was a moving tale of destruction and death.'[23]

Vernon chatted to brigadiers and privates alike, in the same dry, halting phrases; his partial deafness meant he often left their company none the wiser. They, on the other hand, learnt a lot from Vernon. At Myola he popped up again, to record the story of the tribal Biagi people who lived along the track here. The war had forced them into the surrounding hills. When they attempted to sneak back into their village for food, the Japanese were said to have bayoneted many on sight. Later, 56 Japanese corpses were found at the very spot of the slaughter of the tribes, which satisfied Vernon: 'The white man avenged them,' he noted dryly.

The elderly doctor was especially sensitive to the raw beauty of his surroundings. Perhaps his deafness excited his visual appreciation of the natural world. He wrote exuberantly of the flora at Myola: 'The meadows were gay with Alpine flowers, sheets of little blue violets patterning the grass, masses of yellow buttercups, and loveliest of all, shapely bushes of wild Forget-Me-Not, covered with sky-blue florets.'[24] It was an incongruous, perhaps eccentric, observation amid the devastation; but it was how one man chose to record the broken world through which he walked.

Chapter 34
Pursuit

'Dead men were ... sitting in their trenches, with the bones of
their fingers clutched around the triggers of their weapons ...
The equipment and haversacks were still on ... [their] backs'
— *Bill Crooks, 25th Brigade, in* The Footsoldiers

Up ahead, the Australian advance troops — three battalions of the 25th
Brigade and the 3rd Militia Battalion — passed through the aftermath
of Potts's withdrawal. On 4 October, Sergeant Bede Tongs' patrol ascended
Brigade Hill. Near the summit they observed the 'very devastating sight' of
numerous Australian bodies lying about the clearing. Six stretchers lay in a
line, 'holding their skeletal remains. The soldiers in the stretchers had been
either bayoneted or shot. We left the identity discs on the bodies for those
people moving along behind us.'[1]

They passed hastily dug graveyards containing some of Potts's men.
Trench lines had been turned into a makeshift cemetery: 'Several slit
trenches ... had been filled in and a cross or an upturned rifle stuck in the
ground by the bayonet, marked the lonely graves ... moving all to
contemplative silence.'[2]

On the night of 7th the rump of the 25th Brigade camped on Brigade Hill. It was very dark with a wafer-thin moon. The smell of putrefaction lingered because the canopy trapped odours issuing from the jungle floor. It had been in the air 'since we left Ioribaiwa but on this night, high on the ridge south of Efogi, it had become overpowering'.[3] Dawn revealed they were camped amidst the remains of the battle of Brigade Hill. Some had not realised this was the place Potts's battalions were forced off the track. A tangle of Australian signal gear and weaponry — already rusting in the moist alpine air — lay about, and scattered here and there were a few personal items of dead soldiers: the odd letter from a girlfriend or a wife, photos of children.

Patrols dispatched at first light established the extent of Potts's resistance, which stretched from Brigade Hill forward to the hills above Efogi, where the 2/27th had fought: 'Dead men were found in tree tops. Others were sitting in their trenches, with the bones of their fingers clutched around the triggers of their weapons ... In no single case was one of our dead touched or his weapon removed from his hands. The equipment and haversacks were still on the dead men's backs.'[4]

Groups of bodies revealed the closeness of the fighting. Several men had fallen near their commanding officer, Captain Nye; they were cut down as they charged across the clearing in an attempt to reach Potts's headquarters. On the banks of a creek, the bodies of 33 men of the 2/27th battalion were found. Near the southern knoll three Australian mortar crews — ten men — were left dead beside their weapons, while yards ahead lay the crouched body of Captain Langridge, who'd run into the Japanese guns. The Japanese had dug body-deep trenches right up to the edge of Potts's HQ, where troops on both sides had fallen within feet of each other. By nightfall on the 8th, the advancing troops interred 99 corpses, the vast majority Australian. 'The troops dug shallow graves with bayonets and tin hats,' recalled Lieutenant Merv Roberts of the 2/33rd. 'They wore their field dressings over their noses and mouths ... that the Japs could walk past this macabre scene everyday enraged us.'[5]

With no time and scarce dry wood for a ceremonial cremation, the Japanese had buried most their casualties in a mass grave beneath elaborate burial mounds, each marked by a single wooden stake adorned with Japanese characters and surrounded by a little vine fence.[6] After the war the families of veterans repeatedly returned to Papua and New Guinea to find and repatriate the bones of their sons from such sites.

The corpse of General Horii's famously apocryphal 'white stallion' made the last of numerous sightings, in a creek near Efogi, where a horse answering to its description had been unceremoniously dumped. That the Japanese commander's pure white mount — elsewhere described as little more than a grey mule — got so far up the track seems unlikely. This particular candidate for the honour had received neither burial nor cremation. Nor did it appear to have been eaten.

'Jap atrocities reported from ... Ioribaiwa–Nauro,' Allen wrote in his diary on 3 October. '2 Aust soldiers found — one tied to tree, other decapitated.'[7] The arms of one soldier had been cut off, and multiple bayonet wounds were found in both corpses.

The sight of bayoneted, bound Australian corpses revolted the troops then moving up the track, but did not surprise or shock them. The atrocities at Milne Bay and Rabaul were well known. If the Japanese supposed such brutality would frighten or demoralise the enemy, they gravely misread the Australian psyche. The scene of Australian bodies trussed and mutilated merely confirmed the 16th Brigade's opinion of the Japanese. A general hardening resulted; and there would be very few prisoners taken.

Nor were the natives spared. The condition of carriers press-ganged into Japanese service at Rabaul defied belief. Vernon examined a Rabaul man found crawling along beside the track. He'd escaped when the Japanese sounded the retreat and, on hearing Australian voices, dragged himself out of hiding, 'cowed and broken-spirited, the tears welling in his eyes'. Vernon found the man's feet riddled with gangrene, and 'every toe worn to the bone and crawling with maggots'. 'Two bayonet wounds scored his back, the mementoes of two falls with his load.'[8] In a shaking voice the man described how the Japanese kept the carriers moving at bayonet point, working them till they dropped. His was not an isolated case. Ahead were found the bayoneted bodies of several Rabaul natives. They served Kienzle's 'propaganda' purposes, and inspired greater loyalty in the Australian-controlled carriers, many of whom, though scared and exhausted, counted themselves lucky.

———

As the maelstrom swept back the way it came, and the Australians reclaimed previously Japanese-controlled territory, the mountain tribes emerged from the jungle to find their villages destroyed, their gardens plundered and members of their families dead or impressed as carriers.

An Australian situation report on 9 October didn't mention battle. It concerned itself entirely with atrocities alleged by an Orokaiva native who had escaped the Japanese: 'Word of rape of women passed quickly all villages ... Eleven BIAGI natives were bayoneted to death at DENIKI. RABAUL natives dying of starvation from IOROBAIWA [sic] back. Japs also starving to death ... gardens in KOKODA district have been destroyed and thinks Japs will NOT stop at KOKODA due to food shortage and sickness.'[9]

Deeper in the mountains dozens of straggling Japanese troops were found wandering around, or prone on the jungle floor. A medical study of enemy corpses concluded: 'Jap dead very wasted. Evidence of starvation.'[10]

The state of the Nankai Shitai was indeed worse than a beggar's, in Sakomoto's phrase. On the north coast, mosquitoes were feasting on Horii's supply lines. Of the 282 patients in one field hospital, 'the larger percentage has malaria, others have fever or acute inflammation of the large intestine ... beri beri, chest disorders and skin diseases'.[11]

The Japanese were abysmally equipped to deal with malaria. While each man supposedly had ten tablets of quinine, this didn't last long. Malaria wasn't considered a serious disease; nor fully understood. Some Japanese doctors thought malaria contagious through contact with the natives, who were 'separated at the billeting area' to prevent contamination.

Others realised the foe was a tiny parasite borne by the mosquito — but had little means of controlling it: 'There are too many mosquitoes breeding in the streams,' pleaded the Yazawa medical report, 'and we have no defensive equipment against them.'[12]

Those too sick to fight came in at the rate of three to eight per day during October. The coastal hospitals had medical supplies for a month — yet about a third of the troops were unfit for combat by 19 October.[13] It didn't help that wells and streams flowed together with lavatory effluent and contaminated the water supply. Some troops sat 'hip-deep' in contaminated water after heavy rains.

———

Elsewhere the famous Japanese spirit was weakening. A trickle began to desert, or abandon their positions. The rumour spread that a company commander, First Lieutenant Ino, had left his Buna post without permission and returned to Rabaul. Another Lieutenant, Nagano, had relieved himself of his duties. A disgusted Sakomoto wrote that such men were 'unworthy of the Army'. It was unheard of that Japanese officers would simply walk away from battle.

On the Kokoda Track, a rising number of Japanese yielded to their illnesses, and abandoned the fight. The advancing Australians soon encountered more Japanese stragglers stumbling around the forest. 'Many of the Japs,' wrote journalist George Johnston, 'had been eating grass, wood, weeds, roots and poisonous fruits.'[14] Native accounts told of the Japanese 'grubbing in the mud' for a few grains of rice.

Among the few prisoners taken during the counteroffensive was Okino Jiro, of a horse transport unit within the Kusunose Butai, captured between Menari and Efogi. Okino's job had been to take horseloads of wire-cutters, rope and ammunition from Buna to Kokoda. When the animals died, he was himself harnessed as a draught horse and loaded up with grenades weighing 82 pounds. He'd collapsed from exhaustion and disease. The advance troops found him on 2 October sleeping in a native hut, and bound him to a tree, to await the main army.

The Australians looked on this sick, exhausted man, borne aloft through their lines, with loathing and disgust. A half-starved sight, riddled with jungle sores, weakened by dysentery and malaria, Okino lay shaking on his stretcher and gazing indiscernibly at his captors. Two weeks later, he tried to wrestle with his prison guard, but he could not recall the incident when interrogated the next day. It showed nonetheless that he'd regained his physical strength, and the Australians do not seem to have harmed him.[15]

Born in Shikoku, Okino had worked for an Osaka artificial silk manufacturer — so he told his Allied interrogators. He was unusually outspoken, accusing Horii of 'unreasonableness' in forcing the march on Port Moresby, which they were expected to capture, he said, within three days of leaving Kokoda. Coming from an ordinary private, this was extraordinary criticism of a top-ranking officer. It spoke less of general insurrection than personal bitterness: Okino had been refused leave at Rabaul, and complained that his superiors had put the welfare of the horses ahead of the men.

Another prisoner, drawn along by a rifle pull, smiled and bowed to the Australians as they passed. The sight, south of Efogi, of a shallowly buried fellow Japanese soldier, highly amused him: one of the corpse's rigid arms broke the soil, and a blackened finger pointed to the sky, as if showing the way.

Groups of Japanese soldiers were captured sitting in a daze by the track, too weak to continue. They had dropped to the ground to await capture or, preferably, death. One man who called himself Katsukara Kanemidzu, a first class seaman of the Yasuda Special Landing Party, had disembarked with a party of twenty on the beaches near Gona. Sent over the mountains to deliver supplies to Horii's army, they'd got lost.

Katsukara had 'no idea where [the rest of his patrol] went', noted his interrogators. 'For over a month the party wandered from place to place hoping to come across Jap troops. Biscuits ... had long since been exhausted and the men were reduced to eating edible roots.' On 9 October, they 'threw away their rifles being too weak to carry them further'. On 17 October Katsukara, 'exhausted ... and powerless to resist', was marched blindfolded for two hours into a prison camp.[16]

Not all the sick and hungry were abandoned. Some Japanese units tried bravely to carry out the dying, and impressed the natives to shoulder the weakest men, which caused severe delays.

The tail end units blew up cliff sides or log bridges to delay the Australians, 'but the pursuit grew hotter every day until the enemy were close upon our heels', wrote Okada. American aircraft meanwhile strafed and bombed the thin line of retreating men, 'the ratatat of the machine guns, the sound of cannon fire that streamed forth from tails of B-17s — these were nightmares threatening us in our miserable retreat'.[17]

Horii could not rely on airdrops, and the country was denuded of 'Churchill supplies', which had been either spoiled or eaten. Patrols were sent deep into the country in search of native fruit and vegetables. Fields more than six miles away from the track were dug up 'inch by inch', wrote Okada.

The South Seas Detachment had simply 'failed to ... employ adequate numbers of men as beasts of burden'.[18] Nor could they call on the navy for supply drops, as it was increasingly difficult to get ships to the coast as the air war intensified.

A surprising number of Japanese endured these torments — their indomitable spirit would prevail, they told themselves. Such thoughts drove men like machine-gunner Sakomoto, who soon turned to face his pursuers, vowing, incredibly, to fight on.

Chapter 35
Biscuit Bombers

'Unless dropping of 50000 lbs daily ... is assured, complete
revision of plans will have to be made and large proportion of
troops withdrawn to IMITA ridge posn. Any attempt then ...
to occupy KOKODA will be jeopardised beyond all reason'
— *Wire from Major-General Arthur 'Tubby' Allen to New Guinea Force*

About this time Brigadier Selwyn Porter was completing one of his
critiques. It was a document of searing accuracy and unusual candour.
Though of little use to front-line commanders — being more cerebral than
practical — Porter's 'Notes on Recently Expressed Concepts of Tactics: HQ
30 Aust Inf Bde, 11th Oct 1942', helped to explain Allen's tribulations and
offered a glimpse of the thoughts at the top of the Australian army.

'It has been said,' Porter observed, 'that the first feature of our military
organisation at the commencement of hostilities is disorganisation. Why
should we be amazed at this, when we deliberately create our inflexible
monster ...?'[1]

Porter's inflexible monster was alive and kicking. The disorganisation of
supply threatened to blunt the counteroffensive. As the troops advanced, and
the Australian carrier lines extended, so the flow of supplies faltered. Severe

delays ensued, and the usual tantrums convulsed GHQ in Brisbane, where MacArthur persisted in failing to comprehend the enormous difficulties of the terrain. The last resorts of muddle through and trial and error still seemed to govern the supply strategy.

The villages of Nauro, Menari, Efogi and Myola were critical drop zones. Radio signals were meant to guide in the planes and, at the appointed time, bags of food would hurtle to earth. The pilots were instructed to aim for burnt patches of ground, or logs arranged as markings. Their maps were as good as useless. Where the planes missed the marked clearings, hundreds of bags came crashing through the canopy and free fell to the jungle floor. Occasionally they struck the men below — biscuit bombs killed or wounded several Australian soldiers.

Most airdrops still lacked parachutes, and a large percentage of supplies were lost. Virtually all the bags split open, biscuits were reduced to powder and sugar scattered over the jungle floor. 'Many a man would sit down and spoon up as much as he could,' recalls Bill Crooks.[2] Cigarettes were the most sought after commodity: 'The ration of two ounces of Log Cabin fine cut a smoker, a week, fell so short of needs that men took to smoking tea,' said one soldier.[3]

Distributing such scarce resources was a fraught process. Each battalion second-in-command and three helpers were supposed to coordinate the link between the airdrops, the native head and the battalion. Salvaged supplies were thus channelled from the drop zone to the backs of carriers and then on to the battalions, where prized items like food and tobacco were shared out among the sub-units, and finally to the troops. Major Thomas Cotton, for example, of the 2/33rd Battalion, oversaw the distribution of food and cigarettes among his men, 'with all its … arguments, and problems of equitable issue'.[4] Looting seems to have been less prevalent than one might expect.

The inadequacy of airdrops placed a greater burden on indigenous carriers. They shouldered heavy weapons — including the first Vickers machine-guns — as well as ammunition, food, medical gear, signals equipment, and were detailed to retrieve scattered packages from the drop zones.

Despite Kienzle's heroic efforts, sickness and desertions had heavily reduced the number of native carriers north of Uberi.[5] In response,

ANGAU took stern measures to maintain the supply of native labour. They ignored the law — honoured in the breach — that restricted the conscription of tribal carriers above a certain level. Where 8830 native labourers could be contracted for work on the Kokoda Track before the war, ANGAU now maintained some 9270 throughout New Guinea, and somehow had to find a further 4000. Many of these would be required on the Kokoda Track.

Tubby Allen had to ensure that airdrops and carrier teams coincided in time and place in order to feed and arm his 2000 men. In practice, this didn't work, as Allen repeatedly made clear in a series of painful cables to General Herring, Rowell's successor as commander of New Guinea Force in Port Moresby.

In the first four days of October 150 carriers deserted, Allen wrote. At the end of the first week, the counteroffensive threatened to grind to a temporary halt until supplies were brought in.

Allen imagined his demands were being heard, and acted on, in Port Moresby and Brisbane. They were not. It is a dispiriting fact that Allen's men were, for a time, virtually cast adrift in the mountains by the incompetence and ignorance of his superior officers.

We can readily picture Tubby Allen, sitting in his jungle HQ, surrounded by his staff officers, peering at his inadequate maps, and constantly on the field telephone trying to drum up supplies. Back in Port Moresby we can see Herring, anxious to please Blamey, downplaying the supply crisis with long, convoluted messages, written in his tiny, cramped hand. And in turn we can see Blamey, ever anxious to please MacArthur, leavening the sitreps and Herring's missives with a few bland platitudes before dispatching them to GHQ thoroughly rinsed of phrases of alarm and urgency. In Brisbane, the truth underwent its final humiliation: doused in MacArthuresque fantasy, filleted of the barest bones of a fact, the war was presented to the world in the bastardised state of 'Doug's Communiqué', rendered fit for public consumption by dint of its very unreality, through the shattered mirror of the newspapers.

_____

Two messages perfectly captured the void that existed between the reality at the front and the fantasy in the rear. On 7 October Allen sent a clear message to Herring:

> Implementation of air dropping programme causing gravest
> concern ... It would appear that air force cannot supply planes
> necessary to assure dropping of 50000 lbs daily ... 50000 lbs
> covers maintenance only and does NOT repeat NOT provide for
> building up a reserve ... Unless dropping of 50000 lbs daily plus
> additional to build up a reserve is assured, complete revision of
> plans will have to be made and large proportion of troops
> withdrawn to IMITA ridge posn. Any attempt then ... to occupy
> KOKODA will be jeopardised beyond all reason ... Advance of
> whole force jeopardised if supplies can not be maintained by air.[6]

On the same day Blamey sent this update to MacArthur: 'Allen is pushing forward steadily,' he said. 'We may not have a great deal of trouble to get to Kokoda ... Everything is working very happily and co-operatively ...'[7]

Their perceptions of reality were worlds apart. But the defence that Blamey was poorly informed does not withstand scrutiny. Allen's situation reports flowed in daily to Port Moresby, often several times a day. And Blamey, after all, was exceptionally well briefed in other matters. In the same message to MacArthur, he gave a precise summary of the state of the Japanese troops: 'complete demoralisation on the mountain top caused by their considerable sick rate, large number of casualties, and complete breakdown of their supply'.[8]

Are we to conclude, then, that Blamey possessed a more accurate idea of the Japanese supply situation than that of his Australian troops? Of course not: Allen kept Blamey eminently well informed. So why did Blamey ignore or downplay Allen's problems?

It seems simply a case of Blamey the political soldier in action. Where the truth (in this case, the enemy's collapse) redounded to his credit, or appeased GHQ, he let it flow; where it reflected badly on him (Allen's severe supply difficulties) he amended or suppressed it. Ambitious politicians and line managers can be expected to make the facts more palatable to their superiors. This was rather different, however, as the lives of 2000 men relied on the truth — and their supplies — getting through.

The atmosphere got worse, tempers flared and Allen's patience reached breaking point. On the 11th, Brigadiers Eather and Lloyd, commanders respectively of the 25th and 16th Brigades, met Tubby in his tent at Menari. Their main concern was the desertion rate of native carriers — 'whole success depends on efficiency of carriers',[9] noted Allen during this meeting — and the impatience in Brisbane and Port Moresby with the delays.

Allen was in a fraught state. GHQ's confidence in his command was waning, as Blamey made clear that day: 'Your orders [are]... to push on ... and capture KOKODA,' his wire said. 'In view lack of serious opposition advance appears much too slow. You will press enemy with vigour. If you are feeling strain personal relief will be arranged. Please be frank about this. Dropping arranged only at MYOLA 12 Oct.'[10]

The last statement packed the power of a fused grenade. Allen had expressly ordered his supplies to be dropped at Efogi, not Myola, on the 12th. Furious, he wired Port Moresby, and was disturbed to hear from Herring of the last minute cancellation of airdrops at Efogi North. Herring confirmed that no supplies would be dropped at Efogi North 'or any other place other than Myola' tomorrow. Allen protested that supplies to Efogi were 'a vital part of plan'. The sudden cancellation made 'planning in forward area very difficult'.

In case Herring hadn't got the message, Allen added: 'If rations NOT rept NOT dropped at EFOGI NORTH today delay in advance must result ... EFOGI NORTH vital as supply dropping base to supply Bn which will move forward ...' He concluded: 'I hope you appreciate the dangerous shortage of carriers.'[11]

In the event, biscuit bombers dropped 3500 packages at Myola. Allen's requests were completely ignored. They landed well forward of his tactical requirements, all over the swampy lakebed. Blamey himself had made this decision. Later that day some supplies were dropped near Efogi, but well below the required amount.

The counteroffensive stalled, as Allen warned it would. Graver news was in store for him: up ahead Japanese reinforcements were arriving at Templeton's Crossing and Eora Creek.

In Blamey's mind, Allen had become the reason, not the remedy, for the delay. Tubby was now a marked man, maligned by his own commanders in the rear even as he struggled to supply his troops.

He replied to Blamey on 12 October, with a message painfully revealing of his difficulties:

> My outline plan . . . is to capture KOKODA as soon as possible.
> Apparently it has been misunderstood. Nothing is being left
> undone in order to carry out your wishes . . . The most serious
> opposition to rapid advance is terrain. The second is maintenance
> of supplies through lack of native carriers. Reserve supplies have
> NOT rept NOT been adequate . . .
>
> This country is much tougher than any previous theatre and
> cannot be appreciated until seen. From all reports the worst is
> NORTH of MYOLA. The vigour with which we press the
> enemy is dependant on the physical endurance of the men and
> the availability of supplies . . . However I feel somewhat
> disappointed on behalf of all ranks that you are dissatisfied with
> the very fine effort they have made.

Allen couldn't resist a sly retort at Blamey's questioning his fitness: 'Our men have been pleased so far with regard to my personal physical fitness . . . am not repeat not feeling the strain. I never felt fitter nor able to think straighter.'[12]

This did little to appease his persecutors.

'I am very delighted that you are fit and well,' Blamey replied. 'It is essential that you should retain your fitness. Having some knowledge of mountain conditions, I know that great strain under which you are working.'[13] Blamey casually added that Vasey was ready to relieve him, 'after you have done a fair tour . . . and then you could replace him again'.[14]

Blamey's knowledge of mountain conditions had involved a tour of the Greek foothills. He had not seen combat in Greece; on the contrary, he spent a good deal of his time there finding a suitable beach for the evacuation. In any case, the Greek conditions were hardly comparable to the Owen Stanleys. But neither the absurdity of the allusion nor Blamey's disingenuous concern were as infuriating as his oddly puerile game of one-upmanship and political manoeuvring in a time of war.

The next day, after another harassing message from Port Moresby, Allen said: 'I am more afraid of the stab in the back than I am of the Japs.' Rowell had said something very similar before his demise.

By the second week of October, Lloyd's men began the phased relief of the 25th Brigade — the latter had fought the battle of Ioribaiwa and pursued the enemy as far as Efogi.

These men were much diminished physically. Disease ravaged their ranks. Dysentery — from mild diarrhoea to the worst amoebic variety, with the constant passage of blood and mucus — was universal. In Port Moresby some troops had caught malaria and the fever now manifested itself. They lacked adequate food supplies and ammunition.

One battalion's Anglican padre, the tremendously proportioned Donald Redding, had weighed 20 stone (127 kilograms) when he started out; within two weeks he'd lost about five stone.[15]

The brigade's casualty list to 13 October showed the devastation wrought by illness. In battle the unit had suffered 183 killed or wounded (all ranks). Disease, by contrast, had incapacitated or killed 769 men.

Many were mentally spent, and had 'receded into themselves', said Bill Crooks. 'Looking back, I think it was a little psychotic too ... Most were scared of the strangeness and eerie continual darkness ... we felt hemmed in ... beneath us on the track was a slimy ooze of stinking death.'[16]

A few showed signs of total nervous breakdown, but these cases were surprisingly rare.[17] Older soldiers and untrained men were more vulnerable to nervous collapse. 'Our less strong soldiers, many medal winners in the desert, [experienced] total nervous breakdown,' observed Crooks. 'A man could be driven to weeping frustration knowing that he could not keep going. His comrades ... would be looking at him in disgust and abject pity. And they would also feel hate, knowing that there would be one less to help take a turn carrying the section machine gun and ammo, one less to take a turn on the patrols.'

Some men resorted to desperate measures. There were a few cases of self-inflicted wounds, reported battalion medical orderlies in October. A wound in the hand or foot, or 'tattooed with powder marks' was instantly suspicious. Some men were wrongly accused, and medical orderlies were ordered to report, 'FACTS only'. They were 'NOT justified . . . in making or recording any supposition concerning the wound'.[18]

Having relieved most of the advance troops, the fresh 16th Brigade took up the pursuit of the enemy.

Chapter 36
Anthropophagy

'Those who have consumed human flesh — excluding that of the
enemy — will be sentenced to death for committing the worst
possible crime against humanity'
— *Order issued by the Eighteenth Army to Japanese troops,*
10 *December 1944, to clarify official position on cannibalism*

On 13 October a corporal leading an Australian patrol near Templeton's
Crossing discovered two leaf-parcels of meat that aroused 'distasteful
suspicions'. He took them back to the battalion's medical officer for
examination. Captain Donnan concluded: 'One was the muscle tissue of a
large animal, the other similar muscle tissue with a large piece of skin and
underlying tissues attached. I consider the last as human.'[1]

Earlier, there had been speculation about wild animals feasting on
the troops, or fears that tribes might revert to their old head-hunting
ways. George Johnston had written solemnly in his diary, 'In the
Trobriand Islands many of the natives had embarked on rape, pillaging
and even cannibalism within 12 hours of the first Japanese landing. The
same thing might easily happen in New Guinea.'[2] General Morris had
earlier warned, that if 'we lose control of the natives they will revert

immediately to the primeval and it will take us at least 20 years to regain that control.'

Yet, while there were signs of recidivism in the western Highlands, the local Papuans had neither head-hunted nor cannibalised one another for about twenty years.★

The cannibals at Templeton's Crossing were not natives. They were starving Japanese soldiers. The most disciplined army in the world had been reduced to the barbarity of the Stone Age. When the last horses died and the village gardens failed to yield any crops, they had resorted to eating the flesh of Australian corpses.

The shocking thing was not the act itself — which was comprehensible, given the extremity of their condition — but rather the manner in which the Japanese fastidiously prepared Australians for consumption. They cut the flesh in strips from the body, wrapped it in leaves and then fried the neat little parcels — reminiscent perhaps of a plate of sushi — on an open fire. 'The taste is said to be good,' noted Sakomoto, tactfully.[3]

An Australian patrol found the victims' mutilated bodies on 15 October near Templeton's Crossing. They were tied to trees, one with his arms cut off at the shoulders. Their thighs and calves were partially excoriated, and the flesh wrapped in leaves. Uneaten body parts were stored, half-cooked, in the haversacks of dead Japanese troops lying nearby. The findings were confirmed by an Australian medical officer and in a series of situation reports:[4]

> SITREP to 1300. 15 Oct 42
> WITHY reports finding in recently captured area a piece of raw flesh parcelled in green leaves also 2 bodies ... 1 minus arms and large piece of flesh cut from thigh other cuts on lower limbs. Signed report following.

★ The mandate over Papua ceded to Australia after World War I led to the permanent appointment of an Australian governor, part of whose remit was the outlawing of cannibalism and head-hunting, and other practices such as ritual buggery. The teaching of Church missionaries added a gentler form of dissuasion.

SITREP 15 Oct 42. 2/25 bn reports finding in recently captured area piece of raw flesh wrapped in green.

The victims had been 3rd Battalion privates. The leader of their burial party, Lieutenant William Crombie, said at their graves: 'These mutilations were obviously made by a sharp knife, and were not caused by bullets or bayonets. The men's deaths were caused by a burst of [machine gun] fire in the chest and the other in the head.'[5]

Japanese diaries confirmed the practice, and suggest it was quite common. Yasuoka Fumitoshi, of the Tsukamoto Battalion, wrote on 18 October 1942: 'No provisions. Some men are said to be eating the flesh of *Tori* [an abbreviation of *Toriko*, a captive]. It is said to have a good flavour.'[6]

Sakomoto, on 19th October 1942, noted: 'Because of the food shortage, some companies have been eating the flesh of Australian soldiers . . . We are looking for anything edible and are now eating grass, leaves and the pith of the Tako tree . . .'*

It inspired him to write a short poem:

When we ran short of rations,
We devoured our own kind to stave off starvation.[7]

The sight of the mutilated corpses deepened the Australians' loathing of the enemy, which reached a visceral intensity, and partly explained the 'unusually murderous' quality of Australian fighting in coming battles.[8]

'This incensed all our party,' wrote Lieutenant Don Murray, on finding a second member of his battalion partially eaten. The young Australian's upper leg had been almost stripped of flesh, and 'the feeling against the enemy was explosive'.[9] Sixty-two years later, some veterans' feelings remain

---

* An astonished Allied translator asked for two second opinions of his rendering of the passage because of its 'incredible implications'; both agreed with his translation. The Allied Translator & Interpreter Section, set up by MacArthur to translate and analyse captured enemy documents, accepted the diaries as enemy confirmation of cannibalism.

numb. Recalling the incident, one said: 'I have no feelings for the Jap — none whatsoever.'

It mattered little that the motive for cannibalism was survival and not premeditated cruelty. As a 'crime against humanity' it occupies a unique category, the predicate of the most extreme form of physical torment. Whether it represented the Japanese soldier's 'moral collapse between the equally potent tortures of hunger and despair' is a question for the armchair analysts.[10] Conventional morality, banished from the Japanese soldier's mind during his military training, had no purchase in the jungles of Papua. In the grim logic of Horii's army, the practice of eating the dead was an extreme form of military pragmatism, a rational response to his near total logistical failure.

In fact, a few Australian troops also succumbed to the temptation. An Australian patrol, lost and starving for weeks behind enemy lines, cannibalised one of their dead mates, according to research by George Friend and others. Other Australians, if not inured to the latest horror, came to comprehend it. Lieutenant Ken Clift wrote that he and his mates, on seeing partly eaten Australian bodies, 'certainly did not condemn them on this'. Others could only respond with a macabre sense of humour: 'Don't go to sleep!' warned members of the 2/2nd Battalion at night, for fear of losing an arm or leg.[11]

Acts of wanton cruelty, such as the bayoneting of live prisoners for no apparent reason other than training purposes, elicited the deepest loathing. But scenes of cannibalism exacerbated these feelings, and the Australians would retaliate with systematic thoroughness.

Many Japanese who surrendered were subsequently shot (often out of fear of booby traps as much as revenge). There were stories of sudden massacres of Japanese prisoners — dozens were later reported shot by enraged Australian troops. Charles Lindbergh wrote of Japanese being thrown out of planes (though it is unclear whether they were pushed or allowed to jump).

Killing the Japanese seemed to satisfy everyone: many of them preferred to die; the Australians wanted them dead; and the carriers were spared having to carry the wounded or sick prisoners to prison. 'To men with no respect for the humanity of their enemy,' wrote Mark Johnston, 'the practical difficulties of the situation probably made killing them on the spot seem reasonable.'[12]

There was another dimension to the discovery. These were not isolated, frenzied acts of men tearing in desperation at human corpses. The consumption of human flesh was planned and organised, it appears, under a deliberate policy authorised by Japanese command.

For one thing cannibalism was widespread, and the flesh was carefully carved and divided up as though being prepared to feed many troops. The practice became more common as the Pacific War progressed.

Cannibalism was later officially sanctioned as a means of keeping the army not simply alive, but able to fight. This was formalised in an order issued on 10 December 1944 by the Eighteenth Army:[13] '. . . those who have consumed human flesh — *excluding that of the enemy* — . . . will be sentenced to death for committing the worst possible crime against humanity'.★

To eat Japanese corpses was punishable by death, noted one official document (entitled 'Discipline'). In the battles of the beaches, however, and in later campaigns, the Japanese did eat their own troops — though instances were rare. A Formosan prisoner of war, captured at Guadalcanal, told his interrogators that the Japanese had killed and eaten the heart and liver of one of his sixteen-year-old subordinates. He had also seen Japanese troops devour a fellow soldier who had been dead for two days.[14]

Some enemy prisoners apparently feared their Allied captors would eat them, too. A Japanese POW, who seemed to think he'd be cooked alive — perhaps in an open cauldron — 'shot through' when ordered to report to the cookhouse 'without his dixie'.[15]

★ The point is substantiated by the statement of POW Yanagizawa Eiichi, leading private, 239th Regiment, 41st Division, who quotes a speech by Major-General Aotsu Kikutaro, 41st Division Infantry Group Commander: 'On 1 November 1944, in a speech to his troops, Major General Aotsu . . . stated that troops must fight the enemy even to the extent of eating him.' On 10 December 1944, an order was issued from Eighteenth Army Headquarters that troops were 'permitted to eat the flesh of the enemy dead, but must not eat their own dead . . .' On 21 December 1944, at Marujippu, Major Morimoto shared out to his troops the flesh of two Australian soldiers who had been killed in action and joined them in eating it. Some historians believe the Japanese chose to eat human flesh even when other sources of food were in supply: 'The evidence available indicates clearly that cannibalism was frequently practised when there was other food available, that is to say, from choice not necessity. (See also Holt, *From Ingleburn to Aitape: The Trials and Tribulations of a Four Figure Man*, Streamlined Press, Sydney, 1980, p. 205; and recent research on Japanese supply by Keith Richmond, Canberra.)

Chapter 37
Templeton's Crossing

Myola, the burnt-out supply depot, offered a welcome rest to the advancing troops. From here they got ready to attack Templeton's Crossing, where the remnant of Horii's troops were dug in.

The crossing is a single log bridge, dumped over Eora Creek in a setting of Stygian gloom darkened by the high, closed canopy. One has the odd impression it is always raining in this damp, moss-coated world shrouded in mist and filled with the faint odour of vegetative decay.

Along the track to Templeton's, the enemy — now being reinforced from Kokoda — manned clusters of little machine-gun pits, built during the advance and now heavily fortified with logs and camouflaged. Strung along 600 yards of track, they were mutually supporting and connected by fire trenches — letting the gunners move to various positions. The Juki muzzles protruded from firing slits of about six inches deep and eight inches wide. The conditions inside were abominably muddy, wet and cramped; the

Japanese lay glued to their firing slits and nibbling on whatever food they had left in their packs.

Hurling grenades through the firing slits was the only way to destroy the occupants. Air bombardment was of little use in a micro-war fought beneath a jungle canopy, and flamethrowers were not yet available. But first the Australians had to find and stake out the Japanese positions, which involved encircling them, and attacking from the sides. The enemy sat and waited for the Australians to come.

A tiny patrol led by Corporal Terry Campbell walked straight into the machine-gun mounds without seeing them (they were so well camouflaged): 'A woodpecker suddenly opened fire from some hidden position and ... rifles exploded almost in the faces of the patrol.'[1]

That night, 11 October, Brigadier Eather, under extreme pressure to capture Kokoda, held an 'Orders Group' at Myola. Two battalions were to attack next morning and 'clear up Templeton's Crossing'.[2] At 8.00 a.m. the men marched quietly out of Myola, and entered the great halls of vegetation with 'no sight of the sky': 'Although it was early morning, it was strangely dark, like a scene from pre-man. It looked more like the last light in winter than early morning in the tropics. The troops' movement was cat-like. Nobody spoke as they crept over the mud and the soft, springy green mould.'[3]

They planned to surround the enemy in a semi-circular vice using two hundred Australian troops,[4] approaching from either flank. Captain Tim Clowes, brother of Brigadier Cyril Clowes (the victor of Milne Bay) led the flanking unit guided by his compass and 'the run of the ridge'.

There were no maps — this was virgin jungle. Visibility was reduced to a few feet. Over huge fallen trees, down ravines, and up steep slopes they slowly advanced, drawing aside the undergrowth like a curtain, to avoid making a sound.

Clowes reached the agreed point, and soon heard gunfire to the rear — his cue to 'get in it'. He led his men up the last slope and looked back near the top — his men, he wrote, were 'all in single file and gazing up at him'.[5] On their hands and knees they reached the ridgeline where, just twenty yards away, stood a Japanese camp site with a few troops smoking by their lean-tos. It seemed to be the main Japanese HQ at Templeton's.

The shock was mutual. The Australians charged; the Japanese responded with grenades and machine-guns, both sides inflicting heavy casualties before withdrawing. The Australians hunkered down in a ravine, about seventy yards from the Japanese positions, for the night.

Meanwhile, the frontal attack on the machine-gun nests had reached a stalemate. About a hundred Australians[6] attacked a ring of the mini-forts. '[We] became engaged in a bitter and almost eyeball-to-eyeball action,' said one. 'Some of the tougher men got right up to the pits [and] tried to toss grenades into them.'[7]

The Japanese who survived the grenades fled out the back door, and were shot down. But few Australians got within range to toss their grenades because neighbouring pits raked the approaches. Fighting in such close conditions — down a narrow path pocked with dugouts and bound by jungle — was chaotic: 'Men are unable to hear orders, see signals or even their section leaders, so battle dies down quickly into sniping or silence.'[8]

For several nights the Australians ate cold rations in the rain, draped in airdrop bags to keep warm. Sentries sat stationary within forty paces of the enemy foxholes. By this time Japanese reinforcements were coming up to Eora Creek.

Repeated attacks in the next few days slowly dislodged the Japanese at Templeton's Crossing. The gun pits were taken out one by one, and flanking patrols attacked the rear. Perhaps the most lethal was Lieutenant Kevin Power's ambush. On the 13th, Power led 50 hand-picked men along a track due south of a large Japanese encampment. The Australians got right up to the edge of the clearing, and watched the enemy chatting and eating; then charged. It was all over in a few minutes. Sergeant Jack Elliott machine-gunned six where they sat eating rice under a green tarpaulin. Bren gunners mowed down those trying to escape. For one man dead and four wounded, the Australians killed 30 Japanese. Power won a Military Cross for bravery.

The reputation of the super soldier was slowly fading into myth. The Australians used Japanese tactics, attacking at night, and up close. Sergeant Bede Tongs, for example, crawled through the jungle to within ten paces of a Japanese machine-gun. The gunners looked idly away. Tongs held his grenade close to the ground, to muffle the sound of pulling the pin, waited longer than was safe, and threw it. 'The two Japs ... were blown clean out and sprawled one on each other.'[9] He hurled another, and shouted to his platoon, 'Get stuck into the bastards', at which the Australians started 'yelling and whooping' and charged the gun, firing from the hip.

The Japanese tried to confuse the Australians with the old ruse of shouting orders in English, 'Up this way, Jack', 'Hey, Bob, over here, I'm wounded', and 'Cease Fire!' Power responded by yelling in Arabic, bits of which the troops had picked up in the Middle East, e.g. 'Imshi Allah' — 'get out' or 'go!' Soon the forest was a-chatter with Japanese, pigeon–Arabic and broken English.

The Australians reached the banks of Templeton's Crossing on or about 15 October, and camped amidst the bodies of the Australians killed there during Potts's withdrawal. 'The rain poured down in a great deluge and the roar of the creek continued through a bitterly cold night,' remembered Bill Crooks. Most lay awake, he said, 'silently contemplating' the bodies of the men strewn about the area.[10]

Lloyd's 16th Brigade fully relieved Eather's on the 19th, and took over the fighting. Eather had lost a third of his men in a month: 55 dead, 133 wounded and 769 sick. Three died on the day of their relief, in a bad accident: a mortar shell blew up inside the barrel, killing the crew. The shell had been primed for explosion on impact after free falling from a biscuit bomber. One young corporal cried out from the debris — 'there is a letter in my pocket, see that my mother gets it' — and passed away.★

After two days of near constant, close combat, the 2/2nd Battalion drove the enemy out of Templeton's Crossing. The action won three Military Crosses and four Military Medals, and produced some evocative prose: 'As we dug in for the night,' wrote the unit's historian, 'a desolate scene was presented: our

---

★ As at 28 October, total casualties from premature bursting of two-inch and three-inch mortar bombs were eight killed and eight wounded (Allen Papers).

own and enemy dead lying in grotesque positions, bullet-scarred trees with the peeled bark showing ghost-like, our own lads digging silently. And with the coming of darkness came the rain, persistent and cold, and in this atmosphere we settled in our weapon pits for the night. At night we could hear the Jap chattering and moving about.'[11]

Of the 58 Japanese corpses found amid the wreckage, one lay on a little Rising Sun; their determined protection of the Standard had cost the enemy many lives.[12] One sight brought tears to the eyes of some troops: the starved body of a little boy from Rabaul, lying dead on a native bench.

As they searched the camp, a burial party found a grisly discovery: the flesh of Australian soldiers still cooking over the smoking embers of a campfire. More carved corpses lay on the track nearby.

In an official report, the unit's padre wrote: 'I saw an Australian soldier stripped of all clothing with the flesh of his left thigh cut away and a long cut down his calf. There was a razor blade lying on the soldier's body. Another body was also cut about the thigh.' As a lieutenant who accompanied him confirmed: 'Without any doubt this man's body had been mutilated by the Japanese. It can be verified that fresh meat was being cooked in pots.'[13]

Three other bodies were found similarly mutilated, reported Lance-Corporal Allan and Private Connor. Connor's close examination of the enemy camp at Templeton's Crossing found 'small pieces of flesh' on the leaves of nearby trees; while 'dixies 10 to 15 yards away had both flesh and cooked meat in them'.[14]

The memory of the loss of the Philippines tormented MacArthur. The supreme commander had famously promised to return. Only the recapture of the Bataan peninsula would exorcise the demon of that particularly harrowing defeat. For MacArthur, this was curiously personal, and the armies under his command seemed, at times, the mere playthings of the man's immense ego, like the little coloured pins on a military operations board. MacArthur's deepest fear was that his enemies in Washington might find a pretext to remove him before he had a chance to strike back at the Japanese.

So the delay at Templeton's Crossing put MacArthur in febrile mood. His nose for someone to blame alighted once more on Blamey and the

Australian officers. He demanded to know why there was a delay in forcing the Japs back over the mountains.

Blamey did not rush to defend his officers against this stream of American bile. No wonder Allen, Rowell and the brigadiers felt as though they were fighting two wars.★ In a classic display of gutless political cunning, Blamey decided instead to pass MacArthur's attack down the Australian lines of command. General Tubby Allen was the obvious target; Blamey saw to it that the buck stopped with Tubby.

A marked 'Rowell man', Tubby Allen consulted his old friend about Blamey's intentions. Still brooding in his Victorian garden, Rowell replied on a singularly lukewarm note: 'I can't believe the Jap will clear out of Buna unless forced out,' he said. 'You will have a bag full of problems now.'[15]

The confused chain of command added to Allen's frustrations. To whom should he report: Herring, the New Guinea Force commander, or Blamey, the Commander-in-Chief, Allied Land Forces? Both generals were then based in Port Moresby. Allen sent messages to Herring but received answers from Blamey.[16]

'Who was actually commanding in New Guinea at that time?' David Horner caustically inquired. Herring insisted he was in charge, 'but MacArthur believed Blamey was in charge'.[17] This was not simply a question of form — it had tragicomic manifestations. On 9 November the most senior inquired of the second most senior medical officer in the Australian Army, 'Who do you belong to, by the way? The C-in-C or GOC New Guinea Force?'[18]

Allen did his best with scarce resources and a terrible supply line. His HQ, in 'normal' conditions a little transportable village of typists, signals equipment, supply officers, map-readers, cooks and filers, was reduced in the

---

★ 'I just wish,' noted historian Hank Nelson of these shameful episodes, 'that the Australian commanders had been able to back each other instead of being ready to sacrifice those below. Find me a grand gesture of selfless decision-making that puts a career — let alone a life — at risk that matches Kingsbury on the track. I would like Blamey to have said something like this to Curtin: "Mr Prime Minister, Syd Rowell and Tubby Allen are closer to the action than MacArthur and his team, they are much more experienced in battle in this war, they are two of our best officers, and I have every confidence in them. I will back them and their judgment and their troops, and I expect you will do the same for me".' (Interview with Hank Nelson.)

Owen Stanleys to a few tough soldiers running the show out of their backpacks. They fought a rearguard action against severe supply delays and chronic carrier shortages. The least Allen might have expected was Brisbane's encouragement and a swift response to his supply demands. He got neither. Instead MacArthur, acting through Blamey, seemed determined from the start to undermine the man they'd chosen to lead the Allied land offensive.

When Allen reached Myola on 17 October, he received a message from Blamey. It said: 'General MacArthur considers quote extremely light casualties indicate no serious effort yet made to displace enemy unquote.' Allen must capture Kokoda airfield 'at earliest'.[19]

Allen did not share MacArthur's opinion that effort could be measured by the sum of Australian corpses. He replied at once: the 25th Brigade had been 'attacking all day'. The unit's casualties numbered 50 killed, with 133 wounded. The sick numbered more than 700. '...but I respectfully submit,' Allen icily added, 'that the success of this campaign cannot be judged by casualties alone'.[20] On their relief three days later the 25th Brigade's casualties were 68 killed, 135 wounded and 771 seriously ill.

The dispute blew up into another battle of wills, in which Blamey played the role of MacArthur's amanuensis. Blamey's parroted cables conjure an impression of the sender as a rather large, khaki-clad ventriloquist's doll, relaying MacArthur's every word with unconsidered approbation. On the 21st, echoing MacArthur, he insisted: 'Progress on the trail is NOT repeat NOT satisfactory. The tactical handling of our troops in my opinion is faulty. With forces superior to the enemy we are bringing to bear in actual combat only a small fraction of available strength ...'

On the same day came another message from MacArthur–Blamey: 'During last five days you have made practically no advance against a weaker enemy'. MacArthur–Blamey demanded that Allen act 'with greater boldness and employ wide encircling movement to destroy enemy'. Time was critical: 'Capture Kokoda aerodrome.'

Allen instinctively sided with his troops. He drafted an enraged response, accusing MacArthur–Blamey of 'myopic ignorance': 'If you think you can do any better come up here and bloody well try.'[21] Colonel Charles Spry, his senior staff officer, persuaded him not to send it. Instead, Allen wrote that he was 'singularly hurt' to receive General MacArthur's wire, and blamed the country and shortage of carriers for the delay: 'This country does not lend itself to quick or wide encircling movements,' he explained, adding, 'It was never my wish to site a brigade defensively in rear but the supply situation owing carrier shortage has enforced it.'[22]

MacArthur demanded that Allen hurl his entire force at the enemy. Allen knew what was possible, given the terrain and the available supplies. 'I was determined not to murder my men by letting [MacArthur–Blamey] put me in a panic,' he later wrote. Both commanders seemed to think the terrain was 'only undulating and I could have swept around the flanks with a brigade'.[23]

No doubt the Australians outnumbered the Japanese, and were in better shape. But Allen's depleted carrier lines and supply shortages held him back. How could they advance without proper supplies of food and ammunition? However, the delay was getting dangerous: Japanese reinforcements were continuing to move up to Eora Creek from Kokoda.

In fact, a most stubborn obstacle now confronted Allen: a series of entrenched Japanese guns on the high ground overlooking Eora Creek, site of the former Australian field hospital (near the place from which they'd attacked during their advance). It was the perfect position for a small force to put up a strong defence. Allen had to capture it before he could sweep forward to Alola–Isurava and down to recapture Kokoda.

Chapter 38
Eora Creek

'We were ordered to advance across a bridge; there was a machine-gun on the other side. It was a very difficult situation, psychologically. We were terrified. But we did it'
— *Major-General Paul Cullen, commander, 2/1st Battalion*

More Australians died at Eora Creek than in any other battle in the mountains, with the exception of Isurava. For the first time, the Japanese had an overwhelming geographic advantage: the high ridge above the Eora Creek gorge. This country is perhaps the most precipitous in the mountains, with the usual dense jungle cover clinging to steep muddy slopes.

The Japanese reporter Okada recorded his impressions of the place:

One day, towards evening, we came to the ravine. It was in the remotest heart of the great mass of mountains ... and deeper and larger than any other ravine we had passed. The dark path through the enormous cypresses ... seemed to lead down to a bottomless pit. A rumbling sound like drumbeats came, it seemed, from somewhere deep underground.

We rounded a rock, and saw a furious white serpent of water falling from a height of about hundred feet and making roaring noises among the cavernous rocks below.

The branches overhead were so closely interwoven that not a ray of sunshine came through. There was neither day nor night in that ravine; it was always pale twilight, and everything looked as wet as though it were deep underwater.

And in that eternal twilight lay numberless bodies of men scattered here and there ... rotting human bodies lying in all possible postures, some on their faces, some on their backs, some on their sides, some in a squatting position.[1]

Many were casualties from the earlier battle here, during the Australian withdrawal.

Okada had a fine reporter's instinct for 'local colour'. He observed the behaviour of 'maggots crowding in a heap on the belly' of a corpse; and the dead troops' trousers 'lying flat on the ground, their legs having melted away'.[2]

He records a ghastly encounter with one Japanese body, presumed dead. As he passed it raised a hand and managed to mutter, 'Give me something to eat.' Okada put a rice ball into the 'thin hand that trembled like a piece of paper', and then dashed away in horror: 'I ran and ran like one in a delirium as if trying to escape the clutches of death.'[3]

High over the gorge, along the northern rim, the Japanese had set up their guns in log-reinforced bunkers. 'The line bristled everywhere with jukis and light machine guns.'[4] Beyond, lines of carriers bore scores of Japanese wounded back to Isurava and Kokoda, and thence to the field hospitals at Gona and Giruwa, a ten-day journey. The track was congested with walking wounded and the sick. Many had been lying in the area when 'the wholesale retreat began,' reported Okada.[5] Some had been lying in situ since the retreat order; dependent solely on whatever food medics could rustle up in the bush.

Their stretchers were merely blankets or tent-cloths tied with vines to two poles, and carried by four men. Progress was excruciatingly slow. The wounded 'emitted groans of pain at every bump ... the blood from the wounds was dropping through the canvas on to the ground. Some looked all but dead, unable even to give out a groan.'[6]

The heavy footfall of hundreds of Australian troops could be heard as they churned up the track on the southern side of the Eora Creek gorge. Forward scouts had the most dangerous job; most would be killed or wounded by unseen snipers, who waited until they were twenty yards away before firing.[7]

When the 16th Brigade reached Eora Creek on 22 October they halted on a partially exposed spur some 900 feet above the south bank. The Japanese on the north side had a clear view of this feature, waited for the soldiers to crowd up, then shelled and machine-gunned them. The wounded included a battalion commander, Lieutenant-Colonel John Stevenson, who got a bullet through the ear. The Australians withdrew back up the slopes, a mudslide, grabbing tree roots to stop them sliding to the bottom.*

Patrols sent down into the gorge glimpsed through the forest the first of two single log bridges, near a swirling river junction. On the opposite bank, the track followed the creek around a wide horseshoe bend to the right, leading to a second log bridge. On either side the gorge rose steeply up to knife-edge ridges and broad spurs, fortified by Japanese guns.

Brigadier Lloyd chose to split his brigade. Several units would try to outflank the Japanese on a high spur to the west; others would attack across the log bridges. It was the first time the Australian army had attempted an encircling manoeuvre involving so many troops.

The plan did not impress Paul Cullen, commander of the 2/1st Battalion. Cullen argued that the battalion should be concentrated on the high ground, and not divided. He particularly objected to the attack across the bridges, which were directly in the line of enemy fire. Lloyd disagreed, and suggested Cullen hadn't the guts to attack over the log bridges. Cullen, then aged 34 — fifteen years younger than his superior officer — privately dismissed the older man as fighting a jungle war 'with World War One methods'. But he wearily obeyed.

---

* Despite wet conditions, Eora Creek was contaminated and the Japanese had occupied the only water supply on the ridge. The Australian troops resorted to catching rainwater in their gas capes, or sucking water from the roots of trees.

Eora Creek: 22–23 October 1942

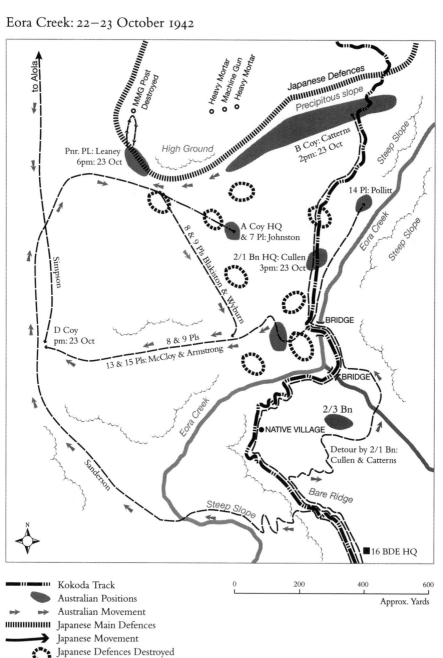

Kokoda Track
Australian Positions
⇒   ⇒   Australian Movement
‖‖‖‖‖‖‖‖‖‖‖‖   Japanese Main Defences
━━━━▶   Japanese Movement
⚬⚬⚬⚬   Japanese Defences Destroyed

0   200   400   600
Approx. Yards

And so, as Lloyd decreed, on 22 October several companies led by Captains Sanderson and Simpson headed up the spur to the west. To get there, they had to descend into the gorge at a safe point further upstream, and then climb 'practically straight up' through dense jungle to the high spur.[8]

Sanderson, a big man who hankered to be a hero, was meant to time his attack with Cullen's assault across the two bridges. But two of his three platoons did not reach the summit, and scouts found no sign of them. They got lost. Nor did Captain Simpson reach the heights above Alola; he seemed to have misjudged the distance (an easy thing to do in uncharted forest).

Sanderson nonetheless ordered his reduced force — a single platoon of seventeen men — into battle. They grumbled at this, to which Sanderson snapped, 'Colonel Cullen expects us to attack and attack we will, now get going.'[9] At dawn on the 23rd his tiny force reached a clearing by a little creek, where a dozen Japanese troops sat chatting loudly and eating breakfast. The Australians charged, spraying the camp with light machine-gun fire; Sanderson used his German Mauser, a trophy salvaged in the Greek campaign.[10]

The Japanese counterattacked, encircled Sanderson's men, and began picking them off. Private Gavin Wynd was hit on the side of the neck. On entry, the bullet left 'a small blue-black puncture', reported Private Ronald Grout, who applied a field dressing. The real damage lay in Wynd's back. Lifting the man's blood-soaked shirt, Grout was shocked to discover a gaping hole the size of a saucer. 'I turned to Captain Sanderson and said, "I can't do anything with that, it's too much for me!" Sanderson gruffly replied, "Soldier, we can do anything, now get that field dressing on."' Grout obeyed. He pushed the flesh back into the hole, 'covered it as best I could with my own field dressing', and propped Wynd against a tree. Moments later Wynd slumped forward.[11] His wound matched the kind inflicted by explosive bullets — a claim refuted by Japanese sources. If so, it was their first recorded use in Papua. Such bullets neatly penetrated the flesh then blew up inside the victim.

As Grout was struggling to save Wynd, a Japanese gunner shouted from the forest, 'Have you had enough, Aussie?' Sanderson swore back, and was riddled with bullets. Three hundred spent Mauser cartridges were later found near his body; bits of clothing and boots were missing from others bodies. From one corpse the Japanese had cut a large strip of flesh. Only four of Sanderson's seventeen men survived.[12]

Back at the two bridges, Lloyd's frontal attack suffered a deeply demoralising start. On the night of the 22nd an Australian reconnaissance patrol led by Lieutenant Ken Burke went down to the bank of the creek. A Japanese machine-gun raked them across the water, leaving thirteen dead or wounded on the bank. Burke refused to go further, according to Cullen. 'Fuck Brigadier Lloyd,' he is reported to have said. Lloyd then summoned Cullen and ordered him — in no uncertain terms — to capture the first bridge 'before daylight!' Cullen set out to do this himself.

A pale moon shone at 2.30 a.m. on 23 October, when Cullen and Captain Geoffrey Cox set off. The pair crawled over the bridge, and found the Japanese gunner on the other bank gone, or asleep. So Cullen seized the moment and ordered his men across before the Japanese realised their mistake.

Little bits of white paper stuck to sticks guided the men down the steep zigzagging track to the creek. A company led by Captain Peter Barclay reached the bridge at 4.00 a.m. They started to cross. The moon lit their way. Many were still crossing the bridge when the Japanese awoke to the threat and fired. But a cloud had obscured the moon, and almost all of Barclay's men made it across (Barclay himself died on the north bank).

The last few men raced across the second bridge as bullets crackled down from above. 'There was a lot of machine-gun fire sweeping the bridge in bursts,' recalls Sergeant Bob Armstrong.[13] Of the entire company, only two didn't make the crossing. But a pile-up on the opposite bank didn't help, recalled Lieutenant Bill Pollitt: 'As this was done in the dark every man was ordered to run across between [machine-gun] bursts and jump to the right as soon as he hit the other side. We did not know that there was a sloping rock there, which meant that everyone finished in the creek.'[14]

Confusion ensued. Several tracks veered off in the darkness. Pollitt took his platoon far to the right, where they found themselves in 'a complete cul-de-sac', hemmed in between the roaring waters of the creek on one side and a vertical rock wall on the other: 'The Japanese [were] dropping hand grenades amongst us,' Pollitt recalls.[15] His men would have died were it not for Lance-Corporal John Hunt, who climbed out of the hole, stalked the Japanese grenade-throwers, and shot them. But the Australian casualties were mounting: the first of two brothers in the 2/1st Battalion, Private Guy Manusa, died in this action; his brother died two days later.

The remarkable Captain Basil Catterns took a different route. He led his company of 100 men straight up the Japanese ridge, directly ahead, under terrible fire. They dug in barely thirty yards from the Japanese guns at the top of the ridge, and scratched out shallow trenches with their helmets. The concave lip near the summit protected Catterns's men from direct Japanese fire. So the enemy bounced grenades down the slope, inflicting many casualties, and sent out night attack patrols. 'At no time during the campaign were any of the battalion in such a miserable condition,' notes the unit history.[16]

The Australians clung to the side of this razorback 'like leeches' for about a week, 'under the very noses of the Japanese'.[17] Most of the wounded couldn't be rescued. They were 'holed in like animals on a precipitous slope'.[18] They urinated and defecated in bully beef tins and hurled the waste down the slope — within sight of the Japanese, who shot at it.

One saving grace was the failure of the Japanese mortars; of 35 two-inch shells fired during one fifteen-minute bombardment only two exploded, the men calculated.

Australian runners — a selection of extremely brave and fit troops — delivered Catterns's ammunition and food each night. The men chosen for these ten-hour round trips fulfilled the most dangerous supply duty of the campaign.

Each delivery involved a four-hour march from HQ, into the gorge, over the log bridges to the base of the ridge, then a rush up the slope under Japanese fire. Darkness afforded their only protection. After depositing food and ammunition, they shouldered any wounded for the journey back. The runners got little more than three hours' sleep every 24 hours, before setting off for another trip.

A flash flood on the 26th dislodged the first bridge over Eora Creek, vital to Catterns's runners. The broken timbers flowed a little way downstream then got stuck against some rocks. In chest-deep rapids, the runners crossed the creek wedged against the logjam. Food and ammunition were borne head high over the rapids.

How they carried the wounded back in these conditions defies belief. One night, in driving rain, they shouldered 27 stretcher cases across the river and up the steep bank, a 300-yard climb. It took six hours. The Japanese fired mortars into the river.

On clear nights, the moonlight on the foaming rapids helped to guide the runners across, but it also lit up the target. At least a dozen runners and their wounded were shot as they crossed.

In the 24 hours that it took the field engineers (2/6th Field Company) to cut and shape a new log bridge, four men were killed and seven wounded during one crossing. Hearing of their ordeal, Padre Charles Cunningham, a Catholic priest of Western Australia who'd just arrived, dropped his pack and headed straight for the rapids to help bear the bodies across; he then buried the dead on the banks.

After a week of this, the runners showed signs of nervous collapse. Several later died from tropical conditions to which, in their exhausted condition, they became peculiarly vulnerable, according to medical reports.

On the ridge over Eora Creek, Horii toasted his officers with cups of *sake*. Though many were gravely ill and hungry, the Shitai had held their ground against a fitter, larger army. Their superb defensive position greatly helped; they commanded the heights, if on a smaller scale, as the Australians had done at Isurava. But Horii knew beforehand that they couldn't hold out, and had pressed for more reinforcements a week earlier. The survivors of the severely depleted Koiwai Battalion, part of the 41st Regiment led by Colonel Yazawa, strongly protested. They had safely landed at Buna in September, but many were wounded or sick in hospitals on the north coast. Now the fittest among them were ordered to march back to join Horii's fighting withdrawal.[19]

Yazawa cabled Horii from Buna to protest that his men were incapable:

Telegram No. 69
    To: Nankai Shitai Comdr
    From: Comdr Yazawa Butai 14 Oct 0700
    Malaria relapses (all officers and men of this unit have had malaria before) and beriberi are increasing . . . We have tried to

supplement food shortage with local potatoes, papayas and coconuts, but they are scarce ... Rations are insufficient even with these.[20]

Telegram No. 77

To: Comdr of the Nankai Shitai

From: Comdr of the Yazawa Butai. 15 Oct 0700

... only four men are healthy enough to be returned ... This is, in reality, no one. Hence it is impossible to carry out the mission of this Tai, ie — despatching one battalion to the Stanley Shitai.[21]

Horii insisted. He assigned great tactical importance to Eora Creek. And so several hundred of these wretched men set off on the ten-day march to join the delaying action. They arrived on the 26th. Horii later sent for further reinforcements. But by the time his request (Operation Order 122 — Stanley Detachment will fortify the Position at Eora Creek as Base for Future Offensive) arrived on the 29th, his men were on the run.

For two days prior, the battle had seized up. Cullen reported that a 'kind of torpor' afflicted his troops. He pressed Lloyd again to unite the brigade, and attack from the high ground to the west. Lloyd refused, relenting days later when he went to the front and was almost killed. Catterns' men, meanwhile, clung to their slope like limpets. Nerves frayed during the lull, and fear crept in. The men had time to think. A few troops, veterans of the Middle East and Tobruk, admitted they were so afraid they urinated in their trousers.

Sergeant Edwin 'Meggsie' Madigan, a 16th Brigade mortarman, was not one of them. When shrapnel tore open a mate's rib cage, Madigan raced to his assistance under fire, dressed the wound and, with the help of stretcher-bearers, lifted him to safety. His was one of many silent acts of selfless courage that constantly occurred and are too numerous to record.

A day later Madigan was severely concussed when a mortar shell blew up in the barrel of his mortar cannon. The same disaster struck Lieutenant Lance Hollingworth's platoon, when a two-inch mortar shell exploded in the cannon, killing his entire staff of six men. Why had nobody warned the mortar crews that airdropped mortar shells were lethal?

The mortar disasters drained morale at a time when the Australians were bogged down without a clear strategy. Three battalions were deployed across a vast area of jungle and mountain, without adequate communication. Brigadier Lloyd seemed unable, or reluctant, to accept the value of Cullen's tactical ideas.

Meanwhile, back at Myola, Tubby Allen, the Australian field commander, was under immense pressure to explain the delay in crushing the Japanese at Eora Creek. His sitreps had become noticeably laconic.

MacArthur and Blamey were similarly reticent. Then on 26th October a MacArthur missile arrived: 'In spite of your superior strength enemy appears able to delay advance at will. Essential that forward commanders should control situation and NOT allow situation control them. Delay in seizing KOKODA may cost us unique opportunity of driving enemy out of NEW GUINEA.'[22]

Allen could no longer complain about supplies: in the third week of October, six aircraft had disgorged 70,000 pounds of food, ammunition, blankets, shovels, picks and medical equipment, the largest single airdrop so far. Of course, what mattered was the amount recovered, not the volume dropped. Allen used 'every available man to search the swamps and jungles'. He reported that losses through damage were 'unreasonably high'. Parachutes were not yet attached to parcels — though crates of mortar shells now mercifully floated to earth.

Nor did Allen have the carriers. The fuzzy wuzzy angels were at a premium, and only 390 were then available. These exigencies did not concern Blamey, who was preoccupied with appeasing the wrath of MacArthur.

Nettled by the lack of progress, MacArthur acted. On the 27th Blamey resumed his role as MacArthur's executioner, and sacked Allen: 'Consider that you have had sufficiently prolonged tour of duty in forward area. General VASEY will arrive MYOLA by air morning 28 Oct. On arrival you will hand over command to him.'

Allen returned 'south for a short break'. On the 28th a plane that could easily have flown Blamey or Herring in to view the situation landed at Myola to collect Allen and deliver Vasey, his replacement (a few planes were now actually landing on the makeshift airstrip by the lakebed, though no wounded were flown out).

Allen lost his job the day before the Australians won the battle of Eora Creek. He later denounced Blamey: 'It is so easy for the senior commander to come forward and see the position for himself [actually, in the Kokoda case, it wasn't], but Blamey didn't do this. He must have known in his heart that he could not have done better than we were doing. Instead he took the line of least resistance and accepted the pressure from General MacArthur who knew even less.'[23]

The sacking of Allen revealed an irksome blend of sycophancy, political opportunism, cowardice and want of loyalty among Australia's top brass, of whom Blamey was the most powerful and shameless example. 'Few divisional commanders in history,' concluded David Horner, 'have been replaced by their army commander without having been visited by ... anyone above the rank of lieutenant-colonel ... Clearly Blamey felt he had to relieve Allen to placate MacArthur. Had Blamey stood up to MacArthur, he would have won the respect of the Australian army. As it was, he did MacArthur's bidding and won the opprobrium of the troops. Kokoda was not captured any faster for his action.'[24]

The Australians prevailed at Eora Creek by doing exactly what Cullen had urged: an attack from the high ground with, at the very least, a battalion of troops. Cullen switched his HQ to the west, and helped coordinate the attack. The 2/3rd Battalion under the fresh command of Major Ian Hutchison led the combined attack.

Hutchison was a short, solidly built young man with a 'bulldog fixity of purpose'.[25] He led three columns, each of 200 men, to the high spur above the Japanese. They charged down, rooting out and killing anyone who barred the way. They struck again at dawn on 28th. Combat 'boiled along the whole Australian front', as Hutchison's columns coursed across the ridge.[26]

'We sailed into them firing from the hip,' said Lieutenant Bruce MacDougal.[27] 'The forward scouts were knocked out, but the men went on

Eora Creek: 28 October 1942

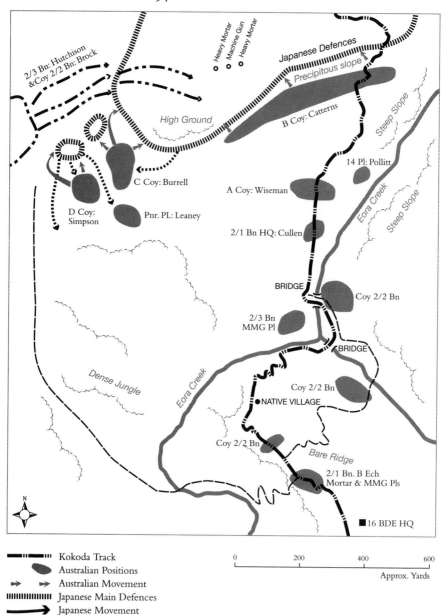

2/3 Bn: Hutchison
&Coy 2/2 Bn: Brock

Heavy Mortar
Machine Gun
Heavy Mortar

Japanese Defences

Precipitous slope

High Ground

B Coy: Catterns

Steep Slope

14 Pl: Pollitt

C Coy: Burrell

A Coy: Wiseman

Eora Creek

D Coy:
Simpson

Pnr. PL: Leaney

2/1 Bn HQ: Cullen

Steep Slope

BRIDGE

Coy 2/2 Bn

2/3 Bn
MMG Pl

BRIDGE

Dense Jungle

Eora Creek

Coy 2/2 Bn

●NATIVE VILLAGE

Coy 2/2 Bn

Bare Ridge

2/1 Bn. B Ech
Mortar & MMG Pls

N

■16 BDE HQ

▬▬ıı▪▪ııı Kokoda Track
Australian Positions
⇒ ⇒ Australian Movement
ıllıllıllıllıllıllı Japanese Main Defences
⟶ Japanese Movement

0   200   400   600

Approx. Yards

steadily advancing from tree to tree until we were right ... into the central position. Suddenly the Japanese began to run out. They dropped their weapons and stumbled through the thick bush ...'

Little Corporal Lester 'Tarzan' Pett — 'five feet of dynamite' — showed his men how to destroy the bunkers. He would race up and hurl grenades through the fire slits; by doing so, he destroyed four single-handedly. His height probably saved his life. The action earned him a Military Medal, though his platoon naturally felt he deserved a Victoria Cross. Pett died of wounds in a separate action two weeks later.

The attack rid the high spur of the Japanese guns, and freed Catterns and other units from their muddy capsules on the forward slopes; they scrambled over the precipice to find the enemy gone.

The Japanese saw the battle differently. Horii construed it as a heroic withdrawal from the jaws of defeat. 'Although the Stanley Shitai was attacked on the 28th along the entire front and a part of the Butai encircled,' he conceded, 'they broke through, taking advantage of the dark, and withdrew.'[28] The survivors headed back to Kokoda and Oivi.

The Australians entered the Japanese camp the next day. They counted 69 Japanese dead — mostly thin, haggard privates, with no food on them except fish paste. Some wore Australian watches. Their bunkers and foxholes 'radiated like a giant wheel from the central hub, about 300 yards across'.[29] Diaries, logbooks, maps and operational orders were retrieved by intelligence for translation. Mortars, machine-guns, rifles and ammunition were salvaged from the smoking mess. Souvenir hunters pocketed Japanese flags and knives. They then resumed the pursuit of the enemy, towards Alola, Isurava and the penultimate prize before the beachhead: the Kokoda airstrip.

Two hundred and ninety one Australians were killed or wounded at Eora Creek, according to Central Army Records.[30] The 'kill ratio' was one dead for every man wounded (Horii sustained a similar ratio of dead to wounded at Isurava). Initially, the Australian troops had shown 'more courage and energy than skill', according to the official historian's diplomatic summary.[31] In the end, they crushingly prevailed. But one fact greatly boosted the morale of the victors: an entrenched Japanese force had chosen to run rather than die fighting.

Old soldiers die hard. More than sixty years after the battle of Eora Creek, Paul Cullen, now Major-General, still clearly remembers that week in October 1942:

> *Major-General Cullen, at Eora Creek you objected to Brigadier Lloyd's plan?*
>
> That's right.
>
> *Do you feel that had you gone around the top, to the high ground, as you suggested, those men would not have died, they would have been OK?*
>
> Absolutely. We were ordered to advance across a bridge; there was a machine-gun on the other side. It was a very difficult situation, psychologically. We were terrified. But we did it.
>
> *Can you remember how you felt when you were crossing that bridge?*
>
> Terrified. Crawling across that bridge with Cox. There were thirteen dead men on the bank. It wasn't encouraging to crawl amongst them.
>
> I mean Brigadier Lloyd was exhausted mentally. He couldn't understand the jungle tactics that we'd learnt in Ceylon.
>
> You've got to get behind the enemy, if only you have the nerve to get behind the enemy, he has no alternative but to fall back. If you have to attack, for Christ's sake, get above him, instead of crawling up and feeling hopeless and useless on your hands and knees. I mean physically, the superiority of being higher up is immense.
>
> Well, the Brigadier looked me in the eye and said, 'If you don't go across that bridge it's because you haven't got the guts.' What else could I tell him? So I did.
>
> *How would you describe yourself, General?*
>
> Reckless, impulsive. But those qualities have served me well.[32]

The Australian field hospital at Myola contained 150 stretcher cases and about 300 walking wounded at the end of October, with dozens coming in every day. Thirty-five required immediate evacuation either by plane — if the light runway on the lakebed was built in time — or over the mountains, needing at least 350 native carriers. Senior medical officers wondered why stretcher cases were forced to wait in a forward post for eleven weeks after being wounded.

The new Myola strip was deemed too dangerous for air evacuation; earlier several planes had crashed. And yet planes were landing daily at Myola in late October — they had delivered Vasey, no less. Why could they not evacuate the most serious casualties, as Allen had pleaded (before being sacked)?

A Lockheed Hudson had comfortably landed and taken off on 21 October. In light of this, Allen requested urgent reconsideration be given to air evacuation of 90 casualties, of whom 21 were seriously ill.[33] His requests were refused. Air force experts advised light aircraft not to use the runway. That included the 'Moth' aerial ambulance for which Allen had been 'clamouring'. The strip was too short, they claimed, and the surrounding hills forced aircraft into a swift climb; the swirling mountain air caused several crashes during take-off and landing. Parer's film *Kokoda Frontline* shows this crater-like 'lip' on the edges of the Myola lakebed.

Yet a plane landed on 27 October to deliver mail, and flew out a severely wounded man, the first to be air-evacuated, without trouble.* News of this prompted 'great excitement' among the wounded. Unfortunately they were doomed to disappointment, and major surgery had to be done in the tent near the tarmac.

When Rupert Magarey urgently requested air evacuation of the wounded, Colonel Kingsley Norris enthusiastically forwarded the request to Allied Air Command, which abruptly rejected it, to Norris' disgust. Even as late as 1 November, after the 2/6th Field Ambulance had built an airstrip at Myola,

---

* Back in Moresby 'nobody seemed to know what to do with [the wounded man] when he landed. Took them all by surprise. Couldn't believe it could be done', according to Lieutenant Fayle's diary (Allen Papers).

and two bombers had successfully landed, the wounded were denied an airlift to safety. The planes that did land were reloaded with stores — while 438 sick and wounded men lay on the tarmac.

Some had been there for months. Norris wrote a damning report: 'In spite of every effort ... air evacuation was neglected. Why this was never adequately undertaken — why, after three years of war no adequate ambulance planes were available — why certain casualties had to remain in a forward medical post for 11 weeks after being wounded — these and many other questions remain unanswered.' [34]

One man, Brigadier William Wallace Johnston, deputy director of Medical Services at New Guinea Force HQ, did attempt an answer. There were no suitable planes, he claimed. Two — a single-engine Stinson and tri-motor Ford — had crashed while attempting to land at Myola. Was the risk worth it? Johnston bleakly concluded: '... air evacuation had become out of the question'.

Indeed, on 30 October, Myola's sick and wounded were ordered to get up and walk back to Port Moresby. Field hospitals along the track would assist them in this agonising ordeal.[35] They were sent back in batches, witnessed Fayle, in his diary on 2 November:

Two arm-wounded men passed us ... one had been shot in the elbow and the arteries cut. They had been tied but the exertion of the fast walk had busted the tyings and he was fast bleeding to death — blood everywhere. Tourniquet applied in double quick time and we carried him in. A few anxious moments when he very often blacked out. After about ½ hour we came to his cobber ... in exactly the same condition ... We got them to Uberi and they lived but only just.[36]

Sufficient numbers of stretcher-bearers were at last obtained for those unable to walk. By now, some patients had lain on the tarmac at Myola for two and a half months. The last wounded arrived back in Port Moresby a day or two before Christmas.

It was a painful Christmas. In total a mere 38 sick and wounded Australian troops were flown out of Myola; by the end of the campaign, more than a thousand would make the journey on foot or by stretcher over the mountains.[37]

The story has a stomach-churning epilogue. In tones that suggest he saw the idea as something of a novelty, Arthur Drakeford, the Minister for Air, wrote to Curtin on 31 December 1942: 'My dear Minister,' he noted, 'The Air Board has just recommended that approval be given for the purchase of 20 air ambulances for the work of evacuation of wounded in New Guinea, a special type of aircraft being necessary in view of ... the mountainous nature of terrain ...'

Asked for his opinion of Drakeford's plan, MacArthur dismissed the need for special air ambulances at Myola: 'Normal aircraft were suitable,' he said.

In short, air ambulances were ordered three months too late for a job that ordinary planes could have done, as MacArthur now blithely acknowledged. In that time, at least 450 seriously ill and badly wounded Australian soldiers lay in Myola within crawling distance of the tarmac.[38]

Chapter 39
Vasey

'We must ... make our mistakes quickly'
— *Major-General George Vasey*

A tall, popular officer with a sharp intellect and sense of humour, 'Bloody George' Vasey flew into Myola on 23 October to drive the offensive forward. Vasey was an unusual general; his quick wit and independent character had happily survived his promotion up the ranks. He seemed cheerfully free of those twin encrustations of power: pomposity and self-importance.

His wit and louche charm were among his most memorable characteristics. Rowell dubbed him Australia's 'most picturesque' general. He was a good-looking man with an irreverent style that might have impeded his rise had not rigid self-discipline and an unyielding spirit formed the core of Vasey's being. He had a genuine concern for, and mingled with, his men, whose names he took the trouble to remember. 'He never lost the common touch,' concluded Raymond Paull.[1]

One anecdote tells, after Vasey's escape from Crete, of the commander loping 'along the quay at Alexandria in the hot Egyptian sunshine ... His head of wiry black hair, parted in the middle, was hatless.' He wore 'crumpled battle dress trousers ... [and] his gaunt leather face, with its clipped black moustache, betrayed nothing of the physical and mental stress immediately behind him. His prodigious vitality seemed unimpaired.'

John Hetherington, the reporter who witnessed this unforgettable sight, asked the brigadier, 'How was Crete?'

'Crete, eh! It was all right. It was perfectly all right, except that it was a bloody fuck-up ...'[2]

Vasey had a swaggering indifference to danger, which impressed the troops. If less forgiving veterans remember him as 'Butcher George', after the bloodbath of Sanananda, most who fought under him deeply admired his courage and honesty. Veterans recall Vasey striding about Sanananda wearing the red hatband of a general, at a time when officers chose not to display marks of rank. Vasey placed military order ahead of personal safety — perhaps unwisely. When Vasey noticed the lack of officers' insignia, he boomed, 'Put back those bloody badges of rank — I don't know whether I'm talking to the cook or my GI!'[3]

Some misread his good humour as a surfeit of calm. On the contrary, he had an inner intensity, which showed in his impatience with fools. Vasey took his huge responsibilities seriously, and the discharging of them was a profound concern behind his effusive exterior.

He was bright, too. His quiet mastery of technical detail distinguished him from his peers, both in the army and in civilian life. Brilliant at maths, he passed in the top five at Duntroon Military College, and later came third in Australia in his accountancy exams. Yet he wore his intelligence lightly.

He neither stooped to cheap political games, nor let himself be provoked by them. He was simply there — smiling, swearing, advising and soldiering — with a brusqueness and candour that warmed his colleagues and marked him as one of Australia's finest generals. Not surprisingly, he had many friends.

Born in 1895, Vasey served on the Western Front as a commander in an ammunition column. He saw the horror of the Somme. Sent into battle nineteen times against the Germans, he served with distinction at Pozières in 1916, where 23,000 Australian soldiers were killed or wounded in seven weeks. Though Vasey's unit had a supportive, not combative, role, his performance won him immediate promotion to battery commander. It was a sign of extraordinary mental toughness in so young a man. He was 21.

In 1921, he met and married Jessie Mary Halbert, whose intelligence and self-assuredness prompted a friend of Vasey's to inquire, 'How are you going to get on married to a blue stocking, George?'

'Don't worry,' Vasey replied, 'I'll soon have the blue stocking off her.'

He was very attractive to women, and 'always made women feel special even when they were somewhat plain,' wrote David Horner.[4] It was his good fortune to be blessed with an adoring family, and a string of entertaining letters to his wife reveals a man of relaxed affection.

There is an amused twinkle in the eye of the older Vasey, and a winning recklessness in the way he spoke and wrote. He seemed to enjoy startling people with his wit, which could be carnal, sometimes cruel, and mostly entertaining. When his little boy 'electrified' British guests by uttering 'a fine string of pungent blasphemies' at a stuffy dinner party in India, Vasey bustled the child out of the room and declared, 'I just can't imagine where these blasted little devils get hold of all this bloody rude language'. He was immediately 'in' with the British, at the officers' course at Quetta, and the anecdote is believed to be the source of his nickname.[5]

The elite Quetta academy did not acknowledge his powers of leadership — they gave him a C. But Vasey revelled in his popularity there, and returned to Australia in 1930 having rediscovered himself: 'friends saw, in this slim, tall man, now thirty-five and nearing his physical and mental prime, not a new Vasey but the old wartime Vasey reborn.'[6]

Religious in a loose, conventional sense, Vasey nodded at the Anglican edifice of belief. He did not attend church. Yet he had a strong sense of right and wrong, and never abused his power. He knew instinctively when the rank and file crossed the line. Dismayed by the loutish behaviour of the Australian troops in Palestine and Tel-Aviv in 1940, Vasey issued orders designed to curb excessive larrikinism and obscenities which, he felt, had brought the army into disrepute. One clause amused the men: 'Obscene language: Strict measures are to be taken to suppress obscene language, the use of which is prevalent both in camps and whilst personnel are on leave.'

It was a touch of sunny self-parody in an otherwise stern list of instructions — Norris remarked that Vasey, 'had the rare gift of transmitting words usually considered foul into terms of endearment'.[7]

In other respects, his personal life was a model of rigorous self-discipline — a template for his behaviour on the battlefield. Vasey's 'Training for War' manual issued on 16 March 1940 promoted the novel idea that a soldier's self-control in peacetime determined his quality in battle: 'An ill-disciplined army can never succeed in battle, and an officer who cannot control his men is a menace. A man who cannot control himself under peace conditions is unlikely to do so in the stress of battle.'[8]

Vasey believed the role of a commander transcended staff work and the ability to make tough decisions under duress. He reckoned a commander needed to be with his men, to lead and be seen to lead. This Vasey did, with exceptional verve and guts, during World War II in the Middle East, Greece and in New Guinea, where he would exceed, to the point of collapse, his own high standards of command and play an indispensable role in defeating the enemy.

Amusing anecdotes tumble from Horner's superb biography of Vasey. During the evacuation of Greece he faced the choice of whether to take two wireless sets or two cases of gin. He chose the gin. Occasionally he cut a dashing, perhaps foolish, figure. Dressed in a white mackintosh, he went within a few hundred yards of German machine-guns during the withdrawal from Greece, 'to see things for himself, as well as to let himself be seen by his soldiers'. Raking fire forced him back on his hands and knees. At Megara, he chatted in his car while German planes strafed the field. He reassured his companions that the Germans would ignore the vehicle, as only an idiot sat in a car during an air attack.

Vasey had a short fuse in the presence of incompetence. But his explosions of rage were not mere punitive gusts of hot air. He taught through his tirades. The object of his anger came away somewhat the wiser.

He had a tendency suddenly to switch from his 'wild jovial ways' into a commander of steel.[9] A lazy staff officer at Australia's HQ during the disastrous Greek campaign had the misfortune to encounter Vasey returning from the front. The officer seemed oblivious to the unfolding catastrophe in the Greek mountains. Vasey let rip with characteristic flair: 'What in the bloody hell do you think I'm fighting with up there? Cream puffs? Get off your big fat arse and I'll show you how to run a war.'[10]

———

Vasey meant to take the fight to the Japanese with every ounce of his energy and brainpower. He stamped his inimitable style on the New Guinea campaign within days. His written orders were admirably brief, and to the point — an eight-line signal outlined a major offensive.

When he took command of the 6th Division on 23 September, he distributed a new set of instructions for fighting 'the Jap'. Distinguished by their unusual clarity and leavened with Vasey's robust prose, they made good sense.

He had a sure grasp of how to deal with the problems that beset Potts, Rowell and Allen, observing, 'The favourite method of Japanese attack is encirclement. To combat this, small formations, which are stationary, must have patrols out and when the Japs are located attack and kill them. To await encirclement will not lead to success ... Because the Jap has established himself in the rear of a unit is no reason to withdraw. Remember that if the Jap has encircled you and got astride your communications, you, also, are astride his' — a direct reference to the disaster at Brigade Hill.

He stated the blindingly obviously on the difficulties of the terrain. That he felt the need to comment at all suggests he sympathised with frustrated attempts by Rowell and Allen to dent the wall of ignorance in Brisbane: 'War in New Guinea is a combination of jungle warfare and mountain warfare,' he observed. 'The Japanese must not be allowed to secure high ground from which he can bring effective fire on our positions.' The best way of stopping them was a matter of 'picquetting the heights which overlook the axis of movement'. In this, he and Cullen saw eye to eye.

Vasey urged every man to carry five days' dehydrated rations, and to act speedily to ensure the Japanese death toll was 'as great as possible' before the December monsoons. In a letter to Herring he wrote: 'We must ... "make our mistakes quickly"'.[11]

Chapter 40
Kokoda Regained

'Occupation of Kokoda is expected by our troops 2nd
November ... The enemy is beaten. Give him no rest and
we will annihilate him'
— *General Vasey to Australian officers, 1 November 1942*

Vasey had flown over the mountains in July, so he knew the scale of the
place; now he confronted the Owen Stanleys on foot. At 47, he
remained fit, but his knee grew 'swollen with fluid' as he climbed the slopes
between Myola and Eora Creek. He ignored his medical officer's concern
until the pain grew intolerable — and each night, in sworn secrecy, Kingsley
Norris re-dressed and bandaged the general's swollen knee joint.

Vasey had a civilian's eye for the beauty of the track: 'In other
conditions it would really be a beautiful walk — forest everywhere and lots
of lovely streams, but at present they merely make mud.'[1] He reached Alola
— recaptured unopposed by the 16th Brigade — sweating and puffing, and
vomited up his first cup of sweet, black tea.

At Alola he provocatively established his divisional HQ just forward of
Eather's, and noted with satisfaction that Eather then resited his brigade HQ
up past his commander's. 'That's the way to keep 'em moving,' Vasey said,

'. . . march divvy headquarters past the brigade and they'll move on.'[2] In such ways, Vasey kept up the relentless pressure on his officers: driving them forward, goading them on, so that a constant sense of the urgency of the advance rippled down the ranks, from the brigadiers to the battalion commanders to the company officers, to the platoon leaders, corporals and private soldiers.

With Kokoda half a day's march away, Vasey cracked the whip. It was thought the Japanese might have abandoned the station too (indeed, a patrol led by Lieutenant Fred Winkle[3] four days earlier had found the airfield deserted — though Allen had not been informed of this). Vasey was determined to recapture the vital airfield within days, and Eather's 25th Brigade was given the honour of doing so. Meanwhile, Lloyd's 16th Brigade, with Cullen's battalion in the vanguard, pursued the enemy north-east, along the track toward the villages of Oivi and Gorari.

Horii had not lost hope. In late October he'd been told to expect an entire division of reinforcements[4] — some 20,000 troops — with which to strike back. The news was electrifying: 'The desire to take Port Moresby blazed up and there were many shouts of joy and exultation,' wrote one soldier.[5]

Their flames were swiftly doused: the order was countermanded on 2 November as the situation in Guadalcanal deteriorated. Most of the fresh division went to the Solomons; those who did attempt to land at Buna faced Allied air raids. The Shitai's morale 'dropped alarmingly', noted one witness.

Of the original 6000-strong infantry of the South Seas Detachment, less than a thousand were fit enough to fight — though this is a relative term. Of his original 500-strong force, the commander of the Koiwai Battalion counted just sixteen fit soldiers — five of whom were engineers.[6] The rest were dead, wounded, sick, starving, or had simply disappeared. Only 176 and 180 'effectives' remained of the Kuwada and Horie battalions respectively, which had lost 568 and 617 men.[7]

Medical officer Hayashi Hiroyuki had charted the Japanese casualty rate in his diary since the retreat from Ioribaiwa:

24 Sept 42: The [Kokoda] Field Hosp will withdraw. At about 1200. . . the sick and wounded would start out.

29 Sept 42: ... Our coy is to proceed to Eora and receive rations. And we are to assist the Engr Tai in taking patients to the field hosp between Giruwa and Kokoda.

8 Oct 42: Our casualties: Aug: 400 killed, 600 wounded; Sep: 200 killed.

11 Oct 42: Up to this date the number of sick and wounded exceeds 3000.[8]

On 1 November, in a jungle clearing at Ilimo, Horii addressed the survivors of the Nankai Shitai. Defiant to the last, he still believed in the possibility of a counteroffensive (and it seems he made this speech in the expectation of reinforcements):

Some time ago, the Shitai was ordered to cross the Stanley Range. With bravery and determination you men advanced as far as Iorabaiwa [sic] in the face of stubborn enemy resistance. We had Port Moresby under our mercy and created terror in the hearts of the enemy.

However, the general situation of the Army forced the Shitai into an unwilling withdrawal. For this reason the Stanley Shitai had to employ defensive tactics at Eora and The Gap ...

... we will withdraw to the Kumusi River area, where problems of supply are comparatively easy, and prepare for a future offensive.

To repeat, our withdrawal will not be the result of the superiority of the enemy. It was aimed to recover the health and strength of the troops. To compare this with defeat shows a gross misunderstanding.

Exert yourselves towards making a healthy recuperation ... prepare for brave and active counter-attacks. To build up our morale and inflexible fighting spirit is the most important thing at present.

It is believed that the enemy, as is characteristic of him, will take this advantage of making further persistent attacks on our front lines. They may also penetrate our flanks and rear. If such an occasion arises, the Shitai will make determined counter-attacks and destroy the enemy.

For the sake of honour, all units, regardless of whether they are combatants, non-combatants or Army employees, are expected to recover their fighting strength spiritually as well as physically, thereby demonstrating the strength of the high-spirited, brilliant Shitai.[9]

His last remark meant, in effect, that the Shitai's medics, transport troops, carriers and HQ staff were to join the infantry as combat troops. None would be spared a role in Horii's lonely Götterdämmerung; the doomed fragment of the Imperial Army would, literally, go down fighting.

Unknown to Horii, the Australians had successfully intercepted Japanese army signals, and knew his approximate strength and the position of some of his reinforcements.

Blamey passed this news to MacArthur on 30 October: 'On 28 Oct . . . Sigs 1 Aust Corps intercepted for the first time the full text of a number of Jap messages . . . in the KOKODA area . . .' It established that three battalions were 'still forward of KOKODA or in that area'. Blamey added that a 'relieving unit', sent to join the Shitai, was sighted moving up the track between Wairopi and Kokoda.[10]

Horii's relieving units were, in fact, fairly substantial reinforcements. They were fresh troops brought up from the beachhead or shipped in from Rabaul, to arrest the retreat and shore up the Gona–Buna littoral. The merged force withdrew to the elevated land on the Kumusi flood plain near the villages of Oivi and Gorari. It astonished the Australian tacticians that Horii chose to make his last act of resistance on the western side of the Kumusi — with his back to the river.

This intelligence was a great encouragement to Vasey, as was the confirmation that the Japanese had abandoned Kokoda. On 1 November, Vasey issued his first 'Order of the Day' to unit commanders: 'Occupation of Kokoda is expected by our troops 2nd November. Congratulations to you and the fine troops under your command for the rapid advance you have made under shocking conditions ... The enemy is beaten. Give him no rest and we will annihilate him. It is only a matter of a day or two. Tighten your belts and push on.'[11] On the 3rd he ordered Lloyd's brigade to move towards Oivi in full strength.

At dawn on 1 November a little patrol led by Lieutenant Albert Black[12] crept into Kokoda unopposed. The Japanese had abandoned the village two days before. The Australian troops jubilantly followed Black's men and on the 4th spread out over the plateau without a single shot being fired.

Three months after the Imperial Army had driven out the 39th Battalion, the Australians reclaimed the airstrip. Vasey magnanimously acknowledged the victory as Allen's — notwithstanding gushing congratulations personally from Blamey, who felt the recapture of Kokoda a tacit vindication of Allen's dismissal.*

That afternoon Vasey raised the Australian flag on the site of the old Kokoda administration building, and held a ceremony of remembrance for those who had died in the mountain campaign. The much-diminished 25th Brigade paraded at the tip of the plateau, where crumbling walls and bomb craters marked the site of the old station buildings.

Bert Kienzle, master of the carrier lines, had fulfilled his promise to the mountain tribes that he would return in time for Christmas. They emerged from the hills and plantations to see his promise honoured, welcoming him 'like a long lost son', wrote Raymond Paull.[13]

The local people were 'bedecked with flowers and shrubs, and all smiles,' Kienzle observed, and happy to be back in Kokoda even as they picked over the obliterated remains. 'They knew they had done well.'

They were put immediately to work, but did not begrudge Kienzle's determination to protect the station. The most urgent task was the restoration of the airfield: 'All available carriers which I could muster were put on during the afternoon weeding the landing ground which was overgrown. The Japs had not used it.'

---

* Vasey, however, did not appreciate being reminded of Allen's role by his staff officer, Colonel Spry, with whom he 'did not hit it off' (Horner, *General Vasey's War*, p. 209).

Kienzle looked in on his plantation at Yodda on the 5th: two farm buildings were burnt down, his own house riddled with machine-gun and mortar fire, and all his possessions removed and destroyed. 'The rubber trees were still standing, a few mutilated . . .'[14]

Vernon, sick with jungle fever, came down the track through the rubber trees where three months ago he'd waited in the mist for the last man to leave Kokoda. On the way he passed a dump of Japanese kit. It was a souvenir hunter's paradise. Amidst the wreckage he noticed 'barrels of a fermented sauce, a first class preventative of BeriBeri. . . a delicacy which seems to follow the trail of the exiled Jap wherever he goes'.[15]

He salvaged a Japanese bicycle, with one pedal and no tyres, 'hopped onto it and the boys shoved behind, highly excited . . .' To whoops of joy from native boys Vernon weaved triumphantly into Kokoda.

He might have arrived on a donkey, such were the tears of happiness in the eyes of the fuzzy wuzzies to whose welfare he'd devoted his waking hours.

Vernon dumped the bike, reported to the ANGAU camp in the Yodda valley, sat back and contemplated the vast serenity around him: 'I had at last got home.'[16]

There were more happy scenes that day. All available carriers assembled on the Kokoda plateau at 4.30 p.m. to receive the gratitude of the Australian nation. Five were awarded medals for outstanding service, and every carrier received an issue of knives and *ramie* (a popular native delicacy).

Vasey, with Kienzle interpreting, thanked the crowds of carriers and stretcher-bearers for their loyal service: 'Without your help,' Vasey said, 'we would not have been able to cross the Owen Stanley Range.'[17]

The tribes responded appreciatively with loud drumming and a traditional chant, which resounded across the Mambare Valley. That night fires were lit and a hot meal with tea served to the troops.

Within two days the airstrip was cleared and refitted, and at precisely 9.45 a.m. on 4 November the first planes flew in a dazzling array of supplies.

The bellies of ten Dakotas yielded American jeeps, ammunition, new weapons, cigarettes, bread and chocolate, fresh meat and vegetables, baked beans, tinned fruit, jam and butter.

The troops gobbled up these delicacies, but their stomachs, so used to army biscuits and bully beef, rejected them, and they lay 'retching and heaving' on the ground.[18] Felt hats were issued, to replace their hot, tin helmets, and new uniforms, boots, socks and blankets were great restoratives.

Kokoda rapidly became a flourishing Allied air base — an indispensable depot in the coming thrust to the sea. The wounded, too, were greatly relieved — for the first time, they could be flown safely back to Port Moresby (though this didn't help the 485 men then lying at Myola, back in the mountains).

The troops' brains were fed as well as their bodies. The day after the capture of Kokoda, Blamey busied himself ordering books for the army's field library. Major-General Victor Stantke, Adjutant-General, Victoria Barracks, Melbourne, obliged by sending up copies of the arresting title, *Savages in Papua*. The Australian Army Education Service thoughtfully added to their library *Headhunters*, by Ion Idriess; *My South Sea Adventures*, by J. McLaren; *My Tropic Isle*, by E.J. Badfield; and Roberts' *Short Stories of the South Seas*.

Blamey backed a new troops' magazine called *Guinea Gold*, for which he requested articles 'dealing with such subjects as birds, butterflies, animals, plants . . . and insects pertaining to New Guinea'. These, he believed, would 'stimulate a very active interest on the part of the men in their surroundings'.★

The Japanese sick and wounded bumped back towards the coast in the hope of evacuation. The fittest had fled the dreadful Kokoda field hospital, and only the bodies of the dead or dying remained under the palm-frond roof. Those unable to walk, or lacking the strength to commit suicide, had been shot in their stretchers.

★ Dr Herber Longman, a botanist from the Queensland Museum, declined Blamey's invitation to contribute, but took great pleasure in showing his collection of Papuan birds to Blamey's commissioning scout, who happened to be called Major C.R. Bird. Longman also acted as a quasi-consultant to Blamey's publishing interests: 'The many New Guinea rodents include giant long-haired rats which are among the largest known species,' he observed. Papua's 'giant bats' were 'quite good to eat in dire emergencies' (Blamey Papers).

When the walking Japanese wounded reached the beachhead they were directed to the ghastly Giruwa Line of Communication Hospital, east of Sanananda. In October this little cluster of huts and tents, set back from the beach, received 1160 new patients. On the last day of that month, Giruwa held a total of 1325 (215 wounded, 1110 sick), 225 of whom drifted in on 26 October. Of 637 patients who belonged to the Naval Pioneers, 520 had acute malaria. By mid-November the 500-bed hospital contained some 2000 patients, most of whom lay about on the jungle floor awaiting treatment.[19] More plodded in every day; and the team of 57 doctors and medical orderlies were soon reduced to a state of utter helplessness.

First Lieutenant Okubo Fukunobo, a Japanese army medical officer at Giruwa, calculated on 31 October that he had only enough food to feed 380 patients for seventeen days. In sum, half a fixed ration for each patient for about a week: 'the quality and quantity of food has gradually declined ... patients cannot be expected to regain their vitality,' Okubo grimly concluded.[20]

His medical fixtures were execrable. The tents were rotting, and 'holes appear simply if you touch the material'. Patients were constantly drenched. The panniers were falling apart from corrosion; the leather straps on stretchers had lost their pliability. The metal parts had rusted and the bases deteriorated. The few surgical instruments were rusting and useless; there were scarcely any painkillers; morphine was non-existent.

None of this deterred the sick and wounded. They came like pilgrims to a religious miracle. In the prospect of evacuation — and it would indeed take a miracle to evacuate them — lay their salvation. Only one boatload of the sick escaped during October, wrote Okubo.

To shelter the hundreds of new patients, the Japanese medical corps built a temporary hospital nearby out of leaking, portable tents. They worked for 46 hours in the 'merciless rain and wind, all were drenched ... Words cannot describe this wretchedness,' Okubo said. He blamed himself and his unit: 'We deeply feel our responsibility and have no excuse for the many regrettable lapses in preparation through our sudden participation in the war and our inability to make a sufficient study of the needs of soldiers ...'[21]

Chapter 41
Oivi–Gorari

'Japan did not lose the ground war in the South Pacific in any
single place. There was no equivalent of Waterloo or Stalingrad ...
Yet if I were to pick one place where the war turned irrevocably
against the Japanese, it was at Oivi–Gorari... The [Australians]
inflicted a massive defeat on crack Japanese troops at small cost to
themselves'
— *Eric Bergerud,* Touched With Fire

Fed up with the insinuations that he was somehow Allen's caretaker, Vasey
now meant to impose his formidable will on the campaign. He had the
comfort of a secure air base and the mountains behind him; the Japanese, on
the other hand, were digging in with their backs to the Kumusi River. This
knowledge made up his mind: Vasey would deploy his entire army in a
single, crushing blow.

He planned to attack on a scale as yet unprecedented in the Pacific War.
No Allied army — in Burma, Malaya or Guadalcanal — had yet committed
two brigades or greater in offensive action. Vasey prepared to surround and
cut off the Japanese with no less than seven Australian battalions — a force

of about 4000 men.* He risked 'having no backstop'; the first time in the Pacific an Allied commander had deployed all his reserve troops in one stroke.

He was racing against time — and not just MacArthur's and Blamey's time. Vasey's army were racked by disease, of which there were more virulent strains near the coast. Every day the sickness rate rose. As they neared the coastal plain, the incidence of malaria shot up (soon it would reach hyperendemic levels). The Australian losses since Myola, 'exclusive of killed', was more than a thousand, Vasey wired Herring in Port Moresby. Companies were amalgamated, they were so thin. Dysentery was endemic, especially in Cullen's battalion as they made their way east.

Ever conscious of the challenge of the terrain, Vasey adopted innovative techniques to get his officers moving — and thinking: 'One cannot accelerate speed of the individual in this climate,' he told Herring. Instead, he asked his officers to accelerate their 'speed of thought and decision'** and 'to take the route where the Jap is not'.[1]

The speed of Vasey's thought alarmed his more cautious staff. When one staff officer wondered whether the huge manoeuvre wasn't a bit risky, Vasey jabbed a finger at the officer's chest and replied, 'I will do anything that [the enemy] will allow me to do.'[2] Vasey knew his own mind, and was superb at thinking on the hop. The staff officer soon came around to Bloody George's way of thinking: 'He knew exactly what he wanted to do. He was quick off the mark, and the clarity of his thought was terrific.'

The combat zone was a rectangular area of grassland, rubber trees and clumps of jungle about three miles long and a mile wide, east to west. On the western end, on higher ground, was the village of Oivi; about a mile to the east was Gorari, the Japanese hub, linked to Oivi by the Kokoda–Wairopi track. About seven miles further east was the Kumusi River. There were perhaps 2500 to

---

* They included the three battalions of the 16th and 25th brigades plus the 3rd Militia Battalion — huge losses to illness and battle casualties had depleted the total, which would have been 7000 at full strength. Most units were at less than half strength. Eather's 25th Brigade had lost 800 men to sickness or injuries since Myola — one battalion (2/33rd) had just sixteen officers and 271 men, while a company of the 16th Brigade had 39 fit troops.

** In the choice of this phrase, Vasey unwittingly foreshadowed the title of Bill Gates's business tome, *Business at the Speed of Thought*, by 60 years.

3000 Japanese troops heavily dug in between Oivi and Gorari. Palm-log reinforced foxholes similar to those at Templeton's Crossing pocked the field.

Vasey had sent one brigade[3] and Cullen's battalion along a track parallel to the Kokoda–Wairopi route, as the southern prong of his vast flanking manoeuvre. The rest of his men were ordered to attack Oivi, to the east. For the first time, the Australians had the numbers and the manoeuvrability to attack effectively on the front and the flanks.

On the 7th, Australian mortars and American bombers pounded the Japanese bunkers at Oivi, followed by a failed attack that claimed 47 Australian casualties. The next morning low-flying American fighters strafed the Japanese bunkers at Oivi and along the track, and dropped eight 20-pound bombs on their bunker fields. The Australian troops noted with relief that the fighters 'didn't hit us on this occasion'.[4]

Vasey had no intention of sending costly 'ram-like thrusts' towards the Japanese front line. His trump card was the wide flanking march of the 25th Brigade and Cullen's battalion. The open terrain helped — this was easier country than Eora Creek. Yet many were sick, and the speed of movement exhausted them. On the 4th, Cullen's men camped on the edge of a razorback, before descending into the Oivi valley: 'That night,' wrote Cecil Traise, 'I was lying across the razorback with part of my legs hanging in space, rain simply pelted down and the smell of rotting leaves gave the impression that I had fallen into a cesspit.'[5]

The next day they entered the village of Sengai, and made a bitterly sad discovery: the skeletons of five Australians dead in their stretchers, with two others, including Metson, lying nearby — final proof of the fate of Fletcher's party.

On the 8th, having gone too far and then been forced to retrace their steps, Cullen's men regrouped at Leaney's Corner with troops of the 25th Brigade. The combined Australian force prepared to encircle the Japanese at Gorari.

Patrols had already clashed for days between Leaney's Corner and Gorari, under sheeting rain, with heavy casualties. These were exceptionally savage. One battalion suffered 37 casualties while fighting along the track to Gorari on the 9th, its costliest day.[6]

Oivi–Gorari: Nightfall, 9 November 1942

Asaki
Kumusi River
Japanese crossing
Wairopi
Asisi
Papaki
Olivi Creek
Illimo
Japanese Retreat
Gorari
Japanese HQ destroyed
2/33 Advance
2/1 Bn
2/33 Bn
2/33 Bn
2/25 Bn
2/33 Bn
25 BDE HQ
Japanese Retreat
Oivi
2/2 & 2/3 Bns
Sengai
Leaney's Corner
3 Bns
Komondo
Pirivi
Kobara
to Awala
Kokoda
to Pitoki!

N

Kokoda Track
Australian Positions
Australian Movement
Japanese Movement
Japanese Defences Destroyed

Approx. Miles
0 1 2 3 4 5

But slowly the Australian trap was being set. To the west, one battalion had wedged itself between the enemy positions at Oivi and Gorari; to the south-east, another blocked any retreat to the Kumusi River; and to the south two more closed in from Leaney's Corner. The Australian troops began to squeeze the Japanese in a three-way vice, from the east, south and west. 'It was clear that the next day or two must bring forth a slugging match. Desperate Japanese would try to fight out of the trap . . .'[7]

The first slugging began at Oivi. The Japanese realised they were cut off from their Gorari HQ — by the Australians sandwiched between the two — and hemmed in by the Australians to the west. Reminiscent of Potts's experience at Brigade Hill — though on a larger scale — Japanese patrols tried to smash through to Gorari. They failed to breach the wall of Australian machine-guns.

Lieutenant Sakomoto, who'd inflicted such damage on the Australian withdrawal at Brigade Hill, sat in his dugout and prepared to face battle. 'The Australian offensive has begun,' he wrote on 9 November. 'They have encircled us, while all morning, their planes bombed and strafed us.'

On the 10th he made his last entry: 'The 1st battalion is leaving Ilimo at 2 o'clock to cover our retreat. Decided to withdraw from this position at 10pm. The Yazawa Butai will be our cover Tai. Situation in the rear is not clear.'[8]

Sakomoto died fighting — a true example of the 'warrior spirit'.

Meanwhile, the Japanese trapped in Gorari tried to blast their way out of the Australian cordon, and wheeled up a mountain gun to the western edge of their perimeter, 400 yards from the Australian dugouts.

Shelled for three hours, the Australian 2/33rd Battalion was almost blown apart. 'With only log cover or bayonet scratched holes, this grim experience shattered nearly all in D company.'[9] Some abandoned their positions — at which the commanding officer pulled his revolver and threatened to shoot the fleeing troops, who were forced back to the front. Eventually the shelling ceased.

On the night of the 11th the Australians 'were gathering themselves for the kill', in the official historian's vivid phrase.[10] The two armies met on that moonless night in pouring rain across a landscape of splintered rubber trees, jungle copses and muddy grass. The Australians crept across the field towards the Japanese perimeter at Gorari village, their main camp. Cullen's men wheeled round to the north of the enemy — utterly confusing them. The other units pressed in from all sides.

Suddenly hundreds of Japanese tried to break out. They rushed for escape routes; suicidal officers ran yelling at Australian guns. Others attempted to bayonet charge their way out. Medieval scenes of hand-to-hand combat flared in the darkness. Tracer fire and exploding grenades flashed on the running shapes. Hunched figures squatted in the mud, clasping wounds; some crawled back to their bunkers. Medics scrambled about to locate the cries of the wounded.

Just as suddenly, the breakout ceased, offering a few hours' respite. The Australians troops waited in the mud for the resumption, '...few slept. Throughout the dark hours fire was heard on all sides, occasionally flaring up to a crescendo. Japanese were heard and seen moving about on all sides.'[11]

Runners sent back with messages lost their way. Often they ran headlong into roaming Japanese. Private George Gates, sent back to his brigade HQ, was later found, bayoneted by wandering Japanese.[12] Another runner, Lance-Corporal Cyril Daniels, was shot dead after walking twenty paces into the scrub. Company commander, Captain Brinkley, lay in the open ground with a gaping stomach wound. Hauled back to safety, he died a short time later.

About midnight a piercing scream stunned an Australian platoon. A Japanese soldier had infiltrated and tried to bayonet Private Bowen, an immensely strong bushman nicknamed 'Yippee'. Yippee grabbed the blade, wrenched both bayonet and rifle out of the Japanese soldier's hand, and hurled it like a spear at his fleeing attacker. The rifle stabbed the Japanese infiltrator in the back.[13] Bowen received deep wounds in his hands.★

The slaughter continued all the next day, beginning with a wave of Australian bayonet charges. At dawn on the 11th, they surprised a group of Japanese troops sitting down for a breakfast of rice and milk. 'It's apparently not etiquette to fight [at] mealtime,' wrote one Australian. 'They were ...

★ Yippee had left his non-combatant unit without permission so that he could join a fighting battalion. He found himself in the 2/1st technically having 'deserted' his original unit, and was later charged with 'firing at the King's enemies without permission' and fined five pounds.

eating their breakfast at the critical moment. The attack became a slaughter and the Japanese were wiped out to a man, with amazingly light casualties to our side.'

The enemy dead were believed to be members of 144th Kuwada Battalion, the unit responsible for the massacre of the Australians at Rabaul. 'So justice was done,' concluded Bert Kienzle, years later, in an address to the 39th Battalion Association Pilgrimage.[14]

Gorari became a mass killing ground. The stupefied Japanese were shot, bayoneted or grenaded without restraint. The scale and fury of the Australian assault shocked even the enemy. Three Australian battalions poured ceaseless automatic fire into the Gorari dugouts. In a cleared hollow, a hundred yards from the main battle, a large enemy group were eating dinner, resigned to death and apparently careless of the battle raging around them. All died where they sat.

Many Japanese refused to surrender. Bullet-riddled soldiers kept running at the Australian guns, brandishing their swords or revolvers: 'I didn't think he would ever fall, and he got within five yards of me before he dropped,' said one machine-gunner. Corporal Harrowby St George-Ryder was changing his magazine when a Japanese officer, waving a flashing sword, charged, knocked off the Australian's steel helmet, and slashed his face and head. In reply, St George-Ryder kneed the Japanese in the groin and the pair wrestled on the ground until another Australian dispatched the swordsman.

The fighting ceased on the night of the 11th, and dawn revealed the extent of the slaughter: 580 Japanese bodies were counted. 'In the jungle area near Gorari,' Blamey informed the Australian Government, 'the enemy left no less than 500 dead. A pleasing feature is that in spite of the closeness of the fighting, our casualties are very much less than the enemy's and our men are definitely superior to them in jungle fighting . . .'[15]

Australian casualties were remarkably light. In the final battle, on the 11th, one battalion[16] suffered just seven dead and seven wounded. The build-up to the entrapment was costlier, with 123 officers and men wounded and 48 killed between 8 and 10 November.

———

A handful of prisoners were taken. A few starving waifs fell into Allied hands — or awoke to find themselves in captivity. Private Yamamoto Kiyoshi, who was caught south of Gorari on 9 November, had acute malaria. He was captured, sleeping at noon. He wept and broke down under interrogation, stating that he'd spent a month in hospital after which he was carried forward on a stretcher to fight.

Of his capture he said he felt 'nothing but the feeling of shame to the Emperor, to the country and to one's family'. He preferred to die rather than return to Japan, 'but if your customs do not permit this I will be a model prisoner'.[17]

Another was Tsuno Keishin, a superior private, knocked out when a bullet struck his helmet. He said he enjoyed listening to Australian radio broadcasts, even though they were officially dismissed as *Dema Hoso* (demagogism).

Australian battalion histories mention only one prisoner, 'a boy, short and dumpy, with a round fat face'. The boy sat on the ground in a daze after 'a terrific thump' to the side of the head from an Australian rifle butt. He was tied to a tree, given a groundsheet and a portion of rice, and left to die.[18]

A trawl through Japanese bodies yielded Australian letters, photos and documents. Captain Sanderson's pay book and his German Mauser were found on one body. The most valuable find was a Japanese plan to inflict the same encircle-and-destroy tactic on the Australians; it delighted Vasey that his speed of thought had outpaced Horii's by a matter of hours.

Milne Bay was the first land defeat of the Japanese. But Oivi–Gorari was the first decisive strategic land victory in the Pacific War. It broke the Japanese hold on the track and forced them back to the coast. One brave American historian dared to suggest it was a 'turning point' in the Pacific War:

> Japan did not lose the ground war in the South Pacific in any
> single place. There was no equivalent of Waterloo or Stalingrad ...
> Yet if I were to pick one place where the war turned irrevocably
> against the Japanese, it was at Oivi–Gorari on November 5,
> 1942... The [Australians] inflicted a massive defeat on crack

Japanese troops at small cost to themselves. Rarely would the Japanese fight Australian troops in open battle in the future. When they did the result was defeat.[19]

The Australian victory drew rapturous praise from Port Moresby. Vasey had delivered the *coup de théâtre*. On the 14th Blamey acknowledged, 'The greatest factor in pressing the continuous advance has been General Vasey's drive and personality.'[20] Herring declared that Vasey had made 'the Japanese dance to his tune'.

Vasey generously passed on their congratulations to his officers and men, and resumed the pursuit. His motto became 'Buna or Bust . . . and we will not bust!'

Chapter 42
Horii

'Tennoheika Banzai!' — 'Long Live the Emperor!'
— *Major-General Horii Tomitaro's last words*

Some Japanese did escape Oivi–Gorari. On 9 November Horii called a general retreat to the Kumusi River. Commanders Yazawa at Oivi and Tsukamoto at Gorari promptly withdrew with their staff and any men fit enough to walk.

Many of the wounded were left behind — with the exception of the Nankai Shitai HQ's walking wounded, who were led out by an extraordinary young lieutenant called Takaki Yoshijo, cannon commander of the 41st Infantry Corps.

Takaki, a graduate of an elite military academy, was ordered to bury his artillery before guiding the wounded to safety, according to Captain Nakahashi's personal memoir. But the 24-year-old artilleryman could not abandon his gun. To be told to bury it was deeply humiliating — a mark of surrender. So Takaki entreated his force commander to be permitted to take his gun out with the casualties.

His commander refused. For Takaki, there remained one course of honour left. After a last goodbye to his men — he was very popular — he buried the weapon, led the wounded to the rear, and returned to the burial spot. He then sat on the mound of soil, withdrew his pistol and shot himself in the head.

Nakahashi, who knew Takaki, wrote: 'The news of First Lieutenant Takaki's final gesture ... did much to lift the flagging morale of the Japanese troops.'*

The Shitai survivors evacuated Gorari by night, along a north-easterly route, guided by vines lashed to trees and candles sheltered in the undergrowth. Horii himself was well back on the western bank of the Kumusi. The troops joined him there on 11 and 12 November.

The Kumusi was in full flood, 100 yards wide and six feet deep at the chosen crossing point, near the village of Binga. Horii ordered Colonel Yazawa, of the 41st Regiment, to take command of the survivors, while he departed on a large raft.

Horii's last words to his men on the bank were, reportedly: 'I will go first.' Then he and his staff officers and a number of 'distressed enlisted men' boarded the palm log raft and drifted away from the shore. They hoped the strong current would carry them to the mouth of the river.

With the grey-haired general fading into the tropical haze, Yazawa contemplated the question of how to transport several hundred men across the river. Allied aircraft had destroyed the wire bridge. They could not swim the swollen current laden with gear and weapons. One officer suggested they build a series of small rafts out of whitewood saplings, six feet long and two inches in diameter, and drift across.

Yazawa agreed. The men loaded their gear and weapons onto the hurriedly built rafts, and pushed off into the current. They clung to the sides, and most seemed to make it across. Extra rafts were built for the wounded and sick, but many of them drowned.

The medical officer Hayashi Hiroyuki 'began to build a raft with two others'. They had not eaten for four days, and one collapsed from weakness.

---

* In 1968, Nakahashi returned to the spot and retrieved the barrel of the gun; its chrysanthemum crest had been removed. The Japanese troops protected their regimental colours with obsessive devotion. When a Lieutenant-Colonel Watanabe lost the colours after his ship, the *Boston Maru*, was torpedoed, he became mentally ill and raved about the loss for weeks, apparently indifferent to the deaths of 600 men.

On 21 November he heard a report that the Australians were five miles away. So they hastily pushed off — of his unit, there were '50 on five rafts'.★

Some attempts failed. At Papaki, in pouring rain, about a third of the remaining strength of the Koiwai Butai drowned when their hurriedly built rafts sank, recalled Lieutenant Watanabe Fukuichi. 'Nearly all lost or threw away their rifles, MGs and ammunition.'[1]

Those who reached the far bank joined a long line of emaciated Japanese troops bumping forward, leaning on sticks, many with blood-soaked, khaki-coloured bandages around their heads or arms. Only those with external wounds — i.e. with a hope of survival — were transported in jeeps. Those with internal wounds were left behind, seen as hopeless cases. The sick were expected to walk. They pleaded 'with anger or resentment in their eyes'[2] for a transport corps to take them part of the way to Giruwa, where they hoped to be evacuated by boat.

One driver recalled, 'Many times I saw soldiers who had collapsed, exhausted on the way, all but dead by the roadside. I wanted to give them a lift but there was nothing I could do ... we were fully loaded with wounded soldiers.'[3]

Imanishi was among the survivors. He wrapped his pistol, shoes, clothes and sword in his tent, placed the bundle on a raft and floated with it down the river. It seems he lost his bundle because he came ashore with only his underwear. In this state, he walked to Giruwa and there salvaged a uniform from a corpse.[4]

Horii's party floated about a mile and a half downstream where the raft caught a large tree and 'smashed into the river bank'.[5] His party went ashore. After a long walk down the East bank, they found a little canoe, in which Horii, his staff officer, Tanaka, and his orderly, Private Fukuoka Shigeji, paddled to the mouth of the Kumusi.[6]

The sequence of events then gets sketchy, and acquires a note of farce. Horii and his comrades 'stupidly put to sea' in the canoe, notes one account.[7] It seems he intended to paddle along the coast to Giruwa and take

---

★ Hayashi reached the river mouth on 28 November, where he found 'nothing to do. Ate and rested on the sand.' He survived on coconuts until, on 10 January, overcome by despair and disease, he wrote his last diary entry: 'Down with malaria again.'

command there; perhaps in his mind's eye he saw himself pulling ashore to the astonished applause of his troops.

Nature intervened. A tropical thunderstorm with gale force winds struck the coast that afternoon, and 'in a flash the canoe was six miles from the shore and capsized ... Staff officer Tanaka could not swim,' writes Captain Nakahashi. 'His head showed above the water once or twice, he then went down and was not seen again.'

Horii and Fukuoka swam for the shore. They made slow progress and, after about three miles, Horii said to his orderly: 'I am exhausted and can swim no further, please report to the unit that Horii died here.'* Horii then raised his hands 'as far as he could above the sea, and called to Fukuoka in a loud voice, '*Tennoheika Banzai!*' — 'Long Live the Emperor!'[8] And then he sank.

Horii's bizarre end was hushed up, but rumours soon spread among the incredulous troops; 'heard that the Detachment commander and Staff had been drowned in Kumusi River', wrote an unknown diarist at Giruwa on 27 November 1942. 'Because of the possible effect on the army this is to be kept a strict secret.'

The Australians reached the Kumusi River at Wairopi, some miles upstream of Horii's crossing point, on the 13th. The empty pylons rose where the wire bridge once stood, and wrecked and half-sunk rubber dinghies and outriggers lined the shores. All along the banks were the carcasses of some five hundred horses.

From a small island they rescued about three hundred terrified Rabaul natives who'd been sheltering there. Many were emaciated and sick, 'others were bloated almost to bursting point from eating abandoned Jap rice supplies', observed Kienzle on 14 November. We can assume they made a swift recovery, because Kienzle had a lot of work in store for them: 'I now had about 1500 natives with the newly acquired Rabaul labour,' he noted.

---

* In an extraordinary twist, the orderly Fukuoka Shigeji survived and returned to Japan after the war, where he became an active member of the New Guinea Association in Kochi Prefecture — and no doubt dined out on the story of Horii's death for many years. In fact, he lived in Motoyama, just down the road from the home of the former mayor Imanishi, veteran of the 144th Regiment.

To Vasey's surprise the Japanese had failed to fortify the eastern bank, and several strong Australian swimmers crossed the river. Vasey himself attempted to wade in at a shallower point, thought the better of it, and took a stroll up the bank with Norris, where they found a little beach on which four dead Japanese had been washed up. One may have been the unit paymaster, as Vasey returned 'with over 500 yen'.[9]

Heavily loaded men didn't stand a chance of swimming, and the division's chief engineer stood on the western bank calculating how to construct a bridge. Days earlier this resourceful man — Lieutenant-Colonel Warren McDonald — had presciently requested airdrops of steel rope and tools. They were flown in on the 14th, and the field engineers set to work, building a bridge of connected logs wedged between forked trunks rammed into the riverbed; two flying foxes were constructed overhead.

These flying foxes enabled 230 men per hour to cross. They queued up in high spirits, and a sort of carnival atmosphere prevailed, 'reminiscent of an old English fair or Irish market day', observed the 16th Brigade diarist. 'Battalions of heavily laden troops in their mud-stained jungle green shirts and slacks, carrier lines with the natives gaily caparisoned in bright coloured lap laps, bedecked with flowers and sprigs of shrubs stuck jauntily in metal bracelets, all mingled as they waited their turn to cross.'[10]

Vasey did not relish river crossings, of which there are many in the Owen Stanleys, usually over single logs. He confided to his wife, 'I'm not too hot at that sort of thing.' Sensing their commander's awkwardness, the men took a close interest in his progress, as Norris observed: 'It was a grand sight to see (and hear!) George's gaunt, lanky frame swaying and swearing across the narrow bridge. As his legs sank into the stream ... George risked letting go with one hand to wave his red cap — this was nearly fatal ...'[11]

Chapter 43
Catterns

'Basil Catterns did something that day which was the bravest thing
I have ever seen a man do.'
— *Major-General Paul Cullen, former commander of 2/1st Battalion*

Brigadier Lloyd, indulging in one of his MacArthur moments, stood on the Sanananda Track 'like Napoleon' and was asked the day's objective. He pointed north and theatrically declared, 'The sea!'[1] (It seemed Lloyd had taken to heart MacArthur's remark about 'the eyes of the Western world' being upon him.) Captain Thomas Silk later wryly noted, 'So the battalion started for the sea.' They marched north towards Soputa, about five miles from the coast.

A little way beyond Soputa, on the road leading north, an enemy mountain gun blocked the forward Australian troops of the 16th Brigade.* As he studied the position — astride a horse he'd bought for five pounds at the Kumusi River — a Japanese mortar narrowly missed Colonel Cullen and flung both man and horse into a ditch.

---

* During the clash, one soldier was shot in the stomach in no-man's-land and cried out for hours — yards from the enemy lines. Unable to bear the sound, Colonel Jim Miller slithered forward through the tall grass with morphine and dressings; later that night, with a corporal's help, the pair dragged the wounded man out. Colonels did such things in this war.

Captain Basil Catterns, Cullen's second-in-command, who was standing beside his superior, was similarly thrown. Cullen raised his head: 'What do you think, Basil?'

'There's only one thing to do,' Catterns said, 'we've got to get that bloody gun.' Catterns volunteered to lead the manoeuvre, because, as he said later, 'I knew it was my turn'.[2]

Sixty years later Cullen still dwells on this episode: 'Basil Catterns did something that day which was the bravest thing I have ever seen a man do.' (Cullen recommended Catterns for a second Military Cross.)

But it was not bravery alone — extraordinary as it was — that distinguished this action. The two-day struggle showed, with terrible clarity, what was required to defeat the invader. Catterns's action combined all the elements that made the infantry war in Papua and New Guinea one of the most savage in military history.

Catterns led a fighting patrol of 90 hand-picked troops (including ten company commanders) to silence the mountain gun. On 20 November, loaded with food and ammunition, they set off on a wide flanking march to the west. They moved all day through jungle and swamp. Late that afternoon they swung east, in accordance with their compass calculations, and came upon a well-used track that led to a watering hole.

At 6.00 p.m. Catterns and Corporal Ralph Albanese crept forward to a clearing. They had expected to find a large gun position. But they had come too far, and stumbled upon one of the main enemy camps, with troops 'huddled over fires cooking their evening meal' in the midst of a group of huts.[3] Through the trees were scores of Japanese troops, milling about, eating, drinking. Unknown to Catterns, there were 1200 Japanese troops in the wider area.

He faced a difficult choice. He could withdraw and report the position. Or he could attack. He was heavily outnumbered; his men had no signals, and could not call for reinforcements. Their medical aid amounted to one field dressing and a stab of morphia per man. They might all die. Yet success held out the prospect of capturing the main track — as wide as a small road here — deep inside enemy lines. Catterns consulted his men, and they agreed.

They moved up in a long line parallel with the track, five paces between each man. Catterns pointed to a large fig tree to the right of the Japanese, as a rendezvous point. Then they set off slowly through the scrub. One soldier compared the adrenal charge with the feeling before 'the football kick off at school'.[4]

Trained in jungle movement, they crept silently forward and drew up, unnoticed, within a few yards of the Japanese. Then they were seen. So great was the shock of their own fire bursting on the clearing it was said a few Australian soldiers fell to the ground. 'And then they were up again ... They smashed through apron fences of vines. They hurdled networks of trenches. They were fighting like wild cats in the very midst of the surprised defenders, some of whom, rallying, manned gun pits and cut swathes through the attackers.'[5]

The stunned Japanese died at their guns. Soon the huts were ablaze, and 'grenades exploded in the fires and scattered sparks. Those of the defenders who were able to do so ran into the bush ...'[6]

No two soldiers have the same memory of battle: 'There was a crash of fire along the whole front as the 18 Brens and 36 Tommy guns, rifles and grenades opened up,' said Lieutenant Don Murray. 'Momentarily some men went to ground but responded to the call, "Keep moving!"'[7]

'Everyone fought like a demon,' recalled Private Allan Gamble. Soldiers fell around him as he ran towards the Japanese camp: 'I grabbed hold of Jack [Hazelton] and dragged him out of the line of fire but he was dead. So I dropped my empty magazine and took Jack's full one. There were running Japanese, screaming Japanese [and] ... fighting Japanese.'

Private John Dyer crashed through the wire fences and raced up to the first bunker, where his Tommy gun jammed. With the help of a platoon sergeant he freed the weapon, which 'spewed into the crowded bunker'.

Murray was among the first to reach the Sanananda Track: 'I quickly placed the few men with me in a defensive perimeter ... I then sent a runner to my company commander "that I was astride the track".'

The Australians cleared the empty enemy foxholes and dugouts, and planted their automatic weapons in a ring around a giant fig. Darkness came, and the firing died. The wounded were laid between the buttress roots of the tree: 'This was a gigantic tree, and the root system ... formed cubicles which were ideal to place the wounded in.'[8] They dug a circular perimeter around the tree and prepared for the counterattack.

Catterns's men waited in the darkness. They could hear talking and shuffling in the undergrowth, as the Japanese noisily encircled the Australians, most of whom were alive. Nothing could be done for the badly wounded, who died during the night: 'Jock is finished. Not quite dead but nearly,' a soldier would call out.

Catterns kept his head. He scanned the area for a break-out route, a better shelter, anything to save his men. Shortly he realised that their position straddled the main Japanese signal lines between the beachhead and the forward troops: '...I saw the maze of heavy telephone cables running north and south ... we were astride the line of communication of a massive defensive position to the south. So I ordered the cables to be cut ...'[9]

This action attracted fresh enemy troops concerned by the breakdown. Their scouts started picking off the Australians in the darkness. Within fifteen minutes two men were shot in a rear bunker: 'Near midnight,' said one soldier, 'we heard noisy chattering ... coming along the track to our rear. We decided to hold our fire and let them have a couple of grenades ... Judging by the screams they were effective.'[10]

At dawn, the Japanese counterattacked with 'a withering mass of small arms fire'. Snipers 'had lined us up from the start', said Gamble. Unceasing firepower splintered the buttress roots — the bullets grazed the protruding heels of the wounded sheltering there, and thudded into exposed corpses.

Gamble recalled: 'The slightest movement anywhere would bring intense fire — the bullets flicking across our backs and touching our shins.' One soldier 'managed to slide in between two large roots, which offered some cover from enemy fire. It hacked at the roots within inches of me all day.'

Sometime — nobody knows when — a heavily built Japanese soldier launched a lone bayonet charge at the fig tree: 'When I first saw him I asked if anyone ... had a weapon but we were all unarmed,'[11] said Corporal Albanese. He quickly found a gun, stood up, carefully took aim and shot down the attacker.

For a whole day the two sides fought yards apart. Private Arnold Varnum 'had his Bren gun going all day' against enemy troops running up to within a few feet in front of him.'[12] Lance-Corporal John Fletcher waited until the Japanese were within fifteen yards of his bunker then leapt out and hurled a grenade among them.

The Japanese retaliated with incessant fire and running mauls; they fought 'like Red Indians circling a covered wagon'.[13] The Australians were being gradually eliminated. Five of Catterns's ten officers were dead and a rising number of troops were either dead or severely wounded.

All day, Catterns and his rapidly diminishing force held their positions until, as night fell, he got a message from a runner: 'Captain Catterns? Paul Cullen wants to see you.' Catterns crawled out, eluded the Japanese, and got back to the battalion HQ. 'So I find Paul in a tent, and he's got a hot billy for me, which was wonderful, and I tell him all about it — and then he says, "How do you feel, Basil? Do you think you could take back [the relieving force]?" That was an order, and all I could say was, "Yes, Paul, I'll take them back".'[14] It was midnight when he departed. Intermittent flashes of lightning guided Catterns and forward patrols of the 2/2nd and 2/3rd Battalions back to his men.

They broke open a line to the tree, where dozens had expired between the splintered remnants of the buttress roots, which were blown apart by the Japanese guns. They rushed in ammunition, biscuits, tobacco and medical supplies. Rain sheeted down through darkness split by lightning as the wounded were ferried out. Twelve stretcher-cases emerged into the waiting care of field medics. The walking wounded came next. Then the men withdrew. Catterns was among the last out. He greeted his commanding officer with his usual high spirits — the two men were close friends.[15]

Out of 91 troops who took part, there were 57 casualties: 31 were killed (including five officers) and 26 were badly wounded. But Catterns's attack cleared a passage to the enemy's coastal strongholds, and captured a great deal of ground. The mountain gun that had held up the Australians was later found buried in the mud.

Chapter 44
Madness

'Major what's-his-name told you the ship's coming. And you took it seriously and came here, didn't you? But look here, it'll never come this way, never! We've been deceived, all of us'
— *Captain Hanai, patient, Giruwa*

One day, on a beach near Giruwa, on the Papuan north coast, the Japanese war correspondent Okada Seizo was sitting staring at the empty horizon, when he heard a rustling sound behind him. He turned to see 'a worn-out shadowy young officer' standing there, smiling faintly and clearly happy to have company on the beach.★

'How do you like it?' the officer asked. 'Wonderful isn't it? I come here every day and look at the sea. Far beyond the sea is my dear old homeland. I come from Osaka where my wife and three children are waiting for me ... I suppose you are waiting for the ship? So am I.'

The young officer surveyed Okada's face, and then asked, 'By the way, have you got any sushi? I'd like to have some ... could you spare me a little? A mouthful if you please.'

★ This dialogue is taken from *Lost Troops*, Okada's extraordinary personal account of the Papuan campaign, translated by Keiko Tamura.

406

The young officer repeated the joke several times.

'Don't joke,' Okada interrupted. 'I haven't had enough to eat for some days, not even sweet potatoes. It's cruel of you to remind me of such a delicacy.'

The officer paused and asked: 'Do you know, there are lots of gold bars along this coast? New Guinea has been famous for its gold mines, as I suppose you know. Did you ever see Charlie Chaplin in *The Gold Rush*? A damned funny picture, wasn't it?'

The officer, Okada noticed, was gazing wistfully out to sea, and kept 'rattling away in a hollow voice':

Funny? Well, everything in the world is funny. How about yourself? Funny, I'm sure. What on earth are you waiting for, hanging around here like a blessed fool? H'm that boss of the hospital, Major what's-his-name, told you the ship's coming. And you took it seriously and came here, didn't you? But look here, it'll never come this way, never! We've been deceived, all of us. And yet you don't know you've been deceived, and are waiting for the ship. Isn't that funny? Oh don't get cross my friend. You're not the only person who looks funny. What do you think about that blockhead at the hospital, Major what's-his-name? No one is more dashed funny than that Major fellow. He's deceived you, but he'd deceived himself too. He doesn't know that he himself has been deceived. By the way, have you got some rice-balls? Oh, I'm sorry, forget rice-balls, my friend. Anyway, I'm not going to be deceived anymore, not I. If the ship comes, let's board it! Don't bother about the gold bars. We must not miss the ship. By Jove, I'm not going to be deceived again. I'm going to stay here until the ship comes. I'm going to wait here for the ship that will take me back to my wife and children. Look here, my friend, the ship will come. Don't you think so? It ... [will] surely come, won't it, my dear friend?

Okada turned away from the young officer, who kept raving in this vein, uninterrupted, until a hospital orderly arrived.

'By God,' the orderly cried at the young soldier, 'I never thought you'd come as far as this. Oh, how I walked about looking for you. The medical officer is very anxious. Come on, sir. Let's go back.'

The orderly led the officer back 'like a mother leading her child', wrote Okada.

The young officer's name was Captain Hanai. Suffering from a violent attack of malaria in the Owen Stanleys, he was carried back to the coastal hospital, where he lay for days tossing with fever. When the fever subsided, he seemed normal. Then he started coming to the beach, and would sit there all day, staring at the horizon, awaiting 'the ship'.

'It's the same every day,' said the medical orderly. 'I always take him back to the hospital at a proper hour.'

Okada watched the pair depart: 'The nurse led the captain away into the wood, gently, with an air of commiseration. The officer followed meekly, with his hand deposited in the nurse's, looking back from time to time towards the sea.'

Part Five
Annihilation

Chapter 45
Gona

'You will tie a bayonet on a pole. Those without bayonets will ...
carry a wooden spear'
— *Yokoyama Hospital Bulletin, order to the sick and wounded,
Gona–Sanananda, November 1942*

In November 1942 the war spilled onto the northern coastal plain of
Papua. The littoral dictated a different kind of fighting. The predatory
manhunt, the war of stealth, became a pitched battle across swampland,
coconut groves, beaches and coarse grassland.

The Allies prepared for a campaign of total annihilation: 'an exercise in
extermination', as decreed by Allied High Command.[1] The Imperial
Japanese Army dictated this outcome: the enemy refused to surrender and
would fight to the last man. Their sick and wounded were ordered to join
the coming battles.

The battlefield was a rough semi-circle about ten miles wide and five
deep stretching from Gona in the west to Buna/Cape Endaiaere in the east,
and inland as far as the village of Soputa. At the centre, on the coast, was
Sanananda/Giruwa, site of the Japanese headquarters and main hospital. War
had scarred the landscape beyond recognition; air raids had ripped apart the

forests and strewn the area with craters. Reverend Benson's Garden of Eden was a wasteland.

The paradise that had bewitched the missionary held little allure for the Australian army. Blamey described the Gona–Buna shoreline as 'about as vile a country as any that exists'.[2] Scraggy jungle and coarse kunai patches; fetid swamps, awash with tidal rivers; pouring rain, steaming heat and nightly mosquitoes — none of these were conducive to human habitation. There were no roads; the tracks that existed were mud, and seemed to empty into swamps, or disappear into tall grassland.

Diseases of the most virulent kind infested the area. In 1942 the swamps were malarial cesspits and the grasslands were home to tiny mites, carriers of scrub typhus. 'It was the edge of the known world,' remarked Frank Taylor, who regularly visits the region today.

The Japanese saw the Papuan beachhead as supremely important to their overall plan. They were determined to hold the Allies there while they fought the American marines at Guadalcanal, an island they vainly hoped to recapture. In early November Tojo personally informed General Imamura, supreme commander of the South East Area Armies, that 'the welfare of our nation depends on this operation, so important is it. Therefore I hope you will make your plans well and ease the Emperor's mind.'[3]

Vasey's 'tiger' was immobilised. The Japanese had their backs to the sea but were extremely well dug in. They had built a coastal fortress of interlocking bunkers, stretching from Gona in the west to Buna in the east. This network of little underground forts locked up the firmer ground. Like clams stuck to a rock pool, hundreds of foxholes pocked the soggy coastal plain. They were an extraordinary feat of engineering. Their frames were of foot-thick palm trunks supported by steel and oil drums packed with sand, and virtually impregnable to mortar, rifle and machine-gun fire. Only a direct hit from artillery or tank shells, or a grenade thrown in through the fire slits, was likely to destroy the occupants. A flamethrower might have roasted the enemy alive, but none was available until later in the war. Air bombardment repeatedly tried, but usually failed, to find their targets.

These formidable structures were expertly camouflaged and well supplied — at least in early November — with enough food and ammunition for weeks of resistance. The bunkers were indiscernible, even at close range; only tiny rectangular fire slits revealed their locations. They were 'so well camouflaged with earth, rocks, palm fronds, and quick-growing vegetation that they could not be detected even from a distance of a few yards'.[4] Bunkers in kunai grass were festooned with bundles of grass; those in palm groves were 'covered with coconut leaves and fallen coconut husks'.[5] Palm fronds obscured the fire slits, and advancing troops often overlooked the pillboxes until they were right on top of them.

The holes were mutually supporting, connected by lateral fire trenches along which, under attack, the Japanese raced to adopt new firing positions. This confused approaching troops who, upon entering the bunker fields, found themselves suddenly trapped by enfilading fire. The approaches were invariably across open grassland, river bank, or through swampland.

The defensive shield was not all underground. In the treetops, heavily camouflaged sharpshooters sat wedged between palm fronds and coconut clusters. Snipers strapped themselves to the trees, and slept there. Caught in this patchwork of invisible artillery and aerial sniper fire, an unsuspecting Allied platoon had little chance of survival.

The Japanese gunners lived in these underground hives for three months; they ate, defecated and slept in the bunkers. The heat was intolerable, the mud floors awash with seeping swamp water. Troops emerged for night attacks, supplies, and to meet reinforcements. Standards of personal hygiene rapidly deteriorated; when forced into daylight, the Imperial Army was barely recognisable as human.

Thousands lay in wait for the Allied armies in such conditions, all along the coast. Estimates of their total strength varied from 5000 to 13,000. Most were fresh troops, landed during the Owen Stanleys campaign. Their actual numbers varied during the three months of coastal fighting. A US army intelligence report, dated 18 November, placed total Japanese strength in New Guinea at the time at 8000.[6] Assuming many of these were at Wau, Salamaua and Lae, the forces at Gona–Buna at that time were probably at the lower end of the range.* But they were being steadily reinforced: on

* Japanese sources put the total at 9600 troops — at 15 November — of whom 2500 were medical units, 'mainly patients' (see Japanese Monographs No 37, p. 33).

17 November a new commander, Colonel Yamamoto, arrived to lead a fresh battalion and reinforcements for the 144th Regiment.

In the Gona–Buna region the Allies slightly outnumbered the Japanese: the Australians fielded four, albeit severely depleted, brigades; the Americans, three regiments. There were in total about 7000 Allied troops.

The enemy lacked air cover; Japanese aircraft in New Guinea numbered just 32 fighters and ten bombers in late November. This made reinforcing the coast extremely difficult; Japanese barges full of fresh troops were sitting ducks for Allied strafing raids.

US intelligence warned, however, of the immense pool of Japanese manpower in the region: they could deploy thirteen divisions to the south-west Pacific without weakening their grip on Manchuria and North China. Some 80,000 men were available to reinforce New Guinea — but only if they regained air supremacy. Hence, it was crucial for the Allies to protect their air bases at Kokoda, Popondetta and elsewhere.

Partly for this reason, MacArthur decided not to bypass the Japanese and let them wither on the vine — 'rot and starve', as one Australian politician later put it.[7] While Blamey favoured 'starving out' small pockets of the enemy,[8] he fully backed the plan to clear the beaches of enemy resistance. The lingering Japanese threat endangered Allied air bases at Kokoda and those under construction at Dobodura.[9] The Allied thrust north depended on unhindered air power, as General Kenney reiterated.[10] The Japanese must be 'destroyed in detail' — and no one better understood this than Vasey, who drove his men with the resolve of a big game hunter.

At Gona, the bunkers formed a perimeter around Reverend Benson's old mission, and ran along the beachfront to Gona Creek, over a distance of about three hundred yards.

In mid-November, flush with their victory at Gorari, the Australian army drew up a few miles south of the coast. It was a dangerous zone. Japanese stragglers were desperately hungry, and at least one Australian soldier was found garrotted in the scrub, with his rations and rifle stolen.

The first to arrive were the advance troops of the 25th Brigade. They encountered a strip of jungle interspersed with palm groves and kunai grass

Blamey, with America's Lieutenant-General Robert Eichelberger at the entrance to a Japanese pillbox near Buna. Eichelberger was sent in to reorganise the chaotic state of the American forces at Buna; many had refused to fight, downed their weapons, and sat loitering by the track in a state of confusion.

General Adachi Hatazo, the commander of the 18th Army, who committed suicide in Rabaul. Tormented by the prospect of his son's death, Adachi had formed a desperate plan to relieve the Japanese troops at Buna, which was foiled by Allied bombing. His son died in Papua.

Charismatic, brave, loved by the troops, Major-General George Vasey inflicted a devastating blow against the Japanese at Oivi–Gorari, a turning point in the Pacific War. Vasey was the longest-serving commander in New Guinea, an experience that reduced this cheerful man to near-despair. He died in a plane crash near the end of the war, prompting an outpouring of national grief.

The fall of Gona, December 1942. Exhausted Australians troops rest after the final charge that cleared the Japanese from the beachhead. The men lie surrounded by dead Japanese.

Near the frontline at Gona, the Australian wounded are treated and placed on stretchers. Hundreds of Australian lives were lost when the troops were ordered to charge Japanese bunker fields across open ground.

An Australian mortar crew works at close range — note the extreme trajectory of the cannon — in destroying the last pockets of resistance at Buna.

Supported by Stuart tanks, the Australian 2/12th Battalion attack Japanese bunkers during the final assault on Buna — a battle in which the Americans had suffered terrible losses. This photo was taken during actual fighting. In the background, troops extricate some Japanese from a bunker destroyed by the tank.

Australian machine-gunners in action at Buna, around 5.30 p.m. on New Year's Day, 1943.
On the left lies the body of Corporal Charles Knight, censored from published versions of the photo at the time.

AWM 014037

The image that shocked America: dead American soldiers lying on Buna Beach. This photo brought home the reality of war in the Pacific to the US public, subjected to the sight of crumpled bodies lying apparently abandoned on an unknown tropical shore.

George Strock/Getty Images

Sanananda is remembered by the few survivors as the worst campaign of the war
— fought in swamps pocked by islands of firm ground, between which the troops
waded into the attack. At dawn, an American soldier surveys what had been a dry
area when he chose it the previous night.

Sanananda, January 1943:
troops of 2/7th cavalry
regiment fire from a platform
surrounded by mud and
swamp, less than 30 yards
from Japanese positions. The
photographer who took this
picture could hear Japanese
soldiers talking, but could not
see them.

The annihilation of the Japanese: all along the shoreline were scenes of slaughter and destruction, strewn with wreckage, riddled with disease and decay, as the Allied armies destroyed the last enemy resistance on the Papuan beachhead.

The few Japanese prisoners captured during the final assault on the beaches told the story of the last days. Starving, abandoned by senior command, many were reduced to cannibalism and so weak they could hardly lift their rifles. Some of the sick and wounded had been ordered back into battle armed with spears.

Single white posts mark Japanese graves near Kokoda. A child's toy car lies abandoned by a native family who fled the Japanese advance. In the background, the Owen Stanleys rise over the airfield.

Anglican minister A.E. Begbie erects a cross at a small burial ground near Gona. Most of the dead buried here were soldiers of the 55/53rd Battalion, who were killed during the battle for Gona. Many were traumatised by charges of cowardice, and sought to erase that slur in suicidal acts of courage.

Major Basil Catterns with his wife Nina study his Military Cross at the start of their honeymoon. Catterns won the honour for his heroism at Eora Creek; his commanding officer, Lieutenant-Colonel (now Major-General) Paul Cullen, recommended him for a bar after Catterns's action at Soputa, which Cullen described as 'the bravest thing I've ever seen a man do'.

clearings. To the west of the village a swamp of sago palms and mangroves merged with Gona Creek, which emptied into the sea.

Perhaps Porter's words resounded in some soldiers' minds, as they surveyed this paludal land. 'It is possible,' he wrote earlier, 'to brave mosquitoes, leeches and mites while wading through them; but there is a limit to the endurance powers of troops, particularly if the swamp is unbroken with dry land on which to rest.'[11]

The battle of the beaches erupted across the whole front on 19–20 November. Japanese positions at Buna, Gona and Sanananda were bombed from the air, and 'softened up' with long-range artillery.

Along the coast to the east a fresh American regiment, dubbed Warren Force, and an Australian independent company, attacked Buna; Sanananda and Gona were left largely to the Australians. For the first time, American troops fought alongside the Australians in a joint Allied action. The troops went into battle expecting a frail adversary, starving and sick.

At the allotted time, a heavily reduced battalion of the 25th Brigade — weary after weeks of fighting in the Owen Stanleys — rose and charged the Gona bunkers. They 'cheered and yelled' as they advanced; and suddenly found themselves enveloped by 'a most intense fire from the front and flank'.[12] Twenty-four men were killed and 42 wounded in that single charge.

It set a depressingly familiar pattern. The Japanese machine-guns repulsed wave after wave. After their victories over the mountains, the Australians 'passed from elation to a sobered ... assessment of the [enemy's] unexpected strength ... to exhausted impotence'.[13]

Within two weeks, the rising Australian casualties drew no less than seven battalions into the Gona maw. They were thrown piece-meal into frontal attacks as they arrived. Brigadier Eather, commander of the 25th Brigade, ordered another attack on 23 November. It, too, was repelled, with 64 casualties. And on the 29th, two 'fresh' units (including the 2/27th, the 'lost' battalion that had been forced into the jungle at Efogi) sustained 87 casualties, for little gain.

Behind these statistics were scores of young men who, on orders to charge, stood up and ran across no-man's-land or waded through swamps into enemy machine-guns. The dead and wounded lay on open ground, within dozens of yards of the enemy. Their bodies could not be retrieved until nightfall; the wounded groaned through the days, a constant reminder of Allied impotence against hidden machine-guns.

Brigadier Eather realised he didn't have the strength to dislodge the Japanese. He decided to contain them, until reinforcements arrived. This didn't always work; the Japanese were prone to creep out of their bunkers at night and launch bayonet charges.

The enemy clung to their positions at Gona with their usual, dogged will. They had little food — less than a handful of rice per day. They scratched crabs and mussels from the beach, and cooked the occasional octopus.

Their bunkers shook and sometimes collapsed under daily air and artillery bombardment. Aerial photos show the bunker fields strewn with bomb craters. Inside these caverns human life somehow persisted. There was a bench, a hurricane lamp — rarely used — dirty piles of rice, if available, and ammunition. The Japanese rotated the manning of the guns, 24 hours a day; sentries sat with field glasses in the fire trenches.

Hysterical orders inveighed against any thought of capitulation. On 19 November, for example, the commander of the Yazawa Butai at Gona told his men: 'It is not permissible to retreat even a step from each unit's original defensive position. I demand that each man fight to the last. As previously instructed, those without firearms or sabres must be prepared to fight with sharp weapons such as knives or bayonets tied to sticks, or with clubs.'[14]

The sick and wounded were ordered to take up arms. Medical officers, incredibly, were given explicit instructions to fight. Yokoyama ordered his medical corps on the day the bombardment began to 'make combat preparations and make up your mind to stick with our patients to the very end. You must not retreat ... Do not be fooled by rumours. Do not give way to hardships ... I pray that you will go down fighting to the last man.'[15]

A field doctor dutifully relayed this order to hundreds of sick and wounded men lying on the ground at Giruwa on 21 November: 'I am filled with sympathy for you who are sick in bed but remember, you are glorious Imperial Japanese soldiers. I pray that you will not be fooled by rumours and that you will not give way to hardships ... The hospital staff will stick with you to the very end.'[16] Later that day the doctor wrote in his log:

'Heavy bombing since dawn. Instructed the patients and staff to expect the worst.'[17]

Worse came on 28 November. The Japanese deemed unfit for combat were ordered to sell their 'pistols, swords and binoculars' to the men of the Nankai Shitai and Yazawa Butai returning from the Kumusi River (many survivors of Horii's retreat had lost their weapons during the river crossing). The wounded were told that their weapons should go to the front 'to take the place of you not being able to go there yourself. You would be doing this for the sake of your country.'[18]

Weaponless and starving, the walking wounded would, if worst came to the worst, 'take up arms and go into combat'.[19] The request defied the realms of medical possibility. At Gona and Giruwa, the troops were to rise, as by a miracle, and fight — their commanders had decreed that the Japanese spirit would triumph over terrible wounds and debilitating sickness. They were told to 'tie a bayonet on a pole. Those without bayonets will ... carry a wooden spear. Everyone must carry a spear and be ready for an attack.'[20] The next page of the Yokoyama Hospital Bulletin is appropriately blank.

Thus the most disciplined army in the world was reduced to carrying primitives weapons. It brings to mind the Nazi *panzerfausts* — boys on bicycles — sent into battle against Russian tanks at the fall of Berlin.

Repeated failure exasperated MacArthur, who showed signs of impulsive, even eccentric behaviour. One of the supreme commander's most erratic moments came in early December, when late at night he sent a message to Blamey via the latter's adjutant, Norman Carlyon.

'One night at Moresby,' recalls Carlyon, 'I was wakened about midnight ... by a despatch rider from MacArthur's HQ about seven miles away. It stated: "Gona will be captured at dawn." I went across to Blamey's tent and woke him.'

A bleary-eyed Blamey shone his torch on the message and exploded: 'Bloody rubbish!' he said. 'I wonder if MacArthur knows what it takes to mount a battle.'[21] Blamey promptly switched off his torch and went back to sleep.

Gona, Sanananda and Buna

Gona: 6 p.m., 6 December 1942

Solomon Sea

Cape Killerton
Waitutu Point
Wye Point
Cape Endaiadere
Strip Point
Giropa Point
New Strip
Old Strip
Buna
Tarakena
Giruwa
Sanananda
Garara
Gona

Sanananda Track
Killerton Track
to Soputa
to Jumbora

Konombi Creek
Giruwa River
Swamp
Swamp
Senemi Creek
Dense Jungle

Australian Positions
Japanese Defences
Swamp

N

0   1   2
Approx. Miles

Waitutu Point
Garara
Patrol 2/14 Bn
Standing Patrol 2/14 Bn
2/14 Bn
Small Ck
2/16 – 2/27 Bn Caro
39 Bn HQ Honner
21 Bde HQ
Gona Ck
Gona
Chaforce Coy 2/16 Bn: Haddy
Chaforce Coys 2/14 & 2/27 Bns

0   1000
Approx. Yards

418

In late November the Japanese blew apart the Allies' rosy scenario. In pouring rain they landed hundreds of reinforcements at Kumusi, bringing their total combat strength in the Gona–Sanananda region to more than 5000.★

On the 29th, with strong air support, four enemy destroyers replete with 800 troops, including a complete battalion[22] and HQ unit, tried to land, but were forced back. Five hundred troops then landed successfully in early December. A new leader, Major-General Yamagata Tsuyuo, was sent on the orders of General Adachi, commander of the Eighteenth Army, in Rabaul.

Yamagata had told his men they were headed for a 'lightning attack' in a battlefield of great hardship. 'The health situation is extremely bad,' he advised. Nonetheless, 'I have not the slightest doubt that you will conquer hardships ... and that with one blow you will annihilate the blue-eyed enemy and their black slaves.' The war in the South Seas, he added, 'will be determined by the success or failure of this operation ... carry this struggle to the end.'[23]

The Japanese moved swiftly along the beach from the west towards Gona Creek. A few volunteers of Chaforce (a unit intended for guerrilla-style activity), led by Lieutenant Alan Haddy, were the only Australians blocking their path. They were based at Haddy's HQ, nicknamed Haddy's village, on the west bank of Gona Creek. His men had held this isolated flank for two weeks; 64 of Haddy's 109 men had already died. Friendly fire hadn't helped; on several occasions Allied aircraft mistook Haddy's village for the enemy, and strafed them; even Allied artillery fired a few shells at him in error.

On 5 December Haddy and his remaining twenty volunteers prepared to face the first 200 Japanese reinforcements then advancing along the coast. Sitting in his dugout under one of the beach huts, Haddy knew the situation was hopeless. If he stayed, he and his men would die. So he sent the sickest back to Brigade HQ, and organised the phased withdrawal of the rest.

Only he and a sentry remained when the Japanese overran Haddy's village. A grenade killed the sentry; Haddy fought on, and died in a hail of

---

★Their attempts to land reinforcements at the mouth of the Mambare River failed miserably, however. A coastwatcher called Noakes managed to wriggle through the mangroves and jungle to the suspected landing site, and found a busy Japanese camp, with supplies and barges. The coastwatchers alerted Allied planes to its precise location, and they destroyed it (for a full account see *The Coast Watchers*, pp. 195–6).

bullets. Later, when the Allies recaptured the position, they found a ring of Japanese corpses around Haddy's beach hut, with his body beneath it. A battalion diary noted, '[He] ordered the withdrawal stating that he would stay to the last ... Haddy was always placing himself in such positions to enable his men to get out ...'[24]

Chapter 46
Koitaki Factor

'My father always said that many men knew they were likely to
be killed in these attacks, but accepted their fate and charged
towards the enemy, because for months they had been incensed
by Blamey's Koitaki address . . .'
— *Dr Richard Honner*

Only a concentrated force of heavy artillery, air bombardment and
infantry would destroy the bunker fields, thought Brigadier Ivan
Dougherty, as he walked toward Gona. The divided Allied army disturbed
the new commander. 'At that stage our forces were split into three pieces —
Gona area, the Sanananda Road, and Buna. At no place did our strength
appear to be sufficient to defeat the enemy.'[1]

Dougherty wanted to throw a full brigade of fresh troops into Gona,
and General Vasey agreed. But who were these 'fresh troops'? They were the
21st Brigade, the 'ragged bloody heroes' of the Kokoda Track. These men,
recovering in Port Moresby, were flown back over the mountains and sent
into battle under Dougherty, their new commander.

They were chosen because Blamey had little faith in the American
troops who were floundering at Buna. At least the Australians would fight,

Blamey thought. After seeming to compare them to running rabbits at Koitaki, he now sang their praises. This was as much political one-upmanship and a dig at MacArthur, as it was new-found admiration for the men.

Blamey's renewed faith in the digger did little to reconcile him to the troops, however. Nothing eased the bitterness sown by Blamey's Koitaki address. The festering memory drew barbs of hatred from among the troops. Did their commanders think them cowards? Had their mates given their lives to be posthumously mocked? Such thoughts profoundly influenced their contemplation of — and performance in — the battles ahead.

Indeed, as they flew into Popondetta, the 21st Brigade felt they had a bitter score to settle — with their commanders and the enemy. Their hatred of the Japanese knew no bounds. Their humiliation at Efogi rankled, and Blamey's 'rabbit' speech rubbed salt into the wound.

Lieutenant-Colonel Ralph Honner dubbed their determination to avenge the past 'the Koitaki factor'. Honner's son Richard wrote:

> My father always said that many men knew they were likely to be killed in these attacks, but accepted their fate and charged towards the enemy, because for months they had been incensed by Blamey's Koitaki address . . .
>
> It certainly appears to me that Blamey's insensitive speech that day was a significant factor in the death of good men. In Ralph's later years, the needless deaths at Gona were one of the recurring themes that he would describe as one of his worst memories from the Second World War.[2]

Dougherty, too, would attribute their extraordinary courage and murderous fighting to a desire to redeem their unit's reputation from the charge of cowardice. A major of the 2/27th told David Horner: 'I claim to this day that some [soldiers] whom we lost at Gona were killed because of the effect of Blamey's . . . criticism.'[3]

Perhaps this was Blamey's dark Machiavellian design: to fire the troops' willingness to fight by impugning their courage. It seems unlikely — the stuff of a conspiracy theorist's dream — yet if so, Blamey judged the psychology of the young Australian soldier with chilling accuracy.

In this febrile state of mind the 21st Brigade re-entered the war. Their new leader, Dougherty, was a 'quiet and experienced soldier'[4] with 'an almost grandmotherly patience'.[5] Born in 1907, in Leadville, New South Wales, some two hundred miles north-west of Sydney, the boy was raised by his mother; his parents split soon after he was born. 'They lived in a slab hut with an earthen floor, and he began his education at a small one-teacher bush school.'[6]

As commander of a battalion in Africa, Dougherty led the attack on Tobruk in January 1941, for which he won a Distinguished Service Order. His unit participated in the doomed Greek campaign, before prevailing — briefly — at Heraklion in the defence of Crete, in May 1941. He was flown to New Guinea in October 1942, to command the re-generated 21st Brigade.

'When morale was low,' David Horner said of him, 'he talked personally with his troops. He was fiercely loyal toward them yet a strict disciplinarian.'[7] Dougherty would win a bar to his DSO for his leadership at Gona.

This battle would test Dougherty to the limit. He started well: his belief in concentrating the force echoed the views of several of senior officers — notably Frank Sublet, the rumbustious commander of the 2/16th Battalion, who was later fiercely critical of the open attacks on enemy machine-guns. Vasey himself later likened the tactical errors of the battle of the beaches to those of the Somme.

On 28 November, Dougherty put his ideas into practice. Heavy aerial bombardment preceded a fresh Australian attack. Twelve fighters each dropped a 300-pound bomb on Gona; Flying Fortresses released eight 500-pound bombs. For two days the Australians pressed toward the Japanese bunkers. Two battalions[8] approached from the east, two more from the south and west.[9] For two days they attacked — moving to the edge of the bunker fields, then charging through smokescreens.

Poor patrolling, nightmarish terrain and stalwart defence thwarted these efforts. From the east, the 2/14th Battalion waded through waist-deep swamp. Heavy Japanese firing, just before dark, pinned them down. In the confusion, Lieutenant-Colonel Hugh Challen, the battalion's new commander, ordered his men to disperse into the brackish water as bullets whizzed overhead and pelted the sludge. Up ahead, intense machine-gun fire cut down his forward patrols, killing or wounding sixteen men. Darkness shut down the attempted advance, and by 2.00 a.m. 32 men were dead or missing in the swamp. An unseen Japanese bunker near Small Creek, 500 yards east of Gona Mission, had ambushed his men. In this unmapped region, reconnaissance was flawed, and not every bunker could be accounted for.

Colonel Cooper's 2/27th Battalion was ordered to run the gauntlet of a 'funnel' of firm ground leading directly into the enemy's machine-gun nests in the heart of Gona village. The charge was fatally delayed by a navigation error, and Japanese machine-guns pinned Cooper's men where the jungle met the sand. Some men broke from the forest and raced up the beach, straight into Japanese guns. A few reached the village, but were forced back; 55 men died in this attempt that gained no ground and scarcely dented the resistance.

The suicidal charges were ordered not by Vasey, but handed down from the top — from MacArthur and Blamey — who were answerable for failure with their jobs. Cooper tried to resist what he saw as mindless carnage. But his repeated requests to harass and starve the enemy rather than waste Australian lives were dismissed. One terse reply ran: 'Canberra must have news of a clean-up and have it quick or we will both go by the boot.'[10] This has been attributed to Vasey, though it sounds uncharacteristically self-serving. It seems more likely to have originated at GHQ in Brisbane. Either way, rarely has a commander's sense of self-preservation so cravenly trampled on the lives of his men.

The Koitaki factor ignited a suicidal courage in the Australians during the attacks in early December. They hurled themselves at the Japanese with a ferocity comparable to the enemy's 'human bullets'. Officers charged into the breach with their men. Privates Maurice Valli and George Thompson and Captain Treacy (who had earlier relayed Buckler's plea for help in the mountains) were among those who dashed along the beach, firing their Brens from the hips; all were shot dead. Captain Joe Cuming and his second-in-command, Captain Justin Skipper, of the 2/27th, were found dead at the foot of a tree, ringed by spent cartridges and Japanese dead. Lieutenant Charles White and Lieutenant George Hicks of the 2/16th both died leading their men into battle.

Not all attacks ended with a swag of posthumous citations. Private Jack Breakey took the lead in blasting into Gona village, after which, forced back, and with his platoon reduced to six men, he swam Gona Creek with four of the wounded and then swam back under fire to retrieve a dying sergeant. For his efforts, Breakey won a Military Medal. Another was Sergeant Reg Roach, of a transport platoon, who, within five days, led a dawn attack, night patrol and machine-gun raiding party, in the course of which he dragged a severely wounded warrant officer to safety and silenced two enemy machine-guns. He, too, got a Military Medal; as did Private Dickenson, who succeeded in killing four Japanese in a Gona hut 'with complete disregard for his own safety'. Though badly wounded, Dickenson 'stood his ground until the order for withdrawal was given'. During a charge across the village of Gona, a platoon led by Lieutenant Leo Mayberry wiped out five Japanese machine-gun posts, for which Mayberry got the Military Cross. Notwithstanding their losses, the 21st Brigade managed to capture a wide section of beach between Gona and Sanananda.[11]

The Koitaki factor played itself out with tragic results. The Australians demonstrated a willingness to die on the Japanese scale, as the order to charge enemy bunker fields exacted a terrific casualty rate. Competent, decent commanders resisted this wanton waste of their men; they were removed, and their careers shattered, as Honner wrote.[12] It was as though the charge of cowardice pursued their men with the relentless momentum of the Furies' in a Greek tragedy. Within five days of fighting at Gona, the 21st Brigade lost 340 men out of 800, with no clear result. The 2/16th and 2/27th battalions were so weak they were amalgamated into a composite unit, under Lieutenant-Colonel Caro.

Though numbers of dead were small, the casualty rate matched that of the huge pitched battles of Europe and later in the Pacific. It was seriously distracting at New Guinea Force HQ. Vasey complained that the casualty rate was too high. The commanders were sending men to die for no reason. Had the Somme taught them nothing? What was the point of charging machine-guns over open ground? But what could they do? Any break in the offensive, any relaxation, let the Japanese regroup and land reinforcements. The prospect of failure met with menacing impatience in Port Moresby and Brisbane. On the 2nd, staring down the muzzle of defeat, three Australian brigadiers — Eather, Dougherty and Porter — met at Gona HQ. They decided once more to throw all they had at the machine-gun nests. They didn't have much. The 25th Brigade had been relieved, with most of the men sick, wounded or exhausted.

The brigadiers needed fresh troops. They decided on one battalion then resting in Port Moresby: the 39th. Once more this extraordinary militia unit, first to fight the Japanese at Kokoda, then to hold the enemy for three weeks at Isurava — and leavened with 100 of the better troops of the 53rd — returned to support the Second Australian Imperial Force. The poignancy of militia coming to the relief of a near-spent AIF brigade was eminently satisfying for Lieutenant-Colonel Ralph Honner, who remained the commander of this unbreakable unit.

Chapter 47
Honner

'Gona's Gone!'
— *Lieutenant-Colonel Ralph Honner, commander, 39th Battalion*

Night lent a freakish quality to the Gona battleground. The field came alive with crawling men — wounded trying to crawl back to cover; stretcher parties trying to find the wounded. Allied sentries sat in trenches filled with rainwater, or on little platforms suspended above the swamp. They waited in the pitch-black for signs of enemy night patrols, which sometimes leapt out of the void with flashing bayonets and awful cries.

Most nights the armies eyeballed one another in the sodden darkness, trying to stay awake. Distant bursts of machine-gun rattled the silence; while overhead, Allied aircraft buzzed the coast and fired great orange flares that 'illuminated the sea and the beaches so that every feature seemed to stand out like an object on a cinema screen'.[1] These 'special effects' were to throw light on enemy barges attempting to land reinforcements, which were promptly bombed. Occasionally, as on 2 December, a low-flying Allied pilot strafed the Australians in error.

It was during this state of 'bewildered desperation' that the 39th joined the first concentrated attack, on 6 December. It was an unmitigated disaster — and told Honner all he needed to know about the chaos at the front: one patrol were up to their shoulders in swamp when the Japanese nailed them; enemy machine-guns then spied Honner's main attack force, under Captain Bidstrup, whose men lumbered into sight through the smoke of bombardment and were shot to pieces. Some, riddled with wounds, lay with unexploded grenades in their hands near enemy positions. One lad, shot twice in the legs, appealed to Lieutenant Doug McClean: 'Sir,' he said, crying, 'everytime I move some bastard shoots me.' He was eighteen. Fifty-eight were killed or wounded, and for the rest of his life Honner remembered that incident with self-loathing — such was his duty of care to his troops. He resolved to force a change of tactics.

Lieutenant-Colonel Ralph Honner, schoolteacher, linguist, lawyer and classics scholar, was that rare spirit: a latter-day Renaissance man, with a touch of knight-errant, who despised war but knew that it had to be won. He gave everything to win it. The citation to the Military Cross awarded for his leadership in the Middle East, North Africa and Greece, reads: 'Captain Honner is the Best Company Commander I have seen in this or the last war.'

He led a company in Crete where he eluded the Germans and escaped the besieged island aboard the submarine *Torquay*. 'He was the coolest man I ever saw,' was the gratifying verdict of one private soldier whose view reflected the consensus.[2] Potts thought Honner's only fault was that 'he was too bloody brave'. Honner led from the front — in the bravest, tactical sense of personally observing enemy positions for himself before sending in his men. In battle he could be dogmatic and infuriatingly stubborn — surely qualities in a man who always applied his formidable brain to the problem.

At heart a romantic, deeply religious soul — he never missed church — Honner loved Shakespeare as a boy, and in his later years wrote lyrical love poetry with not the faintest hint between the lines that the poet had led the 39th at Isurava, Gona and Sanananda. They were poems of love, not of war. But Honner also wrote of war in a way that no Australian soldier has before or since.

———

Dougherty rallied his men for the last push: four battalions — numbering less than a thousand men — were to attack in force; the 39th, the freshest, had the vital job of raiding the village from the south. If they failed, the Australians failed; Gona would have to be blockaded, and starved into submission.

Honner had a pivotal role in planning the attack. In a word, he delayed it. He rejected air bombardment as ineffectual and inaccurate; he refused to attack at night because it led to chaos. He favoured high noon. And he came up with a brilliant innovation: the bombs were fused to detonate eighteen inches underground, in order to maximise havoc in the bunkers. The underground blasts would reduce shrapnel, and allow the men to move right up to the threshold of the bombardment and charge the bewildered enemy.

For a few days a stalemate ensued. The two armies threw everything at each other — in places 30 to 50 yards apart. The Australians' mortar fire came perilously close to hitting their own men because the trajectory was near vertical.

A leaflet drop preceded the bombardment, on 8 December, the first anniversary of Pearl Harbor. Unarmed and acquiescent prisoners were depicted above the caption: 'This is to inform the Emperor's soldiers that thousands of their comrades have already laid down their arms, so you too should surrender.' It was ignored.*

A Japanese soldier in a trench near Basabua wrote: 'Anniversary of the Greater East Asian War. Never thought I would be spending this day in a bomb shelter in New Guinea.'

At 12.30 shells rained down on the fragment of enemy-held coastline. The 39th Battalion was sent in fifteen minutes later — precisely two minutes before the artillery stopped firing. 'I expected [the troops] would take ... a minute to reach the enemy and have a minute amongst them with our artillery still firing,' wrote Honner.[3] His plan relied on highly accurate shelling, just beyond the threshold of the advancing troops; hence the use of ground artillery, not air bombardment. The shells did as he intended,

---

* Leaflet drops were common in the Pacific War. The Far Eastern Liaison Office (FELO) produced Allied propaganda leaflets designed to confuse the enemy and undermine his hopes of victory. They had little effect on the Japanese, according to MacArthur. Japanese leaflets tended to use a sexual theme, with a number warning 'Aussies' that the 'Yank' back in Australia was sleeping with their wives (see Emma Jones' paper on *Propaganda in the SWPA in WW2*, presented to The Asia Pacific Special Interest Group, June 2003).

bursting a foot and a half below ground, where they fell. The blast, a mini-earthquake, shook the bunkers to their foundations. Simultaneously, the Australian infantry charged.

One company crept right up to the edge of the bunker field, and fired as the bombs burst underground, then silenced the bunkers, one by one. 'Our troops commenced the massacre of the still stunned and confused enemy ... before our artillery fire ceased,' Honner wrote. 'They overwhelmed post after post while the enemy were still ... reeling.'[4] A platoon led by Lieutenant Hugh Dalby killed 38 defenders and captured four machine-guns. Sergeant Stan Ellis wiped out four bunkers single-handedly. The Australians had, at last, matched brain with brawn: Honner's brilliant tactical mind with his now veteran militiamen.

One by one the pillboxes were grenaded, and the fleeing occupants cut down. Corporal James Truscott, a quiet, deeply religious Victorian farmer, demonstrated how this was done. After five minutes of concentrated shelling, Truscott rushed into the settling smoke with mortar and rifle grenades. His men 'finally gouged the defenders out of their holes ... and shot them down as they fled along the beach or swam wildly out to sea'.[5]

From 3 to 7 December, Australian units were constantly running at enemy bunkers. Severe casualties — dead, wounded and sick — reduced the 21st Brigade swiftly to a shell force. By 8 December the 2/16th Battalion had only 104 fit men, from a full strength of 800 four months earlier.

By the second week of December, the bunker fields at Gona began to collapse. Surviving Japanese troops appealed to the gods, and to the Shinto spirit. One unknown diarist, prostrate in a Gona bunker, wrote on the 7th: 'We were heavily shelled by the enemy ... It was only through the protection from the gods that some of us were safe ... We could not tell if we could survive tomorrow ... I thought of my beloved wife as well as my younger brothers and sisters ... Everyone expected to die at any moment.'[6] Indeed, they were short of ammunition and grenades, and their daily rice allowance was a quarter of the standard ration. Of the 2500 troops hospitalised, 20 to 30 died a day during December.

General Herring's long, unofficial 'sitreps' to Blamey — candid private letters between old friends — conveyed the triumphal mood among the

Australian troops. 'The enemy garrison or what is left of Gona must be having a rotten time', he wrote on the 6th. 'Our fellows on the west of the creek pick off about six Japs a day ... They look on the successful hitting of a Jap in the same way one might regard the bowling over of a rabbit ...'[7]

A narrow corridor, barely 200 yards wide, across a shallow swamp, offered an apparent escape route inland for some 800 to 900 Japanese troops trapped at Gona. About a hundred tried to run the gauntlet that night, and were destroyed by Australian machine-guns. Another group stole along the shore, and were slaughtered on the sand; the survivors plunged into the water, trying to swim around Basabua Point. They were shot in the water. 'Swimming for the open sea ... phosphorescent water boiled up around them and guided the merciless Australian fire.'[8]

Gona fell on 9 December. The 39th broke into the village and occupied it; two battalions of the 21st Brigade advanced along the beach from the west. Early that morning, Australian forces held the beaches, from Gona Creek all the way to Basabua Point.[9] That day Honner wired his famous message to HQ: 'Gona's Gone!' It headlined an Australian newspaper.

Herring sent a delighted message to Blamey: 'GONA GONE cheered us all mightily, & we are planning ways of making the Japs who are left hate the war more and more.'[10]

Canberra promptly congratulated Blamey on the victory, which owed little to Blamey's tactics of hurling men at machine-guns over open ground, and everything to Honner's smart innovations. But such distinctions eluded Canberra's politicians — Curtin never involved himself in tactical detail, unlike Churchill.

It is fascinating to observe Blamey going about his business at this time. No doubt he was doing everything in his power to deliver the result Canberra wanted. To this end, he had an eye for the bigger picture, the unseen opportunity. Consider his letter to Fred Shedden, secretary to the War Cabinet, on the day Gona fell: 'I am particularly anxious to wind up this campaign in order to get down to discuss the immediate utilisation of the resources of this place. It hurts one to see rubber trees ... and not to be able to bring them into production.'[11]

On a day in which hundreds of his men lay dead or wounded, Blamey busied himself with schemes for harvesting the Papuan rubber crop. Other generals were capable of entering thoughtfully into the world of the ordinary troops — Vasey and Allen, for example. But Blamey remained coldly remote. A greater man, perhaps, might have thought to acknowledge the sacrifice of Gona before lunging for the trophy. But then, a greater man might have missed the chance of bringing the rubber crop into production, something that would aid the Allied war effort. The war effort needed men like Blamey.

And, of course, Blamey had an immense amount to do. He was under great strain. He had strategic responsibility for a vast area, which is often forgotten by troops absorbed in their own exigencies. His letter to Herring on 16 December is revealing of this broader perspective: 'I had a very interesting visitor today, General Van Der Graff, who commanded the division that landed on GUADALCANAL ... He told me that the Americans had cleared the whole of the Southern part of the Island and there only remains 14 miles ... on the Northern end to clear ...'[12] Thirty thousand Japanese troops were killed or wounded in that raid.

It took a further week to destroy the Japanese between Gona and Haddy's village; by 20 December, the Australians had driven the enemy as far as Amboga River. Allied pilots had rebuffed Japanese attempts to land reinforcements — six destroyers carrying 800 troops were sunk or forced back to Rabaul on the 7th.

Yet, the Japanese had successfully landed more men at Mambare Bay, on the 12th, confirming intelligence taken from Japanese bodies.[13] The remarkable Major-General Oda Kensaku, Horii's successor as commander of the Nankai Shitai, was among them. He bypassed Gona and made for the main Japanese HQ at Sanananda, where he took control of the remaining Japanese forces from Yokoyama.

In the end, 750 Japanese were left to fight west of Gona. Of these, 400 were survivors of Horii's retreat, and hence useless due to their physical state. The rest fought with their usual suicidal energy.

There were moments of black farce in the dying days. On one occasion three Japanese officers, including a lieutenant-colonel and a major, were seen strolling down a track with their towels for a swim. They were shot dead on sight by Australian scouts. At Basabua, a Japanese soldier sank his teeth into an Australian corporal's face and bit off a 'large piece of flesh'.[14] The corporal became the only known soldier to be classified 'BIA' — Bitten in Action.

Japanese troops who were not killed committed suicide or tried frantically to escape. A few surrendered. Their last stand at Gona inflicted 129 Australian casualties, of whom the 39th Battalion accounted for 107 (31 dead, 74 wounded, two missing). In two weeks of fighting, the 39th Battalion lost 65 per cent — 228 — of its 350 men. And by early January, the 2/14th Battalion managed to field just 21 forward troops from a usual strength of about 800. Such was the devastation wrought by war and disease.

'As far as we were concerned, the battle was now over,' wrote Private Jack Boland of the 39th. The few survivors trudged back to their HQ and were airlifted to Port Moresby. A satisfying irony was that these men — so derided when first sent to defend Australia in July — had played a critical part in the destruction of one of the toughest pockets of Japanese resistance. They became the 'pivot on which the capture of Gona finally swung'.[15]

The scene of the aftermath at Gona defies the descriptive powers of those who weren't there; Major Bill Russell was:

> The headless palm trunks and few poles of houses [were]
> reminiscent of pictures of the battlefields of France in the First
> World War. The heavy rains seemed not to be able to wash away
> the stench of death. Imagination gave the drinking water,
> obtained by digging sumpholes, a flavour which the chlorine
> tablets couldn't hide. The water in the great craters made in the
> soft earth by the earlier bombings and in the sago swamp beyond,
> was oily and putrid. When the sea rose before the wind it
> uncovered for reburial those whom the enemy had buried too
> close to the water. At night, when the heavy rains blotted out all
> vision ... and the sea blotted out all sound, it seemed that nature

wished to cover her shame. Only in the morning, when in the rain-washed air the great cross which had survived the destruction of Gona Mission gleamed white in the sunlight ... then there seemed room for hope and faith that such sacrifice could not be in vain.[16]

It was 'a shambles with dead Japs and Australians everywhere', wrote the 2/16th diarist.[17] Bloated corpses bobbed to the surface of the swamps and lagoons — some 'nudged past us' when the men tried to brush their teeth, observed Honner.[18]

The Japanese had used bodies as sandbags. Half-submerged limbs provided firing steps; corpses had been 'strewn along the parapet as protection against ... sniping'.[19] Rice supplies, green with mould, were found stacked between rows of the dead, for added protection; to escape the intolerable smell, the Japanese had fought in their gas masks. The air itself was 'sickening to breathe'.[20]

The Australians cleared Gona with appreciable haste. In two days they buried 638 Japanese corpses. Several hundred more were interred along the beachfront. Herring told Blamey: 'It would appear the [Japanese] garrison must have been close to 1000, which makes the achievement of our fellows very satisfactory & the losses suffered by us well justified.'[21] Many survivors disagreed, including Ralph Honner, for whom the battle of Gona was a shocking waste of young men's lives. Frank McLean of the 2/27th Battalion, seriously wounded at Gona, was one of many troops traumatised by the experience: 'For many years ... I could not sleep, recalling this one real experience in my life,' he said.[22] No Japanese troops lived to remember it. The Government congratulated Blamey on the victory, who replied that it was 'necessary to kill every Jap in this area before this was accomplished'.[23]

Chapter 48
Mosquito

Australian casualties from malaria were 9250, compared with
2037 killed and 3533 wounded.
— *Australian–Japan Research Project, Australian War Memorial*

A deadlier foe than aerial bombing imperilled both armies: the mosquito. At night swarms of anopheles mosquitoes — carriers of malaria — swooped on the troops' unprotected skin. Neither army was prepared for this medical catastrophe.

Malaria is caused by a tiny parasite of the genus *Plasmodium*, which is transmitted through the sting of the female anopheles mosquito. As the troops descended from the mountains to the mosquito-infested swamps of the Papuan coastline, exhaustion and hunger overrode their concern about malaria. The disease levelled entire army units.

Blamey miserably failed to take the war to the mosquito. Yet he had ample warning of his tiny new enemy at Milne Bay, for example, where malaria was hyperendemic. Now, on the Papuan beaches, the extreme malaria risk threatened to destroy his army.

The Allies were woefully ill equipped to deal with malaria, but not because medics were negligent or lazy. They lacked suppressant medication, and troops ignored basic preventative measures. The Japanese were even less prepared — or willing — to combat the disease.

With no vaccine against malaria in 1942, quinine and Atebrin were the most effective suppressants. Fortunately the American company Winthrop had a licence to produce Atebrin, because Allied supplies of quinine — derived from the cinchona tree — were finite. The sole source of the commodity in South-East Asia was the island of Java, which fell to the Japanese in early 1942.

The loss of the island handed 1000 tons[1] of quinine per year to the enemy. America would have to make 200 tons, and Britain 50 tons, of Atebrin annually to compensate for the shortfall, 'conditional on [factories] not being destroyed by enemy action',[2] according to an Allied sub-committee on tropical diseases. But this decision was not taken until October 1942.

Meanwhile, a massive consignment of Javanese quinine was lost. On 22 April the Australian army placed a huge order with the Dutch East Indies for £62,500 worth of quinine — Java then produced 95 per cent of the world's supplies. The Australians paid for but never received the consignment, because Japan invaded the country.

To meet the acute shortage, arrangements were made 'to purchase available stocks from drug stores in Australia'.[3] Drug stores were unreliable, and US shipments were held up. On 22 September, 17 million Atebrin tablets awaited shipment for Australia, at a time when the American forces had decided to adopt Atebrin 'for the first time'.[4] Demand soon easily exceeded supply.

Even when it arrived, many Australian soldiers, suspicious of anything the army fed them, refused to take Atebrin. Some even refused quinine. Anti-malarial control measures were 'extremely slack', complained Major-General Sir Samuel Burston, director-general of the medical service.[5]

He blamed 'a very universal idea amongst the troops that ... quinine will cause impotence'. Perhaps bromide-laced chocolate had given them pause for thought. The non-observance of anti-malarial measures, Burston insisted, was an easy way of getting evacuated: 'in fact, a much easier and safer method than a S.I.W. [self-inflicted wound].'[6]

There is no clear evidence to suggest that Australian troops deliberately exposed themselves to malaria to escape battle — although there were probably isolated cases. Rumours of the suggestion infuriated the men, however, and fuelled their simmering hatred of High Command.

As early as 5 October, Burston was alerted to 'the widespread intensity of hyperendemic malaria'[7] in the south-west Pacific. Colonel N. Hamilton Fairley, of the Australian Military Mission in Washington, wrote that no one in the US army or navy realised the gravity of the risk. Nor did the Australians at Gona and the Americans at Buna.

These trans-Pacific negotiations were too late to affect the situation on the ground. Tens of thousands succumbed to malaria in Papua and New Guinea. As the beach battles worsened, Blamey responded to the crisis on 18 December with a set of instructions as perfunctory as they were ineffectual. He recommended giving the troops dummy tablets: '[They] should be trained to take ... dummy Atebrin or quinine tablets ... in order to create in them the habit of taking tablets ...'

Repellents and mosquito nets were 'to be rigidly insisted upon'; 'The wearing of correct clothing should be enforced'; and 'Failure ... to carry out these measures ... should be treated as a serious breach of discipline.'[8]

The mosquitoes did not recognise the new regime. They went about their hungry business, swarming over exposed flesh at night, blackening a man's arm as they feasted. Bare skin drew colonies of the parasites.

By the end of December, some 85 to 90 per cent of the troops complained of symptoms of the disease. Many suffered repeated attacks; their shivering, sweat-drenched bodies and feverish eyes became drearily commonplace. Some form of dire tropical illness racked almost everyone — both Australian and Japanese. Dysentery was simply the norm, and it reduced the men to trouserless spouts of liquid. To have both dysentery and malaria at once was usually a death sentence.

If Blamey's medical supply department needed a live example of the ravages of malaria, they had only to look at Milne Bay. Four months after the battle there, the Australian troops who remained (and who had not been evacuated with malaria) registered a near 100 per cent affliction rate. On 26 December Cyril Clowes, commander of Milne Force, plaintively reported: '... The number of cases of malaria treated is high ... the rate shows NO sign of decreasing, and is, in fact, increasing ... There are cases of individuals having had five attacks, and quite a large number have had three.'[9]

It was too late to start teaching men how to pop pills. The Australian troops, many with incipient symptoms, were expected to fight on. They were sent to the rear only when their temperature passed 103 degrees Fahrenheit.

One Australian soldier described the symptoms: 'You get a fever. You shake like you're going to rattle the teeth right out of your head. You're freezing. Then you're roasting ... You feel like you have to defecate. You try but all you do is dribble some water.'[10]

'First, one is afflicted by an attack of chill tremors,' said Second Lieutenant Rinzo Kanemoto, observing its effects on Japanese troops. 'No matter how many blankets are used, the body shakes uncontrollably. Body temperatures "red line" the thermometer, with 42 degree celsius fevers not uncommon. The liver becomes swollen and the stomach region distended.' In the case of tropical malaria, 'severe diarrhoea results. If this ... continues for four days, the result is almost certainly death. Bodily resistance in soldiers with malnutrition is nil.'[11]

The parasite, which lodges in the red blood cells, can stay in the human system for years. Australian troops experienced bouts of fever more than five years after the war ended. Bill Crooks, of the 2/25th Battalion, later said: 'I had it for about six years, three to four attacks per year. One just lay in bed and sweated it out ... it left one [feeling] like a wet dishcloth with the gutsy threads gone out of it.'[12]

A survey of the prewar malarial victims on the north coast of Papua showed that 75 per cent suffered from the most virulent strain of the disease, which can lead to cerebral malaria and blackwater fever, and was usually fatal.[13]

Malaria was the most devastating of several life-threatening diseases on the Papuan coast. A parasite carried by the aedes mosquito inflicted the debilitating dengue fever, of which throbbing pains in the joints were the chief symptoms. Scrub typhus, borne by tiny swamp mites, was the most feared illness, because it struck an otherwise fit man suddenly, and usually killed him within hours, after violent convulsions and a soaring body temperature. One rare survivor of scrub typhus recalled measuring his body temperature as 108 degrees Fahrenheit.[14] He lapsed into a coma for ten days.

Losses due to malaria — either dead or incapacitated — were staggering. Australian casualties from malaria during the entire campaign were 9250, compared with 2037 killed and 3533 wounded. (Among 14,500 US troops of the 32nd Division, 8600 cases of malaria were reported.[15])

By December 1942, about 5000 of a total force of 15,000 had been treated for malaria, notes Steve Bullard. However, 'practically the whole force' were carrying diseases temporarily held at bay by suppressive drugs.[16]

An alarmed Blamey wrote to Curtin on 4 December: 'It will be quite impossible to maintain the army at its existing strength. The wastage in tropical warfare is immense. At least one third of our force at Milne Bay is already infected with malaria. The Buna area is an equally evil one for this disease.'[17] He belatedly told the War Cabinet that malaria placed the Allied armies 'in a very precarious position'.[18]

So, too, were the Japanese. They mismanaged their Java windfall of quinine, putting it in the hands of a civilian trading company that failed to meet supply targets. The Southern Army was forced to commandeer the factory — and double production rates to 600 tons in the 1943 financial year. That was too late for the troops on the Papuan beaches.

Like the Australians, they knew of the disease's power to kill. It levelled whole units in the aftermath of the invasion of Rabaul. Nearly the entire 1st Battalion of the 144th Regiment was infected. Cases reached epidemic levels due to the complacency of the troops and the failure to take precautions. Many simply did not report the symptoms, partly due to a military culture that frowned on soldiers who succumbed to illness.

In Rabaul, many thousands of soldiers perished, and 'others were left exhausted and prone to recurrences of the disease,' wrote Steve Bullard, of the Australia–Japan Research Project.[19]

Horii's order to leave all non-essential equipment behind — including mosquito nets — to make room in haversacks for ammunition and food, ensured that most of his men got the disease.[20] Others simply threw away their netting and headgear.

Malaria sufferers packed the ghastly Kokoda field hospital during the Owen Stanley campaign: 'These patients were seriously afflicted,' wrote one Japanese officer, 'with many having lost their minds. Their cries and moans in the middle of the night had an other-worldly feel … the faces looked demented, and among them were some who had got up to defecate and urinate but had left their clothes buttoned up. Here and there were rows of freshly dug graves.'[21]

While the Allies eventually contained the disease with emergency measures in December, the Japanese rates of malaria rose. They reached a biblical scale in the final battles, due to the troops' complacency and the indifference of officers.

Chapter 49
Americans

'[There] were just enough savvy professionals to hold together ...
what was, in essence, a children's crusade ...'
— *Eric Bergerud, US military historian*

The Americans arrived on the north coast with the bluster of a conquering army. They streamed into the Allied-controlled villages of Popondetta, Soputa and Pongani to join the final offensive. 'You can go home now,' they told Australian troops beyond Soputa; the Yanks were here to 'clean things up'.

It mattered little that MacArthur's boys were, to use the vivid military phrase, unblooded. None had seen combat; yet many boasted they'd whip the Japs, show the Aussies how it's done, and so on. The enemy, whom they would undoubtedly lick, cowered in holes dying of starvation — so they were told. At this display of braggadocio, the weary Australians sat back and observed their new comrades with wry amusement.

Gung-ho patriotism and youthful naivety no doubt explained the US attitude. Sadly, there was little else to justify it. The Americans had not fought over the Owen Stanleys, or in the Middle East. Some had walked over the mountains unopposed, via Ghost Mountain and the Jaure Track —

parallel to Kokoda — and were tired; others, flown over, were fresh and healthy. A regiment came by boat from Wanigela, on the east coast, landing at Pongani. Very few were usefully trained. During twenty months of jungle training in Queensland rainforests, one American regiment performed a single night patrol.[1]

Most of the Americans at Buna were national guardsmen from the Midwest, whose experience and status roughly corresponded to the Australian militia. They were the ungainly products of America's myopic prewar defence policy, which failed to finance a proper land army; in the late 1930s, it was the size of Belgium's. When war broke out in the Pacific, the prized US marines were sent to Guadalcanal. This fact reflected the relative unimportance ascribed to the Kokoda campaign in the eyes of the American commanders.

The first US troops to arrive were 3000 men of the 32nd Division, raised in Wisconsin and Michigan. Dressed in clean-spun jungle greens, they enjoyed superior rations and always seemed to have an ample supply of cigarettes. They tended to smoke with that peculiarly American swagger; indeed, they looked rugged. Those who walked the Jaure Track were no doubt a little frayed, but compared to the Australians they were models of good health.

In short, the Americans at Buna were good ol' boys from the American backwoods. They marched up utterly unprepared for 'the terrors of jungle warfare so alien to the experience of boys from the clipped green lawns and serene streets of the small-town Mid-West'.[2] Their youth and inexperience troubled their commanders. 'The soldiers,' observed Eric Bergerud, 'although extremely enthusiastic, were very young and very poorly trained ... [There] were just enough savvy professionals to hold together ... what was, in essence, a children's crusade ...'[3]

MacArthur anticipated a swift victory. So did Major-General Edwin Harding, the slightly bewildered American who preceded General Robert Eichelberger as commander of the US forces at Buna. With near total air supremacy, and the possession of airfields at Dobodura, Popondetta and Kokoda, the Allied forces would assuredly destroy the 'shell of sacrifice troops' clinging to the beachhead.[4] Nor could the Japanese get reinforcements through: bargeloads had been bombed and prevented from landing in mid-November. And there was Guadalcanal, where the US marines were in the final stages of wiping out the Japanese forces. Surely Buna would swiftly collapse.

The rank and file at GHQ clung to such comforting notions like children with security blankets. MacArthur himself was openly confident that this would be a 'mopping up' job. In October, the Americans even entertained the idea of delaying their attack on Buna until the Australians in the mountains arrived, so they could share the spoils of victory. 'The belief was prevalent,' on 31 October, 'that the Japanese had no intention of holding Buna; that he had no troops there . . .'[5]

Harding concurred: Buna would be 'easy pickings', he told Lieutenant-General Richard Sutherland on October 14. A ragbag mob of starving and sick Japanese, less than a battalion, supposedly defended the beachhead. Even so, Harding had a small insurance policy, just in case. On 5 November, he'd signed off an evacuation plan, 'Emergency Withdrawal Routes' into the Owen Stanleys, with detailed descriptions of the country. Given the massive Allied build-up and confident posturing, this seemed to smack of alarm.[6]

There were a few dissenting voices. Rowell had growled from his Melbourne garden, in a letter to Allen on 11 October 1942: 'I can't believe that the Jap will clear out of Buna unless forced out . . .'[7] Eichelberger, too, had misgivings, chiefly about the battle readiness of the American troops. He rated them 'barely satisfactory' and incapable of matching the Japanese.

How well prepared were the Allies for the Buna offensive? To Blamey's disgust, they got no help from the US navy. US battleships refused to escort the old fishing craft that routinely plied the coast around Milne Bay to Cape Sudest, carrying Allied supplies. The perils of Japanese strafing attacks forced them to drag canvas assault boats, replete with ammunition, through the surf at night. A big wave sometimes tipped the heavily laden boats, and men had to dive to retrieve the boxes of bullets. Such were the hazards of supplying a roadless front line, without naval support.

Nor were the Japanese defeated in the air. The Zeros still managed some lightning strikes. On 16 November Japanese planes strafed and sank an Allied 'fleet' — three old luggers and a barge — then ferrying US and Australian troops from Pongani towards the Buna front.

The little flotilla happened to be carrying American top brass, in the form of General Harding and Major-General Albert Waldron, who were forced to jump overboard. Their boats were destroyed and 24 troops killed. At least 28 native carriers and Tom Fisher, an Australian war cameraman, were among the civilian deaths. Two heavy artillery pieces, weeks of rations and a huge quantity of ammunition sank or exploded. It was a disastrous loss. Harding and the other survivors swam ashore, badly shaken.

What about air power? Couldn't Allied planes simply vaporise the bunker fields? Certainly General Kenney's 'kids' — the US and Australian pilots — dominated the air; the Japanese 'danse macabre' over Port Moresby had ended. But Allied pilots couldn't see the enemy. Well-camouflaged manholes weren't visible even on clear days, and the technology that produced the lurid metaphors, and loss of life, of the post-Vietnam age — 'carpet-bombing' and 'daisy-cutting' — wasn't available.

A breakthrough of sorts came on 28 November, when a squadron of RAAF Wirraways was deployed as spy planes. These 'slow, almost weaponless'[8] training aircraft were able to fly very low — seeming to hover — over the Japanese positions and report detailed directions to Allied gunners. They were often shot down and forced to land — although one Wirraway actually shot down a Japanese Zero on Boxing Day, a sight applauded by ground troops.

Light Stuart tanks, too, were requisitioned from Milne Bay on 13 November, with the job of shelling and crushing the foxholes. They wouldn't arrive until early December. In tandem, Allied artillery greatly improved. The first howitzers, several Australian 25-pounders, and heavy machine-guns, were flown up to Dobodura. But little of this formidable arsenal arrived in time for the first attack on Buna on 19 November.

Sending troops in without heavy artillery cover was madness, and in early November Blamey demanded naval support. Bombardment of the beaches from ships at sea seemed the best way to 'loosen up' the bunker fields. MacArthur appreciated the 'soundness' of the idea, but replied that the American navy would not assist them. Indeed, the commander of the Allied Naval Forces, Vice-Admiral Arthur Carpender, had been 'unwilling to risk his ships in the shallow reef-ridden waters south-east of Buna'.[9] MacArthur did not enjoy good relations with the US navy.

Blamey replied with undisguised disdain for the American admiralty: 'I regret,' he told MacArthur, 'that I cannot feel very satisfied with [the US navy's] refusal to utilize destroyers.' He added that maintaining destroyers in safe positions when merchant vessels have to take such risks at Buna 'does not appear convincing'.[10]

Australian land troops had fought over mountains where it had been 'extremely difficult to give them the necessary ammunition and supplies to maintain them'.[11] At Buna, the infantry faced a battle where defeat may mean destruction, and the attitude of the [US] navy appeared 'to be to avoid risk', Blamey warned.[12]

His requests met a wall of silence. The navy would not help; heavy artillery and tanks were delayed. And so the American infantry were to march into bunker fields equipped with rifles, a few light machine-guns, and initially no artillery support. 'Can you imagine Nelson's reaction to a Navy that fears to go where the enemy goes regularly?' Blamey confided in his friend, Herring, 'It is their job to transport the Army and to protect it.'[13]

It was, perhaps, one of Blamey's finest hours.

Chapter 50
Buna

'[My] faith in the [Australian] militia is growing, but my faith in
the Americans has sunk to zero'
— *General Blamey to Prime Minister Curtin, 4 December 1942*

A powerful defensive shield locked up the coast at Buna — contrary to reports from Allied intelligence. The battleground, two to three miles of coastal jungle, swamp and coconut groves, ran from Cape Endaiadere in the east to Buna Government Station in the west. The whole area bristled with brilliantly concealed enemy machine-guns and snipers.

A labyrinthine bunker field fortified the Duropa Plantation at Cape Endaiadere, and defended the two runways, New Strip and Old Strip. To the east, scores of foxholes defended the Japanese HQ at Buna Government Station, which comprised a few dilapidated beach shacks situated on a peninsula, just west of Musita Island. Immediately south of the HQ were the so-called Government Gardens — a rough clearing of palm groves — and further inland, a heavily bunkered area known as the Triangle.

Two creeks blocked the Allied advance at either extremity: the swampy Simemi Creek, running between the airstrips to the west; and Entrance Creek, flowing into the Musita lagoon in the east.

The Americans planned to attack from either end of this heavily defended area — and slowly squeeze the Japanese in a vice: Warren Force would attack from the east and clear the airstrips; while Urbana Force would overrun Buna village and the Government Station, from the south-west. The American units were then to unite in a single spearhead, and drive the Japanese into the sea.

The Japanese were clearly outnumbered at Buna. Their commander, Colonel Yamamoto, led two infantry regiments totalling about a thousand men. Well-armed and reinforced, they were veterans of the occupation of Sumatra, experienced jungle fighters and probably the most capable, and resilient, enemy force left on the coast. Nor were they starving.

Amid their ranks were survivors of the Sasebo 5 Special Naval Landing Party, responsible for atrocities at Gona and Milne Bay. This reinforced unit would yield to nothing in the pursuit of victory — as reflected in one soldier's diary during the Buna campaign:

7 Dec: One cigarette was shared by five men this week.

8 Dec: Celebrated the first anniversary of the Greater East Asia War. Received three packets of cigarettes . . .

9 Dec: Our position was bombed and heavily damaged. Company Comdr was killed and the ptn leader wounded.

14 Dec: Suffering from malaria; sent to the rear for treatment.

24 Dec: I have not fully recovered from malaria, but will fight to the very end.[1]

There were perhaps another thousand or so auxiliaries and support troops. Yet American intelligence claimed only 300 starving Japanese occupied the bunkers east of Giruwa River. When Eichelberger arrived he was shocked by the Allies' poor information on the enemy: 'there were about 3000 men there', he grieved.[2]

And so it began.

On 19 November, the first American battalion[3] marched up to the jump-off point, 'joking and laughing, and sure of an easy victory'.[4]

About a mile south of Cape Endaiadere they walked into a thicket of Japanese pillboxes. Machine-guns crackled out of the very vegetation. It seemed they were 'literally surrounded by blazing weapons'.[5] They could not see who was firing, 'but it was dangerous to show even a finger from behind one's cover', recalled Major David Parker.[6] The forward troops were slaughtered, and the badly shaken survivors ran back.

Worse befell the 128th Regiment's III Battalion, which moved along the Simemi Creek, lined by a 'scarecrow growth' of grey foliage, into a bog of oozing swamp and low grass. In the words of Colonel Miller, they were 'stopped cold'[7] in swamp up to their chests, by Japanese machine-guns.

Day after day, the pillboxes cut down the Americans. Within ten days, by 1 December, 492 US troops had been killed or wounded. 'Many others were sick with malaria and dysentery ... They had no flame throwers or tanks and the Japanese bunkers seemed to be proof against bombardment by artillery and aircraft.'[8] Many troops simply gave up, and loitered in a daze in the grass.

The initiation shocked the Americans, and the nightmare continued for weeks. In one attack on the Urbana front, hundreds of troops found themselves wading through swampland towards the Japanese bunkers. Their rifles were wet and clogged, their supply lines 'neck-deep in mud and water'.[9] When they reached the opposite banks they were supposed to climb out of the swamp and charge.

The men lived for three days and nights in that swamp; they complained they could not attack. It did not help that a Major Herbert M. Smith and a Lieutenant-Colonel Herbert A. Smith led the two companies; the Smiths confused US signallers.[10] In any case, General Harding mistook the 'neck-deep' complaint for 'knee-deep' and ordered the Smiths to charge.[11]

Heavy artillery, including Australian 25-pounders, had at last arrived, and supported the two Smiths as they prepared their men for the assault. In the air, no bombers were available, but twelve fighters were expected. Only four showed up, promptly strafed Lieutenant-Colonel Smith's staff in error, and flew off, leaving the Japanese untouched.

The Smiths pressed on without air support. Herbert A. Smith's men feinted half-heartedly in the Japanese direction, and beat a hasty withdrawal. The troops threw away their weapons and 'fell back into the swamp'.[12] Another unit 'dug holes and lay in them with swamp water seeping over them'.[13]

Notwithstanding the Smiths' brave leadership, Urbana Force sat down and refused to fight. It was not surprising: they lacked experienced leadership and their weapons were drenched, 'their mortars fell short because the [propelling charges] were wet. Machine-guns jammed ... Tommy guns were full of muck and dirt.'[14]

General Harding angrily rejected the two Smiths' explanation for the failure. He was a bundle of nerves after his near death at sea, and cut a 'pathetic figure'.[15] His HQ was a shambles, and his men, in Vasey's disdainful phrase, were 'milling around'.[16]

Yet Harding did his best in a dreadful situation. Most of his food and ammunition were sunk, and his men lived hand-to-mouth on emergency rations. Soon nearly half his forces would be recommended for transfer to Australian commanders — a humiliation, in American eyes. At least one battalion was earmarked to go to General Vasey, at Sanananda, which deeply rankled. In the end the Australians declined the American troops — preferring the veterans of the Kokoda Track. Blamey simply refused to believe the Americans would fight. For the Americans, this was a double humiliation.

In the Papuan evenings MacArthur used to stand on the wide verandah at Government House puffing on his corncob pipe, or cigarette holder, and enjoying the gentle breeze that issued up the valley and broke the wretched heat. He had commandeered the large bungalow — the former Australian Governor's residence in Port Moresby — for his New Guinea HQ, and the Bataan Gang moved there on 5 November. He adapted his unorthodox dress sense to fit the occasion. On balmy nights he could be seen striding about in his black satin dressing gown emblazoned with white Japanese characters on the back.

On one particular night — in late November — he looked down on the twinkling lights of the township, deeply preoccupied. The early reversals had made a disquieting impression on the supreme commander. He was fighting a very different enemy from the one he'd supposed. No motley collection of skeletal men, the reinforced Japanese were determined to fight for every inch of Papuan sand. They would never surrender — not until the last Japanese soldier had spilled his blood for the Emperor. How long would it take to dislodge them? What were the consequences for the Allied advance north? Why wouldn't the Americans fight? These were likely MacArthur's thoughts, as he contemplated the consequences of a long war of attrition.

His behaviour became erratic; a spiralling sense of panic seemed to animate his orders. The Japanese resistance threatened the very trajectory of his master plan: the reconquest of the Philippines. On the 20th he burst into Blamey's offices and demanded that the Allies attack the next day. 'ALL COLUMNS WILL BE DRIVEN THROUGH TO OBJECTIVES REGARDLESS OF LOSSES.'[17] He dispatched the same order to his generals on the 21st: 'TAKE BUNA TODAY AT ALL COSTS. MACARTHUR.'

It was the last straw for Harding, who barely knew the location of his men. This was the day earmarked for an all-out infantry assault on the Buna coast. It failed dismally, as did several attacks in coming weeks. The Americans simply sat down, or loitered near the front, as confirmed in the devastating Larr Report by the eponymous US colonel sent to observe progress. Harding was personally battered by these experiences, and he subsequently became dangerously confused and inconsistent.

The frontal attacks would continue, and the casualty rate at Buna soar. All columns were indeed driven through, regardless of losses. It mattered little that High Command tacitly acknowledged the failure of these tactics, insofar as they expedited the delivery of light tanks to the Buna front. Lives were being expended for little or no gain.

Nor did it help that Australian troops seemed willing to fight, which underlined the American failure. MacArthur took this personally; he set great store by the American soldier — marine or national guardsman.

The Americans' inadequacy at Buna came into startling focus when an Australian independent company sent in 50 men under Major Harcourt on 21 November. Americans were ordered to support Harcourt in the capture of Buna airstrip. The Australians crashed through the Japanese bunkers, machine-gunning snipers, who then fell to earth or dangled from the branches. They got within 58 yards of the first Buna strip. But the Americans refused to advance, leaving Harcourt's men stranded; and they were forced back. As so often in the Pacific War, extraordinary individual bravery shone out. One case was Private Stanley Martin, a stockman of Victoria River Downs, who continued fighting after being shot in the arm, the leg and stomach. He withdrew only after receiving direct orders to do so.

MacArthur and his staff were not allowed to forget their earlier contemptuous dismissal of the Australian troops. It was payback time after weeks of American jokes at the diggers' expense. 'The jokes of the American officers ... making fun of the Australian army were told all over Australia,' said one soldier. 'Now it was our turn to rub salt into the wound.'[18]

The salt stung. MacArthur was extremely sensitive to charges of American cowardice. When he requested the US 41st Division, then based in Brisbane, Blamey replied that he would rather send in more Australians. He had the 21st Brigade in mind, then recovering in Port Moresby, 'as he knew they would fight'. (This was the time when these men — the Kokoda veterans — were sent to reinforce Gona.)

Blamey's rejection of the 41st indicted the quality and command of the American division, none of whom had fought on the Kokoda Track. That he chose a battered and demoralised Australian unit reveals the seriousness of the American problem. 'I think it was a bitter pill for General MacArthur to swallow, but he agreed,' wrote General Kenney.[19] MacArthur's secretary observed his boss 'smarting under his own doubt [while] Blamey sat smiling smugly ...'[20] MacArthur grudgingly acknowledged that the Australians were battle-ready in a way the Americans were not.

Blamey reported the American failures in a series of blistering cables smothered in *schadenfreude*. He told the Australian Government on the 30th: 'The Buna area has been assigned to the Americans. We have all been terribly disappointed and ... General MacArthur is equally so at the lack of force and drive shown by the 32nd American Division. They must outnumber the Japs by at least five to one on the Buna front but to date have made no progress ...'[21] (In fact they outnumbered the Japanese at Buna by about three to one.)

The American troops, he told Curtin privately on 4 December, were 'definitely not equal to the Australian militia, and from the moment they met opposition [they] sat down and have hardly gone forward a yard'.[22]

'I am afraid that the bulk of fighting will fall on our troops in spite of the greatly larger numbers of the 32nd US division,' Blamey warned the Prime Minister. Nor, he believed, would the American 32nd Division 'attain any high standard of training or war spirit for many months to come . . . my faith in the [Australian] militia is growing, but my faith in the Americans has sunk to zero'.[23]

In this withering frame of mind, Blamey demanded Australian reinforcements: the immediate return of the 9th Division from the Middle East, the delivery of Australian tanks and the dispatch of the 30th Militia Brigade to Sanananda. And he insisted that Australian officers command some American units, as General Wootten — of Milne Bay fame — would shortly do at Buna.

Blamey's belittlement of the Americans was of a pattern with his earlier dismissal of the Australians: when things went badly, the infantry were to blame. And there were, of course, arch political reasons for this sudden big-noting of his countrymen.

A faint harbinger of hope, a grim reprieve, boosted American morale. On 30 November, Colonel John Mott led a midnight attack on Buna village. A single file of 300 troops, each gripping the shoulder of the man in front, moved into the swamplands south of the objective. It was a moonless night. A signal wire guided them to the jump-off point. Japanese flares illuminated the land, and then a rising tide flooded the swamp. These delayed the attack, and the Americans sat in the brackish water until 4 a.m., when the order came to charge.

'Machine-gun tracers lit the entire area, and our own rifle fire made a solid sheet of flame,' recalled Lieutenant Robert Odell. 'Everywhere men cursed, shouted or screamed . . . Brave men led and others followed. Cowards crouched in the grass literally frightened out of their skins.'[24]

Mott's troops captured the strip of land in front of Buna village. During the mop-up they burst into a hut and shot dead six Japanese officers lying in their bunks. Inside the hut they found exotica from China, Java and the

Philippines — watercolour prints, silks, and painted lacquer boxes — the booty of imperial conquest.[25] The Americans mistook fourteen rolls of thin Japanese writing paper for toilet paper, which they'd lacked for weeks, and gratefully pilfered it. They gathered up a signal box, military documents, medical gear and food, torched the huts and blew up the bunker field.

What of the Japanese during the battle for Buna? How did they react? Their officers had been primed for the fist of god; they got untrained national guardsmen from Michigan.

An intelligence appreciation issued by General Yamagata in late November warned that the Allies had penetrated Buna, Giruwa and Gona and were 'persistently carrying out small attacks'. The Allied air force had established air superiority, and bombed and strafed the Japanese lines daily. 'They seem to be making a determined effort to cause our troops to retire.' He presumed that Allied supply lines were breaking, and that the troops were exhausted. His information was largely derived from interrogation of Allied prisoners of war.[26]

One private, Nakajima of the Moto Butai, observed: 'Enemy frequently use thick smoke screen to cover the front line. Enemy infantry is lacking in attacking spirit.'[27]

The American troops 'believe in certain victory; they have a strong sense of self-interest; this love of pleasure is strong,' noted a Japanese tactical manual found at Buna. It added that American troops were 'most inferior'.[28] The author, it seems, had not yet faced the US marines. Another Japanese report concluded that the Americans were boastful, but apt to carry out their boasts.

The Australian soldier got a slightly better review. He will 'not reveal basic plans when taken prisoner' — a nod, perhaps, at the Australian soldier's resilience under interrogation. In other respects, the Japanese were rather wide of the mark. Under 'Characteristics and training of the Australian soldiers' we learn that he was, on average, twenty years old, typically middle class, kept his rifle's safety catch on at twenty yards, and his rations were mostly 'dry, buttered bread'.

A diary said to belong to First Lieutenant Suganuma revealed the mood in the bunkers during the Allied 'softening up' process. He wrote with that strange mixture of defiance and uncritical resignation that pervaded many officers' diaries; there is a claustrophobic sense of inevitable death, of 'no escape' and 'do or die'. '8 Dec 42: . . . at 0430 each group in bomb shelters bowed towards the Imperial Palace. Bn Comdr lectured us on the meaning of the Great East Asia War . . .'

Suganuma noted the scarcity of coconuts, which had been used to reinforce the bunker walls: 'It is said that a bullet does not penetrate coconut wood.' Yet coconuts were 'about the only local source of food', he added resignedly. Coconuts made up for the deficiency of sugar in his diet, he wrote. As so often in the Japanese army, military exigencies overrode human need.

At dawn on the 11th Suganuma went to prepare breakfast. He found his platoon's mess gear destroyed: 'At 0600 . . . we were bombed and strafed by enemy planes. Well, today we can't eat . . . Everyone is greatly depressed.'

He recorded the shape of the moon — 'brow-shaped' — and looked forward to a new moon in a few days. Japanese soldiers often alluded to the natural world — the sea, the sky and the lunar phases — in little pithy phrases amidst the slow-drip register of their destruction.

On the night of the 12th, 'it rained heavily and I was drenched . . . There was no let up by the mortar fire and airplanes. We entered our trenches dripping wet.' The Allied bombs missed his bunker 'due to our concealed position in a coconut grove . . .'

Three days later Allied planes dropped propaganda leaflets, urging Suganuma to surrender. This provoked a typical officer's response: 'Such impertinence! If and when our infantry arrives we will annihilate the enemy.'[29]

Reinforcements did land, full of optimism. For example, men of the Seibu 34 Butai stepped ashore at Basabua on 21 November, believing that operations at Buna had been highly successful. They found gaunt-eyed, hollow-cheeked soldiers who pleaded for food. The fresh troops were sent to Buna, but most didn't make it, lost their leaders and became 'completely disorganised'. They burnt the unit standard to prevent its capture.

Chapter 51
Eichelberger

'Take Buna or don't come back alive'
— *General MacArthur to General Eichelberger, 30 November 1942*

MacArthur had 'never been so humiliated' when he heard that American troops had dropped their weapons and fled. Harding, he said, had failed, 'and the blame for what happened was his'.[1]

The supreme commander's feelings were heightened by a series of sharply critical reports on the American soldiers' performance. The sharpest was Larr's, which seriously dented MacArthur's faith in American military supremacy. Another, by Lieutenant-Colonel William Robertson, an Australian, tabled a disturbing account of the negligent and increasingly odd behaviour of Harding.

Flying into what he thought was Harding's new HQ at Dobodura, Robertson found the area deserted — a single camp fire burned on the edge of the runway. Around 4.00 p.m. on 29 November, the American general eventually showed. He'd spent the day leisurely walking the sixteen miles from his old HQ. During this jungle stroll, he and his staff had bathed, drunk coconut milk and rested.

Harding presented a sad, shuffling figure. He seemed deeply distracted. He'd had no contact with his forward troops for days: his signals men, finding their wireless set too heavy, had abandoned it. Disconnected from his own men, Harding could offer only the sketchiest account of their infantry positions. Robertson was appalled, and duly informed his superiors.

The slightly sinister General Sutherland — MacArthur's 'eyes and ears' — flew into Dobodura the next day. Profoundly underwhelmed by what he saw and heard, he demanded that Harding relieve two of his most senior officers. One was Mott, a curious choice, since Mott had led the one successful American assault on Buna; Harding refused.

The bitterest pill for Harding was Blamey's open criticism of American troops and refusal to use the US 127th Regiment on the Sanananda–Gona front. Harding was startled,[2] and vigorously defended his men. It was to no avail. Sutherland had already made up his mind: Harding would have to go — the poor man had, after all, insisted on keeping incompetent officers in key posts — and he advised MacArthur accordingly.

A fascinating dialogue between Blamey and Herring rumbled along in the background of these events. Herring, a fastidious barrister who'd succeeded Rowell as commander of New Guinea Force, kept Blamey fully informed with a stream of daily, unofficial, and unusually candid, reports written in the lawyer's dauntingly spidery hand.

Herring, an unapologetic 'Blamey man', obligingly echoed his boss's contempt for the Americans. The American 32nd Division, he wrote on 29 November, 'had still not realised that ... whilst bombing, strafing, mortars and artillery may soften his resistance ... the men who are left will ... have to be taken out & killed in hard fighting. This I was at pains to explain to Harding this morning ... The organisation of [Harding's] HQ is worse than primitive.'[3]

Blamey replied that night, with momentous news: '... I have had a talk with General MacArthur ... and he is now going to take very drastic action. Eichelberger goes over tomorrow to report to you, and has complete authority to remove Harding, all his regimental commanders and several of his battalion commanders ...'[4]

MacArthur's choice of General Robert Eichelberger was propitious. Eichelberger, then relaxing on a sleepy Sunday in Rockhampton, emerges as one of the more impressive figures of the campaign — intelligent, brave, unafraid to visit the front and deeply interested in the state of his troops. He lacked experience as a commander in battle, but he was tough, resolute and a great communicator, who possessed superb organisational skills. Eichelberger, in sum, was a perfect example of the redeeming power of good leadership — but the effort would nearly break him.

He got his orders at midnight, 29 November, and arrived at MacArthur's lavish bungalow late the next day. Ushered past the supreme commander's stony-faced staff, he observed 'fine tropical furniture, a library, and, still more importantly, a breeze'.[5] Of MacArthur's Bataan Gang, only General Kenney 'greeted me with a smile'.[6] Stepping onto a sweeping verandah with sunny views of the hillside, he found MacArthur pacing back and forth, his corncob pipe alight, his face a rock of consternation. The supreme commander got straight to the point:

> 'Bob, I'm putting you in command at Buna. Relieve Harding. I am sending you in Bob, and I want you to remove all officers who won't fight. Relieve regimental and battalion commanders; if necessary, put sergeants in charge of battalions and corporals in charge of companies — anyone who will fight. Time is of the essence — the Japs may land reinforcements any night.'[7]

MacArthur did another circuit of the verandah, and then stopped short of Eichelberger: 'Bob,' he said, 'take Buna or don't come back alive.'[8] Pointing to the nearby Brigadier-General Clovis Byers, he added, 'And that goes for your chief of staff.'[9]

Eichelberger, who'd never led a unit in combat, ruminated on the challenge over his last decent breakfast for months — juice and bacon and eggs — after which, he recalls, MacArthur 'put an arm around my shoulder'.[10] Clearly, there were carrots as well as sticks . . .

MacArthur's carrot, should Eichelberger succeed, revealed a lot about the priorities of the carrot-dangler: as well as a Distinguished Service Cross and a recommendation for high British decoration, MacArthur promised to release Eichelberger's name to the press. Since American officers functioned under a code of strict anonymity — no one back home knew where they were or what they were doing — MacArthur alone had the power to confer immortality on them.

The gift in this case impressed the donor more than the recipient. Eichelberger felt faintly soiled by the experience; the attribution of such self-serving motives impugned his sense of dignity. He later dismissed MacArthur's 'ribbons and publicity': 'neither my soldiers nor I would have stayed a day longer [in Buna] for all the pretty ribbons of all the nations of the world'.[11]

That morning he flew to the front to relieve Harding as commander of the American forces. 'When the stink of the swamp hit our nostrils,' Eichelberger noted, 'we knew that we ... were prisoners of geography. And ... we knew that we would never get out alive unless we fought our way out.'[12] He was under no illusions. Buna, he later wrote, was plainly going to be 'siege warfare ... the bitterest and most punishing kind'.[13] It would drive this strong-willed man to the brink of nervous collapse.

The shock of battle had etiolated the American army. Eichelberger found the men moping about, or sitting in a state of baffled impotence. Instead of a few hundred sick and starving Japanese, the Americans realised they were facing 'large numbers of fresh, well-fed, well-armed troops in seemingly impregnable positions, against whom in almost two weeks of fighting they had failed to score even one noteworthy success'.[14] Military order — leadership, rank, duty, even the salute — seemed oddly surreal, irrelevant even, in the context of this despair. Who will lead us? the men's faces asked. Why have we been sent to fight in this godforsaken place?

When Eichelberger reached Herring's tent at Popondetta, on 1 December, he met blank-faced officers with no idea of what had become of the American regiments. Herring himself could shed little light on the mystery. A senior liaison officer went off to find the errant General Harding, who knew nothing of his men, or their positions.

'When I went to the front on December 2 I couldn't find a front,' an exasperated Eichelberger later wrote.[15] A staff officer apprised him of the state of the American troops at Buna. They were 'deplorable'. They wore long dirty beards; their clothing was in rags, and their boots worn out. Hungry and sick, the men relied on scarce rations and displayed 'little discipline or military courtesy'.[16] Many spent their days eating and sleeping in little groups along the track to Buna.

Eichelberger ordered a cease-fire. He needed a few days to reorganise. The American companies and platoons were 'as scrambled as pied type on the floor of a printing office'. The American patrols were 'dazed by the hazards of swamp and jungle', and the officers demoralised by their failure to advance in appalling conditions. [17]

Eichelberger sent a damning assessment of the situation to MacArthur, and applied himself to the job of transforming the American army. It would take two days to unscramble the regiments. His priorities were then to fix the supply lines and restore order. The return of morale would hopefully follow.

He ensured the troops were better fed, well supplied with cigarettes, and properly armed. He promoted those who showed the right stuff — very young corporals became officers overnight, suddenly elevated to dizzy heights. Harding and other senior officers were formally sacked. Colonel Clarence Martin became commander of Warren Force; Colonel M. C. McCreary replaced Mott as leader of Urbana Force.

The state of the sick and wounded deeply affected Eichelberger. 'The Pacific was a different war,' he wrote. 'In New Guinea, when the rains came, wounded men might drown before the litter-bearers found them. Many did ... Out there I was convinced, as were many of my soldiers, that death was pleasanter in the Temperate Zone.'[18]

He slowly raised the Americans' self-worth from the slough of despond. He gained the mutual trust of his men. Only then would a soldier be prepared to lay down his life. Honner achieved it, as did Vasey, Cullen and Potts. Kusunose, Tsukamoto, Oda and even Horii similarly inspired the Japanese troops. A fragile *esprit de corps* hobbled to life among the American dugouts. The broken American soldier gradually found the inner strength to fight.

Eichelberger proudly informed Herring that 'his boys' were 'getting up the trees and having a go at the Japs'. Since his men had been cared for, 'they have been a different show'. But they were a long way from mounting an effective attack.

———

Meanwhile, on the eastern flank, there was a hubbub of activity. An Australian cavalry battalion was quietly examining ways of breaking the deadlock.[19] It came up with a suicidal plan: to use five lightly armed troop carriers — mounted with machine-guns — as tanks. The US troops would trot along behind these contraptions as they blasted a gap in the Japanese bunkers.

It was another example of 'bewildered desperation'.[20] Troop carriers were meant for troop transport, not attack: 'carriers should not, indeed *could* not, be used as [tanks]'.[21] This was fairly obvious. Their low sides and lack of overhead cover were dispiriting hints to the most casual observer. Nonetheless, these machines were all the cavalry had (their horses long ago went the way of the sabre and musket) — as the tanks were delayed. It was hoped the sight of armoured vehicles might rally the Americans from their torpor.

After a bit of perfunctory aerial bombing, the carriers broke cover on 5 December and drove at a slow walking pace towards the enemy bunkers. Four Australians manned each vehicle; they formed the 'spearhead' of the American III Battalion, which was ordered to creep along behind.

The attack was a complete fiasco, epitomised by the needless death of the young Australian jackeroo Lieutenant Terence Fergusson (whose father, Brigadier Maurice Fergusson, then commanded an Australian armoured brigade). Fergusson's carrier drove into heavy fire from bunkers and snipers. With his driver dead, Fergusson grabbed the wheel, but the vehicle got stuck between two logs. The young man looked back for help, but the American troops were nowhere to be seen, having run away. With his carrier immobilised amid terrific fire, Fergusson called vainly to another Australian driver. A Japanese sniper then shot him through the head. Within half an hour, all five carriers were abandoned or destroyed, their men killed, burnt or badly wounded. Had the American infantry stayed and fought, the result may have been different.

The only good news for the Allies at Buna in early December was the extraordinary performance of the American staff sergeant Herman J. Bottcher, who led his platoon in smashing a path through the Japanese lines to the sea.

Bottcher had a strong motive to succeed. He was born in Germany, and didn't enjoy American citizenship. Strongly opposed to the Nazis, he'd left his country in the early 1930s and spent a year at the University of California. He then rather spoiled his résumé by returning to Europe to fight on Franco's side in the Spanish Civil War, which damaged his hopes of becoming an American.

Nonetheless, he was allowed to fight as one, and in 1942 found himself in Papua at war against an ally of the land of his birth. On the eve of a fresh attack on Buna village, Bottcher approached Eichelberger with an unusual request: would the general secure his American citizenship if he took Buna? Eichelberger agreed to help — anything to get the men to fight. Some were promised a medal; others media fame; but Bottcher fought for a US passport.

This takes nothing away from Bottcher's achievement. He eschewed the futile, frontal attacks on bunker fields. The proud, would-be American beat a path through virgin jungle then outflanked and wheeled around behind the enemy. He reached the sea between Buna village and Giropa Point, in the very midst of the Japanese army and planted his one machine-gun on the beach. His platoon never lost it. When an Eichelberger staffer asked Bottcher's men what they needed to sustain them, a GI bared his backside to Allied binoculars: 'Pants,' he yelled. 'For God's sake, General, pants!'[22] It seemed Bottcher's uniforms were rotting.

The Japanese waded towards him from the east and west, and were mown down 'like wheat in a field'.[23] Every night Bottcher's men could hear the Japanese crawling towards them in the darkness; one night they repulsed fifty shrieking attackers. As casualties mounted, Bottcher's Corner acquired a more fitting name, Maggot Beach, and an American newspaper shocked the nation by publishing images of the carnage. By the time reinforcements arrived, the troops' nerves were shot through. One soldier shook uncontrollably.

Highly decorated for bravery, Bottcher became a captain and an American citizen. He died two years later in the battle for the Philippines. A little statue near Buna village commemorates his courage. 'He was,' wrote Eichelberger, 'one of the best Americans I have ever known.'[24]

___

Sitting in his forward regimental post Eichelberger observed the repeated failures with rising frustration. A pattern had set in. The troops would advance a little, hear the 'typewriter clatter' of Japanese machine-guns, and go to ground. Any man, he promised, who ventured 50 yards down the track would be decorated. Few responded.

Blamey continued, with apparent relish, to inform Canberra of the American refusal to fight. The catastrophe horrified Colonel John Grose, an American World War I veteran who arrived in early December to lead the US 126th Regiment. Grose couldn't believe the state of the men under his command; they had 'simply collapsed from nervous exhaustion, crying like children and shaking from head to foot'.[25]

The American troops, Eichelberger concluded, were cowards, and rather melodramatically he resolved to attack Buna himself if he could find six men brave enough to join him. For a man of his rank, in late middle age, to decide to lead from the front was highly unusual — and clearly a sign of despair. Casualties were likely: Japanese snipers had an eye for any badge of rank, or gesture denoting seniority.

Eichelberger left his observation post with his staff, and shortly came upon a group of young privates loitering by the track. 'Lads, come along with us,' Eichelberger called.[26] And they did; shortly after, he led several units against the bunkers at Buna village.

It was believed to be the most highly ranked fighting patrol in military history. All the troop leaders were pipped and striped officers on Eichelberger's staff. General Waldren was shot in the arm, and a favourite aide was badly wounded and brought in lashed to the bonnet of Eichelberger's jeep. Yet the move achieved its intention, and inflamed American morale. Seeing their commander at the front broke the troops' paralysing fear. Vasey's walkabouts had a similar effect on the Sanananda front.

Even so, Eichelberger knew the Americans would take time to overcome their demons. He understood exactly what was required at Buna: soldiers with solid battle experience. He was forced to acknowledge, like Harding and MacArthur, that only the Australian army had this quality.

In this climate, with MacArthur's incessant demands ringing in their ears, Eichelberger, Herring and the newly arrived General Wootten, commander of the Australian 18th Brigade at Milne Bay, drew up their final plans for the destruction of Buna.

Chapter 52
Tanks

'No thoughts of returning home alive ... Writing in this diary word-by-word, not knowing when a shell may strike and I will be killed'
— *Leading Private Uchiyama Seiichi, in a trench at Buna*

MacArthur's impatience reached boiling point. 'Dear Bob,' he wrote to Eichelberger, on 13 December:

> Time is fleeting and our dangers increase with its passage. However admirable individual acts of courage may be; however important administrative functions may seem; however splendid and electrifying your presence has proven; remember that your mission is to take Buna. All other things are merely subsidiary to this. No alchemy is going to produce this for you; it can only be done in battle and sooner or later this battle must be engaged. Hasten your preparations, and when you are ready — strike, for as I have said, time is working desperately against us.
> Cordially,
> DOUGLAS MACARTHUR
> Allied Commander.[1]

Japanese commanders, no less impatient, sought solace in imperial tidings. Colonel Yokoyama relayed these in a bulletin to his troops on the Papuan coast on 28 November: 'The Emperor visited the Shinto Shrine,' he wrote, 'and expressed gratitude for the achievement of great victories since the outbreak of this war ... He prayed for Heaven's protection over the Imperial Army. Therefore we must perform our duties with diligence to carry out the will of His Majesty.'[2]

American and Japanese methods of raising morale differed, but the effect was the same: the infantry were to be driven harder, hurled at the enemy, with scarcely a thought for their condition or the wastage of life.

The carnage of frontal attacks on bunkers troubled the Australian officers; Herring responded by suggesting they 'go quietly, take out a post here and a post there each day if possible'.[3] Eichelberger's officers, 'torn by the suffering of their troops', similarly argued that attempts to strike at Buna were fruitless, and that they should settle down to 'starve out the Japanese'.[4] Vasey concurred. But MacArthur and Blamey refused to countenance a relaxation of the tactics that had killed so many — 'delay is dangerous', said Blamey — and the troops were sent back in. Tanks were on the way — tacit recognition that the unprotected assaults were ineffectual. But this did not stop Allied commanders wasting many more lives while they waited for the machines.

Nothing enraged Eichelberger so much as the Japanese bombardment of the American field hospital near Buna on 7 December 1942, on the eve of the first anniversary of the attack on Pearl Harbor. The hospital, a series of tents marked with giant red crosses, contained three times the number of patients for whom it was designed. It became a regular target for the few remaining Zero formations. 'There were desperately wounded men on the operating table ... when the bombing began,' wrote Eichelberger. He believed the enemy fighters ignored the front lines and supply line, 'to concentrate on the hospital site'.[5]

Surgeons continued to operate; anaesthetists stayed at their posts. 'But the tent installation was a shambles. There were 40 casualties [and] hysteria among the sick and the wounded.'[6]

Not all Japanese units attacked Allied medical facilities. They pointedly refrained from sinking a hospital ship at Milne Bay. Nor did the Allies show much restraint. They bombed many Japanese medical facilities which, in fairness to Allied pilots, were poorly marked.

One prisoner, Sato Tetsuro, claimed that Allied planes had strafed a clearly marked Japanese field hospital at Buna.[7] One private, Onishi, 23, said the hospital at Buna was bombed at least once, with 50 patients killed. Yet the hospital's only Red Cross insignia was a flagpole at the entrance; there were no large red crosses visible to aircraft on the tent sides. Later, at Sanananda, MacArthur dropped leaflets warning the Japanese to evacuate their field hospital before the final assault.

At last the tanks came. One night in December a large freighter drew quietly into Oro Bay, eastern Papua. In its hold were four light tanks of the 2/6th Australian Armoured Regiment — the first Allied tanks to be deployed in the Papuan war. The operation was highly complex. It had to be done in darkness. The tanks were shifted onto specially built barges, ferried ashore and hidden in the jungle. The next night the barges floated them up the coast to Boreo, near the attack point at Duropa Plantation. Four more tanks followed, in the same quiet stages.

After sunset on 17 December, the tanks rumbled forward, their roaring motors and clanking tracks drowned by a deliberate barrage of mortar fire. About five hundred experienced Australian combat troops walked behind them to the assembly area.

These men formed the 18th Brigade[8] — veterans of Tobruk, who had inflicted the first land defeat on the Japanese, at Milne Bay. Their commander was the bull-headed, thickset Brigadier George Wootten (who would earn a KBE, DSO, CBE, CB, DSC, and be Mentioned in Despatches five times) of whom, when he toured the front lines, the joke ran that he had 'plenty of guts'. Wootten had astonishing energy for so big a man.

'You had to fight Wootten,' observed Colonel Clem Cummings, one of his battalion commanders. 'If he said something outrageous it was to see if you'd come back at him ... he had a terrific bloody brain.' Wootten used to sit through American conferences with his eyes closed: 'You'd swear he was asleep,' said Cummings, 'and all of a sudden he'd bark out, "I don't think that's any good."'[9]

Battle for Buna: 17 December 1942 – 2 January 1943

Track to Sanananda: 24 December

That night, the officers went over Wootten's plan in detail. Up to a thousand Japanese troops were believed entrenched in the Duropa Plantation, defending the two Buna airstrips; aerial bombardment and American raids had failed to dislodge them. The next morning an Australian force of tanks and infantry, working closely together, would find and destroy the Japanese bunkers, one by one.

It was a restless night. The soldiers smoked, had dinner, and tried to sleep. Some lay awake, reading or thinking; a few prayed. They rose at 5.30 a.m., ate a 'scratch breakfast'[10] and formed up.

At 6.50 a.m. every gun and mortar available shelled the Duropa Plantation. Ten minutes later the barrage ceased, and five tanks moved off. They were lightweight Australian Stuart tanks, and could travel up to 40 miles an hour. Not this morning: they rolled forward at the pace of the Australians crouching behind them. Huge cloth bandoleers filled with rifle ammunition were slung on their backs. 'Like race horses harnessed to heavy ploughs,'[11] the tanks clanked into the coconut groves.

The Japanese machine-guns opened up immediately. It was 'a barbarous inferno', said one soldier. 'The roar of the tanks engines added to the crescendo of noise from Vickers and enemy machine-guns … The sky seemed to rain debris as small pieces of undergrowth and bark floated down like confetti … '[12]

The infantry guided the tanks towards the camouflaged bunkers with flares or by hurling grenades. The tanks then rolled up to within ten or fifteen feet of the bunker, aligned their cannons, and blasted away at the crack in the earth, until the whole area was a smouldering ruin. One tank crew member said: 'This usually took 10 rounds.'[13] Then the infantry crawled forward, hurled grenades — including a new kind of phosphorus grenade that created hideous burns — into the manhole, and machine-gunned any survivors. The carnage went on for two hours; then the tanks pulled back to refuel.

The Japanese were 'completely demoralized'.[14] The tank attack had caught them utterly by surprise. Bunker after bunker was targeted, shelled and destroyed. Pockets of enemy resistance recovered and fought back: 'Soldiers were dropping like sacks …' wrote Bill Spencer. 'There were no sounds from the wounded, as the pain of a gunshot wound comes later. The bodies … became sprinkled with leaf and bark litter ripped from the undergrowth by bullets and shrapnel, which somehow softened the starkness of death.'[15]

Many Japanese troops ran at the tanks; they'd leap on top, set fires beneath them or throw grenades at their sides. One soldier disabled a tank by jumping on it and firing several pistol rounds through the driver's slit. 'The man's face was riddled with bullets and steel splinters,' reported Herring.[16] Another tank, struck by a Molotov cocktail, caught fire, but the crew survived. One master sergeant jumped on the tanks eight times in order to destroy them.[17]

To no avail. By nightfall, the Australians had cleared the entire Duropa Plantation of enemy bunkers, and reached the tip of Cape Endaiadere. The resistance was broken. It cost the Australian infantry 181 casualties — 54 killed and 117 wounded — mostly from sniper fire in the treetops. The Japanese fared far worse: virtually the entire force was killed or wounded. Few escaped; there were no reported prisoners. Examination of the ruins revealed that some bunkers were in fact made of concrete, with steel doors. Nothing but tanks at near point-blank range could have destroyed them.

MacArthur's latest communiqué announced a great Allied victory. In fact the action was wholly Australian — in planning and execution — but no one disabused American newspaper readers in Wisconsin, who admired their boys' triumph in the south-west Pacific.

The few Japanese survivors retreated along the coast towards Buna Government Station, their HQ. Disbelief and denial filled their diaries during these final weeks. The unthinkable was happening — they were facing defeat for the first time. Some refused to believe it. Nothing in their training had prepared them for the emotional shock of defeat. Were they not the Emperor's anointed army? Were they not the invincible warriors of Imperial Japan? Most calmly awaited the end, silently clinging to hopes of reinforcements and air support — and, most of all, food.

One was leading Private Uchiyama Seiichi, who sat in a trench in the Buna area in late December. He kept a detailed record of the final days, the resigned tone of which, punctured by searing bursts of emotion, was characteristic of Japanese soldiers' notebooks:

19 November: We are continuously short of rations. Eat only once a day and impossible to walk because of lack of strength.

15 December: ...Enemy plan is to annihilate us before reinforcements come ... we are now completely enveloped. Bombed by enemy planes at dawn, continuously all day. We now only wait for the final moments to come.

20 December: At dawn, enemy bombed the hell out of us. Observe only the sky with bitter regrettable tears rolling down ... Filled my stomach with dried bread and waited for my end to come. Oh! Remaining comrades, I shall depend on you for my revenge.

21 December: Oh! Are you going to let us die like rats in a hole? Sgt Ogawa reported that reinforcements are coming ... one cannot accept such reports except as a temporary relief to one's feelings, or as yet another false rumour. Enemy bombing fiercely and our end is coming nearer and nearer.

December 22: No thoughts of returning home alive. Want to die like a soldier and go to Yasukuni Shrine ... Writing in this diary word-by-word, not knowing when a shell may strike and I will be killed. [At 5.30 p.m. that day:] ...shells dropping all around the trenches. Full moon shining through the trees in the jungle, hearing the cries of the birds and insects, the breeze blowing gently and peacefully ... Gathered twigs and built a fire in the trenches to avoid detection by the enemy. Good news — friendly troops are near ... and friendly planes will fly tomorrow. How far is this true and how far an unfounded rumour?[18]

As hope faded, and rations ran out, the troops appealed to the spirits of Shinto. One soldier wrote, 'We can only wait for aid from the gods ... We may be annihilated.'[19]

The great westward roll of the Australian 18th Brigade, led by the tanks of the 2/6th cavalry and covered by American heavy artillery, ground to a halt at Simemi Creek. How were they to get tanks across a 125-foot log bridge, in which the retreating Yamamoto Shigeaki's men had blown a gaping hole near the approach to the far bank? While the Australians searched for a crossing, American engineers tried to fix the hole, but enemy fire forced them back.

A shallow section of the creek, 400 yards north, was fordable. Australian rifle companies waded over and swooped on the enemy guarding the west bank, who retreated. The engineers then repaired the bridge in peace, and on Christmas Eve the four remaining tanks rumbled onto Old Strip, a mile-long airfield, disused, overgrown and lined with wreckage.

It was heavily defended. All four tanks were knocked out: two by Japanese anti-aircraft guns firing horizontally; the others got bogged down in a bomb crater and swamp.[20]

The troops abandoned the tank cover and ran onto Old Strip, driving the enemy back five hundred yards in the 'bitterest kind of fighting'.[21] American infantry joined the assault. This creeping battle — through swamp and over the airstrip — went on for two days, as if the armies were possessed by demented furies bent on tormenting each other a little longer.

Technology determined the end. When the American howitzer at the Simemi bridge ran out of shells, 25-pound heavy artillery were rolled up to the edge of New Strip. Equipped with armour-piercing projectiles at a range of 1000 yards, the gun tore through the Japanese positions at the far end of the airfield, and took out many of their remaining bunkers.

The battle for the Buna airfields was over. The eastern vicinity of Buna lay in Allied hands. The remaining Japanese, cornered in their foxholes, fought to the last man. The 'mopping up' was ugly in the extreme. Hand grenades tossed into Japanese bunkers were tossed back; Japanese officers came swinging their ceremonial swords through the forest in suicidal charges; snipers scurried up into the canopy — and were shot down; three fell out of a single tree. Many others roamed the jungle, fighting on for weeks.

Chapter 53
Christmas

'Stop any more Xmas hampers coming till we have cleared the position'
— *General Herring to General Blamey, 21 December* 1942

Christmas Eve was a violent night. It poured incessantly. Eichelberger couldn't budge the Japanese at the Triangle, south of Buna Government Station. Many of his men had died in the attempt, and it was the pathos of their deaths that added to the American general's depression.

The black dog had visited Eichelberger often in the past week. He reflected on recent events with near despair. The last bout started a few days previously, when another river blocked his path on the eastern Urbana front: the swift tidal river called Entrance Creek, fordable only by a narrow footbridge. Japanese guns on the opposite bank held the creek and the bridge in their sights.

Heavily weighted Americans troops couldn't swim across. That they were willing to try was an intimation of their new-found courage, tested in circumstances that deeply touched their commander. So many were shot and drowned in the water, Eichelberger ordered the attempt to stop. He decided to try further downstream, at Government Gardens, where the river was shallower and the Japanese presence weaker.

The men needed a rope to drag their boats across, like punts. They were deliberating how best to do this when, on the night of 21 December, an impatient Lieutenant Edward Greene suddenly grabbed the end of a thick rope and, with several of his men, took to the water. He was shot almost instantly, along with others, who drowned. But someone made the opposite bank and secured the rope. All night, under covering fire, the Americans dragged their little dinghies across the river.

Others swam the creek; hundreds gained a foothold on the shore, forced their way into an enclave south of Government Station, and clung on. Meanwhile, the capture of Musita Island, with only slight enemy resistance, opened another flank for the final push to Government Station. Heavy artillery rolled over the little island in readiness for Eichelberger's Christmas Eve onslaught.

The pathetic losses depressed Eichelberger more than the breakthrough cheered him. His men had prevailed. But his scorned troops had tried to swim an unfordable river under fire at night[1] — a nerve-shattering experience even for battle-hardened marines, Eichelberger reflected. On the 22nd their bodies were found bobbing in the stream, and his mind darkened. Depression began to eclipse his judgment.

We can see this thoughtful Teutonic general, in his crew cut and khakis, sitting in his tent clutching his cup of soup, studying his maps and sitreps, his mood swinging between hope and gloom. He expected good news on Christmas Eve. It didn't come. Bad luck, poor reconnaissance, and misadventure dogged his Christmas Eve attack. Once again the Americans were stopped in their tracks, and driven into the mud, with heavy loss. The new commander of Urbana Force, Colonel McCreary, was seriously wounded. Hit in the back by shrapnel, he'd strapped himself to a tree and continued directing his men until he lost consciousness.

Herring was beginning to sound like the chattering monkey on Eichelberger's shoulder. With his usual smugness, and from the safety of Dobodura, he told Blamey: 'Eichelberger's men didn't do very well today, they didn't succeed in taking out the triangle which is a preliminary to a successful attack on the coast ... they found today [it] contained pillboxes ... they should have found this out days ago. Today they rather milled about much to his disgust ...'[2]

In these struggles, the courage of two American sergeants — Elmer Burr and Kenneth Gruennert — deserves a moment's contemplation: Burr saved his unit's commander by smothering a live grenade with his own body, killing himself. Gruennert charged a bunker, blew up the occupants, got wounded, dressed his own wound, refused to withdraw and attacked another bunker with grenades. Enemy snipers then riddled him. Both men won the Congressional Medal of Honor, America's highest award for bravery.

Fraternisation, a brief cease-fire and the singing of hymns have marked Christmas during other wars. On the Western Front in the Great War carols were sung in the trenches; at Gallipoli, a day's peace broke out while the dead were buried. Even at Stalingrad in 1942, the starving German 6th Army sang *Stille Nacht, Heilige Nachte* (Silent Night) in their frozen bunkers.[3]

Not on the Papuan beaches. Only the briefest flicker of recognition of the 1942nd anniversary of Christ's birth interrupted the mayhem. Allied padres did hold services in the rear, with more enthusiasm than hope; soldiers tried to rally something of the memory of Christmases at home. For most, it was another day of slaughter. In fact, on Christmas Day, the war massively intensified at several places along the coast. Both sides launched air, mortar and artillery attacks.

Japanese soldiers vividly described the pounding they received. As Christmas approached, wrote one, 'day after day the number of incoming shells increased greatly. Especially on Christmas Eve ... The stutter of the surrounding machine-guns and the rate of fire increased enormously. In one night alone it must have exceeded 10,000 rounds.'[4]

On or near Christmas, another scrawled: 'As the darkness lifted, yesterday's jungle was no more, and the gaps through which the blue of the sky could be seen had increased tremendously. It would fit the situation to say that the shape of the mountain had changed.'[5]

Holed up at Giruwa, Private Wada Kiyoshi, a signalman, awoke to write: '25th December — Our mess area was blown to bits by enemy artillery fire during the morning ... I suppose the enemy is not having much of a Christmas either. A handful of rice for supper.'[6]

On Boxing Day, he recorded the destruction of a Japanese field hospital: '...terrific artillery fire. The field hospital is the target ... it is certainly a lamentable situation when everyone runs off and not a single person remains to take care of things. Can these men be called soldiers of Japan?'[7]

For their part, the Japanese launched a massive air and mortar barrage on Christmas morning. They meant to demoralise the Allies on their sacred day. The heavy air bombardment awoke Eichelberger at dawn on the Urbana front where he had gone forward to see the state of his troops; he came back severely rattled. That night enemy mortar shells shook his Christmas dinner — a cup of soup — out of his hand.[8]

There were gifts. The Australian troops received a packet of boiled sweets, or a 'table-spoonful each of diced vegies'.[9] The 18th Brigade sardonically applauded their 'sumptuous dinner' of bully beef and army biscuits, their normal fare. Christmas pudding was 'some vile-tasting, lolly-coated Japanese fish balls' salvaged from an enemy bunker.[10]

Some gifts were deeply resented. The few planes that landed at Popondetta on 20–21 December brought Christmas hampers for the Americans, at a time when the Australians were running short of ammunition. Herring politely appealed to Blamey to 'stop any more Xmas hampers coming till we have cleared the position ...'[11]

Elsewhere Christmas was a jolly occasion. At Port Moresby, Blamey and his staff prepared to tuck into a huge turkey; while MacArthur treated his loyal staffers to his favourite: a brace of duck. Blamey invited Herring to fly back for the gang nosh, writing with his usual sensitivity: 'I do not know whether any of you are coming back to eat Xmas dinner with us, but would you let me know ...? [We have] a considerable amount of Xmas fare on hand ... this will include a turkey of about 10 lbs ... It has been in the freezer for some time ...'[12]

It was a very different day for Eichelberger, grimly clutching his cup of soup. The extreme casualty rate, his failure to defeat the enemy, and the sheer wretchedness of the war led him famously to tell MacArthur, on Christmas morning, 'I think the low point of my life occurred yesterday.'[13]

He was wrong. The low point of his life actually occurred at on 28 December. After days of tremendous losses — an entire company were wiped out — Eichelberger learnt that his troops were cut off in enemy territory. The news came in that the men couldn't advance, and were suffering a relapse of severe battle shock.[14] They were trapped somewhere in Government Gardens, beyond Entrance Creek, without relief. Their condition was 'deplorable. The dead had not been buried. [The] wounded, bunched together ...'[15]

'I was thoroughly alarmed,' Eichelberger recalled. 'There was no way to evacuate our units ... I decided to sleep an hour and then go forward. Tossing in my cot, there in the tropical darkness, I remembered my conversation with General MacArthur three weeks before on the verandah at Port Moresby.'[16]

The words, 'take Buna or don't come back alive', were understandably resonant. Buna, Eichelberger feared, would go down as another American military disaster, like the Philippines. He would die with it. At this point he seemed to crack up. The trigger was the utter collapse of another attack from the island, on the 28th. It ended in utter chaos: the bridge adjoining the mainland collapsed, and troops fell into the sea; others simply got lost. Eichelberger 'ranted and raved like a caged lion', observed one colonel. He had indeed reached his nadir, and came very close to being relieved.

But then a remarkable thing happened: there was a startling turnaround. On the morning of the 28th, as yet unknown to Eichelberger, one Major Edmund Schroeder broke through to the US forces in Government Gardens, resupplied them and carried out the wounded. Reinforcements arrived. The effect on morale was inestimable; near lifeless men were reanimated. They turned on the encircling enemy, and secured the Gardens all the way to Entrance Creek. The Japanese in the hitherto impenetrable Triangle were themselves cut off from their northern HQ.

On the 28th, General Adachi, commander in Rabaul, acknowledged the sudden turn of events, and ordered the evacuation of the Triangle, which an American patrol found deserted later that day.

The war crackled on with a terrible momentum of its own. The retreating Japanese — from the west and south — were cornered in the tiny precinct of their HQ at Buna Government Station, with their backs to the sea. Two columns of Allied troops, from the east and south, bore down on them.

It was, in a word, over; but not without a series of last-ditch battles, in which Eichelberger and Wootten — American versus Australian — raced to win the laurels. Lives were expended in this puerile pursuit. On New Year's Eve, for example, Eichelberger issued sudden orders that defied common sense — with disastrous results. Meanwhile Wootten's brigade came crashing along the coast to Giropa Point, sweeping all before them. Wootten eventually prevailed.

At Buna HQ, the naval landing force commander, Colonel Yasuda Yoshitatsu, sent one of his last telegrams to Rabaul at 5.30 a.m. on 28 December: 'Enemy's concentric gunfire keeps destroying our positions one after another; our garrison troops have been continuingly counterattacking ... [but] I have to admit that we will lose Buna probably today or tomorrow. [For] 40 days, both soldiers and civilian employees have made sincere efforts to defend this place ... I pray for the prosperity of the Japanese Empire and everyone's military fortune.'[17]

General Adachi tried to get supplies through from Rabaul by submarine — his only way of eluding Allied air bombardment. This failed, and in their anxiety the dying army threw abuse at the navy: 'You landed the Army without ... food and then cut off the supply. It's like sending someone on a roof and taking away the ladder,' remarked one officer.

Adachi declared that he himself would go to Buna, to lead his troops personally. This was preposterous, roughly equivalent, in the context, to Blamey announcing his intention to charge a bunker field. Adachi's chief of staff, Tsutomu, tried to dissuade him: 'Although one can sympathise with [Adachi's] feelings ... the influence of the GOC would be most important in subsequent operations.'[18] To this, Adachi replied: 'If I don't go, who will save the Buna Detachment? I am not going to look on while my only son is killed in battle.'[19] This unusual softening of severity at the top would only infect the troops, as the illusion of victory faded. Adachi was persuaded to change his mind; his only son died.

The New Year ushered in a final act of desperation. Yamagata, the most senior commander on the Papuan shore, received orders in late December to move along the coast to 'rescue' the Buna garrison. Somehow his very presence — and high rank — would raise the indomitable Japanese spirit. He and his subordinate Colonel Yazawa hatched a plan to evacuate 430 survivors at Buna. They never went. It was too late, and the envelopment, complete. The Allies overran Buna Government Station on New Year's Day.

Yasuda's men — then defending Buna HQ — were ordered to 'retreat from Buna and relocate in Giruwa in order to defend Giruwa district'.[20] The last two telegrams of the Yasuda Naval Landing Force were sent on 29 December 1942: '1515 hours (Outgoing telegram): Four enemy tanks appeared right around the HQ of the Special Landing Force and we are now engaging against them. Now, we are burning up all of the cryptographic documents.' '1710 hours (Outgoing telegram): I am now destroying the communication device.'[21]

Yamamoto and Yasuda — respectively the most senior army and navy officers at Buna, and good friends despite the ill-will between the services — died in a manner befitting Japanese warriors. Theirs were spectacular exits. On New Year's Day, as the Allied armies drew near, the two commanders waited in the Buna HQ bunker with their staff.

In a unique development, the Japanese army and navy — never friends — cooperated closely at Buna. Yamamoto, who succeeded Kusunose as commander of the 144th Regiment, had refused to retreat from Buna. In defiance of orders, he decided to stay with the survivors of Yasuda's Naval Landing Force, who were not allowed to retreat. Then the situation reversed: Yasuda received orders to withdraw and Yamamoto received fresh instructions to stay at Buna until reinforcements arrived (they never did). It was Yasuda's turn to defy orders, and help his friend. So the last army and navy troops at Buna prepared to die together.[22]

Australian grenades were exploding at the northern entrance of their bunker. 'We put a light machine-gun at the entrance and shot the enemy infantry when they tried to come in,' wrote Yamamoto's surgeon. The rest gathered at the south-west entrance. Deep in their surrounded bunker, Yasuda joked to his men, 'I hope we all survive tonight. Because if we die, our families would not be able to celebrate New Year's day from now on.'

They greeted death — now inevitable — as the highest honour. Yamamoto smiled to his men, 'I wish I could eat papaya before I die here.' The unit's surgeon replied, 'Yes sir. Fleshy papaya chilled in the refrigerator would be very nice.'

Yamamoto, who had been wounded on the arm, handed out tobacco and lit the surgeon's cigarette with his healthy arm. The surgeon thanked him: 'Smoking tobacco in the smoke of hand grenades makes you feel better.' Yamamoto replied, 'It will be unnecessary soon.'[23]

A Japanese journalist, Hongo Hiroshi, reported Yasuda's last moments, as told to him by a witness. On 2 January 1943, Yasuda leapt from the bunker with ten men brandishing swords and bayonets, and charged a group of Allied soldiers moving among the palm trees. The witness heard Yasuda's familiar voice shouting, 'Long live the Emperor and the Empire of Japan!!' as he died. 'Then, the enemy ceased fire and the same calmness came back.'[24] Yasuda, who had wanted to study liberal arts at university, received a posthumous promotion to the rank of major-general. [25]

On the same day, Yamamoto emerged from their bunker. He stood with his deputy commander in front of the Australian troops. He shouted, 'Now you are crowing over us. You wasted a great amount of equipment profusely and are about to outmuscle us. But we never wasted a single bullet during the fighting. At some stage, you know Japan will win the war and take over the world! Do not shoot me yet. Long live the Great Empire of Japan! Long live the Emperor! Now, I will show you how Japanese soldiers end their lives. Shoot me.'[26]

Not all the Japanese died fighting. Some fled to Sanananda, and the dreaded Giruwa hospital. A few sick and wounded reached Rabaul on ships that had pulled up at night on the Buna shore, but most did not survive. Suddenly finding themselves safe, a number of the badly wounded 'passed away in their comrades' arms and left their souls for an eternity on Buna Beach . . .'[27]

Hundreds plunged into the sea. All along the coast Japanese troops were seen clinging to boxes and logs, or rowing away in canoes and rafts. Allied machine-guns shot up the surf; Kittyhawks and Wirraways flew in low and strafed the swimming survivors — soon there were none.

The total Allied casualties at Buna were 2817 (excluding the sick) — of whom 620 were killed, 2065 wounded and 132 missing. The American

32nd Division sustained 1954 of these — 353 killed, 1508 wounded and 93 missing. The 18th Brigade lost 267 dead and 557 wounded.

There were some 1400 Japanese troops buried at Buna. Thousands of the sick and wounded died, or killed themselves — the exact number is not known. One Japanese military historian described the Buna defeat as 'the limit of [a] magnificent tragedy'.[28]

There were a handful of prisoners. The Australian forces took one prisoner on 2 January, and eight on New Year's Day, six of whom were Chinese labourers, and technically already prisoners of the Japanese. Chang Yock, 24, a street hawker, had been captured in Hong Kong and employed in Papua carrying timber for bunkers. He accused the Japanese of starving Chinese coolies; he survived by stealing salt and soy sauce.[29]

Blamey and MacArthur received the warmest congratulations from their respective governments, and praised the 'magnificent and prolonged effort' of the troops. The commanders singled out Brigadier Wootten for high decoration, in recognition of his 'soundness and steadiness in control' and 'valour and determination in execution'.

MacArthur personally congratulated Eichelberger. 'Dear Bob,' he wrote, 'I am so glad that you were not injured in the fighting. I always feared that your incessant exposure might result fatally. With a hearty slap on the back, Most cordially, MacArthur.'[30]

The supreme commander later failed to correct the impression that he personally oversaw the victory at Buna, and allowed the idea to percolate that he was somehow involved in a front-line role. An understandably embittered Eichelberger wrote to his wife at the time: 'The great hero went home without seeing Buna before, during or after the fight while permitting press articles from his GHQ to say he was leading his troops in battle.'[31]

Chapter 54
Sanananda

'You will be in action and tomorrow night you might be dead'
— *General Blamey to militia troops on the eve of Sanananda*

The memory of Sanananda lingers in the minds of veterans with the immediacy of a dreadful dream. Singular details — the whiteness of a skull in a village hut; endless mosquitoes; swamp water lapping a gun platform — tend to fix in their memories, and augment the misery of the unsaid, or the unrecalled.

The loss of Sanananda–Giruwa, the main Japanese HQ on the Papuan coast, signalled a larger defeat for the Imperial Army: it was a total moral and spiritual collapse. A raw honesty pervades Japanese diaries during this final maelstrom. The more perceptive troops comprehended the scale of the disaster engulfing them, and charted their own destruction with scorching intensity. Others seemed incapable of comprehending failure, and lapsed into a state of inertia and denial. The unthinkable was happening: the army of the gods was being systematically wiped out for the first time in the Pacific War and, indeed, in Japanese history. There was no reference point in the troops' training for such an event. Men were staggering about without food, and officers abandoning their men and ordering the wounded and sick to fight on.

The high-flown language of General Adachi Hatazo's 'message to the troops' of 26 November horribly demonstrated the gulf between High Command and the men. It had no purchase with the starving ranks on the Papuan beaches: 'The flower of the army and navy,' Adachi declared in a bulletin from Rabaul, 'having organised like iron ... with a spirit like rock, is now trying to smash the offensive power of the US ... It is truly said that the eyes and ears of the world are upon this fight ...What honour you have been given! Isn't this the highest ambition a man can have? ...Now you men with the high fighting spirit! Show the tradition of the glorious Imperial Army in the battlefields ... by a firm unity like iron and stone.'[1]

Sanananda was a bizarre confrontation. The battleground 'looked like a beaded necklace, and was one of the most freakish dispositions of forces in military history'.[2] Picture a raised, narrow road running north–south from Sanananda village, the main Japanese HQ on the coast, to Soputa, a few miles inland, where the Allied armies were massed. Along this road place several Japanese camps, ringed with bunkers and trenches; intersperse these with Australian and American positions, hastily fortified.

A jungle swamp lay on either side of the road, so the camps tended to be on islands of firm ground. At points, the swamp rose and fell with the tide, and the jungle closed around the road like a cowl.

The terrain, wrote a disgusted Lieutenant-Colonel Allchin of the Australian 2/10th Battalion, was 'nothing but dirty, filthy, typhus-ridden jungle and swamp ... walls of green jungle foliage with its drawling roots reaching out into the stagnant pools infested with mosquitoes ...'[3]

Sanananda Road did indeed resemble a necklace or chain, with the difference that the links, instead of connecting, were constantly trying to blow one another apart. Bloody skirmishes flared along the road as patrols tried to reinforce or resupply their troops. To do this they had to creep around enemy camps under the cover of jungle. It was a deadly game of leapfrog. Supplies were hauled up, and wounded carried out, through the trackless swamps on the roadsides. Even by New Guinean logistical standards, it was a unique challenge.

Native carriers were unavailable; they could not work in combat zones, and refused to carry corpses. So the troops acted as stretcher-bearers, carrying the wounded through enemy-held territory. Captain John James spent Christmas Day getting out thirteen wounded, for eight of whom rough stretchers were made. Sometimes the stretchers collapsed, depositing wounded men into the swamp. The harrowing journey exhausted the padre of the 2/7th Cavalry Regiment, Chaplain Francis Hartley, who described the experience:

> Four men were required for each stretcher. These bearers had to
> carry their arms in their free hands ... There were times when, to
> our strained hearing, the noise along the track sounded like a
> herd of elephants crashing through the undergrowth ...
> Whenever there was a stop for rest, armed men would penetrate
> the jungle off the track and watch against a possible ambush.

Around each perimeter the dead served as signposts to approaching stretcher parties. Thus Chaplain Hartley welcomed the gory scene, as he approached the American-held camp called Huggins' roadblock, of 'mangled and rotting Japanese corpses scattered everywhere. Blank-eyed skeletons stared ... from beneath broken shelters. Bones of horses with their saddles and harness rotting around them shone white as the morning sun peering through the creepers caught them in their beams.' It meant that Huggins' was a hundred yards ahead.[4]

The Allied plan was simple: to destroy the southernmost enemy positions around the heavily defended junction of the Sanananda and Killerton tracks; then spread out around Huggins' roadblock, which was halfway to Sanananda village. A great envelopment of the Japanese would ensue, as the Australian and American armies closed on the last enemy bunker fields from the east, west and south. 'Our objective,' noted Blamey, 'is the seizure of the coastal area with the immediate objective of preventing reinforcements landing.'[5]

The ultimate goal was the elimination of every last vestige of the Imperial Army. The Japanese soldier 'has a breaking point,' said Vasey. He ordered 'the complete and utter destruction of the enemy in the Sanananda area at the earliest possible moment'.[6]

Blamey proposed a leaflet drop, for New Year's Day, to give the Japanese 'an opportunity to surrender'.[7] His staff drafted the following:

> To the Japanese Commander –
> Buna has fallen and Gona has fallen. The position held by Japanese troops has been contracted to a small area which is now completely under direct artillery fire from our positions.
> Japanese forces are now isolated and can no longer obtain reinforcements of supplies. Further resistance can only lead to unnecessary bloodshed. To avoid this you are urged to surrender.
> If you are not prepared to accept this invitation . . . I am prepared to allow you to remove your sick and wounded from the area under safe conduct . . .
> If you desire to accept this offer your representatives should proceed southwards on the Sanananda–Soupta [sic] Road starting . . . at 0900 tomorrow morning. The party should be unarmed and should consist of not more than three officers. They should carry a large white flag . . .

Leaflets dropped over Gona and Buna in November had had little effect. It required more than Allied confetti to capture the mind of the world's most indoctrinated army. In any case, MacArthur discouraged the leaflet idea. He bluntly told Blamey:

> I am not in favour of attempting any negotiation with the Japanese in the Sanananda area. If they wish to surrender they are at liberty to initiate such procedure under the customs of war. Their hospitals, if marked, will be carefully respected by our troops. If not marked the responsibilities are theirs. My campaign experience in the Philippines convinces me that it is utterly impossible to negotiate with this enemy and that any attempt to do so will be twisted to our disadvantage. I believe the present operations should go to a definite and positive conclusion unless the enemy initiates unconditional surrender.
> Most cordially, DOUGLAS MACARTHUR[8]

His cordiality was severely strained. Deep friction arose between Blamey and MacArthur in January. It had hit a raw nerve in late December, when MacArthur recommended that a fresh US regiment be sent to relieve the American troops at Buna, and not to Sanananda, as previously agreed.

Blamey refused. Surely it was the Americans' turn to relieve the Australians. The Australians at Sanananda were a skeletal force, many of whom had been driven to fight for almost five months. One battalion had an effective strength of 55, and another 89 (a battalion normally has 1000 men). The militia were on their knees. And the 16th Brigade — veterans of Eora Creek and Gorari — had 198 men left out of an initial strength of 1700; of these, 922 had been evacuated sick,[9] and virtually all of Cullen's battalion were wounded, dead or in hospital.

Bill Jenkins, a sergeant in the 16th Brigade, recalled the sense of careless numbness felt by the men during this final phase of the battle. As he waded through a swamp, he remembered, 'You didn't care what happened to you at that stage, you were so buggered. You didn't care what happened to you. From my battalion of 700 — less than 50 were active.'[10]

Indeed the quality of the Australian troops then fighting at Sanananda was far worse than these statistics suggest. Seriously sick men were being ordered into battle. Hitherto unpublished reports reveal that the 21st Australian Infantry Brigade — veterans of Kokoda, Isurava, Brigade Hill, Ioribaiwa, Gona and now Sanananda — were fighting with temperatures of 104 to 105 degrees Fahrenheit. Those with acute malaria were refused evacuation.

'I have been obliged,' wrote the helpless commander of one battalion,[11] in his 'Most Secret' report, 'to keep men in front line posts for periods up to 3 days with high fever. Some of these men even suffer with hallucinations caused by their fevers and consequent delirium, making them most unreliable and actually a danger to their sub-units ...'[12] He urgently request their relief.

Another top secret dossier revealed that 32 men with chronic malaria and other illnesses had been sent into battle. The authors, Captain Roderick Strang and Major Frank Sublet, recommended their immediate evacuation. 'Already some of the men have died from scrub typhus fever ... The matter is urgent.'[13]

So much for the state of the combined 2/16th and 2/27th Battalion; but during December, three Australian militia battalions[14] were also sent to Sanananda, led by Brigadier Selwyn Porter. Incredibly, one of these was the 39th, veterans of Kokoda, Isurava and Gona. Nothing more poignantly illustrated the despair at the front than this: on 21 December they hobbled up to Huggins' roadblock on the Sanananda Track to relieve an American regiment.

This wasn't relief; it was a case of one group of near-broken men replacing another. Some Australians didn't have boots: they wore bandages around their 'red-raw and white-swollen' feet;[15] all were sick with dysentery or malaria. The Americans were no better off: of the 1400 sent to Sanananda in November, less than 200 men remained 'effective' by mid-December.[16]

Vasey, who'd led the Allied troops for three months — longer than any other commander at the front — noted their pitiful numbers and wretched condition, and ordered the 39th not to attempt 'any large-scale operations'.[17] In this statement of the obvious lay a seam of compassion. Nor did Vasey deserve his new nickname, 'Butcher George'. He openly resisted more frontal assaults, and walked out of at least one officers' meeting in disgust.

Vasey's frustration erupted with a volcanic critique sent to Herring on 24 December, after more failures at the front: 'My experience of the past two months,' he wrote, 'convinces me that for success in jungle warfare, such as is taking place in the Sanananda–Soputa area, the first requisites ... are high morale, a high standard of training, both individual and collective ... and superiority of numbers. I regret to have to report that none of these conditions is present in my command.'[18]

How did they fight? Several militia attacks failed, or dissolved in confusion. One Captain Horace Henderson found himself alone in no-man's-land. He died because 'the remainder of his party left him to the task without aiding him', wrote Porter.[19] The 2/7th Cavalry Regiment fared better, but could not break the Japanese hold on the Sanananda Road.

The affrighted ranks nonetheless threw up extraordinary instances of individual courage. Two cases were exceptional: Captain Henry Cobb, a saddler of Caboolture, Queensland, attempted to crawl along a shallow drain running parallel to the road. The Japanese had this guarded; most of Cobb's men died and he disappeared. The Allies later discovered his body. Mortally wounded, he'd buried his haversack containing valuable maps and documents and then bled to death on top of the burial site.

An undecorated corporal, Ed Connell, a butter grader of the tiny town of Monto, Queensland, was wounded in the open. He yelled at his advancing comrades to leave him alone — in case the Japanese shot them too. But the Australians kept approaching. So Connell 'raised himself from the ground with one last effort to draw the [enemy] fire . . . deliberately threw himself into it and fell dead'.[20]

In a grim echo of the Koitaki factor, the 53rd Battalion[21] was determined to erase the memory of Isurava. What they gave in courage they lacked in experience. After surprising themselves by capturing a Japanese position on the road, they were pushed off it because they seemed unable to use their grenades. Herring blithely remarked: 'This battalion would appear to require still a good deal of training.'[22] Other militia battalions fought with the same untutored courage.

Everyone criticised their lack of training, but no one seemed prepared to do much about it, far less accept responsibility. It was always someone else's job. This was a constant theme throughout this miserable war. Did it vex Herring's conscience that commanders such as he were ultimately responsible for preparing young men for battle? If so, it was too late; the men were dying.

In one day at Sanananda, 7 December, Porter's militia brigade lost 138 killed and wounded, leaving him with an effective strength of 650 (his brigade started at about a third of its normal size). The overall Allied casualty rate soared. Along the Sanananda Road, in December alone, 1932 Australians were removed from battle — dead, wounded or sick. This, from a combined force of about 2500.

Near the end of December, the Australian militiamen at Sanananda were branded 'incapable of offensive action', according to another 'Most Secret' report: 'The trained and resolute leaders have become casualties, and those remaining are not up to the standard of the units.' Seven were arrested 'on charges of cowardice and there were numerous cases in other units'.[23]

Herein lay the blackest farce of Sanananda: severely ill, poorly trained men were threatened with arrest for failing to fight. No top brass were officially indicted for this gross neglect of the troops, the direct result of which was wholesale slaughter, incapacitation and mental collapse.

Consider Brigadier Selwyn Porter. Porter wrote of his own men at Sanananda:

> I regret to report that [the militia] are NOT fit for war under the present conditions ... What success these units achieve ... is due to a percentage of personnel who are brave in the extreme; and, is the result of unskilled aggression. Unfortunately, the latter personnel have been almost exterminated [or] are likely to be exterminated ... The remainder lack confidence in themselves and their weapons, and they lack discipline, due entirely to lack of training and, in some cases, cowardice ...[24]

But Porter was their commander. It was he who nominally led them into battle. It is difficult to conceive of a more disturbing example of unwitting self-incrimination.

Or take Blamey's pep talk to the militia on the eve of Sanananda. The day before they left their Port Moresby barracks, Blamey told the militia units: 'You will be in action and tomorrow night you might be dead.'[25] It was a statement of singular callousness, even by Blamey's vigorous standards. This is not a judgment of today's armchair strategists, or media bleeding hearts. The troops and officers of the time physically recoiled from the man. Colonel Stan Sly described Blamey's remark as a 'shocking theme'[26] with which to send inexperienced troops into battle.

It is intriguing to observe Blamey in his extremity. The Allied land commander undoubtedly had an immense amount on his mind at this time. But his jottings and letters, of which the selection here is merely of rich anecdotal interest, reveal a man at once relaxed and convivial — indeed, one might say, indecently jolly.

He was immensely pleased with himself, of course, and in rude good health, boasting to his brother: 'Even here in this tropical area I find that men ten years younger cannot pace it with me.'[27]

There was Blamey the budding entrepreneur, fascinated by the possibilities of local horticulture. Alerted to a new vegetable strain, he found a colleague's suggestion 're Blue Boiler Pea' very interesting, and the issue of a vegetable after germination 'a new proposal to me'.[28]

And there was the caring Blamey — at least where his mates were concerned. Herring thanked him on 9 January for the delivery of medicated soap and new shoes.

None of these things — Blamey's Christmas turkey, special treats, or fascination with orchids and blue boiler peas — were unreasonable; they certainly weren't illegal. Blamey felt he deserved his perks and saw no reason not to pursue his self-indulgences. Their interest lies in the context. He wrote these snippets — of which there are many examples — during the bloodiest confrontation of the entire campaign. Other commanders, notably Eichelberger and Vasey, were pointedly not self-indulgent or ostentatious. They felt a fellowship of suffering with the troops. Blamey, on the other hand, seemed not to care: a parody of the blundering general, he emerges more Blimpish than Colonel Blimp.

And then he would do something exceptional — such was Blamey's peculiar genius for doing the unexpected. He got the message about the troops' woeful condition, and demanded their immediate relief, forcing MacArthur to back-pedal on the relief of the Americans at Buna. The supreme commander had to mollify his Australian Second-in-Command by saying that his recommendation to send fresh American troops to Buna was advisory only, and not an order. MacArthur did not 'for a moment agree'[29] that he was unduly interfering with land strategy, Blamey's domain. It was agreed: the Americans would go to Sanananda.

And so nearly 4000 fresh soldiers of the 163rd Regiment[30] — well-trained, disciplined combat troops under Colonel Jens Doe — were sent to Soputa, the starting point for the final assault in Papua along the wretched Sanananda Road. On 2 January they were joined by Wootten's 18th Brigade, then thundering along the coast after their victory at Buna. The combined force swung all the strength they had at the last Japanese stronghold by the sea.

Vasey sat and waited for their arrival. He had exhausted his infantry; not a single unit could mount an attack. So a few days of inaction followed, as the American regiment and Wootten's men assembled.

The commanders met on the 4th to hammer out the final plan for the defeat of the Japanese in Papua. Four generals — Vasey, Eichelberger, Herring, and Lieutenant-General Sir Frank Berryman (Eichelberger's chief of staff) — and one brigadier, Wootten, sat around Herring's tent at Dobodura.

They had no accurate estimate of the size of the army they faced, such was the woeful state of intelligence on the enemy: 'we did not know whether there were one thousand Japs at Sanananda or five thousand', wrote Eichelberger soon after the meeting.[31]

They swiftly agreed on a plan. It envisaged a double envelopment of Sanananda village. It was to be a joint American–Australian action, led by the Australian 18th Brigade, supported by MP3 tanks of the 2/6th cavalry, and the American 163rd and 127th infantry regiments — in sum, about 4000 men moving through jungle and swamp.

'New plans were again made to end the ghastly nightmare which the Sanananda affair had become,' the Australian official historian observed. In a striking summary of the campaign, he wrote, 'The primaeval swamps, the dank and silent bush, the heavy loss of life, the fixity of purpose of the Japanese for most of whom death could be the only ending, all combined to make this struggle so appalling that most of the hardened soldiers who were to emerge from it would remember it unwillingly as their most exacting experience of the whole war.'[32]

Chapter 55
Gyokusai

'*Gyokusai*'
— '*A glorious sacrifice for the Emperor*'

'... the only way the Army Commander and his immediate
subordinates could make it all up to the fighting troops and
officers is by committing Hara-Kiri. The stupid fools'
— *Lieutenant Kuroko Toshiro, on the desertion and cowardice of senior
Japanese officers*

In their bunkers on the Papuan shores many of the unquestioning foot
soldiers of the Imperial Army began privately to protest their
predicament. They did not contemplate open mutiny or mass desertion.
But a substantial number criticised, and dared to disobey, their officers.[1] A
sense of defiance, of self-worth, seemed to challenge their military
indoctrination, ironically on the eve of the obliteration of that self-
awakening.

If the Japanese soldier never lost faith in his Emperor, neither was he an
'ignorant automaton' incapable of individual thought. 'He is capable of
criticising what he believes to be erroneous decisions ... misconduct or

dereliction of duty by his superior officers, sometimes in the bitterest terms,' noted Allied intelligence.'[2]

Was the signalman Nada being grateful or sarcastic when he wrote, in early January, 1943: 'Because we succeeded in contacting Rabaul, His Excellency gave us one cigarette each.'[3]

Troops began to wonder why they had shed so much blood for a place of no consequence, at the extremity of the Empire. Rinzo Kanemoto wrote plaintively:

When you look around . . . there is no agriculture. No towns . . . What possible plus can our occupation of such a place offer to our national strength? Yet even given that, here we are, two large groups of white and yellow fighting over the Giruwa area, flinging the fires of war at each other . . . What on earth is all this for? That soldiers . . . had to die so horribly to secure such a completely worthless piece of land! What is the bloody sense of that?[4]

Their greatest complaint at Sanananda and Giruwa was the lack of food, and the perception that officers were being fed while the troops starved. Throughout December and January, hunger, and the greed and cowardice of officers, were recurring themes in Japanese soldiers' diaries.

In January 1943, the rice ration disappeared. Until the end of December, each man had received 300 grams of rice per day; that fell to 30 to 60 grams from 1 to 7 January; and then no rice from 8 to 12 January, according to Lieutenant-Colonel Tanaka.[5] They ate shellfish, coconuts and horsemeat. When they exhausted these, roots and bark, and human flesh — which acquired the nickname 'white pork'.

Morale swiftly collapsed when the food ran out. Arguments flared with officers, who seemed always to be fed. Military order dissolved into 'a snarling scramble for the means of existence'.[6] These were not isolated instances: Borneo, New Britain, Saipan and the Philippines experienced a similar pattern of collapse. The starving men reacted furiously to their sense of abandonment by officers, whose cowardice and greed shed a new light on the sacred myth of Japanese duty and self-discipline. To the abandoned soldier, starving in his bunker, duty seemed a one-way street.

'The indifference and bungling of high commanders,' wrote Lieutenant Kuroko Toshiro, revolted by the failure of the campaign and the desertion of senior officers, 'should be a court-martial offence. Their crimes are worse than desertion, cowardice or running away under fire, but they get off scot-free. If you ask me, the only way the Army Commander and his immediate subordinates could make it all up to the fighting troops and officers is by committing Hara-Kiri. The stupid fools.'[7]

Wada Kiyoshi, an excruciatingly honest private of the 144th Signal Unit, scribbled through his suffering: 'All officers ... eat relatively well. The majority are starving ... the higher officials are not starving. This is indeed a deplorable state of affairs for the Imperial Army.'[8]

In this sense, the officers can be said to have deserted the men at Sanananda.*

The most senior commanders were scorned: Tsukamoto was 'a bawling old buffoon', a crapulent drunk. Lieutenant Watanabe Fukuichi was so disgusted by Yazawa that he told his Allied interrogators, '[Yazawa] had the habit of ordering his troops to advance and hiding himself in a hole like a rat during the action.'[9] The men called him '2nd Class Private Yazawa'.**

For their part, the Japanese commanders severely punished any attempt to retreat. Troops who withdrew without permission were 'sneaking cowards' and should be severely dealt with, instructed Colonel Yokoyama, who shortly evacuated himself without orders.

Even the sick and wounded were ordered to stay at the front. 'Short term casualties were simply carried behind forward positions, to enable them to quickly rejoin their units,' wrote Steve Bullard.[10] Those who withdrew without permission — even the seriously wounded — were severely punished.[11] Illness itself was a disgrace, unworthy of the Japanese soldier. The

---

* Some troops' behaviour became homicidal. One POW despised his superiors because they treated him and his comrades like dogs. During a retreat they buried alive a wounded sergeant major with a reputation for extreme cruelty. Later in the war there were many examples of Japanese troops killing their officers.

** Watanabe was asked to comment on the style and form of an Allied propaganda leaflet; he said the language was too advanced, technical and 'high class' for the average soldier. Asked to write one himself, he declined, not because he thought the act disloyal, but because he felt ill-equipped to cope with a matter of such grave importance.

—

sick were made to feel ashamed of themselves. 'Malaria or diarrheal patients deserting the front line were to be treated as cowards,' instructed the commander of a transport unit.[12]

Desertion, hitherto unthinkable, became a lively option. A disincentive was summary execution under the catch-all Military Criminal Code: 'Notwithstanding the reason or motive the crime will be punished with execution by sword.'[13] Officers whose men deserted were themselves disgraced and severely punished, though usually not executed — they were expected to kill themselves instead.[14]

The Japanese did not desert because they feared fighting. They did so to escape excessive cruelty, or severe hunger. A significant number at Sanananda and Giruwa, unable to take any more, simply staggered towards the Allied lines. Most didn't make it.

Yoshimoto Yoshihiro, eighteen, a first class private in the Yokoyama Advance Force, collapsed with malaria after the retreat across the Owen Stanleys. An officer beat and kicked him where he lay, for 'malingering'.[15] Yoshimoto later said this made him so depressed he got up and walked off. After three days, he surrendered to an Australian camp, and pleaded to be taken prisoner. His Allied dossier states: 'PoW did not want to return to Japan at the end of the war. His presence would shame his folks and the Military Police might even kill him ... PoW said he would like to ... become a citizen of Australia; this was his only wish.'

Another eager deserter was Fusei Iawataro, a labourer, who gave himself up on 3 January. Fusei was 'of extremely short stature ... uneducated but [with] an insatiable curiosity; very talkative and intelligent'. Aged 40, he weighed 93 pounds when captured, and suffered from pleurisy and shell shock. He said that he deserted because he was so disgusted with his treatment at Buna. When he regained his health he grew 'unusually cheerful and co-operative'.[16]

Some resisted the order to fight to the death. One soldier considered this unreasonable; his platoon commander, he said, was the first to disregard it and run. Japan could not win her battles, explained another prisoner, unless 'the men abandoned their suicidal tendencies and the leaders abandoned their heartless attitude towards subordinates'.[17] The irony of an enemy soldier explaining the collapse of the Imperial Japanese Army to Allied interrogators would surely have been lost on his superiors.

Far from the swamps of Sanananda, MacArthur's PR machine fired off a series of victory communiqués. MacArthur's bid for immortality demanded no less. On 8 January, four days before the thrust to the beach, MacArthur returned to Brisbane, having satisfied himself that the job was done. His order of the day issued Distinguished Service Crosses to, among others, Blamey, Vasey, Eichelberger, Sutherland, Willoughby, Eather and Wootten. He thanked 'Almighty God' for His guidance 'which has brought us this success in our great crusade'.[18]

At the same time he issued one of his most fatuous communiqués, declaring, 'One of the primary objects of the campaign was the annihilation of the Japanese Papuan Army ... This can now be regarded as accomplished.'[19]

By now, Doug's communiqués enjoyed the status of a black joke. The Australian officers were wearily familiar with his exaggerated and mendacious interpretation of events. MacArthur's self-serving nonsense — his dismissal of the battle for Sanananda, in the first week of January, as a 'mopping up' operation — was grotesque.*

The battle for Sanananda–Giruwa lasted ten weeks — until the last week of January — and resulted in 2186 Allied soldiers killed or wounded, and 1600 Japanese dead (the number wounded is unknown).[20] Both Blamey and Herring saw Sanananda as the most vital Japanese stronghold, with a deep defence extending well inland. Eichelberger described the fight as 'a completely savage and expensive battle ... siege warfare [of] the bitterest and most punishing kind'.[21] The fatality rate — in percentage terms — approached the heaviest of the American Civil War. Neither side, as a general rule, took prisoners — with the exception, on the Allied side, of a few Japanese stragglers, who lacked the strength or weapons to kill themselves. The battle had to be fought until there was 'not one Japanese left who was capable of lifting a rifle'.[22] The premature announcement of victory, on 8 January, infuriated Eichelberger. It cheapened the duty of thousands of Australian and American troops who were about to give their lives or limbs in battle.

* Eisenhower later told a group of American New Guinea veterans that he'd never heard of Sanananda, because MacArthur always described it as 'mopping up'.

On 12 January the last battle for Papua convulsed the Sanananda beachhead. Wootten planned to ram a passage along the central Sanananda Track; his 18th Brigade would attack on both flanks, and an American regiment, from the west, at Tarakena.

Wootten's men, reinforced with 1000 fresh troops flown in from Australia, marched off at a minute past eight behind three Australian light tanks, which rumbled out of the low mist in single file and headed straight for the Japanese bunkers at Killerton junction. The road was a 'narrow defile through the swamps, the ground flanking its raised surface so soft that no tank could travel on it'.[23] It seemed no tank could U-turn once it entered the battlefield.

The tank crews were commanded, in order of their departure, by the Australians Lieutenant D.A. Heap, Corporal Charles Boughton and Sergeant Ken MacGregor. All were assured the Japanese did not possess anti-tank weapons. They were misinformed. Anti-tank guns fired on all three. Heap's tank was forced into the jungle; Boughton's was ripped apart, though a lance corporal managed an astonishing U-turn, and got the tank back to safety. A fireball engulfed MacGregor's. Japanese suicide squads leapt on the tanks as they rumbled forward, and tried to drop grenades and Molotov cocktails down the turrets.[24]

The infantry, trotting along behind, fared little better. One battalion[25] scarcely made any ground for the loss of 99 men. Six officers including two company commanders (Lieutenant George Jackson and Lieutenant Paul Lloyd) were killed in the attempt to destroy the enemy at Killerton junction, whose bunkers resembled squat humpies laden with vegetation, in which the tiny firing slit was virtually indiscernible.

The apparent failure of the tank charge provoked sharp disagreement at Vasey's HQ. Berryman (Eichelberger's chief of staff) resurrected the worn idea of blockading the Japanese and starving them into submission. Eichelberger conditionally agreed. The meeting ended with Eichelberger favouring another frontal charge, at which Vasey stormed out, 'stating that he would not be party to further murder'.[26] Another stalemate ensued.

The Japanese resolved the disagreement. On 12 January Colonel Tsukamoto — still slurping *sake*, no doubt — ordered the evacuation of the Killerton–Sanananda Road junction. He did so without official authority from Rabaul. His supply lines were wrecked; and his few remaining bunkers unsupportable. His men were shaken by the Australian attack and utterly exhausted — it seemed the Australian charge had been more effective than Vasey realised.

Worse, Tsukamoto had been abandoned by the entire Takenaka Company, who defied the gruff old man's orders to stay and fight. Impossibly outnumbered, and staring down the barrels of Allied tanks, he pre-empted the evacuation order. 'Had he not done that, his men would have been wiped out,' said Shimada. 'If Tsukamoto hadn't give order [sic], his men had no doubt that they would execute a final charge into the enemy and die.'[27]

In this highly unusual case, Tsukamoto withdrew his men to the coast without authority. He saved their lives — but was later scorned by some in Japan for not laying them down.

That day, the remarkable Major-General Oda Kensaku landed at Giruwa, having travelled along the coast from the Kumusi. A powerful spirit with a high-minded sense of duty, Oda was determined to save the coastal garrison and give not an inch to the Allies.[28] He marshalled the surviving soldiers of the Nankai Shitai, whose shocking state deeply disturbed him. Reinforcements here, he realised, were mere cannon fodder, sacrificed as part of a delaying strategy to buy time for the illusory reconquest of Guadalcanal. If Oda tilted at windmills, he did so in the spirit of a true samurai.

In fact, the imperial edifice was crumbling around him. On 17 January Colonel Yokoyama — commander of the first landing party at Gona on 21 July — retreated with 50 troops, also without permission. Oda was furious, and ordered Yokoyama to return to the front. Yokoyama ignored the order, and boarded the boat intended for the evacuation of another commander, Yamagata, to the latter's fury.★ When Oda realised that Yamagata, the most senior commander on the coast, had also evacuated Giruwa without permission, he declared, 'I have been betrayed by Yamagata!'[29]

★ In 1959 Yokoyama was asked to explain his decision to retreat without orders: 'On 17 January,' he said, 'the artillery attack became more severe … we tried to attack, but there were only about ten of us who were mobile … I had a high fever of forty degrees … In front of my men I had to crawl into the sea and stay in the water for about thirty minutes with diarrhoea. On the evening of 17 January … the artillery attacks became more incessant. Thunder and lightning brought drenching rain. Our fox holes were filled with water and there was no boundary between the sea and the ground.' (See *The Human Face of War — Unauthorised Retreat from Buna?* Australia–Japan Research project, AWM.)

Apparently isolated, consumed by a growing sense of abandonment, Oda wired Rabaul pleading for reinforcements. Most of his men were 'without food and too weak for hand-to-hand fighting ... Starvation is taking many lives ... We are doomed.'[30]

'Our duty,' he declared from his battered bunker, 'will have been accomplished if we fight and lay down our lives here on the field.' But that would mean losing 'our eastern foothold in New Guinea ... the sacrifices of our fellow soldiers during the past six months will have been in vain'.[31] For their sake, Oda demanded that reinforcements be landed at once.

Rabaul refused. On the 12th, Adachi gave permission for Yamagata to prepare for a general evacuation — scheduled for 25 January — to the mouths of the Kumusi and Mambare rivers, some fifty miles west of Sanananda, where motor launches would be ready. Adachi personally conceived the plan. To get there, thousands of Japanese troops would have to slip through Australian-held territory, at Gona.

The Allies first heard of the evacuation order from a sick Japanese soldier captured on the 14th. Vasey acted immediately. He sent Wootten's brigade crashing up the Sanananda Road to the Killerton Junction. It was indeed deserted. 'The bugger's gone,' Vasey told Eichelberger.

The Allied commanders seized the opportunity. Wootten struck out along the Killerton Track to the west, the American regiments charged up the coast from the east, and along the Sanananda Road in the centre. Incredibly, the survivors of the 39th Battalion were still busy mopping up in the rear and protecting the supply lines.

'Today, all is optimism,' Eichelberger told MacArthur. 'Vasey, from pessimism, has changed 100 per cent.'[32] Normally a hugely cheerful man, Vasey's dark moods were the consequence of months of immense pressure. And he had malaria.

The approach to Cape Killerton was an abomination. The track simply disappeared into shoulder-deep mangrove swamps. At dawn on the 16th the men waded in; one Australian officer recalled: 'Sometimes the water was over our heads, most times up to our armpits. Our rate of progress was about 100 yards an hour.'[33] They camped in the branches of mangroves, 'perched in the trees like wet fowls'.[34] All the stores, weapons and ammunition were handed over their heads, in a human chain.

On firmer ground, they found a little track running along the shore to Killerton village. Here the Australians shot a group of sunbathing Japanese soldiers, who had not expected an attack from this direction.

Ahead, forward Australian patrols[35] claim to have encountered a remarkable example of Japanese pride in their national standard. Though purely anecdotal, it has a ring of truth, given the ample evidence of Japanese protectiveness towards regimental and national colours. Sprawling across the beach was a large, dead tree; suddenly a Japanese soldier jumped out and hung a Rising Sun flag on a limb, then ducked back behind the tree with a 'defiant yell'.[36] The Australians riddled the flag, and when it fluttered onto the sand another Japanese soldier jumped out, grabbed the flag, and hung it back on the limb. He was shot. Then another soldier leapt out, and raised the flag — he too was shot. 'The grim game of up-flag, down-flag went on for several minutes', until a pile of corpses remained, and no flag.[37]

Resistance at Killerton collapsed. On the 16th Wootten unleashed the broad, westward sweep of the Sanananda area; his three battalions fanned out through swamp and jungle; to the east and south Colonels Doe and George Elms reduced the remaining inland bunkers, and advanced up the road towards the beach. The last Japanese beads in the necklace fell away, and only coastal resistance remained.

The last days of Sanananda entered the realm of the diabolical. A spectacular tropical storm deluged the coast on the night of the 16th. It was fittingly biblical. The black clouds amassed and lowered over the jungle, 'so close that a man reaching out and trying to touch them would not be regarded as in the throes of a malarial nightmare'.[38] Telephone wires were deemed useless.[39]

The rain fell steadily in heavy, monsoonal sheets all night. Twelve inches of rain fell. Water filled the bunkers and trenches. The swamps spilled their banks, rose about the mangrove roots and lapped at the boards on which Allied troops sat. Bloated, waterborne corpses were commonplace. They nudged amidst the mangroves with a ghastly gregariousness. Near the beaches the swamp and tide — whipped up by the wind — merged into a stew of abandoned supplies, palm leaves and human detritus.

During the night two companies of the Australian 2/12th Battalion clung to a narrowing spit of sand between the rising tide and the encroaching swamp — just to the east of Sanananda village. 'The sentries stood waist deep in water looking out into the black void ahead; huddled in their capes but with rifles always ready.'[40] At one point they mistook dozens of bobbing coconuts for Japanese heads; at other times, the coconuts came to life, as Japanese soldiers swam from their bunkers just a few hundred yards away.

With daylight, the storm ceased as if 'cut off by a switch': 'What a scene the early sun revealed,' observed Lieutenant-Colonel Allchin. 'The jungle dripped like a leaking faucet. The sea had cohabited long enough with the swamp, leaving in its wake a trail of dirty foam, wind-wrecked palms, and coconuts strewn along the beach. Bodies of dead sprawling in the reeking undergrowth, rolled with the receding tide ... The battle of the elements over, the battle of the humans ... resumed.'[41]

That day one of Wootten's battalions,[42] under Major William Parry-Okeden, reached the threshold of an undefended section of Sanananda village. They approached via a particularly deep stretch of swamp, which Wootten accurately thought the Japanese would consider an adequate natural barrier; as he expected, it was left undefended.

The Australians waded in, waited for most of the night in the swamp, then attacked at dawn on the 17th. The remnant of the enemy, utterly surprised, offered little resistance, and Sanananda fell that morning — not with a bang but a whimper.

Two Australian battalions[43] encircled a last knoll of Japanese resistance, just inland from Sanananda village. The monsoonal rain and rising swamp water made this push perhaps the most loathsome experience of the campaign. Between 50 and 60 Australians were killed or wounded each day, from 17 to 21 January. On the last day, Lieutenant-Colonel Arthur Arnold, commander of the 2/12th Battalion, 'rang down the curtain' over this 'scene of mud, filth and death'.[44] A prisoner divulged that only the sick and wounded were left — the rest had fled westwards. Arnold's men waded in, through waist-deep swamp, to the island of the dead: 100 Japanese troops fell, 'while swollen and discoloured corpses' of those previously killed 'bumped against them in the swamp water or protruded from the obscene mud'.[45]

The sight sickened Arnold, who wrote with a mixture of morbid fascination and disgust: 'the whole area, swamps and rivers included, are covered with enemy dead and the stench from which is overpowering. It is definitely the filthiest area I have ever set eyes upon. In a great many cases the Japanese bodies are fly-blown and others have been reduced almost to skeletons.'[46]

The Australians reunited with Colonel Doe's American regiment advancing up the Sanananda Road. On 22 January, Doe fought the last battle of the campaign, in which dozens of Japanese troops were slaughtered in the swamp as they tried to escape west, leaving only 'several skeletons walking around' the battlefield.

Of the Japanese survivors, 1200 sick and wounded were evacuated by sea between 13 and 20 January, and about a thousand escaped overland to the west of Gona. More than a thousand fled east — away from their supposed evacuation point — into the tropical ghetto of Giruwa, nominally the main Japanese hospital. It was, on the contrary, the closest thing to hell on earth.

The cornered Imperial Army awaited evacuation on the beach. With Sanananda 'collapsing about his ears',[47] Major-General Yamagata brought forward his evacuation orders from 25 to 20 January, and handed over new orders, in sealed envelopes, to the two remaining commanders: Yazawa, in charge of the coast east of Giruwa; and Oda, commanding west of the village. They were instructed not to open their envelopes until 4.00 p.m. on 19 January.

Yamagata then escaped by barge, at 9.30 that night, with his staff. They reached the Kumusi mouth under heavy bombardment. There are several accounts of his notorious flight. In one version, the sick and wounded crawled to the beach and tried to board his boat. Yamagata's men allegedly threw them in the sea, or abandoned them on the beach, thus securing their commander's safety.

A prisoner who witnessed the general's flight corroborated this: 'When Major-General Yamagata fled ... an attempt was made to evacuate some stretcher cases, but the Major-General ordered this to be stopped and [he] pushed off leaving the wounded on the beach.'[48]

The Australians entered the smouldering village of Sanananda on 22 January. They found signs of organised cannibalism. Human flesh, it seemed, had become part of the Japanese soldier's regular diet. At Giruwa, too, anthropophagy appeared to be routine, confirming Tanaka Yuki's view that cannibalism was sanctioned by the inaction of Japanese commanders. 'We saw little billy tins of human flesh at Sanananda,'[49] reported Colonel Stan Sly of the 55/53rd Battalion. Asked why he thought the meat was human, Sly replied: 'Ohh Well! We were certain there was no other fresh meat around . . . it was just straight out human flesh. I couldn't say that the rest of the body was there.'[50]

The explosive feelings of the Australians can be imagined. When the 18th Brigade found the mutilated corpses of men from their own unit — with the flesh stripped off and wrapped in leaves in tin dixies — they resolved to wipe out every Japanese soldier. The discovery reconfirmed the no-prisoner policy. One officer wrote later, 'This incident sealed the fate of any Japanese we came across. General Vasey was determined that no Japanese should escape from the Sanananda area, and a plan was put into operation that would seal them in and then eliminate them.'[51]

Japanese diaries tell the extraordinary chapter of the final days. In one case, seven troops divided a can of sardines among them; all the horses were consumed; and the rice exhausted. For four days — 8 to 12 January — they ate nothing. The commanders of the last survivors at Sanananda told Rabaul on 12 January that the men were too weak to fight and many were dying of starvation: 'We will be doomed in a few days,' wrote Oda. 'For . . . two months, the men [have been] standing in the flooded and filthy trenches.'[52]

The most famous account of the end of the Nankai Shitai was that of starving signalman, Wada Kiyoshi, whose diary was found floating on a raft and handed over to the Allied forces. 'So it was not surprising that they thought I was dead,' Wada later wrote.[53]

This is the diary of a young soldier on the edge of life — Wada had malaria, dysentery and could barely move — yet somehow he remained sentient, and preserved a basic sense of humanity. His mind conjured soaring appeals to the divine, and reverted as quickly to thoughts of his most basic animal needs (he wrote, for example, 'Caught six crabs and ate them raw'). He guiltily admits to nibbling on friends' rations, although the impression that emerges is of a loyal, selfless, highly articulate young man, deeply concerned about his fellow troops. He was remarkably human:

'Do not lose hope,' Wada tells himself on 21 December. 'Do not forget to be grateful. The foundation for all is based upon military spirit. Loyalty is judged by this.'

22 Dec: I am getting a little better. This must be due to the grateful aid of the gods ... Horita has died. I respectfully pray for his peace and happiness ... I took out the picture of mother and father and thought about home, and I prayed that they may be well.

24 Dec: Seems that there will be no rice today. Supper — coconut, octopus. No rice. Ate snakes.

27 Dec: The enemy shelling from last night was very severe. Since Hagino [Wada's dying friend] is all alone, I cannot very well leave him behind. When shells fall all around us he grits his teeth and bears it ... It is not right to leave wounded comrades behind.

28 Dec: Even though I know we are members of the Imperial Army, there are times when things look very black. I must do my best to the last with the noble spirit of dying for the Emperor ... I could not treat Hagino sufficiently this morning ... Everyone has taken cover in the jungle, but since there is no one to carry and take care of Hagino, I cannot leave him behind.

29 Dec: What a discouraging and miserable state of affairs ... the hospital is in a horrible plight. What is going to happen to us? I pray to the morning sun that our battle situation be reversed. The [hospital] patrol unit has fled and there are only four of us; the platoon leader, Nakano, Hagino and myself. There isn't a single person who will come to help ... I pray only for divine aid.

1 Jan: I greeted the New Year. I spent the last days of 1942 in the jungle amidst bursting shells. I greeted the New Year in the

same way. Received 1 Go of rice ... New Year's Day ended with me still being alive, although with an empty stomach. Prayed for mother's and father's health.

3 Jan: Since eating yesterday's rice I haven't had a single grain to eat. On top of that I had malaria fever last night. I get dizzy when I stand. I must not weaken. I must get well somehow.

4 Jan: Terrific shelling again last night ... I can't nurse Hagino and Kinoshita sufficiently ... forgive me for my body is exhausted.

6 Jan: I dream that I am home every night. When I wake up and realise that I am in the jungle it is exceedingly disagreeable.

7 Jan: We live on borrowed time, but it is a wonder that I can go on living without eating. Our planes do not come over. There are no good stories to tell ... I know I should go to Hagino but I can't. Please forgive me. Wet through from the rain. The three of us made a bed and slept under a coconut tree. No strength left. To do an hour's work requires a whole day.

8 Jan: Died, Hagino Mitsuo. It is regrettable. I did what I could. Please forgive me.

10 Jan: Enemy shelling and bombing everyday. It is about time that we received divine aid. Starvation is a terrible thing. It seems all the grass and roots have already been eaten in the Giruwa area.

11 Jan: Enemy shelling becomes increasingly intense. While I think quietly I feel discouraged and wretched ... But I am a member of the Imperial Army! I will live proudly to the last. If I am to believe General Oda's instructions, the situation should gradually be turning in our favour by now.

12 Jan: It is difficult to control evil thoughts when alone, especially when the rice bag is left by my side when I am so starved. I ate into Kinoshita's and Okasaki's rice rations. Ate the rice raw ... I am a weak character! I am troubled. I am troubled ... Wish I had a thousand yen and could buy a lot of rice.

16 Jan: For the first time in a long while I slept ... on dry ground in the jungle ... I spent a restful night. Fierce rifle fire was heard from the front lines. Stray bullets whizz overhead.

[Wada is sent to the rear to prepare for evacuation.]

17 Jan: We think tonight will be the last night for Giruwa and we talk about swimming together to Lae. We talked about such things. Fortunately the day dawned.

18 Jan: We looked forward to getting on the boat tonight but because the wounded were put on first, we could not get on. It is regrettable. Reinforcements haven't come. There are no provisions. Things are happening just as the enemy says ... I don't think Wakaichi will leave us behind.[54]

Chapter 56
Self-immolation

'I have decided to destroy myself on April 18, 1943, at nine
o'clock somewhere in New Guinea'
— *Nishio Shiro, 33, a doctor and medical captain, to his wife, Mineko*

At the designated time — 4.00 p.m. on 19 January — Major-General
Oda opened his sealed envelope. The last commander of the 144th
Regiment read his new orders. To his shame and disgust, he was to retreat,
and evacuate the men. He felt keenly this stab of betrayal by the Imperial
Army, chiefly Yamagata, whom he accused of abandoning the troops.

Oda was an honourable man — within the strict remit of the Japanese
martial tradition. He subscribed to the warrior code of 'never surrender'. His
memory is revered in Japan — at least among the few who revere war
heroes. 'The strength of the Imperial Army,' Oda famously said, 'is based on
the soldiers' trust of commanders. If I betray that trust, I would not be able
to put my head up before the families of spirits of the war dead.'[1]

On the Papuan beaches Oda lived, and died, according to this personal
rescript. On 19 January he found himself walking through the wreckage of
his army. He'd pressed Rabaul for reinforcements; none had come. The
ignominy of retreat left him only one alternative.

On the 20th — 'X-Day' — he dutifully ordered the general evacuation from Giruwa westwards to Bakunbari, at the mouth of Kumusi River. The withdrawal commenced at 8.00 p.m. and continued through the night. Sixty rounds of machine-gun fire signalled the start.[2]

'At 2000 hours, all units assembled,' one witness recalled. 'Since afternoon, rain had been falling and this continued into the night. This heavy rain deadened the sound of our footsteps and any other noise that we made; furthermore it concealed our attempts to get away.'[3]

The sick and wounded assembled on the beach near Giruwa in the bleak hope of being evacuated. When a few landing barges arrived, the mud and sand seemed to come alive with prostrate forms, scrambling for a place. The stretcher cases or those too weak to walk were abandoned where they lay, and were expected to commit suicide.

'The confusion on the faces of the more serious cases, when told they had to stay behind, indicated their strong desire to live,'[4] reported one Japanese witness. It was a fleeting hope. Most shot themselves — or were shot in their stretchers by obliging troops. The severely wounded were given a grenade each — it was easier to pull a pin than lift a revolver.

A few pathetic cases summoned the strength to fight. 'I cannot even get up and walk,' wrote one very sick soldier. 'I picked up my pistol. Loaded it, and determined to fight the enemy even if I had to do it sitting in that hospital.'[5]

Ohara Kizuchi, a wounded prisoner who'd bitterly watched the officers abandon the sick and wounded, 'cried freely' when describing the sight to his Australian interrogators.[6]

Oda had fulfilled his hated orders, and waited as the last units departed Giruwa into the jungle. Nothing could be done for the stretcher cases, and he visited the men in the Giruwa field hospital for the last time.

'That's the end of that. I'm going to smoke one cigarette,' he told Private Fukuoka Shigeji. He handed Fukuoka all his property, including food and cigarettes, and told him to follow the retreat.

As he smoked, Oda's executive officer, Lieutenant-Colonel Tomita Yoshinobu, asked him what he would do. The major-general answered, 'Of course, I will stay with those wounded men here.'

Tomita replied, 'Then, I will stay with you here, too, sir.'[7]

After the last of the walking wounded were gone, Oda embraced Tomita, laid a cloth on the beach, bowed in the direction of Japan, put a pistol to his head and shot himself. Tomita repeated this performance.

Fukuoka★ heard the pistol shots, returned and saw his commander's body 'lying on a cloak spread out on the ground'.[8] Oda had committed suicide because 'things had shown him he must die', concluded Yoshihara Tsutomu, chief of staff of the 18th Army. 'This sublime conception of duty was the ideal representative of an officer and warrior.'[9]

Oda had always accused Yamagata of betrayal, of abandoning the wounded and refusing to kill himself — the only honourable course for a defeated Japanese officer.

'Under Japanese military custom, Yamagata should have stayed with the men until the end,'[10] said Nishimura Kokichi, the 144th Regiment soldier who returned to New Guinea many times after the war to retrieve the bones of missing soldiers. Yamagata's reputation plunged among the troops, but his actions did not inhibit promotion: after he escaped Papua, he became commander of the 26th Division and died at Leyte Island in the Philippines in February 1945.

In Japanese eyes, Oda's death was exemplary. As the Allies closed in, dozens of officers expired in similar circumstances on the Papuan beaches. Soldiers, too, played out this ritual self-sacrifice that would claim many thousands of Japanese lives in coming months. Many quietly died, like Oda, by their own hand; others gave their lives more usefully — as Kamikaze pilots or human torpedoes, in the later Pacific battles.

Corporal Tanaka died in a suicide squad. His last written words to his unit, the Kusunose Tai, were not encouraging: 'It is now merely a case of waiting for death. Most of the officers have been killed ... The garrison of about 600 has been reduced to 200. . . Sgt Yoshikawa had a stomach ache and went to the toilet 50 times and is very weary. We have not eaten for over a week and have no energy. As soldiers we are ready to die gallantly. Take care

★ Fukuoka Shigeji witnessed the deaths of the first and last commanders of the South Sea Detachment — he was with Horii Tomitaro when he died at sea. Fukuoka survived the war, and lived just down the road from Imanishi in Motoyama-Town.

of yourself and do your best. Excuse my hasty writing. Corp Tanaka.'[11] And off he went.

Younger Japanese were prone to melodramatic exits. The ecstatic quality of the act of self-immolation is captured in one young soldier's diary, in December 1942:

At the time I left my fatherland I pledged that I would never again during this life see the mountains and rivers of my country. But it was 22 November when I resolved to become the soil of Basabua. When I prayed for the eternal life of the Emperor, to my fatherland deities and Buddha, and when I prayed thanks to my parents, wife, brother and sister I felt a high-spirited courage inside of me. It is my great pleasure to die at Basabua. Parents! Wife! Brother and Sister! I have fought with all my strength . . . but now my fighting strength is weakened and I am about to expose my dead body on the seashore of Basabua. My comrades have already died, though my heart is filled with joy because I can become the guardian spirit of my country. I will fight and crush the enemy. I will protect the seashore of Basabua forever.[12]

Few committed *hara-kiri* — perhaps there wasn't time, or they lacked the requisite ceremonial daggers. A bayonet, it seemed, wouldn't do. Or men clung together around grenades and pulled the pins; others shot or obliterated themselves in native huts. Occasionally they tried to blow up their Allied captors, who had to 'root out' the enemy from every trench and bunker.[13] Instead of accepting Allied medical help, a Japanese prisoner nursing a shattered arm pulled the pin of a grenade and tried to kill his Australian doctors as well as himself. Such acts partly explain why so few prisoners were taken. The Australians killed them, often after they had surrendered or been captured, as Major-General Cullen and others confirm.

An Australian patrol gave a trapped Japanese officer until the count of ten to surrender. Ignoring the demand, he bowed three times to the sun, stood to attention and raised a small Japanese flag with his sword. At the sound of 'nine' he shouted 'Out', and was riddled with bullets. Similarly,

Sergeant Lew Scott of the 55/53rd Battalion witnessed a high-ranking Japanese officer die: 'He lifted his head, tried to smile, slowly attempted a salute and ... picked up his pistol ... He placed it ever so carefully to his temple, paused to nod in my direction, and pressed the trigger.'

Many seemed over-eager to kill themselves, and had to be restrained until the right time. The Buna army commander Yamamoto received reports that ten men had survived an Allied attack, and had fought on under Major Kenmotsu, who said he would defend his position to the death. Yamamoto replied via a runner: 'Kenmotsu's death is not permitted yet. He must return to here. This is an order.'[14]

And there were officers abandoned by their men, such as Lieutenant-Colonel Hozumi, commander of the Mountain Artillery Battalion, who collapsed with acute diarrhoea and couldn't go on. When his subordinates refused to help him, he shot himself.[15] Many officers died in similar circumstances.

What became of the Nankai Shitai? The frail, sick old soldier who stood silently in a corner of Asakura Station, Shikoku, in December 1943, watching the caskets of the war dead come home, was Colonel Kusunose Masao, who had led the 144th Regiment against the Australians on the Kokoda Track. Kusunose had fallen seriously ill in Papua and famously issued orders from a stretcher as his troops carried him over the Owen Stanleys. He was later repatriated — and tended to linger near the station watching the ashes of comrades come home.

In December 1945, Allied Occupation Forces summoned Kusunose to testify before the war crimes hearings. Kusunose refused. He walked into a forest on the side of Mount Fuji and, in the freezing winter, starved himself to death — an act of empathy, it seems, with the fate of so many of his troops. In a suicide note he wrote that, as an imperial military officer, he would not accept 'victors' justice'.[16]

Kusunose was deeply mourned. One Japanese soldier, who worked for him for five years, said he never heard him yelling at anyone. 'Colonel Kusunose is a warm-hearted commander.' This became a widely accepted belief among the 144th Regiment in Asakura.[17] 'He never let his men die in vain ... He was the best commander I have ever known,'[18] said Nishimura.

Very few of the Nankai Shitai came home — estimates suggest only 5 per cent of the original 13,000 survived. Only 140 of the 3500 men in Kochi's 144th Regiment returned to Japan after the war.[19]

Warrant Officer Shimada Yuki survived — his last act, he remembers, was to help Private Ôno Nobuyuki, who was badly wounded in the leg during the evacuation of Giruwa. Shimada stayed behind and kept encouraging Ôno during the long march through the jungle to the Kumusi delta. They made it on 28 January and joined a boat to Rabaul. Shimada now lives in Kochi City.

The naked Imanishi survived the raft journey down the Kumusi, scavenged a uniform from a corpse, and fought on at Buna and Giruwa. He refused several offers to evacuate. 'We do not have orders to retreat!'[20] he told friends preparing to escape by barge. He finally withdrew when ordered — he said he felt 'released'[21] — reached the Kumusi and returned to Japan. He became the mayor of Motoyama, a Kochi village where several 144th veterans lived, including Wada and Oda's staffer, Fukuoka.

Some prisoners pleaded for their captors to kill them.* When Lieutenant Inagaki Riichi, 27, a naval paymaster, decided to give himself up at Giruwa, he walked into the Australian lines shouting, 'Shoot me! Shoot me!' One prisoner 'wept with frustration and humiliation' because his Australian guards would not shoot him, according to an account in Johnston's *Fighting the Enemy*. When he bared his chest, an Australian soldier said, 'You stupid bastard, you don't know when you're well off!'

The case of Naka Masao symbolised the self-inflicted destruction of the Japanese army. Naka, a second lieutenant in the 41st Infantry Regiment, was captured near Giruwa on 27 January. Aged 24 and five feet high, he weighed 115 pounds in captivity. His war record tolls out the names of imperial conquest: he'd fought in China, at Nanking and Shanghai; in Malaya, at the

---

* Many Japanese troops committed suicide because they were led to believe they would suffer a barbarous death at Allied hands. In one survey, of POWs, 85 per cent said they had expected torture or execution by their captors. One prisoner quoted the story — for which there is no evidence — of ten Japanese POWs buried in sand up to their necks and then killed by a tank running over them. Japanese prisoners at Finschhafen, and as far north as Alaska, had heard this story (ATIS Research Reports).

fall of Singapore; in Rabaul and New Guinea. His unit had relieved the Kusunose Butai at Ioribaiwa, only to face the mountain retreat.

A member of the Imperial Army's elite, a product of years of martial training, Naka was found lying in the jungle with severe malaria, barely conscious and unable to walk. He had lost his platoon. He lacked the strength to kill himself. Three times during interrogation he formally asked the Australians to kill him, or permit him to kill himself. He repeatedly requested a revolver. He rated New Guinea the worst campaign of his experience.[22]

Some chose life. The deeply rooted human desire to live sometimes conquered — at the critical moment — the Japanese soldier's compulsion to destroy himself.

There were groups of Japanese who surrendered. One unit, led by an English-speaking officer, marched out of their bunkers in an appalling state. The Americans and Australians were amazed that such men, having fought so bitterly, and for so long, were suddenly willing to give themselves up.

'He never wanted to kill himself, and knew of no one who honestly did,' remarked Allied interrogators of one POW. 'He hated war and wanted to live,'[23] they said of another, who had clung to a shipwreck after failing to drown himself with his fellow troops. Apparently he objected to having a loin cloth rammed down his throat.

One soldier simply threw away his rifle and lay down in the long grass. He had a grenade with him when captured, but decided that suicide would be 'foolish'.[24]

Certainly some Japanese troops who were taken prisoner were surprised by their treatment in Allied hands. They presumed they would be tortured or killed; instead they were fed and generally treated in accordance with international law. 'Had he known previous to capture that he would not be killed but accorded good treatment he would have … surrendered at the first opportunity,' said one Allied intelligence officer.[25] There is no reason not to believe this — atrocities against Japanese prisoners were rare — and usually the result of violent spasms of revenge by furious troops. Once in prison, the Japanese tended not to be harmed, for which many were grateful. Few, of course, reached that state of grace.

A poem by an anonymous prisoner beautifully expresses this realisation:

As I cursed the irony of my fate
I received the compassion of a people of an alien land,
And more deeply than in my homeland
It touched my heart.
On a white cot in the hospital
Those who came to comfort me
Were men of a strange country
Who made me weep . . .
Having become a prisoner of war
For the first time I know
The human kindliness of the Australian soldier.[26]

Similarly, probationary officer Watanabe Fukuichi, of the Yazawa Regiment, wrote in captivity on 29 November:

To all in the Australian Red Cross Hospital; I am deeply grateful for the devotion with which you have nursed me . . . when you took an X-ray of me I broke down and cried in front of the soldiers. Your doing all this . . . for an enemy soldier made me think of Florence Nightingale.[27]

Families in Japan knew little of the soldiers' fate. Troops in combat zones generally were not allowed to write home. Instead they committed draft letters to their diaries. Two convey precisely the nihilistic psychology of the last days of the Imperial Army:

A soldier wrote to his wife, on 10 January 1943:

I do not know when I will be going to the next world . . . and I would like to write a few lines before I die. You have a fine soul . . . By chance you married unworthy me and you devoted yourself faithfully to me. I will always be grateful. However, your devotion will have been in vain, as I will soon die for our country. There is no greater glory than this for any man. However, when I think of your sorrow and hardship, how can I die? Be virtuous and bestow the devotion you offered me on your mother and Kunisuke. Your future will be a hard one. My blood and spirit will be carried on by Kunisuke. One of your duties is to look after him and to teach him.[28]

His Australian interrogators described Nishio Shiro, 33, a doctor and medical captain in the 51st Independent Engineer's Regiment, as highly intelligent and, though patriotic and loyal, 'not the usual jingoistic type of Japanese officer'. He maintained constantly that his sole interest was the practice of medicine and that he hated war.

'Beloved Mineko,' Nishio wrote:

As I write my last letter it comes to my mind that we have been married but a short time and so the greatest misfortune has come to you and it is with poignant regret that I shall not again see the face of Toshiko. I have decided to destroy myself on April 18, 1943, at nine o'clock somewhere in New Guinea. Death is the custom for soldiers and therefore I feel you should be prepared for it — take good care of Toshiko ... [29]

Death, for some, was not as light as a feather.

Chapter 57
The End

The Japanese 'lifted brutality to a higher level'
— *Mark Johnston, military historian*

A llied troops silenced the last pockets of Japanese resistance at Sanananda with unsparing thoroughness. This was hardly resistance: the enemy were reduced to a few hundred tottering, barely human, beings who waved their guns or swords in the vague direction of the advancing Allies. Many were partially blind, a symptom of disease and starvation — the 'fog of war' had a literal as well as metaphorical dimension along this wretched shoreline. The coast was strewn with corpses and the air thick with the stench of putrefaction. Burial parties worked in respirators. The gruesome clean-up took until the end of January, under the nervous gaze of Blamey, who made his first trip to the Gona–Buna killing fields on 5 January 1943.

The last days of the Imperial Japanese Army at Sanananda and the nearby Giruwa field hospital is evoked with great courage and honesty in Japanese diaries, written by abandoned troops many of whom were barely able to raise a pencil. Wada recorded that each man's daily rice ration late in January had been reduced to two teaspoons each, 'or only half that. There were many days when there wasn't . . . a single grain.' He observed that most of the men felt death was preferable to life: 'From the point of view of normal society, it was another world, a world beyond all imagination.'¹ 'We are expecting annihilation and do not think of returning home,' said an unknown Japanese officer on New Year's Day, 1943.*

Another soldier, Takita Kenji, witnessed the desperate attempts by the wounded to board landing craft. They 'fell all over each other trying to board, pushing out past the breakers, jostling and crowding each other out'.²

'I think only of home,' wrote Kawano Susumu, who was among the last patients to fight at Giruwa. 'I have hardly eaten for 50 days. I am bony and skinny. I walk with faltering steps. I want to see my children.' Kawano staggered to the Giruwa field hospital where so many dead lay, 'I could not even set my foot down.'³

A particularly disturbing account of the end was that of Lieutenant Inagaki Riichi, 27, a naval paymaster and graduate of Tokyo Imperial University. He surrendered near Giruwa. His Australian interrogators described him as a 'superior type, of good family'. He requested that his answers be kept confidential, on the grounds that if such a report 'ever reached the Japanese people it would be received with horror', according to his interrogator. He displayed genuine distress during the interview, of which the Allied report follows:

The PoW admitted that he had spoken with participants in cannibalism among Japanese troops. [They] admitted having eaten flesh from Japanese as well as Australian corpses ...

The PoW stated that those who had ... participated in cannibalism exhibited extreme and pitiful revulsion of feeling when they realised the full significance of their act. He stated that

---

* Wada survived the war, and wrote this in 1988. Entitled *Painting Over My Shame*, it was part of a collection of 144th Regiment reminiscences (in which he appears to have mistaken Raymond Paull, the journalist who first published his diaries, with Father Benson, the Gona missionary). He adds: 'I am now 72 years old, and in the latter half of my 20s I came home alive. I am now most definitely in the last years of my life, and I feel that I must tell what should be told ... We cannot say that there are not aspects about the war that we do not want to talk about, or that we don't even want to remember [here, he describes his participation in an incident of cannibalism on the Papuan coast]. Yet we, the 144th Regiment, saw absolutely nothing of such horrors as violence against women or atrocities against the locals. Rather we got on very well with the native people and there were many instances where we actually improved their trust in the Japanese. I proudly believe that we were a great regiment who fought well and bravely.'

Japanese troops had been under such conditions that they were not normal human beings at the time . . .

The PoW described these conditions as: continuous standing in swamp water up to the arm pits, suffering from malaria with 40-degrees centigrade of fever, and such lack of food, particularly vitamin B, and to cause Tori Me (Nyctalopia or Night Blindness).

He stated that in this condition troops were unable to see the plainest object except in broad daylight. They were also deaf and reduced to such a state of delirium that their only reaction was to discharge their rifles in the general direction of any sound they might hear.[4]

Of the 7000 or so Japanese troops who had participated at some stage in the Sanananda campaign, 1600 were buried by the Allies, 1200 escaped by barge between November and January, 1000 escaped westward to the Kumusi, and about 3200 were unaccounted for — most probably died of disease or wounds in some dreadful jungle hole or in a later battle. To this day Papuans report the recovery of the occasional skeleton emerging from the swamps after heavy rains.

Their annihilation was total. Yet the Imperial Army's last stand at Sanananda, Buna and Gona must rank among the most courageous, sustained and maddening in the history of warfare, a 'remarkable feat' concluded Dudley McCarthy.[5] A starving, sick, exhausted army, relying on the most fragile supply line, which seized up altogether in January, reduced a far larger Allied force to a state of 'baffled impotence' for three months. This was partly due to the ineffectual American troops; on several occasions, Australian-led offensives were left floundering because the Americans failed to back them up. The Americans' refusal to fight led Blamey to insist on using exhaused Australian troops, who had already fought across the Owen Stanleys or at Milne Bay. But it was ultimately the astonishing courage and determination of the ordinary Japanese troops on the Papuan beaches which led them to resist the Allies for so long — and renders the memory for some in terms redolent of a 'Japanese Gallipoli'.

———

The Japanese deployed 11,880 troops along the Papuan coast, of whom at least 8000 died, according to Japanese sources.[6] Total Japanese war casualties, including wounded and sick, approached 100 per cent on the beaches. In the whole Papuan campaign, the Japanese fielded about 20,000 troops; at least 13,000 of these died, and wounds and disease killed or incapacitated most of the rest. A few thousand escaped and were either killed in later battles in the western Highlands of New Guinea or during the general retreat through the Pacific. Very few actually survived the war — perhaps little more than a hundred.

Horii's men suffered a near complete loss. A Japanese analysis of the Nankai Shitai's casualty rate shows that of the original 5586 troops sent from Kochi to Papua (excluding the 41st Regiment and later reinforcements), 5432 were killed in action — a 'kill rate' of 97 per cent.[7] The 144th Regiment's 3500 men suffered 3264 deaths, 93 per cent of their men. Shimada, Yamasaki and Imanishi were among the 236 survivors of the 144th Regiment's participation in the Papuan campaign — three of the two-digit number to return to Japan when the war ended. These included the sad, solitary figure of Colonel Kusunose, earlier encountered waiting forlornly at Kochi station for the ashes of his men to come home before shuffling off to Mount Fuji to starve himself.

The Nankai Shitai were just one unit committed to the larger battle in Papua and New Guinea. In his memoir, Hoshino Kazuo, a staff officer of the 41st Division, wrote that by the end of the war only 600 troops of the division survived out of an original strength of 20,000 men. Of the 200,000 Japanese troops sent to Papua, east and central New Guinea, 10,000 were alive at the end of the war[8] — 95 per cent did not return home.

The ashes of the dead, when available, were sent to Japan. This custom ceased in Papua after 20 November 1942. Dr Sawatari Zengoro, a medical officer taken prisoner at Giruwa, explained to his interrogators that after that date 'it became impossible in some instances even to bury the dead and no attempt was therefore made to continue cremations'.

'Whenever practicable an entire body would be cremated, but when this proved impossible, a limb, generally an arm, would be amputated. Even this was not always feasible, in which case a hand only, or even fingers, would be utilized.'[9]

The ashes would be placed in the mess tin belonging to the deceased and wrapped in paper for transmission to Japan. When actual remains did not exist, the mess tin of the deceased, if available, with his 'seal' or identity disc, was sent home.

'The fact that the tin did not contain ashes was immaterial, and his relations would consider his spirit was therein,' said Dr Zengoro. He emphasised that the Japanese fully realised that soldiers might be blown to pieces, leaving no trace, and 'in consequence did not expect actual ashes when advised of a death'. Many empty mess tins turned up in Kochi, and other Japanese cities.

The Allies suffered 7500 killed and wounded at Gona, Buna and Sanananda. The Australian 7th Division lost 5905 men in the month between 25 November and 23 December: killed, wounded, missing, or too sick to fight. Precisely 4273 troops were sent to replace them, but these were swiftly reduced, too. In late December Vasey delayed further attacks at Sanananda because he was bereft of men able to raise a gun.

Of the 14,500 American soldiers who served at Buna and Sanananda, 930 were killed and 1918 wounded — a casualty rate of 20 per cent (double that of Guadalcanal).

Total Allied deaths in Papua numbered 3095 and 5418 were wounded — 8513 battle casualties. An additional 8700 US troops succumbed to disease in Papua. This falls slightly short of McCarthy's estimate[10] of total Australian and American casualties — killed and wounded (excluding the sick) — during the campaign, at 8546, of whom the large majority died on the beaches. A total of 625 Australians were killed in the Kokoda Track battles.

During the whole Papuan campaign (including the mountain, Milne Bay and beach phases) — between July 1942 and January 1943 — about 22,000 Australian troops served in combat or support roles. Of these, 2165 were killed, 3500 wounded and 15,575 received treatment for disease: in the great majority of cases, for malaria.

Indeed when the sick are added to the figures — the victims of malaria, scrub typhus, dengue fever, dysentery and assorted tropical conditions — almost every Australian and American soldier who participated in the Papuan campaign can be described as a casualty of war. Curtin told Churchill on 17 February 1943, that 23,000 Allied troops were casualties of tropical diseases in Papua. Most Allied units in Papua suffered a casualty rate (i.e. through death, wounds or sickness) of at least 80 per cent — an astonishing figure — and many suffered over 90 per cent. As Eric Bergerud writes, 'a 30 per cent casualty rate in a combat unit is considered very serious. After that point . . . a downward spiral in fighting spirit often begins. If a rate surpasses 50 per cent, the unit is flirting with disaster.'[11]

To visualise the human reality behind these statistics, consider that 91 of the 2/1st Battalion's 1000 men were left standing after the Kokoda campaign. Their commander, Paul Cullen, was diagnosed with cerebral malaria and had a temperature of 106° degrees Fahrenheit. Most other Australian units were similarly crushed. A tiny trickle of 39th Battalion survivors shuffled out of Sanananda on 23 January: just seven officers and 25 malaria-ridden men, who marched all day to Dobodura and a waiting flight to Port Moresby. Disease was by far the greatest leveller. The Australian dead were usually buried where they fell, or near field hospitals, or in their stretchers, and later exhumed for a proper ceremony at Bomana Cemetery. A tiny number were evacuated by air — a tragic failure of military will.

In fact, the battle casualty rate in Papua was double that of Guadalcanal, which is commonly supposed to have been the more severe campaign. Of the 60,000 American soldiers sent to the Solomon Islands, 1600 were killed and 4245 wounded — a 10 per cent casualty rate. Of course, such crude quantitative judgments mean little to the families and friends of the victims of war. Some perspective is also needed: German 6th Army dead who were caught in the kessel at the concurrent battle of Stalingrad, the worst in the history of human conflict, were 60,000, a 21 per cent casualty rate.[12]

Allied lives were not lost in vain. The strategic importance of the 'battle for Australia', as it is slightly erroneously called, has been grossly underplayed, outside a few Australian texts. Kokoda and Milne Bay — the first land defeat of the Japanese — are not even mentioned in *The Oxford Companion to Military History*. The Australian troops held back a far larger Japanese force and saved Port Moresby, which was the linchpin to the enemy's plan to cut off Australia. The victory delivered Australia not from invasion — the Japanese did not plan to occupy the country — but from isolation. This guaranteed the viability of the only American base in the western Pacific.

Indeed, it is hard to see why the war in the Solomons — which ended with the utter defeat of the Japanese on 9 February 1943 after months of desperate fighting — is viewed as the more important battle. Of course, both Papua and Guadalcanal must be taken together as twin prongs in the Japanese attempt to cut off Australia from Hawaii, and lock up the Asia–Pacific. 'New Guinea was immensely important strategically,' remarks one Japanese history, 'as it was on the right flank of this line and should it fall into the hands of the enemy ... would give them an easy route to the Philippines and other occupied territories.'[13] Guadalcanal's Henderson airfield was less vital, geographically and strategically, than those in Papua. That is why the Imperial Army were so desperate to hold the Papuan beachhead, in the mad hope of launching a second attempt to invade Port Moresby by land. Had they succeeded, the enemy would have captured both a solid airfield and a huge military base on the very cusp of Australia.

Guadalcanal has understandably received a disproportionate share of (American) historical attention. It involved a far greater number of US troops — mostly marines, the pride of the US infantry — and not a few regiments of demoralised, untrained, national guardsmen whose performance generally proved an embarrassment. Guadalcanal was an American success story (14,000 Japanese were killed in battle), which helped to break the spell of Japanese invincibility; Papua, notwithstanding terrific individual exceptions, was an American humiliation.

For the Australians, however, the Kokoda campaign was something of an epiphany. Their stoicism in battle and agonising mountain withdrawal displayed an inner strength touched by the superhuman. The resistance of the 39th at Kokoda and Deniki, against a force varying from six to ten times their size, was a triumph of hope and courage over experience. The Australian troops' bloody stand at Isurava threw Horii's battle plan fatally behind schedule, and helped to cripple his supply lines, which were successively exhausted by Potts's fighting withdrawal despite his defeat at Brigade Hill. Milne Bay punctured Japanese hopes of opening a second flank, and lifted Allied morale.

The counter-thrust over the mountains showed the Allies on the offensive for the first time in the Pacific War. The troops were a wholly

Australian force, who drove a desperately weak enemy back over the same ghastly battlefields through which Potts had come. The defeat of reinforced Japanese units at Eora Creek and Oivi–Gorari destroyed the last vestiges of resistance and forced the enemy back to the beaches. Here, the suicidal courage of the Australian troops thwarted Japanese attempts to reinforce Gona, Buna and Sanananda, MacArthur's greatest fear.

The Imperial Army resorted to dreamy invocations to the Japanese spirit. Throughout February and March 1943 Japanese sub-commanders were still ordering their battered units to conquer New Guinea and attack Australia. On 25 February, Regimental Commander Endo Torahei in the Trobriand Islands, told his men they were 'about to enter decisive battle area of the Great East Asia War ... There is no greater feat than this ... It is our objective to bring the Great East Asia War to a close by suppressing New Guinea and then subjugating Australia, which is our appointed task, thus sealing the fate of our enemy ... Therefore, all officers and men, advance vigorously, fight bravely, and plunge into the jaw of death ...'[14]

On a wider level, Curtin, in securing the return of elements of the Second Australian Imperial Force, played a critical role. The prime minister's refusal to allow their deployment to Rangoon, under overwhelming pressure from Churchill, Roosevelt, Australia's own diplomats in London and Washington, and most of the local media, was an act of heroic political defiance. It demonstrated Curtin's single-minded belief in an Australian future that eluded the mediocrities who surrounded him. It envisaged Australia making its own decisions, without relying on the dubious support of the mother country. If ever a nation experienced a moment of political awakening, of independence from a cosseted, obeisant past, this was Australia's. Curtin brought home the men needed to save the militia at Isurava, and rescued Australia from certain isolation. Of course, the availability of infantry did not assure Australian success: it had to turn to America, not Britain, for deliverance. Yet Britain's failure to help Australia in her hour of need can hardly be cast as a 'great betrayal' when Britain was itself stretched to the limit in confronting both Germany and Japan.

———

The Australians succeeded despite, not because of, the decisions of High Command. Examples proliferate of the ineptitude and illogic of Allied GHQ in Brisbane: the order to build a road over the mountains, and blow up The Gap (even as MacArthur's intelligence chief Willoughby insisted that the Japanese couldn't take Moresby by land); the failure to reconnoitre the Kokoda Track, and train men along it; the dispatch of a mere company of untrained Australian militiamen over the Owen Stanleys — supposedly impregnable to the enemy — thence straight into battle against Japanese shock troops; the gross failure of supply, stranding Potts and Allen in the mountains; the refusal by Blamey to support his own, personally appointed, commanders; and MacArthur's ego-driven reluctance to acknowledge the fighting qualities of the Australians over the Americans. These were some of the disastrous errors of judgment that plagued this wretched campaign.

On a personal level, generals MacArthur and Blamey revealed themselves to be profoundly flawed individuals, captive to the twin sirens of power and fame. They never saw the dismal place into which they were sending demoralised young troops to die; they undermined their own forward commanders with the envenomed relish of the egomaniac; they rewarded themselves with the baubles of high office, with ostentatious disregard for the suffering of the men.

Apologists, in dwindling numbers, believe Blamey and MacArthur were the great helmsmen of the piece, the leaders who extricated their armies from a desperate situation. Blamey's own account of the war, written by his PR department, shamelessly portrays him as the man of the moment whose arrival in Port Moresby on 23 September 1942 transformed the Australian war effort. He did no such thing. Rowell and Potts had exhausted their adversaries before Blamey appeared. To Eichelberger's disgust, MacArthur let it be known that he led from the front — notably at Buna; MacArthur never saw the front.

Indeed, in the eyes of many officers and troops, Blamey and MacArthur actually frustrated rather than furthered the prosecution of the war in Papua. The net effect of their decisions demoralised rather than inspired the men. No soldier and few officers had a good word for either commander. Potts did his best to turn the near annihilation of his undersupplied men into a bitterly fought withdrawal, which sapped Japanese strength; for this Potts was sacked and sent back to Darwin in disgrace, and his men tainted with the charge of cowardice.

Blamey and MacArthur failed to see the point of Potts's action. They never credited the reasons — an acute lack of supplies, ammunition and troops — for his decision to withdraw. He could have retreated. But they never accepted his action as a delaying tactic, designed to draw out the supply lines of a much larger force that he couldn't hope to defeat in combat. No government has since recognised Potts's achievement. No plaque, or rest area, commemorates him. Only the few remaining veterans at diminished reunions, and the pages of battalion histories in libraries, survive to honour Potts as 'this great fighter'[15], 'the warrior of Kokoda'[16] and 'the fighting brigadier of the Kokoda Trail'.[17]

Nor would Brisbane see fit to assist Tubby Allen, who was thwarted at every step. Blamey delayed or failed to fulfil Allen's supply requests. Rowell was repeatedly undermined until he lost his way. It was almost as though Blamey and MacArthur feared their forward commanders would eclipse their own dazzling roles in the rear.

In fact, Allied victory in Papua had little to do with Blamey and MacArthur and everything to do with the prodigious abilities and courage of a few outstanding officers, and the dogged loyalty and bravery of their men: witness Potts and Honner at Isurava, Clowes at Milne Bay, Cullen and Hutchison at Eora Creek, Vasey at Oivi–Gorari, Catterns at Soputa, Honner at Gona, Wootten at Buna–Sanananda, and Eichelberger at Buna. None of these men were satisfied with the way GHQ prosecuted the Papuan war. For many, GHQ and Landops seemed at best ineffectual; at worst, actually disruptive. That criticism found its most bitter expression in Rowell, a proud, talented man, who no doubt deserved to be sacked for withholding, however briefly, intelligence from Blamey. In fairness, Rowell found himself in an intolerable position; Blamey knew his old adversary's Achilles heel, and was determined to snap it.

These conclusions relate purely to the Kokoda campaign, and not to the wider legacy of the war, and the lives of the men involved. Clearly Blamey had rare skills as a staff officer, and was a great military administrator. He held the Australian army together in the Middle East, and Curtin deeply admired his ability to get things done, not least in organising the return of the AIF to Australia.

McCarthy spoke of Blamey's 'unappreciated humanity'.[18] Historian Chris Coulthard-Clark concurs with Horner's generous assessment of Blamey's contribution:

> While [Blamey] had little opportunity to display his ability as a field commander in the Pacific, he quickly grasped the nature of the war: the need to use sea and air, the debilitating effects of climate and terrain, the necessity for thorough training and fitness, and for frequent reliefs for commanders and soldiers, the importance of logistics and the value of accurate intelligence. He did not immerse himself in detail ... but he had at times a clear and at times astonishing grasp of detail ... Blamey did not waste Australian lives. And he always protected Australian interests ... [19]

If so, one is left wondering why so many of Blamey's attributes did not emerge in Papua, where the very absence of training and fitness, the failure of logistics, the denial of seapower, and the waste of Australian lives in the beach battles, were so painfully manifest. As for Blamey's humanity, one wonders how a man who failed so dismally to inspire or elicit the respect of his men, can be so described.

MacArthur's claim to military greatness would await his later victories in the Huon Gulf, and the great rollback of the Imperial Army to the crimson shores of Okinawa. Some believe his greatest legacy came in peace, not war, in the deftness with which he imposed democracy on post-war Japan.

In Papua he failed. He misjudged Japanese plans for a land invasion; he failed to lead the American army to a successful outcome; he viciously disparaged battle-weary Australian troops; he sought scapegoats for his own errors.

Nor did he, as he later claimed, single-handedly rouse Australians to the offensive. It was simply untrue that he switched the offensive from Australia to New Guinea within days of his arrival in Melbourne. If so, why were the AIF withheld in Queensland, futilely building defences? Why wasn't Port Moresby better reinforced? Why were militia troops (the 14th Brigade) dispatched to New Guinea ahead of the AIF, a decision that 'made us weep', said Rowell. Indeed, if it was MacArthur's decision to take the war to New Guinea why were Blamey and Curtin not told? As the official historian writes, 'If MacArthur had a radical change of policy in mind immediately after his arrival, Curtin and Blamey were not made aware of it, and the steps to reinforce Port Moresby were singularly cautious.'[20] In truth, Australia would launch the counteroffensive, when the men and arms were available.

Truth was the first, disastrous casualty of MacArthur's war. Some argued that he was a victim of his own overzealous PR machine, as General George Kenney, the Allied air chief and the supreme commander's close friend, ludicrously suggested. 'His public relations officers invariably adored MacArthur almost to the point of idolatry,' Kenney wrote. 'To them unless a news release painted the General with a halo and seated him on the highest pedestal in the Universe, it should be killed. No news except favourable news, reflecting complete credit on an infallible MacArthur, had much chance of getting by the censors.'[21] Kenney seemed not to understand that it was MacArthur, not his PR hacks, who approved his press releases.

The Japanese defeat was partly self-inflicted, of course. The failure of the Japanese command structure needs little elaboration: clearly many officers let down their men. They dealt brutally with the troops, failed adequately to supply them, and blindly put their trust in the shimmering phantom of the Japanese spirit, when medical care, food, ammunition and reinforcements were needed. When the spirit failed to conquer physical collapse, many officers simply abandoned or deserted their dying troops.

Of course, the ordinary Japanese soldiers' supine obedience to their country's aggressive martial code made them complicit in their own destruction. Indeed, it might be said that the Japanese infantryman fought to die, while the Allied infantryman fought to live. Perhaps herein lies the seeds of the Allied victory — the Australian soldier's fear of death was more powerful than the Japanese soldier's disregard for life.

The Kokoda campaign was a war fought without mercy. Why, warrants a little attention. The Australians hated the Japanese troops with a peculiar intensity. The Japanese were not simply another enemy whom the

Australians blundered into by dint of the Great Game, or on British orders, or through historical accident. Were the Turks so hated? Were the Germans? Not with anything like the visceral, personal loathing felt towards 'the Jap'. One Australian private — a veteran of the Libyan and Greek campaigns — typified the attitude of the Australians at the time: 'My regard for Tony [the Italian] was always impersonal and for Fritz ... tinged with admiration, but none of us know anything but vindictive hatred for the Jap.'[22] US propaganda departments produced lapel buttons; the German version depicted Hitler with the caption: 'Wanted For Murder'. The Japanese version read: 'Jap Hunting License — Open Season — No Limit'. Sociologists may analyse the darker reasons of such extreme antipathy for as long as there are academic tenures in Australian universities.

No doubt some Australian troops were 'racists' who would despise the Japanese in peace and at war. Yet the term racist is inapposite. Most Australians were 'racists' during the war if this defined anyone who believed in keeping Australia white. In 1941, Curtin defended the fight against Japan on the grounds of maintaining the 'principle of a White Australia'. (Australia's White Australia Policy was the first Act on the statute books after Federation in 1901.)

Curtin simply reflected the popular will and civilian fear of the 'terrifying strangeness' of the enemy, in Tom Keneally's apt phrase. 'In my childhood,' said the author of *An Angel in Australia* (a novel set in Sydney during World War II), 'two images of the Japanese were predominant. One moment the rock-jawed digger was worth ten Nips; the next week Australia would be this violable maiden being slavered over by buck-toothed Jap militarists.'[23] The Australian people did not generally appreciate the political exploitation of this fear. When the Curtin Government launched a hate campaign in March–April 1942, the *Sydney Morning Herald* creditably argued that Australians needed no stimulus to fight the Japanese aggressor, and certainly not 'a torrent of cheap abuse and futile efforts in emulation of ... Goebbels'.[24] The hate campaign was opposed by 54 per cent of Australians surveyed in a Gallup poll on the issue. Menzies nobly spoke out against inciting racial hatred as an instrument of war.

It was one thing to frame public policy around a notion of Anglo-Saxon purity; quite another to expect a man to kill for this reason. Most Australian troops were ordinary young men, subjected to terrible circumstances. They were indoctrinated not so much to hate the Japanese as to hold him beneath contempt, as one might regard a hostile animal who must be slaughtered. The process began at Allied army camps where the troops were exposed to the most virulent military propaganda.

This was psychological war at its most thorough. The Japanese had to be dehumanised to be beaten; and Australian commanders found plenty of material with which to achieve this: the Tol Plantation massacres; the emerging horror of Nanking; the atrocities at Milne Bay. The Japanese 'super-soldier' was cast as a subhuman beast, a species of rodent. The Australian soldier was urged to hunt down and kill the 'Nip' with extreme prejudice. At a jungle training school in 1942, Australian recruits were told that the Japanese was 'a cunning little rat ... full of little ruses and tricks'.[25]

Portraying the Japanese as an animal helped to quell fear, and boost confidence — the confidence of the predator. Training and innate prejudice merged into a deep repugnance of the Japanese race. Australian troops were encouraged to think of the enemy as 'bloody little yellow swine', 'semi-educated baboons', 'yellow stinkers', 'filthy monkeys' — these were some of the less vehement epithets. Such attitudes permeated the command structure. Blamey set the most prominent example. The Japanese was 'a subhuman beast', he told recruits in 1942. In early 1943 reinforcements were told that the Japanese were 'a curious race — a cross between the human being and the ape'.[26] General Gordon Bennett, who escaped the fall of Singapore, called the Japanese an 'oriental yellow Hun'. The US Admiral William Halsey perhaps set a new standard for racial vilification during war; referring to the Japanese as 'yellow bastards', 'stupid animals' and 'monkeymen', he urged his men to 'Kill Japs. Kill Japs. Kill More Japs. Get some more monkey meat.'[27]

Not all Allied troops turned into knee-jerk Jap-haters because Blamey or Halsey or an officer told them to. It was the actual experience of war that pitched the Australian mind into a new and unfamiliar place. It took more than propaganda and their commanders to ignite the sort of ferocity unleashed at Oivi–Gorari and on the Papuan beaches.

Indeed, a minority of Japanese troops themselves fully awakened 'the killing instinct' in the Australians, as Mark Johnston shows. The Japanese 'lifted brutality to a higher level'.[28] He argues that the sight of mutilated Australian corpses was crucial to understanding the 'unusually murderous behaviour of Australian troops'. During Milne Bay, Brigadier John Field wrote in his diary, '[t]he yellow devils show no mercy and have since had none from us'. Cam Bennett, of the 2/5th Battalion, wrote that Japanese treatment of captives 'divorced them from any consideration whatever' whenever the Australians had a chance to kill them.[29]

Alas, the actions of thuggish Japanese officers smothered the claim to humanity of many ordinary Japanese footsoldiers, whose diaries reveal the courage and decency of the reluctant conscript, the doctor, the primary school teacher and the peasant, many of whom were bludgeoned into submission by a regime that simply killed dissent.

That side of the enemy barely surfaced, of course. Sergeant Victor Austin, of the 39th Battalion, attempted, and failed, to humanise the Japanese in his unit history, *To Kokoda and Beyond*:

> I have tried to give the Japanese a more human visage but I would say at that time they were still considered to be ... not quite human beings. But as I say I tried to humanise them and obviously they weren't all fanatical brutes. There were sensitive natures even amongst them, but they had a different attitude ... They were part of a society where discipline was something so ingrained and their notion of their honour as soldiers was such that they fought fanatically.[30]

The Japanese soldiers viewed the Australians rather differently. They did not particularise their hatred along racial grounds; the enemy was the enemy, be he Chinese, Filipino, or Australian. The Imperial Army was ordered to destroy any foe, of any race, for whom they felt simply a generalised contempt. True, there was endless propaganda against the white imperialists; just as there was against the Chinese devil. As Warrant Officer Shimada said, 'the Australians were the enemy — it was not racial or anything — we were supposed to hate them. The Australians were just another enemy we were supposed to hate.'[31] Tanaka similarly argued that the Japanese were motivated to kill anyone bearing the mark of the enemy — Chinese or Filipino or British.

Yamasaki remembered: 'I was given an order; I simply knew I had to destroy the enemy.'[32]

Neither side took prisoners, if they could avoid it. The Australians took a tiny number on the Kokoda Track and the beaches; the Japanese took a handful. Both sides killed surrendering as well as captive troops. The policy was in part practical: how were they to cart prisoners back down the trail when they had so few carriers for their own wounded?

In any case, the sight of mutilated Australian corpses sealed the fate of most Japanese who fell into Allied hands. The Japanese simply executed most of those they caught, or who failed to cooperate — troops, civilians, natives. An unusual exception was the Reverend Benson, who survived, it appears, partly because of his collar.

Even the more tolerant, intelligent Australian commanders — Honner, Potts, and Vasey — settled early upon a no-prisoner policy. As Potts wrote to his wife: 'Our little yellow mongrel friends. Did I hope at one time that our crowd could learn to hate? My dear it has happened ... in the future any Jap we meet may kiss himself goodbye on both cheeks. No we didn't take any prisoners, and if I'm ordered to produce one I'll have to swallow hard and do the job myself.'[33]

Sergeant Robert Johns, MM, recalled: 'During our bloody encounters along the Kokoda Trail and at Gona there were few opportunities for taking prisoners. It was that sort of war. In fact through all our campaigns against the Japanese, I can only remember taking two prisoners, one of them badly wounded. It all sounds a bit barbarous now.'[34]

Japanese prisoners airlifted to Port Moresby were hurled out of the planes by Allied aircrews, according to claims by Charles Lindbergh. There is no evidence for this; it may even be that Japanese prisoners were simply free to jump, should they wish. Perhaps some did, such was their shame of being held captive.

While victors can be relied upon not to leave records of their wartime disgraces, it is safe to say the Allies did not mutilate or subject Japanese prisoners to slow, torturous deaths. There were, however, sporadic bursts of Allied rage against the few Japanese prisoners taken; six bound and gagged Japanese troops were gunned down at Wau airfield, for example. An untold number were bludgeoned or shot in the secrecy of the jungle. A handful of bound enemy prisoners were bayoneted to death by members of the

16th Brigade. This was part of the reason why the unit's commander, Major-General Cullen, refused to give evidence at the war crimes tribunal. Cullen spoke out against Allied treatment of prisoners. 'It was my battalion and I felt pretty guilty, but it was understandable. I'm not really critical of the soldiers.'[35]

In January 1943 MacArthur set in train a process — 'by stealth and by the employment of subterfuges that were undignified and at times absurd'[36] — to marginalise Blamey. MacArthur's 'machinations' degenerated into an unseemly scrap for the conqueror's mantle, and it was to Blamey's credit that he chose quiet indifference in response to this American jockeying for power. Nonetheless, the only Australian general on MacArthur's staff was sidelined. Blamey would soon lose his role as commander, Allied Land Forces, as the ground war swept westward along the coast of New Guinea, and north to the Philippines.

In February 1943, the Allied armies turned their attention to the New Guinean highlands and the dense jungle around Salamaua, Lae and Wau, where the Japanese had regrouped. For months, Kanga Force, a tiny Australian guerrilla unit under the command of Lieutenant-Colonel Norman Fleay, had harried the Japanese. Reinforced first by the New Guinea Volunteer Rifles, and now by Allied armies, Kanga Force became part of the final offensive to clear the Japanese from New Guinea. These were short, sharp, ferocious battles, largely forgotten, but critical in driving the enemy out of the south-west Pacific. The three highly decorated battalions of the 21st Brigade — veterans of Kokoda, Gona and Sanananda — again played a critical role. Honner, fittingly, led the 2/14th during the so-called mop-up. Badly wounded, he was returned to Australia, and later became the nation's ambassador to Ireland — one of the outstanding commanders of the war, at whose funeral in May 1994 an uninvited Japanese guest bowed to his family.[37]

The enemy made one last-ditch attempt to reclaim their grip on New Guinea. In the Battle of the Bismark Sea they dispatched 6400 troops from Rabaul to their garrison at Lae, using a convoy of eight troop transports defended by eight destroyers and about a hundred fighter aircraft. It was the Australian air commander, Garing, who convinced Kenney to prepare a massive, coordinated air attack against the enemy convoy. The ships were sunk, and thousands of Japanese strafed in the water as they swam for shore. The US Rear-Admiral Samuel Morison defended this as 'a grisly task but a military necessity since Japanese soldiers do not surrender and, within swimming distance of shore, they could not be allowed to land and join the Lae garrison'. Hundreds made the beach, where the Papuan natives 'had the time of their lives tracking them down as in the old head hunting days', Morison said.[38]

The 39th Battalion was disbanded after the Papuan campaign. But they were not forgotten and, along with their battle insignia — brown over red (or 'mud over blood') — the performance of the Australian militiamen who first met the Japanese on the Kokoda Track gradually became the stuff of legend. It is a legend that withstands the harshest scrutiny.

In 1972 a few 39th survivors — Alf Salmon, Jack Boland, Jack Sutherland, Ron Weakley, Len Murrell, Lloyd Lott, Val Petersen and John Akhurst — joined their Japanese counterparts in a reunion, the only instance of this happening among the Australian armies.

'The Japanese, led by two generals, finished their battle hymn,' reported Alan Downer, a journalist for *The Sun*.[39] 'Then it was the Diggers' turn — with "Waltzing Matilda". The Japanese joined in.' An old Japanese general, Shigeru Sugiyama, 'son-in-law of the once mighty General Tojo', bowed neatly from the waist, and told the Australian reporter: 'Never could we find a time and place to outwit and outmanoeuvre the 39th. And now we have waited 30 years to meet them here and tell them so. To tell them that when our men of the great Nankai Division landed in New Guinea in 1942, they thought they were facing an Australian army some 10,000 strong on the Kokoda Trail. Not, for the first two months of battle, just one battalion of young and untested men — this 39th Battalion — only some 600 strong!'

After the war, Blamey was promoted to field marshal — Australia's only one — the reward for a lifetime's service to Australian arms. If the Papuan campaign tended to blot that record, no one, least of all his annointed disciples in the army and his political friends, were about to say so, and his name now emblazons Australia's military complex in Canberra, part of a questionable legacy.

In George Vasey, we observe a different calibre of man — whom civilian Australia has largely forgotten. In 1945 they knew him well — *Women's Weekly* put him on their cover, and he was hugely popular. Of the top commanders in Papua, Vasey was among the true heroes. He fought with his men at the front for three months — longer than any other commander — under the most dreadful conditions. This is what he said when asked what he did immediately after a battle: 'The first thing I do is call for the casualty list. I go away to my tent ... not to be disturbed ... to be alone with my God and my conscience. It weighs heavily ... [the realisation that] you have no option but to be responsible for creating all these widows, fatherless children, these mothers robbed of sons ...'[40]

True to form, Blamey sought to deny Vasey his rightful place in the eyes of posterity. This appalling man relieved Vasey of his command of the 7th Division, with a lie, according to Vasey's wife, Jessie. Extremely ill in bed, Vasey through his delirium heard Blamey say, 'And don't think because you are lying here, George, anyone is going to ditch you for your job.'[41] Blamey had in fact promised Vasey's job to a rival officer — a day earlier. Vasey died in a plane crash on 5 March 1945; he was 49 years old, and nationally and sincerely mourned.

Far from the fallout of Hiroshima and Nagasaki, after the deaths of millions — in Papua, New Guinea, the Philippines, Saipan, China, Burma, Okinawa and in the Tokyo firebombing — the last Japanese troops in the jungles of Bougainville learned of their country's surrender via floating pamphlets printed from a linocut in August 1945. The linocut was carved from a piece of linoleum taken from the floor of an officer's tent while he was asleep, and hacked out with an army jack-knife by the light of a jeep headlight. The 1st Australian Army Mobile Printing Unit, working three shifts, printed 500,000 copies of the leaflet.[42]

The war in the Pacific was over. In September 2003, Shimada and Yamasaki, as they've done every year since Kokoda, commemorated the 144th regimental reunion with a Shinto ceremony, after which, at a lively reception, they sang old war songs on a karoake machine.[43] Some families still refused to attend, in protest at the failure of the previous organiser

Morita, now dead, to commit suicide while a prisoner at Cowra. The surviving veterans pledge to this day that they never doubted their faith in the Emperor even during the worst extremes of the war.

Horii's body was consigned to an ordinary grave, not the usual general's tomb. Nishimura visited it near Kakogawa City, a depressing experience. 'General Horii's grave was ... built in the joint names with his son. Perhaps it was because he was the defeated general.'

Vernon and Kienzle went about their businesses in Papua; the fuzzy wuzzy angels returned to their villages and gardens. In 1945 they organised a 'very very big feast,' said Havala Laula. 'We killed 25 pigs at Menari. It was a big ceremony, with dancing and singing.'[44]

Vernon had performed a unique service — on par with Simpson of Gallipoli. 'The Australian people ... failed to realise that the fuzzy wuzzy angels' patience, tenderness and fortitude with wounded Australians rewarded, in part, Vernon's unsparing services on their behalf,' is the just summing up of this extraordinary man.[45]

'The Papuans must not be idealised,' wrote Vernon. 'They came into the war unwillingly ... yet a great majority showed up very favourably under the hardship of the campaign. We have expressed much gratitude to the Papuan and by and large they have shown marked loyalty in helping us; let us show it in the future by conserving rather than by exploiting the race.'[46]

Sixty years on little has changed; the fuzzy wuzzies live much as they did then, in villages without sanitation, proper medical care or running water, dependent on their market gardens for food. In fact, their circumstances have regressed; little Australian aid finds its way to their mountain villages, which no longer receive weekly air deliveries of supplies and mail — a distant echo of the shortages faced in very different circumstances by Tubby Allen and Arnold Potts.

The Australian troops returned home in a state of silent wonder that they'd survived. A substantial minority later suffered nervous disorders, alcoholism, broken marriages and career failure.[47] Laurie Howson, who died in 2003, was in and out of psychiatric clinics for years, and eventually developed a novel medical regimen of his own. It seemed to work — he rallied and even found romance in his last few months alive. Others held down jobs and happy long-term relationships. Frank McLean carried shrapnel in his head for decades, suffered eye and neck injuries and recurrent bouts of malaria. Yet he married and raised three children. His biggest regret was losing an eye: 'It's very hard to catch a ball,' he said in 1990, before he died.[48]

Successive Australian governments disgracefully refused to grant 'special consideration' of the medical claims of the 39th, because the men could produce no medical records — the battalion had lost them on the Kokoda Track. Honner, Norris, Steward and other officers pressed the claims of the men; some cases dragged on until the mid-1970s. As late as 1985, Steward was still buttressing his unit's claims, with a letter to officials, which stated: 'Many of these men experienced a variety of mental disturbances, including hallucinations. Because of appalling conditions, few if any medical records were kept by RMOs [regimental medical officers].'[49]

Veterans of the 2/1st Battalion remember one act of homecoming assistance with unbridled delight. When the war ended, Basil Catterns wondered, 'What are the troops going to do when they get home?'

He decided to organise

> ... a little university, or Tafe, where we'd have classes, where some
> of us who know all about sheep farming or know about
> newspapers and someone who knows something about real estate
> or collecting stamps or coins ... we can have that too. We
> discussed everything I could think of, except the one thing I
> knew was on their minds, sex.
>
> So I went and sought a doctor, and said 'Doc, I want you to
> come and address the battalion about sex because it's on their
> minds.' And he said, 'I will not address the unit as a whole,
> individually they can line up and come and see me and I will
> discuss anything with them at all, but I'm not going to do that.'
> I said, 'Have you got any books about it?' And he said, 'No, what
> do you want books for?' I said, 'if I had a book I'd give the
> bloody thing myself.'

There was a library at Wewak, and Catterns hopped in a jeep and headed there. Except 'there were no books at all on sex — only a little book which if I remember correctly was something about the art of love, written of course in the nineteenth century'.

Catterns read this book, assembled the whole battalion, and, in a booming parade ground voice, lectured them on the art of love and sex. 'It worked beautifully. The word "foreplay" had never been invented then but the idea, the message was there, that love is an art and that if you practise and be creative — and I was careful to say "your partner", I didn't say "your wife or your woman", in case there really was someone who was homosexual — it worked beautifully'.[50]

Some years later in George Street, in Sydney, a veteran confronted Catterns: 'Basil Catterns,' he said, 'I was up there at Wewak with you and I remember that lecture you gave about sex, and I remembered it and I got married when I came back and I've now got three lovely teenage children, and it's been a happy marriage all the time, thanks very much.'

Acknowledgments

I am indebted to many people for their help in producing this book. I thank, in particular, the veterans in Australia and Japan who spent hours drawing on distant and difficult memories to assist my understanding of the campaign. Their names are listed in the bibliography. Several were exceptionally helpful: in Australia, Stan Bissett, Basil Catterns, Paul Cullen, and the late Laurie Howson and Phil Rhoden (both of whom died during the writing of this book); in Japan, Imanishi Sadaharu, Shimada Yuki and Yamasaki Yukiharu.

I thank also the soldiers' families for their time and permission to view private papers, diaries and photographs. I'm especially grateful to Gloria Bissett; Angela and Nina Catterns; Eve Cullen; Philippa, Brian and Richard Honner; Rob McLean; and Geoff Steward.

I'm indebted to the Australian Veterans' Associations whose units fought in New Guinea; the Returned & Services League for helping to arrange meetings in Australia; as well as the 144th Regiment Veterans' Association in Japan, who invited me to their annual reunion in Kochi, in 2003.

A few individuals played an essential role in making this book possible. They are: my great literary agent, Deborah Callaghan, who swatted problems I scarcely knew existed; Hajime Marutani, indefatigable translator, interpreter, cultural guide and excellent dinner companion during my journey through Japan; Kitagawa Fumiyuki, the Japanese defence attaché in Canberra, who was vital in helping to arrange meetings in Japan; Dee Johnstone, for her wonderful hospitality during my stay in Canberra; researchers Angela Priestley and Nikki Woloszuk, for whom no task was too difficult; Frank Taylor, of Kokoda Treks & Tours, for a safe and well-informed passage across the Owen Stanleys; and, of course, the people at HarperCollins, notably publisher Alison Urquhart and editors Catherine Day and Neil Thomas.

Many others offered help, advice, criticism or simply the time of day, and I thank them: Georgia Arnott; Drew Blomfield; Dr Steven Bullard; Deborah

Burdett; Cameron Cooper; Dr Chris Coulthard-Clark; Jacqui Crouch; Hugh Fraser; George Friend; Mark Friezer; Emma Harcourt; Dr Carol Hayes; Sarah Heather; Professor David Horner; Emma Jones; Bill James; Michelle L'Huillier; Tom Keneally; Charlie Lynn; Lex McAulay; Kate Manka; Hilary McDowell; Andrew McGeehan; Justin Mclean; Dr Hank Nelson; Rusty Priest; David Rich; Tony Rees; John Rennie; Keith Richmond; Mick Ryan; Pat Sheil; Dr Peter Stanley; Nobby Sugimoto; Keiko Tamura; Tanaka Hiromi; Robyn Van Dyk; Kerry-Anne Walsh; and Geoffrey Wright.

I'm very grateful to the staff of several libraries who dealt imperturbably with the most obscure requests: the Australian War Memorial, Canberra; the Kochi Municipal Library, Kochi City, Japan; the Mitchell and State Libraries, Sydney; the National Archives, Canberra; the National Institute of Defence Studies, Tokyo; the National Library, Canberra; and the Waverley Municipal Library, Sydney. Of all my sources, the monumental research of Peter Brune, David Day and David Horner was especially useful, and I acknowledge my debt to them.

Finally, thanks to my family for their constant interest and encouragement, and to my nine-year old son, Ollie, for an endless stream of unwitting inspiration. Near the completion of this book he produced from the chaotic depths of his school bag a toy soldier. He smiled happily, and proceeded to shoot it. A child's blissful ignorance of the reality of war is at once heartening and immensely saddening, given the thought of what was to happen to similar boys when they became young men, in July 1942.

Bibliography
Primary Sources —
Australian Army

Interviews with Australian veterans, 2002–2004

John Akhurst, 39th Battalion
Stan Bissett, 2/14th Battalion
Harvey Blundell, 55/53rd Battalion
Charlie Butler, 2/14th Battalion
Basil Catterns, 2/1st Battalion (twice)
George Cops, 39th Battalion
Jim Coy, 2/14th Battalion
Paul Cullen, 2/1st Battalion (twice)
Don Daniels, 39th Battalion
Warwick Davis, 55/53rd Battalion
Bill Guest, 39th Battalion
Trevor Harper, 55/53rd Battalion
Laurie Howson, 39th Battalion
Bob Iskov, 2/14th Battalion
Bill Jenkins, 2/2nd Battalion
Keith Norrish, 2/16th Battalion
George Palmer, 39th Battalion
Matt Power, 2/14th Battalion
Phil Rhoden, 2/14th Battalion
Merv Roberts, 2/33rd Battalion
Jack Stevens, 55/53rd Battalion
Frank Sublet, 2/16th Battalion (brief phone conversation)
John Trevan, 39th Battalion
George Woodward, 2/14th Battalion
Roy Wootten, 55/53rd Battalion
Peter Wright, 55/53rd Battalion

Other interviews and discussions

Dr Steven Bullard, director of the Australia–Japan Research Project,
    Australian War Memorial
Angela Catterns, daughter of Basil Catterns, 2/1st Battalion
Dr Chris Coulthard-Clark, historian, Australian War Memorial
George Friend, director of Rising Sun Films
Brian Honner, son of Ralph Honner
Philippa Honner, granddaughter of Ralph Honner
Richard Honner, son of Ralph Honner

Professor David Horner, Australian National University
Bill James, Kokoda trekker and writer
Tom Keneally, novelist
Edward Lewis, grandson of Essington Lewis
Charlie Lynn, NSW Senator, Kokoda tour guide
Lex MacAulay, military historian
Dr Hank Nelson, Australian National University
Rusty Priest, chairman of Kokoda Memorial Foundation, former RSL president
John Rennie, organiser of Isurava Memorial
Peter Stanley, Australian War Memorial
Geoff Steward, son of Major 'Blue' Steward
Frank Taylor, director of Kokoda Treks & Tours
Garry Tongs, son of Bede Tongs, 3rd Battalion

Private papers

Access was kindly granted to the private papers of:
Les Bastock, 55/53rd Battalion
Stan Bissett, 2/14th Battalion
Harvey Blundell, 55/53rd Battalion
Basil Catterns, 2/1st Battalion
Paul Cullen, 2/1st Battalion
Ralph Honner, 39th Battalion
Laurie Howson, 39th Battalion
Bill Jenkins, 2/2nd Battalion
Frank McLean, 2/27th Battalion
D.J. O'Dell, 55/53rd Battalion
Merv Roberts, 2/33rd Battalion
Lew Scott, 55/53rd Battalion
Paul Wright, 55/53rd Battalion
The private papers of Kokoda veterans held in the AWM were also used (see following)

Primary document sources

Australian War Memorial, Canberra

AWM 49 89/9, Letter, Rowell to Hetherington
AWM 54 171/2/48, AWM 54 225/2/5, AWM 54 420/2/2, AWM 54 541/1/4, AWM 54 577/3/1,
    AWM 54 577/6/1, AWM 54 577/6/4, AWM 54 577/6/8, AWM 54 577/7/29,
    AWM 54 917/3/13 [general papers relating to the Papuan campaign]
AWM 54, Report on Operations of the Milne Forces
AWM 54, Australian Imperial Forces Battle Casualties, Owen Stanley Campaign, Kokoda to Imita,
    22 July to 25 September 1942
AWM 54 33/1/4, Official Army File dealing with the action by the Commander-in-Chief
    (General Blamey) in relieving Lieutenant General S.F. Rowell of the Command of New Guinea
    Force, 1942
AWM 54 422/7/8, Notes on Ops Isurava area, 25–31 August 1942
AWM 54 481/12/20, Diary of Sir Rupert Magarey
AWM 54 571/1/2, General Routine Orders by General Sir Thomas Blamey, circa 1939–circa 1945

AWM 54 577/6/8, Report on Kokoda L. of C., Native Carriers during Campaign, Owen Stanley
Range, Kokoda — Buna, Feb 1943, ANGAU N.G.F.

AWM 54 581/7/19, Notes on and lessons from recent operations in Gona and Sanananda areas by
Lt Col R. Honner — Comd 39th Aust Inf Bn

AWM 113 MH 1/160 PARTS 1–10, Weekly Progress Reports of the Chiefs of Staff to the Prime
Minister [War Cabinet Agenda] 1942

AWM 419 14/2, OPS Report by Captain S.H. Buckler, 12 Oct 1942

AWM 419 47/24, John Hetherington, Papers

AWM 419/72/9 PR 85/275, Memoir of Service of Major A.E. Moore of 2/14th & 2/16th Bns

AWM 422/3/94 MSS 701, A.D. Robertson, *Problems of Supply Encountered by the Australian and
Japanese forces on the Kokoda Trail and the Questions of Morale*, MA thesis

AWM 422/3/138 MSS 0739, Horner, D., *Generals in Battle, Problems of Command in the South-West
Pacific Area, 1942–1943*, MA thesis

AWM 3DRL No. 999 AWM file 419/14/2, OPS Report by Captain S.H. Buckler, A Coy 2/14, AIF

AWM 3DRL No. 2381 AWM file 419, Papers of Sir Arthur Allen

AWM 3DRL No. 6643, Papers of General Sir Thomas Blamey

AWM PR00527 Box 10, Papers of Major-General Selwyn Porter

AWM EF 940.54S6 L253, Allied Air Forces, South West Pacific Area, Directorate of Intelligence,
Land–Air Offensive in New Guinea, Kokoda to Gona-Buna, Nov 2nd 1942–Jan 23rd 1943
[photos and maps depicting aerial bombing campaign]

AWM 42/401/142, Combat Efficiency of Army Units, Training and Preparation for Operations, in
Operations Report for Australian Army, 19 July 1942

Mitchell Library, Sydney

ML DOC 2091, WW2 Imperial Rescript — Declaration of War

ML MSS. 614, Gill, E., *Correspondence 1924–46*

ML MSS. 1097, Papers of Damien Parer

ML MSS. 1825, Papers of Alan Watson

ML MSS. 3326, Papers of John Murray

National Archives, Canberra

CRS A373, Disturbances between Australian and American Troops, 1942–1943

CRS A816, Churchill's Speech on Singapore, 23rd April 1942

CRS A816, Organisations of the RAAF — File No. 1, 30/9/44 (RAAF Command Allied Air Force),
1942–1944

CRS A816/1, Cablegrams from Curtin to London concerning return of AIF

CRS A816, Strategical Situation in Far East and Pacific following the Fall of Singapore

CRS A816, Communications Facilities in the SWPA Committee formed by General MacArthur

CRS A816, Review of Production of War Material. General MacArthur's Statement of Priorities

CRS A1608, War Section. Visit of Sir Thomas Blamey to Australia, 1941

CRS A2670, War Cabinet Agenda, 1939–1943

CRS A2671, War Cabinet Minutes, 1939–1943

CRS A2671, Co-ordinated plans for the defence of Australia

CRS A2671 Department of Aircraft Production Progress Reports, 1942

CRS A2676, War Cabinet Minutes without Agenda Files, 1939–43

CRS A2676, Aircraft production policy and administrative machinery for the direction of the aircraft
industry

CRS A2676, Tank production

CRS A2676, Brownout policy

CRS A3052, Running List of War Cabinet and Advisory War Council Agenda

CRS A3300/7 101, Far East Policy, SWPA

CRS A5954, Future Employment of AIF — all files

CRS A5954, miscellaneous files on Army control of New Guinea, troops' pay, New Guinea resources, goldfields, etc

CRS A5954, Sir Frederick Shedden Papers (boxes 532, 537, 573, 587)

CRS A5954 256/3, Inquiries into Looting at Darwin and Port Moresby

CRS A5954 266/1, Dept of Defence — Higher Army Directions of Operations in New Guinea

CRS A5954 473/4, Incidence of Malaria in Forces in New Guinea

CRS A5954 532/5, Operations in New Guinea — Reports by Ministers for Army and Air on their Visits to New Guinea, October '42

CRS A5954 563/4, Policy and Strategy for Conduct of the War in the Pacific

CRS A5954 569/2, Strategical Policy in South West Pacific Area — with special reference to Australia as a base

CRS A5954 573/1–2, Future Employment of AIF — Transfer from Middle East to Far East, 1941–1942

CRS A5954 581/17, Exchange of cablegrams between Mr Churchill and Mr Curtin after the outbreak of war with Japan, 1941–1943; Defence of Australia — appreciation of immediate danger of invasion in force, 7/12/41–30/10/42

CRS A5954 610/1, Australia's overseas defence forces — war correspondents, war records and broadcasters. Press photography in combat areas

CRS A5954 653/7, Dept of Defence Co-ordination — Defence of Port Moresby, Paper by Secretary, Department of Defence, 30 September 1942

CRS A5954 654/26, Department of Defence Co-Ordination: United States Forces In New Guinea Campaign — Assessment by Commander-in-Chief, Australian Military Forces, 4 December 1942

CRS A5954 1300/1, Strategical Plans for Defence of Australia following arrival of General MacArthur, March 1942

CRS A5954 1943/1, AIF & Militia Question of Merging Employment of Militia Outside Australia

CRS A5954, Defence of Australia 1942 — complete files

CRS A5954, AIF and Militia. Question of Merging. Employment of Militia Outside Australia. Amendment of Defence Act

CRS A5954, War in the Pacific, December 1941

CRS A5954, Australia's Overseas Defence Forces, 28/12/39 — 23/2/45

CRS A5954, Mr Curtin's speeches, 1941

CRS A5954, Defence of Port Moresby, 30th September 1942

CRS A5954, Defence of Port Moresby. Master sheets

CRS A5954, Higher Army Direction of Operations in New Guinea

CRS A5954, Criticisms of Australia's War Effort by Hanson Baldwin, New York Times

CRS A5954, Commander Allied Land Forces. Report on New Guinea operations, 23/9/42–23/1/43

CRS A5954, Land Forces in Southwest Pacific Area

CRS A5954, Summary of positions in New Guinea and Solomon Islands, 30th October 1942

CRS A5954, Military Call-up in Papua and New Guinea

CRS A5954, United States Forces in New Guinea Campaign, 4 December 1942

CRS A5954, Procedure in Connection with Correspondence with Commander-in-Chief, South West Pacific Area

CRS A5954, Army administration and policy

CRS A5954, Operations in New Guinea, 23 November 1942

CRS A5954, New Guinea operations. Papuan campaign

CRS A5954, Report on operations — New Guinea Forces, 11 August 1942– 28 September 1942

CRS A5954, Alleged misconduct of troops at Port Moresby

CRS A5954, 1. Pacific Action — Midway Battle. 2. New Guinea Position, 1942

CRS A5954, Operations in New Guinea, October 1942

CRS A5954, Rates of pay and conditions of service, 1945

CRS A5954, Evacuation of essential industry and civil population from coastal areas of New South Wales

CRS A5954/1 230/13, Provision of Aircraft for Air Ambulances in New Guinea, 31/12/42–7/4/43

CRS A12728 Master Sheets of Top Secret Inward and Outward Cables, with WINCH [Winston Churchill], JOHCU [John Curtin], ARDEN [Arthur Fadden] or GORDON [Robert Menzies] prefixes

CRS M100, Personal Papers of Prime Minister Bruce, January–December 1942

CRS M1415–M1416, Personal Papers of Prime Minister Curtin, 11 November 1941–5 May 1942

CRS MP76/3 G254, General Blamey — correspondence [with Army Inventions Directorate] 1942

CRS MP729/7 64/421/38, Pay and Allowances of General Sir Thomas A. Blamey, 1941–1942

CRS MP956/2 103, Reports of the Director-General of Munitions to the Prime Minister for the information of War Cabinet

CRS SP109/1 78/12/51, Film, Mr Curtin Talks for the Talkies

CRS SP112/1, Curtin's broadcast talks over the national network

National Library, Canberra

Map room

Primary Sources — Japanese Army

Interviews with veterans of the Nankai Shitai, at Kochi City, Shikoku, October 2003

Imanishi Sadaharu, 144th Infantry Regiment

Shimada Yuki, 144th Infantry Regiment

Yamasaki Yukiharu, 144th Infantry Regiment

Met and talked with several veterans and family members who have not been named, and who attended the reunion of the 144th Regiment, in Kochi, October 2003

Other interviews and discussions

Dr Steven Bullard, director of the Australia–Japan Research Project, Australian War Memorial

Marutani Hajime, student of Japanese military history, interpreter, in Sydney and Kochi

Professor Tanaka Hiromi, Japanese military historian, in Tokyo, October 2003

Nobohiko Sugimoto, son of Nankai Shitai veteran — several meetings in Sydney, 2002

Dr Keiko Tamura, Australia–Japan Research Project, Australian War Memorial

Japanese soldiers' diaries and notebooks held under Allied Translator & Interpreter Section (ATIS), Australian War Memorial (some may be aliases; full names of individuals and units not always available)

Fujitani Hiroyuki
Hirano, Tsukamoto Daitai
Hisaeda Akiyoshi
Kure 3rd Special Naval Landing Party, notes for unit commanders
Moritomo Yoshiuki
Nada Kozo, Signal Tai
Nagafune
Okajima, 34th Butai
Okamoto Shigeo
Sakamoto, 55th Mountain Artillery
Sato Toshio, Ikeda Tai
Shin Shunji, Tsukioka Daitai (Korean)
Uchiyama Seiichi, Kenmotsu Butai
Sadahiro
Wada Kiyoshi, 144th Regiment signal unit
Watanabe Toshio, Tsukamoto Daitai
Yamada, Umemura Tai
Various diaries and notebooks of unknown soldiers

Interrogation Reports of Japanese POWs held under ATIS, Australian War Memorial (some may be aliases; full names of individuals and units not always available)

Fusai Iwataro, Setsuetai (Pioneer unit)
Ikeda Tomoichi, Tanaka Butai
Katsukara Kanemidzu, Yokosuka No. 5 Special Naval Landing Party (a very unusual name; the sound can mean 'give me your money and water, then we will win' — so it is probably an alias)
Kondo Yuzo
Kunisawa Yuki, Kusunose Butai
Matsuoka Kazuo
Miyaji Chikara
Naka Masao (alias Yamashita Hideo), 41st (Yazawa) Regiment
Okino Jiro
Sakaki Minoru, Kure No. 5 Special Naval Landing Party
Sato Tetsuro
Tsuno Keishin, Kusunose Butai
Yabuguchi, Watanabe Butai
Yamada Kazuo, Kusunose Butai
Yamaguchi Masahiro
Yamamoto Kiyoshi, Yamanaka Butai
Yoshimoto Yoshihiro, Yokoyama Butai
Watanabe Fukuichi, Yazawa Regiment

Primary document sources

Australian War Memorial

AWM 55 ATIS Bulletins 1/1 Nos 1–99 [containing Japanese intelligence assessments, battle orders, unit diaries and notebooks]

AWM 55 ATIS Bulletins 1/2 Nos 100–199

AWM 55 ATIS Bulletins 1/3 Nos 200–279

AWM 55 ATIS Bulletins 1/9 Nos 526–565

AWM 55 ATIS Bulletins 1/10 Nos 566–605

AWM 55 ATIS Bulletins 1/33 Nos 1476–1510

AWM 55 ATIS Current Translations 3/2 [containing Japanese diaries and unit documents]

AWM 55 ATIS Current Translations 3/3 Nos 26–35

AWM 55 ATIS Current Translations 3/5 Nos 51–64

AWM 55 ATIS Enemy Publications 5/1 Nos 1–13 [containing assorted Japanese military documents found on Japanese corpses or in prisoners' possession]

AWM 55 ATIS Enemy Publications 5/2 Nos 14–26

AWM 55 ATIS Enemy Publications 5/2 No. 27, Field Log of Sakigawa Tai

AWM 55 ATIS Enemy Publications 5/2 No. 29, File of Miscellaneous orders and Bulletins 9 November–8 December 1942 compiled by Giruwa L of C Field Hospital

AWM 55 ATIS Enemy Publications 5/2 No. 33, File of Nankai Shitai Orders, 16 August–15 October 1942

AWM 55 ATIS Enemy Publications 5/2 No. 38, File of Nankai Shitai Orders, 13 May–10 July 1942

AWM 55 ATIS Enemy Publications 5/2 No. 39, File of Nankai Shitai Orders, 2 October–7 November 1942

AWM 55 ATIS Enemy Publications 5/3 No. 28, Intelligence Reports Issued by Yazawa Butai HQ

AWM 55 ATIS Enemy Publications 5/4 Nos 44–48 ('True Examples of War Living' in Japan — Contest Winners)

AWM 55 ATIS Enemy Publications 5/6 No. 76

AWM 55 ATIS Enemy Publications 5/8 No. 93

AWM 55 ATIS Enemy Publications 5/22 No. 255, Procedure in Interrogating and Handling Prisoners of War

AWM 55 ATIS Enemy Publications 5/25 Nos 285–302

AWM 55 ATIS Interrogation Reports 6/1 Nos 9, 10, 28, 34, 36, 37, 39, 44, 48, 71 [containing summaries of interrogations of Japanese POWs]

AWM 55 ATIS Interrogation Reports 6/2 Nos 51–80

AWM 55 ATIS Interrogation Reports 6/3 Nos 81–145

AWM 55 ATIS Interrogation Reports 6/4 Nos 146–195

AWM 55 ATIS Information Request Reports 12/1–12/23 [containing specific information sought from Japanese sources and POWs]

AWM 55 ATIS Information Request Reports 12/24–12/36

AWM 55 ATIS Interrogation Spot Reports 7/1 Nos 12, 14, 18, 24, 27, 28, 29, 31, 33, 65, 70

AWM 55 ATIS 'M' Reports 9/1–9/11 [containing reports of Allied covert monitoring of Japanese POWs' conversations and behaviour]

AWM 55 ATIS Research Reports 12/53 [containing detailed analyses of the character of Japanese army, based on information from Japanese POWs commissioned by General MacArthur]:
— Part I: Self-Immolation as a Factor in Japanese Military Psychology, 4 April 1944
— Part II: The Emperor Cult as a Present Factor in Japanese Military Psychology, 21 June 1944

— Part III: The Warrior Tradition as a Present Factor in Japanese Military Psychology, 30 October 1944
— Part IV: Prominent Factors in Japanese Military Psychology, 7 February 1945
— Part V: Superstitions as a Present Factor in Japanese Military Psychology, 24 February 1945
— Part VI: Defects Arising from the Doctrine of 'Spiritual Superiority' as Factors in Japanese Military Psychology

AWM 55 ATIS Research Reports 12/50 Parts 1, 2 & 3, Japanese Violations of the Laws of War, 29 April 1944

AWM 55 ATIS Research Reports 12/89, Infringement of the Laws of War and Ethics by the Japanese Medical Corps, 26 January '45

AWM 55 ATIS Research Reports 12/94, Antagonism between Officers and Men in the Japanese Armed Forces, 19 April '45

AWM 55 ATIS Nankai Shitai Operational Orders for the Invasion of Port Moresby, August 1942

AWM 55 ATIS Spot Reports 2/1 Nos 1–120 [containing translations of brief instructions to troops, notebooks, diaries and interrogations]

The Diary of a Japanese Soldier at Wewak, translated and with an introductory essay by Dr Keiko Tamura, Australia–Japan Research Project

AWM F940.541352 MON 1521, Yoshihara T., *Southern Cross: Account Of The Eastern New Guinea Campaign* (translated by Doris Heath)

AWM 55 492/7/22 MSS 732, Okada, S., *Lost Troops* (translated by Dr Keiko Tamura)

National Library, Canberra

Japanese Monographs [a history of the Pacific War written by Japanese commanders, commissioned by General MacArthur, on microfiche], Reels 24, 33, 34, 37, 45, 96, 127, 143, 146, 150, 152

Library of the National Institute of Defence Studies, Tokyo

South East Area Army Operations, *Lessons learned from battles at Buna and Giruwa and intelligence on future army operations* (extracts translated by Dr Steve Bullard, Australian War Memorial)

Municipal Library, Kochi City

Yukon Kochi-ken Kyodo Senshi, 1 November 1974, Kochi Prefecture

Signals Coy, 144th Regiment (editing committee), Hohei Dai 144 Rentai Tsushin Chutai Shi (History of Signals Company, 144th Infantry Regiment), 1986

For a full list of Japanese Army unit histories, see the bibliography by Dr Iwamoto Hiromitsu, Australia–Japan Research Project, Australian War Memorial web site

General Sources

Essays, articles

Allen, B., and Tamura, K., 'Attitudes of Japanese Troops towards villagers and the supply of food in the inland Aitape-Wewak Campaign, Papua New Guinea, 1942–45', presented at *The 5th Symposium: The Pacific War in Papua New Guinea, Perceptions and Realities*, Australian National University, 7–8 August 2003

Bleechmore, S.J., 'Road Construction in Papua New Guinea in Support of Operations on the Kokoda Track and at Buna-Gona, August 1942 to February 1943', AWM 54

Bullard, S., 'Japanese Medical Corps in the Papuan Campaign 1942–1943', presented at *The 5th Symposium*, as above

Coulthard-Clark, C., 'Blamey: A Commander-in-Chief for the Times', The Blamey Oration to the Royal United Service Institution of NSW, in *United Service*, Vol. 53, No. 2, 2001

Friday, K., 'Bushido or Bull? A Medieval Historian's Perspective on the Imperial Army and the Japanese Warrior Tradition', *The History Teacher*, Volume 27, Issue 3, Pages 339–49, 1994

Grebert, R., *Australian VC Recipients*, 1990

Hiromitsu, I., 'Memories and Realities of Japanese Occupation of New Guinea', presented at *The 5th Symposium*, as above

Honner, R., 'The 39th at Isurava', *Australian Army Journal*, July 1967

Honner, R., 'This is the 39th', *The Bulletin*, 3 August 1995

Jones, E., 'Far Eastern Liaison Office; Propaganda in the South West Pacific Area in the Second World War', AWM Reference Library presentation

Lindsay, P., 'The Lieutenant-Colonel Ralph Honner Leadership Oration', at the Kokoda Track Foundation dinner, 20 August 2003

Marutani, H., 'An Examination of How Race Affected the Far Eastern War', essay, Masters degree, Australian National University

Nelson, H., a brief profile of the life of Dr Geoffrey Vernon (sent to the author)

Nelson, H., 'Kokoda: The Track from History to Politics', presented at the State Society and Governance in Melanesia Project seminar, Australian National University, 19 September 2002

Nelson, H., 'Zentsuji and Totsuka: Australians from Rabaul as Prisoners of War in Japan', presented at *The 5th Symposium*, as above

Phillips, W.H.J., 'The Homefront, 1942–1945', Phillips Publications, Coffs Harbour

Sakaiya, T., 'Hirohito & The Imperial Tradition', *PHP Intersect Magazine*, 1984

Wada, K., 'Painting over my shame', from *The Signals Company Records: 144th Infantry Regiment (Kochi)*, Kobayashi Eijuro (ed.), 144th Infantry Regiment Signals Company Editing Committee, Kochi, 1986

Wyatt, P., 'The Quality of Mercy', *The Spectator*, 1 February 2003

Newspapers, magazines, manuals

Various issues between 1939–1945 (unless otherwise stated)

Guinea Gold
Jungle Warfare 6 Australian Division, Training Instruction No. 11, First Australian Army Press, 1943
Moresby Army News Sheet
The Age
Daily Telegraph (Sydney)
Melbourne Herald
Melbourne Argus
Smith's Weekly
Sydney Morning Herald

Recent press

Sydney Morning Herald, 3–4 August 2002, p. 29
Sydney Morning Herald, 19 January 2004, p. 38
Wartime, official magazine of the Australian War Memorial, issues 19, 20, 21
Weekend Australian, 15–16 June 2002, p. 24
Weekend Australian, 15–16 February 2003, p. 25

Films, videos, CDs, tapes

Hirohito: The Chrysanthemum Throne
Kokoda Front Line, by Damien Parer, 1942
Kokoda . . . the Bloody Track, by Patrick Lindsay and George Friend, for the Australian Army Training Command, 1992
Kokoda . . . the Last Parade, by Patrick Lindsay, Billybob Productions, 1999
MacArthur (Parts 1 and 2), by Austin and Sarah Holt
The Men Who Saved Australia, 'Four Corners', reported by Chris Masters, produced by Jacquelyn Hole, 27 April 1998
Northern Attack: War on Australia, 19 February 1942, produced by Darwin City Council

Australian War Memorial videos, tapes, CDs

AWM F01807, *Blamey's Farewell to Troops*
AWM F01809, *Advance on Kokoda*
AWM F01914, *General Blamey*
AWM F01935, *Blamey Inspects 2/33rd Battalion*
AWM F10250, *The Battle of Buna*
Murdoch Sound Archives [containing transcripts of interviews with troops from various battalions]
Keith Richmond, extensive research on Japanese logistics, on CD

Web sources

Australian War Memorial: www.awm.gov.au, with links to Australia–Japan Research Project (see *The Human Face of War* series on the Japanese army, translated by Steve Bullard and Keiko Tamura)
Unit War Diaries, links on the Australian War Memorial web site
National Archives of Australia: www.naa.gov.au
43rd Bomb Group, 5th Air Force (USA): www.kensmen.com
Various historical web sites concerning the lives of John Curtin, Douglas MacArthur, Thomas Blamey, the Emperor Hirohito and Premier Tojo

Unit reunions attended by the author

Australian infantry

2/14th Battalion, Brisbane, 2002
21st Brigade, Sydney, 2003
55/53rd Battalion, Anzac Day, 2003

Japanese infantry

144th Regiment, Kochi City, October 2003

Secondary sources (Australian and Japanese)

Allchin, F., *Purple and Blue: The History of the 2/10th Battalion AIF,* 2/10th Ex-Servicemen's Association, Adelaide, 1960
Austin, V., *To Kokoda and Beyond: The Story of the 39th Battalion 1941–43,* Melbourne University Press, Melbourne, 1988
Baker, C., and Knight, G., *Milne Bay 1942,* Baker-Knight Publications, Sydney, 1991

Ballard, G., *On Ultra Active Service*, Spectrum, Richmond (Victoria), 1991

Barrett, J., *We Were There: Australian Soldiers of World War II Tell Their Stories*, Viking, Sydney, 1987

Barter, M., *Far Above Battle: The Experience and Memory of Australian Soldiers in War*, 1939–1945, Allen & Unwin, Sydney, 1994

Beevor, A., *Stalingrad*, Penguin, London, 1999

Benedict, R., *The Crysanthemum and the Sword: Patterns of Japanese Culture*, Houghton-Mifflin, New York, 1989

Bergerud, E., *Touched with Fire: the Land War in the South Pacific*, Viking, New York, 1996

Blamey, T. (ed.), *The Jap was Thrashed: An Official History of the Australian Soldier, First Victor of the 'INVINCIBLE' JAP, New Guinea* 1942–1943, Director General of [Army] Public Relations under the authority of General Sir Thomas Blamey

Bleakley, J., *The Eavesdroppers*, Australian Government Publishing Service, Canberra, 1992

Brune, P., *A Bastard of a Place: The Australians in Papua*, Allen & Unwin, Sydney, 2004

Brune, P., *Gona's Gone! The Battle for the Beach-head* 1942, Allen & Unwin, Sydney, 1994

Brune, P., *The Spell Broken: Exploding the Myth of Japanese Invincibility*, Allen & Unwin, Sydney, 1997

Brune, P., *Those Ragged Bloody Heroes: From the Kokoda Trail to Gona Beach* 1942, Allen & Unwin, Sydney, 1991

Brune, P., *We Band of Brothers: A Biography of Ralph Honner, Soldier and Statesman*, Allen & Unwin, Sydney, 2000

Budden, F., *That Mob: The Story of the 55/53rd Australian Infantry Battalion AIF*, Sydney, 1973

Burns, J., *The Brown and Blue Diamond at War*, 2/27th Ex-Servicemen's Association, Adelaide, 1960

Buruma, I., *Inventing Japan, From Empire to Economic Miracle* 1853–1964, Modern Library, New York, 2003

Carlyon, N.D., *I Remember Blamey*, Macmillan, Melbourne, 1980

Carlyon, L., *Gallipoli*, Pan Macmillan, Sydney, 2001

Charlton, P., *The Thirty-Niners*, Macmillan, Sydney, 1981

Charlton, P., *War Against Japan* 1942–1945, Time-Life Books, Sydney, 1989

Clarrie, J., *Angau: One Man Law*

Clowes, C., *The Clowes Report on the Battle of Milne Bay*, 1942, Australian Military History Publications, Loftus, 1995

Connell, D., *The War at Home: Australia* 1939–1945, ABC Enterprises, Crows Nest, 1988

Clift, K., *The Saga of a Sig: The Wartime Memories of Six Years Service in the Second AIF*, KCD Publications, Randwick, Sydney, 1972

Clift, K., *War Dance: The Story of the 2/3rd Aust. Inf. Battalion AIF*, P.M. Fowler & 2/3rd Battalion Association, Kingsgrove NSW, 1980

Conway, R., *The Great Australian Stupor*, Sun Books, Sydney 1971

Cook, H.T. and T.F., *Japan at War: An Oral History*, New Press, New York 1992.

Coulthard-Clark, C., *The Encyclopaedia of Australia's Battles*, Allen & Unwin, NSW, 1998

Cranston, F., *Always Faithful: The History of the 49th Battalion*, Boolarong, Brisbane, 1983

Crooks, W., *The Footsoldiers: The Story of the 2/33rd Australian Infantry Battalion AIF in the War of* 1939–45, Printcraft, Sydney, 1971

Crump, T., *Death of an Emperor: Japan at the Crossroad*, Constable, London, 1989

Day, D., *Curtin*, HarperCollins, Sydney, 2000

Day, D., *Reluctant Nation: Australia and the Allied Defeat of Japan* 1942–45, Oxford University Press, Melbourne, 1992

Day, D., *The Great Betrayal: Britain, Australia and the Onset of the Pacific War* 1939–42, Oxford University Press, Melbourne, 1988

Day, D., *The Politics of War*, HarperCollins, Sydney, 2003

Deane-Butcher, W., *Fighter Squadron Doctor: 75 Squadron RAAF New Guinea 1942*, self-published, Sydney, 1989

Dexter. D., *Australia in the War of 1939–1945 (series I, volume VI): The New Guinea Offensives*, Australian War Memorial, Canberra, 1961

Dixon, N., *On the Psychology of Military Incompetence*, Pimlico, London, 1994

Dornan, P., *The Silent Men: Syria to Kokoda and on to Gona*, Allen & Unwin, Sydney, 1999

Draydon, A. W., *Men of Courage: A History of 2/25 Australian Infantry Battalion 1940–1945*, 2/25 Australian Infantry Battalion Association, Cheltenham, Victoria, 2000

Drea, E.J., *MacArthur's Ultra: Codebreaking and the War against Japan, 1942–1945*, University Press of Kansas, Kansas, 1992

Edgar, B., *Warrior of Kokoda: A Biography of Brigadier Arnold Potts*, Allen & Unwin, Sydney, 1999

Eichelberger, R.L., *Jungle Road to Toykyo*, Odhams, London, 1951

Fearnside, G.H., and Clift, K., *Dougherty: A Great Man Among Men*, Alpha, Sydney, 1979

Feldt, E., *The Coast Watchers*, Oxford University Press, Melbourne, 1946

Franke, C.S., *Mad Mick's Mob: A History of the 15th Australian Field Company (AIF)*, 15th Australian Field Company Engineers Association, Mentone, Victoria, 1995

Gailey, H., *MacArthur Strikes Back*, Presido Press, Novato, California, 2000

Galloway, J., *The Odd Couple: Blamey and MacArthur at War*, University of Queensland Press, Brisbane 2000

Gill, G.H., *Royal Australian Navy, 1939–42*, Australian War Memorial, Canberra, 1958

Gillison, D., *Australia in the War of 1939–1945*, Series 3 (Air): vol. I, *Royal Australian Air Force 1939–42*, Australian War Memorial, Canberra, 1962

Givney, E.C., *The First at War: The Story of the 2/1st Australian Infantry Battalion 1939–45*, Association of First Infantry Battalions, Earlwood, 1987

Graeme-Evans, A.L., *Of Storms and Rainbows: The Story of the Men of the 2/12th Battalion AIF*, 2/12th Battalion Association, Hobart, 1991

Hart, B.H.L., *Thoughts on War*, Faber and Faber, London, 1943

Hartley, F.J., *Sanananda Interlude*, The Book Depot, Melbourne, 1949

Hasluck, P., *The Government and the People 1939–41*, vols 1 & 2, Australian War Memorial, Canberra, 1952

Henderson, J., *Onward Boy Solders: The Battle for Milne Bay 1942*, University of Western Australia Press, Perth, 1992

Hetherington, J., *Blamey: Controversial Solder*, Australian War Memorial, Canberra, 1973

Hicks, G., *The Comfort Women*, Norton & Co, New York, 1995

Hillis, L., *Japan's Military Masters: The Army in Japanese Life*, Viking Press, New York 1943

Hopkins, R.N.L. *Australian Armour: A History of The Royal Australian Armoured Corps 1927–1972*, Australian War Memorial and the Australian Government Publishing Service, Canberra, 1978

Horner, D., *Blamey: Commander-in-Chief*, Allen & Unwin, Sydney, 1998

Horner, D., *Crisis of Command: Australian Generalship and the Japanese Threat, 1941–1943*, Australian War Memorial, Canberra, 1978

Horner, D., *General Vasey's War*, Melbourne University Press, Melbourne, 1992

Horner, D., *High Command: Australia's Struggle for an Independent War Strategy 1939–1945*, Allen & Unwin, Sydney, 1992

Horner, D., and Penglase, J., *When the War came to Australia: Memories of the Second World War*, Allen & Unwin, Sydney, 1992

James, W., *Before Memories Fade: A Trekker's Guide to the Lost Battlefields*, self-published, Sydney, 2002

Jenkins, R., *Churchill*, Pan Macmillan, London, 2002

Johnson, M., *Fighting the Enemy: Australian Soldiers and their Adversaries in World War Two*, Cambridge University Press, 2000

Johnston, G., *War Diary 1942*, William Collins, Sydney, 1984

Jones, F.C., *Japan's New Order in East Asia: Its Rise and Fall 1937–45*, Oxford University Press, London, 1954

Kato, M., *The Lost War: A Japanese Reporter's Inside Story*, A.A. Knopf, New York, 1946

Keneally, T., *An Angel in Australia*, Doubleday, Sydney, 2002

Kennedy, C., *Port Moresby to Gona Beach: 3rd Australian Infantry Battalion 1942*, Colin Kennedy, Canberra, 1992

Kenney, G., *The MacArthur I Know*, Duell Sloan and Pearce, New York, 1951

Keogh, E., *South West Pacific, 1941–45*, Greyflower Productions, Melbourne, 1965

Knightley, P., *Australia: A biography of a nation*, Jonathan Cape, London, 2000

Leary, W.M., *We Shall Return!: MacArthur's Commanders and the Defeat of Japan 1942–1945*, The University of Kentucky, Lexington, 1988

Lewin, R., *The Other Ultra*, Hutchinson, London, 1982

Lindsay, P., *The Spirit of Kokoda: Then and Now*, Hardie Grant Books, Melbourne, 2002

Lodge, B., *Lavarack: Rival General*, Allen & Unwin, Sydney, 1998

Long, G., *MacArthur as Military Commander*, Angus & Robertson, Sydney, 1969

Long, G., *The Six Years' War*, Australian War Memorial, Canberra, 1953

MacArthur, D., *Reminiscences*, McGraw-Hill, New York, 1964

Maitland, G.L., *The Second World War and its Australian Army Battle Honours*, Kangaroo Press, Sydney, 1999

Manning, P., *Hirohito: The War Years*, Dodd Mead, New York, 1986

Marshall, J., *Nulli secundus log*, 2/2nd Australian Infantry Battalion AIF, Sydney, 1946

Mayo, L., *Bloody Buna*, Doubleday, New York, 1974

McAllester, J., *Men of the 2/14 Battalion*, 2/14 Battalion Association, Melbourne, 1990

McAulay, L., *Blood and Iron: The Battle for Kokoda 1942*, Hutchinson, Melbourne, 1991

McAulay, L., *To the Bitter End, The Japanese Defeat at Buna and Gona 1942–43*, Random House, Sydney, 1992.

McCarthy, D., *South-West Pacific Area — First Year, Kokoda to Wau*, Australian War Memorial, Canberra, 1959

McDonald, N., *War Cameraman: The Story of Damien Parer*, Lothian, Melbourne, 1994

McDonald, N., and Brune, P., *200 Shots: Damien Parer, George Silk and the Australians at War in New Guinea*, Allen & Unwin, Sydney, 1998

Manchester, W., *American Caesar, Douglas MacArthur 1880–1964*, Little Brown & Company, Boston, 1978

McKernan, M., *All In!: Fighting the War at Home*, Allen & Unwin, Sydney 1995

McLaren D., *Mates in Hell: The Secret Diary of Don McLaren*

Millar, A., *Orchids of Papua New Guinea*, Timber Pr, Brisbane, 1999

Milner, S., *Victory in Papua*, Office of the Chief of Military History, Department of the Army, Washington, 1975

Minear, R.H., *Victor's Justice: The Tokyo War Crimes Trial*, Princeton University Press, Princeton, 1971

Mishima, Y., *The Sailor Who Fell From Grace with the Sea*, Vintage International, New York, 1994

Monash, General Sir J., *The Australian Victories in France in 1918*, Lothian, Melbourne, 1923

Morrison, I., *This War against Japan*, Faber & Faber, London [undated], written in 1943

Mueller, J., *Guadalcanal 1942: The Marines Strike Back*, Osprey Publishing, Oxford, 1992

Nakahashi, *War History of the Force which was sent to the South Seas*, AWM PR00297, translated by Lt F.C. Jorgensen

National Institute of Defence Studies, Japan, *Official History: Thrust Through the Owen Stanley Range*, NIDS, Tokyo

Nitobe, I., *Bushido: The Soul of Japan*, Tuttle Publishing, Boston, 2001

O'Brien, J., *Guns and Gunners: The Story of the 2/5th Australian Field Regiment in World War I*, Angus & Robertson, Sydney, 1950

Okakura, K., *The Book of Tea*, Kodansha International, Tokyo, 1989

Pacific War Research Society, *Japan's Longest Day*, Kodansha, Tokyo, 1980

Packard, J.M., *Sons of Heaven: A Portrait of the Japanese Monarchy*, Collier Books, New York, 1989

Paull, R.A., *Retreat from Kokoda*, Heinemann, Melbourne, 1958

Perret, G., *Old Solders Never Die: The Life of Douglas MacArthur*, Random House, New York, 1996

Potts, E, and Potts, A., *Yankees Down Under*, Oxford University Press, Melbourne, 1985

Prados, J., *Combined Fleet Decoded: The Secret History of American Intelligence and the Japanese Navy in World War II*, United States Naval Institute, 2001

Prefer, N., *MacArthur's New Guinea Campaign*, DaCapo Press, 1995

Raftery, J., *Marks of War: War Neurosis and the Legacy of Kokoda*, Lythrum Press, Adelaide, 2003

Rees, L., and Akira, I., *Horror in the East*, DaCapo Press, 2002

Rinzo, K., *History of the New Guinea War (Niyuuginia Senki)*, Kawade Shoboo, Tokyo, 1943 (extracts translated by Dr Carol Hayes)

Robertson, J., and McCarthy, J., *Australian War Strategy, 1939–1945: A Documentary History*, University of Queensland Press, St Lucia, 1985

Rolleston, F., *Not a Conquering Hero*, self-published, Eton (Queensland), 1984

Rowell, S.F., *Full Circle*, Melbourne University Press, Melbourne, 1974

Russell, W.B., *The History of the 2/14th Australian Infantry Battalion*, Angus & Robertson, Sydney, 1948

Russell, E.F.L., *The Knights of Bushido, A Short History of Japanese War Crimes*, Greenhill Books/Lionel Leventhal, 2002

Ryan, P., *Fear Drive My Feet*, Duffy and Snelgrove, Sydney, 2002

Saburo, I., *Japan's Last War — Word War II and the Japanese, 1931–1945*, ANU Press, Canberra, 1979

Saburo, S., *Samurai*, I Books, 2001

Scott, G., *The Knights of Kokoda*, Horwitz, Sydney, 1963

Sebald, W., and Brines, R., *With MacArthur in Japan*, Cresset Press, London 1965

Seward, J., *Hara-kiri — Japanese Ritual Suicide*, Tuttle, Tokyo, 1968

Slim, Sir W., *Defeat into Victory*, Cassel, London, 1956

Smith, N., *Kokoda Track Casualties: An Outline History of Australian Involvement in the Campaign with Unit and Full Casualty Listings*, Mostly Unsung Military History Research and Publications, Gardenvale, Victoria, 2001

Smith, M., *The Emperor's Codes: The Breaking of Japan's Secret Ciphers*, Penguin, London, 2002

Somerville, H. and D., *A Taste of Ginger*, Hedley Local History Books, Sydney, 2003

Souter, G., *New Guinea: The Last Unknown*, Angus & Robertson, Sydney, 1957

Spencer, B., *In the Footsteps of Ghosts: With the 2/9th Battalion in the African Desert and the Jungles of the Pacific*, Allen & Unwin, Sydney, 1999

Spencer, M., *Malaria: The Australian Experience 1943–1991*, Australian College of Tropical Medicine, Townsville, 1994.

Steward, H.D., *Recollections of a Regimental Medical Officer*, Melbourne University Press, Melbourne, 1981

Sublet, F., *Kokoda to the Sea: a History of the 1942 Campaign in Papua*, Slouch Hat Publications, McCrae, Victoria, 2000

Takemoto, T., and Ohara, Y., *The Alleged 'Nanking Massacre': Japan's Rebuttal to China's Forged Claims*, Meisei-sha Inc., Tokyo, 2000

Takita, K., *The Pacific Burns (Taiyoo wa moeru)*, Kachoo Shuppan, Tokyo, 1955 (extracts translated by Dr Carol Hayes)

Takushiro, H., *Complete History of the Greater East Asian War*, Masu Shobu 1953, on microfilm, Australian War Memorial Research Centre, Canberra

Tanaka, K., *Operations of the Imperial Japanese Armed Forces in the Papua New Guinea Theater during World War II*, Japan Papua New Guinea Goodwill Society, Tokyo, 1980.

Tann, L., *Unit history: 2/5th Australian Field Ambulance 1940–1945*, 2/5th Australian Field Ambulance Association, Forster, NSW, 1987

Tarlington, G., *Shifting Sands and Savage Jungle: The Memories of a Frontline Infantryman*, Australian Military History Publications, Loftus, 1994

Thomson, J., *Winning with Intelligence: A Biography of John David Rogers*, Australian Military History Publications, Loftus, 2000

Toland, J., *The Rising Sun: The Decline and Fall of the Japanese Empire 1936–1945*, Random House, New York, 1970

Trigellis-Smith, S., *The Purple Devils: a History of the 2/6 Australian Commando Squadron, formerly the 2/6 Australian Independent Company, 1942–1946*, 2/6 Commando Squadron Association, Melbourne, 1992

Turnbull, S.R., *The Book of the Samurai — The Warrior Class of Japan*, Arco, New York, 1982

Uren, M., and Graham, B., *A Thousand Men at War — The Story of the 2/16th Battalion A.I.F.*, Heinemann, Melbourne, 1959

Walker, A.S., *Clinical Problems of War*, Australian War Memorial, Canberra, 1952

Walker, A.S., *The Island Campaigns*, Australian War Memorial, Canberra, 1957

Watanabe. T., *The Naval Landing Unit that Vanished in the Jungle* (edited and translated by Hiromitsu, I.), Tabletop Press, Canberra, 1995

Waugh, E., *The Sword of Honour Trilogy*, Penguin, London, 1984

White, O., *Green Armour*, Angus and Robertson, Sydney, 1945

Wigmore, L., *The Japanese Thrust*, Australian War Memorial, Canberra, 1957

Willoughby, C., and Chamberlain, J., *MacArthur, 1941–1951: Victory in the Pacific*, William Heinemann, Melbourne, 1956

Wilson, D., *Jacksons Few: 75 Squadron RAAF, Port Moresby, March/May 1942*, David Wilson, Canberra, 1988

Wilson, D., *The Decisive Factor: 75 & 76 Squadrons — Port Moresby and Milne Bay 1942*, Banner Books, Brunswick, 1991

Yamamoto, K., *Yokogotoku; Kaigun Yasuda Butai Buna gyokusai no tenmatsu*, Seiunsha, Tokyo, 1985 (extracts translated by Muritani Hajime)

Yomamoto, T., *Bushido: The Way of the Samurai*, Square One Publishers, New York, 2002

Young, M., and Clark, J., *An Anthropologist in Papua — The Photography of F. E. Williams, 1922–139* Crawford House Publishing, South Australia, 2001

Notes

PART 1: LANDING

Chapter 1: Missionary

1 Williams, *An Anthropologist in Papua*, p. 89
2 *Ibid.*, p. 29
3 *Ibid.*, p. 90
4 The Baigona Cult was suppressed in 1912. See Williams, *An Anthropologist in Papua*, p. 90
5 *Ibid.*, p. 28
6 Benson, *Prisoner's Base and Home Again*, p. 20
7 *Ibid.*, p. 20
8 *Ibid.*, p. 21
9 *Ibid.*, p. 21
10 CRS A2671 108/1941
11 Quoted in McCarthy, *South-West Pacific Area — First Year*, p. 40
12 CRS A2671 108/1941
13 Benson, p. 9
14 Okada, *Lost Troops*, Benson's Epilogue, p. 20
15 *Ibid.*, p. 20
16 Benson, p. 22
17 *Ibid.*, p. 22
18 *Wartime*, Issue 21, p. 14
19 Okada, *Lost Troops*, Benson's Epilogue, p. 23
20 *Ibid.*, p. 23

Chapter 2: Yokoyama

1 Interview with Imanishi Sadaharu 18 October 2003
2 *Ibid.*
3 *Ibid.*
4 *Ibid.*
5 Nakahashi, *War History of the Force which was sent to the South Seas*, translated by Lt F.C. Jorgensen, p. 5, AWM PR00297
6 ATIS Enemy Publication No. 27, *Field Log of Sakigawa Tai*
7 In Paull, *Retreat from Kokoda*, p. 50

8 In Horner, *High Command*, p. 218
9 White, *Green Armour*, p. 66
10 Benson, *Prisoner's Base and Home Again*, p. 11
11 White, p. 66
12 Nelson, *Kokoda: The Track from History to Politics* (essay), p. 4
13 In McCarthy, p. 113
14 Horner, *Crisis of Command*, p. 97
15 ATIS Enemy Publication No. 28, *Yokoyama Advance Tai Report*
16 *Ibid.*
17 See Toland, *The Rising Sun*, photograph section
18 ATIS Enemy Publication No. 28, *Yokoyama Advance Tai Report*
19 Nelson, p. 9
20 In McAulay, *Blood and Iron*, p. 41
21 ATIS Enemy Publication No. 27, *Field Log of Sakigawa Tai*
22 ATIS Bulletin No. 218: 'We were forced to transport fodder by manpower,' wrote Second Lieutenant Hirano
23 1 TO = 3.97 gallons; 1 SHO = 0.397 gallons.

Chapter 3: Intelligence

1 There is much literature on Allied code-breakers in WW2. See Smith, *The Emperor's Codes*; Prados, *Combined Fleet Decoded*; Drea, *MacArthur's Ultra*; and Ballard, *On Ultra Active Service*
2 *Herald Sun*, How we turned the tide, 20 April, 2002. Sources: Geoffrey Ballard, Jack Bleakley, Frank Cain, David Horner, John Prados, Michael Smith, Alan Stripp, Barbara Winter, Craig Blair, John Cribbin, Greg Alabaster, National Archives of Australia, Peter Carter and the members of FRUMEL and Central Bureau

3 *Ibid.*

4 *Ibid.*

5 Blamey Papers

6 Smith, *The Emperor's Codes*, p. 173

7 CRS A2671 143/1942 (An Ultra-generated document)

8 *Ibid.*

9 See Feldt, *The Coastwatchers*

10 Feldt, p. 186

11 McCarthy, *South-West Pacific Area — First Year, Kokoda to Wau*, p. 123

12 Milner, *Victory in Papua*, p. 70

13 Interview with Lex McAulay, 30 July 2002

14 *Ibid.*

15 Wilmot, *Observations on the New Guinea Campaign*, in Allen Papers

16 Horner, *Crisis of Command*, p. 82

17 *Ibid.*

Chapter 4: Chocos

1 Interview with Laurie Howson, 30 October 2002

2 *Ibid.*

3 *Ibid.*

4 White, *Green Armour*, p. 48

5 Cranston, *Always Faithful*, p. 29.

6 Barry Report, Paragraph 30

7 Hasluck, *The Government and the People*, Volume 2, p. 175

8 Interview with Laurie Howson

9 Paull, *Retreat from Kokoda*, p. 12

10 White, pp. 47–8

11 Horner, *Generals in Battle, Problems of Command in the South-West Pacific Area, 1942–1943*, MA Thesis, p. 3

12 Editorial, *Sydney Morning Herald*, 2 May 1942

13 Editorial, *Daily Telegraph*, 6 May 42

14 Interview with Tom Keneally, 22 January 2004

15 Alf Salmon's notebook, AWM PR00297

16 In Austin, *To Kokoda and Beyond*, p. 34

17 Interview with Don Daniels, 29 October 2002

18 Australian Military Forces, Notice to Recruits, 14 January 1942

19 Nelson, *Kokoda: The Track from History to Politics*, p. 8

20 Interview with Don Daniels

21 *Ibid.*

22 *Ibid.*

23 *Ibid.*

24 McCarthy, *South-West Pacific Area — First Year, Kokoda to Wau*, p. 44

25 McAulay, *Blood and Iron*, p. 105

26 According to some veterans; others do not recall the cordons

27 Sergeant Keith Irwin, 53rd Bn, in Brune, *Those Ragged Bloody Heroes*, p. 12

Chapter 5: Port Moresby

1 In Brune, *Those Ragged Bloody Heroes*, p. 10.

2 Barry Report, Paragraph 18

3 In Paull, *Retreat from Kokoda*, pp. 14–15

4 In Wilson, *The Decisive Factor*, p. 6

5 *Inquiries into Looting at Darwin and Port Moresby*, CRS A5954 256/3

6 Cranston, *Always Faithful*, p. 155

7 Attorney-General's Dept, *Looting at Darwin and Port Moresby: National Security (General) Regulation 40A*, 18 June 42

8 See *Inquiries into Looting at Darwin and Port Moresby*, CRS A5954 256/3

9 Barry Report, Paragraph 18

10 In Austin, *To Kokoda and Beyond*, p. 23

11 *Ibid.*, p. 44

12 White, *Green Armour*, p. 31

13 In Austin, p. 51

14 Wilmot, *Observations on the New Guinea Campaign*

15 See Fraser, *Quartered Safe Out Here*

16 See Waugh, *The Sword of Honour Trilogy*

17 Porter Papers

18 *Ibid.*

19 In Austin, p. 62

20 Paull, p. 19

21 *Ibid.*, p. 20

22 Porter Papers

23 In Paull, pp. 23–24

24 Paull, p. 26. See also Horner, *Crisis of Command*, p. 336

25 Porter Papers

26 *Ibid.*

27 *Ibid.*

28 Combat Efficiency of Army Units, Training and Preparation for Operations, in *Operations Report for Australian Army,* 19 July 1942

29 Brune, *Those Ragged Bloody Heroes,* p. 15

30 Capt H.T. Kienzle, *Report On Kokoda L. of C., Native Carriers during Campaign Owen Stanley Range, Kokoda–Buna,* Feb 1943, ANGAU N.G.F., AWM54 577/6/8

31 *Ibid.*

32 *Ibid.*

Chapter 6: Kokoda

1 Austin, *To Kokoda and Beyond,* p. 78

2 *Ibid.,* pp. 83–4

3 Horner, *Crisis of Command,* p. 103

4 Austin, p. 85

5 In Brune, *Those Ragged Bloody Heroes,* p. 41

6 Okada, *Lost Troops*

7 McCarthy, *South-West Pacific Area — First Year, Kokoda to Wau,* p. 125

8 Interview with Imanishi

9 McCarthy, p. 127

10 Paull, *Retreat from Kokoda,* p. 55

11 Interview with Imanishi

12 Vernon's diary, p. 8

13 Wilkinson's diary, in Austin, p. 97.

14 Vernon's diary, p. 8

15 Vernon's diary, p. 8

16 ATIS 281, *Nankai Shitai Operational Orders for the Invasion of Port Moresby,* 10 August 1942

17 ATIS Intelligence Report No. 1, Yazawa Butai, 3 August 1942

18 Vernon's diary, p. 8

19 *Ibid.,* p. 9

20 *Ibid.,* p. 1

21 Essay on Vernon, by Hank Nelson

22 *Ibid.*

23 In Paull, p. 65

24 ATIS Enemy Publication No. 28, *Yokoyama Advance Tai Report.* See also diary of Second Lieutenant Hidetaka Noda, ATIS Bulletins

25 Interview with Laurie Howson

Chapter 7: Kokoda Lost

1 Wilkinson's diary, in Austin, *To Kokoda and Beyond,* p. 100

2 Blamey to General Kenney, in Horner, *Generals in Battle, Problems of Command in the South-West Pacific Area, 1942–1943,* MA Thesis

3 Lieutenant Hugh Dalby MC, in Brune, *Those Ragged Bloody Heroes,* p. 52

4 Capt H.T. Kienzle, *Report On Kokoda L. of C., Native Carriers during Campaign Owen Stanley Range, Kokoda–Buna,* Feb 1943, ANGAU N.G.F., AWM54 577/6/8

5 *Ibid.*

6 *Ibid.*

7 Captain Symington in Brune, *Those Ragged Bloody Heroes,* p. 57

8 Captain Bidstrup MC in Brune, p. 59

9 Captain A.C. Dean

10 Paull, *Retreat from Kokoda,* p. 72

11 Bidstrup in Brune, p. 63

12 Interview with Imanishi

13 ATIS Bulletin 87, diary of Watanabe Toshi

14 ATIS Bulletin 218, diary of Hirano

15 *Ibid.*

16 *Ibid.*

17 Boland in Austin, pp. 105–6

18 AWM 577/6/1

19 ATIS Bulletin, diary of Onogawa

20 Austin, *To Kokoda and Beyond,* p. 110

Chapter 8: The Sasebo 5 Special Naval Landing Party

1 Tamura and Allen, *Attitudes of Japanese troops towards villagers . . .*

2 ATIS Enemy Publication 38, *File of Nankai Shitai Orders,* 13 May–10 July 1942

3 Comment based on interviews with Shimada, Imanishi and Yamasaka, and Professor Tanaka, in Japan; plus, Hiromitsu, *Memories and realities of Japanese Occupation of New Guinea* and Tamura and Allen (as above)

4 Hiromitsu, *Memories and realities . . .*

5 ATIS Enemy Publication No. 89, *Message and Instruction for Warriors of South Seas Detached Forces,* November 1941

6 ATIS 5/1 Enemy Publications Nos. 1–13

7 Matthews, *Wartime*, Issue 21, p. 15

8 Murdoch Sound Archive, Canon Charles Sherlock

9 ATIS Spot Report No. 15, diary of Sato Toshio. This is one of several references to the atrocity in Japanese soldiers' diaries.

10 *Ibid*. See also ATIS Research Report, No. 72, p. 23, in *Superstitions as a Present Factor in Jap Military Psychology*

11 ATIS Spot Report No. 105, diary of Shin Shunji

PART 2: INVASION

Chapter 9: Defenceless

1 Dept of Defence Co-Ordination, War Cabinet Agendum No. 422/1941

2 Coordinated Plans for the Defence of Australia, 29 Aug 1941, Appendix A, CRS A2671 286/1941

3 Day, *The Great Betrayal*, p. 15

4 *Daily Telegraph*, 7 June 1940

5 Day, *The Politics of War*, p. 58

6 *Ibid*.

7 For a fuller insight into Australia's unpreparedness, see Hasluck, *The Government and the People*, Volume 2, pp. 4–19; and Day, *The Politics of War, Curtin* and *The Great Betrayal*

8 Hasluck, p. 16

9 Day, *The Politics of War*, p. 171

10 Robertson and McCarthy, *Australian War Strategy 1939–1945*, p. 258

11 Day, *Curtin*, p. 431

12 *Ibid*.

13 McCarthy, *South-West Pacific Area — First Year, Kokoda to Wau*, pp. 30–1

14 Horner, *High Command*, p. 15

15 *Ibid.*, p. 36

16 Day, *The Great Betrayal*, p. 60

17 Day, *The Politics of War*, p. 129

18 *Ibid.*, ch. 11

19 Menzies diary, in Day, *The Politics of War*, p. 110

20 Hasluck, *The Government and the People*, Volume 1, p. 237

21 Moran diary, in Day, *The Politics of War*, p. 237

22 *Official Yearbook of the Commonwealth of Australia*, No. 32, 1939, Canberra 1940

23 Day, *The Politics of War*, p. 9

24 Hasluck, *The Government and the People*, Volume 2, p. 164

25 War Cabinet Conclusions, 8 August 1940, CAB 65/14

26 Horner, *High Command*, p. 38

27 Day, *The Politics of War*, p. 307

28 Hasluck, *The Government and the People*, Volume 1, p. 351

29 Danchev and Todman (eds), *War Diaries*, p. 205

30 Robertson and McCarthy, Document 161

31 Hasluck, *The Government and the People*, Volume 2, p. 3

32 *Ibid.*, p. 81

Chapter 10: Curtin

1 For full account of Curtin's youth, see Day, *Curtin*

2 *Ibid.*, p. 184

3 *Ibid*.

4 Hasluck, *The Government and the People*, Volume 2, p. 56

5 *Ibid.*, p. 58

6 Day, *The Politics of War*, p. 201

7 Hasluck, p. 5

8 Day, *Curtin*, p. 433

9 Letter from Curtin to Roosevelt and Churchill, 23 December 1941, CRS A3300/7

10 Hasluck, p. 39

11 Day, *Curtin*, p. 439

12 See Day and Hasluck for a fuller insight into Curtin's appeals to the Australian people on the eve of war

13 Day, *Curtin*, p. 441

14 *Ibid.*, p. 435

15 Department of Aircraft Production, Progress Report for June 1942, CRS A2671 285/1942

16 Horner, *Crisis of Command*, p. 39

17 Churchill to Curtin, 10 January 1942, Defence of Australia — Appreciation of Immediate Danger of Invasion in Force, January 1942, CRS A5954 581/17

18 Gillison, *Royal Australian Air Force*,
    Chapter 18
19 Day, *Curtin*, p. 444
20 Hasluck, p. 70
21 *Ibid.*
22 Horner, p. 44
23 Robertson and McCarthy, p. 267
24 Secretary of State for Dominion Affairs to
    Curtin, 28 January 42, with extract from
    Churchill's speech to House of Commons
    on 27 January 42. In Future Employment of
    AIF — Transfer from Middle East to Far
    East 19/12/41–13/2/42, CRS A5954/69
    573/1
25 Bruce on 18 February 1942 (see AWM 54,
    541/1/4), Lavarack on 19 February 1942
    (NAA M100) and Page on 19 February
    1942 (AWM 54, 541/1/4) all supported
    Churchill in trying to persuade Curtin to
    divert the fleet to Burma. So too did the
    Australian Chiefs of Staff
26 Curtin to Wavell, repeated to Page, Lavarack
    and Casey, No. 129 of February 1942, AWM
    54 541/1/4 (also in Blamey Papers)
27 Churchill to Curtin, 20 February, NAA
    CRS A5954, Box 573
28 Roosevelt to Curtin, 21 February 1942. In
    Future Employment of AIF — Transfer
    from Middle East to Far East
    9/12/41–20/2/42, CRS A5954/69 573/2
29 *The Argus*, 27 May 1942
30 Curtin to Churchill, 22 February 1942,
    NAA CRS A5954, Box 573
31 In Casey to Evatt, 22 February 1942,
    AWM 54, 541/1/4
32 Day, *The Great Betrayal*, p. 350
33 Churchill to Curtin, 22 February 1942,
    NAA CRS A5954, Box 573
34 Bruce to Curtin, 23 February 1942, NAA
    M100
35 Curtin to Churchill, 23 February 1942,
    NAA CRS A5954, Box 573
36 *Ibid.*
37 Hasluck, *The Government and the People*,
    Volume 1, p. 75
38 For a full account of Curtin's torment
    during this time, see Day, *Curtin*,
    pp. 455–60

39 Day, *Curtin*, p. 457
40 Russell, *2/14 Australian Infantry Battalion*,
    p. 107

Chapter 11: Commanders

1 In Horner, *Crisis of Command*, p. 54
2 *Ibid.*, p. 55
3 *Ibid.*
4 Curtin to Blamey, 20 February 1942,
    Blamey Papers
5 *Daily Telegraph*, 28 March 1942
6 As recorded in several accounts of Curtin's
    views of Blamey
7 Overheard by A.H. Lowe, Secretary of the
    Naval and Military Club, Melbourne
8 Horner, *Blamey*, p. 14. For a full account of
    Blamey's life, see Horner's and
    Hetherington's biographies
9 Interview with McAulay
10 Carlyon, *I Remember Blamey*, p. 42
11 According to Rowell
12 Carlyon, *I Remember Blamey*, p. 96
13 Keogh, *South-West Pacific, 1941–45*,
    p. 472
14 Blamey Papers. Also recorded in
    Hetherington and Horner
15 Horner, *Blamey*, p. 244
16 Interview with McAulay
17 For a full account of their relationship,
    see Lodge, *Lavarack: Rival General*
18 Blamey to his brother Jim, 27 September
    41, Blamey Papers
19 Carlyon, pp. x–xi
20 Horner, *Blamey*, p. 4
21 *Ibid.*
22 Carlyon, p. 18
23 Interview with McAulay
24 For an amusing account of the 'Badge 80'
    affair see Horner, *Blamey*, pp. 75–83
25 Horner, *Blamey*, p. 160
26 *Ibid.*, p. 302
27 *Ibid.*, p. 327
28 Carlyon, p. 95
29 Horner, *Blamey*, p. 268
30 *Ibid.*, p. 98
31 Hasluck, *The Government and the People*,
    Volume 2, p. 158

32 Long, *MacArthur as Military Commander*,
p. 337
33 Hasluck, p. 158.
34 *Ibid*, p. 159
35 *The Bulletin*, 25 March 1942
36 Day, *The Politics of War*, p. 00
37 Brett, 'The MacArthur I Knew', in
McCarthy, p. 20
38 C. Thorne, in *The Australian*, 6 June 1974
39 McCarthy, p. 20
40 *The Argus*, 1 April 1942
41 Horner, *Crisis of Command*, p. 62
42 *Ibid*.
43 *Ibid*.
44 McCarthy, p. 189
45 *Ibid*., p. 190
46 ATIS Spot Report No. 12, Lieutenant-
General Hyakutake's Message to the
Troops
47 The sources for Hyakutake's deception are:
Onda, S., Chapter 2, *Zasetsushita Port
Moresby Sakusen*, in 'Bessatsu Rekishi
Dokuhon — Jigoku no Senjo Kigasen',
Vol. 22 of *Senki* Series, Shinjinbutsu Orai
Sha, Tokyo, 1993; and Onda, S., *Ningen no
Kiroku Tobu New Ginia Sen — Shinko Hen*,
Kodansha, Tokyo, 1988

Chapter 12: Emperor

1 Estimates of the number massacred vary.
But Hank Nelson writes that 160 was the
accurate figure. See his essay, *Zentsuji and
Totsuka: Australians from Rabaul as Prisoners
of War in Japan*, and forthcoming book on
the battle for Rabaul
2 Paull, *Retreat from Kokoda*, p. 27
3 ATIS Research Report 76 (Part III):
*The Warrior Tradition as a Present Factor
in Japanese Military Psychology*, p. 5,
AWM55 12/53
4 Interview with Imanishi October 2003
5 Hisaeda Akiyoshi Papers, AWM 3DRL
4005
6 This poetic tradition is evoked in *The
Diary of a Japanese Soldier in Wewak*,
translated by Keiko Tamura

7 Hisaeda Akiyoshi Papers
8 See *An Examination of How Race Affected the
Far Eastern War*, an essay by Marutani
Hajime
9 ATIS Research Report 76, Appx B, lecture
entitled *The Army of the Gods*, by
Horiguchi Tsugio, Medical Corps, a
veteran of the Russo-Japanese war.
AWM55 12/53 pt1
10 For a Japanese revisionist account of the
well-documented rape and massacre of
civilians at Nanking, see Takemoto &
Ohara, *The Alleged Nanking 'Massacre'*
11 Buruma, *Inventing Japan*, p. 101
12 ATIS Bulletin No. 1478
13 *Umi-Yukaba* (If I were to go to Sea)
written by Yakamochi Ohtomo and
Kiyoshi Nobutoki
14 ATIS No. 43, notebook of Okamato
Shigeo
15 ATIS No. 189, Staff diary, unknown owner
16 ATIS Research Report 76 (Part I), *Self-
immolation as a Factor in Japanese Military
Psychology*, p. 10, AWM55 12/53
17 ATIS Information Bulletin No. 14 —
Part II, p. 19, AWM55 12/53
18 *Ibid*., p. 15
19 ATIS Current Translations No. 216
20 ATIS Current Translations No. 9, p. 31
21 ATIS Research Report 76 (Part I), Appx A
22 ATIS Research Report 76 (Part IV),
*Prominent Factors in Japanese Military
Psychology*, p. 9, AWM55 12/53
23 *Ibid*.
24 *Ibid*.
25 ATIS Interrogation Spot Report No. 6
26 ATIS Research Report 76 (Part I), p. 18
27 *Ibid*.
28 ATIS Interrogation Report No. 36
29 ATIS Research Report 76, Appx B, lecture
entitled *The Army of the Gods*, No. 80, pp.
6–8
30 But they were very few. See *The Warrior
Tradition* …
31 ATIS Interrogation Report No. 18
32 Recorded in several ATIS-translated
Enemy Publications

Chapter 13: The AIF Arrives

1 Horner, *Blamey*, p. 317
2 Rowell, *Full Circle*, p. 111
3 Lavarack to Forde, AWM 33/1/4
4 John Hetherington was Blamey's first biographer
5 Hetherington, *The Herald*, 28 Dec 42
6 Horner, *Crisis of Command*, p. 120
7 *Ibid.*
8 Paull, *Retreat from Kokoda*, p. 165
9 Horner, *Crisis of Command*, p. 126
10 In Bergerud, *Touched With Fire*, p. 137
11 Porter Papers
12 McCarthy, *South-West Pacific Area — First Year, Kokoda to Wau*, p. 141
13 Horner, *Blamey*, p. 293
14 Rowell, p. 117
15 See McCarthy, pp. 6–8
16 Frank McLean, *Recollections & Reflections*
17 Memoir of Service of Major A.E. Moore of 2/14 & 2/16 Bns, PR 85/275, AWM 419/72/9
18 White, *Green Armour*, p. 175
19 *Ibid.*, p. 186
20 *Ibid.*, p. 181
21 *Ibid.*, p. 175
22 Russell, *The 2/14th Australian Infantry Battalion*, p. 3
23 McLean
24 White, p. 181
25 Russell, p. 2
26 Uren, *A Thousand Men at War — The Story of the 2/16th Battalion A.I.F.*, p. 9
27 Burns, *The Brown and Blue Diamond at War — The Story of the 2/27th Battalion A.I.F.*, p. 8
28 *Ibid.*, pp. 6–7
29 Uren, p. 118
30 In Day, *Curtin*, p. 477
31 Sublet, *Kokoda To The Sea*, p. 35
32 AHQ Melbourne, 23/12/41
33 McAulay, *Blood and Iron*, p. 107
34 See Sublet, pp. 35–6
35 Nelson, *Kokoda: The Track from History to Politics*, p. 4
36 *Ibid.* p. 5
37 See Vernon's diary, pp. 3–4, and Nelson

38 Nelson, p. 6
39 Horner, *Crisis of Command*, p. 126
40 *Ibid.*, p. 127.
41 Rowell, p. 122
42 Horner, *Crisis of Command*, p. 127
43 Burns, p. 109
44 Russell, p. 124
45 Of the 2/14th and 2/16th battalions, respectively

Chapter 14: The Track

1 Paull, *Retreat from Kokoda*, p. 103
2 *Ibid.*
3 *Ibid.*, pp. 34–9
4 Nelson, *Kokoda: The Track from History to Politics*, p. 7
5 Interview with Brian Honner, 21 January 2004
6 Paull, p. 35
7 *Ibid.*, p. 37
8 *Ibid.*, p. 34
9 White, *Green Armour*, p. 184
10 McAulay, *Blood and Iron*, p. 109
11 White, p. 188
12 Paull, p. 165
13 Bergerud, *Touched with Fire*, p. 138
14 Raftery, *Marks of War — War Neurosis and the Legacy of Kokoda*
15 In Ralph Honner's paper, *Jungle Lore*
16 From Professor Bryant Allen, Research School of Pacific And Asian Studies, Australian National University

Chapter 15: Nankai Shitai

1 See *The Human Face of War*, Australia–Japan Research Project at the Australian War Memorial (on AWM web site), translated by Steve Bullard
2 Robertson, MA Thesis, *Problems of Supply Encountered by the Australian and Japanese forces on the Kokoda Trail and the Questions of Morale*, 1 June 1973, AWM 422/3/94 MSS.701
3 ATIS Enemy Publications 33 and 39, *Nankai Shitai Operational Orders for the Invasion of Port Moresby*, issued at Rabaul on 10 August 1942

4 Interview with Shimada Yuki, October 2003

5 ATIS Enemy Publications 33 and 39,
Nankai Shitai Operational Orders

6 ATIS Bulletin No. 531

7 ATIS Interrogation Report No. 116, diary
of Warrant Officer Sadahiro

8 McAulay, Blood and Iron, p. 107

9 Nakahashi, War History of the Force which
was Sent to the South Seas, translated by Lt.
F. C. Jorgensen, AWM PR00297

10 McAulay, p. 112

11 ATIS Interrogation Report No. 39, diary
of Watanabe Fukuichi

Chapter 16: Jungle

1 Russell, The 214th Australian Infantry
Battalion, p. 125

2 Interview with Phil Rhoden, 31 July 2002;
also in McCarthy, South-West Pacific Area —
First Year, Kokoda to Wau, p. 195

3 Interview with Rhoden, 31 July 2002

4 Sublet, Kokoda to the Sea, p. 35

5 21st Brigade Report on Operations — Owen
Stanley Range

6 Vernon's diary, p. 4

7 21st Brigade Report on Operations

8 Paull, Retreat from Kokoda, p. 36

9 Russell, p. 127

10 Interview with Rhoden, 31 July 2002

11 Interview with Stan Bissett, 17 July 2003

12 White, Green Armour, p. 190

13 See McCarthy, pp. 196–9

14 Sublet, p. 38

15 Ibid.

16 7th Australian Division messages dealing with
Maroubra Force Operations Kokoda — June to
Oct 1942, AWM54 577/6/4

17 Ibid.

18 Allen Papers

19 Wilmot, Observations on the New Guinea
Campaign Aug 26th–Sept 26th 42, in Allen
Papers

20 Paull, p. 113.

21 21st Brigade Report on Operations

22 McCarthy, p. 199

23 ATIS Enemy Publication No. 28 5/3
Yazawa Intelligence Report, 17 August 1942

24 ATIS Enemy Publications No. 33, Nankai
Shitai Orders 16 Aug–15 Oct 1942

25 Robertson, MA Thesis

26 ATIS Information Request Reports No.
73, 9 Aug 1943 — Spiritual Training,
AWM 55 12/1–12/23

27 ATIS Bulletins 566–605, Diary containing
Nankai Shitai Instructions, owner
unknown, AWM 55 1/10

28 ATIS Enemy Publications No. 255,
Procedure In Interrogating And Handling
Prisoners Of War, AWM55 5/22

29 Interview with Yamasaki

30 In Frank Sublet's vivid phrase

31 McCarthy, South-West Pacific Area — First
Year

32 White, p. 193

33 Ibid.

34 Vernon's diary, p. 10

35 Alf Salmon Papers, AWM PR00297

36 In Edgar, Warrior of Kokoda, p. 139

37 Interview with Keith Norrish, 2002

38 Edgar, p. 71

39 Ibid., p. 101

40 Paull, p. 100

41 McCarthy, p. 195

42 Edgar, p. 64

43 Interview with McAulay, May 2002

44 McCarthy, p. 247

45 Potts to NG Force, 7th Australian Division
messages. . . , AWM54 577/6/4

46 Blamey Papers, AWM 3DRL/6643 2/138

47 Vernon's diary, p.14

48 Porter Papers

Chapter 17: Isurava

1 Bergerud, Touched with Fire, p. 54

2 Ralph Honner, 'The 39th at Isurava', in
Stand-To (Australian Army Journal), p. 9

3 Ibid.

4 Bergerud, p. 54

5 The source of the exaggeration seems to
be that Horii's supply and transport troops
— many of whom remained at the
beachhead — were included as combat
infantry. See Nelson, Kokoda: The Track from
History to Politics, p. 9

6 In Austin, *To Kokoda and Beyond*, p. 130

7 Nelson, p. 9

8 Honner, 'The 39th at Isurava', p. 9

9 39th Battalion War Diary

10 The 53rd were untested in combat, ill-equipped and poorly trained; they were 'battle-ready' only insofar as they were there, and armed

11 Austin, pp. 145–6

12 ATIS Bulletin No. 176, diary of soldier in 5SNLP

13 Austin, p. 135

14 ATIS Bulletin No. 218, diary of Second Lieutenant Hirano

15 ATIS Interrogation Report No. 116, diary of Warrant Officer Sadahiro

16 ATIS Enemy Publication No. 33, *Nankai Shitai Operational Orders*, 16 Aug–15 Oct 1942; the order was from Horii Tomitaro

17 Paull, *Retreat from Kokoda*, p. 123

18 *Ibid.*, p. 124

19 McCarthy, *South-West Pacific Area — First Year, Kokoda to Wau*, p. 201

20 ATIS Interrogation Report No. 116, diary of Warrant Officer Sadahiro, p. 9

21 Honner, 'The 39th at Isurava', p. 9

22 *Ibid.*

23 *Ibid.*, p. 11

24 Paull, p. 125

25 In Brune, *Those Ragged Bloody Heroes*, p. 98

26 *Ibid.*

27 *Ibid.*

28 Interview with Rhoden, 31 July 2002

29 Mentioned in a letter by Harvey Blundell

30 ATIS Bulletin No. 358, diary of Sakomoto, and in Paull, p. 128

31 Budden, *That Mob*, p. 27

32 McAulay, *Blood and Iron*, p. 145

33 Porter Papers, Box 14

34 Honner, 'The 39th at Isurava', p. 12

35 ATIS Bulletin, anonymous Japanese diarist

36 The assorted histories of the battle attribute these events to 28 August. Compare 'The 39th at Isurava', p. 12 with the 2/14th Battalion history, which uses similar phrases to describe the events of the next day

37 Bergerud, p. 258

38 *Ibid.*, p. 302

39 Russell, *The 2/14th Australian Infantry Battalion*, p. 132

40 Honner, 'The 39th at Isurava', pp. 12–15

41 *Ibid.*, p. 13

42 *Ibid.*

43 Interview with George Cops, 29 October 2002

44 Honner, 'The 39th at Isurava', p. 12

45 *Ibid.*

46 Paull, p. 129

47 Allen Papers

48 Paull, p. 133

49 ATIS Enemy Publication No. 33, *Nankai Shitai Operational Orders*, 16 Aug–15 Oct 1942

50 ATIS Bulletin No. 218, diary of Second Lieutenant Hirano

51 Uren, *A Thousand Men At War*, p. 127

52 Interview with Rhoden, 31 July 2002

53 Bergerud, p. 351

54 Interview with Rhoden, 31 July 2002

55 Cameron's 10th Platoon, A Coy, 2/14th Battalion, of about 30 men

56 Russell, p. 134

57 McCarthy, p. 207

58 *Ibid.*, p. 206

59 *Ibid.*

60 Citation for Victoria Cross, in *Australian VC Recipients*, pp. 139–140

61 Interview with Rhoden, 31 July 2002

62 Interview with McAulay, May 2002

63 Interview with Bissett, 17 July 2003; and in Russell, p. 135

64 McAllester, *Men of the 2/14th*, p. 213

65 Interviews with Japanese veterans of the 144th Regiment, October 2003

66 Interviews with Shimada and Yamasaki, October 2003

67 Honner, 'The 39th at Isurava', p. 15

68 Potts was to report 700 casualties to Port Moresby on 2 September — McCarthy, p. 219

69 Honner, p. 14

70 Edgar, *Warrior of Kokoda*, p. 141

71 Brune, p. 113

72 Honner, 'The 39th at Isurava'

73 *21st Brigade Report on Operations — Owen Stanley Range*
74 Blamey Papers
75 Allen Papers
76 Interview with Rhoden, 31 July 2002
77 Bergerud, p. 285
78 *Ibid.*
79 Interview with Howson, 29 October 2002

Chapter 18: Milne Bay

1 In Baker & Knight, *Milne Bay 1942*, p. 104
2 Source for figures: Dr Peter Londey, in 'Roll of Honour' speech organised by the AWM to mark the 60th anniversary of the events of 1942. The 4000 figure is the combat portion of 9500 total Milne Force, including support etc.
3 Smith, *The Emperor's Codes*, p. 174
4 Japanese Monograph No. 37, National Library of Australia, Canberra
5 ATIS Interrogation Report No. 2; prisoner Sakaki Minoru, Hayashi Unit
6 Londey
7 Baker & Knight, p. 147
8 2/10th Battalion, 18th Brigade
9 Allchin, *Purple and Blue — The History of the 2/10th Battalion, A.I.F.*, p. 251
10 Allchin, p. 252
11 Clowes Report, p. 11
12 Allchin, p. 254
13 The 7th Brigade
14 McCarthy, *South-West Pacific Area — First Year, Kokoda to Wau*, p. 174
15 *Ibid.*, p. 176
16 *Ibid.*, p. 175
17 Clowes to Gavin Long, AWM 67 3/74
18 Henderson, *Onward Boy Soldiers: The Battle for Milne Bay*, p. 162
19 *Sydney Morning Herald*, 19 January 2004, Obituary
20 Baker & Knight, p. 287
21 *Ibid.*, p. 286
22 Londey
23 In Baker & Knight
24 ATIS Bulletin No. 44, diary of unknown Japanese soldier found at Milne Bay, September 1942

25 Baker & Knight, p. 438
26 Webb Report, in Allen Papers and Baker & Knight. Two key witnesses were Captain John Stephenson and Captain CW Kendall, 18th Brigade
27 Baker & Knight, p. 438
28 ATIS Interrogation Report No. 2; prisoner Sakaki Minoru, Hayashi Unit
29 Londey
30 Japanese Monograph No. 37, National Library of Australia, Canberra
31 Clowes Report, p. 33

PART 3: WITHDRAWAL

Chapter 19: Wounded

1 White, *Green Armour*, p. 199
2 *Ibid.*
3 Uren, *A Thousand Men at War — The Story of the 2/16th Battalion, A.I.F.*, p. 136
4 *Ibid.*
5 In Steward, *Recollections of a Regimental Medical Officer*, p. 110
6 Diary of Sir Rupert Magarey, AWM 54 481/12/20, p. 6
7 *Ibid.*
8 *Ibid.*
9 See Paull, *Retreat from Kokoda*, pp. 143–53
10 *Ibid.*
11 Wilkinson to Salmon, Salmon Papers, AWM PR00297
12 Steward, p. 112
13 White, *Green Armour*, p. 204
14 *Ibid.*
15 Paull, p. 173
16 Magarey, p. 6
17 Steward, p. 112
18 Interview with Smoky Howson, 29 October 2003; see also Austin, *To Kokoda and Beyond*, p. 170
19 Magarey, p. 6
20 Steward, p.112
21 McCarthy, *South-West Pacific Area — First Year, Kokoda to Wau*, p. 214; see also Paull, p. 176
22 Bullard, 'Japanese Medical Corps in the Papua campaigns, 1942–1943', (essay) p. 2

23 *Ibid.*
24 ATIS Interrogation Report No. 169, prisoner's name unknown, captured at Giruwa, 25 January 1943
25 ATIS 3/1 *Handbook of Hygiene in the Tropics for NCOs and men*
26 Bullard, p. 11
27 Wilkinson to 39th Battalion Association, 5 April 1974, AWM PR87/008
28 Steward, p. 132
29 Salmon Papers
30 Steward, p. 110
31 Bergerud, *Touched With Fire*, p. 484
32 Steward, p. 118
33 Vernon's diary, p. 3
34 White, p. 200
35 *Ibid.*, p. 203
36 *Ibid.*, p. 200
37 *Ibid.*, p. 201
38 Magarey, conclusions
39 In Paull, p. 209
40 Austin, *To Kokoda and Beyond*, p. 176
41 Murie C.F., AWM PR01397

Chapter 20: Fuzzy Wuzzy Angels

1 Interview with Havala, at Kagi, October 2003
2 Interview with Lubini, at Alola, October 2003
3 Vernon's diary
4 McCarthy, *South-West Pacific Area — First Year, Kokoda to Wau*, p. 116
5 Their rations alone cost the Australian Government £425,000 that year
6 Capt H.T. Kienzle, *Report On Kokoda L. of C., Native Carriers during Campaign Owen Stanley Range, Kokoda–Buna*, Feb 1943, ANGAU N.G.F., AWM54 577/6/8
7 McCarthy, p. 116
8 The Australian New Guinea Administration Unit
9 McCarthy, p. 116
10 As told by Frank Taylor, Kokoda Treks and Tours
11 Vernon's diary, p. 13
12 Wilmot, *Observations On Ops Of Maroubra Force, 25–31 Aug 42*, in Allen Papers

13 Interview with Havala, October 2003
14 In Salmon Papers, AWM PR00297; also see Vernon's diary
15 Wilmot, *Observations On Ops Of Maroubra Force*
16 Magarey's diary
17 *21st Brigade Report on Operations — Owen Stanley Range*
18 Paull, *Retreat from Kokoda*, p. 227
19 Barter, *Far Above Battle*, pp. 189–91
20 Magarey's diary
21 AWM Private records collection, Exhibition Documents, 1320179
22 ATIS 6/4 Interrogation Reports No. 157; prisoner Iwasa Koji
23 ATIS Enemy Publication No. 38, *Nankai Shitai Orders*, 13 May–10 July 1942, incl. Notes on the Handling of New Natives
24 *Ibid.*
25 Allen and Tamura, *Attitudes of Japanese troops towards villagers and the supply of food in the inland Aitape-wewak Campaign, Papua New Guinea 1942–45* (essay), p. 7
26 Hiromitsu Iwamoto, *Memories and Realities of Japanese Occupation of New Guinea*, p. 9)
27 *Ibid.*
28 Bullard, *Japanese Medical Corps in the Papua campaigns, 1942–1943*, (essay), p. 3

Chapter 21: Buckler

1 In Russell, *The 2/14th Australian Infantry Battalion*, p. 148
2 See Benson, *Prisoner's Base and Home Again*, and McCarthy, *South-West Pacific Area — First Year, Kokoda to Wau*
3 ATIS Advanced Echelon, No. 1, Subsequent Preliminary Interrogation of POW JA 145118, p. 3
4 McCarthy, p. 218
5 The 2/14th Battalion
6 Buckler's diary, Buckler Papers, p. 20
7 *Ibid.*, p. 16
8 Paull, *Retreat from Kokoda*, p. 160
9 Buckler's diary, p. 26
10 OPS Report by Captain S.H. Buckler, 12 Oct 42, AWM 419/14/2
11 Buckler's diary, p. 34

12 *Ibid.*, p. 38
13 *Ibid.*, p. 43
14 *Ibid.*, p. 68
15 Paull, p. 162
16 From *New York Herald Tribune*, reprinted in *Sydney Morning Herald*, 15 October 1942
17 Buckler's diary, p. 79
18 Colonel Lawrence A. Quinn to Colonel Byers, chief of staff First Army Corps, Brisbane, Buckler Papers, AWM 419/14/2, p. 7
19 *Ibid.*

Chapter 22: Myola

1 Nakahashi, *War History of the Force which was sent to the South Seas*, translated by Lt F.C. Jorgensen, p. 10, AWM PR00297
2 ATIS Enemy Publication No. 33, *Nankai Shitai Operational Orders*, 16 Aug–15 Oct 1942
3 McCarthy, *South-West Pacific Area — First Year, Kokoda to Wau*, p. 217
4 Interview with Keith Norrish, 6 September 2002
5 Interviews with Frank Taylor, October 2003
6 McCarthy, p. 218
7 Blamey Papers
8 McCarthy, p. 219
9 Paull, *Retreat from Kokoda*, p. 190
10 ATIS Bulletin No. 358, diary of Sakomoto
11 *7th Australian Division Messages Dealing With "Maroubra Force" Operations Kokoda — June To Oct 1942*, AWM 54 577/6/4

Chapter 23: Brigade Hill

1 Allen Papers
2 See Carlyon's description of MacArthur wearing his white silk pyjamas and black dressing gown, in *I Remember Blamey*, p. 115
3 McCarthy, *South-West Pacific Area — First Year, Kokoda to Wau*, p. 225
4 *Ibid.*
5 Horner, *Crisis of Command*, p. 150

6 McCarthy, p. 225
7 See Rowell's assessment of the situation in *Full Circle*, pp. 121–3
8 Horner, *Crisis of Command*, p. 155
9 The precise location of Potts's HQ is unclear, but Frank Taylor's calculations place it at the southern end of the summit of Brigade Hill. Bill James, author of *Before Memories Fade*, an excellent historical guide to the battlefields, places it a few hundred yards north
10 Edgar, *Warrior of Kokoda*, p. 163
11 Frank McLean Papers
12 *Ibid.*, p. 166
13 ATIS Bulletin No. 358, diary of Sakomoto; see also Paull, p. 199
14 Burns, *The Brown and Blue Diamond at War — The Story of the 2/27th Battalion, A.I.F.*, pp. 117–18
15 In Brune, *Those Ragged Bloody Heroes*, p. 156
16 Paull, *Retreat from Kokoda*, p. 198
17 Uren, *A Thousand Men at War — The Story of the 2/16th Battalion, A.I.F*, p. 148
18 *Ibid.*, p. 149
19 Steward, *Recollections of a Regimental Medical Officer*, p. 127
20 ATIS Bulletin No. 358, diary of Sakomoto
21 In Paull, p. 199, and ATIS diaries
22 Burns, p. 118
23 *Ibid.*
24 Steward, p. 127
25 Allen Papers
26 Rowell to Vasey, 8 September 1942, AWM 54 225/2/5
27 Allen Papers.
28 ATIS Bulletin No. 358, diary of Sakomoto

Chapter 24: Rout

1 Wilmot, Observations On Japanese Tactics, Kokoda Front Aug 1942. From: APX "B" to 7 Aust Div SG34/4/111, AWM 54 577/7/29
2 Paull, p. 201
3 ATIS Enemy Publication No. 33, *Nankai Shitai Operational Orders*, 16 Aug–15 Oct 1942
4 Vernon's diary, p. 17

5 Ibid.
6 Compared with a normal, combined strength of about 2000; see McCarthy, p. 224, and Uren, p. 151
7 Steward, *Recollections of a Regimental Medical Officer*, p. 128
8 Ibid., p. 130
9 McAulay, *Blood and Iron*, p. 248
10 Paull, *Retreat from Kokoda*, p. 217
11 Ibid., p. 204
12 Porter Papers
13 Steward, p. 132
14 Ibid.
15 Ibid., p. 133
16 Ibid.
17 Memoir of Service of Major A.E. Moore of 2/14 & 2/16 Bns, PR 85/275, AWM 419/72/9, p. 95
18 Ibid., p. 478
19 In *The War Cry*, official journal of the Salvation Army in Australia, Melbourne 9 January 1943; cutting in Moore's memoirs
20 Moore's memoirs, p. 111
21 Ibid., p. 112
22 Ibid., p. 111

Chapter 25: The Lost Battalion

1 Frank McLean Papers, gratefully made available by his son, Robert
2 Burns, *The Brown and Blue Diamond at War — The Story of the 2/27th Battalion, A.I.F.*, p. 124
3 Ibid.
4 See Burns' diary, in *The Brown and Blue Diamond at War — The Story of the 2/27th Battalion, A.I.F.*

Chapter 26: Ioribaiwa and Imita Ridge

1 Horner, *Crisis of Command*, p. 158
2 Horner, *Blamey*, p. 324; and sourced to interviews with Richard and Brian Honner, 2003
3 Wilmot, *Observations on the New Guinea Campaign Aug 26th — Sept 26th 1942*, Wilmot Papers, and in Allen Papers

4 Wilmot Papers
5 Horner, *Crisis of Command*, p. 159
6 Crooks, *The Footsoldiers*, p. 148
7 Ibid.
8 Ibid., p. 144
9 Ibid.
10 Ibid.
11 Ibid., p. 144
12 McAulay, *Blood and Iron*, p. 202
13 ATIS Bulletin No. 358, diary of Sakomoto
14 ATIS Enemy Publication No. 33, *Nankai Shitai Operational Orders*, 16 Aug–15 Oct 1942
15 Paull, *Retreat from Kokoda*, p. 221
16 Porter papers.
17 ATIS Enemy Publications No. 33
18 Russell, *The 2/14 Australian Infantry Battalion*, p. 171
19 Steward, p. 135
20 See Rowell, *Full Circle*, p. 121
21 Ibid.
22 Nakahashi, *War History of the Force which was sent to the South Seas*, translated by Lt F.C Jorgensen, p. 13, AWM PR00297
23 Okada, *Lost Troops*, p. 24
24 Nakahashi, p. 13
25 As mentioned in a letter by General Tanaka to A.D. Robertson, 1973
26 Nakahashi, *War History of the Force which was sent to the South Seas*, translated by Lt F.C. Jorgensen, AWM PR00297
27 Paull, p. 223
28 Vernon's diary, p. 20
29 Ibid.
30 Allen Papers
31 Rowell, p. 123
32 Horner, *Crisis of Command*, p. 155
33 Paull, p. 256
34 Ibid.
35 Ibid.
36 Ibid.
37 Rowell, p. 115; see also AWM 577/3/1
38 Allen Papers
39 Sir Keith Murdoch, chief publicity censor, 22 September 1942, CAB 40, A5954 Box 537
40 Blamey Papers
41 Rowell Papers
42 Horner, *Blamey*, p. 325

43 Dept of Defence, *Higher Army Directions of Operations In New Guinea*, CRS A5954/69 266/1

44 Horner, *Crisis of Command*, p. 166

45 *Ibid.*, p. 155; see also Thomson, *Winning with Intelligence*, p. 156

46 *Headquarters 2/14 Australian Infantry Battalion Report on a Recent Investigation to Ascertain the Standard of Fitness in the Battalion*, 3 October, 1942, AWM54 420/2/2

Chapter 27: Press

1 Blamey Papers, 2/116

2 *Daily Telegraph*, 23 September 1942

3 See, for example, in Paull, *Retreat from Kokoda*, pp. 259–62

4 Blamey Papers, 27 May 1942, 2/115

5 Personal Papers of Prime Minister Curtin, CRS M1415/1

6 William Dunstan VC, general manager of the *Melbourne Herald*, wrote to Rowell to report these words of one of his correspondents.

7 *Daily Telegraph*, 10 Sept 1942, p. 8

8 *Ibid.*, 23 September 1942, p. 6

9 Australia's Overseas Defence Forces, *War Correspondents, War Records and Broadcasters. Press Photography in Combat Areas*, CRS A5954 610/1

10 *Ibid.*

11 Personal Papers of Prime Minister Curtin, CRS M1415/1

12 *Ibid.*

13 Curtin telegraphed the Australian Newspaper Proprietors Association on 28 May 1942, supporting the 'blanketing of speculation', as cited in a letter from Errol Knox of Dept of Army, Director General of Public Relations, June 1942; see Blamey Papers, 2/115

14 Blamey Papers, 2/116

15 Australia's Overseas Defence Forces, *War Correspondents, War Records and Broadcasters. Press Photography in Combat Areas*, CRS A5954 610/1

16 *Ibid.*

17 Okada, *Lost Troops*, AWM 492/7/22

18 *Ibid.*, p. 14

19 ATIS Information Request Reports No. 79, 28 Aug 1943, AWM 55 12/1–12/23

20 *Ibid.*

21 *Ibid.*

22 ATIS Current Translations No. 279

Chapter 28: Blamey and Rowell

1 Horner, *Blamey*, p. 329

2 Horner, *Crisis of Command*, pp. 165–6

3 *Ibid.*, p. 166

4 Horner, *Blamey*, p. 327

5 Interview with Lex McAulay, May 2002

6 See Horner, *Blamey*, p. 327; *Crisis of Command*, p. 170; Hetherington, *Blamey: Controversial Soldier*; and Lodge, *Lavarack: Rival General*

7 Dept Of Defence, *Higher Army Directions of Operations in New Guinea*, Advisory War Council Minute, Canberra 24 September 1942, CRS A5954/69 266/1

8 Horner, *Blamey*, p. 327

9 Carlyon, *I Remember Blamey*, p. 105

10 *Ibid.*

11 Dept Of Defence, *Higher Army Directions of Operations in New Guinea*, Advisory War Council Minute, Canberra 24 September 1942, Dept of Defence Co-Ordination, Minute Paper — Senior Commanders, to Curtin, re: Rowell & Blamey, CRS A5954/69 266/1

12 Carlyon, p. 78

13 Horner, *Crisis of Command*, p. 170

14 *Ibid.*, p. 171

15 Rowell, *Full Circle*, p. 126

16 Carlyon, p. 106

17 Rowell, p. 127

18 See *The Jap Was Thrashed*, written and published by Blamey's PR department

19 Rowell, p. 129

20 Horner, *Blamey*, p. 330

21 *Ibid.*

22 Blamey Papers 2/138

23 Dept Of Defence, *Higher Army Directions of Operations in New Guinea*, Advisory War Council Minute, Canberra 24 September 1942, CRS A5954/69 266/1

24 *Ibid.*
25 *Ibid.*, Blamey to Rowell, 28 September 1942
26 *Ibid.*, Blamey to Curtin and MacArthur, 28 September 1942
27 Rowell, p. 131
28 Horner, *Blamey*, p. 332
29 Correspondence Relating to the Relinquishing of Commands by Lt Gen SF Rowell and Maj Gen AS Allen 1942, Letter Rowell to Allen, 11 October 42, Allen Papers, 3DRL No. 2381 AWM 419/3/1
30 Horner, *Crisis of Command*, p. 318
31 Dept Of Defence, *Higher Army Directions of Operations in New Guinea*, Letter from Rowell to HQ, Australian Military Forces, For CGS, 14 October 42, CRS A5954/69 266/1
32 Rowell, p. 137
33 Carlyon, p. 108
34 Horner, *Crisis of Command*, p. 185
35 Paull, *Retreat from Kokoda*, p. 255
36 Blamey to Curtin, 27 December 42, CRS A5954/69 266/1

Chapter 29: 'Rabbits'

1 Wilmot, *Observations on Ops of Maroubra Force, 25–31 Aug 42 & Observations on the New Guinea Campaign, Aug 26 — Sept 26 42*, Allen Papers, 3DRL No. 2381 AWM 419/3/1
2 Edgar, *Warrior of Kokoda*, p. 196
3 *Ibid.*, pp. 190, 192
4 Blamey Papers
5 Edgar, pp. 192–3
6 *Ibid.*, p. 199
7 Horner, *Crisis of Command*, p. 190
8 Edgar, p. 209
9 Ibid., p. 204
10 Carlyon, *I Remember Blamey*, pp. 110–11
11 *Ibid.*, p. 111
12 *Ibid.*, see also Hetherington Papers, AWM 419/47/24
13 In Brune, *Those Ragged Bloody Heroes*, p. 200
14 Steward, *Recollections of a Regimental Medical Officer*, p. 147

15 Carlyon, p. 111
16 Brune, p. 202
17 Horner, *Blamey*, p. 353
18 Paull, *Retreat from Kokoda*, p. 258
19 According to Carlyon, in interview with John Hetherington, Hetherington Papers, AWM 419/47/24
20 Russell, p. 181
21 Steward, p. 148
22 McCarthy, p. 334
23 *Ibid.*
24 Carlyon, p. 111

PART 4: COUNTEROFFENSIVE

Chapter 30: Civilians

1 Day, *The Politics of War*, p. 263
2 Hasluck, *The Government and the People*, Volume 2, p. 284
3 In Australian newspapers, 17 November 1941
4 Horner, *Blamey*, p. 253
5 *Daily Telegraph*, 31 July 1942, p. 4
6 *Sydney Morning Herald*, 28 July 1942
7 Hasluck, p. 67
8 Day, *The Politics of War*, p. 271
9 Interview with Lex McAulay, May 2002
10 Day, *Curtin*, p. 450
11 Hasluck, p. 10
12 *Ibid.*, p. 271
13 *Sydney Morning Herald*, 4 September 1942, p. 9
14 Hasluck, p. 65
15 *Ibid.*, p. 125
16 McKernan, *All In — Fighting the War at Home*, see chapter 5, 'The Real War'
17 Hasluck, p. 277
18 Phillips, 'The Homefront' 1942–1945, p. 12
19 Hasluck, p. 65
20 See *The Great Australian Stupor*
21 *Sydney Morning Herald*, 4 October 1942, p. 4
22 Hasluck, p. 274
23 *Sydney Morning Herald*, 12 September 1942, p. 7
24 Connell, *The War at Home*, p. 114
25 Hasluck, p. 127

26 *Sydney Morning Herald*, 3 September 1942, p. 3

27 Hasluck, p. 126

28 At the height of the war, NSW provided 17,468 coal miners out of a total of 23,503

29 From 100 strikes in January 1941 to about 180 by the end of 1942 — Hasluck, pp. 604–05

30 Interview with Major-General Paul Cullen, 22 July and 11 September 2002

31 Hasluck, p. 281

32 *Ibid.*, p. 270

33 By June 1942, there were 88,000 American troops in Australia, excluding navy

34 Connell, p. 115

35 Blamey Papers 2/7

36 *Ibid.*

37 'Far Eastern Liaison Office (FELO) — Propaganda in the South West Pacific Area in the Second World War,' paper by Emma Jones, AWM

38 Horner, *Crisis of Command*, p. 50. 'Ek Dum' was a pseudonym used by Malcolm Ellis

39 *Hatred As An Instrument Of War Policy*, Menzies' speech

40 ATIS 5/8 Enemy Publications

41 ATIS 5/4 Enemy Publications Nos 44–48, True Examples of War Living — Contest Winners

42 *Ibid.*

Chapter 31: Hunger

1 Okada, *Lost Troops*, p. 14

2 Japanese Monographs No. 37, p. 18, National Library, Canberra

3 ATIS Bulletin No. 358, diary of Sakomoto

4 Robertson, MA Thesis, *Report on Operations — Owen Stanley Range, 15 August to 20 September*, 1942

5 Okada, *Lost Troops*

6 Paull, p. 227

7 ATIS Enemy Publication No. 33, *Nankai Shitai Operational Orders*, 16 Aug–15 Oct 1942

8 *Ibid.*

9 Okada, p. 15

10 *Ibid.*

11 ATIS Enemy Publication No. 33, *Nankai Shitai Operational Orders*, 16 Aug–15 Oct 1942

12 *Ibid.*

13 *Ibid.*

14 Crooks, *The Footsoldiers*, p. 174

15 *Ibid.*

16 *Ibid.*, p. 175

17 See General Tanaka, in Robertson, MA Thesis

18 ATIS Research Report 76 (Part VI), *The Disgrace of Illness*, AWM 55 12/53

19 *Ibid.*

20 As Yamaguchi Masahiro, a medical orderly with the Nankai Shitai, discovered.

21 ATIS Research Report 76 (Part VI), *The Disgrace of Illness*, AWM 55 12/53

22 ATIS 5/2 Enemy Publications No. 24, *Records of No. 67 Eastern New Guinea Ginuwa L. of C. Hospital*, compiled by Army Medical Officer First Lieutenant Okubo Fukunobo, 10 July 43

23 ATIS Bulletin No. 358, diary of Sakomoto

24 Notes On and Lessons From Recent Operations In Gona And Sanananda Areas by Lt-Col R. Honner — Comd 39 Aust Inf Bn, AWM 54, 581/7/19

25 See www.kensmen.com

26 Allen Papers

27 ATIS Interrogation Report No. 54, 6/2, Inagaki Riichi

28 ATIS, Horie Operation Order No.. 35, in Nankai Shitai report, *Violation of Transport Regulations*, Deniki, 1500 hours, 2 Oct 42

29 Rinzo, *History of the New Guinea War (Niyuuginia Senki)*

30 *Ibid.*

31 According to General Tanaka, in Robertson MA Thesis

32 ATIS Enemy Publication No. 33, *Nankai Shitai Operational Orders*, 16 Aug–15 Oct 1942

Chapter 32: Retreat

1 ATIS Spot Report No. 2, Message of Instruction, Horii Tomitaro, 20 September 1942, Wamai, New Guinea

2 Okada, *Lost Troops*, p. 16
3 *Ibid.*
4 *Ibid.*
5 Takida Kenji, *The Pacific is Burning*
6 Interview with Imanishi Sadaharu, October 2003
7 Okada, p. 17
8 Nakahashi, *War History of the Force which was sent to the South Seas*, translated by Lt F.C. Jorgensen, p. 14, AWM PR00297
9 Okada, p. 17
10 ATIS Bulletin No. 358, diary of Sakomoto
11 For description, see Gower, *Guns of the Regiment*
12 Diary of Sakomoto
13 *Ibid.*
14 Okada, p. 18
15 *Ibid.*, p. 19
16 Nakahashi, p. 39
17 *Ibid.*
18 Crooks, *The Footsoldiers*, p. 182
19 *Ibid.*
20 Diary of Sakomoto

11 *The Kokoda Trail 1942*, by Lieutenant A.N. Black, p. 5; in Papers of Lieutenant A.N. Black, AWM PRO1960
12 Allen Papers
13 Nelson, 'Kokoda: The Track from History to Politics'
14 Horner, *General Vasey's War*, p. 194
15 Allen Papers
16 *Ibid.*
17 McCarthy, *South-West Pacific Area — First Year, Kokoda to Wau*, p. 280
18 *Ibid.*
19 Fayle diary, Allen Papers
20 Capt H.T. Kienzle, *Report On Kokoda L. of C., Native Carriers during Campaign Owen Stanley Range, Kokoda–Buna*, Feb 1943, ANGAU N.G.F., AWM 54 577/6/8
21 *Ibid.*
22 Givney (ed.), *The First at War — The Story of the 2/1st Australian Infantry Battalion*, p. 240
23 Vernon's diary, p. 21
24 *Ibid.*, p. 23

Chapter 33: MacArthur

1 From diary kept for Maj Gen A.S. Allen, 7th Aust Division, by Lieut Fayle ADC, 22 Aug 1942 — 18 Feb 1943, Allen Papers
2 Allen Papers
3 *Report by the Minister for the Army [Frank Forde] on his visit to the New Guinea Theatre of Operations, 1 October 1942 — 4 October 1942*, AWM 54
4 *Ibid.*
5 Fayle diary, Allen Papers
6 Messages and reports, principally between Generals Blamey and MacArthur, on planning and strategy in the recapturing of Kokoda, and build up of allied forces at Milne bay and Wanigela, for subsequent assault on Buna, AWM54, 577/3/1
7 Fayle diary
8 McAulay, *Blood and Iron*, p. 329
9 *Jungle Warfare*, 6th Australian Division, Training Instruction No. 11, pp. 6–14
10 Interview with Major-General Paul Cullen, 11 September 2002

Chapter 34: Pursuit

1 McAulay, *Blood and Iron*, p. 285
2 Crooks, *The Footsoldiers*, p. 190
3 *Ibid.*, p. 192
4 *Ibid.*
5 Interview with Merv Roberts, 24 July 2002
6 Crooks, p. 192
7 Allen Papers
8 Paull, *Retreat from Kokoda*, p. 270
9 Allen Papers
10 *Ibid.*
11 ATIS Current Translation 168, *Medical Report submitted to South Seas Detachment by Yazawa Butai — Soputa — 20 Nov 42*
12 *Ibid.*
13 *Ibid.*
14 Johnston, *War Diary, 1942*, p. 98
15 ATIS Interrogation Report No. 9, Okino Jiro, Kusunose Butai
16 ATIS Interrogation Report No. 18, Katsukura Kanemidzu, No. 5 Special Naval Landing Party

17 Okada, *Lost Troops*, pp. 18–19

18 Bergerud, *Touched by Fire*, p. 139

Chapter 35: Biscuit Bombers

1 Papers of Brig Maj-Gen SHWC Porter, AWM PR00527, Box 14

2 Crooks, *The Footsoldiers*, p. 190

3 *Ibid.*

4 *Ibid.*

5 McCarthy, *South-West Pacific Area — First Year, Kokoda to Wau*, p. 264

6 Allen Papers, AWM 419/3/9 1/7 3DRL No. 2381

7 *Ibid.*

8 Messages and reports, principally between Generals Blamey and MacArthur, on planning and strategy in the recapturing of Kokoda, and build up of allied forces at Milne Bay and Wanigela, for subsequent assault on Buna, AWM 54, 577/3/1

9 Allen Papers

10 Blamey Papers — New Guinea Ops, AWM 3DRL/6643 2/47

11 Allen Papers

12 *Ibid.*

13 Horner, *Blamey*, p. 343

14 See full text, in Horner, *Crisis of Command*, p. 202

15 Papers of Lieutenant A.N. Black, p. 8, AWM PR01960

16 In Bergerud, *Touched with Fire*, p. 240

17 See Raftery, *Marks of War — War Neurosis and the Legacy of Kokoda*, for excellent examination of psychological effects

18 Allen Papers

Chapter 36: Anthropophagy

1 McCarthy, *South-West Pacific Area — First Year, Kokoda to Wau*, p. 271

2 Johnston, *War Diary*, 1942, p. 109

3 ATIS Bulletin No. 358, diary of Sakomoto

4 Crooks, *The Footsoldiers*, p. 210

5 McCarthy, p. 271

6 Paull, *Retreat from Kokoda*, p. 274

7 In ATIS 12/50 Part 1, *Japanese Violations of the Laws of War*, 29 April 1944

8 Johnston, *Fighting the Enemy*, p. 100

9 Givney (ed.), *The First at War — The Story of the 2/1st Australian Infantry Battalion*, p. 288

10 Paull, p. 273

11 Barter, *Far Above Battle*, p. 205

12 Johnston, p. 101

13 ATIS Document No. 80107, Exhibit H, *Japanese Violations of the Laws of War*, AWM 55 12/50, Parts 2 & 3

14 *Ibid.*, Supplement 1, 19 March 1945

15 ATIS Document No. 80107, interview with Japanese soldier in Aitape, north-western New Guinea, 1945

Chapter 37: Templeton's Crossing

1 Crooks, *The Footsoldiers*, p. 195

2 The 2/33rd and 2/25th of the 25th Brigade — see Crooks, p. 197

3 *Ibid.*

4 B & C companies, 2/33rd Battalion

5 Crooks, p. 199

6 C Coy, 2/33rd Battalion

7 Crooks, p. 196

8 *Ibid.*

9 McCarthy, *South-West Pacific Area — First Year, Kokoda to Wau*, p. 284

10 Crooks, p. 197

11 See Wick, *Purple Over Green — The History of the 2/2 Australian Infantry battalion 1939–1945*, pp. 225–7

12 Givney (ed.), *The First at War — The Story of the 2/1st Australian Infantry Battalion*, p. 262

13 Wick, p. 228

14 *Ibid.*

15 Rowell to Allen, 11 October 1942, Allen Papers, AWM 419/3/9 1/7 3DRL No. 2381

16 Horner, *Crisis of Command*, p. 199

17 *Ibid.*

18 *Ibid.*

19 To Blamey from MacArthur, forwarded to Allen, 17 October 1942, Blamey Papers, New Guinea Ops, AWM 3DRL/6643 2/47

20 Blamey Papers

21 Horner, *Blamey*, p. 346

22 Allen to Blamey, 22 October 1942, Allen Papers

23 Allen Papers

Chapter 38: Eora Creek

1 Okada, *Lost Troops*, p. 20
2 *Ibid.*
3 *Ibid.*, p. 21
4 Givney (ed.), *The First at War — The Story of the 2/1st Australian Infantry Battalion*, p. 286
5 Okada, p. 20
6 *Ibid.*
7 McCarthy, *South-West Pacific Area — First Year, Kokoda to Wau*, p. 287
8 Givney, p. 267
9 *Ibid.*
10 McAulay described this as a German machine pistol, commonly called a Schmeisser
11 Givney, p. 268
12 *Ibid.*, p. 271
13 *Ibid.*, p. 270
14 *Ibid.*, p. 269
15 *Ibid.*, p. 269
16 *Ibid.*, p. 278
17 Clift, *War Dance — The Story of the 2/3 Australian Infantry Battalion*, p. 297
18 McCarthy, p. 295
19 Givney, pp. 285–7
20 ATIS Current Translations Nos 26–35, 3/3, Comdr Yazawa Butai to Nankai Shitai Comdr; file containing work and operation orders, dated 30 Sep 42 to 28 Dec 42, belonging to Yazawa Butai
21 *Ibid.*
22 Allen Papers, AWM 419/3/9 1/7 3DRL No. 2381
23 *Ibid.*
24 Horner, *Blamey*, p. 351
25 McCarthy, p. 302
26 *Ibid.*
27 *Ibid.*, p. 303
28 ATIS Enemy Publication No. 33, *Nankai Shitai Operational Orders*, 16 Aug–15 Oct 1942
29 Clift, p. 308
30 McCarthy, p. 306
31 *Ibid.*
32 Interview with Major-General Paul Cullen, 11 September, 2002
33 Allen Papers
34 Paull, *Retreat from Kokoda*, p. 278
35 The 2/4th Field Ambulance, then responsible for the forward areas, had the support of the 2/6th Field Ambulance, the 14th Field Ambulance, and the 2/9th General Hospital at Port Moresby. See McCarthy, p. 277
36 Fayle diary, Allen Papers
37 McCarthy, p. 317
38 *Provision of Aircraft for Air Ambulances in New Guinea, 31 December 42–7 April 43*, CRS A5954/1 230/13

Chapter 39: Vasey

1 Paull, *Retreat from Kokoda*, p. 87
2 Hetherington, 'Bloody George', p. 1
3 Horner, *General Vasey's War*, p. 208
4 *Ibid.*, p. 23
5 In Horner, p. 26
6 Hetherington, p. 8
7 Norris, *No Memory For Pain*, pp. 169–70
8 In Horner, p. 62
9 *Ibid.*, p. 100
10 *Ibid.*, p. 101
11 Herring Papers, 12/9

Chapter 40: Kokoda Regained

1 Vasey to his wife, in Horner, *General Vasey's War*, p. 208
2 *Ibid.*, p. 209
3 Of the 2/6th Independent Company
4 The 37th Division
5 Nakahashi, *War History of the Force which was sent to the South Seas*, translated by Lt F.C. Jorgensen, p. 17, AWM PR00297
6 *Ibid.*, p. 20
7 Of an initial strength of 744 and 797 men respectively — Paull, *Retreat from Kokoda*, p. 289
8 ATIS 3/5 Current Translations Nos 51–64, diary of medical officer, Lieutenant Hayashi Hiroyuki, Tate Butai

9 ATIS Bulletin No. 192, address delivered by Horii Tomitaro at Ilimo, 1 November 1942, found in field diary belonging to Hozumi Butai

10 Blamey to MacArthur, 30 October 1942, Blamey Papers, New Guinea Ops, AWM 3DRL/6643 2/47

11 Horner, *General Vasey's War*, p. 209

12 Of the 2/31st Battalion

13 Paull, p. 287

14 Capt H.T. Kienzle, *Report On Kokoda L. of C., Native Carriers during Campaign Owen Stanley Range, Kokoda–Buna*, Feb 1943, ANGAU N.G.F., AWM 54 577/6/8

15 Vernon's diary, p. 24

16 *Ibid.*

17 Kienzle Report

18 McCarthy, *South-West Pacific Area — First Year, Kokoda to Wau*, p. 321

19 ATIS 5/2 Enemy Publications No. 24, *Records of No. 67 Eastern New Guinea Giruwa L. of C. Hospital*, compiled by Army Medical Officer First Lieutenant Okubo Fukunobo, 10 July 43

20 *Ibid.*

21 *Ibid.*

Chapter 41: Oivi–Gorari

1 Horner, *General Vasey's War*, p. 213

2 *Ibid.*, p. 212

3 The 25th

4 McCarthy, *South-West Pacific Area — First Year, Kokoda to Wau*, p. 323

5 Givney (ed.), *The First at War — The Story of the 2/1st Australian Infantry Battalion*, p. 292

6 The 2/25th Battalion of the 25th Brigade

7 McCarthy, p. 325

8 ATIS Bulletin No. 358, diary of Sakomoto

9 Crooks, *The Footsoldiers*, p. 226

10 McCarthy, pp. 325–8

11 Crooks, p. 225

12 *Ibid.*

13 Givney, p. 302

14 On 18 August 1967

15 Blamey to Shedden, 14 November 1942, NAA A5954 Box 532

16 The 2/31st Battalion of the 25th Brigade

17 ATIS Interrogation Report No. 16, Yamamoto Kiyoshi, farm hand, Yamanaka Butai. He is not to be confused with the surgeon by the same name, who wrote *Yokogotoku; Kaigun Yasuda Butai Buna gyokusai no tenmatsu*, Seiunsha, Tokyo, 1985

18 Givney, p. 305

19 Bergerud, *Touched with Fire*, p. 143

20 Horner, *General Vasey's War*, p. 214

Chapter 42: Horii

1 Nakahashi, *War History of the Force which was sent to the South Seas*, translated by Lt F.C. Jorgensen, AWM PR00297

2 Rinzo, p. 118

3 *Ibid.*

4 Interview with Imanishi Sadaharu, October 2003

5 Nakahashi, p. 41

6 *Ibid.*

7 *Ibid.*

8 *Ibid.*

9 Horner, *General Vasey's War*, p. 215

10 16th Brigade War Diary

11 Horner, *General Vasey's War*, p. 215

Chapter 43: Catterns

1 McCarthy, *South-West Pacific Area — First Year, Kokoda to Wau*, p. 386

2 Interview with Basil Catterns, September 2004

3 McCarthy, p. 389

4 Givney (ed.), *The First at War — The Story of the 2/1st Australian Infantry Battalion*, p. 316

5 McCarthy, p. 390

6 *Ibid.*

7 Givney, p. 316

8 *Ibid.*, p. 319

9 Interview with Catterns, August 2002

10 Givney, p. 320

11 *Ibid.*, p. 321

12 *Ibid.*

13 McCarthy, p. 391

14 Interview with Catterns, August 2002

15 *Ibid.*

Chapter 44: Madness

This chapter draws extensively on dialogue in Okada Seizo's *Lost Troops*

PART 5: ANNIHILATION

Chapter 45: Gona

1 Barter, *Far Above Battle*, p. 197
2 Blamey to Shedden, 30 November 1942, NAA A5954 Box 532
3 Yoshihara Tsutomu, *Southern Cross: Account Of The Eastern New Guinea Campaign*, translated by Doris Heath, AWM F940.541352 MON 1521
4 Austen, *To Kokoda and Beyond*, p. 189
5 War Diary, 2/6 Independent Company
6 Washington to Landforces, Melbourne, *US Army Intelligence estimate of Japanese strengths and capabilities in SWPA as at 18 Nov 1942*, Blamey Papers, AWM 3DRL/6643 2/56
7 Sir Earle Page, in 1945
8 Blamey to Herring, Blamey Papers
9 Eichelberger, *Our Jungle Road to Tokyo*, p. 18
10 '. . . in war today, victory depends on the advancement of the bomber line' — Kenney, *The MacArthur I Know*, p. 120
11 Porter Papers, AWM PR00527 Box 10
12 McCarthy, *South-West Pacific Area — First Year, Kokoda to Wau*
13 *Ibid.*, p. 434
14 ATIS Bulletin No. 47, 1/1, Item 2
15 ATIS Bulletin No. 229, Yokoyama Detachment
16 ATIS 5/2 Enemy Publications No. 24, *Records of No. 67 Eastern New Guinea Giruwa L. of C. Hospital*, compiled by Army Medical Officer First Lieutenant Okubo Fukunobo, 10 July 43
17 *Ibid.*
18 ATIS Bulletin No. 229, Yokoyama Detachment
19 *Ibid.*
20 *Ibid.*
21 Hetherington Papers, 1.12.70, AWM 419/47/24
22 The 3rd Battalion of the 170th Infantry Regiment
23 ATIS Bulletins, Yamagata speech, 25 Nov 1942
24 Appendix to 2/16th Battalion War Diary, in McCarthy, p. 439

Chapter 46: Koitaki Factor

1 McCarthy, *South-West Pacific Area — First Year, Kokoda to Wau*, pp. 423–4
2 Richard Honner, in letter to the author, 7 October 2003
3 Horner, *Blamey*, p. 367
4 McCarthy, p. 422
5 Russell, *The 2/14th Australian Infantry Battalion*, p. 183
6 Horner, in *The Australian*, 20 March 1998
7 *Ibid.*
8 The 2/14th and 2/27th Battalions, AIF
9 The 2/16 AIF and 3rd Militia Battalion
10 Burns, *The Brown and Blue Diamond at War — The Story of the 2/27th Battalion, A.I.F.*, p. 147
11 Examples taken from various battalion histories and war diaries
12 Honner, *The Koitaki Factor*

Chapter 47: Honner

1 Uren, *A Thousand Men at War — The Story of the 2/16th Battalion, A.I.F*, p. 177
2 For a full biography of Honner, see Brune, *Band of Brothers*
3 *Notes on and Lessons from Recent Operations in Gona And Sanananda Areas*, by Lt-Col R. Honner — Comd 39 Aust Inf Bn, AWM 54 581/7/19
4 *Ibid.*
5 McCarthy, *South-West Pacific Area — First Year, Kokoda to Wau*, p. 431
6 ATIS Current Translations Nos 51–64 3/5, diary, unknown owner, found Gona, 8 December 1942
7 Herring to Blamey, 6 December 42, Blamey Papers, AWM 3DRL6643
8 McCarthy, p. 441
9 See Honner, 'This is the 39th'
10 Herring to Blamey, 9 December 1942, Blamey Papers

11 Blamey to Shedden, Blamey Papers

12 Blamey to Herring, 16 December 1943, Blamey Papers

13 *Outline Appreciation Enemy Activity, Mambare–Kumusi–Amboga River Mouth Areas, 15 December 42,* Blamey Papers

14 Russell, *The 2/14th Australian Infantry Battalion,* p. 206

15 McCarthy, p. 448

16 Russell, pp. 207–08

17 War Diary, 2/16 Battalion

18 Honner, AWM 54 581/7/19

19 Paull, *Retreat From Kokoda,* p. 295

20 Honner, *Gona Campaign 39 Bn — An Account by Lieutenant-Colonel R. Honner,* AWM 54 581/7/19

21 Herring to Blamey, 11 December 1942, Blamey Papers

22 Frank McLean's Private Papers

23 Blamey letter to Fred Shedden, Dept of Defence, 15 December 1942, Blamey Papers

Chapter 48: Mosquito

1 Bullard, *Japanese Medical Corps in the Papua campaigns, 1942–1943* (essay), p. 6

2 An Allied sub-committee of tropical disease at a meeting concluded in early October 42, Blamey Papers, 3DRL/6643 84/141

3 CRS A2671 205/1942

4 Blamey Papers

5 Burston to Blamey, 10 December, Blamey Papers

6 *Ibid.*

7 Blamey Papers

8 *Ibid.*

9 *Ibid.*

10 Bergerud, *Touched with Fire,* p. 91

11 Bullard, p. 8

12 Crooks, in Bergerud, pp. 91–2

13 Bullard, p. 7

14 Bergerud, p. 98

15 *Ibid.,* p. 96

16 Bullard, p. 13

17 Blamey to Curtin, Department of Defence Co-Ordination: United States Forces In New Guinea Campaign — Assessment By Commander-In-Chief, Australian Military Forces, 4 December 1942, NAA A5954 654/26

18 Blamey to Shedden, 4 December 1942, NAA A5954 Box 532

19 Bullard, p. 6

20 *Ibid.,* p. 7

21 *Ibid.,* p. 8

Chapter 49: Americans

1 Eichelberger, *Our Jungle Road to Tokyo,* p. 12

2 Eichelberger, p. 22

3 Bergerud, p. 148

4 Milner, *Victory in Papua,* p. 138

5 *Ibid.*

6 *Information on Emergency Withdrawal Routes, Kokoda-Kumusi River-Owen Stanley Area,* with Reference Maps — Submitted by HQ 32 Infantry Division (USA), 5 November 1942, AWM 54 422/7/8

7 *Correspondence Relating to the Relinquishing of Commands Lt Gen SF Rowell and Maj Gen AS Allen 1942,* Allen Papers, AWM 419/3/1 1/7 3DRL No. 2381

8 McCarthy, *South-West Pacific Area — First Year, Kokoda to Wau,* p. 368

9 Horner, *Blamey,* p. 362

10 Blamey to MacArthur, 16 November 1942, Blamey Papers, AWM 3DRL/6643 2/47

11 Blamey Papers

12 *Ibid.*

13 *Ibid.*

Chapter 50: Buna

1 ATIS Current Translations 3/2, diary belonging to a soldier in the 5th Sasebo SNLP, 15 May — 24 Dec 1942

2 Eichelberger, *Our Jungle Road to Tokyo,* p. 20

3 1st Battalion, 128th Regiment, 32nd Division, US Army

4 Milner, *Victory in Papua,* p. 175

5 *Ibid.*

6 *Ibid.*

7 *Ibid.,* p. 176

8 Long, *MacArthur: as Military Commander,* pp. 113–14

9 H.M. Smith and H.A. Smith led the II/126th and II/128th battalions respectively

10 Milner, p. 184

11 McCarthy, *South-West Pacific Area — First Year, Kokoda to Wau*, p. 365

12 Colonel Herbert A Smith to Milner, in Milner, p. 187

13 *Ibid.*

14 *Ibid.*

15 Horner, *Blamey*, p. 363

16 *Ibid.*

17 *Ibid.*, p. 360

18 *Ibid.*, p. 361

19 See Kenney, *The MacArthur I Know*

20 Horner, *Blamey*, p. 361

21 Blamey to Shedden, 30 November 1942, NAA A5954 Box 532

22 Blamey to Shedden, 4 Dec 1942, NAA A5954, Box 532

23 Blamey Papers, AWM 3DRL/6643

24 Odell letter, quoted in Milner, p. 192

25 Mayo, *Bloody Buna*, p. 116

26 ATIS Bulletin Nos. 26–35, 3/3, Yamagata's Address to Troops, 27 November 1942

27 ATIS Bulletins 100–199 1/2, Notes recorded on signal message pad, kept by Nakajima. 30 December 1942, Moto Butai Hq

28 ATIS 5/8 Enemy Publications No. 97, Handwritten notebook containing notes from lectures given at the naval war college to members of Michi force on infantry tactics and combat methods, dated 2 February to 14 May 1943

29 ATIS Bulletin Nos. 26–35, 3/3, Diary presumably belonging to 1st Lieut Suganuma, 3–15 December 42, Buna Area

Chapter 51: Eichelberger

1 Long, *MacArthur: as Military Commander*, p. 115

2 See Milner, *Victory in Papua*, for full account

3 Herring to Blamey, 30 November 1942, Blamey Papers, 3DRL/6643 2/135

4 Blamey to Herring, 30 November 1942, Blamey Papers

5 Eichelberger, *Our Jungle Road to Tokyo*, p. 20

6 *Ibid.*

7 *Ibid.*, p. 21

8 Milner, *Victory in Papua*, p. 204

9 *Ibid.*

10 Eichelberger, p. 21

11 *Ibid.*, p. 22

12 *Ibid.*

13 *Ibid.*

14 Milner, pp. 196–7

15 Eichelberger, p. 24

16 *Ibid.*, p. 25

17 *Ibid.*, p. 26

18 *Ibid.*, p. 34

19 McCarthy, *South-West Pacific Area — First Year, Kokoda to Wau*, p. 375

20 *Ibid.*

21 *Ibid.*, p. 376

22 Eichelberger, p. 32

23 *Ibid.*

24 *Ibid.*

25 Odell's account, in Mayo, *Bloody Buna*, p. 123

26 See Eichelberger's full account

Chapter 52: Tanks

1 Eichelberger, *Our Jungle Road to Tokyo*, pp. 42–3

2 ATIS Bulletin No. 229, Yokoyama address to troops, 28 November 1942

3 Herring to Blamey, 11 December 1942, Blamey Papers, AWM 3DRL/6643 2/135

4 *Ibid.*

5 Eichelberger, p. 38

6 *Ibid.*

7 ATIS Interrogation Report No. 44, Sato Testsuro, shot in right eye at Gona, 18 December 1942

8 Comprising the 2/9th, 2/10th and 2/12th Australian Infantry Battalions

9 Baker & Knight, *Milne Bay 1942*, p. 88

10 *Ibid.*

11 Spencer, *In the Footsteps of Ghosts: With the 2/9th Battalion in the African Desert and the Jungles of the Pacific*, p. 126

12 *Ibid.*

13 *Ibid.*, p. 126

14 Milner, *Victory in Papua*, p. 263

15 Spencer, p. 126

16 Blamey Papers, 3DRL/6643 2/135

17 Yamamoto, Kiyoshi, *Yokogotoku; Kaigun Yasuda Butai Buna gyokusai no tenmatsu*, Seiunsha, Tokyo, 1985, pp. 181–3

18 ATIS Bulletin No. 80, diary of leading private Uchiyama Seiichi, 9 October–24 December 1942

19 ATIS Bulletin No. 195

20 See Allchin, *Purple and Blue — The History of the 2/10th Battalion, A.I.F.*

21 Milner, p. 274

Chapter 53: Christmas

1 Milner, *Victory in Papua*, p. 291

2 Herring to Blamey, 18 December 1942, Blamey Papers, AWM 3DRL/6643 2/135

3 Beevor, *Stalingrad*, p. 313

4 In Nakahashi, *War History of the Force which was sent to the South Seas*, translated by Lt F.C. Jorgensen, AWM PR00297

5 *Ibid.*, p. 56

6 ATIS 3/3 Current Translations Nos. 26–35, diary of Wada Kiyoshi, 144th Regiment signalman, 18 December–18 January 1942

7 Wada's diary

8 Mayo, *Bloody Buna*, p. 155

9 Austin, *To Kokoda and Beyond*, p. 220

10 Spencer, *In the Footsteps of Ghosts: With the 2/9th Battalion in the African Desert and the Jungles of the Pacific*, p. 140

11 Herring to Blamey, 21 December 1942, Blamey Papers

12 Blamey to Herring, 21 December 1942, Blamey Papers

13 Eichelberger, *Our Jungle Road to Tokyo*, p. 47

14 *Ibid.*, p. 48

15 Milner, p. 300

16 Eichelberger, p. 48

17 See the last telegrams of the Yasuda Unit on 28 December 1942, in Yamamoto, *Yokogotoku; Kaigun Yasuda Butai Buna gyokusai no tenmatsu*, pp. 140–2

18 Yoshihara, *Southern Cross: Account Of The Eastern New Guinea Campaign*, translated by Doris Heath, p. 12, AWM F940.541352 MON 1521

19 *Ibid.*, p. 13

20 Comment by Marutani Hajime, translator of military history, on Yasuda telegrams

21 Yamamoto, *Yokogotoku; Kaigun Yasuda Butai Buna gyokusai no tenmatsu*, p. 405

22 *Ibid.*, pp. 247–8

23 *Ibid.*, pp. 185–7

24 *Ibid.*, p. 405

25 *Ibid.*, p. 410

26 *Ibid.*, pp. 162–3

27 Yoshihara, p. 23

28 *Ibid.*, p. 26

29 ATIS 6/2 Interrogation Report No. 51B, Chang Yock, 24, street hawker in Hong Kong

30 Mayo, p. 167

31 In Manchester, *American Caesar*, p. 327

Chapter 54: Sanananda

1 ATIS Spot Report No. 45 2/1, A Message to the Troops by Lieutenant-General Adachi, commander of the Eighteenth Army

2 Bergerud, *Touched with Fire*, p. 370

3 Allchin, *Purple and Blue — The History of the 2/10th Battalion, A.I.F.* p. 325

4 Hartley, *Sanananda Interlude*, p. 35

5 Blamey to Herring, 13 December 1942, Blamey Papers, 3DRL/6643 2/135

6 McCarthy, *South-West Pacific Area — First Year, Kokoda to Wau*, p. 498

7 Blamey to Herring, 31 December 1942, Blamey Papers

8 Blamey Papers — New Guinea Ops, AWM 3DRL/6643 2/47

9 McCarthy, p. 405

10 Interview with Bill Jenkins, 24 July 2002

11 The combined 2/16th–2/27th Battalion

12 Blamey Papers *Confidential and Secret: Condition of Trps at Present Under Comd 7 Aust Div — New Guinea Ops*, 24 December 1942, AWM 3DRL/6643 2/47

13 *Ibid.*

14 The 39th, 55th–53rd and 49th Militia Battalions

15 Honner, 'This is the 39th'

16 Mayo, *Bloody Buna*, p. 170

17 McCarthy, p. 505

18 Horner, *General Vasey's War*, pp. 227–8

19 Papers of Brig Maj-Gen SHWC Porter, AWM PR00527 Box 10.

20 McCarthy, p. 505

21 Now amalgamated with the 55th

22 Herring to Blamey, 19 December 1942, Blamey Papers, 3DRL/6643 2/135

23 *Confidential and Secret: Condition of Trps at Present Under Comd 7 Aust Div*, Blamey Papers — New Guinea Ops, 24 December 1942, AWM 3DRL/6643 2/47

24 Porter Papers

25 Horner, *Blamey*, p. 365

26 Colonel Stan Sly, AWM Murdoch Sound Archive

27 Blamey to his brother Jim, 2 January 1943, Blamey Papers, AWM 3DRL 6643 2/10

28 11 January 1943, Blamey Papers, 3DRL/6643 93/141

29 MacArthur to Blamey, 28 December 1942, Blamey Papers — New Guinea Ops, AWM 3DRL/6643 2/47

30 US 41st Division

31 Milner, *Victory in Papua*, p. 332

32 McCarthy, p. 508

Chapter 55: *Gyokusai*

1 Criticism of officers is a recurring theme in Japanese diaries during December–January, 1942–43

2 ATIS Current Translations Nos. 16–25, diary of Nada, signalman

3 ATIS Research Report No. 122, *Antagonism between Officers and Men in the Japanese Armed Forces*, AWM 55 12/94

4 Rinzo, *History of the War in New Guinea (Niyuginia Senki)*

5 In Robertson, *Problems of Supply Encountered by the Australian and Japanese forces on the Kokoda Trail and the Questions of Morale*, 1 June 1973, MSS701; AWM 422/3/94

6 ATIS Research Report No. 122, *Antagonism between Officers and Men in the Japanese Armed Forces*, AWM 55 12/94

7 *Ibid.*

8 *Ibid.*

9 *Ibid.*

10 Bullard, 'Kokoda: a Japanese Tragedy', *Wartime*, Issue 20, p. 21

11 ATIS Research Report No. 76 (Part VI), *Defects arising from the Doctrine of 'Spiritual Superiority' as Factors in Japanese Military Psychology*, AWM 12/53

12 Rinzo, p. 118

13 ATIS Research Report No. 76 (Part VI)

14 ATIS Spot Report No. 54

15 ATIS Interrogation Report No. 22, pp. 2–9

16 ATIS Interrogation Report No. 55

17 ATIS Research Reports No. 76 (Part 1), *Self-Immolation as a Factor In Japanese Military Psychology*, 4 April 1944, p. 32, AWM 55 12/53

18 Milner, *Victory in Papua*, p. 343

19 Horner, *General Vasey's War*, p. 231

20 McCarthy, *South-West Pacific Area — First Year, Kokoda to Wau*, p. 527

21 Eichelberger, *Our Jungle Road to Tokyo*, p. 57

22 *Ibid.*, p. 51

23 McCarthy, p. 515

24 Nakahashi, *War History of the Force which was sent to the South Seas*, translated by Lt F.C. Jorgensen, p. 37, AWM PR00297

25 The 2/12 Australian Infantry Battalion

26 Horner, *General Vasey's War*, p. 233

27 Interview with Shimada Yuki, October 2003

28 Rinzo, *History of the War In New Guinea (Nyuginia Senki)*

29 Rinzo, p. 22

30 *Ibid.*

31 *Ibid.*

32 Milner, p. 347

33 McCarthy, p. 519

34 Mayo, *Bloody Buna*, p. 176

35 Of the 2/10th Battalion

36 Allchin, *Purple and Blue — The History of the 2/10th Battalion, A.I.F.* p. 323

37 *Ibid.*, p. 324

38 *Ibid.*, p. 325

39 *Ibid.*, p. 315

40 *Ibid.*

41 *Ibid.*, p. 327

42 The 2/9th Battalion

43 The 2/9th and 2/12th Battalions
44 McCarthy, p. 522
45 *Ibid.*, p. 522
46 *Ibid.*
47 Milner, p. 362
48 ATIS Research Reports No. 76 (Part 1),
   *Self-Immolation as a Factor in Japanese
   Military Psychology*, 4 April 1944, p. 31,
   AWM 55 12/53
49 Colonel Stan Sly, AWM Murdoch Sound
   Archive
50 *Ibid.*
51 Spencer, *In the Footsteps of Ghosts: With the
   2/9th Battalion in the African Desert and the
   Jungles of the Pacific*, p. 154
52 Japanese Monograph No. 37, p. 45
53 Kiyoshi Wada, 'Painting Over My Shame',
   a memoir in *The Signals Company
   Records (Memoirs): 144th Infantry
   Regiment (Kochi)*
54 ATIS 3/3 Current Translations Nos. 26–35,
   diary of Wada Kiyoshi, 144th Regiment
   signalman, 18 December–18 January 1942

Chapter 56: Self-Immolation

1 In Yamaoka Sohachi, *Shosetsu Taiheiyo Senso*
2 In Nakahashi, *War History of the Force which
   was sent to the South Seas*, translated by Lt
   F.C. Jorgensen, p. 54, AWM PR00297
3 *Ibid.*
4 *Ibid.*, p. 58
5 ATIS Bulletins 100–199, 1/2, Diary found
   at Giruwa, owner unknown
6 In ATIS Research Reports No. 76 (Part 1),
   *Self-Immolation as a Factor in Japanese
   Military Psychology*, 4 April 1944, p. 31,
   AWM 55 12/53
7 Rinzo, *History of the War In New Guinea
   (Nyuginia Senki)*
8 Yoshihara Tsutomu, *Southern Cross: Account
   of the Eastern New Guinea Campaign*,
   translated by Doris Heath, p. 25, AWM
   F940.541352 MON 1521
9 *Ibid.*, p. 26
10 Interview with Nishimura Kokichi, by
   Marutani Hajime, December 2003
11 *Ibid.*

12 ATIS Research Reports No. 76 (Part 1),
   *Self-Immolation as a Factor in Japanese
   Military Psychology*, p. 6
13 Milner, *Victory in Papua*, p. 317
14 Yamamoto, *Yokogotoku; Kaigun Yasuda Butai
   Buna gyokusai no tenmatsu*, Seiunsha, pp.
   181–3
15 Nakahashi, p. 59
16 The 144th Infantry Regiment Official
   Record, pp. 209–11
17 *Ibid.*
18 Interview with Nishimura Kokichi, by
   Marutani Hajime, December 2003
19 For figures, see The 144th Infantry
   Regiment Official Record
20 Interview with Imanishi Sadaharu,
   October 2003
21 *Ibid.*
22 ATIS Interrogation Report No. 48,
   Lieutenant Naka Masao
23 ATIS Research Reports No. 76 (Part 1),
   *Self-Immolation as a Factor in Japanese
   Military Psychology*, p. 26
24 *Ibid.*
25 *Ibid.*
26 ATIS translated the poem "as a matter of
   psychological interest" (ATIS Serial No.
   141, 29 December 1942).
27 ATIS Current Translations Serial No. 270
28 ATIS 6/3 Interrogation Reports Nos.
   81–145
29 ATIS 6/3 Interrogation Report No. 93

Chapter 57: The End

1 From 144th Infantry Regiment Signals
   Company Editing Committee, *The Signals
   Company Records (Memoirs): 144th Infantry
   Regiment (Kochi)*, 1986. (Extra number
   published in 1988)
2 In Takida, *The Pacific is Burning*
3 ATIS 6/3 Interrogation Report
   Nos 81–145
4 ATIS Interrogation Spot Report No. 11,
   Lieutenant Inagaki Riichi, naval paymaster.
   Signed by Australian officers, Lieutenant
   L.F. Hopkinson and Colonel Sidney F.
   Mashbir

5 McCarthy, *South-West Pacific Area — First Year, Kokoda to Wau*, p. 531

6 See *Yukon Kochi-Ken Kyodo Senshi*, 1974 (in Kochi Prefecture Municipal Library), p. 430

7 *Ibid.*

8 *Nyuginia-sen tsuioku ki*, Memoir of the New Guinea Campaign, quoted by Dr Keiko Tamura, Australia–Japan Research Project, AWM

9 ATIS 6/3 Interrogation Reports No. 86, Lieutenant Sawatari Zengoro, doctor, aged 34, of Rinji Shicho (Provisional Transport Tai), captured at Giruwa, 20 January 1943

10 McCarthy, p. 531

11 Bergerud, *Touched with Fire*, p. 439

12 Beevor, *Stalingrad*, pp. 439–440

13 Japanese Monograph No. 37, p. 64

14 ATIS Bulletin No. 204, 1/3

15 Russell, *The 2/14th Australian Infantry Battalion*, p. 108

16 Edgar, *Warrior of Kokoda*

17 Burns, *The Brown and Blue Diamond at War — The Story of the 2/27th Battalion, A.I.F.*, p. 103

18 McCarthy, p. 591

19 Coulthard-Clark, in his 2001 Blamey Oration

20 McCarthy, p. 112

21 Kenney, *The MacArthur I Know*, p. 241

22 See this and many similar remarks in Mark Johnston's, *Fighting the Enemy*

23 Interview with Tom Keneally, January 2004

24 *Sydney Morning Herald*, March 1942

25 At Caloundra

26 Horner, *Blamey*, p. 381

27 See *An Examination of How Race Affected the Far Eastern War*, an essay by Marutani Hajime

28 See Johnston

29 *Ibid.*

30 Austin, AWM Murdoch Sound Archive

31 Interview with Shimada, October 2003

32 Interview with Yamasaki, October 2003

33 Edgar, p. 192

34 Johns Papers, AWM PR00640

35 In *Sydney Morning Herald*, 23 April 2001

36 Horner, *Crisis of Command*, p. 269

37 See Brune, *Band of Brothers*

38 In Toland, *The Rising Sun*, p. 439

39 Dower, *The Sun*, 27 August 1972

40 Horner, *General Vasey's War*, p. 312

41 *Ibid.*

42 The linoleum is now in the AWM. This anecdote comes from Sergeant Henry Norman Walker of the Far Eastern Liaison Office (FELO); see *Stand-To*, December 1952

43 The author attended the reunion, October 2003

44 Interview with Havala, at Kagi, October 2003

45 Paull, *Retreat from Kokoda*, p. 43

46 Vernon's diary, p. 25

47 See Raftery, *Marks of War*

48 Frank McLean's Private Papers

49 Steward letter, AWM PR 87/008

50 Interview with Basil Catterns MC, 31 August 2002

Index

health (fighting condition) *see also* casualties; disease
  American, 458–459, 485
  Australian, 230, 243–244, 254, 260, 484–487
  Japanese, 432–433
  at Sanananda, 485–487
Heap, Lieutenant D.A., 495
Hedlich, Rev. Vivian, 65
Henderson, Captain Horace, 485
Herring, General Ned, 101, 276, 278, 282, 338–340, 354, 395, 430–431, 434, 445, 456, 458, 459, 462, 464, 472–474, 485, 488, 489
Hetherington, John, 124, 375
Hicks, Lieutenant George, 424
High Command (Horner), 263
Hinchcliffe, Keith, 187
Hirano, Second Lieutenant, 58–59, 164–165, 173
Hirohito, Emperor, 108–109, 115–117, 165, 267, 312–313, 464
Hiromitsu Iwamoto, 217
Hirose, First Class Private, 59
Hisaeda Akiyoshi, Private, 112–113
Hitler, Adolf, 325
Hogan, Captain Allan, 205
Holland, Rev. Henry, 65
Hollingworth, Lieutenant Lance, 365
Hong Kong, 82
Hongo Hiroshi, 478
Honner, Brian, 136
Honner, Lieutenant-Colonel Ralph, 422
  B Company, 167
  Blamey, 250, 282
  career and character, 428
  commands 2/14th Battalion, 530
  commands 39th Battalion, 29, 61, 99, 163, 426
  Gona, 429, 434
  Isurava, 169–171
  medical claims of 39th, 534
  no-prisoner policy, 529
  Porter, 167
  terrain, 140
  views on losses, 136, 200, 202
Horibe, Lieutenant, 145
Horiguchi Tsugio, First Lieutenant, 121
Horii Tomitaro, Major-General

Brigade Hill, 235, 240
  carriers, 217–218
  commands Nankai Shitai, 12–13, 111
  criticism of, 333
  death of, 399
  Efogi, 232
  Eora Creek, 364–365, 369
  grave, 533
  horse, 331
  Hyakutake, 108, 113
  invasion of Moresby, 252, 302–303, 306, 310–311
  Ioribaiwa, 255–256, 300–302
  Isurava, 165–167, 172–173
  judgment, 180–181
  Kokoda Government Station, 154
  Kumusi River, 396–400, 417
  Milne Bay, 195
  Oivi–Gorari, 380–382, 387
  Papuans, 63
  reputation, 107–108
  'South Seas Marching Song', 118
  strategy, 144–145
  supply line *see* supply lines and supplies
  withdrawal, 256, 311–314, 316–317
Hoshino Kazuo, 517
Hosier, Sergeant Jim, 189
Howard, Lieutenant-Colonel, 232
Howson, Laurie ('Smoky'), 21–23, 25, 28, 53, 60, 129, 163, 181, 203, 209, 533–534
Hozumi, Lieutenant-Colonel, 509
Huggins' roadblock, 482, 485
Hughes, William Morris ('Billy'), 5, 10–11, 259
Humphries, Richard, 131
Hunt, Lance-Corporal John, 362
Hunter, Private, 221
Huon Gulf, 12, 17
Hutchison, Major Ian, 367
Hyakutake Harukichi, Lieutenant-General, 12, 108–109, 113

I
Iawarere, 247
Ilimo, 381
Ilolo, 39–40, 51, 135, 208
Ilomo, 222
Imamura Hitoshi, General, 312, 412

suicide (self-immolation), 45, 107, 195, 232, 305, 433, 507–511
suicide squads ('human bullets'), 45, 115, 164, 172, 244, 424, 495, 507
Sumatra, 447
supply lines and supplies
   abandoned, 214, 242
   Allen's, 336–340, 354–356, 366
   Australian, 22–23, 43, 125, 326
   Churchill supplies, 143, 225, 334
   destroyed, 225, 227
   Horii's, 142–143, 217–218, 225–226, 240, 260, 272, 300–301, 303, 309, 334–335, 439
   Japanese, 109, 154–155, 164, 181, 183
   Myola drop zone *see* Myola drop zone
   native carriers *see* native carriers
   native gardens and plantations, 213, 217, 247, 303–304, 315, 332, 334–335
Susuki (interpreter), 10
Sutherland, Jack, 531
Sutherland, Lieutenant-General Richard, 443, 456
Suweri, 222
Sword, Lieutenant, 171, 179
Sydney Morning Herald, 24, 96
Sydney (shelling of eastern suburbs), 289
Symington, Captain, 56–59

T
tactics (Japanese)
   bodies as sandbags, 434
   bunkers and foxholes, 369, 389, 412–414, 419, 444, 446
   encirclement, 378
   machine-gun pits, 349–356
   night attacks, 42, 45, 49–50, 144–145
   singing, 13, 187
   taunts, 170, 200, 224
Takaki Yoshijo, First Lieutenant, 396–397
Takasago *see* Formosan troops
Takenaka Company, 496
Takita Kenji 204–205, 313, 515
Takushiro, Colonel, 109
Tanaka, Corporal, 507
Tanaka Kengoro, Lieutenant-Colonel, 143, 155, 311–313, 398–399, 491
Tanaka Yuki, 501

Tarakena, 495
Taylor, Frank, 227, 412
Tedder, Air Marshal Arthur, 98
Templeton, Captain Sam, 42–46, 53, 155
'Templeton's Crossing' (Eora Creek), 46, 156, 202, 211, 227, 340, 345, 349–356
terrain, 141, 144–145, 148, 162–163, 191, 337, 341–342, 356, 357–358, 378, 388–389, 481
   see also conditions
Thailand, 82
39th Battalion (Australian Militia)
   age of troops, 27
   AIF and, 203
   B Company, 42–44, 46–47, 167
   Blamey, 249–250
   camaraderie in, 28–29
   at Deniki, 55, 520
   disbanded, 531
   formation, 21–22
   at Gona, 209, 426, 428–431, 433
   Honner commands *see* Honner, Lieutenant-Colonel Ralph
   at Ilolo, 208
   at Isurava *see* Isurava
   at Kokoda Government Station, 40, 49–53, 58–60, 520
   medical claims, 534
   in Port Moresby, 22–23, 25–26, 32, 33, 36, 37
   at Sanananda, 485, 497
   Seekamp's platoon, 44–46
   survivors, 519
Thompson, Private George, 424
Thompson submachine-gun ('Tommy guns')
   see weapons
Those Ragged Bloody Heroes (Brune), 263
Tobruk, Siege of, 26, 76, 98, 191, 324, 365, 423, 465
Tojo Hideki, Premier, 12, 82, 85, 289, 412, 531
Tokyo Rose, 26
Tol Plantation massacre, 111–112, 193, 393, 527
Tomita Yoshinobu, Lieutenant-Colonel, 506–507
Tongs, Sergeant Bede, 316, 329, 351–352
Tonkin, Private Kevin, 238
Tori Me (night blindness), 516
Torres Strait, 17